‡ 27⁵⁰
18⁵⁰

8⁹⁵

ra 5/02

BOND OF IRON

BOND OF IRON

Master and Slave at Buffalo Forge

CHARLES B. DEW

W·W·NORTON & COMPANY

New York London

The text of this book is composed in Janson, with the display type set in Bulmer.
Composition and manufacturing by the Haddon Craftsmen, Inc.
Book design and cartography by Jacques Chazaud.

Library of Congress Cataloging-in-Publication Data
Dew, Charles B.
Bond of iron : master and slave at Buffalo Forge / Charles R. Dew.
p. cm.
Includes index.
ISBN 0-393-03616-2
1. Buffalo Forge (Va.)—History. 2. Weaver, William, 1780–1863. 3. Slave
labor—Virginia—Lexington Region. 4. Slaves—Virginia—Lexington Region—Social
conditions. 5. Lexington Region (Va.)—Race Relations. I. Title.
F234.B89D48   1994
975.5′852—dc20   93-6261

ISBN 0-393-03616-2

W. W. Norton & Company, Inc., 500 Fifth Avenue, New York, N.Y. 10110
W. W. Norton & Company Ltd., 10 Coptic Street, London WC1A 1PU

For
Robert C. L. Scott
and
C. Vann Woodward

and for
Robb, Stephen, and Jack

Contents

Acknowledgments   *ix*
Introduction   *xiii*
Prologue: Buffalo Forge, 1858   *3*

PART I: THE MASTER

1 William Weaver, Pennsylvanian   15
2 Mayburry & Weaver: Debt and Disappointment   29
3 Mayburry & Weaver: Dissolution and Division   46
4 Bath Iron Works   63
5 Weaver *v.* Jordan, Davis & Company   83
6 The Master of Buffalo Forge   98
7 William Weaver, Virginian   122
8 Etna Furnace   139

PART II: THE SLAVES

1 Sam Williams   *171*
2 Henry Towles   *187*
3 Tooler   *192*
4 Harry Hunt, Jr.   *198*
5 Henry Matthews   *204*
6 Garland Thompson and His Family   *208*

PART III: BUFFALO FORGE

1 The Late Antebellum Years   *241*
2 The Eve of War   *264*
3 War   *287*
4 Death   *312*
5 Peace and Freedom   *338*

Epilogue   *365*
Notes   *369*
Index   *415*

Photographs appear following page 220.

Maps appear on pages 5 and 245.

Acknowledgments

Many people have helped me at various stages of my work on this project, and I am delighted to be able to thank them for their assistance.

The American Council of Learned Societies provided me with a generous fellowship at an early stage of my research, and a subsequent grant from the National Endowment for the Humanities enabled me to complete most of the work in the primary source materials. I am deeply grateful for this support. Two institutions gave me vital assistance when I came to the writing stage. The Carter G. Woodson Institute at the University of Virginia provided me with an ideal home during the 1989–90 academic year and enabled me to complete a first draft of my manuscript. I wish to thank Armstead Robinson and Bill Jackson of the Woodson Institute for their help in making this fellowship year such a productive one for me. And my wonderful academic home for the past fifteen years, Williams College, gave me a fellowship at the College's Center for the Humanities and Social Sciences in the fall of 1992 that made it possible for me to finish up the writing and make final revisions in the manuscript. All those associated with creating this Center and sustaining its mission—particularly President Frank Oakley and Director Bernie Bucky—deserve the thanks of all of us who have been fortunate enough to enjoy these marvelous facilities. Williams College remains a remarkable place—an undergraduate liberal arts institution that values teaching and scholarship in equal measure.

I owe a special debt of gratitude to Pat and Tom Brady. Without their help, this book could never have been written. I am saddened by the fact that Tom did not live to see the story of Buffalo Forge in print; he died in January 1993. But he read an early draft of the manuscript for me, as did Pat, and seemed to be genuinely pleased that the history of William Weaver and Daniel Brady and the slaves of Buffalo Forge was taking shape. Both he and Pat rendered me every possible assistance, and I cannot say how much their help meant to me. Mary and Bonnie Brady also deserve my warmest thanks. On numerous occasions they welcomed me into their homes and made me feel more like a member of the family than a guest.

I am also deeply grateful to James Thompson for sharing the memories of his family's life at Buffalo Forge with me. I owe him much, and I wish he were here to read the story of Garland Thompson and his family to the extent that I have been able to piece it together. His help played a major part in this process of reconstruction. He was battling cancer when I talked to him, and the disease finally took his life.

Many others have helped at various stages of this book's progress from idea to reality. I would particularly like to thank Bill Abbot, Tom Alexander, Staige Blackford, LaWanda Cox, Gail Godwin, Charles Joyner, Bill McFeely, Jim McPherson, Esther Newberg, Ron Numbers, Willie Lee Rose, Todd Savitt, Anne Firor Scott, John David Smith, Merritt Roe Smith, Ken Stampp, Anne Tyler, and Ben Wall for all they did in my behalf.

No historian can get very far without the aid of archivists and librarians, and a large number of skilled professionals gave me the benefit of their time and energy as I attempted to assemble the materials for this study. I particularly want to thank Michael Plunkett and the superb staff of the Manuscripts Division of the University of Virginia Library for their assistance over the years. Archivists at the Duke University Library, the National Archives, the Virginia Historical Society, the Virginia State Library, the Washington and Lee University Library, and the State Historical Society of Wisconsin also helped me in numerous ways. Lee Dalzell, a peerless reference librarian, and her outstanding staff at the Williams College Library deserve my thanks as well.

I have often used materials relating to Buffalo Forge in my southern history courses at Williams, and a number of students have responded with insight and enthusiasm to the story of slave life at Weaver's ironworks. I am particularly grateful to those who took a seminar with me on industrial slavery several years ago. My thanks to Joe Beach, Robin Bunn, David Kleit, Breck Knapp, Chris Knapp, Duncan Milloy, Matt Waller, and Chuck Willing for all they taught me during our class together.

I had the fascinating experience of seeing a television documentary made on Buffalo Forge before I finished writing this book. Jack Sproat of the University of South Carolina and Ruth Sproat of the South Carolina Educational Television Network made this documentary possible, and I want to thank them for all the hard work they put in to see this project through to completion. William Peters, a talented filmmaker, wrote the script and directed this program with exceptional skill and attention to accuracy and detail. The final product, a sixty-minute documentary entitled *Bond of Iron,* is one of which I am quite proud, and my thanks go to everyone who had a hand in bringing this enterprise to life.

It has been my great good fortune to have had the help of superb typists at every stage of my work on this book. Gail Shirley and the magnificent office staff of the Woodson Institute turned my hand-written pages into a beautifully word-processed manuscript, and Gigi Swift, secretary extraordinaire of the Williams College History Department, prepared the final copy for submission to the publisher. I thank them all, from the bottom of my technophobic heart. To the consternation of all who know me, I still write without the aid of a typewriter or a computer, so I owe special thanks to all of those who have helped me survive into the late twentieth century.

I would also like to thank Ed Barber, my editor at Norton, for accepting my manuscript after reading an early draft and for his help, and his astute suggestions for revision, along the way. He has made the experience of publishing with his fine house a pleasure from start to finish.

Finally, I want to extend my deepest thanks to those to whom this book is dedicated.

Bob Scott was my undergraduate teacher at Williams, and it was he who kindled my desire to learn more about the South. Without the benefit of his teaching, and his example, I never would have gone into the historical profession. He also read this manuscript for me at a time when I very much needed a candid and knowledgeable appraisal of what I was trying to do. Bob provided me with just such a reading, and the book is far better because he was willing to give me the benefit of his mastery of southern history.

Vann Woodward was the best graduate director anyone could wish for. Johns Hopkins was a very special place for all of us who were fortunate enough to do our graduate work there when Vann was a member of the

Hopkins faculty. I know I took to heart his admonition to avoid what he referred to as historical "gerontophagy"—the process of writing history by devouring one's scholarly elders. Do your own research, get your hands dirty in the source materials, and let what you find guide your historical writing, Vann told us. I hope this book will at least approach the high standards he set for us. I owe him more than I can say, both for his help at the formative stage of my scholarly training and for his friendship and support over the years.

No words can adequately express my debt to my family. My wife, Robb, a writer of extraordinary talent and ability and the love of my life, has supported this project from its inception. She has often delayed her own work so that I could pursue mine. She cheerfully went through the arduous process of relocating our family during summer vacations and sabbatical leaves, and she cared for our two sons, Stephen and Jack, while I was spending my days visiting manuscript depositories or combing through records in county courthouses. She is my toughest critic, and it is not the slightest exaggeration to say that without her this book would not exist. With her novelist's eye, she saw the power and potential of the Buffalo Forge story long before I did, and she encouraged me from the very start to focus on William Weaver and his slaves. Stephen and Jack have influenced my work in ways that defy definition. How can anyone measure the experience of being a father? But I can say with absolute certainty that they have made an irreplaceable contribution to whatever merits this study may possess. To Robb, Stephen, and Jack, I simply say thank you for enriching my life in ways that are truly incalculable.

Introduction

———◆———

Every book, of course, has its own history. I began the research for this one
intending to write a very different sort of study. I planned to attempt a
broad-based investigation of slave ironworkers in the antebellum and Civil
War South. This project was a natural outgrowth of my first book, a history
of the Tredegar Iron Works in Richmond, Virginia—the Old South's largest manufacturing facility and a major employer of slave labor both before
and during the Civil War.[1]

I started the research on my new project in 1970 during a year of teaching at the University of Virginia. The Manuscripts Division in Alderman
Library contained several extensive collections dealing with slave-manned
blast furnaces and forges in Virginia, and I systematically worked my way
through all of this material. The most valuable of these collections turned
out to be the Weaver–Brady Papers. These records contained detailed
information on slave ironworkers laboring at William Weaver's Buffalo
Forge, located in Rockbridge County in the Valley of Virginia some nine
miles southeast of Lexington, and at his Etna Furnace, situated in an ad-

joining county, Botetourt, approximately seventeen miles south of Buffalo Forge. These materials also dealt with the period in the late 1850s and the 1860s when Weaver's nephew-in-law, Daniel C. E. Brady, came down from Philadelphia to help Weaver manage his ironworks. During this early stage of my research, Buffalo Forge and Etna Furnace were simply two installations among the many I was investigating.

Subsequent research trips took me farther south—to manuscript depositories in North Carolina, South Carolina, Georgia, and Alabama—and on one of these visits another valuable collection of William Weaver's papers turned up, this one at the Duke University Library. Buffalo Forge was rapidly becoming a first among equals, but at this point my focus was still on the broader picture.

My research plans changed drastically, however, when I discovered a third cache of Weaver–Brady materials in an unlikely place. The State Historical Society of Wisconsin houses a number of collections dealing with antebellum and wartime iron manufacturing in the Valley of Virginia. These materials were originally acquired by the McCormick Historical Association in Chicago because Cyrus Hall McCormick, the inventor of the reaper, got his start in business as a Valley ironmaster. The McCormick family transferred the collection to Wisconsin in 1951 after the Chicago headquarters building was sold as part of an estate settlement. Among the entries in the printed guide to the McCormick Collection was the following item:

> Brady, Daniel C. E.   Journals 1860–1865
> Two home journals kept presumably by Daniel C. E. Brady, nephew [*sic*] of William Weaver, at Buffalo Forge in Rockbridge County, Virginia. These contain a planting schedule; daily entries of work assignments for slaves and hired hands, including farm tasks, hauling coal for the forge, and work at the shop. . . .[2]

The McCormick materials also included the papers of James D. Davidson, a Lexington attorney who was William Weaver's lawyer and closest friend. As soon as I looked through Brady's Journal and examined the Davidson Papers, I knew it was time to rethink my project. Brady's two-volume "Home Journal" contained a day-by-day record of the work done by Weaver's slave force at Buffalo Forge from October 1, 1860, until June 30, 1865; correspondence in the Davidson Papers contained numerous, and exceedingly valuable, references to the use of slave labor at Weaver's ironworks. I was intrigued by the growing possibility that I might be able to take an in-depth look at how the slave system functioned at a single southern manufacturing enterprise. The next stop on my itinerary had to be Rockbridge County, Virginia.

The people I contacted in Lexington, the county seat, could not have been more helpful. The Clerk of the Rockbridge County Court, Harry Wright, showed me the extensive chancery court records filed in drawers covering every wall of the documents room in the courthouse. William Weaver, it turned out, had been a notorious litigator, and all the documentation was there. Since slaves were legally a form of property, Weaver's bondsmen had figured largely in most of the cases in which the master had been involved. A short trip north to the Augusta County Court House in Staunton produced yet another gold mine of records relating to Weaver's slaves.

One of the nicest things Mr. Wright did for me while I was in Rockbridge County was to suggest that I contact the Brady family, who still lived in the area. One phone call was all it took. Mr. and Mrs. D. E. Brady, Jr.—Pat and Mary Brady—generously invited me to stay at their home in Lexington, and Mr. Brady took me down to his basement where he had carefully filed a rich body of Buffalo Forge records—ledgers, cashbooks, and a variety of other valuable materials. Mr. Brady also introduced me to his brother and his brother's wife, Tom and Bonnie Brady, who lived in Richmond. Tom Brady had long been fascinated by the antebellum charcoal iron industry in Virginia, and he had an unparalleled knowledge of forge and furnace sites in the state and of the technology used in nineteenth-century iron manufacturing. He had also inherited William Weaver's desk, and that desk, naturally, had been stuffed with documents, all of which he had preserved and which he readily made available to me. The contents of Weaver's desk included a slim volume labeled "Names, births &c: of Negroes." This was the slave birth and death register kept at Buffalo Forge. I was now fully convinced that the decision I had made in Wisconsin to sharpen my focus to Buffalo Forge was the right one, and my lens has been firmly fixed on that site ever since.

I have been back to Lexington and Richmond frequently since those initial visits, and the Bradys have always welcomed me into their homes with incredibly warm hospitality. I had a similar experience in another Rockbridge County residence when I was looking for the records of the Mount Lydia Church, the Baptist congregation the Buffalo Forge freedmen had organized after the Civil War.

James Thompson, a descendant of the last pastor at Mount Lydia, invited me to stop by his home in Glasgow, Virginia, a small community on the Maury River not far from Buffalo Forge. He did not think he had any church records, but he said he would be glad to talk to me. We were sitting on the couch in Mr. Thompson's living room discussing Mount Lydia when he glanced down at some papers I had spread out between us. One of these documents—an item Tom Brady had found in Weaver's desk—was a Xerox copy of a descriptive list of the Buffalo Forge slave artisans. Daniel Brady had prepared this list for the Confederate government in 1865, and it gave the name, age, height, color, value, and job description of each of the forge workers. Mr. Thompson pointed to the name *Garland* on the list and said, "That man was my grandfather." He not only knew who Garland was, Mr. Thompson also had a rich oral history of his family's experiences at Weaver's ironworks, a history which he graciously recounted for me. James Thompson's stories of his great-grandfather Garland and of his grandfather, Garland Thompson, Jr., provide a dimension and a texture to the story of William Weaver and his slaves that could not have been gained from any other source.

As I assembled more and more of the pieces that made up the mosaic of slave life at Buffalo Forge, I decided I had to return to Charlottesville. I wanted to go back over the Weaver–Brady Papers at Alderman Library. When I had originally examined these materials, I had approached them with my broader study in mind, and I needed to reassure myself that I had not overlooked something that might be important. The always helpful archivists in the Manuscripts Division pulled every one of the seventy-nine ledgers and journals in the collection, and I went over each one page by page. I quickly discovered that the archival description of some of these volumes told only part of their story. A number of them had been used at various times for different purposes. The labels on the spine or front cover—which formed the basis for the entry in the reader's guide to the papers—indicated one thing; the contents, however, frequently contained additional records. Such was the case with a volume identified in the guide as a furnace daybook. On the interior pages lay the first two years of Daniel Brady's "Home Journal." These daily entries covered the period from March 15, 1858, to September 30, 1860. The first volume of Brady's Journal at the State Historical Society of Wisconsin began with October 1, 1860. I now had a daily record of what every black forge worker and field hand was doing at Buffalo Forge during a span of almost eight years that embraced the late antebellum, Civil War, and early Reconstruction eras.

The fortuitous survival of all three volumes of Daniel Brady's "Home Journal" seemed almost to be an omen. I had the same feeling when I was at the National Archives in Washington, D.C., going through the records of the Lexington office of the Freedmen's Bureau. Bureau officers throughout the South in the years following the end of the war constructed marriage registers in which they recorded the unions of local black men and women who had married as slaves. Few of these registers have survived, but the one for Rockbridge County has, and it contains the marriage registrations for most of the former Buffalo Forge slaves. In addition to giving the year they were married, it also lists the dates and places of their birth and the names, birthplaces, and ages of their children. When these records are combined with other sources—most notably the slave birth and death register, documents from chancery court cases in which Weaver's slaves were involved, and postwar manuscript census returns—it is possible to construct the genealogies of many of the Buffalo Forge slave families.

Some Buffalo Forge materials did not survive, of course, and one loss was particularly disappointing. A volume, referred to in other documents as the "House Book," was kept at Weaver's residence and seems to have been a record of the work performed by Weaver's house servants. If this volume had managed to escape loss or destruction, we could have learned much more about the lives of the slave women and girls who worked at Buffalo Forge. And I have often wished that a Virginia Federal Writers' Project historian had made it out to this section of Rockbridge County during the 1930s. State Writers' Project units in the South were interviewing former slaves during the depression, and these narratives, which were finally published in the 1970s, have provided historians of American slavery with an invaluable body of research material. Unfortunately, none of the former Buffalo Forge slaves ever seems to have been interviewed by a member of the Virginia unit.[3]

I have been working on this book for a number of years. Academic life has other tasks besides scholarship, and I have often had to delay research trips and lay my notes and microfilm and Xerox materials aside for months on end because of the press of more immediate teaching and administrative responsibilities. My wife, Robb Forman Dew, was also launching her writing career during these years, and we had two growing sons who needed and deserved our time and attention. But in many ways I do not regret the delays. Time allowed me to decide precisely how I wanted to go about presenting this material, and I had the invaluable, and irreplaceable, experience of being a husband and a father during these years. I cannot say with absolute certainty that this is a better book because of the passage of this time, but I feel in the marrow of my bones that it is. I know that my understanding of the meaning of family has deepened since I first began work on this project, and family lies at the heart of the Buffalo Forge story.

More than anything else, I did not want to rush into print with a half-baked version of the history of Buffalo Forge. The material was too rich to be treated that way. Mies van der Rohe has said of architecture that God is hiding in the details, and so it seemed to me with this research. I hope the contents of this book will confirm in the reader's mind the wisdom not only of my focus on Buffalo Forge but also of my close, sometimes minute, examination of the documentary materials. Detailed presentation of the evidence is often the only way I can carry the reader into the slaves' world as I attempt to re-create the lives of the people, black and white, who once lived there.

BOND OF IRON

Prologue:
Buffalo Forge, 1858

The year 1858 started auspiciously for William Weaver. His ironmaking facilities in the Valley of Virginia—at his home at Buffalo Forge in Rockbridge County and at Etna Furnace in neighboring Botetourt County—were both in excellent shape. He owned a crew of skilled forge hands—Sam Williams, Henry Towles, Harry Hunt, Jr., and a man named Tooler—which was the equal of any gang of slave forgeworkers anywhere in the Valley. His total slave force, close to seventy men, women, and children in 1858, also provided him with almost all the agricultural labor he needed as well as a handful of key blast furnace workers.[1] And in late 1857 and early 1858, he had managed to hire sixty-four additional slaves, enough to ensure that Etna Furnace could be worked to its full capacity that year.[2] If the markets down the James River—in Lynchburg and Richmond—would pay a decent price for his metal, William Weaver stood to make a handsome profit on his ironmaking operations in 1858.

He scarcely needed the money. Weaver would turn seventy-seven in

March of that year. A widower with no children of his own, he was one of
the wealthiest men in the entire Valley. As the largest slaveholder in Rockbridge County and as the owner of over 20,000 acres of land scattered
across Rockbridge and the adjoining counties of Amherst and Botetourt,
there was little else, it would seem, to which he could aspire.[3]

Weaver's carefully cultivated fields around Buffalo Forge were some of
the best farm land in the area, and his large stone house, with its comfortable, sunlit rooms, was a landmark on the road to Lexington, the county
seat, nine miles to the northwest. Whenever Weaver stood on the balcony
that ran the full length of the house and looked east, across North River
toward the majestic sweep of the Blue Ridge Mountains, he could think to
himself that it truly was his for as far as he could see. And one can see a very
long way from the balcony of William Weaver's home.

But making money was second nature to Weaver, and it was unlikely
that it ever occurred to him to stop. He had been doing it for quite a long
time, first in his native Pennsylvania and then in the Valley of Virginia. He
had started out as a farmboy, born in 1781 into a German household at
Flourtown, not far from Philadelphia. He had gone on from there into a
variety of enterprises, principally merchandising, milling, marble quarrying, small-scale textile manufacturing, and, during the War of 1812, blockade running, all in the Philadelphia area.

Another of Weaver's wartime ventures had been his chance investment
in 1814 in the Virginia furnace and forge that later became the central focus
of his life. Those ironworks also became the basis for his fortune after he
moved permanently to the Valley in 1823.[4] He had, over the years, skill-
fully exploited his position in the local iron trade by charging what the
traffic would bear in flush times, then cutting back his iron production and
living off his farms when the iron market was distressed. He had gradually
built up both his slave force and his landholdings until he was, by the 1850s,
Rockbridge County's leading ironmaster. And now, in 1858, things were off
to a good start.

Perhaps nothing was more important to him at the beginning of that year
than the fact that he finally had men he trusted in charge of both Etna
Furnace and Buffalo Forge. Both men were relatives. Weaver did not trust
many people, particularly when his financial interests were at stake, and
the closer he could get to a blood tie, the better he seemed to like it. He had
brought a number of his young relatives down from Pennsylvania over the
past thirty years to help him manage his ironworks, but none had worked
out to his full satisfaction. So in the mid-1850s, he had begun a sustained
and systematic campaign to persuade two men who he hoped would be
among his more talented younger relatives to come to the Valley.

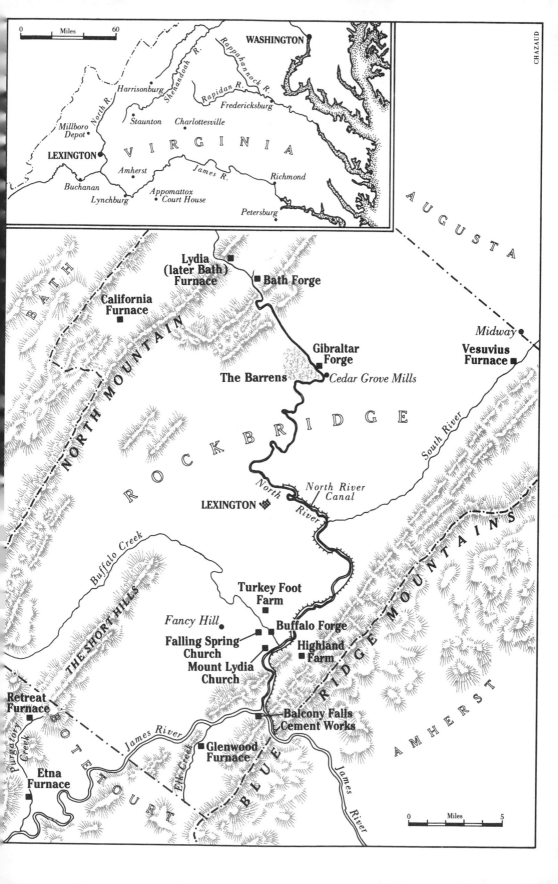

CHAZAUD

Miles
0   60

WASHINGTON

Shenandoah R.
North R.
Rappahannock R.
Rapidan R.
Harrisonburg
Fredericksburg
Millboro
Depot
Staunton   Charlottesville
LEXINGTON
V I R G I N I A
Amherst   James R.
Richmond
Buchanan
Lynchburg   Appomattox
Court House
Petersburg

AUGUSTA

Lydia
(later Bath)
Furnace

Bath Forge

California
Furnace

Midway

Vesuvius
Furnace

Gibraltar
Forge

The Barrens   Cedar Grove Mills

R O C K B R I D G E

South River

North River
Canal

LEXINGTON   North River

N O R T H   M O U N T A I N

B A T H

Buffalo Creek

Turkey Foot
Farm

Fancy Hill   Buffalo Forge

Falling Spring
Church   Highland
Farm

Mount Lydia
Church

T H E   S H O R T   H I L L S

Retreat
Furnace

Balcony Falls
Cement Works

Purgatory Creek

James River

Glenwood
Furnace

B O T E T O U R T

Etna
Furnace

Elk Creek

B L U E

James River

R I D G E   M O U N T A I N S

A M H E R S T

Miles
0   5

The first, a nephew, had come in March of 1856. His name was Charles K. Gorgas, and he was the son of Weaver's favorite sister, Lydia. Young Charley Gorgas had been something of a risk. He was only twenty-three years old in 1856 and still single. But Weaver needed someone reliable and industrious at Etna Furnace, and he thought his nephew might work out. "There is business a plenty here for him if he only attends to it properly, and has the proper head for it," Weaver wrote about Gorgas just before he arrived in Virginia. "Training alone will not [suffice] as nature must do something, in order to make a good Iron Master."[5] Fortunately, at least from Weaver's point of view, nature seemed to have done pretty well by Charley Gorgas, and Etna Furnace was in responsible hands as 1858 began.

So was Buffalo Forge. Charley's older sister, Emma Matilda Gorgas, had married an able man, and Weaver very much wanted his niece and her husband at the forge. Emma's husband was Daniel Charles Elliott Brady, thirty-five in 1856, an aspiring Philadelphia banker. He and Emma were comfortably settled there, surrounded by their own families, and they had started a family of their own. Their daughter, Anne Gertrude Brady, would turn eight in 1856, and they had two sons, Charles Patrick Augustus Brady, born in 1850, and William Weaver Brady, born three years later.[6]

It was one thing for Weaver to talk a young bachelor like Charley Gorgas into moving to Virginia; in that case he needed only to hold out the prospect of a solid business opportunity. It was quite another matter to persuade Daniel and Emma Brady to leave Pennsylvania. But Weaver was a determined man when he set his mind on something, and his mind was made up about the Bradys.

Weaver revealed a good deal about himself in his letters to his niece and her husband. He did not tell the Bradys everything, to be sure. He was too proud and private a person for that, but he probably told them as much as he told anyone, even though they sometimes had to read between the lines to grasp his full meaning. He wrote to them about things that mattered deeply to him and that lay near the core of his emotional being—about his hopes, his fears, his growing physical infirmities, and his mounting loneliness at Buffalo Forge in the years following the death of his wife. Weaver had married late in life; he was forty-nine years old when he and a Philadelphia widow named Elizabeth Newkirk Woodman were married in 1830. The marriage had not been a happy one. She was forty-five at the time of their wedding, they had had no children, and she died in 1850 after a long illness.[7] Clearly Daniel and Emma Brady were dear to him, and it is just as clear that "Uncle William," as they both called him, meant a great deal to the Bradys. The name of their youngest child spoke eloquently enough to that point. Weaver would not rest easy until they were all at Buffalo Forge and Daniel Brady was supervising things there.

"I am old, all but 75—yet 'old *Time*' may be lenient and favor me," Weaver had written Brady in the summer of 1855; "it is one of those cases in which there is no certainty as to the time. One thing is, however, certain, that old people must depart *ere long.*" He asked Brady to "ascertain as to Emma's wishes," to find out if "she could be content to spend her days at this place." This was a critical consideration for Weaver, because he wanted the Bradys to stay if they came. He recognized that "happiness cannot exist without contentment," and he had no desire "to make your family less happy." If it turned out that Emma was discontented in Virginia, they could sell out and leave after his death, "but that would not be carrying out my wishes," Weaver wrote. It was all-important to him that he know how they both felt before he was gone. That was the heart of the matter, and he made no attempt to conceal the reason he was so consumed about their staying. "The great object with me is, that my servants shall remain where they are, and have humane masters," he said simply. "This point is the only difficulty on my mind in relation to my Estate. Giving them their freedom, I am satisfied, would not benefit them as much as having good masters, and remain where they are. You I presume understand my intentions," he told Brady, "—and if you get here I hope they will be carried out. The means will be given you to do so."[8]

His intent was clear. If they would move to the Valley and would promise to keep the slave community together at Buffalo Forge, the Bradys would be William Weaver's principal heirs.

Even so, it was not an easy decision for Daniel and Emma Brady to make. Daniel's banking partnership in Philadelphia was doing well at that point, and he and Emma had recently bought a house in the city. Brady did not feel he could leave in 1855, but Weaver would not give up. He was growing increasingly anxious about his health, and there was, in fact, cause for concern. "Last week in walking to the office, I was very near falling down the steps at the Shoe Shop, and if I had fell [*sic*], it would have been head foremost," he reported to the Bradys in February 1856. "The result in all probability would have been fatal. It was," he admitted, "a narrow escape. I am getting rather old, to attend to the out door business."[9] He had not been able to give affairs at Buffalo Forge his usual attention, obviously a painful experience for him. "I have kept close quarters this winter—on 8th March will be my birth day . . . I will then be 75 years old," he wrote Brady a week later. "It is time to take things easy—which I must do if even property suffers."[10]

Brady, very worried about Weaver, had pressed him for details on his potentially dangerous accident. It was not because his walkway had been neglected or because his sight was failing, Weaver had replied. "It was owing to old age—I was near stumbling owing to a misstep. I have had a hand railing put up, and take care to use it."[11] Weaver knew that death could not be too far off. It did not seem to frighten him, but he wanted to be certain that the enterprise to which he had devoted most of his life would be in good hands after he was gone.

Weaver was also a lonely man. The spacious rooms of his imposing house were empty and silent most of the time. House servants attended to him, of course, but they were not family. "You seem to think your children will be too troublesome to me," he told Emma Brady in March 1856. "You need apprehend no danger on that score. The house is large. In day time I have some business to attend to—and at Night, like all elderly persons, I go to bed. So far from being annoyed, I expect to have a pleasure in your company," he assured her. "I have been set on it for some time—and you must not disappoint me. Just rent your House as soon as you can, and let Dear Daniel bring you to this place."[12]

Late in 1857, the Bradys closed up their affairs in Pennsylvania and moved to Buffalo Forge. Their love for Weaver and concern for his health—and the prospect that Buffalo Forge would someday be theirs—would have been on their minds as they made their decision to come south, but other factors probably influenced them as well. Daniel Brady's banking business had recently suffered some serious reverses, and he was no longer as committed to his partnership in Philadelphia. He and Emma had also experienced tragedy in their own family. Their young son, two-and-a-half-year-old William Weaver Brady, died in the spring of 1856. They had given their next baby the same name, but he had died the same day he was born in August 1857.[13] Perhaps the loss of these boys had a great deal to do with their feeling that it was time to start a new life in the Valley of Virginia. When Daniel, Emma, nine-year-old Anne, and seven-year-old Pat Brady arrived at Buffalo Forge during the latter part of 1857, they had come to stay.

At last, in 1858, Weaver had things lined up the way he wanted them. Charley Gorgas would be managing Etna Furnace, and Daniel Brady would be supervising day-to-day affairs at the forge and the farms. The Bradys' coming must have brought an enormous sense of relief to Weaver, something of that inner peace and security he had been seeking so anxiously these past few years.

The arrival of the Bradys was, if anything, even more important to William Weaver's slaves. It must have relieved much of the fear that would have been building in the quarters as Weaver's age advanced and his health deteriorated. Now there was a clear prospect that the Buffalo Forge slave community would remain intact after Weaver's death, that families would not be broken and friends separated by a division of the master's estate.

Weaver obviously had not consulted his slaves about what arrangements they would prefer. If he had, no doubt he would not have continued to believe that they would rather have "humane masters" to succeed him than to have their freedom. But aside from manumission, there was probably nothing more important to these black men and women than the strong probability that they could all "remain where they are," as Weaver had expressed it earlier, after he was gone. The appearance of the Bradys at Buffalo Forge (and the fact that they already had a son, young Pat, who might inherit the place eventually) would have been the cause for some quiet rejoicing in the slave cabins that dotted the landscape around Weaver's stately residence.

Let the historian celebrate the coming of the Bradys as well. Daniel Brady was a remarkably careful and devoted keeper of records. Soon after his arrival, he began a daily journal noting the work routine for each day—what the weather was like, which slaves were doing what jobs, how much work they did, who was sick, who was pretending to be sick. If a freshet interrupted forge operations or washed out roads and fences, if a snowstorm hit and prevented work, that information also went into his journal. The result is a running description of slave activities at Buffalo Forge that fills three neatly written volumes and covers a span of over seven years, from March 1858 to June 1865.[14] These years, perhaps the most critical in the entire history of the slave South, are the ones through which we can follow the lives of the Buffalo Forge slaves in the greatest and most elaborate detail.

Brady's initial inspection of the forge property would have revealed a well-ordered and self-sufficient community. Weaver's fields yielded large crops of wheat, corn, oats, buckwheat, and rye, all grown and harvested by slave labor. The slaves also raised more than enough hay, clover, and timothy grass to maintain the numerous draft animals needed for farm and forge work. Two large, water-powered mills—a grist mill for corn and a merchant mill for wheat—ground ample cornmeal to feed Weaver's slave force and a large quantity of top-grade flour for sale in the Richmond market. Weaver kept extensive herds of cattle, pigs, and sheep at Buffalo Forge, and he supplemented his own stock with purchases from the Kentucky drovers who worked their way down the Valley every year. Each winter, the slaves would slaughter enough hogs and cattle to fill the big smokehouse and provide a full year's meat rations for the entire population at Buffalo Forge. The gardens produced lettuce, peas, potatoes, and asparagus in abundance. Apples, peaches, plums, cherries, gooseberries, and red currants grew in Weaver's orchards and berry fields.[15] What Weaver could not, or chose not to, produce—things like tobacco, sugar, bolts of cloth, and articles of ready-made clothing—was available at his own well-stocked store at Buffalo Forge. A harness and shoe shop (the spot where Weaver almost fell to serious injury), a carpenter shop, a sawmill, and a large blacksmith shop, all manned by slave workers, provided a variety of important and essential services. Standing in the midst of these buildings was Weaver's office, where he had always gone to post the books, to talk to local customers about iron sales, and to supervise the myriad operations of each day. But now, in 1858, Daniel Brady would be sitting in that office, making out the accounts and religiously filling page after page of his journal with the daily round of events that made up the life of Buffalo Forge.

Brady would have noticed quickly that there was no slave quarter as such. The slaves' cabins, most of them sturdily built log structures, were scattered randomly around the property. Some stood across Buffalo Creek, the wide, swift-flowing stream that cut through Weaver's lands and gave the forge its name. Two substantial brick slave quarters—one a double cabin, the other a single—were slated to go up in 1858 in back of Weaver's residence, probably to house the families which provided the bulk of his cooks, house servants, and dairymaids. This dispersed slave housing arrangement might have struck some whites as a dangerous practice, one that would make supervision more difficult and permit too much clandestine movement from cabin to cabin. But it really had not been necessary to cluster all the cabins together in one place. There is a hill at Buffalo Forge that commands a view of the entire complex. On that hill William Weaver's home stood like a stone sentinel, watching over the generations of black people who lived and worked and died there as slaves.

The hub of this varied agricultural and industrial enterprise was the forge itself, a solid stone building located on the banks of Buffalo Creek. As Daniel Brady entered the forge, he would have seen an impressive, even awesome, sight: charcoal fires burning at white heat, the slave refiner and his underhand working bars of pig iron in those fires until the iron turned into a ball of glowing, pasty metal. The refiner would then sling this semi-molten mass of iron onto his anvil, where it was pounded and shaped under the rhythmic blows of the huge, water-powered hammer. Through successive reheatings and poundings, the refiner removed enough of the impurities in the pig iron to work it into something called an "anchony."[16] Turning out high-quality anchonies was the most important single job in the forge, and Sam Williams was the man responsible for that undertaking.

Weaver himself described an anchony in a court deposition he gave in 1840. It was a piece of malleable iron about six inches square weighing between 80 and 150 pounds, "with a blade of iron about the length of my cane," Weaver noted (his cane measured thirty-two inches); "one end of

the blade has what is called the *tail end,* which contains iron enough generally to make a shovel mould, and out of which shovel moulds are generally
made."[17]

Producing this rather strange-looking item was no easy task. The key
point in the refining process was knowing exactly when the pig iron heating in the fire in the refinery (also referred to as the "finery") had reached
the right temperature and consistency for pounding and shaping on the
anvil block. Bringing the pig iron "to nature," as this was called, was the
most difficult forge skill to learn, and it could only be acquired by many
months of apprenticeship to a master refiner.[18] Sam Williams had entered
such an apprenticeship at Buffalo Forge back in 1838, as a young man of
eighteen. Now, twenty years later, he was William Weaver's master refiner
and the most valued slave hand on the place. Henry Towles, his underhand, was skilled enough to take over the hammer if, for some reason, Sam
could not work. When that happened, Jim Garland, a swing hand who
alternated between agricultural and forge work, usually came in from the
fields to help Towles.[19] In that way, the vital task of making anchonies
could go on even if one of the usual crew happened to be off the job.

Pounding out anchonies was the most critical part of the forge operation,
but it was only the first half of the manufacturing process. The final stage
came when a second group of operatives, the hammermen, reheated the
anchonies and worked them at another forge called a chaffery. The hammermen produced iron bars of various standard shapes, sizes, and
lengths—"merchant bars," in the language of the iron trade—which would
be shipped to the Richmond and Lynchburg markets and sold. Merchant
bars kept the wheels of agriculture turning. Blacksmiths hammered these
bars into the things needed on or off the farm that had to be made out of
iron: horse and mule shoes, wagon tires, nails, tools, agricultural implements, and the like.[20]

The slave hammermen at Buffalo Forge when Brady arrived in Virginia
were an experienced pair. Tooler, the principal hammerman, and Harry
Hunt, Jr., his underhand, had worked together for years. As was the case
with Sam Williams and Henry Towles, there was a swing hand who could
relieve them in an emergency. Henry Matthews, one of the most versatile
of Weaver's slaves, could fill in as a hammerman, a blacksmith, a field hand,
or as a substitute for the forge carpenter. The regular forge carpenter in
1858 was Tooler's brother, Joe, who also happened to be the slave preacher
at Buffalo Forge.[21]

One more slave played an important role in Weaver's forge operations
in the late 1850s. Garland Thompson, a teamster, kept the refinery and
chaffery fires stocked with their daily supplies of charcoal. Thompson's

team of six sturdy mules and his big charcoal wagon were a regular sight on the road to the mountain coaling grounds, across North River, some five or six miles east of Buffalo Forge.[22]

These slave workers had made Buffalo Forge merchant bar a premium article in the Virginia iron trade. In many ways, the "W" hallmark which Weaver's iron carried to market stood more for Sam Williams and his forge crew than it did for the name of their master.[23] These black men would have a great deal to do with Daniel Brady's success or failure as the new manager of Buffalo Forge. He knew it, and, one surmises, so did they. It was a lesson William Weaver had learned a long time ago.

PART I

THE
MASTER

1

———◆———

William Weaver,
Pennsylvanian

William Weaver's character was forged in the crucible of German pietism, a strange beginning for a man who would become one of the largest slaveowners in the Valley of Virginia.

William's family was at the center of one of the most demanding religious traditions of eighteenth-century America. His father, Adam Weaver, and his mother, Hannah Mack Weaver, were both members of the zealous German Baptist sect known as the Dunkers. Hannah's grandfather, the Reverend Alexander Mack, had founded the faith in Germany and in 1729 had led a major migration of Dunker families to the Germantown area of Pennsylvania. Hannah's father, Alexander Mack, Jr., usually called Sander, had taken over the leadership of the Germantown Dunkers in 1749, several years after his father's death.[1]

Under the guidance of these two men, the strongly pietistic church set and maintained rigorous standards of belief and behavior. The Dunkers basically ascribed to the view that the New Testament should be taken literally as a guide to both religious practice and everyday life. They embraced a number of rites mentioned in the Bible and associated with early Christianity—foot-washing, the love feast, anointing the sick with oil, and greeting fellow church members with the kiss of love. They referred to each other as "brother" and "sister," titles which reflected their belief in universal Christian brotherhood. Their distinctive baptismal procedure, immersion by three separate forward actions in a flowing stream, gave the Dunkers their popular name.

Being a Dunker, however, meant much more than trine immersion and the acceptance of the rites of primitive Christianity. It also meant a rigidly ascetic way of life. Clothes should be of the plainest sort. Alcohol and tobacco should never be used, and worldly amusements shunned. Luxury in all its forms should be conscientiously avoided. Since the New Testament served as their law, the Dunkers insisted on total separation of church and state, would not engage in any type of litigation in the civil courts, and were totally committed to the ideal of peace. Like the Quakers, they refused to take oaths or fight in wars. And again like the Quakers, they were unalterably opposed to the institution of slavery.[2]

Into this religious tradition William Weaver was born on March 8, 1781. His birth took place on the family farm near Flourtown, Pennsylvania, in the heart of the area where the Dunkers had planted their faith in America. He was the third child born to Adam and Hannah Mack Weaver. Eventually the family would grow to ten children, four boys and six girls.[3]

William grew to manhood on this farm. Unfortunately we know little about this period of his life, but a strict upbringing stressing God's ever-watchful eye and emphasizing the virtues of thrift and hard work was most likely the experience of all the Weaver children. Certainly that sort of childhood is suggested by the description of William's father that has been passed down within the family. Adam Weaver was "a stern, harsh, and unsympathetic man" according to a relative who recorded the Weaver genealogy in the late nineteenth century.[4] This commentator was silent on the personal qualities of Weaver's mother, but given what we know about his father's character and the family's religious persuasion, it is a safe assumption that young William was not overly indulged as a child.

The anonymous family historian who gave us an unflattering portrait of Adam Weaver also provided the few glimpses we have of William's emerging personality. He was described as "energetic and aggressive from boyhood up," and "so determined . . . to learn that he carried his book with him to the field and in intervals of rest of the plow or otherwise, he would devote himself to it." Industry and seriousness of purpose would have been expected of a boy growing up in a Dunker home, but William seems to have displayed these qualities with exceptional zeal, so much so that his "thrift and economy" rendered him "quite independent" while he was still a relatively young man.[5] Intelligence, energy, aggressiveness, ambition, thriftiness, an acquisitive nature, and a "habit of *taking time by the forelock,*" as one of Weaver's business correspondents would later put it, were all qualities Virginians would come to know, respect, and sometimes fear in William Weaver.[6]

He also grew into a strikingly handsome man. Dark brown hair, a strong jaw, and the straight line of his prominent nose all complemented his eyes, light blue in color, which remained clear and arresting throughout his long life.

Apparently William never joined the church his family had done so much to establish in America. No mention of his membership appears in the family recordbook. There is no way to know why William was not moved to adopt the faith of his fathers, but a possible reason is suggested by the circumstances surrounding the marriage of his parents.

The family history compiled around 1890, simply stating that Adam Weaver and Hannah Mack were married, gives no date for this event. A church historian writing in the same decade, however, listed August 27, 1775, as the day of their marriage, but something was seriously amiss at the time of their union.[7] Hannah Mack was a baptized member of the Dunker church when they married. Adam Weaver was not. So she broke the strict Dunker rule against marrying outside the faith. And that was not the worst of it. Apparently the two young people had managed to meet outside the vigilant gaze of Hannah's father. The result was a serious violation of church conduct, most likely the sin of fornication.

The evidence for this conclusion is indirect and is contained in a single letter Hannah's father, Sander Mack, wrote to a close friend and fellow church member, John Preisz, on February 14, 1776. It is clear from this document that the actions of Hannah and, to a lesser extent, her sister Sarah had caused Sander Mack enormous distress. Preisz had heard something of the family's troubles and had written Sander a comforting letter. In reply, Mack thanked him warmly for his sympathy and told Preisz "it moved me very much that you were made so sorrowful on account of me and my children." Mack then told Preisz some, but not all, details of the trouble. "It is true, my Hannah had thought at first that her sin was not so great because they had been engaged never to leave each other, and both she and her husband indeed intend to prove this," he wrote. "However, she realizes her error and recognizes her misdeed," Mack continued. "She wants me to ask you especially for your forgiveness as she has always held a special love for you, because she believed that you feared the Lord. She would be especially grateful if you prayed to the Lord for her that He might have mercy on her in her condition," Mack told his friend.

Hannah's sister Sarah had also caused the family much anguish, Mack went on, but she had "been spared the kind of shame my Hannah bears." Sarah, like her sister, had married outside the church and she had also broken Dunker rules by obtaining a marriage license and by marrying an apprentice without his master's knowledge or consent. As a consequence, she had been excluded from Communion and from the kiss of love. "My Hannah, however, has been disciplined even more severely, so that we do not even eat with her," Mack informed his friend. "Yet most of the [church] members said that they would be more willing to accept her again if she returned in repentance, in fact they would be more willing to accept her again than they were ready to expell her." Hannah Mack Weaver, in short, had suffered the pain of expulsion from the church and ostracism by her own family for her unnamed sin. Her plea that John Preisz pray for her in the hope that the Lord "might have mercy on her in her condition" reveals the depth of the pain she felt over what had happened to her.[8]

Adam and Hannah Weaver's first child, Alexander, named after Hannah's father, was born June 18, 1776. If Adam and Hannah were indeed married on August 27, 1775, the baby was not conceived out of wedlock. Hannah was subsequently readmitted to both the church and the good graces of her family, presumably as a result of her repentance, and her husband was baptized into the faith in 1783.[9] Yet it is clear that the punishment she received and the sense of shame she had experienced had caused Hannah Mack Weaver great suffering five years before William, her third child and her third son, was born in 1781.

Whether any of this was subsequently learned by William is impossible to say. Perhaps something was revealed during the tragic times when his two older brothers died in the 1790s. John Weaver, born in 1778, died in 1791 when William was ten years old; Alexander, the firstborn, died in 1795 when William was fourteen.[10] If William did come to know something of the troubles surrounding the early period of his parents' life together and of the initial reaction of both church and family to his mother's circumstances, it might well have influenced his attitude toward the stern piety of the Dunker faith.

Although William lived with his parents at Flourtown until his late twenties, he was not content to remain a farmer. He took up a number of occupations in and around Germantown—merchant, miller, textile manufacturer—and seemed to do well at all of them. As a result, he began accumulating enough surplus capital to take advantage of new business opportunities as they arose. When the War of 1812 broke out, William had sufficient means at his command to try his hand at such speculative ventures as running the British naval blockade and iron manufacturing in the Valley of Virginia.

Weaver had been looking for a chance to get into the iron business for some time. As early as 1811, he had tried to buy an ironworks in Pennsylvania at auction. His bid was too low, but his presence at this sale was to play an important role in determining his future. Another unsuccessful bidder for this same property was a Philadelphia merchant named Thomas Mayburry. Mayburry, whose father and grandfather had been prominent Pennsylvania ironmasters, had previously been engaged in iron manufacturing for a short while in Maryland, and he was eager to reenter the business. Weaver and Mayburry did not know each other in 1811, but in 1814 the two bachelors happened to take up lodgings in the same Philadelphia boardinghouse. They recognized one another from the auction three years before. Mayburry was fifty-four in 1814 and Weaver thirty-three, but the difference in age did not prevent them from striking up an acquaintance. They "occasionally conversed together upon the subject of what had occurred at the aforesaid sale," Mayburry later wrote, and "mutually expressed their desire to become the proprietors of iron works."[11] In July 1814, the opportunity came.

Thomas Mayburry's contacts were the key. Five years earlier he and his brother Willoughby had gone to Virginia to look at various iron establishments. They bought no property on this trip, but one of the enterprises they examined was a blast furnace and forge operation owned by a Valley ironmaster named William Wilson. Wilson had erected a forge on a sixty-five-acre tract of timber and farm land in Rockbridge County. This property, known as Union Forge (Weaver would subsequently change the name to Buffalo Forge), stood alongside Buffalo Creek and was about nine miles southeast of Lexington. Wilson also owned two charcoal blast furnaces, named Etna and Retreat, and over 6,000 acres of ore and woodland approximately seventeen miles southwest of Union Forge in neighboring Botetourt County. Wilson was eager to sell, but the Mayburry brothers were wary. Etna Furnace was in serious disrepair, and Retreat Furnace had inadequate waterpower. "Wilson with much apparent candor admitted at that time that the water was not sufficient," Willoughby Mayburry later reported, but the Virginia ironmaster claimed that the summer had been exceptionally dry and that plenty of water would be available to run the furnace by fall. The Mayburrys, unconvinced, left the area the next day.[12]

Wilson persisted. Over the next several years, he dispatched a number of letters to Pennsylvania urging Mayburry and his brother to reconsider. He had brought water from a second stream to Retreat through pipes, he told them, and now the power to operate the furnace was more than ample. One of these letters reached Thomas Mayburry at the Philadelphia boarding-house in the summer of 1814.

Mayburry told Weaver about Wilson's ironworks, and the two men decided to go to Virginia to inspect the property. If they liked what they saw, they agreed to form a partnership, buy the forge and the two blast furnaces, and go into the iron business together.

When they arrived in the Valley in late July, they should have suspected that William Wilson's assurances about the value of his works and the sufficiency of waterpower at Retreat were somewhat exaggerated. Wilson's creditors had had him thrown into debtor's prison. His son John was not incarcerated, however, and he took Mayburry and Weaver on a tour of the property. According to Mayburry's account, Weaver thought the Wilsons had no idea of the true value of their works. "Weaver was much more intent upon the purchase" than he was, Mayburry subsequently claimed, and Weaver "observed . . . in conference that the price which Wilson asked, $27,500, was a mere *bagatelle*." Mayburry may have had his reservations about the deal, as he later insisted, but whatever doubts he had did not hold him back on that July day in 1814. He and Weaver formed a verbal partnership on the spot and agreed to buy the property at Wilson's price.[13]

The purchase agreement, signed on July 30, 1814, revealed clearly that the new firm of Mayburry & Weaver expected to make some quick money in Virginia. With a war on, with iron prices soaring, and with the British blockade still in effect, a successful blast at Retreat Furnace and a vigorous push at Union Forge would surely pay rich and immediate dividends. Weaver and his partner were to pay only $5,000 down, with the remainder of the $27,500 purchase price coming in four annual installments beginning January 1, 1815.[14] As Mayburry put it, he and Weaver figured "that it would not be necessary to raise between them more than the two first payments for the property purchased . . . & $10,000 more for the operations of the establishment, & that out of the profits of the concern they would be enabled to pay off the balance of the purchase money, as it should fall due." Thus, "the sum of $20,000 was . . . supposed to be the requisite amount of advances," with each partner responsible for coming up with half of that amount. Wilson would turn the property over to them on September 1, 1814. That should leave plenty of time for Mayburry & Weaver to get a good supply of pig iron out of Retreat Furnace and then manufacture a substantial amount of bar iron at Union Forge before their next payment to Wilson fell due on January 1, 1815.[15]

On their way back to Pennsylvania, Weaver and Mayburry went through western Maryland to visit Mayburry's brother Willoughby. Willoughby Mayburry owned the Catoctin Furnace in Frederick County, a convenient stopover on their return journey to Philadelphia. They "informed me that they had made a purchase of William Wilson," Willoughby wrote several years later. "I immediately asked them about the water at Retreat Furnace, [and] they replied that she was not in Blast, but that Wilson assured them that by Fall, there would be plenty of water and that they could keep the Furnace in Blast for eight or nine months," he continued. "I laughed at them," Willoughby recalled, "and observed there never was nor never would be water sufficient for even three or four months much less eight or nine."[16]

William Weaver was not a man who enjoyed being ridiculed, and Willoughby Mayburry's laugh turned out to be a very costly one for him. Several years later, Weaver purchased a $4,000 mortgage on the Catoctin Furnace that Willoughby had taken out in Philadelphia. When Weaver subsequently needed money to keep the Virginia enterprise afloat, he foreclosed on this mortgage and forced Willoughby to auction off his ironworks at public sale.[17]

Unfortunately for Weaver and Thomas Mayburry, Willoughby's prediction regarding the waterpower available at Retreat Furnace turned out to be remarkably accurate.

Initially both partners planned to return to Virginia in the fall of 1814, but Weaver was delayed for several weeks in Philadelphia so Mayburry went on alone. He began laying in provisions and accumulating iron ore, charcoal, and limestone at Retreat Furnace and, in his own view, "had progressed very considerably in preparations for a blast" when he was forced to go back to Pennsylvania. Mayburry was having trouble raising his share of the firm's capital, and he thought a trip home necessary. So in December 1814, Weaver went south to replace him at the furnace.[18]

Early the next year, on February 1, 1815, Weaver put Retreat in blast. "After blowing a few days she began to chill," Weaver wrote, and there was no question as to the cause. The "want of water" made it impossible "to give her as much blast as was required," and as a consequence temperatures could not be kept hot enough in the interior of the furnace to make iron. "I immediately sent my compliments to Mr. Wilson and requested his attendance at the Furnace," Weaver reported. Although Wilson "had promised to render us every service in his power" and had long since been released from jail, not surprisingly "he never came near" the furnace.[19] Mayburry was quite right when he referred to this initial blast at Retreat as "a miserable one." It produced only twenty-eight tons of pig iron, a fraction of what the furnace should have made, and, even worse, it resulted in "the loss of several thousand dollars."[20]

Suddenly, Mayburry & Weaver's dreams of quick profits in the Valley evaporated. The two partners were in the unenviable position of owing William Wilson a sizable sum without any local means of making money. They were stuck with one furnace, Retreat, which lacked adequate water-power and another, Etna, which was, in Weaver's words, "in a very dilapidated condition and had not been worked for a number of years." Yet the lack of water at Retreat left them no options; if they were going to manufacture iron in Virginia and settle their debt with Wilson, they would have to rebuild Etna Furnace.[21]

Weaver began reconstruction at once, but it was an expensive and time-consuming process. Just about the only thing left standing at Etna was the furnace stack itself. Before pig iron could be produced there, Weaver would have to put in a new dam, a new bellows, bellows wheel, and bellows house, a coal house, a furnace house, a carpenter shop, a sawmill, new stables, and make various and sundry other repairs, including a massive wooden sluice to bring sufficient waterpower to the furnace.[22]

This work would require a greatly expanded labor force. Apparently Weaver had been using a mixed gang of free and slave workers left over from Wilson's management of Retreat. We cannot be sure of the exact composition of the labor force at this time because most of the records dealing with Mayburry & Weaver's early furnace operations in Virginia have not survived. It is clear, however, that Weaver's initial experience with white workers in the Valley had been something less than satisfactory. He had not been at Retreat very long before he perceived "that no reliance could be placed in the free White laborers who are employed about Iron Works in this country." They were "very poor" workmen in Weaver's view, and in "moments of the greatest pressure & necessity, the proprietor must either make them advances which they will never repay, or they leave his service to the ruin of his business."[23] The alternative, of course, was slave labor.

Weaver seems to have had no qualms about using slaves. His Dunker upbringing inhibited him not at all when it came to the prosperity, if not indeed the financial survival, of his Virginia enterprise. His idea was for the firm of Mayburry & Weaver to begin buying slave workers at once. If each partner contributed an additional $5,000, they could start purchasing key laborers immediately. Annual additions to their work force could be made out of future profits, and eventually a full gang of skilled furnace and forge hands could be assembled. The firm would then be completely independent of free workers and, just as important, he and Mayburry would have acquired an exceedingly valuable species of property.[24]

The plan never got off the ground. Weaver later insisted that Mayburry opposed the idea out of "conscientious motives."[25] In answer, Mayburry insisted just as vigorously that he entertained no "such refined notions" with regard to slaveholding. Mayburry's view was "that slavery in any country is a great evil, & repugnant to enlarged views of moral propriety," but he also believed "that those proprietors of landed estates who reside in a slave country cannot avoid a participation in the general wrong, nor extend any relief to the unfortunate beings who are subjected to the deprivation of liberty by refusing to hold them as property."[26] In other words, given the sad presence of the immoral institution, it was perfectly all right to use it for all it was worth, particularly since no humanitarian purpose would be served by abstaining from slaveownership and business would suffer if one did. Mayburry probably refused to join with Weaver in the purchase scheme simply because he did not have the $5,000 to contribute to it. As events soon demonstrated, Mayburry was not the monied capitalist Weaver assumed him to be.

Without an adequate fund to buy slave workers, Weaver had to hire them. A well-established hiring market existed for surplus slave labor in the counties east of the Blue Ridge. Weaver needed to tap this market extensively in order to get Etna Furnace rebuilt and into production. The construction work called for masons, carpenters, teamsters, and general laborers. Once the furnace was ready for blast, a sizable number of workers would be required for a variety of critical jobs, and almost all these hands would have to be slaves. That was the only way Weaver could avoid the slipshod work and extortion he felt his white laborers had inflicted on him during his first season in Virginia.

Weaver had moderate success obtaining slave workers during a hiring trip in late 1814 and early 1815. He managed to secure approximately thirty slaves, primarily from the Lynchburg area and from Pittsylvania County in the tobacco-growing region along the North Carolina border. Relying primarily on these laborers, he plunged into rebuilding Etna Furnace. He began a new dam across Purgatory Creek, the stream that supplied waterpower to the furnace, he started construction of the huge wooden trunk needed to carry water from the dam to the furnace site, and he put men to work on the various buildings and fixtures that had to go up before Etna could return to production.[27]

Weaver remained at the furnace supervising this work until the summer of 1815. In July of that year, he had to return to Pennsylvania to attend to pressing family and business matters. His father was seriously ill, and his various enterprises in and around Philadelphia had suffered during his absence. It was also becoming increasingly obvious that more money would have to be pumped into the Virginia operation. Mayburry was still well short of his expected contribution to the firm's capital, and that left the financial burden squarely on Weaver's shoulders. Mayburry & Weaver had been able to put off the January 1815 payment to Wilson because Wilson had not been able to obtain a clear title to the forge tract. There was no way of knowing when Wilson might be able to rectify this difficulty, however, and when he did, they would have to come up with the $5,000 due him. They also needed funds to tide them over until their furnace and forge could start earning them some sort of return on their already sizable investment. The new construction took money, and supplies had to be purchased to maintain their workers. Payment for the hire of their slave hands would not be due until the end of the year, but at that time the masters would have to be paid in full and in cash. Thus, for a variety of reasons, Weaver felt it was mandatory for him to go back to Philadelphia in July and for Mayburry to take over for him at Etna. He planned to rejoin his partner in Virginia as soon as he could.[28]

But eight years passed before Weaver got back to Virginia for much more than a brief visit. Growing family responsibilities held him in the North. In 1813, Weaver's sister Margaret, two years younger than he, had been abandoned by her husband. Margaret Weaver Davis had five children, two boys and three girls, and her youngest daughter was less than a year old when her husband, the bankrupt Stephen Davis, deserted the family. William Weaver, in his early thirties and already the most successful of the Weaver children, immediately assumed responsibility for Margaret and her family. He paid for the children's education and continued to support the family for a number of years.[29] In the late 1820s, he would bring Margaret's two sons, William Weaver Davis and Abram Weaver Davis, to Virginia and launch them on what turned out to be turbulent careers as Rockbridge County ironmasters.

Margaret's difficulties were only the start of a period of anguish for the Weaver family and mounting personal obligations for William. In 1815, his parents were both in failing health, and William's return from Virginia in July of that year preceded his father's death by only a matter of weeks. Adam Weaver died on August 30, 1815. Less than eight months later, on April 6, 1816, Hannah Mack Weaver died. And the following year, William's only surviving brother, Abraham, passed away. The death of Abraham Weaver, who was only thirty-two, left William as the sole surviving male in his immediate family. William, unmarried at thirty-six, became the executor of Abraham's estate and the guardian of his brother's two sons. Thus between 1813 and 1817, the period in which he and Mayburry were inaugurating their Virginia enterprise, William acquired seven wards and became the head of his family, a family which now consisted of himself and six sisters, two of whom were still unmarried in 1817.[30]

Even so, Weaver by no means neglected the Virginia ironworks. One step in particular proved to be exceedingly important in determining the future course of his affairs in the Valley.

In October 1815, Weaver bought his first slaves. Mayburry had written early that month to tell him that John S. Wilson, William Wilson's son, would probably be coming up to Philadelphia to make Weaver a proposition. Young Wilson had apparently hired a number of slaves to Mayburry & Weaver to help meet the firm's labor needs at Etna Furnace and Union Forge in 1815. John Wilson subsequently told Mayburry that he was willing to sell some of them, and he and Mayburry had been haggling over the price. Wilson had offered Mayburry a slave woman named Mary and her two youngest daughters for $700.[31] Mayburry replied that $600 was his top price for the woman and the two children. Wilson soon grew tired of dickering with Mayburry and decided he would be better off talking to the partner who obviously controlled the firm's finances. In late October, John Wilson traveled north to Philadelphia to talk to William Weaver.

Weaver might have known the slaves under discussion through his six-month tour supervising operations in Virginia between December 1814 and July 1815. It is highly unlikely that Weaver would have bought any slaves sight unseen, particularly given the amount of money he and Wilson were discussing. Weaver's acquaintance with Wilson's servants is also suggested by the fact that Weaver was willing to go well beyond the limits of the deal Wilson had originally proposed to Mayburry in Virginia.

On October 24, 1815, Wilson and Weaver completed their negotiations. Weaver agreed to pay $3,200 for eleven slaves divided into two quite distinct groups. The first parcel consisted of a valuable ironworker, his wife, and their four sons. This family had not come up in Wilson's earlier discussions with Mayburry, but Weaver was clearly out to obtain furnace and forge hands, and he apparently persuaded Wilson to part with these six slaves. The man, named Tooler, was about forty years old, and he possessed a wide range of ironworking skills. Rebecca, his wife, came with him in the sale as did their four boys: Bill, seventeen; Robert, seven; Tooler, four; and Joe, two years of age.

The second group of slaves Weaver bought from Wilson contained no males at all. This parcel was made up of Mary and her four daughters (as opposed to the two girls Wilson had offered to sell Mayburry): Sally, thirteen; Amy, ten; Louisa, six; and Georgianna, two. The ages given on the bill of sale for Rebecca's and Mary's children were all approximations, a common practice in transactions of this sort. Since slave marriages had no standing in law, there was no requirement that births of slave children be legally registered. In the absence of such certification, the owner's estimations of the ages of the children were often given. "Sally aged about 13 years, Amey about 10 years, Louisa about 6 years, & Georgianna about 2 years" was the way this bill of sale read when John Wilson listed Mary's four daughters.[32]

The purchase of these slaves would be at least a modest beginning toward the solution of Mayburry & Weaver's labor needs in Virginia, but it was essentially a long-range remedy. Tooler and his oldest son, Bill, promised an immediate return to the firm since their services would be available without delay. Not for several years, however, could Robert, young Tooler, and Joe enter the work force. But since they were all boys, there was a strong likelihood that they would become productive ironworkers.

Such was not the case with Mary and her girls. Mary could cook, wash, and serve in the house, and she was in fact exceedingly valuable as a cook at Etna Furnace in the years ahead. Her daughters might help in the kitchen, act as nursemaids, or do various chores around the house until they grew old enough for full domestic work. But work at a blast furnace or forge was clearly beyond them physically. Raking leaves to cover smoldering hardwood at charcoal pits was about the only task slave women ever performed around ironworks in the antebellum South.

In acquiring Mary and her daughters, Weaver was looking toward the future needs of his ironmaking venture, but in a far different manner from the way he viewed the acquisition of Tooler and his family. Mary would provide his ironworks with a "breeding woman," to use a phrase Weaver himself employed on another occasion to describe a similar situation, and probably Mary's four daughters would bear children someday too.[33]

A "breeding woman" to Weaver meant a slave woman who had already borne children. It did not imply interference on Weaver's part with the marriage choices or the sex lives of his slaves. It did imply a careful eye set toward the future and knowledge that the natural increase of his slave force could be a vital element in the financial health of his Virginia operations, a return on invested capital that would occur in the normal course of slave life.

When Weaver bought Tooler, Rebecca, and their four sons, he was obviously maintaining the integrity of this slave family. Such was not necessarily the case, however, with Mary and her daughters. The bill of sale made no mention of Mary's husband, and there is no indication in the surviving records that he was ever acquired by either Weaver or Mayburry individually or by their firm. Yet Mary's continued presence at Etna Furnace may have kept her family intact as well. She probably lived at the furnace during the period when John Wilson was helping to manage his father's iron business, and her husband could have lived nearby or worked at the furnace regularly as a hireling. The evidence for this is indirect: After she was sold to Weaver, Mary gave birth to at least five more children, including twins who did not survive. These children were all born at Etna between 1816 and 1825.[34] So there is a fairly good chance that Mary's husband was able to maintain contact with his family at the furnace.

One thing is certain. In the years ahead, the eleven original "Wilson negroes," as Weaver and Mayburry referred to them, and their children, would provide the nucleus around which Weaver would build his extraordinarily able crew of black ironworkers. Sam Williams, master refiner, Henry Towles, his underhand, Tooler, the chief hammerman, Joe, the skilled forge carpenter, and Henry Matthews, forgeman, blacksmith, carpenter, and jack-of-all-trades at Buffalo Forge in 1858, were all there because Weaver had spent $3,200 on a black man, two black women, four black boys, and four black girls over forty years before. And there were almost two dozen other slaves at Buffalo Forge in the late 1850s who could also trace their ancestry directly back to the "Wilson negroes." In a life filled with successful deals, Weaver probably looked back on the purchase of these eleven slaves as one of the best bargains he ever made.

The agreement he struck with John Wilson in 1815 also revealed a good bit about the way Weaver did business. First of all, he did not pay for the slaves totally in cash. "I rec'd for the ... negroes a Whitmore patent still & fixtures valued at fifteen Hundred and seventy five dollars, and drafts on different Merchants in Philadelphia for about sixteen hundred and twenty five dollars," Wilson reported in 1825. "The stills I have never been able to sell although I have frequently offered them for seven Hundred dollars. They are at this time unsold in ... New Orleans," he added.[35] For Weaver, it was quite a bargain indeed.

There was another intriguing and even more revealing aspect to this 1815 purchase. When Weaver bought the slaves, he had the bill of sale made out to him personally rather than to the firm of Mayburry & Weaver. He did this, he assured Wilson at the time, because he thought Mayburry "might have some religious scruples" about owning slaves.[36] Weaver clearly had no such scruples, and Mayburry did not discover his partner's delicate concern for the health of his soul until 1823, eight years after the sale. In 1825 when Weaver moved to dissolve their partnership, he insisted that Mayburry surrender the entire Wilson slave force. To back up his claim, Weaver could show a bill of sale that gave him full and exclusive ownership of the original "Wilson negroes" and, as a consequence, all of their offspring as well.

Nothing is more indicative of the distance William Weaver had traveled from the fierce German Baptist piety of his family than his purchase of these slaves in October 1815. William's father, Adam, had been dead less than two months at the time of the sale, but his mother was still alive. Her death did not come until April of the following year. As subsequent events demonstrated, William made every effort to keep his purchase of these slaves a secret from the rest of his family. They might not see things as he saw them or understand his vulnerable labor situation in Virginia, the difficulties inherent in operating a profitable ironworks with free labor in a slave country. The Dunker stand against slavery was absolute. It allowed for no exceptional circumstances. Yet William felt no recorded twinges of conscience over ownership of the "Wilson negroes." As he so artfully told John Wilson, those sentiments were Mayburry's problem, not his. On the other hand, William did not want it known in Pennsylvania that he had become a slaveholder. It would do him no good at all if word got around Philadelphia that William Weaver, the grandson of Sander Mack and the great-grandson of Alexander Mack, the founder of the Dunker faith, now possessed human chattel.

2

Mayburry & Weaver:
Debt and
Disappointment

At the same time Weaver was becoming an absentee slaveowner, Thomas Mayburry was struggling to finish the renovations at Etna Furnace, make substantial repairs at Union Forge, and get both facilities into production. He had his hands full.

Etna, like Retreat, had a waterpower shortfall. Purgatory Creek had enough water, but unfortunately the stack itself stood on a site that made it difficult to get sufficient power to the furnace. Constructing the large sluice to correct this error was an extremely ambitious undertaking. As late as October 1815, the trunk remained unfinished. "The quantity of timber hauled for it exceeds all belief," Mayburry wrote Weaver, "enough to build a little *Town.*" Finally, by the end of the month, everything was completed, and on November 1, 1815, Etna was blown in.[1] After months of arduous work and the expenditure of thousands of unanticipated dollars, Mayburry & Weaver finally had a blast furnace back in production.

Etna Furnace in blast was a spectacular sight. The furnace itself was impressive enough—a massive stack built of roughly finished, rectangular-shaped pieces of limestone, each weighing several tons. It stood thirty-five feet high and had an interior nine feet across at its widest point. The process of blowing in started with slave workmen filling the furnace completely with charcoal. It was lighted at the top and took several days to burn to the bottom. When the fire reached the base of the furnace, slaves refilled the stack with charcoal and the fire gradually worked its way back up to the top. At this point, the furnace was charged, always from above, with measured quantities of iron ore, limestone, and charcoal, and the manufacture of iron began.

The burning charcoal supplied the heat needed to melt the ore, the limestone provided the flux that carried most of the impurities in the ore to the top of the mass of liquid iron, and molten iron gradually accumulated in a hearth at the base of the furnace. Blasts of air, needed to sustain temperatures high enough to melt the ore, were forced into the interior of the furnace by huge bellows operated by a waterwheel—thus the essential requirement of adequate waterpower at any furnace site. When enough molten iron settled in the hearth area, the furnace was tapped, usually twice a day, and the iron drawn off into sand molds and cast in one of two ways. Sometimes it was made directly into hollowware, items like skillets, pots, pans, kettles, and the like; more frequently, it was cast into pigs, which required further processing in a forge before they could be worked into usable articles (the term "pig" originated in the resemblance of the casting bed to a sow suckling her young). The refining and chaffery stages of the forge operation took out enough of the impurities present in the brittle pig iron to render the metal malleable, and therefore ready to be worked by a blacksmith into useful articles.

Once a furnace was blown in, it operated almost continuously, day and night, until the blast was completed. Blasts at southern furnaces frequently lasted for six to nine months, with stoppages normally occurring only when repairs were necessary or when the hired slave force returned home for the traditional Christmas holidays. Since farming operations were also conducted at most southern ironworks, including Mayburry & Weaver's newly acquired installations, a constant interchange of workers between industrial and agricultural tasks took place at furnaces and forges throughout the South and allowed ironmasters to employ their extensive labor force year-round.

Slave workers played a major role in practically every phase of pig iron production at Etna and throughout the South, from the initial construction of the stack to the completion of a successful blast. Slave masons often quarried, cut, and fitted the heavy blocks of limestone used to build the furnace. Slave carpenters and laborers erected furnace buildings from timber cut by slave woodchoppers and sawed into lumber at slave-manned mills. Slaves built the extensive dams required to obtain waterpower to run the furnace. Dam construction was a particularly difficult and demanding process, and slave dam builders usually received a daily whiskey ration for working in the cold, swift-running streams—one of the rare occasions in the antebellum South where slaves were voluntarily given alcohol by their employers.

Once the stack, dam, fixtures, and structures were all in place, slaves filled many important positions in the furnace labor force. Some white men were invariably present—the furnace manager, one or two clerks, and usually, but not always, the founder, who had responsibility for the day-to-day operation of the furnace itself (slave founders were not unknown at antebellum blast furnaces, but they were the exception rather than the rule in the Valley). The potters, who cast the hollowware, were often itinerant white workers who traveled from furnace to furnace and were employed when ironmasters wanted to turn out small, specialized types of castings.

In almost every other area of furnace work, however, black labor predominated: as keepers, the founder's principal assistants, who frequently kept the night watch and supervised furnace operations in the founder's absence (Tooler, one of the "Wilson negroes," was a keeper, which was undoubtedly the reason Weaver was so anxious to buy him in 1815); as fillers, who charged the furnace with its alternating, carefully measured layers of ore, limestone, and charcoal; as guttermen, who drew off the molten iron into the casting beds; as miners and ore pounders, who dug and blasted the ore and limestone flux and prepared them for the furnace; as choppers, who felled the trees and cut cord after cord of hardwood for the coaling pits; as colliers, who converted this wood into the thousands of bushels of charcoal required for a successful blast; as teamsters, who were skilled enough to handle the large teams and heavy wagons needed to haul charcoal, ore, and limestone over primitive roads to the furnace (Tooler's son Bill was a furnace teamster at Etna); and as furnace carpenters, pattern makers, blacksmiths, and general laborers.[2]

A furnace could be kept in operation with a relatively small slave force of twenty hands or so, but larger gangs of between fifty and one hundred slaves were more common. The length and success of a blast were directly related to its personnel and their skills.

Nothing proved the interdependency of Maybury & Weaver's fortunes and slave labor more than the closing of Etna Furnace at the end of 1815. The furnace had been blown in only on November 1, but even so Maybury shut it down in mid-December so that the slave hirelings could be home by Christmas Day.[3] Virtually all activity would cease at the furnace, and work could not be resumed until these, or other, slaves were hired for the next year's blast.

Christmas to New Year's Day was a customary holiday for almost all southern slaves, and ironworkers were no exception. It took the consent of both master and slave to keep a hired slave worker at a furnace over the Christmas break, and the agreement of both parties was not easy to come by. Masters wanted to see how their bondsmen had fared during the year, and slaves were eager to return home to be with their families and friends over the holiday season. So Mayburry had no choice but to close Etna down and hope the firm would be able to secure an adequate force for the year ahead.

As early as September 1815, Mayburry had begun pressing Weaver to return to Virginia for the traditional end-of-the-year hiring season. "Do not fail to be here in time sufficient to go after negroes," he urged. Weaver should be in the prime hiring area of Pittsylvania County by December 10 if possible, December 15 at the latest. "Bear in mind, and rest assured that it is all important to us—for without negroes we can do nothing here," he continued. Mayburry had heard rumors that another Valley ironmaster would bid to hire away some of their best workers. Weaver should reach the slaveowners in Pittsylvania earlier than the competition. "I am importunate on this subject because so much depends upon it," he added. "And if I were to go it would be like a stranger[,] the introduction and all the difficulties attendant to go through," he pointed out, whereas in Weaver's case "the ice is broke and you are known. . . . I therefore say again," Mayburry wrote in conclusion, "do not fail."[4]

Weaver agreed with Mayburry about the importance of acquiring an adequate work force, but he was reluctant to return to Virginia during the latter part of 1815. The death of his father in August and his mother's frail health probably had a good deal to do with his desire to remain at home, but there were other important reasons as well. Weaver's ability to raise money in Philadelphia was all that kept their Virginia operations going. He secured a bank loan for $2,000 in mid-September 1815 and forwarded the money to the Valley. These funds allowed Mayburry to complete the critical renovations at Etna Furnace. In early December, Weaver borrowed an additional $1,950 so that the firm could pay its Negro hire, and $1,900 during the first week of January 1816 probably for the same purpose. Failure to meet their hire bonds would have been disastrous, because that would have made it virtually impossible for them to acquire hands for the year ahead, and possibly for several years thereafter. Word would spread quickly among slaveowners, and a reputation as defaulters would take a long time to live down. By the spring of 1816, Weaver had taken out bank loans for another $1,650. So in less than nine months, he had raised $7,500 for Mayburry & Weaver, and he might have to secure additional funds at any time.[5] Mayburry would have to do the best he could hiring Negroes in Virginia.

Weaver's partner did not give up easily, however. In mid-December 1815, Mayburry made a final effort to persuade Weaver to make a hiring swing through eastern Virginia. If he could just get to Fredericksburg and the Spotsylvania County area, only a three-day trip from Philadelphia, Mayburry thought Weaver might obtain fifteen or twenty hands. Since Weaver had not previously hired in this region, Mayburry cautioned him to take letters of introduction and to make certain he arrived one or two days before January 1, the traditional hiring day in Spotsylvania County. Mayburry would do what he could in Pittsylvania County, but he had been sick and this had prevented him from getting an early start. "I fear we shall have difficulty in getting the necessary number," he warned Weaver.[6]

Mayburry's fears were not groundless. Weaver did not get to the Fredericksburg area, and Mayburry failed to obtain all the hands he wanted. He did hire enough slaves to make a three-month blast at Etna, which was "great for Virg-ª," he told Weaver in February 1816, but if they "had negroes enough I should not despair of making a Pens-ª blast." The renovations at Union Forge were almost complete, and that facility would soon be ready for full-scale operations.[7]

A shortage of forgemen and the lack of a good manager were their most pressing manpower needs at Union Forge in 1816. Mayburry lacked a full complement of slave forge hands in Virginia. He evidently retained some or all of the forgemen Weaver had hired the previous year, but they would not be enough once all the forge improvements were finished and full production of bar iron began. As a consequence Weaver did some recruiting in Pennsylvania. "I am happy to hear that you have succeeded in getting a good & *steady* hammerman—such an [*sic*] one we much need," Mayburry wrote on March 31, 1816. If Weaver could also "get two good refiners it would be a great acquisition." Mayburry was convinced that without "Pen-ª Forgemen" and either himself or Weaver "on the spot," Union Forge would never be a profitable enterprise.[8] A week after Mayburry wrote this letter, Weaver's mother died. Although he was able to send an occasional white workman down, there was little chance Weaver could take up residence at the forge in the immediate future.

Certainly in good part Weaver stayed anchored in Philadelphia owing to his mounting financial obligations, most of them incurred on behalf of the firm of Mayburry & Weaver. These debts forced him to keep his Pennsylvania businesses profitable.

Weaver's textile factory near Germantown and a marble quarry in Montgomery County, Pennsylvania, were his most important enterprises in the area in the late teens. His brother Abraham had been operating the marble quarry, and when he died William had taken it over. Now he continued to run this business both as a service to his brother's estate and because quarrying turned out to be a highly profitable venture. Weaver did not want to give it up.[9] With all the money he owed in Philadelphia, he could hardly afford to.

In 1816, Weaver also entered Pennsylvania politics. He supported the winning candidate for governor in 1817, and he may have caught a touch of political fever himself. He ran for a seat in the state legislature from Philadelphia, won election to the lower house, and served in three consecutive sessions between 1818 and 1821.[10]

As with almost everything else he undertook, Weaver's interest in politics had a financial motive as well. He tried very hard to obtain a gubernatorial appointment to a three-year term as an auctioneer for the City of Philadelphia, a commission which, as one contemporary observer reported, "was said to be worth $10,000 per year." Weaver did not get the post and thereby lost his best opportunity to make money from his brief political career. Weaver himself lamented that he would have been far better off if he had "gone to Virginia" and not "gone to the Legislature."[11]

Weaver's Pennsylvania affairs were now quite tangled. The marble quarry in Montgomery County, so long a source of income, had spawned a dangerous lawsuit. Weaver's valuable concession to raise marble there was jeopardized when his brother Abraham's widow and her father objected to the way Weaver was managing both the estate and this particular piece of property. The father accused Weaver of literally trashing the quarry— failing to haul out the rubble as it accumulated—and of damaging the sides of the pit by using powder to blast the marble loose. The ultimate object of the suit they brought against Weaver was to have him removed as the executor of Abraham's estate.[12] Loss of this position would cost Weaver a great deal more than his marble concession.

After he assumed control of Abraham's inheritance in 1817, Weaver had begun using substantial sums of money from the estate to sustain the Virginia ironmaking venture. Weaver felt this was a sound investment, or at least he claimed that it was, but the use of his brother's funds in this way made it absolutely necessary that he stay in Pennsylvania and defend his position there.[13]

This was particularly so since Mayburry's need for fresh capital seemed to be the one constant factor in their Virginia operations. Mayburry & Weaver had managed to avoid paying William Wilson most of the money

due him in 1815 and 1816 for their ironworks because of Wilson's continuing difficulties over the title to the forge property, but he could not be
held off forever.[14] Once he secured a clear title to the land, Wilson had an
unquestioned claim on them for the balance of his purchase money. In
addition, Mayburry constantly asked Weaver for funds to meet day-to-day
expenses—money for pork, money for grain, money for slave blankets and
clothing—and to pay off their annual bill for Negro hire.[15]

Only the forge produced any real income in 1816. Pig iron sales from the
blasts Mayburry conducted during the year were extremely disappointing,
and sales of bar iron from the forge had fallen short of the expected level.
Mayburry reviewed the forge's difficulties in a long letter to Weaver written two days before Christmas 1816. Two forgemen Weaver had sent down
from Pennsylvania earlier in the year had been a large part of the problem.
"Murphy left us long since, and I depend on Niece to draw iron, who got
drunk after drawing about one ton and left us," Mayburry complained
bitterly. "If our forge had been in good repair, and we had had forgemen, so
that we could have made 150 to 200 tons iron p year, we should at all times
have had a great sufficiency to conduct the works with ease, and the surplus
pig when sold would have been more than enough to pay up Wilson," he
continued. But, as luck would have it, pig iron had been a drug on the
market all year. "It is the Devil to be poor," Mayburry added, a refrain that
would echo through his correspondence with Weaver for the next six
years. Mayburry would be heading to Southside Virginia very shortly to
hire slaves for the coming year's work. Perhaps things would be better in
1817 than they had been in the year just passed.[16]

Any optimism Mayburry might have entertained about the immediate
future evaporated almost at once. "We are doomed to misfortune and
disappointments," he wrote Weaver on January 9, 1817. "I have just returned from Pittsyl[a] [County], after a long and most unpleasant trip, unsuccessful. I have failed in getting a supply of negroes," he went on; "all I
could procure, with all the industry I am master of was 7 hands to wit 4
men 1 woman & 2 boys for which I pay $440." He had wanted to hire a
minimum of twenty men, more if possible. Hirelings simply were not available, however, and Mayburry's observation that "this system of hiring
negroes is a very bad and uncertain one" was a complaint his partner
clearly shared. Uncertainty over their labor supply had led to Weaver's
purchase of the "Wilson negroes" back in 1815. Mayburry had hoped to
put the forge in good order "and get if possible a set of good, steady
workmen," but now it would be "at least another year" before their ironworks could be producing at anything like their full capacity.[17]

From Weaver's perspective, it must have seemed as though his partner had an unerring knack for making gloomy predictions come true. A severe shortage of woodchoppers impeded operations early in the year. When Mayburry finally obtained enough ore, charcoal, and limestone for a fairly decent blast, the year was almost over. "We shant be able to blow longer than Christmas as hands are very scarce," he told Weaver in November. Most would be leaving, as usual, in mid-December, and without every available hand, the furnace would have to be blown out. "At present we can scarce make out," Mayburry added.[18]

Things were just as bad along the banks of the Buffalo. "We are badly hampered at the forge for the want of hands, particularly forgemen," Mayburry reported to Weaver in August 1817. Their best white hammerman, a man named Brien, had gone home to Pennsylvania, ostensibly to move his family to Virginia. Mayburry pressed Weaver to look the man up "and urge his immediate return—and endeavor to get one or two good refiners to come with him." They also needed an experienced forge carpenter. "We shall never be able to do a good business without a new set of hands," Mayburry lamented. He had been unable to secure enough slave refiners and hammermen to fill out his forge crew, and most of the white hands working at Union Forge were, in Mayburry's estimation, totally unreliable. That was why the absent white hammerman was so important; he was a conscientious workman. "Don't fail to see Brien," Mayburry repeated in a postscript, "depend upon it [it] is of material consequence to us that *he* returns—and some hands with him if possible."[19]

Mayburry & Weaver's entire Virginia investment was in jeopardy, and a major reason for their difficulty was their failure to assemble, either by hire or by purchase, a full gang of skilled slave forgemen: a master refiner and his underhand, a chaffery forge hammerman and his underhand, a forge carpenter, a forge blacksmith, and enough swing hands to fill in at any of these positions if a primary worker or his assistant were sick or injured. As a consequence, they were forced to rely in large part on white forge workers, most of whom were "idle half their time drunk," Mayburry complained bitterly in the summer of 1817.[20] William Weaver had a long memory, and he did not forget the threat which even a partial reliance on free labor posed to their operations. The slave system was there to be used, and he would use it to the fullest extent possible after his move to the Valley in 1823.

Better forge management would also have helped the situation, but Weaver simply could not leave Philadelphia in the late teens and early twenties. He sent several men to Virginia to serve as forge managers and clerks with generally disappointing results. Four different men managed Union Forge between late 1814 when Mayburry & Weaver acquired the property to the summer of 1823 when Weaver finally took over the forge. None proved satisfactory. Mayburry dismissed one for impertinence and general incompetence and told Weaver not to send the man back down to Virginia under any circumstances. The firm could not afford to pay him "a *pension* of $500 p an^m," Mayburry wrote.[21]

Part of the difficulty hindering the acquisition of good management at the forge was Mayburry's adamant refusal to try any local ironmen in positions of authority. As a consequence, all the managers had to be brought in from the North more or less sight unseen. Mayburry had a decidedly negative opinion of the business acumen, as well as the moral fiber, of his neighbors in the Valley. When the store at Etna Furnace was broken into and robbed of several hundred dollars' worth of merchandise in 1816, Mayburry immediately blamed the theft on "some worthless whites in the neighborhood." A new clerk at Etna, a Pennsylvanian who seemed reasonably efficient, prompted Mayburry to express his assessment of most of the local population. Taking "all things into view I prefer him to getting a V[irginian] of whom I have a poor opinion," he told Weaver. "I know of none that can be had, at any rate—they are generally gentlemen, gamblers, drinkers &c &c." "As to employing a Virginian," he wrote Weaver on another occasion, "it is my honest belief that the most of them would run us in debt, if left to their own controul."[22]

But that was just the problem: Mayburry & Weaver's ironworks were sinking farther and farther into debt, and Mayburry seemed powerless to halt the downward slide. Weaver grew apprehensive and was obviously having second thoughts about the entire Virginia investment. He expressed his doubts to Mayburry in the fall of 1817, and Mayburry's reply went to the heart of their dilemma. "The Works have been much more expensive than I ever calculated, as well as yourself—And as you say, I agree with you, could I have foreseen it I should never have entered into the business," Mayburry wrote. But "it is now too late to look back—our only alternative is to struggle through." There was some cause for guarded optimism, however. The forge was in excellent shape, "and all we want is good workmen to enable us to make bar iron pretty fast." But then there was that other ever-present difficulty, which Mayburry touched on in closing: "If I have any luck—in getting negroes at Christmas . . . after this year we shall be through the worst, and god knows it is now bad enough."[23]

Weaver agreed with Mayburry that they had invested so much in their ironmaking operations that they could not get out without taking a disastrous loss, but he was unquestionably irritated that almost all of the capital at risk was his, and his family's. The two partners had originally expected to put approximately $10,000 each into the business, $15,000 at the outside.

Part of the money would be used to make their $5,000 down payment to Wilson, part would be used to renovate the works, and the rest would serve as working capital. Once the furnace and forge were producing, they had anticipated that enough profits would accumulate to pay Wilson his annual installments and give each partner some sort of return on his investment.[24]

None of these things had happened. The business had, by the end of 1817, already required more capital than they had originally estimated, and Mayburry had not been able to come up with anything like his share of the money. He wrote his brothers in Maryland and Pennsylvania and asked them for loans. "Mr. Weaver has already supplied more than his proportion of capital to the works," he told one. His brothers could offer no help. Mayburry had expected to make a considerable amount of money when he closed up some business interests in Pennsylvania; "the miserable way" these affairs turned out deprived him of funds he had intended to invest in Virginia.[25] The result was that Weaver had been called upon to sustain the financial side of the partnership almost single-handedly, and he had borrowed very heavily to do so, not only from Philadelphia banks but from his brother's estate as well. Weaver's sizable investment, and the lack of any return thereon, would profoundly influence his reaction to Mayburry's management.

Prospects seemed never to improve in Virginia. In late 1817, Mayburry had three hundred tons of pig iron lying on the banks of Purgatory Creek, not a ton of which he could sell. There was simply no market for it in the depressed postwar economy. Chances for the sale of merchant bar were better; farmers were always in need of wrought iron for things like wagon tire, horse and mule shoes, plow points, and agricultural implements. But bar iron, which could be sold, was not coming out of the forge at a satisfactory rate because of bad management and bad workmen.[26] And that was not all. William Wilson, who was being hounded by his own creditors, in November 1817 claimed to have obtained the long-delayed titles; if this proved true, Mayburry & Weaver would owe him close to $12,000. Wilson was expected at the forge any day, Mayburry wrote on November 10, and he did not have a dollar to give Wilson. What, Mayburry asked, were they going to do?[27] There really was only one answer. Put Wilson off as long as possible, press on with their business, and hope for better times in the year ahead.

"I shall set out next Sunday to hire negroes," Mayburry told Weaver on December 19, 1817, "(a business not much more agreeable than raising money in Ph^a)," he added. He gave Weaver the results of this expedition early the next year. "I returned from hiring negroes about the 6 of Jany, & I had but little success in getting hands," he wrote. "I hired but 13—

including men, women, and children.—In consequence of the demand for tobacco, there is a thorough revolution as respects negroes—there are few to be had at any price," he continued, and "those that are to be hired their masters generally object to their being taken out of the County." Still, he had done better than the previous year, and he had managed to retain four or five choppers at the forge, enough for charcoaling operations there. The thirteen slaves he had hired in Pittsylvania County could be put to work at various jobs around the furnace. In late March, he reported that he had fourteen hands cutting wood, certainly a respectable chopping force.[28] Their worries were by no means over, but things were definitely looking brighter.

Then disaster struck. During the last week in March 1818, Maybury rode over to Union Forge from his home base at Etna. When he arrived at the forge, "the Buffaloe was uncommon high," he reported to Weaver, and "about 1 o'clock pm I had the mortification to witness the loss of our new forge dam—which was carried away by the freshet—scarce a vestige left." He had begun rebuilding right away, but the work would, of course, be expensive. In addition, Wilson was still pressing Maybury for his money. Weaver would have to come up with some cash both for the new dam and for William Wilson. "I had flattered myself that we had just escaped from our worst embarrassments—and that I had in view a prospect of better times, when this sad calamity has befallen us," Maybury lamented.[29]

The loss of the forge dam was a serious blow. In addition to the expense of rebuilding, destruction of the dam halted forge production and deprived the partners of their only real source of income. Maybury had to put most of his slave force to work on the dam, and, as he told Weaver, this "puts us back at the furnace, as hands are scarce." The slowdown in accumulating furnace stock delayed the anticipated spring blast until the summer, and when the summer months arrived, they had to face a recurring difficulty: low water. It would be September at the earliest before the blast could begin, and Maybury was short in some critical furnace positions. "We shall commence coaling . . . next week, if I am not again disappointed in a [master] collier," Maybury explained to Weaver in mid-July; "the fact is there is very little reliance to be place[d] on the *greater* part of people in this Country." Ample unsold pig iron remained from previous blasts to begin making bar as soon as the new forge dam was finished, but once again forge operations were crippled by an ever-present problem. "We are in great want of forgemen[—]refiners—if you could find one or two it would be a great acquisition," Maybury wrote, in what was almost an endless refrain in his correspondence with Weaver.

Unfavorable weather conditions continued into the fall and raised yet another specter. "In my last I informed you that we were suffering here under an uncommon drought, which unfortunately still continues," Mayburry reported in late November 1818; "my principal fear now is that the cold weather will freeze us up." Union Forge, as usual, badly needed a new manager, and although the reconstruction of the dam had long since been accomplished, the forge was "doing but little for want of *water.*"[30] Nothing seemed to have gone right in 1818. Once again, it was a case of wait until next year.

The approach of January not only brought with it thoughts of a fresh start; it also brought nearer the most critical season of the ironmaster's year in Virginia and throughout the South. "I must call your attention to the subject mentioned in my last—which is all important, to wit, hiring negroes," Mayburry wrote Weaver on November 29, 1818; "if we fail in getting them we can do little or nothing here next year—for white hands are not to be had." Mayburry would make his annual trip to Pittsylvania County at Christmas "to *try* to hire, but prospects there are gloomy.—As I said before, it is the heart of a tobacco country, and but few to be had there.—Don't judge it by what you know of it," he warned Weaver, "things have undergone an entire change since you were there."

Mayburry again was convinced that Spotsylvania County in eastern Virginia offered "our best, and almost only chance of getting negroes for the ensuing year," and he once more pleaded with Weaver to obtain letters of introduction and visit slaveowners in Fredericksburg and the surrounding region. If Weaver could not come south over the holidays, perhaps he could do something in Pennsylvania that would help relieve their shortage of skilled workers. "I understand German Redemptioners can be purchased in Ph.ª at about $60 to $80 for three years," Mayburry noted; "—if they are good they would be preferable to negroes which can't be had under $100 for one year—and the advantage of having them for a considerable time would be great." Weaver should also be on the lookout for blacksmiths and carpenters, "two of each, much wanted." But one way or another, their labor problems had to be dealt with. "It must be evident to you that without hands nothing can be done here—with them I think I could make a good blast," Mayburry concluded.[31]

Weaver again was unable to make the trip south and he forwarded no German servants to the Valley. Mayburry, for his part, reported on his trek through Southside Virginia in a long, gloomy letter to his partner in late January 1819:

> I was absent, in pursuit of negroes near 3 weeks—rode between 3 & 400 miles, was in ten counties—took letters to two gentlemen—was pre-

pared to give good security for the hire—and used all possible industry—notwithstanding all this, I did not hire a single negro.—The people over the mountain are crazy about making tobacco—negroes hire from 120 to 170—and not permitted to go out of the county.

Fortunately Mayburry had sent a furnace assistant into central Virginia, and he had hired four slaves in Louisa County for $120 a piece. These hands, plus three slaves hired by another employee for forge work, would probably give Union Forge an adequate number of hands. But his total work gang at Etna consisted of two of the "Wilson negroes," Tooler and his son Bill, along with three other slaves and one white man. Tooler was a skilled furnace keeper and an excellent workman and Bill was an able teamster and general furnace hand, but Mayburry had been forced to send them along with the remainder of his small force into the woods to chop so that charcoaling could commence. Several white men in the vicinity of the furnace had promised to do some woodcutting, "but there is little dependence to be put in them," Mayburry believed. The best hope for the dismal-looking furnace situation lay in the considerable amount of stock left over from the previous year, when low water had curtailed operations for a number of months.[32]

The weather situation in 1819 looked inauspicious, however. The furnace had frozen up in January, as Mayburry had anticipated, and when mild temperatures arrived, the water was too low in Purgatory Creek to run the furnace. Inadequate waterpower held production at Union Forge to about 50 percent of capacity. "It seems as if the very elements had conspired against us," Mayburry ruefully observed. "At present I am extremely hard run," which undoubtedly came as no surprise to Weaver, "and it is tight scuffling to get along," but as soon as their waterpower was restored and he could get the furnace in blast, "I hope to be relieved in great measure," Mayburry wrote. "If it were not for hope," he asked in conclusion, "what should we do"?[33]

Things had been running on hope and William Weaver's money for over four years. "I know full well that you have been strained to furnish the means of going on here," Mayburry acknowledged in the fall of 1819, "but situated as I am what is to be done?" Mayburry subsequently admitted what Weaver undoubtedly knew. "Wilson got a very extravagant price for his Iron Works, more than any person in *that* country [the Valley] would have given him for them," Mayburry wrote Weaver in 1821. The word in the neighborhood was that Mayburry & Weaver had paid no less than twice what the works were worth. Wilson, from the confines of his cell in debtor's prison, had outfoxed the Pennsylvanians in 1814. The price had turned out to be anything but the "mere *bagatelle"* Weaver had called it at the time. Mayburry came much closer to the truth when he observed that he and Weaver "were strangers and were taken *in.*"[34]

Just how far Weaver had fallen in financially was revealed by a detailed statement Mayburry drew up in 1821. Weaver needed a precise accounting of the money he had put into the Virginia enterprise in order to convince the court in Pennsylvania that the money in his brother Abraham's estate was safely invested. His brother's will had placed over $22,000 in Weaver's hands, money that he, as executor, was responsible for safeguarding and managing until Abraham's two sons, Abraham and William, reached their maturity. Since young Abraham Weaver, Jr., and William Weaver, Jr., as he was called, would not turn twenty-one until the 1830s, Weaver would long have use of these funds, unless the court intervened. It seems almost certain that Weaver sunk a considerable portion of his brother's estate into the ironmaking operations in the Valley. Weaver told Mayburry to give a full statement of the value of his investment, including the slaves he had purchased from John Wilson in 1815, but he was careful to instruct Mayburry to "say nothing about owning negroes."[35] Given the religious tradition of his family, this was a prudent omission. Weaver did not want his relatives, or the court, in Pennsylvania to know about his slaveholdings in Virginia, and he concealed this information from them for as long as he could.

Mayburry's statement, forwarded to his partner on October 1, 1821, showed Weaver owning one-half interest in Etna and Retreat furnaces, Union Forge, a gristmill, two sawmills, an ironmaster's residence, and various and sundry other buildings. Weaver's investment stood at $39,242.43. This sum included any profits Weaver had earned because he had taken nothing out of the partnership in its seven years. Mayburry was careful to make no mention of the "Wilson negroes," but he included the value of these slaves when he recorded the total amount of Weaver's investment.[36]

Fortunately for Weaver, he was allowed to remain as the executor of his brother's estate. Auditors appointed by the court to go over Weaver's books accepted his evidence that he had handled Abraham's assets satisfactorily. And the court, in turn, decided in 1821 that he was a competent agent to trust with the financial future of Abraham's heirs. The suit against him, triggered by his management of the marble quarry, failed, and with its failure a major roadblock standing in the way of his going to the Valley disappeared.[37]

In fact, the day was rapidly approaching when Weaver would have no choice but to move to Virginia. His financial commitment to the partnership had swollen far beyond his original intentions, but there was no way he could extricate himself from the ironmaking venture without suffering very serious losses. In addition to his liability for the funds in his brother's estate, Weaver was also personally responsible for the substantial bank loans he had taken out in Philadelphia to keep the firm going. He had managed to delay repayment of these notes, but they could not be put off forever.[38] Something good would have to come out of the Valley before too long, or his entire range of business interests in Pennsylvania might well be in jeopardy.

Weaver's family situation in Pennsylvania was also changing during the early 1820s. His youngest sister, Lydia, married in 1822 at the age of twenty-five. Her husband, Peter K. Gorgas, hailed from a prominent Dunker family in the Germantown area, and William must have felt relieved to see Lydia finally settled. That left only one of his sisters, Sarah, unmarried, but Sarah was twenty-eight years old in 1822, and William apparently felt that there was no need for him to remain in Philadelphia solely on her account.[39]

A letter from Mayburry written in June 1822 said it all: "I don't expect much money has been made there for the last 2½ years," he noted.[40] The lack of profits, and the firm's unwavering reliance on Weaver's ability to come up with the necessary funds, never seemed to change.

And news from the Valley remained bad. Consider the fall of 1822. On September 25, Mayburry notified Weaver that "our black boy Bill ran away, in company with a negro man hired in Louisa County." According to Mayburry, the two men fled because they had been caught stealing and they "apprehended correction." He would have told Weaver about it sooner, Mayburry added, but he did not think the two men would try to leave the vicinity of Etna Furnace, where they both had been working. However, "subsequent circumstances induces the belief that they will attempt to escape out of the State, probably Pen.[a] and Ph[a] will be their aim." Bill, Tooler's oldest son, was one of the "Wilson negroes." Standing five feet nine inches tall at about twenty-five years of age, Bill had a small scar on his breast, Mayburry wrote. The hireling, a blacksmith named Cato, was six feet tall and darker than Bill. Mayburry was providing Weaver with a physical description of the two men so that he could identify them if they reached Philadelphia.[41]

The runaways never got out of Virginia, but they did succeed in getting out of the Valley. On October 2, 1822, Mayburry informed Weaver that the two men were in jail in Cumberland County, about one hundred miles east of the furnace, well over the Blue Ridge Mountains. Two weeks later, Bill and Cato were back at Etna.[42] Mayburry did not say whether a "correction" had been administered, but it probably had. Runaways rarely escaped the lash.

This episode must have profoundly disturbed Weaver. Bill and the rest of the "Wilson negroes" were Weaver's most valuable assets in Virginia, and the most marketable, should he have to raise some cash in a hurry. They were also his exclusive property. He had made certain of that when he bought them back in 1815. And the possibility, as reported by Mayburry, that Bill and his accomplice might have been trying to reach Philadelphia was especially worrisome. They were probably heading north in quest of freedom, but there was also a chance that they were trying to get to Weaver. It was not at all uncommon at Virginia ironworks for hirelings or slave hands belonging to absentee owners to try to get back to their masters if they had been overworked, abused, given inadequate food or clothing, or otherwise mistreated. Mayburry said Bill and Cato had been caught stealing, but how was Weaver to know? Perhaps they were trying to steal food because they were hungry. Mayburry seemed to be mismanaging most things in Virginia; maybe he could not manage slaves either.

It did not take long for Weaver to receive another lament from Mayburry, one with an old, familiar ring to it. "I am now in a most anxious, & ... unpleasant situation," he wrote Weaver on November 14, 1822. He was, as usual, out of money. He would need $1,500 to pay their Negro hire at Christmas, bigger debts were looming on the horizon, and he was looking in the usual place for help; "of course, remember our dependence is upon you," he told his partner.[43]

Their financial situation had, in fact, become critical, for they once again faced a familiar adversary—William Wilson. Mayburry, using funds supplied by Weaver, had managed to string Wilson along for several years by making partial payments, and the firm's indebtedness to Wilson had been reduced to just over $6,000. But he had clear titles to both the furnace and forge tracts in hand, and his legal position was unquestionably strong. Wilson ultimately tired of their delaying tactics; in 1821 he filed suit against Mayburry & Weaver in chancery court charging them with fraud and demanding his money. The court, acting with uncharacteristic speed, ruled in Wilson's favor the following year.[44] Mayburry immediately appealed the decision in hopes of delaying matters still further, but he was not sanguine about either the outcome of the appeal or the amount of time it might buy. "I am sorry to observe that you still appear so much pressed for money," Mayburry wrote; "if you can't remit, we may bid good bye to the works." Mayburry, who had been carrying the burden of responsibility in Virginia by himself for over seven years, seemed rather piqued with his partner, particularly after Wilson proposed a settlement that would require them to pay only $3,000 that fall with the balance not due for another year. "You certainly can in a case wherein you are so deeply interested, by some financial scheme or other raise this sum," Mayburry chided Weaver. "I hope you will not after wading through difficulties, which to look back upon are appalling, give up, when so small a sum comparatively will extricate us—when our goal may be said to be almost in view."[45]

Weaver's irritation more than matched his partner's. His answer was that Mayburry should return to Pennsylvania and come up with the funds himself. Mayburry refused. "As to my coming on, what could I do in Ph^a with not a penny in my pocket, & no property or credit to raise money on," he replied.[46] Weaver knew full well by then that his partner had no capital of his own and no way of obtaining any. And Weaver also knew that he would have to go to the Valley and try to salvage his investment there. His line of credit with his Philadelphia bankers was not yet exhausted, so he could deal with Wilson's judgment against Mayburry & Weaver if their appeal failed. But he was unwilling to sink any more capital into their ironworks without being there to oversee its use himself.

The next summer, in early July 1823, Weaver left for Virginia. Still a bachelor at forty-two, he came south with every expectation of returning to Philadelphia once he had straightened out affairs in the Valley. Accompanying him on his journey was a fourteen-year-old boy named John Weaver Danenhower.[47] John Danenhower was one of William's nephews, the son of his sister Rachel. He was also the first in a long line of Weaver's young relatives who would come to Virginia over the next four decades to assist their "Uncle William" in the ironmaking trade. If this young man had known what lay ahead of him in the Valley, he probably would never have left Philadelphia.

3

—◆—

Mayburry & Weaver: Dissolution and Division

Weaver's arrival in the Valley came none too soon. With their debt to William Wilson still unpaid, with large loans outstanding in Philadelphia, with their furnace and forge earning them precious little income, and with farmers around Etna unwilling to sell grain and meat to them except for cash, the fortunes of Mayburry & Weaver had fallen low indeed. Just how low emerged in a conversation Weaver overheard between his partner and a white hammerman working at Union Forge. The forgeman remarked that he knew of an ironmaster in New Jersey whose I.O.U.'s "passed like Bank Notes" in the neighborhood of his works. Mayburry replied that "Mayburry & Weaver's orders would not pass at Jenkin's still house for a half gallon [of] whiskey."[1] Weaver was not amused.

It took Weaver several weeks to get his bearings. He had not lived and worked in Virginia for almost eight years, so the area was almost totally new terrain to him. One of his first moves was to install John Danenhower at Etna as a clerk, a step that may have been prompted by Weaver's desire to have someone he trusted keep an eye on Mayburry's activities.[2] Weaver divided his own time between the furnace and Union Forge. He had to go over the books carefully and acquaint himself with the day-to-day operations of both the forge and the furnace. He also wanted to visit the major markets for their iron "down the country," as people in the Valley referred to the area east of the Blue Ridge Mountains. There he planned to talk to commission merchants in Lynchburg and Richmond to see if he could substantially improve the sales of their pig and bar iron in these two markets.[3] The Richmond and Lynchburg trade was particularly important because these commercial centers were just about the only places where their iron could be sold for cash. Almost all the sales around Union Forge itself were barter transactions.[4] That was usually fine for obtaining part of their supplies, but it would not meet their annual bill for Negro hire, nor would it pay off their debts.

Before he could get to Lynchburg or Richmond, however, he went briefly back to Pennsylvania in the fall of 1823 to look after his business interests there. While in Philadelphia, Weaver used his own funds to purchase a substantial stock of goods for the Union Forge store. Weaver was convinced that some of the firm's local debts could be paid off through sales of this merchandise, and he was right. The articles he sent south were, in John Danenhower's words, "sold at a handsome profit," and this helped relieve some of the immediate financial pressure on the forge.[5] But measures of this sort were only temporary expedients. The major problems remained. Weaver needed a way to settle the firm's debts and reverse the downward slide of their iron business. To achieve these ends, Weaver soon concluded that it would be necessary to get Thomas Mayburry out of the picture.

Mayburry should have seen what was coming. In the course of going over the firm's accounts, Weaver informed Mayburry that the books at Etna should carry an entry for the hire of the "Wilson negroes" who had worked there over the years. The eleven slaves he had purchased in 1815 and all their offspring were his personal property, Weaver said, because he had taken title to them in his own name when he bought them from John Wilson. Mayburry professed to be stunned by this information. "They were always considered partnership property," Mayburry insisted, just like the handful of slave forge workers Mayburry had bought over the years with the firm's money. It was true that Mayburry had not contributed so much as a dollar toward the purchase of the "Wilson negroes," but he refused to acknowledge the legality of Weaver's claim.[6]

Mayburry did demand, however, that if Weaver claimed title to the Wilson slaves, then Weaver should take the Wilson slave children living at

Etna Furnace over to Union Forge, and he wrote Weaver to that effect in the summer of 1824. He "was unwilling to be at the expense of raising negroes for [Weaver's] benefit," was the way Mayburry put it. Weaver replied that "he . . . would take large & small & provide for them, but if [Mayburry] kept the large ones he must also keep the small ones." When Mayburry pressed the subject, Weaver responded angrily that Mayburry "should not dictate to him which of the Negroes he should keep at the Forge."[7] The children remained with their mothers at Etna, but Weaver made sure that the books kept at Union Forge indicated that he was the sole owner of these slaves. He posted entries showing that the firm was indebted to him personally for the hire of the entire Wilson slave force.[8]

This argument foreshadowed the much larger dispute between the two men that resulted ultimately in the dissolution of their partnership. The fight was long, acrimonious, and all but Dickensian. Both men ended up hurling scurrilous charges of fraud, dishonesty, and deception at the other. They frequently couched their attacks in the most heavy-handed sarcasm. And because their battle landed in the tortuous machinery of the Virginia chancery courts, it dragged on for years. Their sworn testimony was almost always in direct conflict, and it is usually impossible to tell who was giving an accurate account of motives and events. One suspects that neither man was overly scrupulous about the truth when his vital interests were threatened. But much more was at stake than their reputations for veracity or the fate of their ironworks. They were fighting, among other things, over the ownership of the "Wilson negroes." The outcome of that controversy would determine the course of over two dozen black lives.

"I was desirous of ascertaining that year [1825] how the Iron business would answer," Weaver said later, "with a determination if I could not make money at it that I would quit it at the end of the year or as soon as possible."[9] His attempts to turn things around were unexpectedly bolstered in the winter of 1823–24 when William Wilson suddenly died. Weaver found Wilson's heirs easier to deal with than "old man Wilson" had been, and he arranged for a gradual repayment of the money due the estate out of the profits of the works. This relieved the immediate threat of foreclosure, gave Weaver more time to settle this sizable debt (which, with interest added on, now totaled almost $7,000), and freed up whatever capital he could still raise in Philadelphia to invest in the business itself or to fend off his northern creditors.[10] As far as Weaver was concerned, Wilson's death had been a stroke of great good fortune.

That still left Thomas Mayburry on his hands, but Weaver was preparing to move on that front as well.

By the end of 1824, Weaver was convinced that his partner was lazy, dishonest, and incompetent. Weaver's examination of the books at Etna revealed that Mayburry had secretly paid himself a salary of $1,000 a year for superintending the furnace in addition to living off the works. Since Weaver had not taken a cent out of the partnership in the ten years the firm had been in existence, he considered Mayburry's action "most extraordinary, and highly unjust." And, according to John Danenhower, Mayburry was anything but vigorous in his conduct of affairs at Etna. He "breakfasted late," Danenhower reported, and "lived as comfortably and enjoyed as much ease as any person I have ever known who was in business of any kind." Danenhower may well have been telling Weaver what he wanted to hear, but the young man still maintained that Mayburry "did not use that exertion I have generally known men of business to do." Finally, and perhaps worst of all in Weaver's eyes, Mayburry's duplicity and sloth had been compounded by what Weaver called his partner's "improvidential management" of the firm's affairs for years. That, Weaver insisted, was the main reason their business was mired so deeply in debt.[11] If his efforts to make money in 1825 were to succeed, Weaver felt, Thomas Mayburry would have to go.

Extricating himself from the partnership would not be easy, however, because Weaver knew Mayburry would oppose a dissolution which gained him little or nothing. So Weaver proceeded step-by-step. In March 1824, he fired the forge superintendent, who happened to be a nephew of Mayburry's, and took over management of Union Forge himself. The following month, he brought John Danenhower over from Etna to assist him at the forge. He next offered to buy the forge property for $6,000. Mayburry refused. Finally, in late December 1824, Weaver proposed a rental arrangement that would put him in control of Union Forge and its profits for three years and place Mayburry in charge of Etna Furnace and its profits for a similar length of time.[12] This would not dissolve their partnership, but as far as Weaver was concerned it was a major step toward the achievement of that goal.

Mayburry later insisted that he had no idea Weaver was setting the stage for an end to their association. As Mayburry put it, Weaver "was entitled to greater credit for discretion than for candor. It would certainly have been more *ingenuous,* if not so *ingenious,* had [Weaver] . . . communicated his sentiments" at the outset. Mayburry likened his partner to "the watchman who cries 'all's well,' though he sees a house on fire, or is about to break into it himself."[13] These sentiments were voiced in November 1825, but Mayburry's bitterness would last much longer than that and would ultimately affect the lives of many of the "Wilson negroes."

On December 28, 1824, Mayburry and Weaver signed a rental agree-

ment. On the surface, it looked like a straightforward, sensible arrangement, which was undoubtedly the reason Mayburry was willing to affix his
signature to the document. Each man would concentrate his time and
energy on one facility and keep the profits earned at that place for himself.
Weaver would rent Union Forge for three years and pay Mayburry $600
per year for his half interest in the forge property. Mayburry, in turn,
agreed to provide twenty-eight tons of Etna pig iron for the forge during
each of the next three years as a rental fee for Weaver's half interest in the
furnace. Such additional pig iron as Weaver might need he could buy at
Etna for $27.50 per ton, a price higher than the prevailing price of pig iron
in the Valley at that time. The advanced price was stipulated because
Weaver expected to pay for this pig iron in the way ironmasters cus-
tomarily did business with one another, by barter. He would trade merchant bar for pig, and Mayburry could sell or barter this bar iron wherever
he could find a market for it. All the personal property of the partnership
then at the forge would be sold to Weaver at a fair price.[14]

This agreement was misleading, however. As was often the case when
Weaver proposed a deal, he knew something the other party did not,
namely that iron was poised on the brink of a significant price rise. He had
visited Richmond in early December, before Mayburry agreed to rent him
the forge. While he was there, word arrived of a sharp increase in the price
of iron in England. Such news generally presaged a similar movement of
prices in the United States, and Weaver had, in fact, managed to secure
orders for merchant bar iron from several Richmond commission houses at
substantially higher prices than those that had previously prevailed there.
In addition, these Richmond merchants promised large orders in the future
if the quality of Union Forge bar proved satisfactory. Weaver arrived back
in the Valley before the news of the price hike filtered in from the east and
struck his deal with Mayburry. He said nothing about his new orders until
after the rental agreement had been sealed.[15]

Weaver believed the losses on behalf of the firm, coupled with what he
perceived to be his partner's dishonesty, laziness, and general ineptitude,
gave him the right to seize the main chance when he saw it coming. Mayburry believed he had been duped. Matters between the two men deteriorated rapidly from that point on, and by early February 1825, Mayburry
was sufficiently fed up with Weaver's maneuverings to agree to a dissolution of their partnership. He would take control of Etna Furnace, Weaver
could work the forge, and they would go their separate ways. That, of
course, was exactly what Weaver had wanted all along.

Before the assets of the firm could be divided and arrangements made for
the settlement of Mayburry & Weaver's debts, however, certain critical

points had to be resolved. The central matter at issue was the status and future ownership of the "Wilson negroes."

We have a graphic picture of the two white ironmasters fighting over who would own these slaves. The scene was described in detail by several men who were at Union Forge on February 8 and 9, 1825, to appraise the value of the personal property there and help arbitrate any points of disagreement that might arise as Mayburry and Weaver terminated their affiliation. Since Weaver had agreed to compensate Mayburry for his partial ownership of all the firm's personal property at the forge—slaves, horses, mules, tools, fixtures, pig iron, anchonies, and the like—a price had to be placed on everything of this nature that would go to Weaver. During the ten years he had been in Virginia, Mayburry had used partnership funds to purchase a few slave hands for the forge, and two of these men, Phill Easton and Billy Hunt, were valuable ironworkers.[16] Weaver would have to buy Mayburry's half interest in these forgemen. The "Wilson negroes" were another matter, however, and one of the arbitrators, a Rockbridge County justice of the peace named Charles B. Penn, told what happened when the subject of these slaves came up on the evening of February 9.

Weaver, Mayburry, and the arbitrators were gathered in the front room of Weaver's residence at Union Forge. A rough draft of the agreement dissolving Mayburry's and Weaver's partnership was read, corrections were made, and both partners agreed to the wording. At this point, while the final copy of the document was being prepared for their signatures, Mayburry suddenly walked out of the room and stood on the front porch. He called to Penn to join him, and Penn did so. Mayburry was uneasy, Penn said, because the agreement "included all the negroes at the Forge belonging to the late concern and there being several of the negroes then at the Forge called the Wilson negroes it might by implication compromise his interest in those negroes." Mayburry asked Penn to go back inside and state his position.

When Penn returned to the front room and raised the question of Mayburry's right "to one half of the Wilson negroes," Weaver exploded. He "replied immediately that the negroes were his and that if [Mayburry] ... did not give up all claim to them that the arrangement was at an end." Mayburry would face dire consequences if he did not concede the point then and there. Weaver said if he had to "go to Law he might as well go for the whole [of Mayburry's property] as for the negroes." Mayburry had a clear choice: He could surrender his claim to half ownership of these slaves or he could face Weaver in chancery court. And if Weaver had to sue for complete ownership of the "Wilson negroes," he would sue for every piece of Mayburry's partnership property he could get his hands on in order to satisfy Mayburry's indebtedness to him and to the firm's creditors.

Penn went back outside to tell Mayburry what Weaver had said. The two men remained on the porch a long time. Mayburry did not want to give in. The slaves were joint property, he insisted, and he had a just claim to half their value. Penn warned him that he was "largely indebted to the concern of Mayburry & Weaver," and that "a suit in chancery wou'd be ruinous to him."[17]

At this point, William Ross, one of the arbitrators who had been inside with Weaver, stepped out onto the porch. Ross was a well-known ironmaster in the Valley, and his opinion carried considerable weight. Ross "joined Mr. Penn in urging Mr. Mayburry to yield," and repeated Penn's warning that a suit against him in chancery court "wou'd be ruinous."[18] Mayburry finally, and with great reluctance, consented to give up his claim. He did so "to save himself from a chancery suit and to have the business amicably adjusted" between himself and Weaver. The arbitrators went back inside and informed Weaver of Mayburry's decision.

The final agreement dissolving the firm of Mayburry & Weaver was speedily completed and was signed by both men later that same evening, with the arbitrators serving as witnesses to their signatures. The document contained no specific provision for the disposition of the "Wilson negroes," a tacit acknowledgment that they belonged solely to Weaver.[19] And they were not appraised with the rest of the partnership property at the forge— like Phill Easton (at $600) and Billy Hunt (at $500)—that went to Weaver.[20]

The most interested parties had no say in this entire affair, of course. They were the "Wilson negroes" themselves. By 1825 the original group of eleven slaves purchased from John S. Wilson ten years before had doubled in size. They were, by a wide margin, the largest group of slaves working for Weaver and Mayburry in 1825, and they were divided between Union Forge and Etna Furnace at the time the partnership was dissolved.

Most of Tooler's family was with him at the forge. Tooler worked at the chaffery hammer drawing bar iron for Weaver, and Billy Hunt served as his underhand. Rebecca, Tooler's wife, was in charge of the cooking and housekeeping at Weaver's residence; two of her boys, Tooler, Jr., fourteen, and Joe, twelve, helped Rebecca with various kitchen and household chores, but Tooler, Jr., would soon be joining his father in the forge as an apprentice hammerman and Joe would later train as a blacksmith and forge carpenter. In addition to these two sons, Tooler and Rebecca also had two younger children with them at Union Forge who had been born after the original sale of the family to Weaver in 1815. Their two oldest boys, Bill and Bob, twenty-seven and seventeen, respectively, were working at Etna Furnace in 1825.

Almost all of Mary's family lived at Etna at the time the partnership dissolved. Mary was there along with two of her older daughters, twenty-three-year-old Sally and sixteen-year-old Louisa. Mary had given birth to at least five children in the ten years Weaver had owned her, three of whom were still living in 1825: John, born in 1816, Hamilton, born in 1823, and Ellen, "an infant at the breast" in 1825. Sometime in the late teens or early twenties, Mary had borne twins, but both these babies had died.

Sally, Mary's oldest daughter, was married to a slave ironworker at Etna and had begun raising a family there. Her husband was named Sam Williams, and they had three children at the time Mayburry and Weaver dissolved their firm: Mary, born in 1817, Sam Williams, Jr., born in 1820, and Elizabeth, born in 1825.

Louisa, Mary's sixteen-year-old daughter, also had a child at the time the firm broke up. Her baby, a boy, had been born two years earlier, and was named Wilson Botetourt King.

Two of Mary's older daughters who were part of the original sale to Weaver in 1815 were not with her at Etna Furnace in 1825. Amy, who was twenty, and Georgianna, twelve, were both living at Union Forge, where they worked as house servants and helped with the kitchen duties. Amy had two young boys with her at that time, Henry and Charles Matthews.

Mary and her children and grandchildren represented no fewer than fourteen slaves in 1825, all but four of whom were living with her at the furnace. Tooler's family represented eight slaves, six of whom were living at the forge. The eleven "Wilson negroes" of 1815 had become the twenty-two "Wilson negroes" of 1825; twelve were at Etna Furnace, ten were at Union Forge.[21]

Weaver himself did not know the names of all the slave children at the time the partnership split, but he certainly knew what they meant to him. They represented both present wealth and a future source of recruits for his forge and fields. Not all these slaves were destined to play major roles in the history of the place he would soon rename Buffalo Forge, but a surprisingly large number of these children of 1825 would profoundly influence Weaver's fortunes in the years that lay ahead.

Weaver could have brought all the "Wilson negroes" living at Etna Furnace over to Union Forge in 1825. Mayburry had surrendered his claim to them. But their February 9 agreement left Mayburry in control of Etna Furnace, and he had promised to keep the furnace in production at least until the end of the year. This was a matter of no small concern to Weaver. He was dependent on this furnace for much of the pig iron he needed to run his forge, and the sale of any surplus pigs in the rising iron market of 1825 could help pay off the debts of the late firm of Mayburry & Weaver. Thus Weaver had a significant stake in Mayburry making a successful blast at Etna that year. So when Mayburry requested that all the "Wilson negroes" then at the furnace be allowed to remain for the balance of the year, Weaver agreed, with one exception. He insisted that one of Tooler's sons, Bob, who was working at Etna, be sent over to help out in the forge. Mayburry returned him to Weaver. But Bill, Tooler's other son at the furnace, stayed at Etna and so did Mary, Sally, Louisa, and their young children.[22]

Given Mayburry's earlier complaint about the expense of raising slave children for Weaver's benefit, his request to retain these slave women might on the surface have appeared odd. But Mary, Sally and Louisa were the only house servants at Etna; they had worked there for Mayburry and his family for ten years. Thomas Mayburry had married a local woman after he moved to the Valley in 1815. His wife, Eleanor, was considerably younger than he (Mayburry was fifty-five in 1815), and was a widow at the time of their marriage, with a young daughter.

The Mayburry family relied heavily on the three slave women, Mary in particular. She cooked not only for the Mayburrys but also for the "boarding room" for the white workers at the furnace, and she tended the cow herd and kept the dairy there as well. According to one observer, both Mayburry and his wife considered her a "verry valuable" servant and stated "that they could not do without her." Sally helped her mother with the cooking and dairying, and Louisa served as the "waiting maid" for Eleanor Mayburry's daughter and accompanied the little girl when she visited neighbors or took walks to the nearby village of Pattonsburg.[23] Weaver saw no pressing reason to take immediate possession of these slaves, so he acceded to Mayburry's request that Bill and the three women be allowed to stay at Etna. And, as he had done earlier, Weaver insisted that if Mary, Sally, and Louisa were to remain, their children should remain with them.

Weaver's failure to take possession of all of the "Wilson negroes" in 1825 proved to be a serious mistake. The bitterness between Weaver and Mayburry did not evaporate with the signing of the February agreement dissolving their partnership. Mayburry felt himself to be the injured party, and when the chance came to strike back at Weaver, he took it.

Weaver was truly vulnerable at only one point. Union Forge had little pig iron other than that from Etna Furnace. Only one other furnace was in blast in the area in 1825—Lydia Furnace twenty-five miles away in northern Rockbridge County—and it was owned by ironmasters who ran their own forge.[24] Transportation from that part of the county to Weaver's place was difficult and expensive. Although Etna was across the county line in Botetourt, it was only seventeen miles from Union Forge and the roads were better. Weaver needed Etna pig iron, and Mayburry controlled Etna. It did not take long for Mayburry to begin putting pressure on his former partner.

Weaver thought his supply of Etna pig iron was perfectly safe. The February dissolution agreement contained a clause which would provide his forge with at least a portion of its pig iron. It stipulated that if Weaver, using his own money, paid off any debts of the former firm then he was "entitled to demand from said Mayburry pig iron for the amount at the rate of $27 50/100 pr ton which said Mayburry on his part hereby agrees to deliver at the furnace when demanded."[25] Weaver would be paying off creditors; he would have to do so in order to protect his position at Union Forge, and Mayburry was obligated to provide enough metal to cover these payments. Such additional pig iron as Weaver might need he expected to receive under the usual bar-iron-for-pig-metal barter arrangement that generally prevailed between forge and furnace owners. The agreement did not specify this arrangement, however, a serious and uncharacteristic omission on Weaver's part. Perhaps it was the lateness of the hour on the night of February 9 when he and Mayburry finally finished their quarrel over the status of the "Wilson negroes." Perhaps he was too concerned over other matters covered in the agreement, things like the long clauses outlining the conditions under which the property belonging to the late firm could be sold by either partner. Or perhaps he simply underestimated Mayburry and failed to recognize the degree of bitterness and resentment Mayburry harbored against him as their partnership dissolved. Whatever the reason for the omission, Mayburry recognized the loophole and soon moved to exploit it.

First, he began selecting the lowest-grade pigs to turn over to Weaver to compensate him for the payments Weaver was making to pay off the firm's old debts. This was a serious matter for Weaver because poor pig iron would seriously damage the quality and reputation of his bar and threaten pending sales in Richmond and Lynchburg. Next, Mayburry insisted that Weaver pay cash for any additional Etna pig iron.[26]

In the spring of 1825, Mayburry rode over to Union Forge to press his demand. Shortly after this visit, Weaver wrote Mayburry a decidedly conciliatory letter outlining what was discussed at their meeting. The tone of this letter, dated May 12, 1825, contrasted sharply with that of the earlier heated exchanges between the two men, and the new note of amicability on Weaver's part may well have been prompted by his dependence on Mayburry for much of his pig iron.

> I have made up my mind, in future to communicate freely with you, whenever the nature of our business shall require it—this appears to me the only correct course and one that I shall not deviate from hereafter, unless a contrary disposition is evinced by yourself—This is a point we both agreed to when sitting in the garden—I there told [you] that money at this time was scarce—but anything I had, that you could use for the benefit of the business at Etna was entirely at your service—I now repeat the same thing to you—that you may use my Iron freely, which is the only thing I have, but if I should get cash, the latter shall be given as freely—

Weaver would exchange bar iron valued at $100 per ton for pig iron valued at $27.50 per ton. "The above is as low as a Forge owner can sell at, when pigs are $27.50 per Ton—and what I should think correct between you and me, *or even brothers*," Weaver wrote.[27]

Whatever Mayburry may have thought of Weaver's new and friendlier tone, he did not think much of Weaver's proposition. No cash, no pig iron, was Mayburry's final position, and he refused to budge. Unless Weaver met his terms, he would provide no more Etna metal for Union Forge.

Mayburry should have known better than to play this game with Weaver. He had neither the financial resources nor the guile to engage Weaver in a protracted struggle, and he was still vulnerable to a suit that would tie up his property until all the debts of Mayburry & Weaver were settled. Since Weaver had been the major financial contributor to their firm, the court might well decide that he owed Weaver a considerable amount of money in addition to his shared liability for the partnership's outstanding debts. Mayburry took a great gamble in cutting Union Forge off from its regular source of pig iron. It did not take long for Weaver to retaliate.

In the fall of 1825, Weaver filed suit against Mayburry in the Superior Court of Law and Chancery. He was prepared to push his case for all it was worth. The dissolution agreement of February 9, 1825, which Mayburry had signed in order to avoid a chancery suit, was a dead letter as far as Weaver was concerned. Weaver undoubtedly thought about the "Wilson negroes" still living at Etna Furnace before hauling Mayburry into court, but he was not unduly concerned about this issue. The bill of sale was in his name and his name alone. In addition, Mayburry had agreed to surrender all claim to these slaves in front of several reputable witnesses back on that February evening at Union Forge. Weaver's position regarding the "Wilson negroes" appeared unassailable.

Since Weaver had broken their February agreement by filing suit against him, however, Mayburry saw no need to honor his pledge to give up his interest in the Wilson slaves. First, the pledge had been a verbal one. The document he and Weaver signed on February 9 mentioned these slaves only in passing and did not refer to them either individually by name or collectively as the "Wilson negroes." In the section dealing with Mayburry's continued operation of Etna Furnace for the balance of the year, the agreement simply gave him permission "to use the stock of all kinds (including provisions) now on hand and belonging to the concern at said furnace, together with all the negroes, horses, waggons &c, now attached to the said establishment."[28] Second, Mayburry had a plan which might establish in the eyes of the court his contention that the "Wilson negroes" were indeed partnership property.

Weaver probably anticipated a fight over the Wilson slaves. But he apparently did not foresee Mayburry's strategy of obtaining a lengthy and damaging deposition from John S. Wilson, the man who had sold Weaver the original eleven slaves ten years earlier.

John Wilson remembered the transaction quite well. "The . . . negroes were sold to Wm. Weaver in the City of Philadelphia for the firm of Mayburry & Weaver, of Virginia, who had some time before Bought Iron Works of my Father," Wilson reported. "I considered the Sale made to the firm and it was a consideration with me at the time I made the Sale, that I expected & believed that the Negroes would be well and humanely treated by Tho..ˢ Mayburry, the then acting partner of the firm of Mayburry & Weaver in Virg..ᵃ," he continued. "The reasons assigned by Wm. Weaver for not taking the bill of sale in the name of the firm was that he thought Thomas Mayburry might have some Religious scruples, and I believe the Bill of Sale was made in his own name," Wilson recalled.

At this point in his testimony, Weaver's lawyers asked Wilson why he "considered the sale made to Mayburry & Weaver & not to William Weaver?" Wilson replied that "Wm. Weaver told me at the time I made the sale to him in Philadelphia that they were bought for the firm of Mayburry & Weaver."[29] After reading this deposition, Weaver no doubt regretted fobbing off that "Whitmore patent still & fixtures" on John Wilson back in 1815.

The dispute between Weaver and Mayburry was a fairly typical chancery court battle in antebellum Virginia. After Weaver brought suit against Mayburry, elaborate documentation was filed with the court, lengthy depositions were taken on both sides, and the whole thing dragged on for over ten years. It was not resolved until the two men reached a final out-of-court settlement in 1836. But before this agreement was reached, the court, drawing heavily on John Wilson's detailed deposition, had ruled that the "Wilson negroes" were partnership property.[30] Mayburry eventually lost the war with Weaver, but this particular battle he won. He still had a legal right to a portion of the Wilson slave force. Since a sizable number of these slaves—primarily Mary, Sally, Louisa, and their children—had remained in Mayburry's possession during the eleven years the case of Weaver *v.* Mayburry was before the court, Weaver clearly would have to contend with Mayburry's claim before a final settlement could be reached.

The two men who talked to Mayburry on Weaver's front porch on the night of February 9, 1825, had warned him to avoid a chancery suit at all costs. This turned out to be sound advice. When Mayburry later referred to chancery court as "the great gulf," he spoke from painful and bitter experience. "We had a long law suit of his own seeking and making, and I believe it was because he had got a good deal of my property into his possession and wished to keep it as long as possible," Mayburry commented in 1839; "the suit appeared to be interminable," he continued, and "by this means he was grinding me into the very dust with poverty."[31]

Mayburry was in desperate financial straits, and as a result he signed two very unfavorable out-of-court agreements with Weaver, the first in 1827, the last in 1836. In the initial document, dated January 19, 1827, Mayburry sold his half interest in Union Forge to Weaver for $4,000, payable *after* their chancery suit was settled.[32] This 1827 document effectively gave Weaver undisputed possession of Union Forge, but it left unresolved the issue of the "Wilson negroes." The same week this agreement was signed, Weaver changed the name of the property to Buffalo Forge, the name it would carry from that time on.[33]

The final agreement, signed on August 3, 1836, completed Weaver's acquisition of the entire landholdings he and Mayburry had purchased back in 1814. Since their chancery suit was still undecided and Weaver had not yet paid Mayburry for the forge, the new document was drawn up to cover both Buffalo Forge and Etna Furnace. Mayburry, hard pressed by other creditors, felt he had no choice but to accede to Weaver's terms. The price for his half interest in the two ironworks and all the adjoining land was "the paltry sum of $5,000," as Mayburry phrased it. Truly a mere bagatelle. Twenty-two years earlier, Mayburry & Weaver had agreed to pay William Wilson $27,500 for the same property. In 1839, three years after the "final" agreement was signed, Weaver was still withholding $3,000 of the $5,000 purchase price from Mayburry on the grounds that Mayburry had not provided a good title to all the land. As a consequence, Mayburry had been forced to sue Weaver in chancery court for the balance of his money. And chancery court, Mayburry observed bitterly, was like "the sleep of death."[34]

More than the land and the works that stood alongside Buffalo and Purgatory creeks was at stake in the agreement signed on August 3, 1836. One other matter had to be settled: "The Wilson negroes now in possession of said Mayburry."

For eleven years, the slaves Weaver had left at Etna Furnace in 1825 had remained with Thomas Mayburry. They lived at the furnace during 1826 and 1827; Mayburry rented Weaver's half interest in this property and operated the blast furnace on his own account during those two years. In 1828, however, Mayburry launched a new ironmaking venture in northern Rockbridge County. He acquired Gibraltar Forge, located on North River five or six miles downstream from Bath Forge, and erected a new blast furnace, which he named Vesuvius, at a site he had purchased on South River near Steele's Tavern, just below the Augusta County line. Mayburry moved his group of "Wilson negroes" to Vesuvius when he established his residence there in 1828, and then, after he sold the furnace in 1833, he took them to Gibraltar Forge. They were living at Gibraltar in the summer of 1836 when Mayburry and Weaver reached their final agreement.[35]

At the time Weaver had originally filed suit against his former partner in 1825, the number of Wilson slaves with Mayburry at Etna had stood at eleven: Tooler's Bill, Mary and her three youngest children, Sally and her three children, and Louisa and her one child. Now, in 1836, there were nineteen "Wilson negroes" at Gibraltar Forge. Eight, or possibly nine, of the children born to these slave women in the ensuing eleven years were still alive and were living with their mothers at "Mayburry's Forge," as Gibraltar was sometimes called.[36]

One of Mayburry's friendly witnesses in the suit brought by Weaver, a furnace employee named James Brawley, claimed as early as 1826 that the labor rendered by the "Wilson negroes" hardly compensated for the cost of maintaining the adults and providing for the children. The cooking, house-keeping, nursing, and dairying of the women, plus whatever work Bill was able to perform, were more than offset by the expense of "feeding, clothing, and raising the young negroes born at Etna Furnace," Brawley insisted. He underlined this point by referring to the cost of "the lying in, doctors bills &c" associated with the births of "eleven or twelve" slave children, "eight or nine of them now living." At this point in his deposition, Brawley was asked if there were "any of the children belonging to the Wilson negroes that died except Mary's twins." "I believe there was four died," Brawley answered, "all very young."[37] His matter-of-fact reply was a response to only one of the almost countless instances in the suit where Weaver and Mayburry grappled with each other over who owed whom and how much. No testimony was taken regarding the feelings of the mothers involved, or the fathers. Considerations of this sort had no bearing on the tilt in the balance of accounts between the two men and consequently were of no interest to the court.

Mayburry, who felt that he had been financially damaged and exploited by Weaver, was not about to surrender the entire Wilson slave force. Once the court accepted John Wilson's testimony that Weaver had bought the slaves for the firm, Mayburry had a powerful lever to use against his former partner on this issue, and use it he did.

Mayburry wanted to retain the services of Mary, his longtime cook, house servant, and dairymaid, and secure sole ownership of Mary's three young children. According to the evidence offered in the suit, Mary was an exceedingly valuable slave. The Mayburrys had earlier remarked how much they depended on her, and their positive assessment of her was confirmed by John Danenhower, Weaver's young nephew who had met Mary during his first days at Etna Furnace in 1823. "Mary the cook was one of the best slaves I have ever known," Danenhower testified in 1830.[38] Mary's relatives at Buffalo Forge would provide a much more eloquent testament to her in the years that lay ahead.

The article of agreement Weaver and Mayburry struck on August 3, 1836, divided the "Wilson negroes" between the two men. "The said Mayburry is to keep Mary and her three children viz John, Hamilton and Ellen for which said Weaver is to give him a title," the agreement stipulated; "the balance of the negroes viz Sally & her children and Louisa and her children are to be given up by the said Mayburry to Weaver on the 1st day of January next."[39]

This document made no mention of Tooler's son Bill. There is a chance that he managed to escape (as he had attempted to do in 1822), but such evidence as we have suggests that he may have been the victim of an accident. In 1825 Mayburry noted "the infirmity of the boy for several years," and another witness reported that for some time after he was purchased in 1815, Bill had been "a cripple and incapable of work."[40] He was alive in 1828 when Mayburry moved to Vesuvius Furnace, but he may well have died before the 1836 agreement was drawn up.[41]

This agreement was also silent as to Sally's and Louisa's husbands. Sam Williams, Sr., Sally's husband, did come to Buffalo Forge at some point because his name appears subsequently in the records kept there. Whether the father of Louisa's children also came into Weaver's possession is unknown. He may have, since Louisa had children at Buffalo Forge after 1837. The other possibility, of course, is that the children born to her there were the result of a new union.

The division took place as scheduled at the beginning of 1837. Mary's family was broken as Weaver took possession of her daughters Sally and Louisa and their thirteen children—Mary's grandchildren—on New Year's Day, 1837. Mayburry retained, as the agreement stipulated, Mary and her three youngest children: John, who was twenty; Hamilton, thirteen; and Ellen, eleven.

One other slave was involved in this arrangement, as Weaver described in a later deposition outlining the terms of the settlement. "Mayburry had held over during the contest between him and me up to the compromise about 20 negroes: four of the negroes I gave Mayburry under the compromise, and the balance were returned to me, except one which was in possession of Mrs. Weir, a daughter of Mrs. Mayburry, for which negro I deducted $400 out of the first payment under the compromise," he reported in 1842. Weaver went on to note that this $400 represented "the value of a negro girl" and "was applied towards taking up a note for $2500 which I endorsed for Mr. Mayburry immediately after the compromise."[42] Chances are this slave girl was one of Louisa's daughters; Louisa had served as the "waiting maid" for Eleanor Mayburry's daughter when the little girl was growing up at Etna Furnace. The forced division of Mary's family thus provided each man with a portion of the human assets of their former firm and allocated an additional slave to a member of Thomas Mayburry's family.

As far as Weaver was concerned, things had turned out remarkably well. He owned Buffalo Forge and Etna Furnace, and he had finally dissolved the last remnants of his ties to Thomas Mayburry, something Weaver had been seeking for over a decade.

Weaver also had undisputed ownership of the overwhelming majority of the "Wilson negroes" who had been living with Thomas Mayburry and his family for the past eleven years. Mayburry ended up with four of these slaves and Weaver got fifteen, which was about the way things usually turned out between the two men. Weaver undoubtedly used Mayburry's sizable indebtedness to him and other creditors in striking this lopsided bargain. But perhaps Mayburry drew satisfaction from the fact that Weaver had not gotten away with all the "Wilson negroes." Whatever Mayburry's sentiments may have been, it is almost certain that the settlement between the two masters brought deep sorrow to the slaves involved.

The dissolution of Mayburry's and Weaver's partnership involved them intimately because it divided Mary's family between the two men. Subsequent events were to show, however, that Mary and the children who remained with her were not forgotten by those family members who went to Buffalo Forge in January 1837. Every generation of children born to her descendants there had a girl named Mary, and there were quite a few Johns, Hamiltons, and Ellens as well. If the names given to these children tell us anything at all about the lives of the slaves at Buffalo Forge, it is that they bitterly resented the destruction of their family that occurred on that winter day early in 1837. By exercising an element of their precious and limited autonomy—the right to name their own children—they acknowledged and preserved the memory of a tragic moment in their family's history.

4

Bath
Iron Works

Thomas Mayburry's decision to choke off Weaver's supply of Etna pig iron in the summer of 1825 had created a critical situation at Buffalo Forge. Weaver responded to this crisis by purchasing small lots of pig metal from other Valley blast furnaces, but the distances involved and the chance that these sources of supply might also prove unreliable prompted him to make a major investment in a new ironmaking enterprise.

In September 1825 he bought Lydia Furnace, located on Big Calf Pasture River, a tributary of North River, in a remote and rugged section of Rockbridge County some twelve miles northwest of Lexington. It was the only blast furnace in operation in the county at that time, which made it even more desirable in Weaver's eyes. He changed the name of the furnace to Bath, a move confirming its new ownership and also reflecting the proximity of the furnace site to a local spa known as Rockbridge Baths.[1]

Weaver needed a manager for his furnace, and he thought he found a good one in the person of John Doyle, a Pennsylvanian who had come to

Rockbridge County in 1825. Weaver later described Doyle as "a man of great address and considerable intelligence" who had "represented himself ... as a man of experience in the iron business ... and fully understood the management of a forge and furnace."[2] Just to be on the safe side, Weaver sent his nephew John Danenhower up to Bath to act as Doyle's assistant.[3] Weaver again appears to have been placing Danenhower in a position where he could observe and report on the activities of one of Weaver's business associates. If such was the case, Weaver was to be disappointed in young Danenhower's performance on this occasion.

Doyle put Bath Furnace into production almost immediately in the fall of 1825.[4] With his own source of pig iron now guaranteed, Weaver moved ahead vigorously to maximize both production and profits at the forge. His timing could not have been better. With his costs low and with iron prices climbing, he was finally able to realize the extraordinary profits he had anticipated back in 1814 when he and Mayburry had made their original investment. Merchant bar commanded a cash price of between $100 and $112 per ton in Lynchburg, and Weaver made even more on local sales. During the mid-1820s, his forge was the only ironworks in Rockbridge County producing ample quantities of bar iron, a monopoly Weaver had no qualms about exploiting.[5]

Local customers, needless to say, were not pleased. "We have been thinking for some time past that the Barter trade existing between you and ourselves is a very unequal one," a mercantile firm in nearby Lexington wrote Weaver early in 1829. "But we believe it is only necessary for the case to be fairly stated for you to see the propriety of making an alteration on your price," they went on. "Whilst we are selling you our goods at the lowest cash price, ... we are paying you about 25 pr cent more for your Iron than it is worth elsewhere." These Lexington merchants obviously thought plain talk was called for, so they did not mince words:

The fact is Mr. Weaver that Iron has always been sold *too high* in this country. It is a stubborn fact that whilst the farmers & mechanicks in the neighborhood of Lynchburg 50 miles from where the article is made have been buying their Iron for several years past @ 5 cts pr lb the same class of men in the very *Iron region* have been compelled to pay from 6 to 7 cts per lb. ... You may rely upon it sir, that among the intelligent farmers of this country this difference of price has been a cause of heart burning and has produced a feeling of hostility towards the Iron manufacturers which to say the least of it has been of no advantage to them—The Iron manufacturer who first makes this change, which sheer justice requires at your hands to say nothing of patriotism or the disposition to favour ones own section of the country at least as much as another, will turn the tide of opinion in his favor and in our humble sentiment gain by it in the end.[6]

Goodwill was not a currency in which Weaver placed much value, however. He held his price at 6 to 7 cents per pound on local sales, which brought him between $120 and $140 per ton on iron delivered to customers in the neighborhood of Buffalo Forge.[7]

Ample supplies of Bath pig iron and a growing crew of skilled slave forgemen produced a dramatic increase in the tonnages of iron hammered out at Weaver's forge in the mid-1820s. In 1825, with pig iron in short supply thanks to Mayburry's maneuverings, the forge turned out only 160 tons of merchant bar. The next year, with Bath metal arriving regularly, production jumped to 225 tons. In 1827, Buffalo Forge turned out 250 tons of iron. With prices holding at $100 per ton and over during this period, William Weaver made a small fortune during his first three years without Thomas Mayburry. He cleared over $5,000 on his forge operations in 1825, $6,000 in 1826, and $7,000 in 1827.[8]

According to his manager at Bath, Weaver's blast furnace did just as well. "At that time there was no competition in the Iron business here, castings were in great demand, and I sold $10,000 worth of castings at high prices," Doyle recalled later. "I sent 100 or 150 tons of pig metal to Richmond or its vicinity for which from $40 to $43 per ton was obtained," he noted.[9] Part of the pig iron sold in the Richmond market was cannon metal purchased by John Clarke, the proprietor of the nearby Bellona Foundry, and cast into ordnance at that facility.[10] Pig iron of this description always commanded a premium price and helped establish the general reputation of a furnace for high-quality iron, which helped the sales of lower grades of metal.

High prices had been accompanied by low costs. The hire of an able-bodied slave for a full year "did not exceed $50," Doyle reported, and accumulating ample supplies of iron ore and charcoal fuel for the furnace had been accomplished with an absolute minimum of trouble and expense. "The ore . . . was easily raised, was near the surface, and the timber [for charcoal] was convenient," he explained. Maintaining their slave force had also cost them very little because corn and pork were both plentiful and cheap in the Valley during these years. According to Doyle, the profits realized at Bath Furnace during 1826–27 had been "something over $14,-000."[11] Weaver later disputed this figure, but Bath clearly made a considerable amount of money during the initial period of Weaver's ownership. Thus during his first three years in the Valley manufacturing iron on his own account, William Weaver made in the vicinity of $30,000. He was able to settle with William Wilson's heirs, pay off his debts in Philadelphia, including those incurred from his brother's estate, and still have capital available for the purchase of additional land and slaves.[12]

Weaver had, in fact, managed to catch the wave of economic prosperity that was building all across the country during the middle and late 1820s. These flush times stood in stark contrast to the depressed economy Thomas Mayburry had faced in Virginia following the War of 1812, but that was the way things always seemed to go with these two. Weaver might not like the political situation that was developing nationally as Andrew Jackson swept to presidential victories in 1828 and again in 1832. Like most ironmasters, he had nothing but disdain for the Democratic party and its low tariff views. But there was no denying that the Jacksonian years were, by and large, prosperous ones, and William Weaver was certainly a man who knew how to seize the day.

With business booming, Weaver undertook a major expansion of his manufacturing facilities. In 1826, he purchased over 5,000 acres of ore and timberland along North River, some two miles downstream from Bath Furnace, and the next year he decided to erect a new forge on this property, a logical decision. He was working Buffalo Forge to its full capacity, and he could still not satisfy the demand for his iron. A second forge would give him added production and increased profits, and he had the money to build it. Buffalo Forge really could not be expanded because its waterpower would not drive a larger forge, but North River had ample waterpower available where Weaver's land was located.

Putting a forge near the blast furnace made sense in several others ways as well. Pig iron could be brought by wagon the short distance from the furnace to the forge, worked into bars, and then hauled nine miles to Cedar Grove, the head of navigation on North River. There the bar iron could be loaded onto light, flat-bottomed bateaux and shipped directly to Lynchburg or Richmond. So in the latter part of 1827, Weaver authorized Doyle to erect a forge on the land he had acquired near Bath Furnace the previous year. Bath Forge went into production in December 1828, and from this time on, Weaver's furnace and forge complex on North River carried the name Bath Iron Works.[13]

Operating two forges would require a significantly larger force of skilled ironworkers. Weaver, as always, bought slave forgemen whenever they came on the market, hired others when they could be found, and then shuttled these artisans back and forth between Buffalo Forge and Bath Iron Works as the occasion demanded. Once again, however, he was forced to take on a number of white forgemen—mostly new men, recruited in Pennsylvania—in order to maintain a satisfactory level of production at both installations.[14]

His experience with white labor in the 1820s was a virtual replay of the difficulties he had encountered at Etna and Retreat furnaces during his first months in Virginia in 1814 and 1815. Alcohol consumption was heavy among the white laborers at Bath, and in one case a drunken worker "on his return from the Stillhouse to his family got drowned," as Doyle put it, leaving "a widow with a parcel of children."[15] The white workers were also too "fond of novelty," in Weaver's view, and were liable to be off "on a Frolic" when most needed. Sometimes they just refused to work or feigned illness. These deficiencies, as Weaver perceived them, only confirmed his prejudice against employing free labor in a slave country.[16]

The acquisition of Bath Furnace and the construction and operation of Bath Forge put Weaver back into the slave hiring market in a major way. Not only did he need forgemen, he had to have hands to quarry stones, move the massive rocks on sleds to the forge site, build roads, help construct the large forge planned for Bath, and erect various support buildings and a dam across North River.[17] Then he would require a large number of slaves for the operation of Bath Iron Works once construction was finished. During the late 1820s and early 1830s, he regularly hired sixty or more slaves to man his two ironmaking facilities.[18] These men, plus his own black forgemen, formed the backbone of the labor force at both Bath Iron Works and Buffalo Forge year after year.

Acquiring more than sixty slaves every year was by no means a routine affair. In mid or late December, Weaver would cross the Blue Ridge Mountains and ride to the hiring centers in eastern Virginia, particularly Spotsylvania, Orange, and Louisa counties. There he would compete with farmers, canal builders, gold miners, Richmond industrialists, and other Valley ironmasters for slaves whose masters were willing to hire them out for the year.[19]

Weaver had to convince the owners that he was a good credit risk and that he would treat their valuable human property well during the year, and he often had to convince the slaves of his good intentions as well. Employers who abused their hirelings, who fed them poorly, or who drove them excessively hard soon got an unsavory reputation among the slaves themselves. When employers of this stripe returned to the hiring markets to obtain another year's labor, they frequently found slaves hard to come by. Weaver wanted no trouble of this sort. Without an adequate force of slave workers, he could not run his iron business. Over the years, Weaver received enough letters from slaveowners to convince him that cultivation of a certain amount of goodwill among his hirelings was essential. In December 1828, he wanted to hire a slave owned by a Spotsylvania County woman and managed to bond for him. The hire was tentative, however, because the woman insisted on learning the slave's wishes before sending him on to Weaver's ironworks. On the last day of December, she wrote Weaver the outcome of her consultations:

> Enclosed you will receive your bond, as our agreement was, if Brandus was not willing to go to you, I should not force him and on seeing Mr. Brawley, who says the boy is anxious to remain with him, therefore I cannot think of compelling him to go any where it is not his wish, as that has always been my rule, as I told you he could have his choice.[20]

Initially, Weaver's reputation as an employer seems to have been a good one. The owner of a slave who was returning to Buffalo Forge for another year's labor told Weaver "I must confess that I had rather have seventy five dollars on you than ninety . . . on one half of the people and therefore you must have him for seventy five dollars."[21] It is obviously more difficult to document how the slaves themselves felt about Weaver, but such evidence as we have suggests that slave hirelings considered Weaver a decent man who treated his workers well. Robert Crutchfield, a Spotsylvania County man who was helping Weaver hire in the late 1820s, wrote that he was sending Weaver an extra hand for 1829 because the slave was "so anxious to come to you."[22]

Several months later, the same agent reminded Weaver of a revealing incident that had occurred when Weaver had been on his hiring swing through eastern Virginia earlier that year. Among the hands Crutchfield had sent Weaver was a Negro named Davy. Weaver complained several weeks after the workers arrived that he did not want to give a hire bond for Davy because he was "a free Man." Crutchfield replied that "in order to prove to you that I did not intend to impose him on you as a slave, you will recollect that when you left my house in passing the yard gate, I introduced Davy to you as one of the hands then hired [by] you." At that time, Weaver had "recognized him as an old acquaintance & made no objection to him." Crutchfield concluded the matter by advising Weaver to "let his hire rest upon the contingency of his serving you faithfully (for that is what he promised most confidently)." The fact that Weaver remembered the man "as an old acquaintance" and the black man, who was free, would choose to go to Weaver's place to work for the year as a hireling suggests strongly that Weaver was known among blacks in the prime hiring areas of eastern Virginia as an employer who did not abuse his workers.[23] Weaver could ill afford to lose that reputation.

In 1830, however, Weaver's reputation was placed in some jeopardy. The seriousness of the situation was outlined in a letter he received in early

January of that year. William Staples, a hiring agent in neighboring Amherst County, had bad news for Weaver:

> I am sorry to inform you that one of the men I hired you (Isaac) has expressed such an unwillingness to return to you that I feared should I send him over he would run away, and perhaps be of little or no service to you during the year. I therefore thought it best to hire him in Amherst where he is willing to stay. . . . I am very sorry this has happened as perhaps it may put you to some inconvenience, but I hope not much. When I hired him I was under the impression he would be willing to serve you, but I find he is not. Sam has requested me to ask the favor of you to permit him to stay at the establishment at which you live; he says he greatly prefers it. He also was unwilling to return; but says he would have no objection, provided he could live at your own establishment. I hope, if it will not put you to much inconvenience, you will grant his request.[24]

Amherst County was an important source of workers for Weaver. So was Spotsylvania County, and the word from there was not good either. One of the key workers Weaver wanted to rehire for Bath Iron Works for 1830 "was unwilling to return to you," Robert Crutchfield, his Spotsylvania hiring agent, reported later in January. The slave's owner "gave him his choice & he I am informed will go to Mr. Mayburry." Weaver could not have been pleased with this last bit of information, but that was not the worst of it.

> I have not been able to get you any hands in consequence of their being unwilling generally to go over the Mountains (as they call it). You will not take it unfriendly when I say to you in candour that some of the hands (I know not whom) have made somewhat an unfavourable impression on the negroes in the neighborhood as to the treatment at the place for which they were wanting.[25]

In every instance, "the place for which they were wanting" was Bath Iron Works.

Weaver should have seen this trouble coming. Conditions at Bath had deteriorated badly in 1828 and 1829. Periodic shortages of food and clothing had occurred there during both years, but the situation had been particularly bad in 1829. Most of the supplies for the isolated Bath works had to be hauled in from Buffalo Forge, some twenty-five miles away. Bad weather, poor roads, a shortage of wagons, poor planning, and sometimes low stockpiles at Buffalo Forge had led to real suffering among the Bath laborers, both slave and free.[26] "We have been out of leather for 5 weeks & our Shoemaker & all our people barefooted & the whites . . . really grumbling," Doyle told Weaver in the summer of 1828.[27] Shoes again were in short supply in the fall of 1829, and this shortage was particularly critical because of the rough work required around the furnace and forge. Slave miners, for example, were forced to work in water as it became necessary to dig ever deeper into the pits in order to raise the ore needed to feed Bath Furnace.[28]

An even more serious situation developed at Bath during 1829. Much of the slave housing at both the furnace and forge had always been, in the words of one observer, "very indifferent"—earthen-floored cabins, twelve by fifteen feet, with clapboard roofs and wooden chimneys, all "built in the roughest style."[29] In the summer and fall of 1829, one of these cabins was abandoned by John Doyle "in consequence of the dysentery having got among the negroes in it." The outbreak of dysentery at the works in 1829 took the lives of six hired slaves.[30] No wonder slave hirelings in eastern Virginia did not want to go back "over the mountain" to Bath Iron Works in 1830. Not surprisingly the number of runaway slaves from Bath shot up during 1829 as well. Weaver blamed his manager, John Doyle, for most of the troubles, and the statements of some of the hirelings confirmed this view. A master in Amherst County returned a runaway named Abram to Weaver in the spring of 1829 with the information that "his principle complaint seemed to be lodged against your overseer." Abram's owner had "chastised him severely" for running off, and he requested that no further punishment be inflicted on him.[31]

Weaver ultimately came to the conclusion that he had another Thomas Mayburry on his hands. Weaver later claimed that he found evidence suggesting Doyle's duplicity when he went over the books at Bath in early 1828 and discovered that Doyle had posted all of the castings made at the furnace twice. The sale of hollowware had been one of the most lucrative aspects of the furnace's operation, and this double counting had inflated the profit figures considerably, according to Weaver. Doyle had reported the profits on his first two years as furnace manager as $17,000; since his contract with Weaver called for Doyle to receive any profits above $14,000, he stood to gain $3,000 if Weaver accepted his accounting. Weaver admitted that he did not know if the error on the books "was done by design or not," but when he called it to Doyle's attention, the manager "became much exasperated, urged that he was poor and would have nothing left for his services." Weaver agreed to give him $1,400 out of the profits on the furnace.[32] Even more important, he left Doyle in charge of Bath. The two men had a contract calling for Doyle to manage the furnace through 1829, though it seems unlikely that Weaver would have honored the terms of that agreement if Doyle had not been making money at Bath. But Weaver was determined to introduce new management at Bath Iron Works as soon as Doyle's contract expired. He told Doyle late in 1829 to close up the books at Bath and vacate the property by January 1, 1830.[33]

The two men did not part amicably. Doyle called Weaver "a damned scoundrel" and insisted that Weaver had cheated him. He filed suit against Weaver in chancery court claiming, among other things, that Weaver had told him that Bath pig iron could not be sold above $26 a ton in Richmond while Weaver was actually selling between 100 and 150 tons of the metal at prices ranging from $30 to $33 per ton.[34] Weaver replied that this was none of Doyle's business, called him a "rascal," and claimed that Doyle had mismanaged Bath and run up unnecessary debts during his final two years there.[35] The suit, a fairly typical chancery court suit in antebellum Virginia, was finally decided some twenty years after it was filed. The court ruled that Doyle owed Weaver $88.09.[36]

Doyle's anger, like that of Thomas Mayburry, did not abate with the passage of time. When he was asked his opinion of Weaver ten years after he departed from Bath, Doyle replied, "I despise him most cordially, and I believe that he is despised by nine tenths of the men who ever had any dealings with him."[37] There is no way to know if Doyle's assessment of Weaver's popularity, or lack thereof, is correct, but it is certain that the master of Buffalo Forge created another bitter enemy in the Valley iron trade when he dismissed Doyle from his post at Bath Iron Works.

Weaver was not without his defenders in this confrontation, however. Shortly after Doyle left Bath, one of Weaver's commission merchants in Lynchburg wrote to congratulate him on "getting rid of Mr. Doyle. I do not at all doubt that it is like getting your neck released from a Mill Stone," the merchant added.[38]

Weaver knew whom he wanted to appoint to replace Doyle at Bath. William Weaver Davis and Abram Weaver Davis, his sister Margaret's two sons, had been in Virginia for several years helping Weaver run his iron business. Abram had come down in 1826, William had followed him two years later, and each had spent time at both Buffalo Forge and Bath Iron Works as clerks and undermanagers. John Danenhower had been in the Valley since 1823 and he had served Weaver in a number of capacities, including a stint as Doyle's principal assistant at Bath. Weaver apparently did not hold Danenhower responsible for troubles at the furnace and forge in Doyle's time, or if he did, he was willing to give his nephew a second chance. All three were young men. William Davis would be twenty-four, Danenhower would turn twenty-one, and Abram Davis would be only twenty years old in 1830. Weaver later claimed to harbor fears about the youth and good judgment of both John Danenhower and Abram Davis, but William Davis had demonstrated considerable capacity, first as the manager of Weaver's cotton factory near Germantown and then as the principal clerk at Bath Forge in 1829.[39] And Weaver was counting on a fourth partner joining them at Bath Iron Works.

The other partner was also relatively young, but he already had an impressive background in the iron business. He was Samuel F. Jordan, twenty-five years old in 1830, and the son of Colonel John Jordan, Weaver's chief rival in the Valley. John Jordan had built a furnace and forge in Alleghany County, west of Rockbridge, in 1827. This substantial ironworks, known as Clifton Forge, had emerged as Weaver's most serious competition in his efforts to dominate the local iron trade. Sam Jordan had been a partner in his father's firm since its inception, and he would have been a most unlikely partner for Weaver's nephews except for one thing. In 1828, Sam Jordan had married Hannah Davis, the sister of William and Abram Davis and a frequent visitor at Buffalo Forge prior to her marriage. Weaver wanted Sam Jordan at Bath with the Davis boys and John Danenhower, and late in 1829 Jordan agreed to join them.[40]

Weaver hoped to accomplish several things by placing his nephews and Sam Jordan at Bath Iron Works. First and foremost, he wanted to ensure a regular supply of pig iron for Buffalo Forge. Bath Furnace produced a high-quality metal, and Weaver believed that the firm of Jordan, Davis & Company could operate the blast furnace successfully, keeping his interests, and his need for pig iron, firmly in mind.

Second, Weaver seems to have gone into the new arrangement with the idea that the Bath property would ultimately belong to the Davis boys, John Danenhower, and Sam and Hannah Davis Jordan.[41] Weaver, still single, would be forty-nine years old in March 1830, and he had been responsible for the welfare of William and Abram Davis since 1813. William had been seven and Abram only three when Weaver became their guardian, and Weaver had paid for the boys' schooling in Philadelphia and supported the family, including their sister Hannah, during the ensuing years.[42] Now he had a chance to set the boys up in a way that would also work to his advantage at Buffalo Forge. John Danenhower, at work for Weaver during the seven years they had both been in Virginia, was eager to go into the iron business on his own account.[43]

Finally, Sam Jordan, in addition to being Hannah Davis's husband, would bring both capital and much-needed experience into the Bath enterprise. It looked like an ideal situation for both Weaver and the four young men who would make up the partnership known as Jordan, Davis & Company.

Weaver insisted from the outset that his object was to serve the interests of his young relatives, not his own. As Sam Jordan later recalled, Weaver told them "that he had a plenty to live on without that property, that he had no family of his own, that he intended his property for his relatives at his death."[44] In somewhat more direct language, the young men referred to Weaver in their private conversations as "an old bachelor, reputed to be wealthy," and they viewed the Bath opportunity as a way to enhance their own wealth and station. Sam Jordan described Weaver as "urgent" in persuading him to sell out his interest in his father's ironworks in Alleghany County, and said Weaver assured him that "it would be to his advantage" to come to Bath "even if he should get nothing for his interest in the firm of Jordan & Irvine" which operated the Clifton Forge works.[45]

The contract between Weaver and Jordan, Davis & Company did not spell out any of these promises, however. Indeed it did not spell anything out in writing at all. The contract was an oral one, a method that was perfectly satisfactory, Weaver later maintained, because all parties well understood what was involved and because the boys "had known him long enough to have confidence in him."[46] Of such oversights great lawsuits are made.

The contract called for the four partners to buy Bath Iron Works from Weaver for $30,000, but no date was set for the payment of this money. Instead, Jordan, Davis & Company were to pay Weaver interest on the purchase price annually at the rate of 6 percent. The firm was to buy the personal property at the works as of January 1, 1830—tools, fixtures, supplies, stocks of pig and bar iron, and so forth—and provide Weaver with "a sufficiency of pig metal to make 150 tons bar iron per year until all the personal property was paid for."[47] That was it, an apparently simple, straightforward verbal agreement between relatives and men of goodwill, clearly understood by all.

At least one interested observer thought it was not quite so simple, however. John Jordan, Sam's father, did not like the looks of the arrangement from the outset. He wondered why Weaver was calling at his son's home prior to the agreement, and when he heard what was afoot, he did not want Sam to go to Bath. John Jordan "thought that there was not a sufficiency of ore to make a permanent Iron Establishment," and that "without ore the property would not even be worth fifteen thousand." Sam "was determined to go," however, and he ignored his father's wishes. When John Jordan subsequently asked Weaver about the deal, Weaver repeated the assurances he had given to Sam and the others earlier, "that the [$30,000] price was merely nominal, and that he never expected to have a family himself, and designed the most of his property for his nephews and nieces." John Jordan was unconvinced. "I told [Weaver] that I thought he was making [the boys] a *Scotch Present,*" he later recalled.[48]

Weaver had an additional reason for wanting his young relatives settled in at, and operating, Bath Iron Works in 1830. Weaver was contemplating matrimony. On his visits to Pennsylvania in the late 1820s, he had been courting a Philadelphia widow named Elizabeth Newkirk Woodman. Weaver thought he was keeping all of this more or less a secret, but at least one of his nephews in Virginia had a good idea what was going on. Abram Davis remained at Buffalo Forge in 1830 to help manage the business and then to run things when Weaver went north in the early spring of that year. He was planning on joining the partnership at Bath Iron Works in 1831 after his twenty-first birthday. "I suppose that ere this the *auto-da-fe* is accomplished, the *nuptiale-de-celebratione* is passed, & the delights of married life (if so they may be called) are now yours," Abram wrote his Uncle William on July 24, 1830; "you might have told me before you departed, or at least have mentioned the fact (for I was aware of it six months ago) it would have shown that you had placed a confidence when it would never have been abused." Abram's speculation that the wedding had already taken place was a bit premature. William and Elizabeth were married on August 5, 1830; Weaver was forty-nine, Eliza, as she preferred to be called, was forty-five. They honeymooned at Saratoga Springs and then returned to Philadelphia, where Weaver had rented a house for the winter.[49]

Speculation regarding Weaver's future business plans was rife in Virginia following his marriage; "there is a great clamour in this country & Lynchburg about your not intending to reside here," Abram wrote his uncle on October 22, 1830. Owners of the slaves hired to Bath Iron Works and Buffalo Forge who were due to be paid at the end of the year appeared to be particularly worried. "I should presume that here [at Buffalo Forge] we should have about 800 Ds Hire to pay but as you say *that* at Bath Works will be heavy, and we must assist them," Abram continued. He advised Weaver to be sure to settle these hire bonds in order to protect the credit of both installations.[50]

Whatever Weaver's plans may have been immediately following his marriage, he did not abandon Buffalo Forge. He was back in the Valley before the year was out, and his wife, Eliza, came with him.

As these changes were occurring in Weaver's personal life, William Davis, John Danenhower, and Sam Jordan were pushing ahead at Bath Iron Works. Much work needed to be done. Bath Furnace had to be completely rebuilt, a new furnace dam had to be constructed across Big Calf Pasture River, extensive repairs had to be made to Bath Forge, a turnpike built across a portion of the property, and farm land had to be cleared and fenced. These improvements required eight to ten months of hard and steady work, almost all of which was performed by slave labor.[51]

A force of over fifty slaves toiled at Bath Iron Works in 1830. They cut, hauled, and fitted the massive stones for the new furnace stack, worked in the cold running water of Big Calf Pasture River building the new furnace dam, erected cabins, stables, and furnace buildings, built Weaver's turnpike, and cut the timber, made the charcoal, and mined the ore and limestone needed to put the new furnace in blast. Once the manufacture of pig iron commenced at Bath Furnace on October 1, 1830, their labor was vital to the successful operation of both furnace and forge.[52]

When asked about the proportion of free and slave workers employed at Bath by Jordan, Davis & Company, one observer reported that "Much the largest portion of it was slave labor. I think at least about four fifths of it." And most of these slaves, he noted, "were principally hired from the East of the Blue Ridge."[53] He might also have added that almost all of these slaves had been hired by Weaver, who had visited the principal hiring areas in eastern Virginia at the beginning of the year.[54] His reputation would be on the line if any difficulty developed with these hands.

Trouble began almost at once. Two slaves hired in Amherst County ran away in early March, and before the month was out another slave had fled from Bath.[55] "The Negroe man named Ben has come home this morning and complains of being very unwell also of his fare at your Iron Works," the slave's owner, Elizabeth Mathews, wrote Weaver from Louisa County on March 29, 1830; "he says he left your Service on Friday the 19th of March in consequence of not being fed well & other harsh treatment," she added. Since Ben was "not willing to stay" at Bath, she intended to allow him to remain at home.[56] This letter was addressed to Weaver, but he may well have left for Philadelphia by the time it reached Buffalo Forge.

Weaver's absence and his preoccupation with his marriage were undoubtedly the major reasons he neglected the situation developing at Bath. He relied on letters from Jordan, Davis & Company and from twenty-year-old Abram Davis at Buffalo Forge to keep him apprised of what was going on in Virginia, and these communications contained no hint of difficulties over slave labor at Bath Iron Works, or anywhere else, for that matter. The only mention of the Bath slaves came up toward the end of the year when they reminded Weaver that he would have to pay much of Jordan, Davis & Company's large bill for Negro hire.[57]

A letter dispatched to Buffalo Forge in late October also mentioned the flight of the slave Ben, and although it was addressed to Weaver, once again he may not have seen it. He and Eliza were living in Philadelphia during much of 1830, and he did not return to Virginia until late November or early December 1830. James Dickinson of Louisa County, a friend of

Weaver's who regularly hired a large number of slaves to him, had acted as Elizabeth Mathews's agent in the hiring out of Ben, and he sent a message to Weaver about this slave on October 21, 1830. "I wrote to your Nephew about Mrs. Mathis [sic] negro—& have never got an answer," Dickinson noted. As a consequence Ben had remained at home, as Mrs. Mathews had indicated that he would, and his services had been lost to Jordan, Davis & Company that year.[58]

Weaver gave no indication that he received this letter or knew of possible labor difficulties developing at Bath. In December 1830, he again set out on his annual hiring swing through Louisa and the other counties in central and northern Virginia where he traditionally secured most of his hired slave labor. And once again he was seeking to obtain a sizable labor force for Bath Iron Works as well as a few hands for woodchopping and farm work around Buffalo Forge. Sam Jordan accompanied him on this trip.[59]

A number of factors made the lives of the slaves at Bath particularly difficult. The furnace and forge lay in rugged terrain in a sparsely settled area of Rockbridge County that did not produce abundant stocks of grain and meat. As had been the case during John Doyle's tenure at Bath, most of the supplies for the works had to be brought in by wagon from Buffalo Forge. This invariably led to hardships for the workers there. Shortages of beef, bacon, flour, shoes, and clothing occurred periodically throughout the year.[60] Some of the slaves may also have resented the eating arrangements at Bath. "Our Forge hands eat in one kitchen collectively," one of the partners wrote, "its being so convenient we can oversee the whole."[61] This setup subjected the black forge workers to continued white supervision at a time of day slaves traditionally viewed as their own and may have been a source of additional dissatisfaction.

Housing was another problem. A few of the slave cabins at the forge were comparable to the housing used by the white workers there, but some of the slave houses had dirt or unfinished board floors and were missing chinking in the log walls. Overall, the slaves' quarters at Bath Iron Works seem to have been poor to begin with and to have deteriorated badly while Jordan, Davis & Company held the property. It was particularly bad at the ore bank near the furnace. Of the seven cabins there, two were described by one observer as "very small & rough, not larger than a common size chicken coop."[62]

Slave miners working at the ore bank faced a number of adverse circumstances. Doyle had largely exhausted the high-quality ore near the surface of this mine in the late 1820s and had been forced to open deep pits in order to raise enough ore to keep Bath Furnace in operation. Jordan, Davis & Company inherited this situation, just as Sam's father had foreseen, and had to go deeper and deeper for their ore, eventually taking these pits to a depth of twenty-five feet or so. Most ironmasters in the Valley could dig the ore needed to keep their furnaces in blast using a white supervisor and four or five slave miners. It took ten slaves to work the ore bank at Bath, plus a slave boy who ran a mule-drawn windlass used to raise the ore to the surface.[63]

Mining iron ore in deep pits would have been hard labor under any circumstances, but there was yet another problem at Bath. During the wet season—which usually ran from November to March but could stretch as long as nine months—water ran through these pits. Two wooden pumps operated constantly in a losing battle to keep the ore bank dry, "and very frequently, when the pump would be out of order, all hands employed in the bank, would have to assist in bailing out with the Bucket," John Hill, the chief miner at Bath, reported. In an effort to drain the mines, the slaves dug two extensive ditches, one two hundred yards long and eighteen to twenty feet deep, the other fifty yards long and ten to fifteen feet deep. These ditches "were very difficult to open being deep, and the water running down them," Hill explained. "There were some very large rocks to break up, and throw up, on to the scaffolds, and then over the bank." At one point blasting power had to be used. One of the white employees at Bath Furnace succinctly summarized the situation at the mines when he described the raising of ore there as "an ugly job."[64]

Mining was not the only "ugly job" around Bath furnace. When Jordan, Davis & Company began reconstructing the furnace in 1830, they noticed a thick coating of sulfur on the inwalls of the old stack. The presence of sulfur in the iron ore meant that once the furnace was rebuilt and blown in, some of the slaves working there were assigned a most unpleasant and undoubtedly hazardous duty. The task was described in detail by James Lowe, the founder at Bath, in his answers to a series of questions about the various difficulties the firm encountered at the furnace:

> QUESTION. "Is not the sulphur very troublesome at this furnace after she is in blast five or six weeks?"
> ANSWER. "Yes, after she blows two months it has to be knocked off before the iron will be fit to make castings."
> QUESTION. "Does not the sulphur injure or destroy a good deal of the metal made after six weeks?"
> ANSWER. "It will if it is not knocked off. . . ."
> QUESTION. "Is it not a very ugly and dangerous job to get the sulphur off when the furnace is in blast, in consequence of it making the hands very sick that are engaged in it?"

ANSWER. "It is an ugly job but not very dangerous; it makes the hands faint sometimes."[65]

Lowe no doubt never consulted the slaves who did this "ugly job" before rendering his opinion that it was "not very dangerous."

A final complication faced the slave workers at Bath. Sam Jordan, who supervised most of the new construction there, did not handle slaves well. Such, at least, was the view of his father. When he was asked if Sam were "as well qualified to superintend a gang of hands, and direct the building of a stack, and also to erect it to as great advantage, as any man within your knowledge," John Jordan replied, "I think he is as to the mechanical part— but not altogether as much so as to the contrivance and management of hands."[66] The problem was Sam Jordan's fiery temper, a trait he recognized in himself, and of which he was not proud, but which he claimed he was largely unable to control. "I am aware that I am easily excited, it is my nature, I cannot help it," he admitted some years later.[67]

Life was never easy for slaves in the Old South, but for many of those working at Bath during the tenure of Jordan, Davis & Company, it appears to have been particularly hard.

Weaver was spending a lot of time in Philadelphia during the early 1830s, and he may not have known very much of what was going on at Bath Iron Works. He may not have cared. Perhaps it was enough for him that Bath pig iron began arriving more or less regularly at Buffalo Forge in the fall of 1830.[68] As long as relations between the various members of the firm appeared cordial, Weaver gave no indication that he was unduly concerned about the way Jordan, Davis & Company were conducting their affairs at Bath.

Despite some disappointment over the early pace of production at Bath, Weaver was generous with his nephews and Sam Jordan as their first year of operations came to a close. The new furnace had not gotten into blast until October and had been forced to shut down in mid-December, for the usual reason. "We had thought [of] blowing through the Christmas holy days and going on as long as possible," Jordan, Davis & Company wrote Weaver on November 24, 1830, "but as our white hands are few and the most part of the blacks will be going home and the few remaining not willing to be closely confined we have concluded to stopup for a short time during Christmas and blow as long as possible."[69]

Because of the time taken to renovate the works and this relatively short blast, Weaver received just over twenty-two tons of pig iron from Bath that year, far short of what Buffalo Forge needed to operate at anything like full capacity. Nevertheless, Weaver waived their 1830 interest payment of

$1,800 on the purchase price of the Bath property and paid their sizable bill for Negro hire when it came due at the end of the year. As a consequence, Jordan, Davis & Company fell in debt to Weaver to the extent of $2,693 during the initial year of operations at Bath Iron Works, a sum Weaver was content to carry forward in anticipation of much larger deliveries of pig iron in the future.[70]

Weaver was generous in other ways as well. He had periodically sent slave artisans from Buffalo Forge up to Bath Iron Works during the years John Doyle supervised operations there, and he continued this practice when his nephews and Sam Jordan took over. Like Buffalo Forge, Bath ran with a mixed crew of white, free Negro, and slave forgemen during the early 1830s, but most of the skilled labor there was slave, and most of these slaves belonged to Weaver. Tooler and Harry Hunt and his brother Billy Hunt were among Weaver's skilled and experienced black forgemen who did tours of duty at Bath for Jordan, Davis & Company.[71]

Harry Hunt was a particularly valuable slave. He had received his training at a famous ironworks in Campbell County, not far from Lynchburg. The Oxford Iron Works had been developed in the eighteenth century by David Ross, a legendary ironmaster of the Revolutionary and post-Revolutionary eras and one of the wealthiest men in Virginia in his time. Ross had operated his blast furnace and forge almost exclusively with slave labor, and his works had served as a training ground for some of the best slave artisans of that day. Ross's death in 1817 and the subsequent breakup of his estate sent a number of his most skilled furnace and forge hands across the Blue Ridge Mountains and into the Valley, where the Virginia iron industry was moving during the first decades of the nineteenth century.[72]

Hal Hunt, as he was often called, had come into Weaver's possession in 1827 and had worked regularly at Bath Iron Works in the late 1820s. Weaver allowed him to remain there when Sam Jordan and the Davis brothers took over. Hal and his wife, Gilly, lived in a cabin near Bath Forge, where Hunt held the important post of master refiner. In 1832, their first child, a boy, was born at Bath, and was named Harry after his father.[73] Hal, Gilly, and Harry Hunt, Jr., were to play a critical role in the relationship between Weaver and the members of the firm of Jordan, Davis & Company.

The first hint that something might be wrong among the partners at Bath Iron Works came in the summer of 1831. Weaver and his wife had returned to Pennsylvania earlier that year to the house Weaver had rented in downtown Philadelphia, and there he received some unsettling news. "With respect to Jordan Davis & Co., I have merely to say that they dissolved partnership a few days since, and have formed a new concern," Abram

Davis wrote from his post at Buffalo Forge on June 10, 1831. "They are waiting anxiously for your arrival, as the business is suffering for want of aid, John having left there," he continued. "You say you will come out by harvest. I would be glad if you could come sooner," he added.[74]

At the end of May, John Danenhower had sold out his interest in the firm of Jordan, Davis & Company and had left Bath Iron Works. His departure came shortly before Abram Davis arrived at Bath. Abram had remained at Buffalo Forge until he became of age in 1831, but when he turned twenty-one, he was eager to take his promised place in the firm. There was money to be made at Bath, and Abram did not want to be left out. He joined the partnership at Bath Iron Works in the summer of 1831.[75]

As Danenhower later described it, Abram's anticipated move to Bath marked the end of his welcome there, such as it had been. "I was induced to believe from the first to the last, that it never was the wish nor the intention of the parties concerned that I should remain with them longer than they could use me to their advantage or until Abram became of age," Danenhower wrote in 1835; "from their subsequent conduct towards me I was convinced of this, and rather than be in the way of their *family* arrangements, I concluded that if I could get anything for my Services I had better take it & be off." The decisive moment came when "Wm Davis told me the proposal for me to quit had been urged by you and as your word was my law what could I do," he told Weaver. Was "it any wonder that I became careless of business [and] willing to leave them," he asked in conclusion?[76] He received only $660 for his interest in Jordan, Davis & Company but was released from any responsibility for debts incurred by the firm. He was also homesick and wanted to see his family again in Pennsylvania. Danenhower returned to Philadelphia, where he obtained what turned out to be a tenuous position in a dry goods establishment.[77]

Weaver later claimed that he had doubts from the very beginning about the maturity and level-headedness of both John Danenhower and Abram Davis, but it is unlikely that he encouraged the other partners to drop Danenhower from the firm. Danenhower himself admitted that he had become "careless of business" before he left the works, but he attributed this laxity to the shabby treatment he claimed to have received at the hands of the other partners at Bath.

Danenhower may, in fact, have been his own worst enemy during his years at Bath Iron Works. As he acknowledged in a letter to Weaver, his poor work habits there predated the formation of the firm of Jordan, Davis & Company. "In my former connections with you I have been placed in situations apart from your person," Danenhower wrote Weaver in 1833. "I am anxious to have a trial under your immediate observation, or in other words I wish for an opportunity to regain the good opinion I flatter myself you once entertained of me," he continued. "I was too young (when thrown upon the world) to be aware of the deception and vice to which I was exposed, the peculiar situations in which I was placed and the designing persons with whom I lived, have led me into many, very many errors," he admitted. "I am convinced that had I been with you the four years I was the dupe of that worst of men *Doyle,* my course of conduct would have been altogether different and I might now have enjoyed the reputation of a respectable citizen in society." Danenhower went on to say that he was facing dire prospects in Philadelphia, that his job was in jeopardy, that his father was trying to "wring from me every penny of my earnings," and that he was anxious to come back to Virginia and work for Weaver.[78]

For whatever reason, Weaver did not bring his nephew back to Virginia. Nor did he seem overly concerned at the time that Danenhower had left the firm. Sam Jordan was the key man at Bath in Weaver's eyes, and Danenhower's departure had been followed closely by Abram Davis's arrival, so there were enough managers to look after business there. John Danenhower had had his chance and had not taken advantage of it. It was time, Weaver seemed to feel, for the young man to look after himself.

"I have been out of a Situation for two months in debt and as poor as Job's turkey & without a friend to . . . councel or assist me," Danenhower wrote his Uncle William mournfully on January 7, 1835; "what I shall get at God only knows." He eventually got to Cincinnati, where he wrote Weaver in 1854 to say that he was taking a trip east that year and hoped to come down to see Weaver. Danenhower did not mention his line of work in this brief letter, but the tone of this piece of correspondence clearly suggests that he and his Uncle William had reconciled their differences. He visited Weaver at Buffalo Forge and the two men spent several weeks together there and at Etna Furnace.[79]

Danenhower's departure from Bath in 1831 caused not a ripple in the operations of Jordan, Davis & Company. Hiring problems eased once the construction of the new furnace and forge was completed, although Bath never seems to have been a favorite location among the slaves in eastern Virginia. Those who had a choice invariably chose Buffalo Forge over Bath Iron Works, but Weaver and Sam Jordan, and the other partners, were still able to hire furnace gangs of forty or more hands from 1831 through 1834.[80] With the works newly rebuilt and renovated, and with Weaver's slave artisans assisting at the forge, Bath Iron Works was realizing the potential Weaver had hoped it would yield when he set his nephews and Sam Jordan up to run the property in 1830. Bath Furnace averaged blasts of six or seven, and sometimes eight, months of the year, despite continuing difficulties encountered raising a sufficient quantity of good iron ore. Weaver's supply of pig metal for Buffalo Forge finally seemed assured as he received ever-increasing tonnages of Bath pig over the years—72 tons in 1831, 143 tons in 1832, and 317 tons in 1833–34.[81]

Problems still cropped up at Bath. Occasional shortages of food and clothing occurred. The iron ore in the deep pits at the furnace was becoming sandy and more and more difficult to raise. And there were those continuing signs that "the contrivance and management of hands," as John Jordan put it, was not all it might be. Runaways plagued Jordan, Davis & Company throughout their years at Bath, although the numbers were never great enough to threaten operations at either the furnace or the forge.[82] Weaver seems to have shrugged off the runaway situation among the hired hands as part of the normal price of doing business at an ironmaking establishment located in a remote and rugged region of the country.

Weaver, keeping his usual careful watch on the accounts, continued to assist the partners with their slave hiring, stood as security for their notes, offered advice on business affairs, and advanced them funds when needed.[83] Jordan, Davis & Company in return sent a steady supply of pig metal to Buffalo Forge. Three years into the firm's tenure at Bath, Weaver had little cause to doubt the wisdom of establishing his nephews and Sam Jordan in business there. He and Eliza spent a considerable amount of time in Pennsylvania during these years, and aside from the brief flare-up of difficulty at the time of John Danenhower's departure in the spring of 1831, things seemed to be working out pretty much as Weaver had hoped.

5

Weaver *v.* Jordan, Davis & Company

The year 1834 marked the beginning of yet another stormy episode in William Weaver's long and litigious career as a Virginia ironmaster. And once again his slaves were at the heart of the controversy.

The smooth surface among the principal partners at Bath during the first three years of the firm's operations turned out to be deceptive. Sam Jordan, the man Weaver believed was essential to the success of Bath Iron Works, was having trouble with William and Abram Davis. The nature of the problem was unclear, but while Weaver was away in Philadelphia early in 1834, he was informed that Sam and Abram Davis had a falling out. As a result, Jordan sold his interest in Bath to the Davis brothers for $5,000 and moved into Lexington.

Weaver objected strenuously to this arrangement. As soon as he came back to the Valley in the spring, he rode up to Bath Iron Works. Abram was away when Weaver arrived on April 1, 1834, but William Davis was there and assured Weaver there would be no difficulty about Sam rejoining the firm. Weaver remained at Bath for two days waiting for Abram to return. When he did, the three men discussed the situation fully and, according to Weaver, Abram agreed to leave the partnership so that Sam might come back in.[1]

With Abram's status apparently resolved, Weaver and William Davis rode into Lexington to talk to Sam Jordan. Jordan wanted no part of their proposition, however, and steadfastly refused to go back to Bath. At this point in their discussion, Weaver laid down an ultimatum. He would either hold Jordan and his nephews responsible for the purchase price of the ironworks, or take back the property immediately. Negotiations followed. Sam backed away from his position that he would have nothing more to do with Bath, and Weaver gave up his insistence that they pay for the property or surrender it at once. A compromise was worked out, an agreement drawn up, and Weaver, Sam Jordan, and William Davis signed the document on April 4, 1834.[2]

The agreement called on Jordan, Davis & Company to continue at Bath until the end of the year. They agreed to take good care of the property and keep the ore bank in good shape prior to turning the works over to Weaver on January 1, 1835. All matters of dispute were to be decided by one or more arbitrators familiar with the iron business. The amount the firm owed Weaver for the use of the property for five years and the amount he owed the partners for the improvements they had made were also to be settled by arbitration. Weaver agreed to buy the personal property at the works at a fair evaluation. And finally, Jordan, Davis & Company agreed to let Weaver have as much pig iron as he might want, if they could spare it.[3]

There was one hitch in all of this, however. Abram Davis had not been privy to the negotiations that produced this agreement, and when he was presented with the document, he refused to sign it. As he later explained, he thought he perceived Weaver's "sinister designs" in the terms of the agreement.[4] His stand prompted Sam Jordan and William Davis to reconsider their positions. As a result, they withdrew their consent, and the entire settlement fell apart. Subsequent negotiations between Weaver and the members of the firm failed to produce a new agreement. All of this activity produced one significant result, however. Sam Jordan returned to Bath Iron Works. The argument with Weaver had reunited the members of the firm of Jordan, Davis & Company.[5] But the failure of both sides to resolve their differences in the spring of 1834 had moved their dispute onto new and treacherous ground.

The explosion was not long in coming. On June 16, 1834, Jordan, Davis & Company notified Weaver that, because of the debts they would have to pay off by the end of the year, they would be sending him no more pig iron from Bath Furnace. Buffalo Forge would have to look elsewhere for a supply of metal.[6]

Sam Jordan and the Davises could have done nothing to anger Weaver more. Thomas Mayburry had made that very same mistake exactly ten years before and Weaver had forced Mayburry to pay a very heavy price for his errant ways. Mayburry had compounded his error, in Weaver's eyes, by attempting to claim slaves Weaver considered his alone. Jordan, Davis & Company, Weaver soon came to believe, had committed this sin as well.

During the extensive negotiations that followed the collapse of the April 1834 agreement, Weaver spent a considerable amount of time going over the accounts at Bath Iron Works. One day during the course of this examination, he discovered that entries had been erased from the books which showed that Harry and Gilly Hunt and other property on loan to Bath belonged to him. Weaver was furious at what he perceived to be a blatant attempt at theft.[7] If Sam Jordan and William and Abram Davis were going to try to play this sort of game with him, it mattered not that the Davises were his nephews and former wards and that Sam was married to his niece. They could either meet his terms for a settlement or face him in chancery court.

The opportunity for cordial negotiations and a friendly resolution of differences had evaporated. In November 1834, Weaver notified Jordan, Davis & Company in writing that he would insist on the execution of the agreement that he, Sam Jordan, and William Davis had signed on April 4, 1834. These were now the only terms Weaver would accept.[8]

There was one critical matter not covered in this agreement, however. It had made no specific mention of Harry Hunt and his family. The reason for this omission, and for the erasures on the books at Bath, lay in a tangled web of circumstances surrounding the ownership of these slaves. William Davis later adamantly claimed that Weaver had given Harry, Gilly, and Harry Hunt, Jr., to him. Weaver insisted just as adamantly that he had done no such thing. Once Weaver discovered the alterations in the books, however, the status of Harry Hunt and his wife and son became very much an issue.

Weaver had made a grave error ten years before when he allowed Mayburry to retain control of a significant number of the "Wilson negroes." He did not intend to make the same mistake twice.

The situation regarding Harry Hunt and his family came to a head just before Christmas 1834. Late in the evening on December 23, Harry Hunt, riding one of William Davis's horses, arrived at Buffalo Forge. Joseph Barker, who had taken over as Weaver's manager at the forge following Abram Davis's departure for Bath Iron Works, described in detail what happened the next day. "On the morning of the 24th Mr. Weaver sent for me to come up to his house, and stated to me that Harry Hunt was very anxious to leave Bath Iron Works," Barker reported. Weaver wanted to send his slave Billy Hunt up to Bath with Harry to assist his brother "in getting his family away," but Weaver thought it unsafe for them to go by themselves because "they were both inclined to drinking, too much at times." Weaver asked Barker to go with them. "At lenght [*sic*] I told him I would go," Barker noted, and he added that Weaver gave explicit instructions about how they were to proceed. Weaver was particularly concerned that, on their arrival at Bath, they scout the area "to see if there was any person about the Forge, who would be likely to resist the attempt to remove the negroes."[9]

The three men set out from Buffalo Forge around the middle of the day on Christmas Eve, Barker and Billy Hunt on two of Weaver's horses, Harry on the horse he had ridden down from Bath the previous day. On their way up, Harry Hunt informed Barker that William Davis was away from Bath, which was undoubtedly the reason Harry had chosen this moment to go to Buffalo Forge and talk to Weaver. "We proceeded on till we got to Bath Iron Works, through the Country called the Barrens," Barker continued. They arrived about an hour after dark and, following Weaver's orders, halted some twenty yards from Harry's cabin at Bath Forge. "Harry Hunt directed his brother Billy to go into his house," Barker observed, "to see if there was any person in who would give information about their going away." Billy returned a few minutes later and reported that there were two other Negroes in the house besides Harry Hunt's wife and child, and that he had instructed Harry's wife to dispatch them. After the two visitors left, Barker, Harry, and Billy Hunt, all "very wet and cold," entered Harry Hunt's house.

Gilly Hunt "had a good fire made," Barker said, and the three men "sat and warmed and dried ourselves for some time." Harry "directed his wife to get us something to eat," Barker added, and Gilly brought them food and warm coffee. "After done eating, we then commenced packing up, and preparing to start: about which time it commenced snowing," Barker reported. Some two hours after the men had arrived at Bath, the little party set out—Harry, Gilly, little Harry Hunt, Jr., Billy Hunt, and Joseph Barker on the three horses the men had ridden up from Buffalo Forge earlier that day. Barker carried some of the Hunts' clothing with him as they rode away from Bath Iron Works.

Barker's description of what happened next made it clear that they soon found themselves in a very perilous situation:

We got some distance into the Barrens, probably two miles or more—got off our road, into the bushes, and lossed [*sic*] our way as the roads were covered with the snow then falling. We wandered about for some time, and at lenght [*sic*] got into an old field—proceeded on, and in a short time arrived at a house—called up the owner and requested him to let us in to warm, as we were suffering with cold. He readily admitted us, and made a fire—we sat some time and warmed ourselves. We requested him to direct us into the road heading from Dr. Campbell's Mill to Lexington that we had got lossed. After remaining about an hour, we set out again, but could not succeed in finding the road owing to the heavy falling of the snow, and the bushes being bent down. We returned to the same House, and staid till day break. We then set out at day light and found our way into the main road, continued our journcy, and got to Buffalo Forge about 3 o'clock in the afternoon of the 25th.[10]

Their safe arrival at Buffalo Forge on Christmas Day 1834 must have given all of them great cause for rejoicing.

Weaver was probably just as pleased as they were. He had devised a plan to spirit Harry Hunt and his family away from Bath under cover of darkness. The heavy snowfall on Christmas Eve had made their journey through the Barrens much more dangerous than he had anticipated, but all of that was now behind them. The plan had worked. Harry, Gilly, and their son, Harry Hunt, Jr., were back at Buffalo Forge, and Weaver was determined to see that they remained there.

The departure of Harry Hunt and his family from Bath Iron Works further embittered relations between Weaver and members of the firm of Jordan, Davis & Company. When Weaver made a final offer of settlement to his nephews and Sam Jordan on February 12, 1835, he was careful to include the stipulation that "The Family of Negroes, ordered home must be considered as mine—."[11] When Jordan, Davis & Company rejected Weaver's offer twelve days later, they just as vigorously insisted that "the negroes taken from this place on the 25th of December last, viz: Harry, Gilly and their boy Harry," had to be considered personal property belonging to them. Under the terms of their counterproposal, Weaver would have to repurchase these slaves along with the horses, mules, wagons, tools, farm implements, and other such items at Bath Iron Works.[12]

Weaver had had enough of such proposals and counterproposals. In April 1835, he filed suit in chancery court against Sam Jordan and William and Abram Davis. "Your Orator during the negociation [*sic*] was willing to take back the property if the terms could have been satisfactorily arranged," Weaver told the court. "But having been under the necessity of appealing to law to secure his rights—he would now be unwilling to rescind the [oral] contract [of 1830]—The timber has been much exhausted and the ore bank is from the operations of five years necessarily much exhausted & mining rendered more difficult." Weaver would hold Jordan, Davis & Company to the original contract, the one, he insisted, that required them to pay him $30,000 plus interest for Bath Iron Works and a separate sum for the assorted personal property at the furnace and forge at the time they purchased the works. Harry Hunt and his family played no part in the 1830 contract at all, Weaver maintained. These slaves were his exclusive property and had been so all along.[13]

The suit of Weaver v. Jordan, Davis & Company achieved legendary status in the annals of the Superior Court of Law and Chancery for Rockbridge County, Virginia. It involved the taking of hundreds of pages of depositions from the major participants in the case and dozens of expert witnesses. Tempers flared as the plaintiff and the defendants battled one another and examined and cross-examined friendly and hostile witnesses. The most heavy-handed sarcasm was employed, long-standing grievances were aired, old hatreds bubbled to the surface, and character assassination became a regular means of combat. The suit dragged on for over twenty years. Along the way, much attention was focused on who actually owned Harry, Gilly, and Harry Hunt, Jr.

The central point at issue in this phase of the suit was whether or not Weaver had given Harry Hunt and his wife and child to William Davis. Davis insisted that he had, although he could produce no documentary evidence to show that Weaver had legally passed these slaves over to him. His case rested on the testimony of several witnesses who claimed that Weaver had made a gift of Harry and Gilly Hunt and their son to Davis at the time he married Ann Dickinson, the daughter of Weaver's longtime friend and hiring agent in Louisa County, James C. Dickinson.

On December 2, 1832, James Dickinson had written Weaver that a wedding would soon be taking place that would bring their families together. William Weaver Davis and Ann Overton Dickinson were planning to be married on New Year's Day, 1833, and Dickinson invited Weaver and his wife down for the wedding. Eliza could stay at the Dickinson's home "whilst you are engaged [in] hiring all the negroes that you can hire in our section of the country," Dickinson added.[14]

Weaver arrived in Louisa County prior to the wedding in a generous mood, Dickinson reported. Weaver told him he had already given William and Abram Davis, John Danenhower, and Sam Jordan the Bath property, and that the Davis boys and Sam "had purchased out Danenhower's interest" and now held the works "as their own." Weaver went on to say that he "regretted only one thing, that the house [at Bath] was too small for William's wife." Weaver "then pulled out a piece of paper on which the plan of a large house was drawn, and said if I would send my man Guy and make the brick he would put up the house and it should not cost William a dollar, except the sawing of the timber. I then replied to him that this house is too large for young beginners, that it would take a thousand dollars worth of furniture to furnish such a house," Dickinson recalled saying. Weaver replied to this by repeating his earlier offer: "you send up your man, make the bricks and help to lay them, and it shall cost William nothing," he said. The whole conversation, Dickinson said later, struck him "as an inducement to the marriage undoubtedly."[15]

That was not all Weaver claimed he had done and would do for the young couple, Dickinson went on to say. At this point in their discussion Weaver raised the subject of Harry Hunt and his family. "He said he had given . . . William Davis this old man, as he called him, and his wife and child, and that he had given . . . [Sam] Jordan [a slave named] Manuel and his wife and some children, and that he wished me to give . . . William a breeding woman, that he might stand on equal footing with Mr. Jordan and that as soon as Abraham [*sic*] Davis got married, he . . . would buy a negro man and his wife for him, that he might stand on the same ground with the rest."[16]

Mary Dickinson, the bride's mother, remembered Weaver telling her much the same thing, but in slightly more delicate language. "He said he had given Harry (a Forgeman) and his wife to . . . William Davis," she recalled. "He stated also that he had given . . . [Sam] Jordan a family of negroes, more valuable than those he had given William."[17]

Weaver had given Hannah Davis Jordan a slave family at the time of their marriage, but he steadfastly denied that he had given Harry, Gilly, and Harry Hunt, Jr., to William Davis or to Jordan, Davis & Company, for that matter. If William owned these slaves, where was his title? Weaver received confirmation of his position from an unexpected source. "I *distinctly* remember making an entry of Harry Hunt's family . . . to your credit on their [Jordan, Davis & Company's] Books," John Danenhower wrote Weaver in October 1834. "The negroes . . . I had always considered as the property of Buffalo Forge."[18]

Weaver had acted to reclaim the slaves only after he "discovered that the price entered on the books for the Negroes Hall & Gilly . . . [had] been erased," he noted in his bill of complaint against Jordan, Davis & Company. Weaver had every reason to believe that the firm "intended to claim these negroes," and that after a lapse of five years, his title of ownership to them might be questionable. He "sent up his manager to bring him the negroes—

They were brought and are now in possession of your Orator," Weaver succinctly informed the court.[19] He clearly had learned from his experience with Thomas Mayburry and the "Wilson negroes." If possession were to figure largely in the eyes of the law, the prudent course of action was to leave nothing to chance.

There is no way to be certain if the conversations described by James and Mary Dickinson actually took place, but chances are they did. At least one other witness claimed that Weaver had said that William Davis had been a good boy to him, that Davis had managed a cotton factory for him in Pennsylvania, and that Weaver felt obligated to give him something.[20] Weaver probably did intend originally to give Harry Hunt and his family to Davis. Weaver probably did tell the Dickinsons that he *had* given the slaves to him. But Weaver then held back on the final step—granting Davis a title to these slaves—until he could be absolutely certain that things would work out to his full satisfaction at Bath.

Such a scenario—expansive promises followed by cautious deeds—is suggested by the circumstances under which Sam Jordan and Weaver's nephews went to Bath in the first place. Several witnesses reported that Weaver said on more than one occasion that he intended to give the Bath property to the young men, that the $30,000 purchase price was a "nominal" one, and that he had "designed the most of his property for his nephews and nieces."[21] John Jordan, Sam's father, had asked Weaver why, then, had he never given the boys a title to the works? "His first reasons [*sic*] was in consequence of the unsteadiness of John Danenhower," Jordan quoted Weaver as saying. "His second reason in consequence of the unsteadiness of Abraham [*sic*] Davis."[22]

Weaver was a very careful man when it came to the conduct of his business affairs. It was one thing to make generous promises; it was quite another to allow valuable assets to pass permanently into the hands of others. Not until Weaver was quite sure of the "steadiness" of his young relatives, and of their unwavering willingness to work in his interests, would he take the final, legal steps to transfer property to them, be it landed or slave.

There were two key moments in the case of Harry Hunt and his family. The first came when Weaver discovered the erasures on the books at Bath. The second was when Harry showed up at Buffalo Forge two days before Christmas in 1834 and asked Weaver to help him get his family away from Bath Iron Works.

Abram Davis admitted in his testimony before the court that he had altered the books at Bath. He insisted he had done so "before any difficulties had arisen with" Weaver. According to young Davis, he "received the impression from a communication made to him by [Weaver's] sister . . . that he intended said negroes &c. as a present." As a consequence, when he was "engaged in posting the books, coming across the entry," he "erased the sum at which the entry was extended, leaving the entry as a memorandum for any future occasion."[23] Abram did not say which one of Weaver's sisters had given him this impression, and her name did not surface in any of the voluminous depositions taken in connection with the suit.

When Abram described the erasures as "negroes &c.," he failed to mention what the *et cetera* stood for, but Weaver was not silent on this point. The deletions consisted of "a negro man Hall and his wife Gilly, a mule team, a log wagon and another wagon and two cutting boxes." No one besides Abram Davis ever claimed that Weaver had given these latter items away. Harry and Gilly Hunt and these other pieces of property belonged to him but were simply at Bath when Jordan, Davis & Company took over, Weaver insisted.[24] His anger when he discovered the erasures, and the attempted thievery he thought they represented, played a major role in precipitating the suit.

Weaver told the court he had no doubts whatsoever about the propriety of spiriting Harry Hunt and his family away from Bath Iron Works. He was, he said, simply regaining possession of his property. If that were the case, Sam Jordan wondered, why had he done so at night in the cautious and secretive manner Joseph Barker had described? Jordan asked Weaver's forge manager just such a question as Barker was completing his testimony. "Why did you not go in daylight, and demand these negroes of [the] Defendants?" Jordan inquired. "I went agreeably to the instructions of Plaintiff [Weaver]" was the only reply Barker could give.[25]

Clearly from Barker's evidence Weaver wanted the slaves back, and he did not want anything—like William Davis's refusal to allow them to leave—preventing their return. Harry Hunt's unexpected visit to Buffalo Forge on December 23, 1834, and his information that Davis was away from Bath Iron Works, triggered Weaver's response.

The dispute over the ownership of Harry Hunt and his wife and son was only one of numerous points of contention between Weaver and the members of the firm of Jordan, Davis & Company. They argued over the specifications of the oral contract that had put the partners in control of Bath, over the value of the improvements they had made there, over the way in which they had cut timber and mined ore on the property, over their maintenance of the various buildings scattered about the works, and over a host of other issues, large and small. One bitter fight—over the amount of profits the firm had taken out of Bath Iron Works—illustrates the nature of the charges and countercharges that flew back and forth between the litigants. Two family members in Pennsylvania reported that the Davis boys had bragged on more than one occasion that they had made a profit of some $20,000 or $21,000 on their operations during the years they held the property.[26] John Doyle examined their books as an expert witness, much to Weaver's dismay, and estimated their profits at $8,602.-25.[27] Weaver went over the same books and claimed their profits were $69,573.76.[28] And so it went.

The first of what turned out to be several decrees handed down by the Superior Court of Law and Chancery for Rockbridge County came on April 21, 1838, almost three years after Weaver had initiated the suit. The court ruled that the initial contract calling for Jordan, Davis & Company to purchase Bath Iron Works for $30,000 could not be enforced, primarily because it had been a verbal agreement. But the court did mandate that an account be drawn up that would settle the financial affairs between the parties. Weaver should receive a fair rent for the years Jordan, Davis & Company had held the property, less the value of the permanent improvements the partners had made there. This accounting would require that a commissioner conduct an elaborate review of the books and take depositions to resolve a host of difficult questions. What was a fair rent? How much were things like the new dam and the rebuilt stack at Bath Furnace worth? To what extent had the property been damaged by timber cutting and ore exhaustion? What was the value of the supplies and cash advances Weaver had sent Jordan, Davis & Company? What was the value of the pig iron they had sent to him? This initial ruling of the court did not mention Harry Hunt's family, which left Weaver in possession of these slaves. But it did rule that the partners had to surrender the property at once to Weaver.[29]

Weaver retook possession of Bath Iron Works on May 2, 1838.[30] Abram Davis had pulled out of the firm earlier and returned to Pennsylvania, where he was "going to school, attending to writing & arithmetic to qualify him for a store," one of Weaver's relatives wrote from Philadelphia in 1835.[31] William Davis and Sam Jordan, operating under the new name of Jordan & Davis, ran Bath until they turned the works back over to Weaver in the spring of 1838.[32]

Weaver was dismayed when he saw the property. Bath Iron Works was, as he termed it, in "a state of dilapidation." The forge roof was almost totally gone and, as a consequence, much of the machinery there was badly damaged and had to be extensively repaired or replaced completely before production could begin.[33] An ironmaster who visited Bath shortly after Jordan & Davis pulled out described the forge as being "in horrid order."[34] Bath Furnace was in a similar state of disrepair. The furnace stack was badly cracked, and a number of buildings around the furnace were without roofs or had totally collapsed. Fences were down everywhere, the fields were overgrown and choked with weeds. In Weaver's words, Bath looked like "a sheriff had had that property under execution for some three or four years."[35] Weaver made minimal repairs at both the furnace and forge and operated the works intermittently for several years, but Bath had seen its best days.

On March 14, 1840, following two years of lengthy depositions and careful study of the books, the commissioner appointed by the court handed down a report that was very much to Weaver's liking. The report did not fix a sum Jordan, Davis & Company owed Weaver; that would be done by the chancery court after it examined the commissioner's report. But on point after point, it sustained Weaver's position. Particularly welcome was the finding concerning Harry Hunt.

"The defendants are charged by your Commissioner with five years hire of negroes Hall and Gilly," the report read. As soon as Weaver heard these words, he knew the commissioner had decided that the Hunts belonged to him. The commissioner found the testimony of James C. and Mary Dickinson less persuasive than the physical evidence contained in the records: "an erased entry on the books of the defendants would indicate a purchase." The report quoted the entry from the daybook verbatim:

"1831 February 1   Furnace to Wm. Weaver Dr for negro Harry and Gilly his wife and 1 six horse mule team. log wagon &c. on hand 1 January 1830, and not taken in inventory   00": an erasure of two figures having been made from the left hand side of the cyphers.

The final sentence of this paragraph settled the matter of ownership: "The legal title to the negroes appearing to be vested in the plaintiff, he is allowed hire for them at the rate of $180 per annum."[36] Weaver's regaining possession of these slaves had, in fact, been critical. His experience with Thomas Mayburry and the "Wilson negroes" had been instructive, and no one ever accused Weaver of being a slow learner.

Two years later, the chancery court came in with a dollar amount Jordan, Davis & Company owed Weaver. The decree, handed down on September 22, 1842, required the partnership to pay him a total of $6,177.88 and to reimburse Weaver for all costs he had incurred in the prosecution of the suit.[37]

Sam Jordan and William Davis decided to carry the case to the Virginia Court of Appeals. The commissioner's report had erred in a number of critical areas, they felt, and the size of the judgment against them was formidable. The decision to appeal was not a casual one. It required them to submit a printed copy of the reports and decrees and all the depositions and documents submitted in evidence in the suit. If the appeal failed, they would be out hundreds of dollars more, at minimum. But they thought the risk was worth taking.[38]

In February 1843, the appeal and supporting documentation went to the printer: 1,037 handwritten pages, 286,709 words, clerk's fees for making up and copying the record, $477.85.[39] Twelve years later, on April 23, 1855, Sam Jordan and William Davis finally received confirmation of the wisdom of their decision to appeal.

"The Judge came into the Court this morning with a Decree against you in the Case of Weaver vs J. D. & Co.," Weaver's lawyer and close friend, James D. Davidson, wrote on April 23, 1855. The Court of Appeals had agreed with a number of exceptions Jordan and Davis had entered against the earlier decrees against them, particularly their claim that the commissioner had erred in the principles he had employed to calculate the rent they owed Weaver. The appellate court sent the case back to Rockbridge County with instructions to the chancery judge to revise the monetary award in light of the higher court's ruling. The judge's verdict on April 23, 1855, "shows a balance against you, in favor of Defendants of $594.04 on the 1st of May 1838," Davidson went on. The good news was that the court had granted Weaver almost $550 in various credits against this judgment.

If matters had stood there, the end result of twenty years of litigation would have been a virtual draw between the plaintiff and the defendants. But Weaver was charged with some $400 in interest plus court costs of over $800, so when all the additions and subtractions were tallied up, the court ruled that Weaver owed the former members of the firm of Jordan, Davis & Company a grand total of $1,321.30.[40]

Weaver had some cause for satisfaction in all of this, however, and one suspects that Harry Hunt and his family shared Weaver's sentiments in this matter. The Court of Appeals had rejected the claim of William Davis that Harry, Gilly, and Harry Hunt, Jr., belonged to him. The slaves would remain at Buffalo Forge.

Weaver delayed payment for as long as he could, and no money actually passed from his hands until 1857. On November 28 of that year, William W. Davis acknowledged on behalf of the firm the receipt of $456.40 from Weaver, and the next month Weaver gave Davidson $580 to give to Sam Jordan's lawyers to apply toward the bill for court costs. Weaver was not one to give up a fight of twenty years' duration without a final bit of obstinacy, however. After making these payments, there was still a balance of $284.90 in court costs due, but that amount was being "controverted by Weaver."[41]

Not surprisingly, the lengthy court battle over Bath Iron Works left a residue of bitterness and ill-feeling among the participants and their families. Weaver's and the Davises' relatives in Pennsylvania took sides during the dispute, with some praising Weaver for his years of magnanimous behavior toward the boys and their mother and others censuring him for his long-standing and shameful neglect of their welfare. One of the more vituperative members of the latter group roundly condemned Weaver for providing the boys with an inadequate education in Pennsylvania and then bringing them to Virginia "to drive Negro's or any other menial service."[42]

The bitterness between the principal parties seemed to fade with the passage of time, although it took somewhat longer in the case of William Davis. The reconciliation between Weaver and Sam Jordan was undoubtedly furthered by a tragedy that struck Sam's family in 1843. Hannah Davis Jordan, Sam's wife, died in childbirth that year, and the grief that accompanied her death must have brought the two men closer to each other. The willingness of both parties to forgive past mistakes and move on was probably strengthened when Sam subsequently married another of Weaver's Pennsylvania nieces, a young widow named Elizabeth Leibert Keen who had lost her husband and three children. Sam Jordan and Elizabeth Keen, who was fourteen years younger than Sam, were married in 1846, and they were regular visitors at Weaver's residence in the 1850s and 1860s. William and Ann Davis were also invited back to Buffalo Forge in the late 1850s.[43]

All indications are that Abram Davis and Weaver also managed to put their differences behind them. Abram's return to Pennsylvania in 1835 was subsequently followed by another move south, and in 1852 he sent Weaver a deeply emotional and moving letter from his home near Oakland in north-central Mississippi:

> It is now nearly seventeen years since I left Virginia to follow the fortunes of my dear wife and her family to the South, one by one they have all dropped off, my dear wife having departed this life some weeks since leaving with me three sweet little daughters to mourn her loss, her dying moments being cheered with the hope of immortality hereafter. On today I received a letter from brother William in reply to one I had written him enquiring after your health. He informed [me] that you were still living at Buffalo Forge, and now my dear Uncle, as the late sad event of the death of my dear wife has brought vividly to my memory the scenes of my youth, I cannot let the time longer pass, without asking your forgiveness for any cause which I may have given for the unhappy differences which existed between myself and my brother and you before I left Virginia. I have often and often regretted the painful occurrence and bitterly and deeply have I wept over it, and often intended writing to you on the subject, but I did not know how you would receive it. I can never

forget the kind and fatherly care you extended to myself and my brother and sisters when we were left fatherless in our infancy, and although *we* can never repay you for it, Heaven will do it. Nor can I forget the many kind attentions and the instruction you bestowed upon me at Old Buffalo. Be reconciled to my dear old Mother and my brother if any unpleasant feeling still exists. And as your years are declining and hers too, let the grave close over each and all of us with no unkind or painful family reflection. I have written this because I love you yet as much as ever my dear Uncle.

And now when the shadow of death shall be closing around you, may your last moments be cheered with the bright hope of meeting your sainted Mother in the realms of bliss is the earnest prayer of,

Your affectionate nephew,
Abram W. Davis

P.S. Please answer this and direct to Oakland, Yalobusha Cty Mississippi.[44]

Weaver did answer, and although we do not know the contents of his letter, he apparently shared Abram's desire for a reconciliation. Such, at any rate, is suggested by a brief sentence in the daily time book kept by Weaver's manager at Buffalo Forge in the early 1850s. Under the date of Sunday, September 5, 1852, a line reads: "Davis of Mississippi called on Mr. Weaver today."[45]

The departure of the firm of Jordan & Davis from what was left of Bath Iron Works in the spring of 1838 led to one more significant consequence. Almost a year to the day after they left Bath, the actions of William Davis and Sam Jordan intersected with and closed, at least for the moment, another circle in the rings of controversy and litigation that spread out from Weaver during these years. On May 7, 1839, Jordan & Davis bought Gibraltar Forge from Thomas Mayburry.[46]

Sam Jordan's and William Davis's partnership did not last very long. After an acriminous dispute, they dissolved the firm in late 1842, with Davis buying his partner's half interest in the forge and Jordan going on from there to become one of the area's most successful iron manufacturers, most notably at Buena Vista Furnace on the eastern edge of Rockbridge County.[47] William Davis remained at Gibraltar Forge during the remaining antebellum years.

But Jordan & Davis's purchase of Gibraltar Forge in 1839 allowed Thomas Mayburry to close the book on his star-crossed career as a Valley ironmaster. The sale of his forge property meant that he could finally pull out of Rockbridge and launch a new ironmaking venture to the east in Louisa County. As Mayburry and his family crossed the Blue Ridge and headed "down the country" in 1839, Mary and her sons John and Hamilton and her dauther Ellen—Thomas Mayburry's portion of the "Wilson negroes"—were with them.

6

The Master of Buffalo Forge

From his earliest days in the Valley, William Weaver believed that the financial health of his ironmaking enterprise would depend on the extent to which he could acquire and successfully utilize skilled slave labor. The twin problems of assembling a forge crew of slave artisans and motivating them to work with speed and care occupied much of Weaver's time and attention during his first years in Virginia and throughout his long career as Rockbridge County's preeminent ironmaster.

He started with an excellent nucleus of able workmen at what was then called Union Forge. Included in the personal property he purchased from Thomas Mayburry in 1825 were Phill Easton and Billy Hunt, both of whom were skilled ironworkers.[1] Phill Easton, a master refiner, was widely regarded as one of the best slave artisans in the Valley. He could also take a turn at the chaffery hammer when needed. Billy Hunt served as an underhand at both the chaffery and refinery forges. In addition to these two men, Weaver also had Tooler and his son Bob available for forge work. Tooler, like Phill Easton, was an exceptionally versatile ironworker. He had been a key man at Etna—a furnace keeper—but he could also handle the chaffery hammer with more than adequate skill. Bob could apprentice at his father's side until he was an accomplished hammerman, which was undoubtedly the reason Weaver made Mayburry send him over from Etna in 1825. And two of Tooler's younger children, Tooler, Jr., fourteen, and Joe, twelve, would be potential recruits for the forge crew before very long. But until these boys grew up and were trained, or until Weaver could buy additional black forgemen, he would have to use free white, free black, or hired slave labor to supplement his own skilled workers.

Weaver's early crews were, in fact, about as throughly integrated as any work force at any industrial establishment in the Old South could be. At least three white men worked in his forge in 1825 and 1826, all of them Pennsylvanians: William Norcross, the principal hammerman until the fall of 1826, and James Bryan and William Nevil, also chaffery forgemen. A free black named William Empy, who lived close to the forge, served both as a master refiner and chaffery hammerman during these same years. And Weaver hired three slave forge workers over the same period: Harry Hunt, Billy Hunt's brother and a master refiner, and Solomon Fleming and Sam Templeton, both hammermen. Thus on a typical working day at the forge in the mid-1820s, white, free black, hired slave, and Weaver's own slave artisans would all be working alongside each other.[2]

This was not a situation Weaver particularly liked, however. The mix of free and slave workers created no apparent friction, but Weaver always felt vulnerable in Virginia depending on white workers who had freedom of movement and ready access to alcohol. Hiring skilled slave workers was also a risky proposition. There was no guarantee that their owners would send them to the same ironmaster year after year, and the slaves themselves might decide they did not want to return. Since their services were much in demand throughout the Valley, their masters would have no problem at all hiring them out to a different ironworks. Weaver wanted to own a full complement of forge workers, and by late 1827 he had achieved this goal.

In 1826 and 1827, Weaver was able to purchase all three of the hired slave forgemen who had been working for him over the past couple of years. He first bought Sam Templeton and his wife, Jenny, whose combined price was six tons of bar iron valued at $100 per ton. He next acquired Solomon Fleming from a prominent Valley ironmaster named Moses McCue whose family was associated with Mossy Creek Furnace and Forge in Augusta County, just north of Rockbridge.[3] Harry Hunt, who also belonged to McCue, was the man Weaver wanted most, however, and by the fall of 1827 he had him as well.

A single slave artisan could make a critical difference in forge operations. Weaver revealed his thinking on this point quite clearly in an exchange of correspondence with John Doyle, then his manager at Bath Furnace, shortly after he purchased Hunt. "I bought a Forgeman for which I have to pay 300 D in cash and . . . 2 tons castings," Weaver informed Doyle on October 12, 1827. "I should not have bot [*sic*] him at this time when money is much wanted but I have been endeavoring to purchase him ever since I have been in the Country." The purchase of Hunt was particularly important because Thomas Mayburry and his partner at Gibraltar Forge, Thomas Jolly, had been seeking to buy this slave, and John Jordan, the proprietor of Clifton Forge, had been after the man as well.[4]

Doyle agreed with Weaver that he had been "fortunate in getting the Forge man negro," particularly since "it goes to prevent Jordan from getting him." Doyle considered Jordan "our only rival," the one competitor "from whom any material injury can be calculated on." Doyle's only regret was that Weaver had been forced to part with some much-needed hard currency in the transaction; "if you can by any means raise a little cash so as to enable me to pay the triffling old acts. & give the hands a dollar or two upon an emergency I shall be able to dash on with spirit and have nothing to fear from Monsour Jordan," Doyle wrote from Bath.[5]

"I viewed the purchase of the negro pretty much as you have done, but considered it important to get him for he is the only one I know of—for sale—and such a negro in reality, will be worth two common hands," Weaver replied. "I shall now have 6 Forgemen of my own—I need hardly say it is all important particularly in this country." The fact that "the negro took 300 D . . . was unavoidable," Weaver added.[6] With Phill Easton, Billy Hunt, Tooler, Sam Templeton, Sol Fleming, and now Harry Hunt at Buffalo Forge, Weaver felt that he was in a position to meet John Jordan, or any other competitor for that matter, head-on.

Six forgemen, it turned out, were not quite enough. The completion of the new forge at Bath Iron Works in 1828 meant that Weaver would have to assemble yet another crew of refiners and chaffery hammermen. Once again he had to go back into a tight hiring market, and, even worse from his point of view, he had to turn to white artisans as well.

Neither prospect appealed to Weaver. White forgemen were hard to find, they were prone to leave without notice, and, almost to a man, they showed an excessive fondness for alcohol. When the manager of an extensive ironworks in neighboring Botetourt County was questioned in 1826 about whether he preferred free or slave labor, he answered in words that Weaver himself might have chosen. "I would rather have slaves," he said, "they are less trouble."[7]

Hiring slave artisans was also a decidedly risky business. The number of skilled slave forgemen available for hire was limited, and the competition for these men was fierce. Weaver managed to acquire some forge workers from a familiar source, Moses McCue of Augusta County, for 1829—the first full year of production at Bath Forge—but in the summer of that year, McCue wrote Weaver that his use of the men in 1830 was by no means guaranteed. "On reflecting on the conversation we had a few days past, respecting my forge men now with you, lest any thing that passed between us should be improperly understood, I have thought proper to drop you a few lines relative thereto," McCue wrote Weaver on July 3, 1829. "I told you, I should prefer your having the Boys upon equal terms with any other applicant, but at the same time, wish it to be understood, I shall be at liberty to take the highest offer made me; I think *you* would do the same," he added. "I think you had better say . . . the highest you will give for the Boys, so that I may act consistently with other applicants—One bid from each, will be sufficient to decide the matter."[8]

Weaver's vulnerability was graphically illustrated in the early 1830s when he confronted an old adversary. The difficulty, as it was related to Weaver, arose after Weaver's agent in Spottsylvania County bonded for three slaves, including a valuable ironworker Weaver was particularly eager to hire. "Afterwards Mayburry went there bribed both Negro & Master hired the main hand that you wanted and left the other two for you," Weaver's correspondent informed him.[9] The slave in question would be working at Gibraltar Forge instead of Weaver's ironworks during the coming year. Weaver's heavy investment in Buffalo Forge and Bath Iron Works could not be allowed to rest on a labor force that was so uncertain.

Weaver was constantly on the lookout for good forgemen, and he particularly wanted to buy artisans who had received their training at the Oxford Iron Works, the blast furnace and forge complex formerly owned by David Ross. Three of Weaver's best forgemen, Phill Easton and Harry and Billy Hunt, were former Oxford workers, and Weaver thought very highly of these men. He wanted more Oxford slaves if he could possibly obtain them.

It obviously was not easy to come by David Ross's former bondsmen. In February 1828, Weaver contacted an agent in Lynchburg about the possibility of buying a man named Aaron, who had worked at the chaffery forge at Oxford. Weaver undoubtedly had heard about Aaron from Phill Easton or the Hunt brothers, and he wanted to add this hammerman to his crew of slave forgemen. The agent replied that he had "been down to see Black-smith Phill," an Oxford-trained slave who was working in the Lynchburg area, and that Blacksmith Phill "informs me that Aaron has gone to the western country" and therefore was not available. This Phill had given him a lead on another Ross slave, however. "Ben Gilmore is in the neighbor-hood and is a stout old man sufficiently strong to draw iron pretty well," the agent reported, and he advised Weaver to "consult Phill [Easton] about his qualities, and let me hear from you as I shall probably hear from Ben's master shortly whether he can be had."[10]

His master was willing to sell, and Weaver subsequently purchased Ben Gilmore and brought him to the Valley to work at Buffalo Forge. A letter Weaver received on February 22, 1830, describes what eventually hap-pened to this slave:

> Campbell Feby 22nd 1830
>
> I understand from your man Ben Gilmore that he has leave from you to purchase himself and that if [he] does so it is his wish to return to this part of the country, this under the laws of the state he cannot with safety to you or himself do without some person to represent him in the character of an owner—he has requested me to serve him in that way. I have only to say that if his statements be true with regard to your willingness to give him such permission I will consent to represent him for one year at least and should nothing present itself to prevent perhaps longer. Should you approve his choice you will forward me the necessary authority. I have thus far presumed to address a stranger at Bens instance which is the only appollogy I have to offer.
>
> Respectfully yours,
> Wm. C. McAllister[11]

Since this letter was hand-delivered to Weaver by Gilmore, it is clear that Weaver had given him permission to go back across the Blue Ridge to Campbell County to look for a place where he could live and work while he attempted to earn enough money to buy his own freedom. Ben Gilmore was sixty-seven years old in 1830, but his age clearly had not weakened his desire to be free. The surprising thing is that Weaver, given his need for forgemen, granted Gilmore the privilege of buying himself. The slave undoubtedly presented Weaver with a strong case, but Gilmore's argument was probably less persuasive than the fact that Weaver had been able to buy two additional forge hands by the time Ben Gilmore left the Valley: John Baxter, a master refiner, and Garland Thompson, a chaffery forgeman whose feats of physical prowess during his years at Buffalo Forge would take on almost mythical proportions.[12]

Weaver had an opportunity to acquire a particularly versatile slave workman in 1828. This man, like Phill Easton, Ben Gilmore, and Harry and Billy Hunt, was also a former Oxford hand, and the circumstances surrounding his appearance at Buffalo Forge are intriguing and illustrate the complex give-and-take that sometimes occurred between master and slave, particularly when the bondsman possessed much-needed skills. The slave's name was Billy Goochland, and he was owned by David S. Garland, who lived in Amherst County, across North River from Rockbridge. He wrote to Weaver about Billy Goochland on May 23, 1828:

> I have recd your esteemed favour of the 19th Inst. in which you inform me that you wou'd be pleased to purchase my man Billy Goochland that formerly belong'd to Ross's Estate.
>
> It being Holliday times the fellow has concluded to visit his friends own'd by you and to see you also, in order that he may make up his mind how far he wou'd be pleased with an exchange of residence. He is an exceedingly valuable man and was appraised the highest of any negro in Ross's Estate except one. He has been brought up to the wheel wright and mill-wright trade and is a good workman at either. He is an excellent hand at stocking plows making harrows, hames, &c. and a good common carpenter. In addition to these qualifications, he is honest, sober and industrious and punctual in the observance of orders, and very attentive to his business in the absence of his master. Upon the whole I regard him to be one of the most valuable negroes that I was ever acquainted with. But still my want of money makes me willing to sell him.

The owner authorized Weaver to keep the slave at Buffalo Forge "a day or two" if Weaver should "wish to obtain information as to the fellows skill and capacity." The notation on the front of the letter, "pr. Billy Goochland," indicates that the slave delivered the letter to Weaver himself when he came to call.[13]

The most interesting aspect of this episode is the reciprocal nature of the inspection that went on. Weaver had the right to satisfy himself about Billy Goochland's qualities, but the slave would be looking over Weaver and Buffalo Forge as well. It is doubtful that very many slaves in the antebellum South had the right to veto a proposed sale, but Billy Goochland had such a right, and he may well have exercised it on this occasion. It is also possible that Weaver was disappointed with the slave's work or perhaps he did not offer his owner enough money. Whatever the reason may have been, Billy Goochland did not join Weaver's slave force.

The detailed description of Billy Goochland's work habits and personal characteristics in this letter highlights a concern that was shared by Weaver and ironmasters throughout the Valley. How would a slave perform at a blast furnace or forge after he was purchased and trained in the arts of ironmaking? Much depended on a slave's physical ability and the level of skill he was able to acquire, but that was by no means the whole story. In his testimony given in Weaver's suit against Jordan, Davis & Company, John Jordan emphasized "the speed and fidelity of the hands" when he discussed the factors that went into making a forge operation successful. "How many days, weeks or months are Forges usually stopped by high water, breaking hammers, helves &c. about the Forge—low water, freezing up, hands sick, drunk, and other causes known to iron men?" Sam Jordan asked his father at this point. "I think if I were to say one third of the whole time, I would not be far wrong," John Jordan replied, "as it would depend very much on the fixtures, faithfulness of the hands, sufficiency of the stream at all times, &c. &c. &c."[14]

In both word and deed, William Weaver demonstrated over the years that he fully agreed with Jordan's assessment. Of course a forge had to be well designed and well built and have adequate waterpower, but ultimately nothing was more important than the "faithfulness of the hands." The master of Buffalo Forge went to elaborate lengths to try to ensure that "the speed and fidelity" of his slave hands would be second to none.

The process began with a careful examination of a slave's work habits and personal qualities prior to purchase. Weaver considered much more than price when he was thinking about buying a slave. "Granville a boy belonging to Miss Sarah McDowell wishes me to buy him," Weaver wrote his lawyer, James D. Davidson of Lexington, in 1852; "if he can be had for about 700 Ds I will purchase—make inquiry as to character and if it answers make the purchase for me."[15] Weaver often bought slaves he had hired for a year, or sometimes for several years, and he seems to have liked this arrangement in many ways. It gave him time to see how well they would work and how they would fit into the larger slave community at Buffalo Forge.

If Weaver needed any confirmation of the value of his policy of making "inquiry as to character" before buying a slave, he received it in 1854. "W. W. Davis wants to sell you negro man, a carpenter named Dick," James Davidson wrote Weaver on December 21 of that year.[16] Six days later, Davidson told Weaver the results of his investigation of the slave's qualities. William W. Davis, Weaver's nephew, had revealed "that his man Dick, is a fellow of bad character—& that he had incestuous connection some 4 months since with his own daughter, who is now with child by her own father & that the girl says the connection was by force. Mrs. Davis is unwilling that he shall remain upon the premises," Davidson went on. The slave was "about 40 years old," and the price was $1,000. Davis could not vouch for his honesty. Dick was "always cunning enough to cover up his tracks," Davis maintained, and "nothing but his cowardice, restrains him from violence (which makes him the more dangerous.)" Davidson concluded this letter by advising Weaver that he "should not have such a negro about you. He would not only trouble you—but would pollute your other negroes."[17] Weaver did not have to be given such a warning. He had followed a policy of screening his slave purchases as carefully as possible over the years, and he was not about to change. Dick was sent to the Richmond slave market, where he was sold for $800.[18]

Weaver looked for two other qualities besides "character" when he was seeking recruits for his skilled work force. First, he wanted slaves who were willing to apprentice to one of his refiners or hammermen. Weaver revealed his thinking on this subject in the fall of 1849 when James Davidson sent a slave named Terry out to Buffalo Forge to talk to Weaver about possibly becoming an ironworker. "I sent him to the Forge to see how he would like the business," Weaver subsequently wrote Davidson; "he returned to me and told [me] he would like to be a Forgeman."[19]

The purchase of Terry was complicated by the fact that he had a wife who lived some distance from Buffalo Forge, and in the end he did not join Weaver's forge gang. But it is highly significant that before Weaver would consider buying the man, he had Terry go down to the forge and watch the refiners and hammermen at their jobs and then decide if he wanted to train as a forgeman. The episode with Terry was only one incident, but there can be little doubt that Weaver followed a similar practice whenever he considered assigning a new slave apprentice to one of his master workmen. Voluntary consent, a feature not normally associated with many aspects of slavery in the antebellum South, was very much a part of the process by which Weaver recruited his slave forge workers.

The second thing Weaver looked for in potential forgemen was a talent for ironmaking. Perhaps the most revealing statement he ever made about his approach to the problem of making high-quality bar iron with slave labor came in a letter he wrote to James Davidson in 1852. Weaver said that one of his slave artisans "belongs to a family that produces good mechanics."[20] Weaver clearly believed that if fathers or uncles had demonstrated a capacity for mastering ironmaking skills, then the chances were good that their sons or nephews would possess a similar ability. An older brother or cousin who had become a refiner, hammerman, blacksmith, or forge carpenter suggested to Weaver that younger relatives coming along might make excellent additions to his skilled labor force. It was no accident that three sons of Sam Williams, Sr.—Sam, Charles, and Washington—filled important forge positions for Weaver in the decades prior to the Civil War. So did Tooler, Jr., his brothers Joe and Bob, Harry Hunt, Jr., and Jim Garland and his brother Garland Thompson, Jr. Many of these slaves traced their ancestry back to the "Wilson negroes" purchased by Weaver in 1815; others were the sons of forgemen acquired by Weaver after he moved to the Valley in 1823. All belonged, in Weaver's words, to families that produced "good mechanics."

By the end of 1840, Weaver had managed to eliminate all white workers from key forge positions. "My forge refinery men (slaves) belong to me," he reported proudly in December of that year, and the production records kept at Buffalo Forge show that the last white hammerman stopped drawing merchant bars at the chaffery forge on November 23, 1840.[21] After Weaver retook possession of Bath Iron Works in 1838, he operated Bath Forge intermittently in the 1840s and early 1850s exclusively with slave labor.[22] He would shuttle his refiners and chaffery forgemen back and forth between Bath and Buffalo Forge as needed; the manager and a clerk would generally be the only whites around either forge unless Weaver himself stopped by to check on production or issue instructions.

According to John Doyle, Weaver's first manager at Bath Iron Works, there was an economic downside to the use of slave forgemen. "I have no doubt but it costs more to refine a ton of iron with slave labour than it does with white labour," he testified in 1840; "the reason is that they, slaves, do not understand it and they waste more metal and coal to greatly overbalance the difference in other respects. I was forcibly struck with this difference soon after I started Bath forge," he added, and Doyle went on to illustrate his point.

> I procured a workman, a free man from the North, who put up a refinery fire in which he made an anchony that would go 18 [hundredweight] to the ton with about 12 bushels of coal; he remained there but a short time. When he left I put Hal Hunt, a slave, to the same fire who took from 20 to 25 bushels to make the same quantity of iron.[23]

William Norcross, a white chaffery hammerman who had worked alongside Harry Hunt and Phill Easton at Buffalo Forge during the 1820s, agreed with Doyle's assessment. Slaves "were not as good workmen and do not take as good care or as much pains as good white workmen," he claimed.[24]

Weaver clearly believed that the advantages of using slave labor far outweighed any disadvantages, but Doyle and Norcross had a point. What they failed to offer, however, was an explanation for the difference in the levels of knowledge and skill they observed. David Ross, the owner of the Oxford Iron Works, understood the situation far better than Weaver's two employees. His slave forgemen at Oxford "were as good workmen 20 years ago as they are now—they have had no chance to improve—they have not

[had] an opportunity of travelling to see other works and the annual improvements [made there]," Ross wrote in 1812. His "Iron Works people ... have remained as it were stationary," he observed.[25]

The problem, as Ross recognized, was the institution of slavery itself, not the innate talents and abilities of his Oxford workers. He knew they were "good people," but they had had "no chance for improvement—there is no emulation—the father and son joggs on in the old way[.]" "I wonder they do so well," he added.[26] Unlike free artisans in the North, slave ironworkers had little opportunity to travel widely, visit other industrial establishments, learn new techniques, witness technological innovations, and acquire scientific knowledge.[27] Small wonder, as Ross put it, that his slave forgemen "remained as it were stationary." Much the same situation seems to have prevailed at Weaver's ironworks.

In the end, however, even Doyle acknowledged that the ironmaster who *owned* his forgemen had a cost advantage over installations that used free or hired slave labor, even though slave workers might be more wasteful in their use of charcoal and pig iron.[28] Doyle's position—that a proprietor needed to own his slave artisans—had been Weaver's conviction all along, and by 1840 he had achieved that goal.

Subsequent purchases in the 1840s and 1850s added blacksmiths, teamsters, woodchoppers, and field hands to Weaver's labor force, but his forge gang was essentially complete by 1840. From that point on, he relied largely on recruits from the ironworking slave families at Buffalo Forge to replace forgemen who were growing too old or were becoming too infirm to stay at their jobs. By 1860, William Weaver owned sixty-six slaves: twenty-eight adult men, fifteen women, fourteen boys, and nine girls. His core forge crew in that year had all grown to manhood at Buffalo Forge: Sam Williams, master refiner; Henry Towles, refinery underhand; Tooler, Jr., chaffery hammerman; Harry Hunt, Jr., chaffery underhand; and Henry Matthews, forge carpenter. All these men had served their apprenticeship at Buffalo Forge, and often they had trained alongside their own fathers. All belonged to families that had an impressive history of turning out highly skilled artisans.

Assembling a full crew of skilled forgemen and maintaining their number as death and injury thinned the ranks of his original force were formidable challenges for Weaver. These were not, however, the ultimate challenges he faced as a southern ironmaster. Even more imposing was the task of motivating these slaves to work, and work well, at the art—for that is what it was—of ironmaking.

Weaver, of course, had considerable coercive power at his disposal. He could punish any recalcitrant or troublesome slave, but if he had relied on the whip to achieve satisfactory levels of production, his career as a Virginia ironmaker would have been very short-lived indeed. Excessive use of force certainly would have backfired, and a whipping administered to a skilled slave would, at minimum, leave the man sore and incapable of work. It would probably leave him seething with anger as well and looking for ways to get back at the master. Acts of industrial sabotage could be accomplished with relative ease around a forge. To cite only one example, the huge wooden beams that supported the 500- to 600-pound cast-iron hammerheads in the forge—"helves" was the name given to these beams—occasionally broke in the normal course of operations and had to be replaced. The forge would shut down for at least a day, sometimes more, while the forge carpenter installed a new helve. Weaver's forgemen could break these helves intentionally whenever they wished, and who could say whether it was or was not deliberate? Another alternative would be for the slave to burn the forge down. On any working day, live charcoal was there to do the job. The slaves, in short, were in a position to do considerable physical and financial damage to Weaver's interests, even if they limited their activities to passive forms of resistance like work slowdowns or slipshod performance of their duties. Not surprisingly, there is no indication that Weaver ever whipped one of his slave forge workers at any time during his forty years in the Valley.

A far greater threat to the slaves was the possibility of sale. Even skilled slaves who tried to run away or who carried their resistance beyond Weaver's level of toleration could be turned over to slave traders and readily sold. Yet no ironmaster would want to part with a trained slave ironworker, as Weaver's delight over acquiring his sixth forgeman in the fall of 1827 suggests. Buying or training an immediate replacement would be difficult, if not impossible, and trying to hire skilled slave forge workers was, as Weaver well knew, both uncertain and expensive. It was far better, from Weaver's point of view, to avoid the use of physical coercion to the fullest extent possible and to turn to a weapon like the sale of a slave only in the most extreme circumstances.

The alternative to force was positive incentive. From his earliest days in Virginia, Weaver paid slaves who did extra work. Weaver's artisans had a daily or weekly task to perform, but he compensated them, either in cash or in goods from his store at Buffalo Forge, for anything they turned out over and above the required amount. Payment for "overwork," as this system was called, was a common practice at slave-manned manufacturing establishments throughout the antebellum South, and it was a feature of the labor regimen at southern ironworks as early as the mid-eighteenth century.[29] The task for slave refiners at Buffalo Forge, and everywhere else in the Valley, was a ton and a half of anchonies per week for a forge worked in the customary fashion—two-handed by a master refiner and his underhand. Chaffery forge hammerman throughout the Virginia iron district were required to draw two "journeys" of 560 pounds of bar per day. For a two-handed forge, again the usual method of operation, this meant a total daily task of 1,120 pounds. Choppers cutting wood for charcoal pits had a task of 1 1/2 cords per day—9 cords for a six-day workweek.[30] All these tasks had been the customary quotas for years in the Valley, and they did not change during the forty years Weaver lived at Buffalo Forge. They were in place when he arrived, they were there when he died, and he never, as far as we know, made any attempt to alter them.

The unchanging nature of these tasks over time suggests that both master and slave regarded them as a traditional standard, and these quotas seem to have been set at levels that an average worker could reach by putting in a day, or week, of steady labor. They were not pegged at an excessively high point for good reason: The whole intent of the task system was to encourage slaves to produce a set amount of output in a given time and then to work beyond that minimum point in order to earn compensation for themselves.

Pay for slave overwork was identical to the pay given free artisans for doing the same job. In the 1830s and 1840s, for example, the rate for refining anchonies with free labor was $8 per ton in Virginia, for drawing bar iron $6 per ton. Thus, a slave master refiner and his helper would start earning overwork, at the rate of $8 per ton, for all the iron they produced after they had met their weekly task of 1 1/2 tons of anchonies. The $8 would be divided between the refiner and his underhand on the basis of the level of skill the helper possessed. The same thing held true for the two slaves working at the chaffery forge. The hammerman and his assistant would split the overwork payment of $6 per ton for any iron they made over and above their combined task of 1,120 pounds of bar per day.[31]

The practice of paying for slave overwork at the same rate given free labor for performing similar duties was not limited to the forge operatives. The same principle applied to less skilled positions as well. Slave choppers in the early 1830s were paid at the going rate of 33 1/3 cents per cord for all the wood they cut over and above their weekly task of 9 cords. By the late 1830s, the rate had climbed to 40 cents a cord. Slaves who performed common labor on Sundays, holidays, or at night were paid the standard wage of 50 cents per day. The overwork system embraced almost every conceivable job around Weaver's ironmaking installations. Colliers could stand watch over the charcoal pits during their time off; ore bank hands could mine and wash extra ore; teamsters could haul iron exceptionally

long distances or work on Sundays; slaves could weave and sell the standard-sized charcoal baskets used to charge both blast furnaces and forge
fires with their fuel. Weaver paid slaves who used their own time to cut the
flexible wooden hoops used to band his flour barrels (the price was 25 cents
per 100 "hoop poles," as they were called). Other slaves earned money by
going into the woods during their off hours and felling trees for Weaver's
sawmill (the price was 12½ cents for each "saw log").[32] Several hired
teamsters who did not return home for the customary Christmas break
were paid $5 yearly in the late 1830s "for staying here during the holidays."
And some slaves received what amounted to a regular wage for performing
their jobs satisfactorily. A hireling named Isaac, for example, was paid $1.50
per month in 1830 for serving as the forge "stocktaker"; his responsibility
was to keep the forges supplied with iron and charcoal. "Allen Collier," a
slave belonging to Weaver, was given the same amount monthly for super-
intending the production of charcoal at the Buffalo Forge coaling
grounds.[33]

Weaver also extended the opportunity for overwork to his agricultural
hands. Large numbers of slaves grew corn on plots Weaver set aside for
their use, and he would buy whatever they did not wish to keep for themselves at the current market price; he paid 42 cents per bushel for corn in
the early 1830s, 50 cents per bushel later in the decade. Field hands regularly received $1, sometimes more, in "harvest money" after the crops were
brought in. Some of Weaver's slaves were able to raise their own poultry
and livestock and sell Weaver their surplus chickens, hogs, or calves.[34]

Special situations frequently provided the slaves with the chance to earn
overwork: cutting ice from the pond behind the forge dam and filling
Weaver's icehouse in the winter; fighting fires that had broken out in the
coalings; pumping water out of flooded mines at night; rebuilding roads
and fences damaged by storms; repairing the dam after a freshet. Anything
that was above and beyond normal duties, Weaver was willing to pay for.[35]

Weaver's use of the overwork system was so extensive and so nearly
all-embracing that it is difficult to see how it was anything other than a
conscious design on his part to try to make his slaves, both those he owned
and those he hired, more willing workers. His intent, clearly, was to give his
slaves a stake, however modest, in the success of his operations, to try to
motivate them to work for, rather than against, his interests. His goal was to
make his slaves disciplined and productive laborers without having to resort constantly to the use of physical coercion. Force—the possibility of
punishment, the threat of sale, the strength of law that relegated human
beings to the status of chattel property—was the cement that ultimately
held slavery together, at Buffalo Forge and throughout the antebellum

South. But some means had to be found to prevent the constant intrusion of physical compulsion into the day-to-day commerce between master and slave. Slavery was inherently a brutalization of the human mind and spirit, but it could not function as a labor system—particularly as a skilled, iron-making labor system—if that brutality became a daily, physical presence in the lives of the slaves. The overwork system acted to minimize the use of force at Buffalo Forge, and thus it served well the needs of the master. But it also served the needs of the slaves, for they took the system and used it to enhance the quality of their own lives in ways Weaver probably could never imagine.

Weaver, like masters everywhere in the antebellum South, provided his slaves with certain basic necessities—food, clothing, housing—and the available evidence indicates that he did not try to skimp or cut corners when it came to maintaining his labor force.

Weekly distributions of food, weighed out by the forge clerk as part of his regular duties, consisted of a peck of cornmeal for each slave and a meat ration of beef or pork. Weaver reported in 1840 that he used bacon about seven months of the year and that seven pounds of pork converted to bacon was his standard allowance for each hand. These figures compared favorably with the weekly rations provided slaves at other ironworks in the Valley.[36]

Each slave also received an annual allotment of clothing. Included in the winter issue were a shirt, heavy pants, a coat, yarn socks, shoes, a wool hat, and a blanket. The summer issue consisted of a shirt, lighter-weight pants, and shoes. "Negro clothing," as it was called, was generally made out of coarse, strong fabric like jeans cloth or tow linen. Weaver's slave women were given petticoats of homemade linsey. Slaves expected these items—all of them—to be distributed at the appropriate times every year, and Weaver corresponded regularly with his commission merchants in Lynchburg and Richmond to ensure that the necessary articles would arrive punctually.[37]

The manuscript census returns for Rockbridge County listed eighteen slave dwellings at Buffalo Forge in 1860. We know from photographs, sketches, and physical survivals what this housing looked like. The best slave cabins are still standing today; they are two substantial brick structures—one double and one single cabin—built in 1858 fairly close to the rear of Weaver's residence. The normal slave house at Buffalo Forge was a sturdily built log cabin with a stone chimney, a singled roof, and well-chinked walls. One of these cabins was a large two-story structure that may well have served as a bunkhouse for the unmarried men and the handful of slaves hired annually to work at Buffalo Forge. As mentioned, Weaver

owned sixty-six slaves in 1860—twenty-eight men, fifteen women, fourteen boys, and nine girls. If his slaves were dispersed more or less equally
among the eighteen cabins, each house would have provided a home for
three or four people.[38] That was, in fact, about the way it turned out. The
normal unit of slave housing at Buffalo Forge was a single-family cabin in
which a father, a mother, and their children made their home.

The food, clothing, and housing furnished by Weaver at Buffalo Forge
certainly met the average standard of maintenance provided by most nineteenth-century southern slaveowners, and the housing may well have been
superior to that available to slaves in wide areas of the South. It is not
likely, however, that Weaver's slaves were overwhelmed by a sense of
gratitude for the master's largesse. They probably saw these items exactly
for what they were—basic necessities, adequate to sustain life but insuffi-
cient to accomplish much more than that. To bring modest luxury to their
tables, to add an article of fine clothing to their wardrobes, to improve the
furnishings in their cabins, Weaver's slaves turned in overwhelming numbers to the overwork system. Along the way, one suspects, the slaves gained
something much more valuable than the material goods they obtained.

The skilled forgemen were certainly in the best position to exploit the
overwork system. Weaver's need for a high-quality, attractive product to
send to key markets across the Blue Ridge gave these slaves considerable
leverage—an edge, as it were—in their dealings with the master. "Some of
the dealers complain that your iron has too many flaws & that you don't
draw it sufficiently nice—the quality is approved of & only a little more
nicety in drawing is required," Lewis Webb & Company, Weaver's principal commission merchants in Richmond, wrote in June 1828.[39] "Bar iron
goes off slowly @ $90," the same firm informed Weaver the following
March. "The article is plenty & as the competition in the sale of it is great
you will do well to make yours nice." The merchants then added a message
that was bound to get a rise out of Weaver: "We observe Jordan & Irvine [at
Clifton Forge] sends their Iron down in better order than yours."[40]

Weaver heard a similar refrain from every merchant with whom he did
business. "I hope your Hammerman will be particular in drawing this
parcel nice and I think it probable I will on receipt order more," one wrote
in February 1830.[41] "As I keep no iron but yours, if a man gets a bad piece
of me he can not mistake the works it comes from," another told Weaver
later that same year.[42]

Weaver's fortunes as an ironmaster depended on his ability to sell his
iron at a good price, and he took these admonitions seriously. To Lewis
Webb & Company in Richmond, Weaver replied that he expected to do a
better job drawing iron in the future, and a subsequent shipment of bar to

this commission house elicited a much more favorable comment. "The thin flat Iron sent on the last boats . . . is much approved of," the Richmond merchants wrote Weaver in June 1829, and they added that "we still want well drawn tire."[43]

The production of "well drawn tire" and bar that was "much approved of" rested more than anything else on the skill of Weaver's forge hands and their willingness to work with speed, care, and attention to detail. High-quality iron could not be whipped out of them; they had to be encouraged to make it.

One of Weaver's principal commission merchants in the 1820s and 1830s, a man named John W. Schoolfield, had clerked for Weaver prior to setting up a mercantile business in Lynchburg. Schoolfield knew the Buffalo Forge operation well, and he knew the Buffalo Forge slaves. "You may promise Sol that if he will draw iron nicely to suit my orders and quick after they are received that I will give him a beautiful callico dress for his wife Christmas," Schoolfield wrote Weaver in July 1829. Sol Fleming had been the principal hammerman at Buffalo Forge since Weaver had purchased him in 1826. In the same letter, Schoolfield placed a large order for wagon tire, one-half inch thick and ranging from two to three inches in width, and he asked Weaver to "make Sol gage [*sic*] them or else people will not have them"—a clear indication of the exacting work slave forgeman were frequently called on to turn out.[44]

Schoolfield's promised present for Sol's wife came back to haunt him. Sol inquired about the dress as Christmas approached, and the reply he received was clearly not the one he expected. "Tell Sol that I had not forgotten the Dress I promised him but he has not done any thing for me to earn it," Schoolfield wrote Weaver in early December. Schoolfield's orders for some specific sizes of bar and light tire had not been filled, and as a consequence he refused to send the gift. Sol "must not expect me to give him a Dress promised on a condition with which he did not comply," Schoolfield added in closing.[45] It may have been totally coincidental, but four months later, the Lynchburg merchant was complaining about the "bad Iron" he was receiving from Buffalo Forge. "If you can have me supplied from Bath I should be very glad," Schoolfield added somewhat ruefully.[46]

The overwork system was absolutely crucial to the functioning of Weaver's ironmaking enterprise and slave-manned industrial establishments throughout the antebellum South. Weaver's need to both discipline and motivate his slave workers required that a rather delicate balance be worked out between the demands of the master and the wishes of the slave. The words "delicate" and "balance" are not often used to describe any aspect of the slave regime, and the chances for misunderstanding and misinterpretation here are obviously legion. No sane person would deny that the scales were weighted far more heavily on the side of the party that possessed the power to inflict brutal punishment on, or put on the auction block and sell, a recalcitrant worker. But it still seems fair to say that southern ironworks employing slave artisans had to develop a labor system that brought the requirements of both master and slave into some sort of harmony. The long-standing traditions of a reasonable task for each worker and the practice of paying all slaves who exceeded their tasks or performed any sort of extra labor were critical elements in achieving this balance of needs and wills, however rough and inherently unequal it might be.

Entries in the Buffalo Forge "Negro Books," as the overwork ledgers were called, indicate that most of the slave hands, both skilled and un-skilled, used the system to earn compensation for themselves. Traditional practice allowed slaves to choose whether they would take payment in cash or in goods from the ironmaster's store. If they chose cash, they could use the money to shop at other country stores, and this seems to have afforded the slaves a measure of protection against price gouging by the local store-keeper. One knowledgeable observer reported in 1840 that good profits were made on "the furnishing of supplies . . . where the iron works are operated entirely with free labour, but where the works are carried on principally with slave labour the amount of profits is very limited."[47]

If the slaves did opt for payment in merchandise, they could draw on their overwork immediately for things like coffee, sugar, tobacco, molasses, cloth, or articles of clothing. The one item conspicuous by its absence in the list of slave purchases was alcohol. Weaver tried, not always success-fully, to keep whiskey out of the hands of his slaves. Only on special occasions would he issue a whiskey ration to slaves who had performed difficult work under arduous circumstances, such as cutting ice from the frigid waters of Buffalo Creek or dam building.[48]

Admittedly, in the process of earning overwork compensation, the slaves were in one sense doing the master's bidding: They finished their required tasks before they began working for themselves and thus responded posi-tively to Weaver's attempt to motivate them. But on another level the slaves were being very much their own men. They could do extra work if they wished, or they could take their time off as leisure. Even in the simple act of accepting or rejecting the overwork system they were achieving, in at least one small phase of their existence, some measure of self-choice. If they did choose to do additional labor, the sums they earned were theirs to control, and they gained an even greater measure of personal initiative.

One of the most significant things about the overwork accounts is the way in which they suggest how a sizable number of Weaver's slaves took advantage of the system to carve out something of a private and individual life for themselves. Opening these ledgers and turning page after page with the names of slaves written across the top is very much a process of opening a window into a hidden past. The "Negro Books" afford a rare glimpse into the lives of antebellum southern slaves because they tell us what slaves chose to do with resources they themselves controlled. They worked exceedingly hard to accumulate the sums recorded on the credit side of these ledgers. The debit side reveals how they spent these precious resources, and by tracing their expenditures we can learn a surprising amount about their values and priorities, about what was important to them and, frequently, to their families.

For example, Phill Easton, one of Weaver's master refiners at Buffalo Forge, built up impressive amounts of overwork earnings from 1839 to 1840. His account opened on April 1, 1830, with a transfer of $65.27 to his credit from an earlier "Negro Book" (which unfortunately has not survived) against a debit account of only $40.34. Phill regularly bypassed Weaver's annual clothing allotment for both himself and his wife, Betsy, and for each year that he did so he was credited with $15 (except for 1834, when the figure was $13.50) on the books as a payment in lieu of clothing. He raised a calf every year, which he sold to Weaver for $2 through 1834 and for $3 thereafter, and he made extra tonnages of iron over and above his weekly task of 1½ tons of anchonies.

Weaver, like all ironmasters in the Valley, paid $8 per ton for iron refined by free labor or by slaves as part of their overwork, and Phill received either $4 or $5 per ton for his extra iron; the rate depended on whether he worked two-handed at his forge with a skilled or less skilled helper. When fully trained refiners like John Baxter or Billy Hunt assisted him, the $8 fee was split evenly.

By his ironworking and calf raising and by choosing to forgo his annual issue of new clothing, Phill regularly put between $20 and $30 in overwork credit on Weaver's books each year during the 1830s. On February 29, 1840, when his account was totaled up, he showed a balance in his favor of $100.28½. Included in this sum were two exceptionally interesting items. One, dated August 18, 1837, was for 44¾ cents "By Wm. Empy for Cooking for him." Bill Empy, a free Negro forgeman who occasionally worked for Weaver, had apparently taken meals with the Eastons and was paying Betsy for the cooking she had done on his behalf. The other was dated February 29, 1840, the date Phill's account was balanced. This entry read: "By 14 months Interest your former Duebill . . . $6.72." Phill apparently held Weaver's I.O.U. for a substantial amount of overwork credit and was drawing interest on this note.[49]

The debit side of the ledger is even more revealing. Phill Easton's most frequent use of his overwork credit was for the purchase of coffee and sugar, for which he clearly had a taste, as did, in all probability, his wife. Phill regularly bought cloth, such as "6 yds Fancy Calico for Betsy $3.00" in September 1831, "3 yds Jeans $1.87½" in December 1833, "8 yds Flax linen $3.00" in June 1834, and "3½ yds. Casanet $3.50" in January 1838. He occasionally bought items like handkerchiefs and new shoes, and there are a number of small charges for mending shoes for both himself and his wife, a reflection of his decision to opt for the clothing credit instead of new clothing each year.

In addition to his regular purchases of sugar and coffee, he occasionally used his overwork to acquire a gallon of molasses or a barrel of fine flour. He also bought items for the home: "1 sifter 1 Sett knives & forks $3.00" on June 4, 1830, and "1 Sett cups & saucer .50¢" on August 13, 1831. He sometimes drew cash from his account, sums ranging from as little as 50 cents to as much as $5. There is an intriguing entry dated August 11, 1838, debiting his account 25 cents for "postage on letter from Columbus" (a black hammerman named Columbus worked for a time at Buffalo Forge in the mid-1830s). And there are almost always Christmas entries: for coffee, sugar, shoes, and withdrawals of cash, which he, or Betsy, could use to shop at one or more of the stores that dotted the countryside around Buffalo Forge. After Phill left the forge, probably as a result of infirmities brought on by old age, he continued to earn money by raising and selling calves to Weaver, who by the early 1850s was paying $5 for each calf.[50]

It does not take a great leap of the historical imagination to grasp the importance of the overwork system to Phill Easton. He clearly used his earnings to improve the quality of life which he and his wife were able to enjoy, but he also seems to have used his overwork to stake out some precious independence—some psychological breathing space—in the midst of a system that theoretically held him totally bound to the will of his owner. Phill's decision to take primary responsibility for clothing himself and his wife is particularly telling in this regard, since it broke with a traditional form of slave dependence and substituted his own work, sweat, and skill for the master's beneficence, such as it was. The clothes on his back he put there himself, and the same held true for his wife. The fact that his purchases included expensive fabrics like fine calico and cassinette also meant that Betsy Easton would be wearing something other than coarse "Negro cloth" as the result of his efforts.

There are other hints that point to Phill's sense of pride and self-worth: his holding Weaver's note and collecting interest thereon, for example, or a brief entry to his credit dated December 23, 1839: "By 8 lbs Iron he sold &

said it belonged to him .50".[51] His Christmas purchases certainly must have given him considerable satisfaction; to be able to buy presents for himself and his wife at a traditional time of gift giving would mean, at minimum, that he and Betsy would not have to depend on Weaver's noblesse oblige for their holiday celebration.

Phill Easton lived on well into the 1850s. The last entry under his name in the Buffalo Forge "Negro Books" reads:

> Uncle Philip Easton
> Died Nov. 20, 1856 and
> Burried Nov. 21, 1856

He was seventy-five years old at the time of his death; his wife evidently had died before him. He had been born in 1781, the year of Weaver's birth, and one suspects that Phill Easton, like William Weaver, was a proud man. It also seems fair to say that he had great faith in his own abilities and that he used his talents as best he could to benefit himself and those he loved.[52]

Much the same could be said about Sol Fleming. Sol did not receive a credit instead of his annual clothing allowance, but in every other way his overwork account bears a striking resemblance to that of Phill Easton. Sol earned substantial sums of overwork income by turning out extra tonnages of iron at both the refinery and chaffery forges, and, to cite one particularly impressive example, on December 24, 1838, he was credited with $25.80 for refining "3 [tons] 4 [hundredweight] 2 [quarterweight] 7 lb over Iron By Your Self 8 Dols Pr Ton." He made additional sums by splitting rails, working nights in Weaver's sawmill, and operating the threshing machine both at home and on neighboring farms. Like Phill Easton, his most common use of his overwork was for sugar and coffee, but he also bought molasses, tobacco, fabric, handkerchiefs, and household items like a "picher," for which he paid 62½ cents in December 1831. Unfortunately, his accounts can be traced in detail only after April 1830, so it is impossible to know if he used his overwork to buy a dress, or fabric to make one, in December 1829—that was the month J. W. Schoolfield wrote from Lynchburg that Sol would not be receiving the present for his wife that Schoolfield had promised earlier. Sol's regular purchases of calico, linen, checks, and bleached cotton during the 1830s suggest that he may well have substituted his own gift for the one his wife failed to receive that Christmas.[53]

If a slave had a credit or debit on the books when Weaver balanced their accounts, that sum was simply carried over to the following year. John Baxter, for example, regularly spent more than he earned in any one year on items like coffee, sugar, molasses, calico, and nice articles of apparel for both himself and his wife. Among his clothing purchases were "1 pare Casimer Pantaloons & making do 5.00" in February 1836 and "1 Silk Hat 4.00" later that same year. Baxter's purchases in 1836 and 1837 totaled $38.76½, but his earnings for this two-year period—all for extra tonnages of iron—amounted to only $12.08¾, leaving a "Balance Due from you" on December 24, 1837, of $26.67¾. Over the next year, Baxter significantly reduced his indebtedness to Weaver by cutting back (but not totally eliminating) his new purchases, by increasing his forge overwork, and by returning his silk hat, for which he received $4 in credit. When his accounts were balanced on Christmas Eve 1838, he owed Weaver only $3.44, and that sum was posted to his debit as his account for 1839 began.[54]

John Baxter's experience was by no means unique at Buffalo Forge, and his account and others similar to it suggest the possibility that Weaver may have allowed his slaves to run up considerable debts against future over-work earnings in order to pressure them into subsequently increasing their output of iron or, in the case of non-forge workers, doing other extra labor for him. Here, in other words, may have been a way for Weaver to make some members of his labor force literally work like slaves, meeting their tasks and more on a regular basis, without his having to turn to the whip or the threat of sale in order to motivate them to labor of this intensity. But the same factors that kept Weaver from beating or selling his slave artisans would have acted to restrain the effectiveness of the "debt to the company store" technique as well.

Weaver really had no choice but to rely on the labor of these men, and they were not easily replaced. They also had the ability to hurt Weaver's operations in a great many ways, if they chose to do so. Thus he had no real way of collecting these debts other than encouraging the slaves to meet their obligations. If at some point he tried to force them to settle their accounts or if he denied them the right to make additional purchases until their debts were all paid off, he would be running much the same risks he would entail if he decided to apply the whip to the backs of his forgemen: They could feign illness, or engage in work slowdowns, shoddy workmanship, or outright sabotage.

The fact that Weaver allowed workers who had debts to continue to obtain store items and to carry their negative balances from one year to the next suggests that he did not want to resort to a day of reckoning with these slaves. The cost might be too high. It is interesting to note that in 1838 when John Baxter returned the silk hat he had purchased early in 1836, he was credited with the same sum he originally paid for the hat, $4. Baxter may never have worn this hat, but the chances of that are remote. He probably decided on his own to give the hat back in order to reduce the overwork he owed Weaver, and Weaver probably decided all parties would be well served if he made no reduction for any wear and tear the hat may have received while in Baxter's possession.

The carryover of debit balances from year to year was a privilege largely limited to Weaver's own slaves. Hirelings returning home for Christmas almost always had their accounts totaled up just before they departed for the holidays. During the week preceding Christmas, the "paying of hands" would take place at Buffalo Forge and at ironworks throughout the Valley. Almost every hired slave who had worked for Weaver received cash and occasionally merchandise for the overwork credit they had on the books as the year drew to a close.

Absolom, for example, a hireling employed at Buffalo Forge in 1833, sold Weaver 13 bushels of corn he raised that year, and on December 20 was paid $5.46 for his crop. Jim Derest, a teamster who worked for Weaver in 1836, earned $4.87½ in overwork by hauling 27 loads of metal at 12½ cents per load and growing 3 bushels of corn; he spent 75 cents for two handkerchiefs and 25 cents for a pair of suspenders during the year and at Christmas took home the balance of his overwork credit of $3.87½.

Jack Holmes, another hireling, made $11.62 in one year by raising a hog (sold to Weaver for $3), growing 8⅝ bushels of corn ($3.62), and weaving twenty-two small charcoal baskets ($5). He was paid his $11.62 "Cash in full" on December 23, 1837.

Major Watson, a hired slave who worked at the coaling grounds that same year, earned $14.83, all of which he took in cash at year's end, by growing 29 bushels of corn and "watching on Sundays" (at the rate of 40 cents per day) to make sure that fire did not break out in the smoldering charcoal pits.[55]

Major Watson's pay for tending the coalings on Sunday seems to have created a very interesting situation up in the mountains where black colliers made the fuel for Buffalo Forge. These men worked on their own, without white supervision, some four or five miles east of the forge. As mentioned, they were directed by one of Weaver's slaves named Allen, who was listed as "Allen Collier" in the overwork ledger covering the 1830s. Allen received a regular wage of $1.50 per month for acting as the master collier, and his duties included seven-day round-the-clock responsibility for the coaling pits once they were fired and the process of making charcoal had begun. Yet Sunday was a traditional day of rest for slaves throughout the South, and some of the colliers, like Major Watson, were being paid for standing Sunday watches. Allen seems to have come to the conclusion that his Sunday responsibilities deserved additional compensation as well, and he took the matter up with Weaver.

The production of charcoal was an extremely important part of Weaver's ironmaking enterprise, and Allen was a first-rate master collier. When the forge manager wrote Weaver in the fall of 1830 to tell him that "our coal houses are both full/nearly/of good coal," he called it such "a fine thing in the routine of an ironmasters business" that "it might be termed a phenomenon."[56] Allen was largely responsible for this phenomenon, and Weaver could not afford to lose his cooperation. In the late 1830s when Allen apparently raised the subject of back pay for his previous years of Sunday labor, he obviously caught the ear of the master. Weaver made the following notation on a page in the "Negro Book" containing Allen's overwork account:

> 6 years Sunday work
> @ 12 Dollars per annum
> up to 1st Jany 1838

Weaver credited Allen with the extraordinary sum of $72 for six years of *past* service on the Sabbath. This brief entry is a very small part of the copious manuscript record describing antebellum life and labor at Buffalo Forge, but there are few items that reveal more about the complex nature of slavery at Weaver's ironworks.[57]

The overwork system was only one of the techniques Weaver employed to make Buffalo Forge a profitable enterprise, but, as the experience with Allen suggests, it was a critically important element in his approach to the challenging task of making high-quality bar iron with slave labor. By systematically building up his crew of skilled slave artisans by purchase and by allowing younger slaves to apprentice alongside his experienced operatives, Weaver eliminated his dependence on free forge labor and placed himself in an advantageous competitive position in the Valley iron trade. Reliance on overwork as a principal means of motivating his forge workers allowed both Weaver and his forgemen to find that elusive middle ground where at least the minimal demands of both the master and the slaves could be brought into some sort of balance.

Weaver generally got what he most wanted and needed from his slave force—a sufficient quantity of high-quality iron produced at a cost that allowed him to earn a profit on his sizable investment in land, ironworks, and labor in Virginia. Weaver could have been a slaveowner without the extensive use of the overwork system, but he could not have been the successful ironmaster that he was—the master of Buffalo Forge—without it.

The slaves, as always, got much less out of the bargain. Only one, Ben Gilmore, seems to have gotten what slaves universally in the South wanted above all else, a chance at freedom. But they did earn recognition and limited reward, they gained considerable protection for themselves and their families against sale and abuse, and they secured the chance to do something tangible to improve their own lives and the lives of those they loved. Considering the limits imposed by the always degrading and frequently brutal system of southern bondage, these were not insignificant achievements. They could give a man a sense of pride and accomplishment and the wherewithall to stand up against the dehumanizing aspects of chattel slavery, and that was an achievement of a very high order indeed.

7

—⧫—

William Weaver, Virginian

During the 1820s and 1830s, Weaver periodically toyed with the idea of selling out in Virginia and moving on—to Mississippi on at least one occasion, or, more often, back to Pennsylvania. The closest he came to leaving probably occurred in the years immediately following his marriage. Eliza seems to have had a decided preference for Philadelphia, and Weaver bought a house there and he and his wife spent much time in the city during the early 1830s.[1]

By the 1840s, however, Weaver was no longer talking of leaving the Valley. He turned sixty in March 1841, and he clearly decided at some point during that decade that Buffalo Forge would be his home for however many years he had left. "Tis a good thing to go abroad occasionally—the effect of it is, that I love Virginia the more," he wrote in June 1848 to his lawyer and closest friend, James D. Davidson of Lexington. "I love her mountains, her Valleys, and above all, I love the Farmers old fashioned fire side hospitalities—the string of their latch is always out, and the hinges of there [sic] doors never screak—they are greased with the oil of kindness and welcome," he went on. "No place like home, however homely it may be be. I have seen no spot, that pleases me as well as my old Buffalo place," he told Davidson. "In my sojourns, I have envied no man. Some of my friends in Phila wondered why I did not reside amongst them—I replied—at home I was but a small person, but that I was somebody—the people knew me—and in crowded Phila I should be nobody."[2]

William Weaver was much more than "a small person" in the Valley, as well he knew. As early as 1830, a fellow ironmaster had told Weaver that he could be a bank director in Lynchburg any time he wanted to be, and Weaver's growing wealth in land and slaves placed him at the pinnacle of Rockbridge County's elite during the late antebellum decades.[3] Weaver was being much more accurate when he wrote that he "was somebody" in his adopted region, that "the people knew me." The problem, if indeed Weaver considered it a problem, was that a large number of those who knew him in Virginia did not like him very much.

Even relatives who obviously admired Weaver admitted that he had a complex personality. "He was an exceedingly handsome man, shrewd and well informed, a genial and companionable one with friends but blessed with strong prejudices, an implacable foe, tho' an open one," was the description provided by the anonymous family historian who earlier had sketched the portrait of Weaver's boyhood diligence and thrift.[4] Some of those who worked closely with Weaver after he came to the Valley, such as Thomas Mayburry and John Doyle, clearly would have considered this assessment of his character overly generous.

Yet there is much truth in the family's reading of Weaver's personality. He was "shrewd and well informed"; if he had not been, he never would have succeeded as an ironmaster. Weaver followed various occupations during his lifetime and seems to have made money at all of them, but he could say "without hesitation it required more capacity and judgment to conduct an extensive ironwork establishment to advantage than any other business in this section of the country."[5] Men who were well acquainted with furnace and forge operations in the Valley agreed with Weaver on this. They described ironmaking as "laborious" and "a very precarious business," and these observers could tick off the names of almost two dozen local ironmasters who had failed, some of whom were "utterly ruined." Those who had made money could be counted on the fingers of one hand, and Weaver was among the successful few.[6]

The family historian's comment that Weaver was "blessed with strong prejudices" also seems to be on target, although one might ask if Weaver's "strong prejudices" were always a blessing. He was a very stubborn, opinionated man with firm ideas on how things should be done. When people did not do what Weaver expected them to, he reacted swiftly and often angrily to their behavior, sometimes at the expense of his own long-term interests.

Such was the case in 1828 and 1829 when Weaver got into a bitter dispute with a man in eastern Virginia over some slave hires. Slave hands were not difficult to obtain in the traditional hiring areas during these years, but Weaver knew that the goodwill of slaveowners could be a crucial factor should a tight hiring market recur. Nevertheless, Weaver engaged in a running argument with a master from whom he had hired slaves, and the cause of the disagreement appears to have been Weaver's fiery temper and an almost compulsive niggardliness.

In 1827, Festus Dickinson of Bowling Green in Caroline County hired out two slaves, Dennis and Manuel, to Weaver; the price was $90 for the two men.[7] The slaves worked at Bath Furnace and then returned home at the end of the year for the usual Christmas holiday. Later, on his annual hiring trip, Weaver spoke with Dickinson and arranged to rehire the men for 1828, although no final price was agreed upon.

Dickinson initially seemed satisfied with this rather uncertain financial arrangement and quite pleased that Dennis and Manuel would be working for Weaver again. "When you come down next winter I shall be pleased to see you at my house and think it probable I can assure you of several additional hands from my county," Dickinson wrote Weaver on February 12, 1828.[8] The difficulty arose because Dickinson had trusted Weaver to set a fair hire for one of the men. The full text of Weaver's letters to Dickinson have not survived, but Dickinson quoted Weaver's language in one of his replies to Weaver's earlier correspondence. Dickinson's three letters to Weaver deserve to be quoted virtually in their entirety. No where else in extensive documentary record of Weaver's affairs is there a more revealing picture of what it was like to do business with William Weaver when his temper flared and he held the upper hand.

Dickinson's first letter was dated March 8, 1828:

> From the high estimate which I had formed of you from the opinion of others and the slight personal acquaintance I had with you, I do not know when I have felt more mortified and disappointed than when I examined the note which you inclosed me for the hire of my two men Dennis & Manuel for the present year. I understood the contract for Manuel for this year as being fixed by us . . . at the sum of $50. for which you offered then to execute your note and although you manifested a repugnance to hire Dennis again, yet I concluded of course that you would certainly be willing to give me within the neighborhood of the price which I could get

for him in my own County. Thirty five dollars was the least sum which I could have supposed you would offer. As this however was left entirely at your option and convenience I shall be compelled to abide by the price which you have agreed to give. But it will be an additional warning to me hereafter, to trust to the liberality of no man, or in other words never to place myself in the power of any man, to fix his own price upon my property. Seventy dollars for two strong able bodied negro men! Why I understand you pay Mr Cole Dickinson $60 each for his hands. I am receiving much better hires for my hands in my own county than you agree to give me, and would any person suppose I would send them 150 miles from home for the same price. I shall insist on your paying the sum of $50 for Manuel as stipulated and as I had placed it in your own discretion to fix the price of Dennis I shall abide by your decision, but shall expect them to return at the expiration of the year.[9]

On January 15, 1829, Dickinson used much stronger language to express his dismay at Weaver's conduct.

Your note of the 24 ult from Chilesburg requesting me to call on Lewis Webb & Co of Richmond for the hire of my two negro men Dennis & Manual for the last year was recd. The Doctors bill for attending Dennis was also recd and I could but feel indignant at the manner in which you treated me after my placing such implicit confidence in you as a high minded, liberal gentleman. I put it to you as a man of good sense whether or not $25 was a fair & just equivalent for the services of Dennis for twelve months, and then to bring in a medical bill reducing his hire to the pitiful sum of $15. "Shame where is thy blush!" You the year proceeding gave me $45 for his hire. I was offered $40 for him before I started him back to you, and I have hired him out this year for $50. How can you reconcile these things to the pitiful sum at which you valued him, having me completely in your power. Delicacy at least should have induced [you] not to have made so great a reduction of his hire from what you gave me the preceding year. I should have been well contented with a reduction of some five or ten dollars as you manifested some reluctance to hire him again. You however thought you could make him useful upon your farm, and men for similar service hired in my own county from $40 to $45. Moreover you forfeited your positive agreement about the hire of Manuel. You must certainly recollect that you expressly stipulated to pay me $50 for his hire and I so informed you by mail after the receipt of your letter sending the bond for their hires, which letter you have thought proper not to notice.

I recd. of Mssrs Webb & Co. $60 16/100 and gave them in your bond, and I sincerely hope it may terminate all intercourse between us. I felt it due to my own injured feelings and that confidence which you have forfeited to let you know that this conduct of yours was noticed by me, and if you ever get another gentleman in your power as I have been to caution you how you treat him.[10]

What was almost certainly Dickinson's final letter to Weaver was written on February 2, 1829:

I did not calculate when I addressed to you my letter of the 15th ult. that the injury therein complained of would be addressed by you; for after your prior treatment to me about the hires of my two slaves, Dennis and Manuel, I could not consistently have made any calculation based upon your liberality or your disposition even to do justice to me. The only object I had in view was to let you know that I felt injured & that you had forfeited my good opinion. This I never fail to communicate to any man who treats me badly. But I did not suppose that your answer to that letter would have added insult to injury. In your reply to that letter you say "Your letter of the 15th Inst has just been recd. I also recd. one the beginning of the year, which I considered a very *extraordinary production*, and such a one as I should not have expected from its author. It satisfied me at the time that you wished to have the best of the bargain, and my rule is, when I discover a person wishes to take the *advantage* of me I cease dealing with him." There is something in this language to which I am unaccustomed. . . . I am still at a loss what there was *extraordinary* in that production. Your insinuation of a disposition on my part to take *advantage* of you I throw back as false and unfounded. You Sir by my misplaced confidence in you had all the bargain in your own hands, and you did not fail to use the advantage which I had thus given you. . . . I should not have noticed your late communication [but] for the supposition that you might construe my silence into an acquiescence in the correctness of your statements. This letter will close (I hope forever) my correspondence with you.[11]

We have only one side of this correspondence for the most part, so there is no way to judge Weaver's actions in this case with any degree of certainty. But if Festus Dickinson ever crossed paths with Thomas Mayburry, the two men undoubtedly would have had a subject for mutual discussion.

Weaver's temper, it seems fair to say, rested on a hair trigger. A Rockbridge County farmer whom Weaver suspected of shortchanging him on a promised delivery of wheat reported that "Mr. Weaver was cursing me for a Raskel" (the farmer, it turned out, had delivered the full quantity).[12] In a land title dispute, Weaver outlined his position and then instructed his lawyer to brook no compromise; "we are entitled to it and will have it— and no more *Tom foolery*," Weaver told James Davidson.[13] When the integrity of Weaver's expert witnesses was challenged during the suit against Jordan, Davis & Company, Weaver responded immediately with a vigorous defense of his own witnesses and a witheringly sarcastic attack on those of the opposition. "Cannot Mr. Walkup write an order to a merchant without murdering the King's English . . . ?" he asked. "How is Joseph Bell regarded in his neighborhood laying his money bags aside?" he inquired. "Cannot a wood-chopper possess knowledge and judgment equal to a fat grazier who deals in bullocks?"[14] There is no question that Weaver was, in the words of the family historian, "an implacable foe, tho' an open one." Even the most cursory examination of the antebellum chancery court records of Rockbridge and Augusta counties amply demonstrates the accuracy of this description.

The family chronicler did not say all that might be said about Weaver's personality, however. No comment was offered regarding the hard-edged, almost ruthless, quality that characterized Weaver's ceaseless pursuit of wealth and success. He appears to have been, in many ways, a driven man who was willing on more than one occasion to ride roughshod over those who stood in his way.

No one knew this side of Weaver better than John Doyle and Thomas Mayburry. These two men were hardly unbiased observers of Weaver's character; both claimed to have suffered heavily and unjustly at Weaver's hand. Whether Weaver had cause to haul them into court is not the issue here. The point is the depth and intensity of feeling that Weaver's conduct engendered in his two former colleagues. Their antagonism almost leaps off the pages of the depositions they gave in Weaver's suit against his nephews and Sam Jordan.

In both instances, Weaver sought to discredit their testimony by questioning their impartiality. "Have you not been for some years, are you not still, upon the most unfriendly terms with the plaintiff?" Weaver asked Doyle on February 5, 1840. Doyle's reply, mentioned earlier, merits fuller quotation here:

> I could have hoped that the plaintiff for his own sake would have foreborne to ask such a question but as he has done it I shall be compelled to answer it. I despise him most cordially, and I believe he is despised by nine tenths of the men who ever had any dealings with him. But bad as I know his character to be, and cordially as I despise him, those circumstances would not make me swerve one iota from the truth when testifying under oath.[15]

In some ways, Thomas Mayburry's comments were more powerful because they were more restrained. Mayburry gave his deposition in April

1839. He was seventy-nine years old that year; Weaver had just turned fifty-eight. The most revealing exchange between the two men occurred at the end of Weaver's lengthy cross-examination of Mayburry's testimony. Weaver concluded by asking Mayburry three questions:

> WEAVER: "If you yourself had a question of great magnitude to be settled, would you consider it correct that your antagonist should call on your avowed enemy for his opinions in adjusting the matter."
> MAYBURRY: "I do not know who has done it."
> WEAVER: "Are you not at variance and on bad terms with the plaintiff?"
> MAYBURRY: "Yes, but not without cause."
> WEAVER: "Have not the defendants for sometime past known that you are on bad terms with the plaintiff?"
> MAYBURRY: "I do not know, but I presume they did, as it seems to be in the neighborhood a matter of public notoriety."

Following this exchange, Sam Jordan began his reexamination of Mayburry by asking a question of his own.

> JORDAN: "If the defendants were allowed to take the depositions of those only who are on friendly terms with the plaintiff, might they not find some difficulty in obtaining the evidence of respectable persons who stand fair before the community?"
> MAYBURRY: "I think they would, for I believe his friends are few indeed."[16]

Weaver seems to have taken delight in the sparring and legal combat that went on almost continuously during his years in Virginia. His chancery court suits were the major arenas for this activity, but there were minor scuffles as well over things like evicting squatters from his property or withholding permission to cross his land. Weaver had a long memory when it came to anything or anyone that had injured his interests, as indicated in a letter he dispatched to John Jordan on December 15, 1851.

> Shortly after succeeding your Son & Wm W Davis in the possession of Bath Iron Works, they gave me notice not to pass over a corner of their land lying behind Bath Forge. They fell[ed] trees across the road. I acquiesced, and went to considerable expense in getting a new route. As you are the Father of S. F. Jordan, and this appears to be the Jordan doctrine when they have power, I presume they are ready and willing to extend it to others. I therefore notify you not to haul across my lands lying back of James Paxtons.[17]

When Jordan protested Weaver's action, Weaver could hardly contain his glee. "I am getting the Jordan Dander up to fever heat," he wrote James

Davidson the following February; "with such people I neither consider property or that which is more dear, character secure."[18] An "implacable foe" indeed, and certainly "an open one."

The anonymous family historian touched on a final, more positive, aspect of Weaver's character, that he was "genial and companionable ... with friends." If we are to believe John Doyle and Thomas Mayburry, that was practically a moot point, and Weaver himself acknowledged in a touching letter to James Davidson written in December 1852 that there was some truth to their charges that he was a man not widely liked in the Valley. He was seventy-one years old when he told Davidson, "I feel as if my age would reach Par—if so it is highly probable I shall see many of my friends depart before me—wrong again. I said many—I have but few—but the more esteemed on a/c of being scarce."[19]

The one dimension of Weaver's life about which we know very little is his relationship with his wife, Eliza Newkirk Woodman Weaver. The family recordbook contains a single sentence on this subject. According to the nameless chronicler of the family's history, Weaver "married for money and was disappointed but had no children."[20] The oral tradition among Weaver's descendants is that the marriage was not a happy one, and this view is supported by fragments of documentary evidence. Two letters written to Eliza during the first years of her marriage to Weaver suggest that she felt lonely and isolated at Buffalo Forge from the very start and that she shared none of Weaver's affection for their Virginia home. In 1830, one of her nieces living in Philadelphia wrote that she had "heard that Uncle is [the] greater part of his time from home," and she urged Eliza to return to the North. "I think you would be just as happy here with your friends and have him gone as to be there and have him gone," the niece observed.[21] The next year, another Philadelphia relative, also a niece, expressed her pleasure at having heard from Eliza but added that she was very sorry to learn "that you dislike the place so."[22] Eliza's distaste for life at Buffalo Forge was tempered during the early period of her marriage by the frequent trips to Philadelphia she and Weaver made, but these extended visits grew less and less frequent as the decade of the 1830s wore on.

Weaver became increasingly preoccupied with his business and legal affairs in the Valley in the late 1830s and the 1840s. The failure of Jordan, Davis & Company to operate Bath Iron Works to Weaver's satisfaction, the long-running suit against his nephews and Sam Jordan, and the necessity of being in Virginia to supervise operations at Bath and Buffalo Forge were the critical factors holding him in the South during these years. Eliza sometimes traveled to Philadelphia by herself in the 1840s; she was there when Weaver, at Buffalo Forge, wrote his letter to James Davidson in June 1848 praising the qualities of Virginia's humble but hospitable farmers and extolling the virtues and pleasures of life in the Valley and at "my old Buffalo place" in particular. Eliza clearly did not subscribe to those sentiments.

It certainly would not have been uncharacteristic of Weaver to marry for money. His acquisitive skills were well honed, and whenever the chance presented itself to make or save a dollar, or two, he invariably took it. A brief statement he made in 1850 effectively summarized his attitude toward the pursuit of wealth: "It is my Principle to collect Interest," Weaver told a man who owed him some money; "if not paid, it is my Interest to collect Principle [*sic*]."[23] There would be nothing at all surprising about Weaver approaching matrimony with some attention to the pecuniary advantages of a union with the widow Woodman. The surprising thing, if we are to believe the family history, is that he "was disappointed" in realizing the anticipated financial windfall.

Eliza apparently had no children by her first marriage; she had married a fellow Philadelphian named Constant Woodman in 1816 when she was thirty-one and he was thirty-four. Her first husband died in 1825, and five years later she married Weaver.[24] William was forty-nine and she was forty-five at the time of their wedding, and again no children were subsequently born. These circumstances tell us very little about their marriage other than the obvious fact that if his wife predeceased him, Weaver would have no immediate heir to the substantial fortune in land and slaves he was accumulating in Virginia.

One area where Eliza may well have exerted some influence over Weaver was in matters of religion. The documentary record of Weaver's life is almost totally devoid of reference to religious faith. It is possible that his rejection of the Dunker tradition into which he was born led him so far away from Christianity in general that he was uninterested in trying to regain any lost theological ground. After he married, however, Weaver begain attending Sunday worship services with his wife.[25] Eliza Weaver was a devout Presbyterian and a member of the congregation at Falling Spring Church, not far from Buffalo Forge.[26] Whether faith accompanied Weaver on these Sunday outings is impossible to say. In a letter written in December 1850, he referred to "the great god of nature" who was "as lavish to those who are born in a hovel as to those who receive their birth in a palace: he neither knows nor makes a distinction in the bestowment of his munificent gifts."[27] Certainly no evangelical fire breathes from this passage. We would seem, in fact, to be much closer here to the deistic, clock-maker God of the Revolutionary generation than to the stern, all-powerful deity of mid-nineteenth-century southern Protestantism.

It is perhaps a commentary on their life together that the record of

Eliza's death is considerably fuller than the story of her twenty years as William Weaver's wife. She was sixty-five when she died at Buffalo Forge on Thursday, October 31, 1850. Later that day, Weaver sent a letter to James Davidson containing measurements for a coffin and asking Davidson to "order a decent one to be made." The coffin should be at Buffalo Forge early on Saturday "—the Ladies say they ought to [be] busy at 10 o'clock Saturday morning—" along with a shroud, a cap, a pair of white gloves, and a bottle of chloride of soda, all of which Weaver requested Davidson to purchase in Lexington. "I send a Tub and if you have Ice please send it," Weaver added.[28] The brief obituary which appeared in the Lexington *Gazette* shortly after her death noted that "Mrs. Weaver was born in the city of Philadelphia, where she spent the greater part of her life." For the past twenty years she had lived at Buffalo Forge, the death notice read, where "she had the care of a large household, the comfort and happiness of which, it was her constant study to promote." The obituary concluded by noting that Eliza Weaver's "last illness was protracted during near twelve months," and that "she had been a consistent member of the Presbyterian Church" for many years prior to her death.[29] Her burial took place approximately a mile from Buffalo Forge in the cemetery of the Falling Spring Presbyterian Church.

When the sixty-nine-year-old Weaver came to record Eliza's passing in her family Bible, there was no room left on the page set aside for deaths. So he crossed through a heading on a page marked "Births," wrote "Deaths" above it, and made the following notation (which I have reproduced exactly as he wrote it):

> Eliza Weaver
> Died October 31st 1850
> at 3 oclock P.M.
> (Thursday) and was
> and was buried Saturday
> on Saturday 2d November
> Buffalo Forge Rockbridge
> County Virginia

Immediately under this entry, he drew a line and wrote:

> William Weaver
> was Born March
> 8th 1781 - in the
> County of Philadelphia
> Pennsylvania[30]

Although Weaver would grow increasingly infirm and suffer his share of sickness during the 1850s—"disordered bowels" and "a Bilious attack," to cite two examples—he had a remarkably robust constitution.[31] He would outlive his wife by almost thirteen years.

There are a few additional brief bits of information on William Weaver's wife. Tradition among Weaver's descendants who still live at Buffalo Forge today is that Eliza "was very strict and was feared by the slaves." The oral tradition among the descendants of William Weaver's slaves states the case in considerably stronger terms. According to James Thompson, whose grandfather and great-grandfather were slaves at Buffalo Forge, Eliza Weaver was "an evil mean lady" who was unhappy in her marriage and who took out her anger and frustration on the black people unfortunate enough to come under her thumb. Black folklore holds that she paid for her sins in the afterlife, however. An elderly black woman—almost certainly a former Buffalo Forge slave—called at the residence in the early years of the twentieth century and asked "if old 'Miss' still walked in the big house." James Thompson tells a similar tale of Eliza's ghost ascending the stairs and prowling the attic of Weaver's mansion after her death, her movements clearly marked by the clanking of the chains that shackled her restless soul.[32]

The picture of Weaver that emerges from the black oral tradition in Rockbridge County is considerably more generous than the portrait painted of his wife. James Thompson describes Weaver as a decent man who was spoken of without animosity by Thompson family members who passed down numerous stories of slave life at Buffalo Forge.[33] This image is reinforced by a few pieces of scattered evidence that give us some indication of Weaver's attitude and behavior toward his slaves during his early years in Virginia. John Danenhower described an incident which occurred as Weaver was preparing to leave on a business trip to Philadelphia in the fall of 1823. When Weaver visited Etna Furnace prior to his departure, the "Wilson negroes" living there "called on him for some present, and I believe he gave a dollar to each or something near it," Danenhower reported. He added that Mayburry "laughed heartily" at Weaver's extravagance and observed that Weaver "humored his negroes more than was necessary." Danenhower contrasted Weaver's treatment of the "Wilson negroes" with that of Mayburry, who cursed them as Weaver's slaves whenever he became angry or provoked at any of them.[34] And it is suggestive that Phill Easton, one of the skilled ironworkers at Buffalo Forge, regularly asked to be remembered to Weaver whenever Weaver was away from home for any length of time.[35]

These isolated incidents do not tell us very much, of course, and they can be interpreted in a variety of ways. The slaves might well have been trying to appeal to, or even stimulate, a sense of noblesse oblige in Weaver that they could exploit in various ways for their own benefit or protection. They could have been playing on whatever kind instincts they read in Weaver's character in the hope of receiving better treatment in the future than they had recieved in the past, perhaps at Mayburry's hand. But the possibility also exists that these incidents reveal at least minimal levels of kindness and consideration on Weaver's part when he dealt with the black men, women, and children under his control. If we accept the tradition handed down in James Thompson's family that Weaver was a decent master, it would seem fair to say that many of the slaves who lived and worked at Buffalo Forge probably thought more highly of Weaver than most of the whites who did business with him during his forty years as a Virginia ironmaster.

There was, however, a darker side to Weaver's career as a slavemaster. It revealed itself when he spoke of a female slave of demonstrated childbearing ability as a "breeding woman." Such a slave he considered an ideal wedding present for a young white couple because the slave's children would both add to the white family's wealth and provide slaves for its work force. He gave such a "breeding woman," and her husband, to his niece Hannah Davis and Sam Jordan when they married, and he contemplated making similar gifts to William and Abram Davis in the 1830s.

Weaver gave away slave children as well. In 1849, he presented Mary Davidson, the infant daughter of his close friend and lawyer James D. Davidson, with "a certain Female slave named Matilda, aged about 17, together with her future increase." As the deed of conveyance read, Mary Davidson was "to enjoy the use of said Slave & her increase for & during the natural life of the said Mary for her sole, separate, & peculiar use & benefit."[36] The next year, Weaver gave Davidson's newborn daughter Clara a twelve-year-old slave girl named Eliza, "together with her future increase." The terms of enjoyment were the same as those laid out in Mary's document the previous year.[37] Both deeds were recorded in the Rockbridge County Court House to guarantee their unquestioned legality.

Lexington, where Mary and Clara Davidson would grow up, was only nine miles from Buffalo Forge, and James Davidson and his family visited Weaver's home frequently. Weaver went to extraordinary lengths in both deeds to outline his future wishes with regard to the slave girls and any children they might have. Matilda and Eliza would be the exclusive property of James Davidson's daughters and would pass on to the daughters' children or next of kin when Mary and Clara died. If the Davidson girls should subsequently marry, the slaves would not be "in any wise, subject or liable, to the debts, control, or interference of any husband," and Weaver underlined this point later in each deed by repeating his "intention that no future husband . . . shall have any right to the enjoyment of the said property, during coverture, or to take as survivor after [Mary's or Clara's] death."

The gift of the two slave girls was clearly an act inspired by Weaver's deep affection for James Davidson and his family; Matilda and Eliza were given in love—William Weaver's love—to little Mary and Clara Davidson. It is also possible that Weaver secured the consent of Matilda and Eliza and their parents to the transfer, although there is no evidence to demonstrate this one way or the other. But almost nothing he did in his long career as a Virginia slaveholder demonstrates more vividly his acceptance of what slavery in essence was—the ownership of human beings as chattel property by other human beings. Weaver, on this and several other occasions, was more than willing to exercise the power conveyed to him by his status as the owner and master of his slaves.

Weaver clearly revealed his unquestioned acceptance of the slave regime when his bondsmen attempted to run away or committed some other serious breach of discipline. The power of the few lines recording the fate of these slaves is not diminished by the brevity of the entries. In the time book kept at Buffalo Forge in the early 1850s, Weaver's forge clerk made the following notations:

Thursday,	December	2	Jno Wilson run off
Friday,	"	10	This day heard of Jno Wilson
Monday,	"	27	James Watkins to Amherst after Jno Wilson
Wednesday,	"	29	Watkins returned from Amherst Sold John for $850[38]

Two months earlier, the time book contains these entries:

Saturday,	October	23	[Constable] This arrested Arch for stealing
Sunday,	"	24	Arch confined in irons all day
Monday,	"	25	Watkins to Lynchburg with Arch
Wednesday,	"	27	Watkins from Lynchburg[39]

The final items relating to Arch appear in two large ledger books which were part of the extensive financial records kept in the stone building down the hill from Weaver's house which served as the office at Buffalo Forge. In the Forge Journal, Weaver posted the following entry on November 8, 1852:

> Lee & Johnson
> For proceeds Arch $1175.00[40]

Lee & Johnson were Lynchburg commission merchants. A few days earlier, on October 29, James Watkins, the manager at Buffalo Forge, had been paid $5, presumably for taking Arch across the mountains to Lynchburg.[41] This slave was twenty years old and "a good blacksmith," in Weaver's estimation, but his skills and his value to Weaver as part of the Buffalo Forge work force failed to save him.[42]

Another party at Buffalo Forge received money in connection with Arch's arrest, confinement, and sale. One of the Buffalo Forge "Negro Books," the volumes in which the records were kept of slaves who did extra work, has an item under the name of the principal slave blacksmith at Buffalo Forge dated the day Arch was apprehended. This reads:

> Henry Matthews
>   Cr
> Oct/23/1852   By making Hand Kuffs for Arch   .50[43]

Weaver sold slaves only for what he considered just cause; there is no record of his selling one of his bondsmen simply for the profit such a transaction would bring. But he dealt severely with slaves who stole, who tried to run away, or who were chronic disciplinary problems. Slaves who did something that went beyond the bounds of Weaver's tolerance were simply sold off. It was the only way, he clearly believed, to maintain a well-ordered community of slave workers on his estate.

Weaver needed a reliable slave force for agricultural as well as industrial labor at Buffalo Forge. One of the secrets to his success as an ironmaster was his practice of using his own fields to provide most of the corn and meat needed to sustain his slaves. Weaver had 1,500 acres under cultivation around Buffalo Forge and at Highland Farm, a mountain property across North River where he had cleared and planted land that most farmers in the area considered too poor to invest in. Weaver paid $2 an acre for the 800-acre Highland site, converted the wood on the property into charcoal, rooted out the stumps, and grew abundant crops of corn on thin mountain soil that sloped at angles from twenty to fifty degrees. His scientific farming techniques attracted notice beyond the borders of Rockbridge County. He employed a sophisticated system of crop rotation, renewed his fields by planting clover and applying plaster to counteract the acidity in the soil, and used substantial quantities of manure from his own stables as well as imported guano to fertilize his land. Large herds of cattle, pigs, and sheep were fed from grain raised on the property; Weaver "crushes all his corn for stock-feeding in the ear, and he considers his crushing machine as the most profitable on his estate," noted an admiring observer in an article published in Edmund Ruffin's *Farmers' Register* in 1842.[44] In 1853, he had a McCormick reaper shipped in from Chicago and gave it a trial, but his wheat fields were too hilly for the machine to operate effectively.[45]

It was not uncommon for Weaver to harvest as much as 8,000 bushels of corn, 2,500 bushels of oats, and 2,000 bushels of wheat from his land.[46] The wheat he ground in his own mill at Buffalo Forge into high-quality flour, which sold well on the Lynchburg and Richmond markets. "His is what I would call very energetic and successful farming," wrote the author of the piece in the *Farmers' Register.* "Is it excelled, or even equalled, by any other farmer in the United States, under any thing like similar circumstances?" he asked.[47] Weaver's impressive crops were all planted, cultivated, and harvested by slave labor.

Weaver's agricultural and industrial interests clearly complemented one another. He easily combined a Jeffersonian love for life lived close to the land with a Hamiltonian desire to wrest as much wealth as possible from the riches that lay under the soil. When it came to politics in the 1830s and 1840s, however, Weaver displayed no trace of divided loyalty. He was a confirmed Whig. His involvement in iron manufacturing made the Whig positions on things like the tariff and the need for internal improvements highly attractive to him.

Only once did he seek political office after he came to the Valley. On April 8, 1845, he announced that he was running as a Whig candidate to represent Rockbridge County in the Virginia General Assembly. Weaver took this step after the regular meeting of local Whigs had already nominated a ticket to fill the county's two seats in the lower house. Weaver's statement of candidacy did not give his reasons for entering the race as a latecomer, and press reports of a meeting held in Lexington on April 12 to hear his explanation only noted that "for a 'first appearance' he showed no little tact and spirit."[48]

Canal politics—specifically issues involved in the management of the James River and Kanawah Canal and its extension from Lynchburg to Buchanan in Botetourt County, just south of Rockbridge—appear to have been Weaver's principal motive for declaring his candidacy. A subsequent attack on Weaver by an anonymous correspondent in the Lexington *Gazette* charged that he wanted the state to embark on "a grand and untried scheme of buying an immense number of negroes, and putting them under an overseer to carry on the work" of building the canal. This same writer also claimed that Weaver was interested in a political career because he was enamored of the sound of his own words. "Did any man ever happen to pass a night in the same room with him without being kept awake two thirds of the night by the sweet sounds of his musical voice?" this writer inquired; "we never heard of him talking *a little* in his life, if he could find any body to talk to."[49]

Weaver lost the election to the regularly nominated Whig candidates, and thus ended his major foray into the political life of Rockbridge County.[50] The next year he announced that he was running again for the legislature, but he withdrew from the race a week later when he learned "that the next session of the legislature would be a very protracted one."[51]

Canal affairs drew Weaver back into the public arena in 1850–51, but this time he limited his activity to letter-writing in the local press. He attacked John Jordan and others for pushing the idea of building an expensive canal up the North River from Balcony Falls to Lexington. Weaver noted that Jordan and other Lexington interests, who were loudly proclaiming the necessity of the canal, had purchased precious little stock in the enterprise. Too many of the canal supporters were "100 dollar Nags," Weaver wrote, referring to their niggardly stock subscriptions. "It reminds me of an observation made by his Satanic Majesty, when he sheared the Hogs," Weaver went on. "Great noise and little wool." Lexington would reap most of the benefits of the North River improvement, Weaver concluded, while the rural taxpayers of the county would end up shouldering most of the cost of the project.[52] The canal was subsequently built, but Weaver did succeed in altering the original plan, which called for construction on the project to begin in the middle and work both ways from that point. He had to petition the legislature in order to force this change, however.[53]

When Weaver had made his initial investment in the Virginia ironworks in 1814, the nation was at war with Great Britain and James Madison was president. Weaver came to Virginia in 1823 during the presidency of James Monroe, a period marked by peace and enough domestic political tranquility to prompt a Boston newspaper to dub the Monroe years an "era of good feelings." Seven years later when Weaver married, Andrew Jackson occupied the White House and opposition was mounting that would soon provide Weaver with his political home, the Whig party. By 1850, the year

Eliza Woodman Weaver died, the United States had fought a successful war with Mexico, and the country was in the grip of a bitter debate over the extension of slavery into the western territories. The unity of the nation, which had seemed so secure following America's victory in the War of 1812, would become increasingly fragile as the 1850s wore on.

Weaver, like the country, had also undergone a marked transformation during these four decades. Certainly by the mid-1850s, he no longer thought of himself as a Pennsylvanian. "At home, the place that suits me best," Weaver wrote after he returned to Buffalo Forge following a short trip in 1856.[54] By then, William Weaver had become a Virginian in every sense of the word but birth. His slaves, his lands, his home, and his attitudes all made him part of his adopted state and region. If the sectional conflict building in the 1850s should lead to something more than political infighting and rhetorical combat, there was no question where his sympathies would lie.

8

Etna Furnace

To keep Buffalo Forge operating as a profitable enterprise, William Weaver had to overcome two major and recurring obstacles. The first was to find and retain an able crew of skilled forgemen. The second challenge was no less daunting: to secure a steady source of pig iron. Given the important role played by the "Wilson negroes"—the eleven original slaves purchased from John Wilson in 1815 and their descendants—throughout Weaver's long career as a Virginia ironmaster, it is not at all surprising that these slaves figured prominently in Weaver's efforts to solve both these problems.

The connection of these slaves to Weaver's labor needs was, of course, immediate and direct. From his earliest years in the Valley, he employed Tooler and his sons as ironworkers, and the division of that portion of the "Wilson negroes" held by Thomas Mayburry brought Weaver additional recruits for Buffalo Forge. When he took possession of Sally and Louisa and their children in 1837, he gained ownership of young men like Sam, Charles, and Washington "Etna," as Weaver originally listed the children of Sam and Sally Williams in the Buffalo Forge "Negro Books," and these slaves would help man Weaver's refinery and chaffery forges throughout the late antebellum decades.[1]

Weaver's search for an adequate supply of pig metal involved the "Wilson negroes" as well, but in this instance, the slaves were not those who had arrived at Buffalo Forge on January 1, 1837. Weaver's ongoing efforts to guarantee that Buffalo Forge would have enough pig iron brought him back into the lives of Mary and John, Hamilton, and Ellen, the four slaves taken by Thomas Mayburry when he and Weaver finally reached the agreement that dissolved their partnership and divided the firm's chattel property.

Following the sale of Gibraltar Forge to Sam Jordan and William Davis in 1839, Thomas Mayburry left the Valley and settled east of the Blue Ridge in Louisa County. He was initially drawn there by reports of discoveries of rich veins of iron ore along Contrary Creek north of the town of Tolersville. In July 1838, he purchased a large tract of land lying on Contrary Creek containing both ore and a seat for a blast furnace, and subsequent land acquisitions in 1839 and 1840 brought additional ore banks under his control. In 1839, at the age of seventy-nine, Mayburry began building a blast furnace on his Louisa County property. His new stack, which he named Victoria Furnace, was in full operation when Thomas Mayburry died in July 1840.[2]

Mayburry owned eight slaves at the time of his death, four of whom were his portion of the "Wilson negroes": Mary, the Mayburry's longtime cook and house servant, who was in her mid-fifties; John, age twenty-four, by this time a trained forgeman and blacksmith; Hamilton, at seventeen just beginning to take his place as a full-time ironworker at Victoria Furnace; and Ellen, a girl of fifteen. Mayburry left no will, but he did leave sizable debts. As a consequence of his dying intestate, the Louisa court named an administrator to pay off Mayburry's outstanding debts and to oversee the sale of whatever assets might be necessary to settle all claims against the estate.[3]

Mayburry's assets, it turned out, were not large. Victoria Furnace and his Louisa County lands were already encumbered by heavy mortgages, so this property passed immediately out of the estate. All that was left, in the words of the administrator, were the "eight negroes, . . . some bar iron (if received . . .), and about three thousand dollars." Since Mayburry's debts totaled well over $3,000, his creditors were looking toward the slaves as the chief means by which their claims could be met.[4]

One of the first steps the administrator took was to hire out those of Mayburry's slaves who were not already committed to other parties for the year. Fortunately, two of Mary's children, John and Hamilton, were hired out at the time of Mayburry's death. John was back in the Valley in 1840 working for a Rockbridge County ironmaster named Matthew Bryan. Bryan owned Vesuvius Furnace, where Mary and her three children had lived from 1828 to 1833, so John, in a sense, had gone home (or at least to one of his homes) to work for the year. Hamilton was hired out to John Hunter and William Stout, two prominent Louisa County men who had advanced Mayburry most of the capital needed to build Victoria Furnace and were legally in charge of the furnace when Mayburry died. Thus both John and Hamilton were out of the reach of Mayburry's creditors, at least for the time being. Such was not the case with Mary, Ellen, and the remainder of Mayburry's slaves. The administrator believed there was a very real chance that some of the creditors would try to force an immediate sale of these slaves, a step which would leave other creditors with no means to satisfy their equally legitimate claims. By hiring out all of Mayburry's slaves, the administrator was buying time for an orderly liquidation of Mayburry's assets and a fair settlement of all debts owed by the estate.[5]

The administrator's quick action proved to be a godsend for Mary and Ellen. It prevented them from going under the auctioneer's hammer at a Louisa County sheriff's sale and prepared the way for them to rejoin John back in the Valley. Hamilton was eventually to follow the same path back to the more familiar surroundings of Rockbridge County.

Matthew Bryan wasted no time hiring Mary and Ellen. Mary's skills as a cook and house servant were well known at Vesuvius, and Ellen could help her mother with various chores. Hamilton was an experienced furnace hand after his work at Victoria, and Bryan hired him as well as soon as he became available. In 1841 and 1842, Mary, John, Hamilton, and Ellen were all working as hirelings for Bryan.[6] It was a fortunate turn of events in the lives of four people who had only the most fragile hold over their own destiny.

On September 16, 1842, the Louisa chancery court ruled that it was time to proceed with the steps necessary to settle the estate. The court instructed the administrator "as soon as he can after the end of the present year" to "convert into money all the slaves and other personal property belonging to the estate of the said Thomas Mayburry dec.ᵈ."[7] Once the new year arrived, the administrator wasted little time executing this order. On January 2, 1843, he sold Mary, John, and Hamilton to Matthew Bryan of Vesuvius Furnace; John brought $859, Mary and Hamilton together sold for $640. Ellen went to another party, however. She was purchased for $338 by none other than William Weaver and a man by the name of Constant W. Newkirk.[8] Ellen, who would turn eighteen in 1843, was destined for

Bath Iron Works, where she would act as a cook for the Newkirk household.

Constant Newkirk was Eliza Newkirk Weaver's nephew. He had come down from Philadelphia in the early 1840s, and Weaver had installed him at Bath in order to place the furnace and forge under the supervision of a trusted family member. Weaver was counting on Bath for the pig iron he needed to run Buffalo Forge, and he hoped Newkirk could manage the property successfully. In November 1843, Weaver gave Newkirk, free of charge, a one-third interest in Bath "for & in consideration of the natural love & affection which he bears unto his said Nephew, Constant W. Newkirk." Weaver confirmed the gift in an indenture filed with the Rockbridge County Court, and this document contained a final sentence relating to other property: "And the said William Weaver doth hereby further grant, confirm, & release unto the said Constant all his the said Weavers interest in the slaves Ellen & Tom, now in the possession of said Constant."[9] From this point on, Ellen's fate would largely be tied to the fortunes of Constant Newkirk as the principal proprietor of Bath Iron Works. A year later, Newkirk became the only proprietor at Bath. On November 28, 1844, the Lexington *Gazette* carried a notice signed by Weaver informing the public that he was no longer involved in the operation of the Bath property and that hereafter the works would "be under the sole management and control of . . . C. W. Newkirk."

In the opinion of John Doyle, Weaver's first manager at Bath in the 1820s, Newkirk's personal qualities did not equip him for the ironmaster's trade. The problem, as Doyle put it, was that Newkirk "was a man of education and a gentleman so far as I know, but had no business capacity." It was Doyle's view that Newkirk also "ruined every hand [he] had for want of exercising a proper system of management."[10] Whether Doyle's assessment of Newkirk's lack of business and managerial talent was accurate or not is impossible to say. But by early 1847, Newkirk was ready to go back to Philadelphia. Weaver would have to find someone else to run Bath Iron Works.

Weaver thought he knew just the party. In 1845, he had sold Etna Furnace in Botetourt County to a partnership of Pennsylvanians headed by a man named Samuel Sherrerd.[11] One of these partners had confided in Weaver that Sherrerd and his brother John had inherited a large sum of money from their mother—reportedly $10,000 each—and Weaver had also received word from Pennsylvania "that S Sherrerd and his Brother received a considerable estate in ground rents in Philadelphia through their Mother."[12] Believing the Sherrerds to be men of capital, Weaver had no qualms about selling Samuel Sherrerd and his partners Etna Furnace.

Then when Newkirk pulled out of Bath and Samuel Sherrerd expressed a willingness to sell his interest in Etna to his brother John and buy Bath Iron Works, Weaver accepted his offer.

In the purchase agreement signed on February 1, 1847, Sherrerd agreed to pay $25,000 for Bath, payable in pig iron at the rate of 200 tons per year with the pig priced at $20 per ton. Included in the personal property sold with the works were, as Weaver noted later, "two Negroes, one a very valuable House Servant."[13] Ellen was undoubtedly the house servant to whom Weaver referred; the other slave was probably Tom.

Weaver realized he had put "a great many Eggs in Sherrerd's Basket," but he thought the brothers' reputed wealth made them safe bets to take over the operation of the two ironworks.[14] Weaver would have the pig iron he needed for Buffalo Forge without having to go to the trouble and expense of running either Bath or Etna furnace. With Newkirk heading back north, it looked like an ideal solution to Weaver's long-standing problem of obtaining regular supplies of metal for his forge.

The sale of Ellen and Tom to Samuel Sherrerd along with the Bath real estate would have been nothing out of the ordinary from Weaver's point of view. Ellen had lived at Bath for four years, she was Constant Newkirk's property, and Newkirk was selling out. Sherrerd would need a cook and house servant when he went there, so she and Tom went to Sherrerd along with the rest of the personal property at Bath.

Etna Furnace and Bath Iron Works, it turned out, were not in the hands of the moneyed capitalists Weaver thought they would be when he sold the properties. He learned this in 1849 as he waited for Samuel Sherrerd to comply with the terms of his contract, which called on him to supply Weaver with 200 tons of pig iron per year. Weaver's patience, never a prominent component of his personality, wore thin, and in the spring of 1849, he instructed James Davidson to file a chancery court suit against Sherrerd. "The time has arrived for energetic action," Weaver wrote his lawyer on May 6, 1849, and energetic action was not long delayed.[15] Sherrerd could not afford a lengthy suit, and on August 15, 1849, he resold Bath Iron Works to Weaver for the token sum of $5. As a result of this settlement, Weaver's suit against Sherrerd was stricken from the Rockbridge chancery court docket the following month.[16]

These legal and financial maneuverings placed Ellen at great risk. She was Samuel Sherrerd's property and a valuable asset at a time when Sherrerd was hard-pressed for cash. Weaver heard a rumor in January 1850 that she had been "sold and sacrificed, Bought I believe by an agent of some body," and that she was "to go to Etna."[17] This report apparently was true. In 1851, she was the property of John Sherrerd, who had purchased Samuel's interest in Etna Furnace in 1847. We know John Sherrerd owned her in 1851 because she, along with Etna Furnace, was advertised for sale early in the year. John Sherrerd had gone bankrupt, and his property was slated to be sold at public auction.

"A Valuable Negro Woman For Sale," read the advertisement which first appeared in the Lexington *Gazette* on February 6, 1851. The ad did not mention the woman by name, but she was described as "twenty-six years of age, and said to be a good Cook, and has a very good character." Ellen, born in 1825, was twenty-six years old that year. John Sherrerd's agent handling the sale, a prominent Rockbridge lawyer and former state senator named Samuel McDowell Moore, noted that he preferred "to sell her privately, as she has a husband in the county, and as the persons entitled to the proceeds of the sale are in want of money immediately, I will sell her low for cash." In the event a private buyer could not be found, "she will be sold at auction in Lexington, on the first day of March court next." This advertisement, which was typical of thousands of such ads that appeared with great frequency in antebellum southern newspapers, contained one additional piece of information which provided a clue as to Ellen's fate. It noted that she was "now at Matthew Bryan's in this county."

Ellen's husband, a slave teamster named Harry who belonged to Bryan, had driven Ellen to Vesuvius almost a month before this advertisement was published. "I have permitted Harry to take his wife down to your place, which I presume you have no objection to," Samuel McDowell Moore wrote Bryan on January 9, 1851. "I wish on account of her good character and Mr. Sherrerds good feeling towards her, to sell her privately," Moore went on. "If I can get her a good home I will take five hundred dollars for her." It took Bryan several weeks to come up with enough cash, but he did manage to buy Ellen before she was scheduled to go on the block at the March meeting of the Rockbridge County Court. Ellen was thus reunited with her husband and her other family members who were living at Vesuvius in 1851. Apparently she and Harry had no children. Moore mentioned in his letter that Ellen had "some affliction of the womb," but he assured Bryan that "she lost very little time" because of her condition.[18]

It was a brutal fact of life for all slaves in the South that one could never rest easy. A master who would buy a slave one day and reunite her with her husband and members of her own family could just as easily die the next. It did not happen quite that rapidly, but in April 1854, three years after he purchased Ellen, Matthew Bryan died. Like almost all ironmasters, he was heavily in debt; his estate would have to be sold to satisfy a long list of creditors waiting to be paid.

On April 28, 1854, appraisers arrived at Vesuvius Furnace to inventory

Bryan's personal property. No woman named Mary was listed among the slaves.[19] It seems almost certain that she had died sometime between 1843, when she was purchased by Bryan, and 1850. The entries under Bryan's name in the manuscript slave census for 1850 show only three slave women living at Vesuvius in that year, the oldest of whom was thirty-five.[20] If Mary did indeed die at Vesuvius in the middle or late 1840s, she would have lived into her early sixties and would at least have had the comfort of spending the last years of her life with some of her children. John was on the estate inventory, valued at $900, the highest figure given for any male slave and a sum that reflected his skills as a blacksmith and forgeman. Ellen was there as well, valued at $450. There was no slave by the name of Hamilton on this inventory; he was apparently hired out at the time Bryan died and was not at the furnace on the day the appraisers made their rounds.

A number of other slaves were listed, however:

Mary Ann & her 3 children	$1,200
Charles a Boy	500
Solomon	725
Rosey	350
Dick	750
Jerry	375

The appraisal continued until all the slaves at Vesuvius that day—the final tally was twenty—were enumerated.[21] Hamilton's hire would be up at the usual time, just before Christmas, so he and several other slaves who were also hired out could return home for the inevitable sale at the end of the year.

There was no man named Harry among the slaves appraised as part of Matthew Bryan's estate, and his name appears on none of the subsequent documents dealing with the final disposition of Bryan's property. Whether Ellen's husband had died or been sold prior to Bryan's death is impossible to say; the surviving records are silent as to his fate.

The headline on the advertisement announcing the estate auction had a familiar ring to it: "Valuable Slaves and other Personal Property for Sale." It was published in the *Gazette* on November 23, 1854, and informed potential buyers that the sale would occur on December 15, 1854, "at the late residence of Matthew Bryan, in Rockbridge County." Scheduled to be sold were "about 20 slaves, 10 or 12 of whom are valuable men, three or four women, and the residue boys and girls," along with eighteen mules, ten or twelve horses, some cows and hogs, a number of wagons, and various farm implements. The advertisement appeared over the name of Samuel McDowell Moore, administrator of Matthew Bryan, deceased.

The auction took place as scheduled at the appointed time and place. John, whose full name was given as "John Sims" on the sale bill, was purchased by a friend of Weaver's, a man named Henry A. McCormick, who lived at Steele's Tavern in Augusta County, not far from Vesuvius; the price was $720. Ellen went for $600 to Lorenzo Shaw, Matthew Bryan's business partner and a prominent Valley ironmaster who lived at Mount Torry Furnace in Augusta County, north of Vesuvius. Hamilton was sold to a former Augusta County resident named John Crobarger. In 1849, Crobarger had purchased a 260-acre farm on the headwaters of Mechum River in western Albemarle County just across the Augusta County line, and he seems to have been in the market for a prime field hand. Crobarger paid $800 for Hamilton, and he also purchased Mary Ann and her three children (for $1,910), which suggests that "Ham," as he was listed in the sale bill, and Mary Ann were married and that the "3 Children" were theirs.[22]

All of these slaves apparently remained in the hands of these owners throughout the remainder of the decade. The antebellum manuscript slave census schedules do not list slaves by name—only the age, gender, and color ("black" or "mulatto") were recorded. But the 1860 returns show John Crobarger of St. Ann's Parish, Albemarle County, Virginia, owning two male slaves, ages thirty-seven and twenty-seven, two female slaves, ages thirty and twenty-four, and seven slave children ranging in age from one to thirteen. This certainly suggests that Crobarger owned two slave families in that year, and Hamilton, who was born in 1823, was thirty-seven years old in 1860. One of the women might have been Mary Ann, and the presence of seven slave children on the Crobarger farm again indicates the possibility that Hamilton and his family were bought by Crobarger at Matthew Bryan's estate sale in 1854 and that they remained together six years later.[23]

Lorenzo Shaw moved his operations from Mount Torry west to Estilline Furnace, also in Augusta County, in 1855, and Ellen probably went with him. Estilline was located on the headwaters of Little Calf Pasture River, north of Bath Iron Works and not far from the Rockbridge County line. The manuscript census lists Shaw as the owner of seven slaves in 1860: a woman of thirty-five, three men (forty, fifty, and fifty-six years old), two girls (ages seven and eleven), and a boy (age nine). This woman may have been Ellen, whose age in 1860 was thirty-five.[24]

We can speak with absolute certainty about the whereabouts of John. Beginning in 1855, Henry McCormick, John's new owner, regularly hired him out to the man who had originally purchased John's mother in 1815, William Weaver. And Weaver just as regularly placed this slave at a site John knew only too well. From 1855 through the start of the Civil War, "John Sims" was a hireling at Etna Furnace.[25] It seems particularly ironic that after years of uncertainty and forced movement, beginning with the division of the "Wilson negroes" in January 1837 and culminating in the final dispersal of John, Hamilton, and Ellen at Matthew Bryan's estate sale in December 1854, one of Mary's children should end up back at the place of his birth. John was born at Etna in 1816 and spent the first twelve years of his life there. He returned to Etna in January 1855 because William Weaver was once again looking to this furnace as the prime source of pig metal for Buffalo Forge.

Weaver's repurchase of Bath Iron Works from Samuel Sherrerd in the summer of 1849 had done little to solve his pig iron problem. Although Weaver continued to tout the superior quality of the iron ore on the Bath property, this was largely empty rhetoric intended to lure prospective buyers out to Rockbridge County. An advertisement offering the Bath estate for sale placed in the Richmond press in January 1854 stressed the use of Bath metal in cannon produced at Bellona Foundry and the premium price such iron commanded. Weaver failed to inform the public that the easily raised and readily accessible ore at Bath had long since been exhausted.[26] If the property had been as good as Weaver's advertisement claimed, he would have worked it himself. After intermittently operating Bath Forge from 1849 to 1852, Weaver finally decided to abandon any attempt to make iron there. The books at Bath were closed for good on April 1, 1852. From that point on, the cattle turned out to graze on the Bath land represented the only activity regularly going on at what had once been a thriving industrial enterprise.[27]

In the fall of 1853, at the age of seventy-two, William Weaver was ready to get back in the blast furnace business in a big way. He had been one of the buyers of Etna Furnace when that property sold at public auction in January 1851, and he had leased his interest in Etna to his co-purchasers, John and Thomas Cartmill of Botetourt County, in March of that year.[28] Two personal inspections of the 8,000-acre site in 1853 convinced Weaver that he should buy out his partners. He discovered an abundance of high-quality iron ore on the property at the site of Retreat Furnace, the stack Weaver had been forced to abandon for lack of waterpower almost forty years earlier. A six-mile wagon road connected this ore bank with Etna, but Weaver had something much more efficient in mind: a railroad, ten miles in length, between Retreat bank and Etna Furnace, over which mule-drawn carts could be run to keep the furnace well supplied with ore.[29]

In the late summer of 1853, Weaver wrote his nephew Constant New-kirk in Philadelphia about his plans to regain complete control of Etna, build the railroad, and put Etna back into full production. He wanted Newkirk to manage this ambitious enterprise. Newkirk admitted that Weaver's offer was "considerable better than I am doing at present," but he tried nonetheless to argue his Uncle William out of the whole undertaking and even wrote James Davidson to ask him to intercede with Weaver. As Newkirk told Davidson, "the kind feelings and favours conferred on me by Uncle" prompted him to speak frankly to Weaver. "I was induced to write him opposing his starting of the Furnace, on the grounds that he is now perfectly easy, out of debt, and an independent man, and there is very few that can say that in the Iron business," Newkirk wrote. He thought Weaver would have to sink between $18,000 and $20,000 in the property to do everything he proposed, and there was no reason in the world Weaver should be launching such a scheme at his age.[30]

Newkirk's letter only prompted Weaver to look for a new manager. Weaver's nephew failed to realize how excited Weaver had become over the prospect of making Etna profitable once again. Others had tried and almost all had failed over the years. Newkirk offered his Uncle William sane, sober, and affectionate counsel, but such advice meant little to Weaver when his blood was up, be it over a chancery court suit or a major entrepreneurial challenge.

Etna would be a challenge, there was no mistaking that. The charcoal iron industry in Virginia and throughout the South was under heavy pres-sure from cheaper northern and British iron in the 1850s. The report issued by a Miners and Manufacturers Convention meeting in Richmond in De-cember 1850 called the condition of the iron trade in the state "depressed and discouraging" and predicted that "the mountain works near the James river" with an annual capacity of 25,000 tons of pig iron would produce no more than 2,500 tons in the year ahead.[31] Blast furnaces in Pennsylvania using anthracite coal for fuel could produce pig iron for far less than the charcoal-fired stacks in the Valley, and modern rolling mills springing up across the North, and Great Britain, were flooding southern markets with merchant bar that consistently undersold the iron drawn at facilities like Buffalo Forge. Even up-to-date southern rolling mills using more expen-sive charcoal pig iron were finding it hard to compete with northern and British manufacturers. The Tredegar Iron Works in Richmond, for exam-ple, priced its merchant bar iron at $85 per ton in the late 1850s; at the same time, top English refined bar could be purchased for $75 per ton in Rich-mond, and common English bar could be had for $65 a ton.[32] This was the iron market into which Weaver was preparing to plunge as he considered the acquisition of Etna Furnace.

On October 20, 1853, Weaver bought out the Cartmills' interest in the Etna property and began immediate preparations to put the furnace in blast.[33] He hired an experienced furnace manager, a local man named James K. Watkins who had served as the founder at Vesuvius Furnace under Matthew Bryan, had worked at Etna under the Sherrerd regime, and had managed Bath Forge for Weaver prior to its closing in 1852.[34] Weaver gave Watkins and another agent written authorization to hire slaves and sent them across the Blue Ridge to comb the hiring markets in central and Southside Virginia for the manpower needed to operate the furnace during the coming year. The books would open at Etna on January 1, 1854.[35]

Weaver felt some initial unease over their hiring prospects. Despite the decline in the iron trade in Virginia, other employers had entered the hiring market in substantial numbers in the 1850s. Railroads, canal companies, coal mines, and urban factories were all seeking hirelings and offered stiff competition for Weaver and other Valley ironmasters. Weaver became particularly anxious when late January came and he still had not heard from one of his hiring agents who was responsible for obtaining between ten and twenty hands. "He has either fallen in with a widow or become deranged," Weaver wrote Davidson on January 23, 1854.[36] His anxiety lifted, however, as slaves secured by this agent in Southside Virginia began arriving at Etna in late January and early February. Weaver obtained a force of over forty hirelings to work at the furnace in 1854, but the price his agents had been forced to pay was sobering. Hands Weaver could have hired for $65 to $70 in the mid-1830s were now going for $125 to $150.[37] Things would get no easier as the decade wore on.

Much work needed to be done before Etna Furnace could begin to make pig iron. The most important task was the construction of the railroad from the furnace to Retreat bank. Work on this project began in mid-February, and, although slowed by inclement weather, occupied a sizable force of slave hands for the balance of the year. Tunneling began at the bank—deep shafts would have to be sunk to reach the richest ore—new hearthstones were cut, dressed, and installed at the furnace, fields around Etna were planted and cultivated, and slave woodchoppers and colliers began the laborious task of preparing the fuel needed to put Etna back in blast.[38]

The amount of wood required to sustain production at a charcoal-fired furnace was staggering. In 1854, fifteen slave woodchoppers, a standard-sized gang for an antebellum Virginia blast furnace, worked in the mountain forests around Etna cutting and stacking thousands of cords of wood for conversion into charcoal.[39] Ironmasters counted on each hireling for approximately 400 cords of wood. Time was always lost in January as the slaves traveled on foot from their homes to the Valley furnaces; they would come from as far away as Orange and Spottsylvania counties in central

Virginia—a six-day walk to Etna—and owners would frequently delay their departure if there was snow on the ground or if the weather was intensely cold. Additional travel time would be needed in December to allow the slaves to return home by Christmas Day. Then there were always some days during the year when the weather was too bad to go into the woods, and sickness was also a possibility. Adding all of these things together, ironmasters figured hired woodchoppers would generally put in some 44 or 45 weeks a year; with their task set at 9 cords a week, this translated into 400 cords.[40] Fifteen choppers at Etna in 1854 meant that Weaver and his manager were looking for approximately 6,000 cords of wood from this gang. If that much wood were stacked end to end in the standard cord configuration—a pile eight feet long, four feet broad, and four feet high—it would stretch for over nine miles, half the distance from Etna to Buffalo Forge.

Weaver came down frequently during the year to check on the progress of the formidable project he had launched. He clearly found the entire experience exhilarating. "I feel about 5 years younger since I have been at Etna," he told James Davidson in May 1854.[41] Weaver did not seem to be unduly worried that his capital flow was all in one direction that year. The furnace could not begin making iron until the tramway to the ore bank was completed, and that job would not be finished until the spring of 1855. Perhaps the riskiness of the venture quickened his pulse and took him back to those days thirty years before when he had come to Virginia and reversed the decline of Buffalo Forge. "Etna will be a first rate establishment to judge from your outlay, & no doubt will pay you handsomely," Daniel C. E. Brady, Weaver's nephew-in-law, wrote from Philadelphia in August after Weaver had described the work under way at the furnace. "I hope your ore bank will turn out as wished for," Brady added.[42]

It was essential that Weaver's slave force work well in 1854 as construction of the railroad proceeded and the furnace was prepared for a blast. A great deal was riding on their performance. One incentive employed by Weaver was to allow some of his woodchoppers to take some time off in the spring. "Booker went to see his wife in Pittsylvania April 12*th*, 1854—and returned April 28, 1854," read an entry in the time book kept at Etna; "Byrd went to see his wife April 12, 1854, and returned Ap 20th." Both Booker and Byrd had been hired from a Bedford County slaveowner named James Callaway, and permission to leave the furnace was unquestionably granted because the two men had put in a good winter's work.[43]

Another technique Weaver used is indicated in a document titled "Memorandum of Cash Due Negroes" and dated December 1854. This two-page listing suggests very strongly that Weaver promised to reward those slaves who did their jobs well during the year with cash payments to be given out before the hirelings returned home for Christmas. The amount paid to each slave probably reflected the difficulty of the work that was done and the diligence with which it was performed. Any slave who attempted to run away during the year would certainly have lost whatever payment he might have had coming to him. According to the furnace time books, no runaways occurred at Etna that year. In all, forty-two hirelings were paid at the end of 1854, with some receiving as much as $10 and none receiving less than $1. The total amount distributed that December was $259.50, an average of over $6 per hand.[44] Once again, Weaver turned to the overwork system in an effort to motivate and discipline his slave work force.

He may have had another motive in mind as well. The fierce competition for hirelings in the 1850s meant that an employer's reputation became an extremely important element in his ability to secure hands from one year to the next. In November 1854 when Weaver wrote an agent in Orange County asking him to assist with the coming year's hiring, the man agreed to do so and added that he would also be seeking slaves for another ironworks in the Valley "but that will make no in[ter]ference as persons let their [hands] go pretty much where they please."[45]

A woman in Amherst County told Weaver much the same thing the following month. "I address you a few lines on the subject of hiring our negroes Joe Abner & Farley," Mary E. Gregory wrote Weaver on December 29. "We are willing you should have them, provided you will give what we have been getting for them. . . . I know we can get good prices for them on this side of the mountain," she went on. "But we have heard that you are anxious to hire them and they are willing to live with you again." She was "not willing that they should go on the rail road," she told Weaver, "and wee [*sic*] greatly prefer their living in the Country." One of her slaves who had been hired to another employer the past year might also be available: "Henry has not come home yet and wee do not know whether he is willing to leave his present home or not if he is you can have all of them that is if you are willing to give a fair price for them. . . ."[46]

Price and working in the country, as opposed to working on the railroad, were obviously important considerations for this woman, but the slaves' preference would also have a great deal to say about where they would live and work in the coming year.

Weaver was not the only ironmaster who was told that slaves would not return to employers who mistreated them. "I find it impossible to hire hands until they get home as the owners are antious [*sic*] to see them first," an agent informed Francis T. Anderson, the owner of Glenwood Furnace in Rockbridge County, in December 1855. "I saw Mr. Winn yesterday & he promised me not to hire his hands until he saw me or you; if his hands are pleased you will get them," he told Anderson.[47] This was the sort of pressure that made incidents like the one that occurred at Etna in the summer of 1854 so critical.

A fairly regular interchange of slave labor took place between Buffalo Forge and Etna Furnace during the year. Several of Weaver's men worked at the furnace in 1854 as blacksmiths, teamsters, woodchoppers, and farm hands, and two of Weaver's slave women, Rebecca and Sophia, served there as well, probably as cooks.[48] Occasionally some furnace hands would be sent up to Buffalo Forge. One such Etna worker was a woodcutter named Anthony. This man and another woodchopper named Frank were both hired from a Pittsylvania County slaveowner, Peter R. Griggs.[49] Weaver apparently needed some additional choppers for the forge, and Anthony was chosen, either by Weaver or by one of the furnace managers, to go to Buffalo Forge. At this point, serious trouble developed. The circumstances surrounding this incident were described by John K. Watkins, a clerk at Etna and a relative of furnace manager James Watkins. On Sunday, July 30, John Watkins relayed the following information to Weaver:

> Anthony was told Saterday evening to start to the forge this morning—I waited till about 10 oclock and finding that he had not started I asked him the reason he said it was Sunday and that he was not going till tomorrow—with some other impudence to me I collared him & he resisted & struck me—I struck him on the head with a rock. You please will see about the matter.

Watkins closed his letter with a revealing postscript: "He said that this was Sunday and his day and that he was not going to take it up in going to your place."[50]

James Watkins then penned his own comment to Weaver at the end of this letter:

> I have taken the libty to look at the letter John wrote to you I see he has had Impudence & abuse from the negro Anthoney I insist that you have him corrected as he deserves please let me know by the first opportunity if you have had him corrected.

Unfortunately, there is no information in the surviving records that reveals whether Weaver inflicted further punishment on this bondsman. All we know is that in November 1854, Weaver asked to rehire Anthony

and Frank for the coming year, and Griggs agreed and promised to assist
Weaver with his hiring in Southside Virginia.[51] Neither Anthony nor
Frank returned to Etna in 1855, however, and Griggs did not act as a hiring
agent for Weaver in the Pittsylvania County area.[52] In all probability,
Anthony and Frank told Griggs when they got home that they did not want
to go back to the furnace, and that ended the matter.

The fight that occurred between Anthony and John Watkins in July 1854
showed clearly the determination of one slave to preserve Sunday as his
day of rest and probably speaks for a view that was universally held by
southern slaves, industrial and otherwise. Weaver certainly would have
been alarmed by this potentially explosive altercation and its effect on slave
discipline at his ironworks. But he would have had to worry about the
impact of something like this on his hiring situation as well. Hirelings
would note Weaver's response, and their reaction could influence his ability to secure an adequate labor force for the coming year. As 1854 ended,
the railroad to Retreat bank was still under construction and Etna Furnace
was not yet in blast. Weaver stood to suffer sizable losses if he came up
short during the end-of-the-year hiring season.

He had to worry about price as well as supply. With hire rates climbing
and the iron market uncertain at best in Virginia, ironmasters looked for
ways to control their labor expense. "Sam Jordan told me that the iron men
here are trying to make an agreement not to give more than $100- for
hands: and that Crenshaw [a prominent Richmond commission merchant]
has written to him that with the prices of metal in prospect, iron men can't
afford to give more than $100-," James Davidson in Lexington wrote
Weaver on December 17.[53] In an effort to secure an adequate force at
reasonable cost, Weaver arranged for his nephew Constant Newkirk to
come down from Pennsylvania so that he could have a trusted agent on the
ground in eastern and central Virginia at the earliest possible moment.
Weaver dispatched a second hiring agent, Thomas Cartmill, formerly a
co-owner of the Etna property, to Southside Virginia.

The first reports that filtered back to Buffalo Forge were highly encouraging. "I understand Negroes are hired by C & N for me at 100 Ds.,"
Weaver informed James Davidson on January 10, 1855. "I shall leave to-
morrow for Furnace it is probable I shall get 90 or 100 Negroes." If that
turned out to be the case, "I shall be kept busy in having matters organized.
That," Weaver added, "is not much for a person of my *age*."[54]

As the first hirelings began arriving at the furnace, however, Weaver's
near euphoria gave way to a more cautious assessment of the year's prospects. He still had not heard directly from his nephew, although hands
secured by Newkirk reported upon reaching the furnace that he had gotten

"over his complement at low prices." Thomas Cartmill "did not do as well[—]the people in Pittsylvania adhered to the high prices," Weaver wrote Davidson from Etna on January 18. His tone was much more somber than it had been the week before. "I am not for a large number—times will not warrant it," he continued. He planned, nevertheless, to press on at the furnace. "I shall be enabled in all probability to make 1000 or 1200 Tons Metal—I shall however make all I can, and if it is low hold on [to it]." Once his tramway was finished and Etna was in blast, Weaver thought he could produce pig iron for $15 per ton, a very low figure for a charcoal-fired stack.

> I will run the Forge, and can probably sell some little, and with the aid of the Farm I shall be able I hope to get along—and let the metal remain on hand, or at least the greatest part. Hard times cannot last very long in this country—and when business revives metal will command a fair price. I must let my profits remain in metal—work the Farm and make supplies.[55]

Weaver, in short, would fall back on a strategy he had used successfully for years. He would simply refuse to sell his pig iron on a depressed market. He would hold on to most of his metal, sell such merchant bar from Buffalo Forge as he could, farm his land, "make supplies," and wait for prices to go up. Waiting out the market was a luxury few ironmasters in the Valley could afford; Weaver was one of those who could.

When Newkirk's letter, written from Philadelphia and dated January 4, 1855, finally reached Weaver, it did not bring good news. "I hired in all 24 Hands averaging $112 2/3." So much for the ironmasters' plan to pay no more than $100 per slave. "I left for this place on the night of the 1st heartily sick of Negro Hiring," Newkirk continued. "Hands did not want to come and Masters held the price from $125 to $150. I was fearful at one time that it would be slim chance for hands, as there were but few for hire." Three other Valley ironmasters had been in Louisa County at the same time looking for hirelings, and they "did not get half the quantity they wanted . . . , so we all left down in the mouth as to quantity & price." Newkirk's average price was as low as it was only because he had "hired a couple of boys able to do mens work but hired them as cart boys, one . . . named Billy for $80, and the other . . . named Tom for $60." He closed this discouraging report by noting that $5 of his expenses he had "paid out in change to the Hirelings."[56] Newkirk did not say whether this money was for travel or for bribery, but since most of the slaves walked to the mountains and carried their provisions with them, chances are it was offered as an inducement to enter Weaver's employ.

Weaver ended up with a hired slave force of just over fifty men at Etna in 1855.[57] This was hardly the ninety to one hundred hands he had predicted in early January, but it was a number sufficient to do the work that needed to be done and certainly a number sufficient for the times, as Weaver commented to Davidson back in January.

The completion of the railroad to Retreat bank in the spring meant that Etna Furnace would soon be in blast. The first mule-drawn cars, each of which carried two tons of ore, arrived at the furnace on April 24, 1855. Slaves began charging the furnace with ore, charcoal, and limestone at once, the furnace was fired on the evening of May 7, and ten days later the blast was put on. After almost a year and a half of hard work and heavy expense, Etna Furnace was making pig iron.[58]

As Etna began to achieve a steady and impressive rate of production, Weaver could hardly contain his enthusiasm. "Furnace is working quite well as I could wish," he wrote James Davidson in the summer of 1855. "She will make I have no doubt 50 tons this week." True to his word, he was in no hurry to sell pig metal. "I was offered 30 Ds pr ton for 150 Tons," he told Davidson; "I refused, asked 35 Ds."[59] If anyone could make money on a charcoal blast furnace in the Valley of Virginia in the decade prior to the Civil War, William Weaver was the man.

The work of his slave labor force was as important in 1855 as it had been the previous year. The construction phase at Etna largely ended with the completion of the tramway, but then the production of pig iron had begun in earnest, and Weaver intended to keep the furnace in blast right up to the last possible moment. Overwork was, once again, a key element in the labor system at Etna. Almost all the slaves hired to work at the furnace earned overwork income for themselves, and we can learn a good deal about these men by looking at their accounts in the Etna Furnace "Negro Books."

Among the slaves secured by Weaver's hiring agents in eastern Virginia were five men belonging to a Colonel Camack of Caroline County.[60] These slaves, whose names were Ben, Dick, Dudley, Reubin, and Tom, were all listed in the Etna "Negro Books" under the last name of their owner. Four of the five Camack slaves earned substantial amounts of overwork in 1855, generally by working on Sundays at the standard rate of 50 cents per day. They used some of the credit they accumulated during the year to buy various items, but they also were clearly anticipating their return home at Christmas. Dick Camack, for example, earned $20 by Sunday furnace labor and was paid $10 for hauling on Sundays. His purchases during the year included a coffee pot and relatively small amounts of coffee, sugar, and flour. In late November, however, he bought a shirt for $1.50, a yard of flax linen for 25 cents, a pair of boots for $4, and, most significantly, a silk dress for $10. He spent an additional 50 cents for three yards of cotton cloth on December 13, and then closed out his account by drawing $10 in cash.[61]

Three of the other Camack slaves did much the same thing. They bought coffee, sugar, flour, and sometimes tobacco throughout the year, and then made Christmas purchases and drew the balance of their credit in cash. Dudley Camack went home with seven yards of calico, two and a half yards of gingham, and $4.13; Reubin Camack with a comforter, four yards of cotton cloth, and $7.41; Tom with six yards of bleached cotton and $5.[62] It seems reasonable to surmise that in every case these men returned to Caroline County with presents for their wives and with cash to spend over the Christmas holidays and perhaps beyond.

Only four of the Camack slaves would be going home for Christmas, however. The fifth man, Ben, drew on the store at Etna for modest amounts of tobacco, coffee, and sugar during the year, but before he could work off his debt, he became seriously ill. His last purchase, a half pound of sugar, came on September 30.[63] On December 8, Ben died.[64] His owner apparently did not hold the managers at the furnace responsible for Ben's death. The Camack slaves returned to Etna later in the decade, and it seems unlikely they would have done so had their master believed that Ben had died because of the negligence of Weaver's white employees.

Mary's son John, purchased by Henry McCormick at Matthew Bryan's estate sale in December 1854, worked at Etna as a skilled furnace hand throughout 1855, and McCormick would hire him out to Weaver for the next six years as well. John's overwork earnings and expenditures were typical of dozens of such accounts in the Etna Furnace "Negro Books." He began buying tobacco, sugar, and coffee almost as soon as he arrived at the furnace, and he continued these purchases throughout his years there. He worked off most of his debt by Sunday labor and carried any amount he had not discharged over to the next year. His account suggests strongly that John, who was thirty-nine years old in 1855, was married. He regularly bought calico, cotton cloth, and tow linen during his first year's work, and in December 1856 he paid $2 for a shawl. John's duties at Etna appear to have centered initially around the casting operations at the furnace. He was given $2 in December 1857 for "fixing Foundry," and the chief molder at the furnace, a white artisan named Henry Rodenheizer, occasionally put sums of as much as 50 cents into John's account.[65] John Sims, as he was sometimes referred to in the records, would be a key worker at Etna throughout the seven years he lived there.

On December 14, 1855, Etna Furnace "blowed out, with a vengence," the clerk noted in the time book. The year's production of pig metal stood at 829½ tons, short of the 1,000 to 1,200 tons Weaver had predicted back in January, but a very respectable showing nonetheless. Weaver could draw

considerable satisfaction from the fact that he had finally solved his seem-
ingly endless search for a reliable source of high-quality pig iron for Buffalo
Forge. His slave teamsters had started hauling Etna metal as soon as the
first pigs cooled back in May, and they continued to freight iron to the
forge throughout the year.[66] For the first time since the early 1830s when
a friendly Jordan, Davis & Company had taken over Bath Furnace, Weaver
could feel completely confident about his pig iron supply.

True to his word, Weaver refused to sell his pig at a price he considered
inadequate. "Furnace continues to do well keeping the metal at Furnace
expect better prices next spring," Weaver wrote Daniel Brady, his nephew-
in-law in Philadelphia, in August 1855.[67] The Etna ledgers show almost no
deliveries of pig iron to any party other than Buffalo Forge during 1855.[68]
Weaver's slave forgemen—Sam Williams, Henry Towles, Tooler, and
Harry Hunt, Jr.—converted his metal into merchant bars, and Weaver sold
this iron to local customers in the Valley and made regular shipments to
Lynchburg, where his high-quality "mountain iron" continued to command a good price. Etna Furnace represented a heavy investment, but
Weaver was holding his own in the Virginia iron trade. "You can make Iron
for a less price than any other man," Weaver's Lynchburg commission
merchants told him in the late 1850s. "You have most of your labour and
raise almost every thing."[69]

It was true that Weaver owned almost all of his forge and farm labor, but
furnace hands were quite another matter. The hiring market was absolutely
critical to Etna operations, and the hiring market was turning into a mare's
nest. Weaver had three agents out in late 1855, one of whom was his friend
Henry McCormick. "They are asking $135 to $150 for good hands, no one
can tell what the price will be, until new years day," McCormick wrote
from Spottsylvania County at the end of December. "You have no idea of
the trouble there is in hiring hands here, at this day, there is all sorts of
trickery and management," McCormick went on. "I don't expect to be able
to hire more than thirty or forty hands, we may get fifty, but I can assure
you, the prospect is very gloomy."[70]

McCormick barely made the low end of his predicted range.[71] "Our
force will be small this year . . . which is a disadvantage, but must put up
with it—what cannot be cured must be indured," Weaver wrote Daniel
Brady in March 1856.[72] Just over thirty hirelings worked at Etna that year,
and, to make matters even more problematic, Weaver had installed a new
and largely untested manager at the furnace.

During the mid-1850s, Weaver brought a fresh wave of his younger
relatives down from Pennsylvania to work at Etna and at Buffalo Forge.
The first to arrive were two brothers, William Weaver Rex and John A.
Rex, who took over managerial positions at the forge in 1854. Will was

twenty that year, John was twenty-two; both were the sons of Weaver's niece Mary Ann Davis, who had married a man named Samuel V. Rex. Will Rex subsequently moved on to Etna, and John served as a clerk at Buffalo Forge. Once again, Weaver had decided to give some members of the Davis family a chance at the ironmaster's profession. Mary Ann Davis was the older sister of William W. and Abram Davis, the two young men who had been original members of the ill-fated firm of Jordan, Davis & Co.[73]

In 1856 Charles K. Gorgas, the son of Weaver's sister Lydia, would join the Rex brothers in the Valley of Virginia. Weaver wanted Charles to take over the management of Etna, but that was not his only motive for bringing him down. "I wrote to Charles to come on as soon as possible, and go direct to the Furnace. I want him to be there a short time before William [Rex] leaves," Weaver told Daniel Brady in Philadelphia on March 4, 1856. "I am pleased he is coming on another a/c it will relieve his father and mother, who would have more or less anxiety about him if he went to the West."[74] Later that month, Charles arrived at Etna. He had visited the furnace in the summer of 1854 in the company of his "Uncle William," but now, at the age of twenty-three, he would be taking charge of that complex enterprise.[75]

Under normal circumstances, Weaver probably would not have run the risk of placing an inexperienced man in charge of Etna Furnace, no matter what the family considerations might have been. But Weaver's age was advancing, his health was deteriorating, and he was concerned about both the ultimate disposition of his slaves and the fate of his ironworks. It was during this same time that he began urging Daniel and Emma Brady to move their family to Buffalo Forge.

"What think you of quitting House keeping this coming summer—rent your establishment and let Emma and the little one spend the Summer here," Weaver urged Brady on March 4, 1856. "Tell [Emma] she shall do just as she pleases at her end of the House, and she must let me do just as I please, and go and come when I please. Those are the Terms—all she has to do is to say *Yes*—and come on as soon as possible—you perceive I am turning Democratic," quipped Weaver, a thoroughly partisan Whig, "every one do as they please."[76] Several days later, Weaver, who earlier had admitted to Brady that he had come very close to a potentially fatal fall and had been forced to keep "close quarters" that winter, wrote that he had to get over to Etna soon. "There is something wrong [with me] either too old or too Lazy—either has a bad effect on business," Weaver observed. "I must however submit till such times as the young men can manage to get along."[77] Weaver clearly was worried about trusting so much responsibility for his affairs to his three young relatives.

Daniel Brady was the man he really wanted in Virginia. Brady turned thirty-five in March 1856, he and Emma had been married for ten years, and he was an experienced Philadelphia merchant and commercial banker.[78] Weaver considered himself an excellent judge of business capacity, and he was convinced that Daniel Brady had a good head for business. If the Bradys would move down, Weaver could rest easy, or as easy as it was possible for a man of his makeup to rest. Weaver knew time was not on his side. He celebrated his seventy-fifth birthday with a dinner at Buffalo Forge on March 8, 1856. Five days later, he urged Brady to sell—not rent—his house in Philadelphia. "Bring Emma and the small Fry this way, an[d] we will take care of them. Need not bring any servants with you," Weaver added, "we have plenty."[79]

Weaver's "servants"—his slaves—had been on his mind all along. He had made that point clear to the Bradys from the start. "The great object with me is, that my servants shall remain where they are, and have humane masters," Weaver had told Daniel Brady in August 1855. He had gone on to say that this was "the only difficulty on my mind in relation to my Estate," and that he was convinced that "giving them their freedom . . . would not benefit them as much as having good masters, and remain where they are."[80] The Bradys eventually did sell out and move to Buffalo Forge, but they did not reach that decision until 1857. Charley Gorgas would have to manage Etna Furnace in 1856 without the reassuring presence of Daniel Brady at Buffalo Forge.

Gorgas had his work cut out for him. An inadequate slave force, a slack market for pig iron, and a diminishing ore supply faced the twenty-three-year-old Philadelphian. The availability of good iron ore was vital to the success of the furnace operation, but the situation at Retreat bank was deteriorating rapidly by the spring of 1856. In May, Weaver sent Will Rex to Pennsylvania with instructions to hire a German miner who had experience working underground. Rex could "find but two Germans," he wrote Weaver, and only one of the men was willing to come south and then only if Weaver would pay him $1.50 per day, a figure well above the dollar a day Weaver was offering.[81] Weaver would have been well advised to pay the man's price.

Three entries in a time book kept at Etna described what happened at Retreat bank in the summer of 1856:

July 3   Commenced working tunnel night & day

July 22   Within 10 ft of ore in old tunnel sand fell in and oblige to give up but will try to go through by striking to the left & going over.

July 26   All wrong oblidge to give up working Tunnel on a/c of caving in sides.[82]

Gorgas was forced to strip the face of the bank and rely on the extensive use of blasting powder to loosen the ore. Masters were understandably wary of hiring out their valuable slave property to work around blasting powder, and the situation at Retreat bank eventually created a potentially serious labor problem for Weaver.

Gorgas made only a short blast at Etna in 1856. The furnace did not begin making metal until July, and total production amounted to only 430 tons, almost exactly 400 tons less than the previous year's blast. But fate smiled on Charley Gorgas in one all-important regard. The pig iron market moved upward during the year just as Weaver had predicted that it would. Gorgas kept Buffalo Forge well supplied with pigs, but he also sent substantial tonnages of Etna metal to Shields & Sommerville, Weaver's commission merchants in Richmond. Sales of this iron brought in over $9,000 in much-needed cash by the end of 1856.[83] If this market continued, if the hiring went well, if the ore held up, and if Gorgas could make a longer blast at the furnace, the Etna operation stood a good chance of making some money again in 1857.

The hiring did go well—over fifty hands—a more experienced Charley Gorgas got the furnace into blast in March, and Etna pig sold well again on the Richmond market.[84] Only the ore bank situation threatened the new-found prosperity of Etna Furnace.

Among the slaves hired to work at Etna in 1857 were three men from Orange County, Robert, Prince, and William, belonging to a woman named Mary C. Towles. Thomas R. Towles, the family member who had arranged the hire, wrote Weaver on November 11, 1857, that some very disturbing intelligence had reached him about one of these slaves:

> I received a letter from some one with no name to it saying that Robert had left you and the reason assigned was that your [furnace] manager wished him to work in the Ore Bank and it was so dangerous that all your white hands had quit on that account, if so I am surprised for I had always thought you a different man and had always represented you as being one of the safest men to hire to as regards the treatment in the Vallie and besides I have always hired Robt William & Prince as wood choppers and I have no doubt it was done without your knowledge. If Robt has left please let me hear from you immediately as I dont want the Boy to give either of us any trouble.[85]

Weaver's long-standing reputation, in Towles's words, as "one of the safest men to hire to as regards the treatment in the Vallie" was clearly on the line. Weaver immediately asked Gorgas for a detailed explanation and received a full account of the difficulty concerning Robert:

> On inquiry I find there is something in relation to Bob from which a tale could be manufactured, to wit. On Tuesday a week William [W. Rex] requested Bob to go to the Bank (he picking him out on a/c of being near his wife's) William thinking all [was] right left, but afterwards finding that he did not go up, saw him again on Tuesday last at which time Bob said very imputantly that you had a letter at the forge to the effect that a particular understanding was made that he (Bob) was not to work in the Bank. If that is the case (says William) I dont expect you to work there. He William at the same time requesting him (Bob) to come [to the] Furnace stating to Bob that he would write to you & if it was not in your hands he bob might expect a punishment. That was all that was said & the last & Bob is now away. Of course there is not one word of truth in regard to white hands in [the] bank & *no danger there either.*[86]

Several days later, Gorgas reported that he had removed all but three slaves from Retreat bank and asked Weaver if it would be all right for him to arrange with a white contractor to raise ore there. "Did you get a suitable answer from Towles?" Gorgas inquired.[87]

Weaver seems to have gotten a partially satisfactory answer. Prince was rehired to Weaver for 1858, but Robert and William, who were brothers, were not. In all probability, Prince was willing to go back to the Valley, Robert and William expressed a reluctance to return to Etna, and the Towles family honored all of their wishes. And Prince worked at Buffalo Forge, not Etna Furnace, in 1858. Most important of all from Weaver's point of view, Robert's running away late in 1857 did not have an adverse effect on the hiring for 1858. Weaver's agents obtained almost sixty slaves to work at the furnace during that year.[88]

The tight hiring market and the all-important role played by slave labor at Etna probably lay behind some significant changes in the overwork system at the furnace in the middle and late 1850s. Weaver had to be able to secure hands each year, and the slaves had to work well when hired. Harsh treatment and unsafe working conditions would create very difficult problems for him; he needed, in fact, to try to inculcate a certain amount of goodwill among his hirelings in order to sustain his reputation as a decent employer and produce satisfactory levels of work. In an effort to accomplish both these ends, Weaver in 1856 expanded his practice of paying slave workers at Etna a regular "allowance" if they performed their assigned duties well during the year. Ore bank hands, furnace workers, colliers, teamsters, woodchoppers, and the slaves who drove the ore carts received $1 a month, and they could also earn additional sums by cutting extra wood, weaving charcoal baskets, raising chickens and hogs, working nights, Sundays, and holidays—all the activities that over the years had earned slaves overwork compensation. One hired slave, a keeper named Joshua Crews, was paid $5 a month for his supervisory work at the furnace; his "allowance" for 1857 was $60. Over fifty slaves received cash payments in December 1857, and Joshua Crews closed out his lengthy account by buying an overcoat for $10 and drawing $20 in cash.[89]

Weaver also allowed hirelings to buy time off, if they wished to use their overwork credit in this way. In May 1858 three slaves, Dabney, Jack, and Jim Willoughby, returned to their home in Spottsylvania County for short visits. All were debited 50 cents a day, the standard rate for working nights or Sundays, for each day they were away from the furnace. Dabney and Jack were gone for ten days, Jim for two weeks. These visits by no means exhausted their overwork credit, however. All received cash at the end of the year—Dabney $2.25, Jack $7.25, and Jim the extraordinary sum of $25. A fourth Willoughby slave, Bill, who chose not to go home during the year, received $10 in cash. In subsequent years, all four of these men returned to work for Weaver at either Etna Furnace or Buffalo Forge, and when they came back to the Valley, three additional Willoughby slaves came with them.[90]

Etna Furnace was by no means immune from runaways and serious disciplinary problems. Two hirelings fled from the furnace in the summer of 1855, and one of these men got over the mountains into Campbell County before he was captured.[91] And the Etna Time Book recorded an infraction in 1856 that threatened a slave with serious punishment:

June 20   Moses stole Obenchain [an Etna clerk] corn

June 25   [Moses] To be whipped this day—if we catch him[92]

But events such as these seem to have been rare, or at least they were infrequently noted in the extensive records kept at the furnace.

One might be tempted to argue that the relative absence of this sort of activity indicates that slaves were "bought off," as it were, by the opportunity to acquire items like coffee, sugar, and tobacco during the year and to return home with money in their pockets at Christmas. There may be an element of truth in this interpretation. It would not be surprising for men who were systematically deprived of small "luxuries" of this sort to use the chance provided by the overwork system to enjoy the pleasure of a cup of coffee or a chew of tobacco. But an interpretation of the slaves' response to the overwork system that stops here would be woefully deficient. At the very least, such a reading would ignore the importance to a slave of being able to arrive back home in December with presents for his loved ones and cash to spend as his family celebrated the holidays. As these men departed from the furnace, they could anticipate the pleasure their gifts would give their wives and children. If they were able to bring some joy to their families, they had every reason to take pride in their achievement.

An interpretation that sees mainly evidence of slave accommodation in the Etna records is shortsighted in other ways as well. The few references to overt acts of resistance like running away and stealing are testimony only to the grave risks attendant to such activity. More subtle forms of resistance were available, the kinds of things that would not normally warrant an entry in the furnace time books. Slaves could feign illness, for example, or could do the absolute minimum amount of work necessary to avoid punishment. Will Rex wrote a revealing letter in 1862 describing two Etna slaves who were engaged in actions of this sort:

> You ask about Griffen. I consider him a triffling hand.—He laid up here very often & for long periods—but it was only when we worked him about the Furnace[;] he laid up so often that we had finally to take him away. Par objected to changing so often. tell him that you will put him in the wood chopping when he gets well, & I will guarantee he will soon be out—that is his object now is laying up. I found that he laid up very seldom when he could get a chance to run to his wife.[93]

There were doubtless many more instances of this type of resistance at the furnace; there certainly were at Buffalo Forge, as Daniel Brady would note with great frequency in the journal he began keeping at the forge in March 1858.

When Etna blew out in December 1857, Weaver could look back on the year with considerable satisfaction. Charley Gorgas had proven himself to be a more than capable ironmaster. The furnace had produced 734 tons of metal in the blast that began back in March, over 300 tons more than Etna had made in 1856. Weaver could anticipate ample supplies of pig iron for Buffalo Forge in the years ahead, particularly since the use of blasting powder and open pit mining had straightened out Etna's ore problems, at least for the time being. He had weathered the difficulty over Robert, the

runaway slave, and the anonymous letter charging Weaver with irresponsi-
ble exposure of hirelings to dangerous working conditions at Retreat bank.
The market for Etna metal had continued strong in 1857. Sales in Richmond during the spring and summer had brought in almost $8,000, and
although Weaver was not getting the $35 per ton he wanted, his metal was
selling at a price—$29 and $30 per ton—that was well above his cost of
production.[94] Perhaps the most satisfying thing that had happened during
the year, however, was the achievement of a goal Weaver had been seeking
for a very long time. Late in 1857, the Bradys decided to accept Weaver's
long-standing invitation to move to Buffalo Forge.

The decision was a difficult one for Daniel and Emma Brady. Both were
native Philadelphians. Daniel had been born there in 1821; his father, an
Irish immigrant, had settled in Philadelphia in 1801 and had married Daniel's mother, Leah Cecilia Elliott, in 1811. Emma was the daughter of
Weaver's favorite sister, Lydia, and her husband, Peter K. Gorgas. Emma
was born in 1826 and had married Daniel Brady twenty years later. All of
these family connections bound them to the Philadelphia area, and they
had purchased a house there in 1854 and had begun raising a family.[95] If
Daniel's business partnership with an uncle had not gone sour in 1856, they
might have remained in Pennsylvania.

Daniel went to work in his Uncle Patrick Brady's mercantile firm as a
clerk in 1843. He eventually became a partner in this concern and continued his association with his uncle when they converted their partnership
into a banking business in 1855. After six months of profitable operations,
things began to go wrong. First, a clerk Patrick had insisted on hiring
defrauded the firm of a sizable sum of money through unauthorized stock
speculations. Then in 1856 Patrick married, withdrew some $25,000 in
capital from the partnership, and, in Daniel's opinion, began neglecting the
business.[96] While all this was going on, Weaver was pressing the Bradys to
come to Virginia and was promising to place his considerable estate in their
hands should they do so. Charley Gorgas, Emma's younger brother, had
already moved down and was running Etna Furnace. Relocating in the
Valley, a place Daniel and Emma had visited on several occasions, looked
increasingly attractive to them.

Deaths that touched the Bradys deeply surely influenced their decision
to leave Philadelphia as well. Daniel's mother died in 1854, and Emma's
father, Peter Gorgas, died two years later following a long illness. These
losses were only two of the many Daniel and Emma Brady suffered during
these years. Death also struck down four of their own children. Among
these were the first baby named for Emma's Uncle William, in May 1856 at
age two and a half, and the second namesake, who died on the day of his

birth, August 30, 1857.[97] During the fall, the Bradys decided to come to Virginia.

Daniel and Emma and their two remaining children arrived at Buffalo Forge in early November.[98] Their daughter, Anne Gertrude Brady, was nine, and their son, Charles Patrick Augustus Brady (called "Pat"), was seven.

In January 1858, Daniel Brady took up his new duties. Weaver's word was doubtless still law, but Brady was responsible for the day-to-day management of the forge and the agricultural side of things, and he started posting the books at Buffalo Forge as the new year began. In early February, he and his daughter, Anne, returned to Philadelphia for a short stay; Brady probably had some final business affairs to settle and Anne may have wanted to visit friends and relatives. It took Brady about three weeks to do what needed to be done there. On March 4, 1858, he and Anne departed from Philadelphia.[99]

They would miss Emma's birthday. She turned thirty-two on March 5, but they arrived at Buffalo Forge in time to help Weaver celebrate his seventy-seventh birthday three days later. The next day, March 9, Daniel Brady turned thirty-seven.[100] It was quite a confluence of birthdays, and it was surely one of the happiest such events Weaver had experienced in some time.

Weaver's long quest for capable family members to help him manage his iron business had finally reached a successful conclusion. He now could view the future with considerable pleasure and equanimity. The fall of 1857 had been marked by a commercial and financial panic that continued into 1858, but Weaver was not overextended even with his sizable investment in Etna Furnace. He had survived economic storms of this sort before, and he would ride this one out as well. The important things for him were that Brady would be looking after Buffalo Forge, that Charley Gorgas would be managing Etna Furnace, and that his home, or at least the Brady's end of it, would constantly be filled with new life and people he loved. There was, of course, one other consideration: Weaver's desire for his slaves to "remain where they are, and have humane masters." He was counting on Daniel and Emma Brady to fill that role as well.

There was a cloud on the horizon in March 1858, but Weaver seems to have paid it little attention. The Lexington papers that month carried lengthy excerpts of the acrimonious debate in the United States Senate over the admission of Kansas as a slave state.[101] Sectional tension over the subject of slavery in the territories had been mounting ever since the Mexican War and the 1846 debate over Pennsylvania congressman David Wilmot's soon-to-be-famous Proviso that "neither slavery nor involuntary servitude shall ever exist" in any territory that might be obtained from Mexico. The Compromise of 1850 had edged the country back from the brink of sectional division over the slavery issue, but that calm, such as it was, had been shattered four years later when Senator Stephen A. Douglas introduced the Kansas–Nebraska Act in Congress. Douglas's legislation called for the settlers themselves to decide the fate of slavery in these two territories, and his initiative had immediate and far-reaching consequences for American politics. The Republican party was born later in 1854, the Whig party was effectively destroyed as a national political institution, and guerrilla warfare broke out in Kansas.

The status of slavery in Kansas was still before the Senate when Daniel and Anne Brady arrived at Buffalo Forge in March 1858. Later that same year, Abraham Lincoln would give his "House Divided" speech in which he would state his belief that "this government cannot endure permanently half slave and half free." In the fall, Senator William Henry Seward of New York would refer to "an irrepressible conflict" between the forces of slavery and freedom that would result in the United States becoming "either entirely a slaveholding nation or entirely a free-labor nation."

These events seemed very far removed from the lives of William Weaver, the Bradys, and the slaves of Buffalo Forge, however. It was easy enough to imagine that the outside world would never be able to intrude on the pace of life and labor in the Valley, that forces demanding change were no more tangible than the mists that perpetually hung over the peaks of the Blue Ridge. The daily work routine went on at Buffalo Forge as it had for years, Sam Williams and Henry Towles pounding out anchonies at their refinery forge, Tooler and Harry Hunt, Jr., drawing bars under their chaffery hammer, Henry Matthews making needed repairs about the forge, Garland Thompson bringing his daily wagonload of charcoal from the coaling grounds, and the agricultural hands planting, cultivating, and harvesting rich crops from Weaver's carefully tended fields.

The only difference in 1858 was that Daniel Brady was on hand to record these daily events. In mid-March, he began writing down a day-by-day summary of work, weather, and anything unusual that happened at Buffalo Forge. These entries were relatively brief, straightforward summaries. Brady did not normally embellish his text with his own thoughts or reactions to what was going on around him, but his "Home Journal," running from March 15, 1858, to June 30, 1865, is nevertheless an exceedingly valuable document.[102]

Brady's "Home Journal" embraces a period of extraordinary significance in the history of the South and of southern slavery. And, perhaps most important of all, it affords a rare glimpse of individual slaves as they went about their daily tasks. We can follow them during the late antebellum years when the slave system reached its zenith. We can trace their activities as war engulfed the region and the sound of Union cavalry shattered the tranquility of the Valley. And finally we can see them as peace returned to Buffalo Forge and changed their lives forever.

PART II

THE SLAVES

1

———◆———

Sam Williams

$\mathbf{E}$arly in 1855, Weaver's nephew John Rex, the twenty-two-year-old clerk at Buffalo Forge, had a minor problem on his hands. Sam Williams, the master refiner at the forge, and Henry Nash, a free Negro cooper who lived nearby and produced barrels for Weaver's flour, had made a wager and had asked Rex for assistance in settling the question under dispute. Rex, it turned out, needed some information before he could deal with the issue at hand, so on February 25 he proceeded to write James D. Davidson in Lexington. "I wish to ask you one question whether Sam Williams can draw his money from the Savings Bank or if he cannot," Rex inquired of Weaver's lawyer. "As Sam and Henry Nash has got a bet for his watch against the said Nash['s] watch. It is my opinion that he can draw his money if he gives the Directors of the Bank 10 days notice," Rex continued. "After he receives the money he wishes to show it to Henry Nash, and then he will return the said money back to the Bank again." The young forge clerk closed by noting that he "was witness to the said bargain."[1]

Obviously Sam Williams had said something about owning a savings account, Henry Nash had questioned the existence of the account, and the wager had followed. Sam Williams, a slave, bet his watch against the watch of Henry Nash, a free Negro, and John Rex, the white forge clerk, was, in effect, holding the bet. His letter to Davidson followed.

James Davidson was an experienced attorney, but it is unlikely that he had ever confronted the issue of how a slave should handle his savings account. The same day he received Rex's letter, he wrote a short reply instructing the clerk "to confer with Wm. Weaver" about the matter.[2] Perhaps the master could decide how a man who was himself legally property should deal with his own property, in this case an account in a major Lexington financial institution.

What action Weaver took is unknown. Nor do we know if Sam Williams ended up with Henry Nash's watch. But if Weaver allowed the bet to go forward and assisted Sam in proving his claim, then Williams would have become the owner of two watches. He did indeed have a savings account in 1855, and a sizable one at that. The story of how Sam Williams managed to acquire such an asset tells us a good deal about him and about the way slavery functioned at Buffalo Forge in the decades leading up to the Civil War.

Sam Williams was born at Etna Furnace in 1820. His mother, Sally, was one of the original "Wilson negroes" purchased by Weaver five years earlier. Sally was thirteen years old at the time of the sale, and she had come to Weaver with her mother, Mary, and her three sisters, Amy, Louisa, and Georgianna. Around 1817, Sally had married a man named Sam Williams, who was one of the skilled ironworkers Weaver and Mayburry were constantly seeking to add to their labor force. Sam and Sally Williams had their first child, a girl, in 1817, and they named her Mary, undoubtedly for her grandmother. Three years later, Sally gave birth to another child, a boy this time, and the new baby was named Sam after his father. Other children followed during the 1820s: Elizabeth, born in 1825, Washington, born two years later, and Charles, born sometime after 1828.[3]

Very little is known about Sam Williams, Sr., because most of the records dealing with Mayburry & Weaver's early ironmaking activities in Virginia have not survived. According to a slave register compiled by Daniel Brady during the Civil War, Sally's husband was born in 1795, but that date was probably a rough approximation.[4] An evaluation of the Buffalo Forge slaves made in 1863 listed Sam Williams, Sr., with a string of zeros following his name—he had no dollar value—which suggests that he was physically or mentally incapacitated and unable to perform useful work at age sixty-eight or so. The probability that he was disabled is reinforced by the fact that other slave men of similar age had values of $200 to $300 beside their names on this document, and Sally, Sam's wife, who was sixty-one in 1863, was valued at $500.[5]

Other fragmentary evidence suggests the cause of his disability. In 1832 when Jordan, Davis & Company were in desperate need of a master refiner at Bath Iron Works, William W. Davis spoke to Sam about taking a turn at the forge. Sam refused; "he objects [because of] his eyes (which is in fact a very great objection might in all probabality [*sic*] loose [*sic*] them if continued in the forge)," Davis told Weaver.[6] Forgemen were in constant danger of eye injuries from sparks and flying bits of red-hot metal, and Sam Williams, Sr., seems to have suffered such an injury, or perhaps a series of them. Clearly his eyes were badly damaged while he was still a relatively young man; he would have been in his middle or late thirties in 1832 and, if sound, still in his most productive years as a slave—a "prime hand," in the language of the trade. He may well have been blind by 1863 when the entry "Sam Williams Senior 0000.00" was made on the list evaluating William Weaver's slaves.

Sam Williams, Jr., spent the first eight years of his life at Etna Furnace. He went with his mother to northern Rockbridge County in 1828 when Thomas Mayburry moved his portion of the "Wilson negroes" first to Vesuvius Furnace and then, in 1833, to Gibraltar Forge.[7] If his youth was spent like most slave boys who grew up around ironmaking facilities in the South, he probably had no regular duties until he reached age eight or so, when he would have been expected to assume some light chores such as helping to look after the younger slave children during the day. By age twelve or fourteen, he would have entered the regular labor force, perhaps doing odd jobs around the furnace or forge, working as a field hand, tending livestock, raking leaves at the charcoal pits, or acting as a cart boy. He does not seem to have had any training as a forgeman, however, prior to his arrival at Buffalo Forge on January 1, 1837.

Sam was sixteen when the division of the "Wilson negroes" took place that New Year's Day. Sam's mother and his brothers and sisters also came to Weaver as part of the deal Weaver and Mayburry struck to settle their differences. The ironmasters' out-of-court settlement saw Sam's grandmother, Mary, and John, Hamilton, and Ellen go to Mayburry, but the division reunited the Williams family.[8] Sam Williams, Sr., was already in Weaver's possession, as the 1832 letter about Sam's failing eyesight shows, so the arrival of Sally and her children at Buffalo Forge had at least one happy consequence.

The exact size of Sally's family at the time of the division is unclear. The records show only that Sally, her sister Louisa, and thirteen of their children were turned over to Weaver under the terms of the settlement.⁹ We know Sam's younger brothers Washington and Charles went to Weaver because their names subsequently appear in ledgers kept at Buffalo Forge. Sam and his brothers did not at first carry their father's last name; they were entered on Weaver's books as "Sam Etna," "Washington Etna," and "Charles Etna."¹⁰ The reason seems clear. The "Etna" designation clearly identified the boys as coming from that portion of the "Wilson negroes" born at Etna Furnace and previously held by Thomas Mayburry. It was easier for the clerks to write "Sam Etna" than "Sam Williams, Jr.," and if you identified the oldest brother in this way, why not do it for the younger ones as well? Washington was nine years old at the time of the division, Charles seven or eight. Like Sam, both of these boys would later take their place as ironworkers in Weaver's forge. And Sam would eventually reclaim his father's name, although it took a long time—sixteen years—before "Sam Etna" became "Sam Williams" on the pages of the time books and ledgers kept at Buffalo Forge.

Sally's daughters Mary and Elizabeth and perhaps additional children of hers went to Weaver as part of the 1837 division of the "Wilson negroes," but we cannot be sure. Weaver's "House Book" in which the work and the overwork of the slave women were recorded has not survived; the loss of this source makes it extremely difficult to trace the lives of most of the female slaves at Buffalo Forge throughout much of the antebellum era.

Young Sam Williams's first duties for Weaver were primarily agricultural. He was paid $1 in "harvest money" on December 18, 1837, and received an additional $2 on Christmas Eve that year, his first at Buffalo Forge.¹¹ There is no indication that he did any ironworking during his initial twelve months with Weaver. But Sam came from "a family that produces good mechanics," as Weaver liked to say, and Weaver was probably waiting for Sam to reach his full growth. In 1838, when Sam was eighteen, he began his training as a forgeman.

In addition to his family background, Sam had two other qualities that made him a likely recruit for Weaver's forge gang. First, he had the necessary size and strength to handle the demanding physical labor required of a refiner. When he achieved his full stature, he stood five feet ten inches tall, which made him one of the tallest slave hands at Buffalo Forge. Second, his color suggested to white southerners of that time and place that he was likely to possess intelligence and good judgment as well. A physical description of Sam and the other forge workers drawn up during the Civil War listed his color as "Yellow."¹² Sam had, at some point in his ancestry, a strong component of white genes.

Where this miscegenation occurred in the Williams family remains a mystery. Since he took the elder Sam Williams's name as his own, one assumes that both his mother and father were slaves, and his grandmother, Mary, was certainly enslaved. It could be that his maternal or paternal grandfather was white; perhaps there was white ancestry on either or both sides of his family going back several generations. The records are silent on these points. Whatever the case, William Weaver obviously knew he had a likely candidate for his ironmaking crew when Sam "Etna" grew into his full manhood at Buffalo Forge.

Weaver undoubtedly had Sam go down to the forge and watch the black refiners and hammermen at their jobs before deciding whether he wanted to apprentice to one of the master workmen. This was Weaver's usual practice, and there is no reason to suspect that he did things differently this time. Sam's father had suffered eye injuries in the forge, and that might have given young Sam pause, but he also would have been well aware of the advantages forge work would bring him. In making himself indispensable to Weaver's ironmaking operations, he would be gaining a significant amount of influence over his own fate. There was no sure guarantee against punishment or sale; like all southern masters, Weaver could do pretty much what he wished in the way of punishment, and if he should fall deeply into debt or die suddenly, his slave force could be dispersed by either sale or the division of his estate. Barring that sort of catastrophe, however, Sam would be in a much stronger bargaining position as a skilled ironworker than in any other occupation at Buffalo Forge. If he trained as a refiner and showed an aptitude for the work, he would have talents Weaver would need for many years into the future. There was, of course, another advantage as well. Of all the slaves used by Weaver in various agricultural and industrial pursuits, the forgemen were in the best position to earn substantial sums for themselves through their overwork. Sam could materially improve his standard of living if he could master the ironmaker's art.

Sam's first year in the forge, 1838, was a period of apprenticeship. He served as an assistant to John Baxter, one of Weaver's slave refiners at Buffalo Forge, and under Baxter's guidance, Sam learned to put up and maintain the special refinery fire, to heat the pig iron and bring it "to nature," and to pound the red-hot metal under the huge, water-powered hammer into those oddly shaped anchonies. Sam undoubtedly cost Weaver some money that year in wasted pig iron and excessive use of expensive charcoal, but the only way to learn was by doing. Like most of the slaves at Buffalo Forge, he shifted to agricultural work at harvest time, but on December 24, 1838, Sam was credited with his first earnings as an ironworker, $2 for "1/2 Ton over Iron with J. Baxter." That plus his $1 in harvest money put his total for the year at $3, the same amount he had received in

1837, but there was a major difference this time.[13] He had begun his forge apprenticeship and had taken the first steps toward gaining those skills which he could use to make his life a little more comfortable and perhaps a bit more predictable and secure.

In 1839, Weaver sent Sam up to Bath Iron Works. Weaver had reclaimed the property from Sam Jordan and William Davis the previous spring and had resumed operations at Bath Forge. Sam served there as an apprentice to Harry Hunt, one of Weaver's most skilled slave ironworkers, before returning to Buffalo Forge and John Baxter's refinery hammer in the summer. He was paid small sums for overwork with both Hunt and Baxter and received additional money for weaving eight charcoal baskets for Weaver. His total earnings for 1839 were just over $3.50, very much in line with what he had made the previous two years.[14] He would not be content with earnings of this sort the following year, however.

Sometime in 1840, at age twenty, Sam Williams married a slave named Nancy Jefferson, twenty-three, who was also owned by Weaver.[15] The wedding may have occurred in the fall. In September, Sam bought two dress handkerchiefs for $1 and spent $10.50 on a store order that was not spelled out in detail; this store purchase was by far the largest single expenditure he had ever made. On October 10, he used his overwork credit to buy five yards of calico and three and a half yards of bleached muslin.[16] These acquisitions suggest that Sam and Nancy were married in September 1840, and that Sam bought the calico and muslin the next month as a present for his new wife, probably for her to sew into a dress and petticoat.

Sam and Nancy's marriage was not a legal one, of course. Slave unions had no standing in Virginia law, or that of any other state. But time would clearly show that Sam Williams and Nancy Jefferson viewed themselves as man and wife. The date of their marriage was not recorded in the journals and papers kept at Buffalo Forge, but they knew the year was 1840 and they never forgot it.

The birth of their first child did appear in the Buffalo Forge records, however, and for good reason. The birth of a new baby in the slave quarters meant an addition to the master's wealth and potential work force. So, when Elizabeth Williams came into the world late that year, note was taken of the event. Elizabeth, or Betty as she was more frequently called, was undoubtedly named after Sam's younger sister, Elizabeth, who would have been fifteen years old in 1840.[17]

Sam Williams's marriage and the birth of his daughter gave him added incentive to exploit the possibilities opened up by the overwork system. Early in 1840, he began devoting much of his spare time to "tar burning." He would begin by collecting the heart of fallen pine trees in the woods around Bath Iron Works, where he worked during most of 1840. After stacking the wood on a low, hard-packed mound of earth with gutters running out from the center, he would cover the resinous pine with dirt and light it. As the wood smoldered, the gum would flow out as tar through the trenches cut in the earth. Sam would collect and sell this "tair," as it was spelled in the Bath Forge books. The managers at Bath were willing to pay 25 cents a gallon for it—pitch and tar were always needed around installations dependent on waterpower—and Sam's long hours in the woods produced fifty-nine gallons of tar before the year was out.[18]

He also did something else in the year he was married that he had not done during the three previous years—he worked through the Christmas holidays. Forges almost always closed down for the holidays, but there were plenty of other things to do—stock to be fed and watered, firewood to be cut, roads and walks to be cleared if it snowed. Sam worked five days out of the seven-day Christmas break in 1840 and earned $2.50 for his labor. The rate at which he was paid for his forge overwork—$2.50 per ton—indicates that Sam was still serving as an underhand that year; he received a total of $7.30 for his extra production of iron. His tar burning brought him $14.75, and he earned $2.18 for three and a half days of "Sunday work" at Bath Furnace and for "attending to team" during his off-hours while he was there. His total overwork earnings for 1840 came to $26.73, well over seven times what he had made for himself in any previous year at Buffalo Forge or Bath Iron Works.[19]

There is no way to be certain why Sam worked so hard in 1840, but it seems safe to assume that his efforts were spurred by a desire to be able to do more for his wife and his baby daughter. During the summer, he bought a set of crocks, for household storage, and his other purchases during the year included molasses, sugar, and coffee, as well as the large store order and the cloth he obtained for Nancy in the fall. On January 15, 1841, he spent 40 cents for two yards of calico. Perhaps Nancy used this cloth to make a garment for herself or for their little girl.[20]

Sam completed his apprenticeship and entered the ranks of Weaver's master refiners during 1841. He continued to work at Bath during most of 1841 and part of 1842, and his ironworking now brought him $4.50 per ton for any anchonies he produced above his weekly task of one and a half tons. He continued his tar burning in 1841, but on a reduced scale. Given the rate at which he was now being paid, it made more sense for him to spend his extra time in the forge rather than in the forests which surrounded Bath Iron Works. His purchases during the year again suggest that he was buying things his wife and daughter could use—sugar, bed ticking, striped drill, and calico cloth—and on December 17, 1841, he paid $1.25 for a silk handkerchief.[21] Almost certainly this was a Christmas present for Nancy.

Their family grew steadily over the next several years. In 1842, a second daughter, Caroline, was born, and she was followed by two more girls, Ann, born in 1843, and Lydia, born the next year.[22] Thus in the first four years of their marriage, Sam and Nancy Williams had four daughters. The births of these four girls would complete their family. Their marriage lasted a great many years, but no children were born to them after Lydia came into the world in 1844.

Sam's growing prowess as a refiner and his continued support of his loved ones are apparent in his overwork accounts during the next few years. He and his family moved back to Buffalo Forge in the spring of 1842, but slave overwork records are missing for that year and for 1843. In 1844 he earned $31, most of which he made at his forge. Sam's five tons of extra anchonies translated into a credit of $24 when Weaver totaled up his overwork compensation in December. The debit side of the ledger is incomplete for 1844, but some of his purchases were listed, particularly his holiday buying at the end of the year. On December 21, he bought four pounds of sugar for his mother, Sally, undoubtedly as a Christmas present (the cost was 77 cents). Three days later, on Christmas Eve, he took $1 in cash from his account, spent $2 for eight yards of calico, and drew against his overwork credit for $20 for a "Blue Coat Fine."[23] Sam could have used the dollar in cash to buy treats for the girls; he almost certainly gave the calico to Nancy; but the "Blue Coat Fine" was his, and it was purchased for a very special reason.

Earlier that December, Sam Williams had stood before the members of the Lexington Baptist Church. This church had been founded in 1841 by sixteen white residents of Rockbridge County, including William W. Davis and his wife, Ann, and Samuel F. Jordan and his wife, Hannah. As was the case in Baptist churches throughout the South, slaves were eligible for full membership. If they submitted a letter of transfer from another Baptist church or if they claimed that they had received the Holy Spirit through a conversion experience, they could appear before the congregation and seek admission. "At a church meeting held on the 1st Lords Day in Dec 1844, Samuel, a colored man of Mr. Wm Weaver presented himself and after examination by the church was received and will be considered as a member of this church when baptized," noted Sam Jordan, the church clerk, in recording the minutes of this meeting.[24] The blue coat was undoubtedly the coat in which he intended to be baptized.

Christianity, an enormously powerful force in slave life prior to the Civil War, had clearly touched Sam Williams. We have no way of knowing the nature of what he went through prior to his appearance before the membership of the church; the minutes are silent on details of this sort. But chances are he underwent a profound ecstatic conversion experience of the sort often described by many blacks who entered the Baptist faith. Those who had had such experiences described the process as one of rebirth. They talked of having "come through," of having "passed through death to a new life." They spoke of having been touched by God and receiving "the essence or spirit" of the Almighty and retaining "that thing" inside them forever. And they described themselves as "free at last," a liberating freedom of the soul granted by God for all eternity that could not be constrained by the absence of physical freedom.[25]

It is extremely difficult to document the existence of the Christian faith in a specific slave community like Buffalo Forge, but we have some hints that point toward the religious life of the black men and women who lived there. In late August 1834, the chaffery forge shut down because the forgemen had gone to a camp meeting.[26] Probably a large number of Weaver's slaves attended this gathering, because the forge was generally the last activity to be halted for any reason other than necessary repairs or agricultural work that required all hands. The descendants of the Buffalo Forge slaves also describe prayer meetings that moved from cabin to cabin in the slave quarters.[27]

Sam Williams, as a recognized member of a regularly constituted church, may have helped lead these services, or they may have been conducted by Joe, a skilled forge carpenter and blacksmith and a son of Tooler and Rebecca, two of the original "Wilson negroes." Daniel Brady occasionally noted in his journal that Joe was "praying" or was "reading his bible," and a clerk at the forge once described Joe as "Joe Gentleman with his linen coat on." This coat may have been the formal clothing Joe wore when he preached the Gospel or conducted wedding services for the slaves, as he appears to have done.[28] Sam Williams was the only slave belonging to Weaver who sought formal membership in the Lexington Baptist Church, but it is clear that Christianity was a presence in the lives of many of the Buffalo Forge slaves.

As Sam gained additional skill and experience as a refiner, his forge overwork earnings grew. In the late 1840s and early 1850s, he was regularly making over $50 per annum. Sam did some of this overwork with one of his brothers. Both Charles and Washington "Etna" had followed Sam into Weaver's forge. By the late 1840s, Sam's two younger brothers were both earning overwork compensation as forgemen, and on January 1, 1849, Sam was credited with $7.50 for making anchonies with Charles, who was serving as Sam's underhand. Charles was given $4.50 for his overwork on the same day. A year later, Sam received $40 for eight tons of overwork iron, and Charles was given $3 per ton for his work on the same quantity of extra metal. These rates—$5 per ton for Sam, $3 for Charles—again show that Sam was acting as the master workman and Charles was assisting his older brother at the refinery forge.[29]

Charles's accounts in Weaver's "Negro Books" are lengthy ones, running from 1848 to 1857. The entries under "Washington Etna" are much briefer. After receiving $3 "Cr over work 1 Ton" on January 1, 1850, and drawing 50 cents in cash twelve days later, Washington's account abruptly stops. No evidence exists that reveals why he suddenly disappeared from Weaver's records, but the most logical explanation would be that Washington died sometime in early 1850.

The things Sam Williams did with his overwork earnings in the 1840s and 1850s tell us a good deal about this man and his attitudes and priorities. He supplemented Weaver's standard rations of pork and cornmeal with regular purchases of flour, sugar, coffee, and molasses, and he frequently bought cloth for Nancy to sew into garments for the family. His overwork kept him, and perhaps Nancy as well, supplied with tobacco. And his gifts to various members of his family continued. His mother received fifty pounds of flour from him in February 1845, and he gave his father a pound of coffee in April 1846—to cite two instances where the items were specifically mentioned in the records as going to his parents. Nancy, as might be expected, received a number of presents: a pair of buckskin gloves at Christmas in 1848; a shawl in May 1849; and a very expensive—$12—gift of fabric in October 1851 that included silk and four yards of "Bolt Clothe." One of Sam's special purchases for his children that is clearly identified in his account came in 1853. On June 22 of that year, he spent $1.75 for "8 ¾ yds [cloth] for Annie for Bedspread." His daughter Ann turned ten in 1853, and the bedspread may well have been a birthday present for her.

Sam also bought items of apparel for himself during the mid-1840s. There was nothing that could match his blue baptismal coat, but he bought a pair of "Fine shoes" for $2.50 and a "Summer Coat" for $4.50 in May 1845, probably to wear when he attended church services in Lexington. He added "1 Fine Hat," priced at $4, to his wardrobe the following November.

The most fascinating items that he acquired during these years were the articles of furniture he bought for the cabin that he, Nancy, and the girls shared. His major Christmas gift to the family in 1845 consisted of a table ($3) and a bedstead ($9), both of which he purchased at the Buffalo Forge store on Christmas Eve of that year. He added significantly to the cabin's furnishings six years later when he apparently attended an estate sale held in the neighborhood. In April 1851, he made two acquisitions "at Blackford's Sale": a set of chairs, for which he paid $7.25, and probably his most revealing purchase of the entire antebellum era, "1 looking glass," priced at $1.75.[30]

There are many reasons why any family would want to own a mirror—perfectly natural reasons, such as curiosity about one's appearance or a touch of vanity, perhaps. Sam and Nancy Williams had growing daughters, too. Betty was eleven, Caroline was nine, Ann was eight, and Lydia was seven in 1851. But the purchase of a mirror by a *slave* suggests something more. It indicates a strong sense of pride in one's self and one's family that transcended their status as slaves. Why else would Sam spend that kind of money on such a purchase? One dollar seventy-five cents represented the sweat and sore muscles that went into several hundred pounds of overwork iron. One almost suspects that the looking glass, packed carefully in a wagon and hauled home from "Blackford's Sale," stood as a symbol of Sam and Nancy's feelings about themselves and their children. And there were other signs of pride as well, the most notable of which occurred in 1853.

Sam was thirty-three years old that year. He and Nancy had been married for thirteen years, they were raising their four girls, and he was a member of the Lexington Baptist Church. As the master refiner at Buffalo Forge, he was the most important single artisan in Weaver's employ. His overwork earnings exceeded those of any other hand on the place. If Weaver wanted to try a new brand of pig iron at the forge, it was up to Sam to make a couple of anchonies with the metal "to see how it worked."[31] Sam's judgment determined whether Weaver would or would not place an order for the iron. Sam was also in charge of the annual slaughter of hogs at Buffalo Forge and was responsible for cutting up and salting the pork that served as the primary source of meat for almost all of Weaver's slaves. He and Nancy cultivated their own garden and corn lot, raised chickens and hogs, and regularly sold Weaver sweet potatoes, poultry, pork, and bacon, as well as the brooms Sam managed to find the spare time to make. When he was not pounding out anchonies at his refinery hammer, he was almost always engaged in some other type of productive labor: repairing the forge; cutting logs at Weaver's sawmill; driving a herd of cattle down from Bath Iron Works or over to Etna Furnace; working with the field hands at planting, fertilizing, and harvest times.[32] It was time for Sam to get his own name back.

On the page in the Buffalo Forge "Negro Book" covering his work for the year 1853, his name appears two ways: as "Samuel Etna" and as "Sam Williams." On January 12 and 13, 1853, the clerk keeping the time book at the forge wrote: "Sam Williams & hands sowing plaster in the big field." Several days later, the clerk reverted to the old form. "Sam Etna & Hands sowing plaster," he wrote, and in June he noted that "Sam E" was among the five or six slaves who had come down with the mumps. But mistakes of this type became increasingly rare in the records kept at Buffalo Forge. As the year drew to a close, it was "Sam Williams" who drew $5 in cash against his overwork credit and bought 3¼ yards of expensive cassinette cloth for Nancy on Christmas Eve. Four days later when all hands went to work cutting blocks of ice from the pond behind the forge dam to fill Weaver's icehouse, it was "Sam Williams" who received a day's wage and a whiskey ration for his part in seeing this project through to completion. And when his overwork account was totaled up at the end of 1853 and his expenditures ($36.58) were subtracted from his earnings ($63.50, for more than twelve tons of overwork during the year), his credit balance of $26.92 was posted on a new ledger page carrying only one name, "Samuel Williams."[33] From this point on, as far as the records were concerned, he was almost always identified as "Sam Williams." His father was "Sam Williams Senior."[34]

The most logical explanation for this change is that Sam himself wanted it made. By this time he was certainly important enough to Weaver's operations to get his way in a matter of this sort, particularly since his request must have struck Weaver and the forge manager and clerk as a fairly minor one. One suspects that Sam viewed the subject quite differently.

During 1855 and 1856, the last two years for which his complete accounts are available, Sam's overwork earnings reached levels that were extraordinary by any measure. In 1855, he made $92.23. The next year, his earnings went even higher. His credit account for 1856 contained only four entries, but when added together they reached a very impressive figure:

June 20	8 chickens	1.00
Sept 2	8 chickens	1.00
Oct 5	½ Bush Sweet Potatoes	1.00
Dec 10	By Over Iron 20 tons @ 5.00	100.00[35]

For the first time, Sam earned over $100 in overwork in a single year. The extent of his overwork income for that year can perhaps best be appreciated if these earnings are translated into present-day dollars: The $103 he made in 1856 would equal the purchasing power of over $1,600 in 1992.[36]

In 1849, Sam began making fairly frequent cash withdrawals against his overwork account. Some of this money he certainly used to buy items at rural stores that dotted the nearby countryside, places like Saunders' Store, which stood just across Buffalo Creek from the forge. But he was not spending all of it in this way. The individual withdrawals were small at first, a dollar or two generally, but they soon added up: $24 taken out in cash in 1849 (as opposed to $6.75 in 1848, $5 in 1847, and $1.50 in 1846); $23.25 in 1850; a jump to $41.16 in 1851, followed by a one-year falloff to $16 in 1852; and then a sharp increase to almost identical sums of $51 in 1853, $57 in 1854, $56.87½ in 1855, and $57.81 in 1856. In 1857, the last year in which the withdrawals can be traced in full, he took out $25.50 in cash.[37] Thanks to the bet Sam and Henry Nash made in February 1855 and John Rex's letter to James Davidson regarding their wager, we know where at least part of this money was going.

We also know the size of Sam's savings account. Just over a year after Rex wrote Davidson about the bet and asked him how Sam could go about withdrawing his money, James Davidson drew Sam's funds from the bank. On April 22, 1856, Davidson rode out to Buffalo Forge carrying Sam's savings of $91.31. He also brought with him $61.96 belonging to Sam's wife.[38]

Nancy Williams had a savings account, too, and in her own name. Since she was in charge of the dairy operations at Buffalo Forge and did a good deal of housework at Weaver's residence, she clearly had opportunities to earn overwork pay in her own right. Without the house accounts it is impossible to say exactly how she made all of this money, but we can identify some of the things that resulted in payments to her. Weaver sometimes noted in his cashbooks why certain sums were paid out, and occasionally these entries show Nancy as the recipient. During the 1850s, she received money for raising calves, for a stone pitcher she sold Weaver, and for indigo she grew in her garden. She was given money on one occasion to buy starch, which indicates that she was ironing at Weaver's residence.[39] And she also kept her own hogs at Buffalo Forge which were weighed, slaughtered, and put up in the smokehouse in her name when hog-killing time arrived.[40] Some of this meat could have been sold to Weaver. By these means and other forms of overwork we unfortunately cannot identify, she had managed to accumulate savings that were fully two-thirds the size of her husband's. Between them, Sam and Nancy Williams had $153.27 in cash in 1856, the 1992 equivalent of approximately $2,500.[41]

What were they saving for? No evidence exists to show that Weaver had given them the right to buy their own freedom or that of their children, so self-purchase apparently was not the reason. The fact that they were saving at all suggests that they felt their material standard of living was adequate to the family's needs; if it had not been, they probably would have spent much more than they did on various food items and cloth, and they would not have sold Weaver items like chickens, pork, and sweet potatoes if they had needed them for their own table. The most logical explanation for their extraordinary, and substantial, bank accounts would seem to be that they both had extra overwork funds and they simply put their money in a safe place where it would earn interest for them. The safest place they could find was apparently the Lexington savings bank.

For some reason, Davidson transferred their funds to Buffalo Forge in the spring of 1856. Perhaps the bank directors felt uneasy about holding, and paying interest on, money belonging to slaves after Sam's bet with Henry Nash brought the subject up. Or maybe Weaver decided it would be better to handle their accounts in some other way. For whatever reason, Weaver replaced the bank as the holder of their savings. He also became the payer of interest on their funds.

Special entries were made under their separate names in a private ledger kept at the forge on April 22, 1856, the day James Davidson brought their money out from Lexington. Neither Sam nor Nancy made any withdrawals during the next twelve months, so exactly one year after their initial deposits, Weaver credited both accounts with interest on the full amounts. Sam's $91.31 earned him $10.96, and Nancy's $61.96 made $7.44 for her. The interest rate in both instances was 12 percent.[42]

In the years just ahead, Sam and Nancy would follow quite different courses in handling their savings. In the spring and fall of 1858, Nancy made fairly systematic cash withdrawals of $4 to $5, and in 1859 she used the remainder of her money for substantial purchases at Buffalo Forge and at two neighboring country stores. On October 27, 1859, she closed out her account by spending $4.82 at Saunders' Store. Sam, on the other hand, kept exactly $100 on deposit throughout these years and into the 1860s. He withdrew the interest each year, in either cash or goods, but kept the $100 principal fully intact. Weaver regularly credited him with interest on his $100, figured after 1860 at 6 percent, and Sam just as regularly drew off his $6 a year (for some reason, two interest payments were made in 1862, so Sam took out $12 that year). His account was not closed out until after the Civil War.[43]

The picture that emerges from this story of two slaves with savings accounts is by no means a simple one. On the surface, one might be tempted to argue that Sam and Nancy Williams simply swallowed more of the bait Weaver offered to induce his black laborers to work like slaves and that their behavior indicated a placid acceptance of their status and condition. Since they had to complete their required tasks before they could start earning money for themselves, they obviously were turning out a considerable amount of work for their master. Yet they were doing a great deal for themselves as well, and for their children. They were improving the material conditions under which all of them could live, and they were protecting themselves against the fearful threat that hung over them all—the breakup of the family through sale. Weaver would be very reluctant indeed to part with workers like this man and woman, who meant so much to the smooth running, and the success, of his ironmaking and farming activities. Nor would he want to run the risks he would face if he tried to sell Sam and Nancy's daughters off Buffalo Forge. Through their overwork, both Sam and Nancy could help to shield and provide for each other and for their children. The psychological importance of this to them—the added access it afforded Sam to the traditional responsibilities of a husband and father, and Nancy to the role of wife and mother—cannot be overemphasized. Their feelings and emotions can be shared by anyone who has ever tried to make a good and descent life with another person and has helped to bring children into a fragile and uncertain world.

Early in 1858, Sam and Nancy Williams became grandparents. The exact date when their oldest daughter, Betty, married was not entered in the Buffalo Forge records, but it was probably sometime in 1857. Betty was seventeen then, and she and a man named A. Coleman, who apparently belonged to a neighboring slaveholder, became husband and wife. On February 18, 1858, Betty gave birth to her first child, a boy, and they named him Alfred Elliott Coleman.[44] The baby was probably named for his father, but since we only know the initial of his father's first name, we cannot be sure.[45] Weaver's family physician, Dr. Daniel Morgan, was at Buffalo Forge on February 18 and was paid $5 "For visit to Betty & subsequent visits"; almost certainly he was there to help deliver the baby and then returned on two or more occasions to see how the mother and the infant were doing.[46] Neither Betty nor the baby seems to have experienced any problems at the time of birth or in the weeks that followed.

The birth of Alfred Elliott Coleman early in 1858 came at a time when the Bradys were just settling in at Buffalo Forge. There is no way of knowing if the baby's middle name was prompted by the arrival of Daniel Charles Elliott Brady and his family, but we can be reasonably certain that the Bradys' coming brought a welcome sense of stability to life at Buffalo Forge. Three generations of the Weaver family were in residence now. Weaver's heirs were in place, and he could face the future with much greater equanimity.

The stakes were even higher for Sam Williams. The birth of his grandson meant that four generations of the Williams family would be living at Buffalo Forge. Sam had seen his family broken once before. It had been over twenty years since Thomas Mayburry had taken Sam's grandmother and three of her children away, but there was no way Sam could forget that event. Now, with Betty's new baby, Sam Williams had even more reason to do whatever he could to shelter his family and try to protect all of them—his mother, his father, his wife, his children, and his grandchild—from the worst aspects of the slave regime. The years ahead would soon demonstrate, however, that there were some things that were beyond his control, indeed were beyond the control of any man, free or slave.

2

Henry Towles

In February 1840, John Doyle gave a detailed description of the work performed by various types of slave forgemen. He was testifying in the case of Weaver *v.* Jordan, Davis & Company, and the counsel for the defense was trying to establish the cost of producing bar at Bath Forge during the time Sam Jordan and the Davis brothers were operating the works. "Cannot an under hand be made out of a good common hand in a short time?" the lawyer asked. "Yes, they are made to answer for that purpose here," Doyle replied. He went on to state that there were "two descriptions of under hands." The first was "the inferior kind . . . called a *melter;* he does nothing but melt the pig metal and carry it in" to the refiner. The second was very close to the master refiner himself in terms of the abilities he possessed. This type of underhand not only could melt; he could also bring the pig iron "to nature and make a loop, and does make blooms about with the master refinery man: the only difference between him and the master is that he cannot handle his iron at the hammer nor put up nor keep his fire in order."[1]

Henry Towles never worked at Bath Forge, but he was definitely a refinery underhand of the second description. Indeed, his abilities were such that if John Doyle had seen him working with Sam Williams at Buffalo Forge in the late 1850s, Doyle might have wanted to expand his descriptive analysis to include a third category: an underhand who was capable of substituting for the refiner in emergencies and who was so good at what he did that his status, and his compensation, approached that of the master refiner himself.

Henry Towles was considerably younger than his forge partner. Henry was born at Buffalo Forge in 1836 and was less than a year old when Sam came into Weaver's possession on New Year's Day, 1837. Sam was sixteen at the time the division of Thomas Mayburry's group of "Wilson negroes" occurred. Henry's parents were Prince and Sally Towles, two slaves owned by Weaver whose cabin stood on the far side of Buffalo Creek.[2] Exactly when Weaver acquired Henry's father is unclear. A Louisa County slave-owner named David Tinder offered to sell Weaver a man named Prince in 1828, and Weaver and Tinder appear to have agreed on a price for the man. The deal may have fallen through, however, since Prince's name—identified as belonging to "Tindar Louisa"—appears on a list of slaves hired to Bath Iron Works in 1829.[3]

Weaver may have purchased the man in the early 1830s, or perhaps Henry Towles's father was another man named Prince. Whatever the case, Prince Towles was working for Weaver from at least the mid-1830s on, and records kept at Buffalo Forge show that he was a woodchopper and an agricultural laborer as well as a skilled basket weaver. In a two-year span during the mid-1850s, he made and sold to Weaver sixty-six charcoal baskets.[4]

The background of Henry's mother is equally obscure. Sally Towles might have been the daughter of Amy, one of the "Wilson negroes" who lived at Buffalo Forge throughout the 1820s. Slave girls were rarely given their mother's name but were frequently named after aunts. Amy was Sally Williams's sister. Sally Towles was probably in her mid-teens when Henry was born in 1836, which would place her birth around 1820. If her mother had indeed been Amy, then her baby and Sam Williams would have been first cousins once removed. Henry appears to have been the Towles' first child, but he was soon followed by other children, all boys: Charles, born in 1838, Edgar, born two years later, Constant, born in 1842, and Prince, Jr., born in 1845.[5] All would eventually take their place in Weaver's work force.

In the descriptive list drawn in 1865, Daniel Brady listed Henry Towles as twenty-nine years of age, gave his height as five feet seven inches, and listed his color as black. Charles and Edgar were approximately the same height as Henry and were also described as black.[6] Unlike the case of Sam Williams, there was no visible addition of white blood in the Towles family.

Henry went into the forge in 1852 at the age of sixteen. He replaced Charles "Etna," Sam's brother, as the underhand at Sam's refinery forge. Charles's reason for leaving the forge is unknown. Quite possibly he had suffered an injury and could not, or did not want to, continue there. Whatever the reason, he earned his last overwork payments for ironmaking in 1851. All his earnings in subsequent years were for corn and pork sold to Weaver.[7]

Henry Towles was a quick learner. His overwork account for 1852 shows him receiving small sums of cash—fifty cents or $1—identified as "per order Mr. Weaver" throughout much of the year, but when his "over iron" was added up just before Christmas, he was credited with $31.80 for heating just over ten tons of pig metal. He was, at this stage of his training, still a "melter," to use John Doyle's term, but he had earned an impressive amount of money for himself nonetheless. The "per order Mr. Weaver" designation suggests strongly that Weaver made incentive payments to Henry during his apprenticeship before he actually began doing any overwork. By year's end, however, Henry's earnings covered these initial payments several times over, and he had become a first-class refinery underhand.[8]

Henry bought small amounts of sugar for himself in 1852 and early 1853 and drew out small sums of cash—usually 50 cents—but in the spring of 1853, he made his first major purchase. On May 14, Weaver noted that Henry took out $3 "Cash to buy pants." Henry was buying clothes for his wedding. A week later, on Saturday, May 21, he married Ann, a young slave woman belonging to Weaver. Henry was seventeen, Ann was fifteen, and they would soon be starting a family.[9]

The records give two different dates for the birth of their first child, a boy they named Joseph. A register of slave births compiled by Daniel Brady in 1864 lists Ann Towles giving birth to "Joe" on July 10, 1853.[10] William Weaver, however, reported to the county clerk that Joseph, son of Ann, was born on June 22, 1854, and this date was recorded in the Rockbridge County Register of Births.[11]

If their son was indeed born in July 1853, Ann would have been seven months or so into her pregnancy at the time of her marriage. Customs surrounding slave courtship did not place a taboo on sex before marriage. Accepted practice did require the couple to enter into matrimony after a child was conceived, however, and to remain together and be faithful to each other for the rest of their lives. If Joseph Towles was born in June 1854, however, as Weaver indicated, then his mother and father would have been married for more than a year.

Henry Towles stepped up his overwork following his marriage, just as his forge partner, Sam Williams, had done during his initial year of married life. Henry's earnings rose to $38.42 in 1853, most of which he made by helping to produce more than twelve tons of "over iron" with Sam; Henry was paid at the rate of $3 per ton, Sam was paid the master refiner's rate of $5 per ton. Henry used his earnings in 1853 and 1854 to buy flour, sugar, and coffee, and he drew substantial sums of cash from his account on several occasions. One, for $5, came on Christmas Eve, 1853. Two other similar withdrawals—$5 in May and another for $10 in June 1854—came during times that had special significance for him: the anniversary of his wedding and the (probable) birth of his first child. Ann made major contributions to the family's income as well. In January 1855, Henry's account carried the notation "Cash for Pork Annas 6 00," six months later "Cash for Annas Pork .50," and in December "117 lbs Pork 6.43 ½," which may have been hers as well. Henry continued to make extra iron with Sam in the forge, and when his and Ann's account was balanced in the spring of 1856, it showed that their earnings for the past two years totaled $93.58.[12]

These years also witnessed the birth of their second child. Hannah Frances Towles was born on May 26, 1856, but she did not live long. She was stricken with what appears to have been an attack of measles and died less than a month after her birth.[13] As that year drew to a close, Henry used some of his overwork credit to help his family celebrate the holidays. On Christmas Eve, 1856, he took $5 in cash from his account and, for $3.50, purchased a half barrel of flour.[14]

The new year brought an upturn in the fortunes of Henry Towles and his family. On July 10, 1857, Ann gave birth to another daughter whom they named Cornelia, and this time the baby came through her first months in good health.[15] That year was also marked by further recognition of Henry's growing skills as an ironworker. On December 10, 1857, Henry was credited with $53.40 for making just under eighteen tons of extra iron; he was paid at the usual rate of $3 per ton. His account shows, however, that on the same date, Sam Williams gave Henry $5 in cash out of his own pocket. Apparently Sam thought that his assistant's work warranted additional compensation, and he may have suggested to Weaver that an adjustment be made in their pay scales that would reflect the full extent of Henry's contribution to the refinery operation.

Daniel Brady, who arrived at Buffalo Forge in late 1857, posted the next set of entries in the "Negro Book." On January 8, 1858, he recorded a credit

for Henry for making 11 ¾ additional tons of overwork; this time, however, he was paid at the rate of $3.50 per ton, which resulted in $41.13 being
added to his account. On the same date, Brady made a similar entry under
Sam's name: "By overwork 11 ¾ tons." Sam's compensation for making
these anchonies was $52.87; his pay scale for this work was $4.50 per ton.[16]

Henry was much more than a "melter" now. He was well on his way to
mastering the art of turning pig iron into anchonies. On those days when
Sam was not at his post at the refinery forge, Henry was fully capable of
substituting for him. He could also help out at the chaffery hammer if
Tooler or Harry Hunt, Jr., were absent and Weaver needed a skilled underhand to fill in there.

Henry Towles would turn twenty-two in 1858, he had a wife and two
young children at Buffalo Forge, he and Ann were earning very impressive
amounts of overwork compensation, and, like Sam Williams, he had made
himself an indispensable part of Weaver's forge operation. The skills he
had acquired were of a high order, and he undoubtedly knew that the
acquisition of those skills had given him about as much mastery over his
own fate as the system of slavery would allow. Henry Towles was a forgeman. William Weaver had always needed able hands at his refinery and
chaffery forges. There was no reason to expect that this master's needs
would be any different in the future than they had been in the past.

3

Tooler

Ironworking was a strong tradition in Tooler's family. His father, Tooler, Sr., had been a keeper at Etna Furnace and then worked as a chaffery hammerman at Buffalo Forge. Tooler's brothers, all of them, were either furnace or forge hands. Bill had worked at Etna until an injury disabled him, Bob was a chaffery underhand, and Joe would later become a forge carpenter and blacksmith for Weaver. There was no question that this family was one that produced "good mechanics."

Tooler, his mother, father, and three brothers had all come into Weaver's possession in 1815. They were among the eleven slaves Weaver bought from John Wilson that year, and young Tooler was four years old at the time of the sale. He grew up at Buffalo Forge, helped his mother, Rebecca, with her household chores at Weaver's residence during his early years, and then, probably at age seventeen or so, went into the forge to train as a hammerman.

By 1830, when the surviving overwork records begin, Tooler, Jr., was a fully trained chaffery forge hand. It is highly likely that he served his apprenticeship with his father. Tooler, Sr., drew iron for Weaver at Buffalo Forge during the late 1820s, and the transmission of skills from slave father to slave son was a common practice at Virginia ironworks. The emergence of Tooler, Jr., as a skilled hammerman probably paved the way for his father to leave the forge. "Old Tooler," as he was sometimes called, was a woodcutter at Buffalo Forge throughout the 1830s, but he appears to have trained his son well.[1]

Young Tooler was only nineteen in 1830, but on December 30, when he was credited with $3.45 for making iron "during holidays" and $13.70 for overwork metal turned out earlier in the year, he was paid at the rate of $3 per ton. This was the pay scale for the master workman at the chaffery, the man who actually drew the bar under the rhythmic pounding of the forge hammer. Tooler's brother Bob served as the underhand and received $2 a ton for his part in producing this metal. "Tooler Junr.s" account had opened in April of that year with a transfer from an earlier "Negro Book," so it is clear that he had been working as a forgeman prior to the spring of 1830.[2]

So had Bob. He was three years older than Tooler, and probably preceded his brother in the forge by that length of time. Bob frequently worked alongside Tooler, Jr., during the decade of the 1830s, and then in 1840 Weaver transferred Bob to Bath Iron Works. He served as Harry Hunt's underhand at the chaffery forge there before moving over to Bath Furnace in 1841. Joe, who was two years younger than Tooler, did a brief stint in the forge in the late 1830s, but he did not remain there very long. He had trained as a blacksmith, and he combined his expertise in this field with woodworking skills that made him an ideal choice for the position of forge carpenter.[3] He filled that position for Weaver from the 1840s until his mysterious death in the fall of 1860.

Both Tooler's mother and father lived at Buffalo Forge during the years following his forge training. Tooler, Sr., was well into his fifties by 1830, but apparently he still possessed great strength; he chopped wood in the forests around Buffalo Forge until 1840 or so. During 1834, while a white hammerman was employed briefly at the forge, young Tooler joined his father as a woodcutter for several months. Tooler, Jr., returned to the forge before the year was out, but his father continued on as a woodchopper, and his overwork accounts indicate that Rebecca was still alive during the 1830s. With money that he made by cutting extra wood, raising corn, and making hoop poles, Tooler, Sr., bought coffee, sugar, and a considerable amount of cloth—calico, checks, stripes, cassinette—that was undoubtedly for his wife.[4] The date of Rebecca's death does not appear in Weaver's records, but her husband's passing was noted in the time book kept at Buffalo Forge.

On Saturday, March 25, 1844, "Tooler Died and was beried [*sic*]."[5] He was probably close to seventy years of age and had lived and worked at Buffalo Forge for almost thirty years. By the time of his death, the son who carried his name was one of the slave artisans whose diligence and workmanship largely determined the course of Weaver's ironmaking enterprise.

Young Tooler's overwork account, filled with line after line of book-keeping entries, reveals much about him, and about his priorities. In his case, however, we can also see something of the life he lived beyond the confines of Buffalo Forge.

Tooler's account opens in 1830 like most of these records with modest amounts spent on coffee and sugar and an occasional withdrawal of small sums of cash. Very soon, however, he began using most of his money to buy clothing: a vest, a pair of fine shoes for $2, a pair of "pantaloons & trim-mings" for $7, a coat for $3.50, a handkerchief, and cloth to be sewn into shirts.[6] Tooler was probably courting.

The date of Tooler's marriage is unknown, but we do know that he married a woman who did not live at Buffalo Forge. Evidence for this exists in the time and production records kept at the forge, in his overwork accounts, and, after 1858, in Daniel Brady's journal. The wedding may have occurred in the summer of 1832. Tooler was twenty or twenty-one that year, and in August he bought "1 yd check," perhaps to use as a tablecloth, and a half dozen plates. The possibility certainly exists that this was a wedding present as Tooler and his wife began trying to establish some sort of household for themselves. Some of his purchases the following year suggest strongly that he was married: 3 ½ yards of fine muslin bought in October 1833 and a Christmas Eve order consisting of 7 ¼ yards of calico, 2 yards of muslin, 1 ½ yards of checked cloth, and a pound of sugar.[7] It seems almost certain that these were gifts to take with him when he went to visit his wife for the holidays.

Tooler's wife lived in Lynchburg, which normally would have presented the couple with a serious problem. Lynchburg was on the other side of the Blue Ridge Mountains and was not easily reached by land. But Weaver maintained a fleet of bateaux to carry his iron and flour to market and owned a crew of slave boatmen who made regular trips down the James River to Lynchburg and Richmond. Tooler apparently was no stranger to Weaver's boatyard; his overwork account shows he drew some cash there in 1836, and he undoubtedly rode Weaver's bateaux to Lynchburg when-ever he went to visit his wife and, one can surmise, his children.[8]

Since his wife was not one of Weaver's slaves, any discussion of Tooler's family involves a good deal of guesswork. His overwork account, however, offers some clues. On December 2, 1836, Tooler paid 37 ½ cents for

"Leather for Par Small Shoes." On September 23, 1837, he spent $1 for "Leather for a Pair Shoes for wife." Two months later, he bought "Leather for 2 Pair Small Shoes" for 50 cents. And on September 27, 1839, he again spent for "Leather for a Pair Shoes for wife." The small shoes were most likely for a child, or perhaps two children. Large store purchases and cash drawn just before Christmas in the late 1830s and early 1840s were almost certainly used to obtain presents for his family.[9]

Forge work was dangerous business, and Tooler incurred more than his share of injuries. Chaffery records show that he hurt his hand on numerous occasions, suffered a leg burn that kept him from returning to his hammer for several days in 1837, and sustained a serious arm injury in 1852.[10] But perhaps most significantly, his eyes do not seem to have been damaged as was so often the case with forgemen. He kept on drawing iron throughout the antebellum decades, which was probably the reason Weaver allowed him to carry substantial debit balances from one year to the next throughout much of the time he worked at Buffalo Forge.

Tooler earned fairly large sums for his overwork iron during most of the 1830s—yearly amounts in the $15 to $25 range were common—and he sometimes supplemented his forge wages by weaving charcoal baskets and selling them to Weaver. But he just as regularly overspent his income on sugar, coffee, cloth, leather, and occasional expensive items like a $4 silk hat bought on July 2, 1836, and "2 ¼ yds Broad Cloth & trimmings for Coat" purchased for $14.05 the following October. His debt, which stood at $6.34 ½ at the beginning of 1831, rose to almost $16 by the end of the decade; this was money he owed Weaver after his overwork earnings for the year were subtracted from his yearly purchases plus the negative balance he had brought forward from the previous twelve months.[11] A gap in the overwork records from 1840 to 1844 makes it impossible to say precisely how Tooler and Weaver dealt with this situation, but chances are Weaver was not overly concerned. This was a relatively small price to pay for the reasonably steady work of a skilled slave hammerman.

Tooler certainly does not seem to have worried about his overcharges. He had the skills he needed to wipe out his debt whenever he chose to do so, as he demonstrated conclusively in the mid-1840s. By January 1, 1845, he had turned his debit into a credit balance of $4.18, and the following year, he did even better. He made his normal purchases throughout the year, and in December he bought a gallon of molasses, two pounds of coffee, and spent $4 on a Christmas Eve store order; he had earned $35 on almost twelve tons of overwork iron in 1845, and he carried a credit of $10.23 over to the next year's account.[12]

The unmistakable impression one gets looking at Tooler's accounts during the 1830s and 1840s is that he made extra iron when he wanted to and then at other times simply chose not to do additional work. Yet he was able to maintain his standard of living at a relatively high level throughout the entire period. His frequent purchases of cloth, leather for shoes, and Christmas orders like four yards of cotton flannel and a pair of gloves on December 24, 1847, would suggest that he continued to provide many items for his family as well.[13]

We can speak with some precision about Tooler's use of his overwork earnings to benefit his family in the late 1840s and early 1850s. On May 2, 1849, he spent $6 for "1 Dress for wife," and two weeks later he paid $2.59 for a calico dress and a "vest & trimmings." It is possible that the calico dress and the vest were items Tooler purchased for his children. On March 16, 1850, he made a $5 withdrawal from his account labeled "Cash to send to his wife."[14] Other occasions where Tooler clearly relied on his overwork to assist the family came as he prepared to head down the James River to see his wife.

Weaver, who recorded production figures at the chaffery forge, sometimes gave the reason Tooler was absent from his post. "Tooler visiting his wife," Weaver wrote in the iron book on July 3, 1847; several days earlier, Tooler had taken $1 in cash from his account. He was "absent to his wife" the week of February 12, 1848, and just before he left for Lynchburg, he drew on his overwork credit for $3 in cash plus a $5 store order. When he went to visit his wife in the spring of 1851, he carried $5 in cash with him. The forge time book shows Tooler taking a four-day trip to Lynchburg from October 23 to October 27, 1851; he took $2.25 from his account prior to his departure from Buffalo Forge. And for 1852, the debit side of his page in the "Negro Book" carries the following entries:

April 17	Cash for trip to Lynchburg	2.00
July 3	Cash for trip to Lynchburg	2.00
Sept 2	Cash trip to Lynchburg	2.00
Dec 26	Cash trip Lyncbg, per order	1.00[15]

The "per order" notation on the last entry probably indicates that Weaver instructed the forge manager, James Watkins, to make this payment. Tooler was running a negative balance at the time, but Weaver apparently was unwilling to cut Tooler off from compensation as he left to visit his family for the holidays.

The length of time Tooler was away from Buffalo Forge varied considerably. His April 1852 trip lasted nine days; the one he took the following July was only four days long, however, and the September visit was almost as brief. He left Buffalo Forge on Friday, September 3, and returned on Wednesday, September 8. While he was away, other slaves would often fill in for him at the chaffery hammer. Harry Hunt, Jr., who was Tooler's regular underhand, and Henry Matthews frequently drew iron in his absence; sometimes Jim Garland came in from the field gang to help out.[16] Weaver did not normally allow the forge to shut down just because Tooler was away.

Tooler's versatility and Weaver's dependence on his skills as a forgeman were clearly demonstrated in 1853. Weaver wanted two refinery fires in production that year, and that left him short one master refiner. Sam Williams was there, of course, but Henry Towles was not yet ready to take charge of the other fire. That job fell to Tooler. He spent almost the entire year refining anchonies at Buffalo Forge while Henry Matthews and Harry Hunt, Jr., manned the chaffery.[17]

Tooler's earnings never reached the levels of some of the other Buffalo Forge slaves, most notably Sam Williams. This seems to have been by choice. Tooler could make large sums when he chose to do so, as he once again demonstrated in the latter half of the 1850s. By then Weaver was paying Tooler $3.50 per ton for extra metal, and Tooler's almost thirteen tons of "over iron" in 1856 earned him close to $45. He also raised hogs that year and sold Weaver 260 pounds of pork in December, which brought him an additional $15.60. His total compensation for the year was over $60. His purchases in December came to $21.60, by far the largest sum Tooler had ever spent just before Christmas. When Daniel Brady balanced Tooler's account on January 8, 1858, he had a credit of $13.56.[18]

Tooler was forty-seven years old in 1858 and had been working in Weaver's forge for close to thirty years. For most of that time, he and his underhands had regularly met their quota of two journeys of bar iron per day when the forge was running smoothly. And for most of that time, Tooler seems to have set his own pace when it came to doing overwork. Weaver had no choice but to go along. The last white hammermen to draw iron quit work in the fall of 1840.[19] From that point on, Weaver's forge was totally dependent on slave ironworkers, and Tooler was the best chaffery forgeman William Weaver had.

4

—◆—

Harry Hunt, Jr.

The Hunt family was one of the oldest ironworking families in Virginia. Harry Hunt, Jr., was born in 1830 or early 1831 at Bath Iron Works; his father and mother, Harry, Sr., and Gilly Hunt, were living at Bath then and working for Jordan, Davis & Company. Harry Hunt, Sr., had been born in 1788 at the Oxford Iron Works in Campbell County, Virginia, not far from Lynchburg, and had trained there as a refiner. His brother Billy, born in 1787, had also worked at Oxford as a refinery hand. They were the sons of "Old Hunt," a limestone miner at Oxford Furnace born in 1747, and Nanny Hunt, born in 1757. Nanny Hunt, in turn, was the daughter of an Oxford slave named "Old Belinda," born in 1731, and Belinda was most likely the wife of an Oxford worker (whose name does not appear in the surviving records).[1] When Harry Hunt, Jr., began his apprenticeship at Buffalo Forge in the late 1840s, he was in all probability the fourth generation of his family to follow the ironworker's trade.

Harry's boyhood at Bath Iron Works did not end with the family's perilous night journey through the snow-covered "Barrens" of northern Rockbridge County on Christmas Eve, 1834. There was, however, a three-and-a-half-year interruption in his time at Bath. His father had gone to work for Weaver as a refiner in January 1835 following the family's return to Buffalo Forge, and Harry Hunt, Sr., continued to make anchonies there until the spring of 1838. His brother Billy frequently acted as his underhand, and Harry, Jr., probably spent a considerable amount of time around the forge watching his father and his uncle at their jobs.[2] On May 1, 1838, however, Harry, Gilly, and Harry, Jr., returned to Bath. Weaver had reclaimed the works from Sam Jordan and William Davis that spring and was anxious to get the forge back into production. Harry Hunt, Sr., served as the master refiner there, and nineteen-year-old Sam Williams was among the slaves assisting him during 1839. Young Harry Hunt's name appears in the Bath "Negro Book" in 1838, but only to indicate that he had received his shoes, socks, shirt, and hat as part of the regular winter clothing issue to the slaves; little Harry was eight or nine years old that year.[3]

Harry and his father and Sam Williams returned briefly to Buffalo Forge in the spring of 1841, but the occasion that brought them down was a sad one. Billy Hunt became gravely ill in late March, and on April 5, 1841, he died, at the age of fifty-four. The Hunts and Sam came down for his funeral the following day and were there as Billy Hunt's body was lowered into a grave at the slave cemetery at Buffalo Forge.[4]

The Hunt family remained at Bath Iron Works until the early or mid-1840s. Extant records are not clear as to the exact date of their return to Buffalo Forge. The Bath "Negro Book" shows Harry Hunt, Sr., buying "calico for Gilly" in the summer of 1841, purchasing coffee, sugar, tobacco, and molasses throughout the remainder of the year, and then buying a pair of suspenders, a pair of gloves, and two pounds of coffee in January and February of 1842 just before his account was carried to a new Bath Forge ledger, which unfortunately is missing.[5]

A January 20, 1843, entry in the Buffalo Forge time book possibly refers to Harry Hunt, Sr. It notes that "Henry comenst drawing iron at Buffalo." Since Harry Hunt, Sr., and his son were frequently referred to as "Hal" or "Henry" or "Henery" in the records, this may well be the approximate date the family came down from Bath. Harry Hunt, Jr., was only twelve or thirteen years old in 1843. The Buffalo Forge "Negro Book" for the early 1840s is missing, but an account was opened for Harry Hunt, Sr., in a new book in January 1845. It shows him earning $24 for six tons of overwork iron at Buffalo Forge in 1845 and 1846 and using his credit to buy coffee, sugar, molasses, flour, tobacco, a half bushel of peaches (for $1), and cloth which was clearly intended for his wife: satinet, muslin, and canton flannel.

He also spent $3.37½ for nine yards of bed ticking for himself and Gilly in the spring of 1845.[6]

Harry Hunt, Jr., took his apprenticeship at Buffalo Forge. He apparently began his forge work in 1847 when he was about seventeen years of age.[7] Young Harry was about the same size as Henry Towles when he grew to his full stature; Towles was five feet seven inches tall, and Harry, Jr., was five feet seven and one-half. This may be the reason the younger Harry Hunt, like Henry Towles, worked primarily as an underhand in the forge. All the refinery and chaffery hammermen whose height was noted by Daniel Brady in 1865 stood five feet ten inches or taller (no description of Tooler or Henry Hunt, Sr., was recorded; Tooler was exempt from the slave draft because of his age, fifty-four in 1865, and Harry Hunt, Sr., who was seventy-seven that year, had long since given up forge work). As in the case of Sam Williams, miscegenation had taken place at some point in the Hunt family's history; Brady had indicated that Sam Williams was "Yellow"; Harry Hunt, Jr., was listed as "Brown."[8]

Young Harry Hunt assisted at both the refinery and chaffery forges in the late 1840s and early 1850s. His first overwork account—"Harry Hunt (little)" was the name written at the top of the page—shows him being paid $14.25 on January 1, 1848, for "over work to this time." He had made over four tons of "over iron" and was paid at the rate of $3 per ton, the refinery underhand's pay scale. The next year, however, he earned $14.50 for "over work chaffery." He served at the chaffery forge for part of 1850 as well, earning $11.84 for this work on August 5, but then he shifted again; on January 1, 1851, he was paid $6.90 for "Over Work at Finery" during the latter part of the previous year.[9] Harry Hunt, Jr., like many of Weaver's slave artisans, was trained so that he would possess multiple skills as a forgeman.

His early use of overwork credit was typical of most of the slave workers at Buffalo Forge: small cash withdrawals and purchases of sugar and various articles of clothing—a vest and pants for $2.80, a "fine shirt" for $1, a pair of gloves bought at Christmastime in 1848. In the early spring of 1850, he made some impressive acquisitions that reflected his growing purchasing power as his abilities as an ironworker increased: a pair of pants for $4 and a "Blue Coat" that cost him $18. Perhaps Harry had admired a similar coat Sam Williams had purchased prior to his baptism some six years earlier. Harry Hunt, Jr., would turn twenty years old in 1850 and must have taken a good deal of pride in being able to outfit himself in fine clothes. Just before Christmas in 1853, he again spent $18, this time for "1 fine suit (coat and pants)." Harry Hunt's marriage to Charlotte Wade, a slave woman who did not belong to Weaver but lived close to Buffalo Forge, came in 1856, probably in the early fall. On September 10, Harry spent $13.14 on a large order at a nearby store, probably one that lay near his wife's residence. Charlotte was eighteen at the time of the wedding, Harry twenty-five or twenty-six. Their first child, a boy whom they named Wilson, was born in 1857.[10]

His marriage and the birth of his first child were undoubtedly among the happiest moments Harry Hunt experienced during this period of his life. He had other moments that were far from pleasant.

In November 1852, he was working with Henry Matthews at the chaffery forge when an accident occurred. "Hunt eye Burnt" was the description entered in the Buffalo Forge iron book. The time book carried similar messages: on Wednesday, November 17, "Hunt laid up with eye"; on Friday, November 19, "Hunt sore eye." He and Henry Matthews resumed work at the chaffery on Monday, November 22, so the injury apparently did not threaten his sight.[11] But these brief entries nevertheless tell a grim tale of the risks the slaves incurred as they pounded white-hot metal under the massive forge hammers.

This sort of injury may, in fact, have put an end to his father's career as a forgeman, as seems to have been the case with Sam Williams, Sr. There is no indication in Weaver's records that Harry Hunt, Sr., was engaged in forge work after his $24 credit for "over iron" was posted at the end of 1846. He was fifty-eight that year, an age that did not usually mean a refiner or hammerman was too old to continue ironmaking. Subsequent credits entered on his account—small items like a dollar "Harvest money" in 1852, 50 cents for helping to fill the icehouse at the end of 1853, and two pounds of coffee for "Christmas work" in 1854—were few in number and were all for non-forge labor.[12] It is quite possible that his sight deteriorated badly in the late antebellum years and that he totally lost his ability to see early in the 1860s.

A year after his 1852 eye injury, Harry Hunt, Jr., had another experience that probably stayed with him for a long time. "Henry Hunt goes up to town as a witness, so soon as the court is done with him will you please start him home," Weaver wrote James Davidson on November 2, 1853.[13] Harry had been summoned to testify in a murder case. The previous month, a dispute had broken out between two slave boatmen. The men had been playing cards in a bateau on North River, and one of the slaves, a man by the name of Jim Gooch, had been losing heavily to the other, a man named Sam belonging to William and John Poague. Sam won all of Jim's money, but Jim wanted the game to go on so that he could have a chance to get his money back. Sam insisted that Jim put up something of value before he would continue playing, and Jim claimed there was an item in a chest he had on board that he would bet. They played another hand, Jim lost again, and Sam demanded his winnings. At this point, the two men got up and moved toward the head of the boat where Jim's chest was located. Jim claimed the item was missing; Sam responded that if that were the case, he would take Jim's chest. A scuffle broke out and, according to witnesses, Jim plunged a hunting knife into Sam below his right shoulder. The blade cut an artery. Dr. Daniel Morgan, Weaver's physician, was summoned, but before he could get to Sam, he bled to death. Jim Gooch was immediately arrested and charged with felonious and willful murder "with malice afore-thought."[14]

Harry Hunt was called in an effort to establish the fact that Jim had threatened Sam a week or so before the killing. Harry testified that on "Saturday of the big meeting of Falling Spring Church"—the date was October 9, 1853—he was at Miller's Landing, the point where Buffalo Creek enters the North River. Sam and Jim Gooch were also there, and Harry had heard Jim tell Sam "that he intended to kill him; and that seven years was not too long a time to do it in."[15] Harry's testimony was crucial in establishing the "malice aforethought" charge and unquestionably played a role in determining the severity of the sentence the court handed down. Jim Gooch was to "be hanged by the neck until he be dead." Counsel for the defense asked that the sentence be commuted to sale and transportation out of the state; the court refused and ordered the Auditor of Public Accounts to pay Jim's owner, a man named Creed Taylor, $350 as compensation for the loss of his slave property.[16]

The slaveholders of Rockbridge County could not have been pleased by what they heard at this trial. Several white men called as character witnesses for Jim Gooch described him as "peaceable" and a "good negro." A man who had hired Jim in previous years stated that he had "whipped him occasionally, but never heard anything against him till now." Finally, his current employer testified that he had known Jim for some time and considered him "one of the most humble and biddable negroes" who had ever worked for him.[17] Yet clearly an enormous amount of anger had been building inside of Jim Gooch, a smoldering resentment which no white man had detected. When it burst forth, he had taken the life of a fellow slave, but the thought must have crossed some white minds in the courtroom that it could just as easily have been someone whose skin was not black, brown, or yellow.

The trial took place on a Wednesday. Harry Hunt, Jr., returned to Buffalo Forge when it was over, and on Friday, November 4, 1853, he was back working at the chaffery forge with Henry Matthews.[18] The two men continued to draw iron together for the rest of the year, and in January 1854,

Henry Matthews moved over to the blacksmith shop and Tooler returned to his usual job at the chaffery hammer. Harry Hunt, Jr., seemed to suffer no permanent effects from his eye injury. He served as Tooler's principal underhand for all of 1854, and except for the usual shift of the ironworkers to agricultural tasks during various times of the year, he worked steadily in the forge throughout the remainder of the decade. He filled in where most needed, alternating between the finery and chaffery hammer with no apparent difficulty. When necessary, he could take over for one of the teamsters, men like Garland Thompson, Jr., who usually made the daily trips to the coaling grounds to pick up the forge's supply of charcoal.[19] On the eve of the Civil War, Harry Hunt, Jr., was one of the most versatile of William Weaver's slaves.

He was also one of the most valuable. When Daniel Brady drew up his descriptive list of black ironworkers in 1865, he estimated Harry's value at $8,000, the highest figure accorded any member of the slave force; only Henry Towles was listed as having the same market value.[20] An appraisal of the value of Harry's father made two years earlier stood at the opposite end of the spectrum. A string of six zeros was entered after the name of Harry Hunt, Sr. Like Sam Williams, Sr., he was judged to be of no dollar value whatsoever, even in the inflated Confederate currency of the day. Gilly Hunt did not appear on this 1863 list.[21] Her death, which probably occurred sometime in the late 1840s or early 1850s, had stricken her name from the roster of William Weaver's slaves.

5

Henry Matthews

If William Weaver ever needed
confirmation of the wisdom of his decision to purchase the "Wilson
negroes," all he needed to do was walk down to the forge during the 1850s
and watch Henry Matthews at work. He might be making anchonies at the
finery or helping to draw iron at the chaffery forge. He could be doing the
principal carpentry work as a broken helve was taken down at either hammer and sound timber was installed in its place. He might be putting in a
new anvil block—the chaffery usually needed two a year, the refinery at
least one—and if the iron bands that girded the anvil needed to be repaired,
he could take them over to the blacksmith shop and do that job as well. On
any given day, in fact, he might be at the smith shop doing any number of
things—ironing a wagon, making horse or mule shoes, fixing tools or farm
implements, repairing Weaver's threshing machine. If agricultural work
was the order of the day, he might be leading a plow gang or taking a crew
of field hands to a site that needed to be cleared of cockle.[1] Among a slave
force characterized by great versatility, Henry Matthews was the ultimate
jack-of-all-trades.

His first heading in the Buffalo Forge "Negro Books" tells us who he was: "Henry Amey's son." His mother was one of Mary's daughters, Amy, who had been about ten years old when Weaver bought Mary and her four girls in 1815. Amy had grown up at Buffalo Forge—she was not one of the "Wilson negroes" Thomas Mayburry had kept for many years—and she had given birth to two sons during the early and middle years of the 1820s, Henry and Charles. Her husband was a slave identified in the records only as Cosby.[2] His last name was probably Matthews, since that was the family name Henry took as his own. There is no indication whether Henry's and Charles's father was owned by Weaver.

"Henry Amey's son" soon changed to "Henry Blacksmith" and finally, in 1846, became "Henry Matthews" in Weaver's "Negro Books."[3] Like his cousin Sam Williams, it took Henry Matthews a number of years to get his name in the records the way he wanted it to be entered. That was not all he had in common with Sam. He was exactly the same height—five feet ten inches—and his color was yellow.[4] Henry was the older of Amy's two sons. Charles was born in 1827, Henry was born two or more years before that. Charles eventually became a teamster for Weaver; he was variously listed as "Charles Amey's," "Charles Waggoner," and "Charles Cosby" in the books kept at Buffalo Forge.[5]

Henry's training as a blacksmith and forgeman occurred both at Weaver's home place and at Bath Iron Works. His overwork account indicates that he was doing skilled smithshop work at Buffalo Forge by 1839, when he was in his late teens. Weaver sent Henry up to Bath at the start of 1841, and he worked there initially as a blacksmith. Twists of chewing tobacco and "fir hats" stand out among his initial acquisitions during these early years.[6]

By the mid-1840s, however, Henry was expanding both his ironworking skills and his range of acquisitions. He served as Sol Fleming's underhand at the Bath refinery forge at various times during 1846 and worked in the smith shop there when he was not helping Sol make anchonies. In November 1846, he bought two items—a comforter and four yards of calico—that suggest he was, or was about to be, married.[7]

Henry's wife, Frances, one of Weaver's slaves, was at least five years younger than her husband. A list of Buffalo Forge slaves compiled by Daniel Brady in 1864 gives 1830 as the year she was born, 1825 as the year of Henry's birth. Henry was almost certainly born somewhat earlier than Brady indicated on this roster; a number of the birthdates he gave for the slaves were far off the mark, some by as much as nine or ten years. Brady probably recorded the birth of their first child accurately, however. According to his listing, a boy named Wash Alexander Matthews was born to Frances on July 24, 1852.[8]

By this time, Henry and his wife were back at Buffalo Forge. In 1848, he was credited with a substantial sum of overwork, $18.10, for helping Tooler at the chaffery hammer, the first indication that Henry had added the art of drawing bar iron to his already impressive range of skills.[9] His purchases of muslin, calico, silk, cassinette, canton flannel, and diaper cloth in the late 1840s and early 1850s as well as his acquisition of household items like iron skillets and a spice mortar show that he, like the other bondsmen at Buffalo Forge, was using his earning power for the benefit of his family. Two days after his son Wash was born in the summer of 1852, he bought two pounds of coffee and two pounds of sugar, and surely Frances shared in this purchase. Henry spent $4 for a barrel of flour in October of that year and, the next month, $1.80 for "Loaf sugar." His overwork credit compiled at the end of 1852 showed him receiving $10 for refining two tons of overwork anchonies (the rate at which he was paid, $5 per ton, was the pay of a master refiner), making $5.82 for drawing overwork iron with Tooler and Harry Hunt, Jr., and earning a small amount for one blacksmith job that unquestionably stirred deep and powerful emotions in him: "By making Hand Kuffs for Arch .50."[10]

The next year, 1853, was one of both loss and growing accomplishment for Henry Matthews. The loss came in the late autumn. "Charles very sick—Dr Morgan all night," forge manager James Watkins noted in the time book on November 1. Henry's brother had a severe pulmonary infection, and the doctor could do little for him. "Charles Cosby died about 8 o Clock last night—(Nov 2d)," Watkins wrote on Thursday, November 3. Charles's burial took place that same day in the slave cemetery at Buffalo Forge. Dr. Daniel Morgan duly reported the death to the clerk of the court in Lexington, but the entry in the county records was not totally accurate. According to the Register of Deaths, "Charles Crosby" of Rockbridge County, a slave belonging to William Weaver, had died of pneumonia in October 1853. He was the child of "Crosby & Amy"; Charles had been twenty-six years old at the time of his death.[11]

Henry Matthews's forge and blacksmith overwork earned him $26.78 in 1853, more than he had made in any previous year at either Buffalo Forge or Bath Iron Works. On December 24, he took $5 in cash from his account, undoubtedly to help his family mark the holidays. Yet the loss of his brother, coming less than two months before Christmas, probably robbed the season of much of the joy that usually accompanied relief from work and holiday celebrations.[12]

In subsequent years, Henry and Frances Matthews marked milestones in the family's history in the way that probably had more meaning for them than any other—the names of their children. When their second child, another son, was born on February 21, 1855, he was given the name Philip Cosby Matthews. As he had done at the time of his first child's birth, Henry once again drew on his overwork earnings: 25 cents in cash taken out on February 22 and two pounds of sugar purchased the following day. When he took his now customary $5 in cash from his account at Christmastime in 1855, he and Frances had two healthy boys, and she was expecting another child early the next year.[13]

A girl, Mary Ellen Matthews, was born in February 1856.[14] Her name clearly reflected a critical moment in the lives of so many of the black men and women at Buffalo Forge: The time when Thomas Mayburry had gained full ownership of Mary, her daughter Ellen, and her sons John and Hamilton, and had taken these four away from the rest of the family. Mary was Henry Matthews's grandmother, Ellen was his aunt. The new baby's name almost certainly was chosen to honor them.

Mary Ellen Matthews did not survive the year of her birth. She died on September 1, 1856, and when Weaver reported her loss to the county authorities, he cited worms as the cause of her death.[15] Tragically, parasitic infestations were all too common among slave children in the Old South, and Buffalo Forge was no exception.[16] The Matthews' baby would not be the last infant to die this way in the slave quarters there.

Henry Matthews spent fewer working days at the refinery or chaffery hammer as the 1850s wore on. Henry Towles had developed into a first-rate finery underhand by then, and Tooler and Harry Hunt, Jr., usually teamed up to draw iron. The blacksmith shop afforded Matthews continued opportunities for overwork, however, and he supplemented his earnings there by raising corn and hogs and selling any surplus to Weaver. And when he did take a turn at the chaffery hammer, either as the principal hammerman or as Tooler's helper, he was as capable a forgeman as he had always been, as his overwork production showed to be the case.[17]

When Daniel Brady took over as manager at the beginning of 1858, Henry was about in his middle thirties and was a first-rate blacksmith, carpenter, and forge hand. Brady would have great need of Henry Matthews's talents in the trying years that lay ahead.

6

Garland Thompson and His Family

The experience of the Thompson family was typical of that of a number of slave ironworking families at Buffalo Forge. Weaver's initial purchase of Garland Thompson, a powerfully built slave forgeman, was followed by his marriage to one of Weaver's slave women, the birth of children, and the maturing of a second generation of skilled workmen to help operate the forge, till Weaver's fields, and drive his wagons. In one significant way, however, the Thompsons' experience was quite different from that of most of the Buffalo Forge slaves. Weaver, who almost invariably held on to valuable ironworkers once he managed to acquire them, subsequently sold Garland Thompson. The story of this slave family is an intriguing one, and it is made all the more fascinating by the presence of a rich oral history among Garland Thompson's present-day descendants in the Valley.

Weaver seems to have purchased Garland in the mid-1820s. The year of his birth appears to have been around 1805, which would place him in his early twenties at the time he was acquired by Weaver. In the early 1830s

when the overwork and forge production records begin, Garland was serving as Tooler's regular partner at the chaffery forge. He was a melter, the
man who heated anchonies in the forge fire and carried the metal over to
Tooler's hammer, where they would draw the iron into merchant bars.
From 1830 until 1848, Garland was the principal chaffery underhand, regularly earning impressive amounts of credit on Weaver's books for "over
work with Tooler." And he was almost always referred to simply as "Garland" in the records. His full name seems to have been given only once;
among the slaves receiving shoes at the summer distribution in 1850 was
"Garland Thompson."[1]

Garland's wife was one of Weaver's slaves, but the documentary evidence does not reveal her name. We know she belonged to Weaver because
he owned her children, and southern law accorded the ownership of a slave
child to the master who held title to the mother. Garland Thompson and
his wife had at least six children in their years together at Buffalo Forge.
The oldest, a girl named Eliza, was born about 1826. She was followed by
Jim, born in the late 1820s; Garland, Jr., born around 1830; Matilda, born in
1832; Bill, born between 1838 and 1840; and Sam, born in the early 1840s.
In 1849 when Matilda Thompson was seventeen years old, William
Weaver gave her to nine-year-old Mary Davidson, the daughter of James
D. Davidson.[2]

Like most slave husbands and fathers at Buffalo Forge, Garland Thompson used his overwork earnings to improve his family's standard of living
and to buy gifts for them when the holidays arrived. The first page of his
account in the surviving "Negro Books" shows him buying coffee, sugar,
cotton cloth, a pitcher, and, on December 24, 1830, spending $13 on
"Goods &c for Christmas." Sometimes he bought items for himself—pantaloons, a vest, a "Fine silk hat" for $3. But more often than not, he pur-
chased things for his wife and children. In the spring of 1834, he used $6 of
his credit to buy "4 yards Cassimire, ¾ yds muslin 2 Skiens Silk." Two
years later during the spring and summer months, he bought 4 yards of
cassinette, 16 yards of calico, and "3 yds strip for Jim," his firstborn son. At
Christmastime in 1836, he purchased two pounds of sugar, a pair of pantaloons, and "leather for small shoes," and on December 21 he drew $10.60
"Cash in full" to settle his account for the year.[3]

Garland's overwork records suggest that his wife may have died sometime during the mid-1840s. His last purchases clearly intended for her were
made just before Christmas in 1844, when he bought sugar, a handkerchief,
and eight yards of calico.[4] We cannot be sure about her death; it is not
mentioned in the surviving Buffalo Forge records, and the county death
records do not go back beyond 1853. But her passing is suggested by several

things. Garland remarried in the 1850s, and divorce among slave couples was a very rare occurrence. The names eventually given the Thompson children on Weaver's books are also suggestive. The normal pattern was to begin identifying slave children through their mother's name—"Amey's Henry" or "Amey's Charles," for example—or to refer to them by place of birth, as in the case of Sam, Charles, and Washington "Etna." In the case of Garland's children, however, they were identified through their father. Jim, Bill, and Sam were all eventually given their father's first name as their family name; they became "Jim Garland," "Bill Garland," and "Sam Garland" at Buffalo Forge.[5] Garland Thompson, Jr., started out as "Little Garland," and as he grew older, became simply "Garland."[6] Their daughter Eliza married Wilson Botetourt King, the son of Louisa and one of the "Wilson negroes" who had been born at Etna Furnace in Botetourt County. She became "Eliza King" on the roster of Buffalo Forge slaves. Her maiden name did not emerge in the records until 1866, when she and her husband went in to Lexington to register their marriage. Wilson King, age forty-three, and Eliza Thompson, age forty, reported that they had been man and wife since 1850.[7]

The sudden cessation of the elder Garland Thompson's apparent purchases for his wife at the end of 1844 was followed in succeeding years by a number of special presents specifically earmarked for his children. He paid to have a coat made for Jim on December 13, 1845; his oldest son would have been in his mid-teens then. The next spring, he bought Jim a "fine Hat" for $4, and in December he spent some of his Christmas money on "trimmings for Sam." On September 20, 1847, Garland's account shows him spending $3.75 for five yards of green cloth and $1.25 for "Making Suit for Little Garland."[8] As in the case of his brother Jim a couple of years earlier, Garland Thompson, Jr., would have been in his teens at the time his father paid to have this clothing made for him. The unmistakable impression conveyed by these expenditures is that a rite of passage was taking place, that the boys were growing into men and that Garland Thompson, Sr., was marking the occasion by providing appropriate articles of clothing for them.

The tradition passed down among the descendants of Garland Thompson, Sr., is that he was an imposing figure of a man, courageous and unflinching when confronted by white authority and capable of prodigious feats of strength and workmanship. According to his great-grandson, James Thompson of Glasgow, Virginia, Garland Thompson, Sr., stood six feet six inches tall and weighed 270 pounds.[9] Unfortunately, he was not at Buffalo Forge in 1865 when Brady recorded the physical descriptions of the slave ironworkers there, but his four sons were present. Garland, Jr., at five feet eleven and a half inches, was the tallest slave on the property, and his brother Jim, at five feet eleven inches, was nearly as tall. Bill, who stood five feet seven inches, and Sam, who was five feet four inches tall, were not as large as their two older brothers. In the column marked "Color," Brady wrote "Black" after all four names.[10]

Very few people would trifle with Garland Thompson, Sr., James Thompson recalled. When the slaves were gathered for a party without the master's permission and the Rockbridge County slave patrol—the hated "paddyrollers"—showed up to disperse the illegal gathering, "people would be jumping out the windows and things trying to get away," but Garland "would just walk through the front door . . . pushing them [the paddyrollers] aside and say 'Watch out I'll slap you presently' and go ahead." Given his size and strength, no one wanted to run the risk of even trying to stop him, much less attempt to administer a whipping.[11]

The extraordinary prowess Garland Thompson, Sr., possessed as a worker has come down in the family as a woodcutting story. The slaves "had to get their quota in the stacks by Saturday—a certain number of cords," James Thompson remembers his father telling the children as they were gathered around a wood stove on chilly winter evenings. "Everybody else would go ahead and work Monday . . . up until Saturday noon," but not Garland. "He'd lay in the shack all the week until Friday morning, and then he would go out Friday morning, but at 12 o'clock Saturday, his quota was in the stacks like everybody else."[12]

A fascinating dimension to this particular story is that an even more impressive version of it has come down among the descendants of the masters at Buffalo Forge. Douglas E. Brady, a grandson of Daniel Brady's, remembered being told that one of the slaves, a man named Garland, "could complete his woodchopping task in a half day."[13] Garland's feat, impressive enough when accomplished in a day and a half, was now being done in even less time. Chopping nine cords of wood—the slaves' weekly quota—in half a day seems beyond the reach of anyone, but the accuracy of this and other tales of Garland Thompson's life as a slave is not of primary concern here. The point is the sense of pride and the image of strength, resistance, and manhood these stories convey, a tradition that was passed down to succeeding generations of his own family and that impressed white members of the Buffalo Forge community as well. As James Thompson put it, his family "never felt inferior to anyone," and that attitude began with his great-grandfather, Garland Thompson, Sr.[14]

All of Garland Thompson's children entered Weaver's work force as they came of age. Eliza, the oldest child, became a cook and assisted Louisa—one of the original "Wilson negroes"—who was in charge of the kitchen at Buffalo Forge. Jim—"Jim Garland" on Weaver's books—went to the forge. He started at the chaffery hammer in the spring of 1848 when he was in his mid to late teens. His father almost certainly played a role in his training, as did Tooler. On December 20, 1848, when his overwork was totaled up, he was credited with $5.50 for his part in helping Tooler draw iron that year. In 1849, his chaffery forge earnings jumped to $17.50.[15]

Jim used a substantial portion of his initial income the same way many of the young men at Buffalo Forge did. On March 21, 1849, he bought a "Blue Coat" for $14.82[16]; one suspects that these coats were almost a badge of honor worn by the slave forgemen there. Indeed, the blue coats purchased by Weaver's ironworkers may well have been inspired by clothing David Ross prescribed for his most skilled slave artisans. In 1813, Ross told one of his managers at the Oxford Iron Works to provide his blast furnace hands, blacksmiths, and forgemen with "a coat of blue cloth and waistcoat of scarlet flannel with sleeves," and he specifically instructed that the blue cloth used for these coats was to be "of good quality."[17] Given the presence of former Oxford slaves—men like Harry Hunt, Sr., and Billy Hunt—in Weaver's work force, the idea that an expensive "blue coat" was an article of apparel appropriate for a skilled forgeman could certainly have originated at Ross's ironworks in the early years of the nineteenth century.

The "Blue Coat" was not the only costly item Jim bought in 1849. Just before Christmas that year he paid $6 for "1 pr. casimir Pants," and he was able to make similar purchases during the 1850s as his versatility as an ironworker, and his earning power, increased. In 1850 and 1851 he took turns as an underhand at both the finery and chaffery hammers and gained sufficient levels of skill at both operations to become an ideal "swing hand": someone fully capable of substituting for men like Henry Towles, Henry Matthews, or Harry Hunt, Jr., if they were sick, injured, or absent from work for some other reason.[18]

Jim's development into a first-rate underhand in the late 1840s and early 1850s was undoubtedly a primary factor in Weaver's decision to send his father up to Bath Iron Works. Weaver was making one of his periodic efforts to get Bath Forge back into operation, and he could spare Garland once young men like Jim and Harry Hunt, Jr., were fully trained and had demonstrated their capacity for forge work. Garland's move to Bath proved to be a turning point in his life. It led to his second marriage, his eventual sale by Weaver, and, if family tradition is to be believed, a potentially explosive run-in with Weaver's manager at Bath Iron Works.

As James Thompson told the story, he did not know what his great-grandfather had done, "but he had done something wrong, so he was going to be whipped with the old big whip." The overseer, a man named "Obenchain," told Garland "to meet him down at the barn at . . . daybreak," but Garland arrived at the barn early—two o'clock in the morning—and waited for Obenchain to arrive. Garland "was in one of these rages," James Thompson said, and "the overseer saw him . . . and decided then that he'd rather not go down." Garland "stayed down there two days waiting on him to come down, . . . he was so angry he just stayed down there." Obenchain never did show up. He had no interest in trying to whip a furious man who was "six six and 270."[19]

James Thompson did not place this incident at Bath Iron Works, but Weaver's manager there between February 1849 and August 1850 was a man named George Obenchain, so it seems highly likely that Bath Forge was the locale where Garland Thompson refused to allow himself to be whipped.[20] And James Thompson added one other detail to the story that almost certainly confirms Bath as the site. Garland was finally calmed down by the only person who "could go close to him" when he was mad; that person was his wife, a "tiny 97-pound lady, . . . Great-grandmother Dicey," James Thompson said.[21]

Reconstructing the history of Garland Thompson and Dicey is not an easy process, but fragmentary evidence suggests the broad outlines of their story. Garland had worked regularly as Tooler's underhand at Buffalo Forge through the month of December 1847. After that, except for brief stints at Tooler's chaffery hammer in May 1848 and February 1849, he largely disappears from Weaver's books. His overwork account at Buffalo Forge was balanced as of January 1, 1848, and the only other entries under his name are small sums of cash—25 or 50 cents—paid out to him at Buffalo Forge between December 29, 1850, and April 7, 1851. At this point, his account ends and a new account for "Little Garland" begins.[22] Garland Thompson had been working primarily at Bath Forge, and it was almost certainly during his time there that he met Dicey.

Dicey was thirty years younger than Garland Thompson, Sr. She was born in 1835[23] and was the personal servant of Mary Dickinson of Louisa County, Virginia, the same Mary Dickinson who had testified about the ownership of Harry Hunt and his family during Weaver's suit against Jordan, Davis & Company. Ann Overton Dickinson Davis, Mary Dickinson's daughter, was the wife of William W. Davis. During the late 1840s and early 1850s, the Davises were living at Cedar Grove Mills in Rockbridge County, not far from Gibraltar Forge, the ironworks on the North River that William Davis was operating at that time. Gibraltar Forge and Bath Forge, where Garland Thompson was working, were separated by only five or six miles. When Mary Dickinson came to see her daughter in Rockbridge, her maid accompanied her. "Dicey sends her love to all of you—white & coloured," Mary Dickinson wrote Ann Davis on August 22, 1848, following a visit to the Davis home.[24] It was almost certainly on one of these visits that Dicey and Garland Thompson met. Dicey was thirteen years old in 1848, Garland forty-three.

Sometime in the early 1850s, William Weaver sold Garland to Mary Dickinson.[25] Weaver might not have been willing to part with him if he had been short of forge workers, but Weaver had closed down Bath Iron Works for good in 1852, and younger slaves like Garland's son Jim were coming along to fill the ranks at Buffalo Forge. Mrs. Dickinson undoubtedly bought Garland at Dicey's urging, and the chances are reasonably good that Dicey and Garland were married before the sale took place. Slaves often pleaded with their owners to complete transactions of this sort, particularly if a sale would unite husband and wife. And it is clear from her correspondence that Mary Dickinson was concerned for Dicey's welfare. "Dicey has been confined to bed nearly 3 weeks with Hemorage of the Bowels," she told Ann Davis in 1848. "She is much better & I hope she will soon be well."[26] In 1852, Mary Dickinson wrote her daughter that she was putting off a visit to Rockbridge County because Dicey was not well enough to travel. "Dicey's health is very precarious she is constantly with the menses so that she is much weakened & suffers much *pain at times,"* Mrs. Dickinson noted. "The doctor says it is owing to her time of life."[27] When Mary Dickinson made out her will in 1855, she instructed that "the sum of Ten dollars" be held "For the benefit of my servant woman Dicey."[28]

Garland's sale to Mary Dickinson meant that his skills as an ironworker would hereafter be employed at Gibraltar Forge. He worked there as a hireling in both 1854 and 1855, and Mary Dickinson received $100 each year for his services.[29] He apparently impressed William Davis and his oldest son, James Cole Davis, who managed the forge and did much of the hiring for Gilbraltar during the middle and late 1850s. On January 5, 1856, Cole Davis wrote his father from the Dickinson home in Louisa County that he had again hired "Grandmama's . . . Garland." The price was $75, and Cole added that "The old Lady put him at that this year but would not knock off a single cent for last year."[30] Apparently Garland had missed considerable work time the previous year, perhaps because of trips to Louisa County to visit Dicey, and Mrs. Dickinson agreed to reduce his hire for 1856 but would make no reduction on the previous year's bond. A document containing the names of all the hired slave hands at Gibraltar Forge drawn up in February 1856 lists Garland as a "melter" and indicates that his annual hire was $75.[31] As the year drew to a close and Christmas approached, Mrs. Dickinson sent word to the Davises that she wanted Garland sent down to Louisa County for the holidays.[32]

As long as Mary Dickinson was in good health, Garland and Dicey Thompson had an owner who seems to have been genuinely interested in them and who would see that their marriage was protected. But Mary Dickinson's health was growing increasingly precarious as the decade of the 1850s advanced, and in late 1857 and early 1858, a crisis came. "I know by this time you have heard of the death of our own Dear good Mother," Ann Dickinson Davis wrote her husband on February 4, 1858. She was at "Seclusion," the Dickinson family homestead in Louisa County, where she had gone to be with her mother during her final illness. Dicey was there as well, and her services had been much needed during this sad and critical time. Mary Dickinson's last days, and nights, had not been easy ones. "My mother has not slept in her bead [*sic*] half of any one night since I have been down," Ann wrote, "she has not been well at all she sat up in her big Chair all day I could not persuaide her to lye dow[n] in day light Dicy & myself sleept in her room when we slept at all. we would all waise [*sic*] help her up to get in her Chair which was often through the night I could see that she was waisting away very fast." Ann closed this portion of the letter by saying how grateful she was that she had been there at the end. "I fccl glad that I did not divide my time much with any one," she said.[33]

Ann Davis then turned to other, more practical matters. "Brother Roscoe wishes the estate to be settle[d] up before he leaves & he is compelled to leave soon," she informed her husband. Her mother had made no provision in her will for the distribution of her slaves among various family members and had even instructed that no inventory be taken of her estate.[34] The heirs would share equally in her property settlement. "All of the persons who have any interest in it at all thinks that the servants will have to be sold at publick sale . . . and when this is done traders will have a chance to buy as much as any." She would write "as soon as I can hear when you must come down & you will have to bring Garland with you," she added.[35] Mary Dickinson seems to have served Garland and Dicey reasonably well while she was alive; Mary Dickinson in death was quite another matter.

The loss of their mistress brought Garland and Dicey Thompson to the moment all slave couples feared most. Their fate was almost totally beyond their control. Escape—particularly the joint escape of a slave husband and wife—was virtually impossible, and capture would result in almost certain sale. The only weapons at their disposal were their pleas and whatever sympathy they could elicit in Ann and, to an even greater extent, her husband. If Mary Dickinson's slaves mounted the auction block, William Davis would be the one to decide whom they would buy.

There is no way to know if the views of the son were the views of the father, but James Cole Davis revealed an attitude toward several individual slaves that was nothing less than chilling. Aside from William Weaver's reported reference to a "breeding woman" during the 1830s, there is nothing in his voluminous correspondence that is even remotely comparable to some of the things Cole Davis wrote his father in the 1850s. "Do pray let Old Fannie go for 500$," he told William Davis in December 1854. "I would rather let her go for nothing than keep her on the place to spoil the younger negroes: and I (and I suppose you too) am tired of drinking mean coffee & hearing so much talk about it. She is not the only settled woman in the State." He went on to say that Daniel and Louisa, two of Mary Dickinson's obviously less favored slaves who had worked at the Davis house the previous year, would be coming back to Rockbridge County to work during 1855 even though they did not want to return. "Grandmama says that if Daniel and Louisa dont go back she is determined to sell them: so you may look for them back: then we will salt Daniel up *for pork:* have ready the salt & cutting instruments. We need pork anyhow."[36] A youthful attempt at humor perhaps, but Cole Davis was twenty-one years old in 1854. If his father considered this passage funny, however, Garland and Dicey Thompson could expect little sympathy from William Davis.

The slave woman Louisa did not end up back at the Davis home that year. She was hired out in Richmond without Daniel during 1855, and her experience there prompted young Davis to offer additional commentary on this couple's situation. "Old Louisa . . . gave birth to a boy the other night. Mirabile dictu! Will wonders ever cease. So much for her being hired in Richmond. All things for the best. She is now worth $300 more than any one thought her a year ago," he wrote his father on January 7, 1856. If it were up to him, Cole Davis added, "I should advocate her being hired in R. again. Either this or her separation from Old *Eunuch* Daniel."[37] Two days earlier, difficulties he had encountered when he attempted to rehire a slave for Gibraltar Forge led him to pass a somewhat more philosophical thought on to his father. "This negroes perversity is but another instance of the assimilation of the negro to the dog," he commented. "In order to make a dog like and follow you, you must whip him occasionally & be sparing of favors, or he will turn at last & bite the hand that feeds him."[38]

We do not know if William Davis shared his son's remarkably callous and insensitive attitudes, but Garland and Dicey Thompson had several qualities that would have prompted W. W. Davis to view their acquisition as an attractive proposition. Garland was a forgeman, Davis needed forge workers, and Garland's age—he was fifty-three years old in 1858—meant that his price would be relatively low. And the fact that he had been hired for several consecutive years prior to Mary Dickinson's death indicated that Davis was satisfied with his performance at the Gilbraltar chaffery fire.

Dicey was a trusted and experienced house servant, but her chief claim to William Davis's sympathy and resources probably came through his wife, Ann. Dicey had helped Ann Davis nurse her mother until the very end, had slept in Ann's mother's sickroom and had been there with Ann as Mary Dickinson's final illness turned into a death watch. Ann was willing to plead with her husband, beg might not be too strong a word, in order to save those slaves about whom she felt strongly. Dicey and any of her family were clearly among those slaves.

Ann Davis made her point forcefully in the letter to her husband telling him of her mother's death. She had earlier helped raise nine slave children from her father's estate, and she named them all in case her husband needed reminding: Jenny, Nelson, Emily, Frankey, Kate, Edgar, Albert, Allen ("the boy who was killed by the horse"), and "poor Margarette who was small when we got her." Ann used this experience and the time and effort she had devoted to those children to argue that her wishes should count for something when it came to the disposition of all the Dickinson slaves:

> I nursed them when sick I saw that there [sic] Clothes were washed and I pached [patched] for them with my own hands yes I have pached for Jenny just before I left to keep her from suffering .... I had to act as a Mother even in giving them a piece of bread when hungry yes many & many a time I have given Nelson something to eate [sic] when I gave my own. Children must be attended to white or black and now I want to ask you why *I did it all* Did you not tell me from your own lips that they were for our *Children* ... did I not nurse Edgar with the fever when very low too low to be raised from the bead [sic] to the pot .... Yes Dear William I done it for my Children[39]

Garland and Dicey came to William and Ann Davis when the Dickinson slave force was broken up. Whether or not these slaves were auctioned off is unclear. Mary Dickinson's stipulation that no inventory be made of her estate prevented the slaves from being appraised and a record posted of their disposition in the Louisa County will books, as had been done in the case of Thomas Mayburry's slaves. But the census of 1860 showed a male slave, age fifty-five, black in color, a female slave, age twenty-six, also black, and seven slave children, all black, ranging in age from nine months to eleven years among the eighteen slaves owned by William W. Davis of Rockbridge County, Virginia.[40] Daniel Brady noted in the diary he kept at Buffalo Forge that on Saturday, May 17, 1862, "Sam & Bill Garland went to W. W. Davis'," and in the margin beside this entry Brady wrote "Sam & Bill

Garland to their fathers."[41] In February 1864, Ann Davis was visiting in Louisa County, and she wrote her husband to "ask Garland to put manure around our tree."[42]

The manuscript census of 1870 reported that Garland Thompson (listed as "John G. Thompson"), his wife Dicey, and two sons, Frank, age twelve, and Samuel, age seven, were living in the Walkers Creek Township district of Rockbridge County, the area in which both Gibraltar Forge and Cedar Grove Mills were located.[43]

Three of Garland Thompson's children who remained at Buffalo Forge began raising families of their own during the 1850s. Eliza and Wilson King's first child, a boy named Charles B. King, was born in 1851, and another boy, James, most likely named for his uncle, Jim Thompson, was born two years later. Eliza gave birth to her first daughter, Isabella, in November 1856.[44] Wilson King was Weaver's personal servant and carriage driver, and he made frequent trips to Lexington with and without his master. He also worked as an occasional farm hand and woodchopper at Buffalo Forge and earned considerable amounts of overwork credit raising hogs and selling both pork and corn to Weaver in the middle years of the 1850s. His use of overwork earnings—cash withdrawals at various times during the year and at Christmas and the purchase of flour—followed the pattern of many of the Buffalo Forge slaves.[45]

James Thompson—"Jim Garland" on Weaver's books—married when he was in his early twenties. His overwork account suggests a spring wedding in 1851: $5 spent on "4 yards casinet" and "trimmings & making coat" on April 12.[46] His wife, Betsy, was not one of Weaver's slaves, but she appears to have lived close by; she was five years younger than Jim. Their first children were both girls: Rachael, born in 1851, and Alice, born two years later.[47] In addition to his role as principal substitute for the regular forge workers, Jim was a first-class woodcutter and field hand. His combination of skills was reflected in his overwork credit for 1856: a total of $37.21 earned for "Over Iron Refinery," "Over Iron Chaffery," 8½ bushels of corn sold to Weaver, and twenty extra cords of wood.[48]

Garland Thompson, Jr., did not follow his father and his older brother into the forge. He became one of Weaver's teamsters and regularly traveled the road to the coaling grounds in the mountains east of Buffalo Forge.[49] His marriage to Ester Boldock, a slave woman who belonged to one of Weaver's neighbors, came in 1852 or 1853 when Garland was in his early to mid-twenties; Ester was three or four years younger than her husband. When Garland and Ester Thompson registered their marriage in 1866, they reported that they had been man and wife since 1852.[50]

A document preserved in Weaver's papers suggests that they may have been married a bit later than that. "My Boy Garland is smitten by one of your Lasses, and nothing will content him but matrimony," Weaver wrote Alfred Douglass, whose farm lay close to Buffalo Forge; "he has my consent, if it meets your approbation."[51] This brief letter, dated October 7, 1853, contains an element of amused condescension on Weaver's part that Garland undoubtedly would not have appreciated. He was seeking the master's permission to marry, and an all-important phase of his life hung on Weaver's words. According to their grandson James Thompson, Garland and Ester had thirteen children during the course of a marriage that lasted almost forty years.[52] Their first three—John, born in 1853; Ruben, born two years later; and Adeline, born two years after that—came into the world prior to the Bradys' arrival at Buffalo Forge at the end of 1857.[53]

William and Samuel Thompson, the elder Garland Thompson's two youngest sons at Buffalo Forge, also became teamsters when they were old enough to enter Weaver's regular work force in the late 1850s. And, like almost all of the Buffalo Forge slaves, "Bill Garland" and "Sam Garland," as they were listed on Weaver's books, did field work when agricultural tasks were pressing.[54] Their appraised monetary worth in 1865—$6,250 for Bill and $6,000 for Sam—indicates that Daniel Brady considered them among his more valuable hands, in the same league with Henry Matthews, who was valued at $6,500 at that time. Garland Thompson, Jr., Brady's best teamster, he estimated to be worth $7,000.[55]

According to his grandson James, Garland Thompson, Jr., followed the biblical example of Sampson and would not let a razor touch his face.[56] A photograph of Garland and Ester Thompson and their family taken after the Civil War shows a man and woman seated next to each other surrounded by their children and grandchildren. Garland's beard is a full one, and he is dressed in a coat, trousers, and leather shoes. Ester's full-length dark dress has a bow at the neck, and she is wearing a white kerchief around her hair. One of her hands is folded in her lap, the other rests on the head of a little girl seated at her feet. Garland's right arm encircles the waist of a young boy, and his left hand touches the shoulder of a small girl standing just in front of him. A two-story log cabin with a stone chimney and a shingled roof forms a backdrop to this family portrait. Garland and Ester are looking straight into the camera. His eyes are deep-set, his features sharply chiseled. Her face is rounder, her complexion slightly lighter than his. But the look in both their faces is the same, one that conveys a clear and unmistakable impression of dignity and pride.

Photographs

Portrait of William Weaver by an unknown artist.
Courtesy of D. E. Brady, Jr., photo by Thomas C. Bradshaw, II.

William Weaver in 1860. This ambrotype shows Weaver at the age of seventy-nine and was taken by an itinerant photographer named D. H. Placker. Daniel Brady wrote in his "Home Journal" on November 12, 1860, "Placker left after breakfast, having charged a damed heavy bill for his pictures." A notation on the rear of the case holding these pictures reads "D. H. Placker $3.50."
Courtesy D. E. Brady, Jr.

Another ambrotype of William Weaver taken by Placker on his trip through Rockbridge County in the fall of 1860.
Courtesy D. E. Brady, Jr.

A view of Buffalo Forge in 1860. This ambrotype was also taken by
D. H. Placker in November of that year. Weaver's house dominates
the left background; the flour mill is the multi-story structure in the
left center. Weaver's office is located just to the right of center, and
the handrail which Weaver had erected in 1856 is clearly visible
along the walk leading to the office. This railing continues on to the
harness shop, the small two-story structure just down the hill from
Weaver's office. A stable, clearly identifiable from the piles of
manure near the back wall, is in the right foreground. The
whitewashed building between the harness shop and the stable is
the Buffalo Forge store.
Courtesy D. E. Brady, Jr.

A view of the Buffalo Forge property from across Buffalo Creek. This ambrotype probably dates from the Civil War era. A log slave cabin with a stone chimney can be seen in the right foreground. The roof of Saunder's Store is visible to the right of this cabin. Smoke is rising from the chimney of the guest cottage, which is located to the right of Weaver's residence. The forge building was not caught in this picture, or in any of the other nineteenth-century photographs of the property. It was located to the right of this view, on the same side of Buffalo Creek as Weaver's house.

Courtesy D. E. Brady, Jr.

Daniel C. E. Brady.
Courtesy D. E. Brady, Jr.

Emma Gorgas Brady.
Courtesy D. E. Brady, Jr.

Emma Brady (far left) and her mother (far right) and sisters.
Courtesy D. E. Brady, Jr.

Garland Thompson, Jr., his wife, Ester, and their children and
grandchildren. This photograph was taken after the Civil War and shows the
family posing in front of their home. According to James Thompson,
this house was located at the ore bank near Glasgow in Rockbridge County, Virginia.
Courtesy D. E. Brady, Jr.

James Thompson, the
grandson of Garland
Thompson, Jr., and
the great-grandson of
Garland Thompson.
*Courtesy South Carolina
Educational Television.*

A log slave cabin at Buffalo Forge
as it appeared in the 1930s.
Courtesy D. E. Brady, Jr.
photo by William D. Hoyt.

The brick slave cabins at Buffalo Forge built in 1858.
Courtesy South Carolina Educational Television.

Another view of the brick slave cabins. The chimneys of Weaver's residence
are visible beyond the roof of the single cabin. The Blue Ridge Mountains
are in the background.

A close-up view of the double cabin.

An interior view of
one of the brick cabins.
*Courtesy South Carolina
Educational Television.*

The spring house
at Buffalo Forge.

Ruins of the flour mill
at Buffalo Forge.
Weaver's residence can
be seen up the hill.
*Courtesy South Carolina
Educational Television.*

Weaver's house at Buffalo Forge as it appears today.
Courtesy South Carolina Educational Television.

Weaver's library at Buffalo Forge.
Courtesy South Carolina Educational Television.

Gravestones of William
and Eliza Weaver in
the cemetery at
Falling Spring Church.
*Courtesy South Carolina
Educational Television.*

View of the Blue Ridge
Mountains from the site
of the slave cemetery
at Buffalo Forge.

Limestone grave marker at the slave cemetery at Buffalo Forge.
Courtesy South Carolina Educational Television.

Gravestones in the freedmen's cemetery at the site of the Mount Lydia Colored Baptist Church.
Courtesy South Carolina Educational Television.

Close-up view of one
of the gravestones at
the Mount Lydia cemetery
*Courtesy South Carolina
Educational Television.*

Another view of one of
the gravestones at Mount Lydia.

Ruins of Etna Furnace. The author is standing in
what was once the interior of this stack.
Courtesy South Carolina Educational Television.

PART III

BUFFALO FORGE

1

The Late
Antebellum Years

In the spring of 1858, James David-
son informed Weaver that yet another Valley ironmaster had gone under.
B. J. Jordan & Company, the owners of an extensive furnace and forge
enterprise in Alleghany County just west of Rockbridge, were bankrupt
and their entire property was scheduled to go under the auctioneer's hammer. "The news of B. Jordans failure does not disappoint me," Weaver
replied; "he has always been to[o] reckless in business." Weaver was, however, surprised by the extent of this firm's indebtedness—"90,000 D is a
heavy Burthen to travel under," he remarked. "There has been no money
made at Furnaces the last three years, and time I fear will make more
developments—among the Iron Men," Weaver went on to say. "I fear
there is to be great distress for money in this country for some time [to
co]me." Weaver had heard a rumor that William Alexander, the operator
of another large Alleghany County ironworks, was also about to fail. "If so
the Iron gentlemen are retiring rapidly," he told Davidson. "There is only
two ways of getting out of the business Dieing out or [c]ashing out. The
latter is the customary plan."[1]

With ironmasters "cashing out" all around him during the late antebellum years, Weaver plowed ahead as if no such developments had ever occurred. From his actions, one would never guess that "no money" had been made at blast furnaces in the Valley "the last three years."

As 1858 began, his chief worry had been hiring enough slave workers to keep Etna in full production during the forthcoming year. Davidson had dropped Weaver a note back on January 6 to tell him that masters in Spotsylvania County were holding out for high prices for their slaves and that "I fear they will be higher than was expected—and if you have limited the boys to $100—you may not get a supply."[2] Weaver wrote back the next day to assure Davidson that he had given "The Boys"—Charley Gorgas and Will Rex—"instructions to hire—at high prices if they could not succeed at low prices."[3] And the boys did very well indeed, hiring sixty-four slaves, all but a handful of whom were headed for Etna Furnace.[4]

Despite Weaver's forebodings over "distress for money" as the economic downturn of the second half of 1857 extended into the new year, life at Buffalo Forge reached a remarkable level of stability in 1858. The Bradys were all in residence by early March, so Weaver's line of succession was clearly established. Charley Gorgas's able management of Etna Furnace meant that Weaver would not have to worry about his forgemen exhausting their supply of pig, and there was always the chance that manufacturers in Richmond and Lynchburg would turn to Etna metal when they needed high-quality charcoal iron for foundry or rolling-mill use.

Weaver's forge crew of Sam Williams and Henry Towles at the finery and Tooler and Harry Hunt, Jr., at the chaffery hammer produced an iron of superior quality that was holding its own in local markets in the Valley and over the Blue Ridge Mountains in Lynchburg despite stiff competition from northern and imported bar iron. Weaver's forgemen could usually fill orders on reasonable notice for assorted types of hammered iron—scalloped, shovel, hoe, horseshoe, wagon tire—that never seemed to want for customers. The market might be slack, but there was always some sort of demand for the iron that came out of Buffalo Forge, bar that one Botetourt County commission merchant described as "the *very best* Iron made," and even when sales were slow, Weaver kept his forge in production.[5] There were too many stoppages for things like repairs and low water in the normal course of forge business. He held his price at $90 per ton for iron delivered in Lynchburg, stockpiled what he could not sell, and waited for the inevitable upturn. In the meantime, he "made supplies," as he liked to say.

During the late antebellum years, the seasonal cycles of planting, cultivation, harvest, and planting once again moved across the landscape at

Buffalo Forge with all the inevitability of nature itself. Clover and oats were generally sown in early March, the first crops to be planted. Spring plowing began in earnest that same month, and when the corn was due to go in, even some of the forgemen shifted over to agricultural tasks. Tooler and Harry Hunt, Jr., joined the plowmen during the last week of March and the first week of April 1858 when Brady had as many as ten plow gangs turning the soil in the fields surrounding the forge. Plaster was sown over the cornfields prior to planting, and when the seeds went into the ground, ashes and plaster were dropped into each hole to fertilize the crop. Two fourteen-year-old girls assisted with this planting in 1858: Lydia, the daughter of Sam and Nancy Williams, and Amy, the daughter of Warder and Frances Banks, joined the field hands on Wednesday, April 14, as Brady made an all-out push to get the corn crop in while the ground was moist from earlier rains but still dry enough for the work of planting to proceed.[6]

Once Weaver's cornfields were finished, the plow gangs moved on to the "boys lots," as Brady called them, those areas set aside for the slaves to cultivate their own crops. These fields were plowed on Thursday, Friday, and Saturday afternoon, April 15–17, and a week later, Brady noted in his journal that the "Boys planted their lots in P.M." The corn crop was now all in, and the field hands could turn to other tasks—planting potatoes, making rails and erecting fences, and building new roads in the nearby coaling grounds, a job that occupied a full week of their time in late April and early May. While this work was proceeding, two of Weaver's teamsters, Warder Banks and Charles Towles, were hauling bricks for the two new slave quarters, a single and a double cabin, that were slated to go up just to the rear of the kitchen that stood alongside Weaver's residence.[7]

The month of May brought a new cycle of field work. Small crops of sorghum and millet were planted, but the big job was working the massive corn crop that Weaver relied upon to feed his slave force at both Buffalo Forge and Etna Furnace. The cornfields had to be cultivated continually, and Brady usually had ten hands at this job, sometimes supplemented by Lydia Williams, Amy Banks, and an occasional forgeman. When Sam Williams was "laid up with sore arm" for a day, on Monday, May 24, Henry Towles was one of thirteen slaves—eleven men and the two girls—who were "working corn in the big field." A week later, on May 31, Garland Thompson took his mule team and wagon up into the mountains across North River on the first of what would be almost daily trips to the coaling grounds. "Garland brought a load of coal" was a phrase Daniel Brady repeated over and over again as he recorded the work regime of the Buffalo Forge slaves.[8]

June was a time to thin and continue working the corn crop, to mow and
rake the hay fields, and to begin harvesting the rye planted the previous
fall. Brady sent Tooler and Harry Hunt, Jr., out to join the field hands on
Wednesday, June 16. It would be six weeks—the completion of the wheat
harvest—before they would return to their chaffery forge. Sam Williams
and Henry Towles remained at the finery, as they would throughout most
of that year. Not until the late fall and early winter, when the time for
slaughtering cattle and hogs arrived, would Sam and Henry leave their
normal posts.[9]

Occasionally the Valley would be swept by a violent summer storm,
leaving in its destructive wake added labor for Weaver's slaves. A thunder-
storm accompanied by torrential rains began at 2:30 in the afternoon on
Thursday, June 24, 1858, Brady noted in his diary. "The creek rose fear-
fully & by 4½ PM the water was running 5 feet over the bridge" spanning
Buffalo Creek. "All the branches were swollen more than known for 25
years," he went on. "The water washed away a great many of our fences.
Washed down wheat oats & rye, & done considerable damage." The storm
halted all field work but created extra tasks for the next day. "All hands
working at bridge & road," Brady wrote on Friday, June 25. "The road is
washed from both ends of the bridge. The river too high for Garland to
ford." Saturday was clear and warm, and the slaves returned to the fields
to cradle rye and make hay. By the end of the month, both crops were
harvested and the work force turned to Weaver's substantial fields of wheat
and oats.[10]

Slaves had sown the wheat crop the previous autumn at a farm across
Buffalo Creek known as Turkey Foot. Oats had been planted at the same
site back in March. On July 1, 1858, Brady had a gang of fourteen slaves—
six men cradling wheat, eight gathering and hauling—at Turkey Foot, plus
one of Weaver's slave women, Martha, cooking for them so that they could
remain in the fields all day. Four days later, he divided this force and
started on the oats as well. All the wheat was cut by noon the next day, July
6, and all hands turned to the oat crop. Eight cradles swung as Weaver's
men moved through the field the remainder of that day and for several days
thereafter. Constant Towles, a blacksmith, and Joe, the forge carpenter,
spent Friday, July 9, in the blacksmith shop fixing Weaver's threshing
machine, which would be hauled to the fields early the next week. It took
almost two weeks to thresh Weaver's sizable crops of wheat, oats, and rye.
The wheat crop alone—some 2,500 bushels annually—produced enough
grain to make approximately 500 barrels of flour in the merchant mill at
Buffalo Forge.[11]

Little rain fell at Buffalo Forge in late July and early August, and the

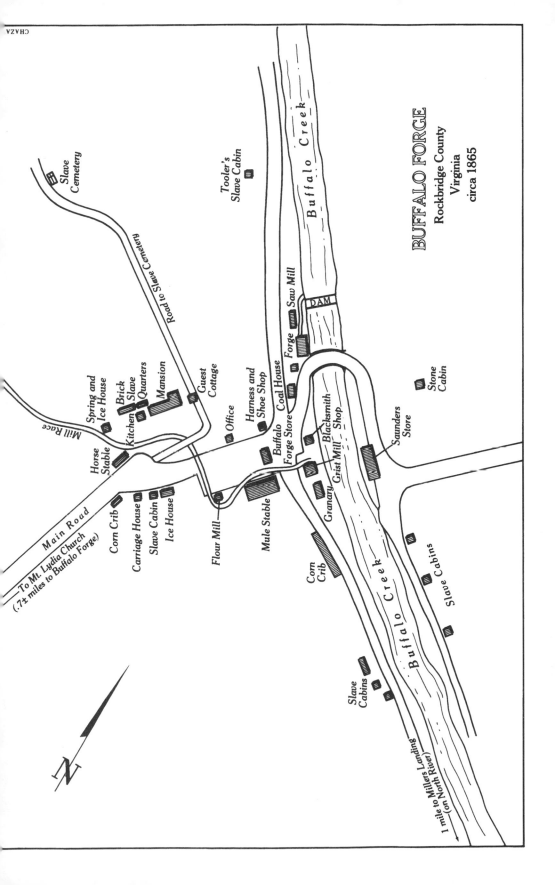

BUFFALO FORGE

Rockbridge County
Virginia
circa 1865

Slave Cemetery

Road to Slave Cemetery

Tooler's Slave Cabin

Buffalo Creek

Mill Race

Spring and Ice House

Brick Slave Quarters

Kitchen

Mansion

Guest Cottage

Harness and Shoe Shop

Office

Buffalo Forge Store

Coal House

Forge

Saw Mill

DAM

Stone Cabin

Horse Stable

Main Road

To Mt. Lydia Church
(.7± miles to Buffalo Forge)

Corn Crib

Carriage House

Slave Cabin

Ice House

Flour Mill

Mule Stable

Blacksmith Shop

Granary

Grist Mill

Saunders Store

Corn Crib

Slave Cabins

Buffalo Creek

Slave Cabins

N

1 mile to Miller's Landing
(on North River)

succession of clear, warm days made the ground too dry to plow but facili-
tated another task the forgemen undoubtedly took no pleasure in performing. On Saturday, July 31, Brady noted that Sam Williams, Henry Towles,
Tooler, Harry Hunt, Jr., and four other slaves were cleaning out the mud
that had built up behind the forge dam. Once this job was finished and some
minor repairs were completed, work resumed at both the finery and the
chaffery in early August.[12]

Low water—a frequent problem during the summer months—often
meant that the refinery and chaffery forges would have to operate alter-
nately; there simply was not enough power to drive both forges at the same
time. Such was the case on Monday, August 9, 1858. "Sam Williams had to
stop on account of water," Brady wrote. "In the P.M. he fell into the water,
& hurt himself very much." Brady failed to record the exact nature of Sam's
injury, but a week later he noted "Sam Williams arm not well." Jim Garland came in to work with Henry Towles while Sam recuperated, but
Sam's recovery was slow. By Tuesday, August 17, he was well enough to
joint shingles, and he assisted with some major forge repairs at the end of
that week and the beginning of the next. On Wednesday, August 25, he was
back at his refinery hammer with Henry Towles, and no doubt Weaver and
Brady were greatly relieved.[13] The iron market in Lynchburg was recovering nicely in the second half of 1858, and Buffalo Forge could ill-afford to
lose its most valuable slave artisan.

During the late spring and throughout most of the summer—from May
26 until August 13, 1858—a period of intense agricultural work at Buffalo
Forge, not a pound of hammered iron had been sent off to Lynchburg. The
dispatch of three tons of bar in mid-August to Weaver's commission merchants there inaugurated a period of renewed iron production intended to
earn some much-needed cash.[14] A sizable bill for Negro hire—over
$8,000—would fall due at the end of the year, and Weaver and Brady could
use every dollar their forgemen could bring in.[15]

"Both hammers going at forge" became a monotonous entry in Brady's
journal during the early fall. Brady could not have been pleased when
Tooler laid up with a "sick head ache" on Monday, September 13, but he
was back at work the following day, so little production was lost. Much
more serious was a hand injury Tooler suffered on Tuesday, September 21,
as he and Harry Hunt, Jr., were installing a new helve at the chaffery
hammer. Tooler's "lame hand" kept him off the job for almost two weeks.
Brady shifted Henry Matthews over from the blacksmith shop to the forge,
and he and Harry Hunt drew iron until Tooler returned to work on Monday, October 4.[16]

The leverage Weaver's skilled forge hands possessed was clearly reflected in the drop-off in production that occurred while Tooler was recovering. During a four-and-a-half-day period in late August and early September, he and Harry Hunt had drawn 5,707 pounds of bar, easily making their task of two journeys of 560 pounds of bar per day. During four days in late September and early October when Harry Hunt and Henry Matthews were manning the chaffery forge, production reached only 3,195 pounds, well short of their combined task of 4,480 pounds for this four-day period.[17] The lesson contained in these production figures could not have been lost on Daniel Brady. If Tooler missed a day now and then with a "sick head ache," so be it. That was a price masters had little choice but to pay when they relied on skilled slave workers to operate their industrial establishments. This lesson surely was not lost on Tooler, either.

Tooler's return to work was followed by an immediate jump in hammered iron production. His first week back on the job, October 4–9, saw 5,261 pounds of iron drawn at the chaffery forge. The next week, October 11–16—a five-day workweek because of the loss of one day for repairs— Tooler and Harry pounded out 6,193 pounds of iron: ten journeys plus close to 600 pounds of overwork. The following Monday, October 18, Tooler told Brady he was sick and took the day off.[18]

The day lost for chaffery repairs the week of October 11 had been Friday, October 15. Both the chaffery and refinery hammer helves had broken on Friday and for the same reason. A "white frost," as Brady described it, had fallen overnight, and neither forge had been adequately thawed before work had begun. New helves would have to be installed, and while these repairs were going on, Henry Towles hurt his hand. The injury was not as serious as the one Tooler had suffered the previous month, but it was bad enough to keep him off the job all the next week. Jim Garland came in from the fields—the corn harvest was well under way at this time—to work with Sam at the finery, but on Wednesday, October 20, Sam reported that he was ill. "Sam and Henry on sick list still," Brady recorded at week's end. Both men returned to work on Monday, October 25.[19]

For the field hands, the late summer and early fall had been a period of almost constant labor. Rebuilding the fences destroyed by the June 24 storm continued well into August, and during the last two weeks of that month, the slaves cut the large clover crop planted back in March and threshed enough clover to provide seed for the next year's planting. A gang—including Lydia Williams and Amy Banks—went through the corn-fields regularly in late August and early September topping the plants while plow gangs prepared other fields for their crops of rye and winter wheat, both of which would be sown from mid-September until mid-October. In the middle of September, the corn harvest also began. For the next month and a half, slave crews would move through the fields harvesting the corn as it ripened, and slave teamsters would haul load after load of this crop to Weaver's barns, cribs, and grist mill. On Monday, September 20, a clear, warm day in the Valley, Nancy Williams and three slave girls went over to Highland Farm and spent the day picking apples. Forty cattle that had been fattening at Highland were driven across North River to Buffalo Forge on October 12, and two days later, a white drover set out for the Richmond market with a herd of fifty head: Weaver's forty, nine owned by the drover, and one steer belonging to Wilson Botetourt King. By mid-October, so much corn had been brought in that it was necessary to extend the slave's workday beyond the normal hours of dawn to dusk. "Shucked at night," Brady recorded on Thursday and Friday, October 14 and 15, and for most of the next two weeks, "All hands" were "shucking in evening," he noted.[20]

November was a time for chopping wood for the winter fast approaching, for hauling firewood and kindling to Weaver's residence and the slave cabins scattered around Buffalo Forge, for making rails and building fences, for fattening hogs for the December kill, and for an occasional extra day of rest. It rained hard all day on Tuesday, November 2, and it was, in Brady's opinion, "Too wet for any out door work." As a consequence, all the field hands were "idle except for a few minutes work." "Snow on the mountains for the first time," Brady wrote on Monday, November 8, and a three-hour snowfall at Buffalo Forge the afternoon of Saturday, November 27, sent all hands indoors where they spent the remainder of the workday grinding axes. The last corn planted the previous spring, that belonging to the slaves, was brought in during November, and on Saturday, November 13, Brady noted that "Sam, Henry, & Wilson killed their hogs."[21]

The weather had little impact on the forge regimen, however. Work went on there day in and day out unless repairs were needed. When Harry Hunt, Jr., became ill on Friday, November 12, Jim Garland took over as Tooler's underhand and spent a week at the chaffery forge. Harry returned to work on Wednesday, November 17, but he went to the finery to serve as Henry Towles's helper. Sam Williams was busy cleaning out meat casks that day prior to the slaughter of ten cattle Brady had driven over from Highland Farm at the beginning of the week. Sam and Henry Matthews spent Thursday, Friday, and Saturday, November 18–20, cutting up meat that would help feed the slaves at Buffalo Forge and Etna Furnace in the coming months.[22]

Early December brought a time of great sadness to the Brady family. "Emma sick. Dr. Morgan all night," Daniel Brady wrote on Friday, December 3. Emma was pregnant, and she and her husband had been looking forward to the arrival of the first of their children to be born at Buffalo Forge. Thomas Forest Brady, born December 3, 1858, died December 3, 1858, according to an entry in the family recordbook.[23]

Emma's loss of her child stood in marked contrast to the experience of two slave women who gave birth at Buffalo Forge that same year. Betty Coleman, Sam and Nancy Williams' oldest daughter, had her first child, Alfred Elliott Coleman, back on February 18; he was Sam and Nancy Williams' first grandchild. On October 6, 1858, Eliza Thompson King had given birth to her fourth child, a girl, and according to the register of slave births later compiled by Brady, the baby's name was Anne Gertrude King. Anne Gertrude Brady, Daniel and Emma's daughter, was ten years old in 1858 and was often called Nan or Nanny. When Wilson and Eliza King registered their marriage in 1866, they gave "Nanny" as the name of their daughter who had been born in the fall of 1858.[24]

December was traditionally the time for the annual slaughter of hogs at Buffalo Forge, and 1858 was no exception. With Sam Williams once again in charge of the butchering operation, hog killing began on the morning of Thursday, December 9. The temperature was twenty-one degrees at 7 A.M., and by three o'clock that afternoon, forty-three hogs had been slaughtered. The next day the weather was also just what it should be, clear and quite cold—seventeen degrees on that Friday morning. By the end of a full day's work on Saturday, December 11, Sam and his crew had completed the job of cutting up all the pork.[25]

The week that hog killing took place, Tooler and Harry Hunt, Jr., put in their best six days of the year at the chaffery forge. They drew eleven journeys (one journey had long been an acceptable task on Saturdays) totaling 10,095 pounds; this produced 3,375 pounds of "over iron," and it was probably no coincidence that this output came shortly before Christmas. When the forge's total production for the year was added up just before the holidays, it came to just over 77 tons, certainly an acceptable figure from Weaver's point of view given the weakness of the market for hammered iron during the early months of 1858. Chaffery overwork totaled 19,795 pounds, just short of nine tons, most of which was credited to Tooler and Harry Hunt, Jr. Brady made no deductions for those days, generally Mondays, when Tooler was out because of a "sick head ache" or for some other cause. Sales of bar iron to various commission merchants in Lynchburg and the Valley between August 13 and December 15 had brought in close to $2,000 in cash and negotiable paper. Total sales of bar iron in 1858 amounted to well over $6,000.[26]

Sam Williams was probably back in the forge following the completion of his hog-butchering duties, but Brady did not make his usual journal entry entry on Monday, December 13. He only noted that he was off to Lynchburg on a business trip that would keep him away from home until the end of the week.[27]

Brady's final description of a workday at Buffalo Forge in 1858 came on the Saturday just after he returned from Lynchburg. "Clear & pleasant," he wrote on December 18, "All hands making fence & hauling wood." He also noted that he had taken sixty head of cattle over to Highland Farm that day; these steers were part of a herd of 113 purchased from a drover for $2,000 back in October to replace the cattle sold in Richmond that fall. The next day, Sunday, Charley Gorgas came up from Etna Furnace, and on Monday morning, December 20, he and Brady set out for Spotsylvania County on the usual year-end mission: hiring slaves for the coming year for Etna Furnace.[28]

Etna pig iron sales had been disappointing for much of 1858. Gorgas had gone down to Richmond in October, and, after calling on the proprietors of the Tredegar Iron Works and a number of other potential customers in the city, reported back to Weaver that "the iron market looks gloomy."[29] Before the year was out, however, a major purchaser for Etna metal surfaced closer to home. In December, F. B. Deane, Jr., & Son, a major Lynchburg foundry, bought 150 tons of pig iron at $25 per ton, and Weaver's principal commission merchants in Richmond seemed to be on the verge of an even larger order.[30] As Daniel Brady and Charley Gorgas rode down to Spotsylvania County to hire slaves for 1859, they could anticipate a much stronger demand for the products of both Etna Furnace and Buffalo Forge in the year that lay ahead.

The pace of life—and death—at Buffalo Forge in 1858 had been typical of many years that had gone before. The seasonal imperatives of Weaver's agricultural system and the steady pace of forge work, followed by stoppages for repairs or sickness or inadequate power or field labor or hog killing, and then a return to production until the next interruption occurred, had been the work regimen at Buffalo Forge for as long as anyone could remember. Infant mortality, a dreaded specter in the house of both master and slave in the Old South, had struck down a white child at Buffalo Forge in 1858, but the slaves had not been spared in the past and they would certainly not be spared in the future.

No matter how unchanging life might seem at Buffalo Forge, the world was closing in inexorably on the Valley of Virginia and indeed on the entire South during the late 1850s. "The Atlantic Telegraph was completed today," Brady wrote in his diary on August 5, 1858.[31] Far more important to William Weaver, Daniel Brady, and the Buffalo Forge slave community, however, were a series of events taking place across the North which Brady failed to mention in his journal.

Saturday, August 21, 1858, was a day largely devoted to extensive forge repairs, cutting clover, and hauling wood and charcoal at Buffalo Forge. It was also the day Abraham Lincoln and Stephen A. Douglas opened their race for the United States Senate by engaging in the first of a series of debates that would transform Lincoln from an obscure Illinois politician into a figure of national prominence.[32]

On Friday, August 27, it started raining at Buffalo Forge about six in the morning and continued until noon; Brady had the agricultural hands doing indoor chores until the weather cleared, and then they went into the fields to finish threshing the clover crop while the forgemen completed their repairs and got ready to resume production. That same day, Stephen Douglas virtually destroyed his chance of leading a united Democratic party into the 1860 presidential election. In his debate with Lincoln at Freeport, Illinois, Douglas argued that the Supreme Court's recent Dred Scott decision, which seemed to extend the right to southerners to take their slaves into the territories, could have no practical effect "for the reason that slavery cannot exist a day or an hour anywhere, unless it is supported by local police regulations." Since these regulations could only be established by the local legislature, Douglas maintained that his concept of "popular sovereignty" was still valid as a means of deciding the question of slavery in the territories.[33] Douglas's "Freeport Doctrine," as it was soon called, made him a totally unacceptable presidential candidate to much of the southern wing of his party and helped pave the way for the Republican victory in 1860.

Wednesday, October 13, 1858, was a good day for field work, Brady noted—clear and warm. The slaves shucked corn in the forge field, and the teamsters hauled sixty bushels of corn to Weaver's grist mill. The forgemen were at their jobs. In his debate with Douglas at Quincy, Illinois, on that date, Lincoln referred to slavery as "a moral, a social, and a political wrong."[34]

Lincoln lost his race with Douglas in 1858, but that was just about the only major setback the Republicans suffered in the fall elections. The Lexington press reported sweeping Republican victories in state after state that November, a precursor of the triumph the "Black Republicans" would achieve in the presidential elections two years hence.[35]

The new year did not begin auspiciously for Weaver. On January 8, 1859, Will Rex reported to Weaver that he was finding it very difficult to obtain more than a handful of slaves locally for work at Etna Furnace. "I hired Cartmills hands, Bill was willing to come—as long as he is satisfied he is not hard to manage," Rex wrote. He had been able to secure one additional hand in the neighborhood, but that was about it. The recent failure of Shanks & Patton, the firm operating Grace Furnace in Botetourt County, had put a chill on the local hiring market. "I was up at Fincastle on New Years day, but did not hire any," Rex continued. "They are unwilling to hire to Furnaces." Masters were hiring their slaves out to farmers for $125 to $135 for the year, but slaveowners in Botetourt, some of whom had lost as much as two years' hire when Shanks & Patton went under, were not interested in any proposition Rex might offer. "They say . . . that S & P Debts will reace [sic] near $100,000," he added, and this firm had "borrowed a great deal of money about Fincastle."[36]

Weaver's two principal hiring agents fared little better than Will Rex. One of James Davidson's sons, Greenlee, an up-and-coming lawyer in Lexington, happened to run into Weaver's two emissaries as they came through Lexington on their way back to Buffalo Forge. "Mr. Brady & Charley Gorgas passed through here yesterday, on their return from negro hiring," Greenlee told his father on January 9. "They were the worst used up and the most disconsolate looking persons you can imagine. Although they used every exertion in their power they only succeeded in hiring 15 hands," young Davidson reported. "They dreaded meeting Mr. Weaver," he went on; "they feared that he would become excited, & that it might have a bad effect upon him." Two other Rockbridge ironmasters, Sam Jordan of Buena Vista Furnace and Francis T. Anderson of Glenwood Furnace, had fared no better. "Gorgas says that none of the Iron men obtained more than a half force," Greenlee wrote. "The Tobacco Factories & rail road Contractors monopolized the market."[37]

If Weaver suffered a fit of apoplexy when Brady and Gorgas got back to Buffalo Forge, it was not a fatal one, and indeed things were not quite as grim as Davidson reported. Buffalo Forge was adequately manned by Weaver's own slaves, and there were some free labor options at Etna Furnace. "We are having a strong force at present in the chopping," Charley Gorgas assured Weaver on February 3: "16 . . . chopping 3 more go in to morrow." It was a mixed force of slave hirelings and local whites, and the problem, as Gorgas put it, was "the want of dependence in them staying— (the wht hands)."[38] Hiring white men to do a black man's traditional job— in this case woodcutting—was always a high-risk proposition in the Old South, and Gorgas's doubts about the reliability of his white woodchoppers eventually turned out to be well-founded.

From Weaver's point of view, the makeshift labor situation at Etna was an unfortunate one because the demand for his iron was increasing at the same time many of his local competitors were falling by the wayside. "In reference to Iron Masters, we have to say, if they continue to go out of the market in the next 12 months in proportion to the past year say three a year,—we shall have none to begin 1860 with, as three more will include you," Lee, Rocke & Company, Weaver's principal Lynchburg commission merchants, wrote on January 8, 1859. "Your prospects in the Iron business is [*sic*] certainly looking much brighter," they went on. They included an order for five tons of Buffalo Forge bar and asked Weaver to consider a modest financial adjustment; "if you could possibly put your price at *85*$ when for 5 tons or more and $90 if under 5 tons, we verily believe that we could control nearly the whole of the hammered Iron trade in our city," they continued. "You can make Iron for a less price than any other man.— You have most of your labour and raise almost every thing." Lee, Rocke & Company closed by reminding Weaver of the exceptional status he enjoyed with their firm: "you only pay half the Commission for selling that other men pay.—all the others pay 5%."[39]

The fact that Weaver had managed to cut a favorable commission deal with these merchants was typical of the man and the way he did business. So was his response to their request for a price adjustment. Indeed the chances of Weaver lowering his price in a reviving iron market were about on the same order of probability as the spontaneous disappearance of the Blue Ridge Mountains. The odds grew even longer, if that were possible, when other Lynchburg mercantile houses began inquiring about his metal. "Iron is in demand here and by Keeping 2 or 3 Tons on hand we could frequently effect sales," the firm of Irby & Saunders wrote Weaver before the month was over. "We think it would be safe to send us say about 2 Tons or more every week."[40] Weaver was more than happy to oblige, and the price was the same to all the Lynchburg commission houses, $90 per ton. Weaver charged merchants in the Valley, where competition was less keen, $92.50. For individual buyers with small orders who called at the forge, the cost was 5½ cents per pound; that worked out to a price per ton of $123.20.[41]

Sales of Etna pig iron were also picking up. In early February, Weaver's commission merchants in Richmond reported that William S. Triplett of the Old Dominion Iron & Nail Works had purchased 100 tons of Etna iron for $26 per ton and was in the market for an additional 100 tons. In March, F. B. Deane, Jr., & Son, the Lynchburg founder, placed a substantial order for Etna metal, and Weaver soon received inquiries about his pig iron from other Lynchburg and Richmond parties, including the Tredegar Iron Works.[42] It was not a good time for labor troubles at Etna Furnace.

"One of our boys (named Aaron Stuart) has ran away," Will Rex reported to Brady on February 18, 1859; "he left the Coaling last Monday night. Old Daniel met him on Tuesday morning 3 hour[s] before Day." Rex thought Stuart, who was a hireling, had run off because he could not make his quota of wood and Rex believed the slave might be headed for

Buffalo Forge. "Please writ [sic] me weather [sic] Aaron is there," he told Brady the next day. "I think he is making for home (he is a triffling nigger)."[43]

It was bad enough when a hired slave tried to flee, but it was even more serious when discipline broke down among Weaver's own slaves. The exact nature of the offense committed by Lawson, a coaling hand belonging to Weaver, is unclear, but it was serious enough to prompt an irate reaction from Charley Gorgas. The final entry under Lawson's name in the Etna Furnace "Negro Book" reads: "the Son of a bch." The curse is in Gorgas's handwriting, and it is written in heavy bold strokes.[44] Whatever Lawson did, he paid a heavy price for his transgression. He was placed in the hands of J. E. Carson, an Augusta County slave trader, and sent south.

"I have just got rid of your man Lawson," Carson wrote from New Orleans on March 12, 1859. "I had sold him twice before this but he was returned on my hands both times." In a market where prime field hands were selling for $1,500, Carson had managed to get only $500 for the man, and he had "sold him the last time with out any guarantee accept [sic] the title." The slave trader described Lawson as "the hardest selling negroe I ever sold and the worst talker he stuck out to the last that he was not healthy."[45] Lawson had resorted to the only means at his disposal in his efforts to get back at Weaver. He had talked down his price and had made it as difficult for the slave dealer to sell him as he possibly could. Weaver had instructed Carson to sell the man, and Carson did so, but Lawson had refused to go quietly.

There was a lesson here for Weaver if he chose to see it, but like most masters in the Old South, he closed his eyes to unpleasant truths concerning slavery, and his own slave hands in particular. He held firmly to the belief that the great bulk of his slaves were loyal and devoted "servants," as he usually preferred to call them, and that any who behaved otherwise were aberrant cases who had to be removed from his work force before their bad example could corrupt others and lead them astray. Whatever Lawson had done that prompted Gorgas to call him a "son of a bitch," it was serious enough for Weaver to take swift and decisive action to excise the man from his labor force and remove him from the vicinity, even if it meant selling Lawson for what amounted to a cut-rate price.

Before Carson returned from the Deep South, Weaver experienced more trouble with his slaves who were living at Etna Furnace. Again, the record does not show the nature of the actions that prompted Weaver's anger and his decision to sell, but Carson's correspondence with Weaver reveals some of the details. "I will try and buy the negroes you wrote me about if we can agree on the price and you have not disposed of them," the

slave dealer wrote Weaver in late May after his return from New Orleans.[46] Carson came out to Buffalo Forge on Monday, June 6, and gave
Weaver a check for $415.90 "for negro Lawson."[47] The slave trader spent
the night at Weaver's residence and then rode over to Etna the next day to
examine the slaves Weaver wanted to sell. Carson returned to Buffalo
Forge on Wednesday, June 8, and his presence there seems to have had a
deleterious effect on the health of three of Sam Williams's daughters. Perhaps it was only coincidence, but on the day Carson came back from the
furnace, Brady noted in his diary that Betty Coleman and Lydia and Caroline Williams were all sick, out of the work force, and presumably confined
to their cabins. Carson's departure after breakfast on Thursday, June 9, may
have been the reason Betty and Caroline recovered from their illnesses that
day; Lydia returned to work on Friday, June 10.[48]

Carson apparently liked what he saw at Etna. "As soon as your harvest is
off if you are still in the notion of selling your negroes if you will write me
I will come and buy them," the slave dealer told Weaver in late June. "I can
sell one of my weemen [sic] that I have at home and would like to get an
other to put in her place." Carson's slave woman would be sold to the man
who owned her husband, but she would have to be replaced; "if your
wooman [sic] is a good cook and you do not object to her staying this near
to you I will buy her and sell mine but if you wish your wooman to go out
of the country I will send her off," he added, and "the man if I should get
him I will send him off of coarse [sic]."[49] The man, a slave named Millin,
may well have been a runaway. What the woman had done to incur
Weaver's wrath was not mentioned in this or in subsequent letters.

"You can have the woman and children whenever you please at $1,500,"
Weaver replied on July 2. "I have no objection to her remaining at yr
place." Millin had apparently been recaptured, and Weaver offered him to
Carson as well. "The boy you can have at 1150 in about a months time, as I
should be through thrashing by that time," Weaver wrote.[50]

Carson came for the woman, and possibly her children as well, in early
July. He did not conduct a minute physical examination of her while he
was at Buffalo Forge, but he wasted little time doing so once he was away
from Weaver's place. He left Buffalo Forge with her on July 8; the next day
he wrote from Lexington that he wanted to reopen the transaction. "Your
wooman did not soot [sic]," Carson told Weaver. "She has bad teet says she
has brest [sic] complaint says Dr McClung attended on her at one time and
blistered her she has a blister mark on her brest. I can not give the price," he
continued. "I am willing to buy her at what she is worth You can keep the
check until I come up for the boy."[51]

Before the month was out Carson was back at Buffalo Forge. "I will be at your place the 28th for your man if you are through thrashing and can spare him," the slave dealer told Weaver on July 25. He also indicated what Millin's fate would be: "I expect to start a few negroes south next week."[52] Carson showed up at Buffalo Forge on the appointed day and mixed a bit of social intercourse in with the business at hand. "Carson came to tea, & all night," Daniel Brady noted in his journal on July 28. Brady did not indicate whether the woman and her children, whose names were never mentioned in any of this correspondence, accompanied the trader on this occasion. The next day, July 29, "Carson took off Millin," Brady wrote, and the day after that, Weaver's manager posted an entry in the cashbooks kept at Buffalo Forge: "J. E. Carson for Negroes $3,650."[53] The slave trader apparently kept the woman and children, bought Millin, and may have made additional purchases as well. The amount of cash Weaver received on July 30 was $1,000 more than the total price he had earlier indicated he would accept from Carson for the man and the woman and her children.

Millin went south in August 1859; Weaver went to the springs. His friend Henry A. McCormick had been trying for several weeks to persuade him to take a short vacation. "You & myself can not be hear [sic] long, by the course of nature," McCormick wrote Weaver on July 21. "We had just as well spend a few Dollars of what we have as to devise it to some one els[e] to spend after we are gone from time to eternity." McCormick added tactfully that "whatever you may give friend Brady he will try to take care of."[54] Weaver left Buffalo Forge to join McCormick at a nearby spa on August 19.[55] With Brady looking out for affairs at home, and with the sale of his slaves to Carson recently negotiated, Weaver felt free to indulge himself in a brief holiday.

Weaver clearly sold his slaves in 1859 for what he considered "just cause." Attempts to run away or behavior that created disciplinary problems and disrupted life in the slave quarters had to be met head-on, Weaver had always believed. J. E. Carson provided a ready solution, one that Weaver undoubtedly hoped would have a salutary effect on the conduct of those slaves who continued to live and work at Buffalo Forge and Etna Furnace. Later in 1859, Henry McCormick offered to buy Weaver's "old woman, Louisia, at Etna, . . . providing you will sell her to me at what she is worth." McCormick acknowledged that the slave woman was "getting old" but thought "perhaps she will live long enough, for my wife & me."[56] Louisa, who was one of the original "Wilson negroes," had done nothing to prompt Weaver to sell her, and he refused McCormick's offer despite the long-standing friendship between the two men.

The difficulties Weaver experienced with his slave force at Etna in 1859 were more than matched by the problems created by the employment of a sizable number of white workers at the furnace that same year. "We have no Meat in Smoke House now," Charley Gorgas told Weaver in late March. The white workers were "complaining very much on a/c of the beef—it spoils before the week is out—warm weather," he explained. "Am afraid if we are to push through your two hhds [of beef packed in brine]— we will lose our White force."[57] A week later things had not improved. "It is taking all our management to get off that beef & to keep them in good humor—they want money to buy bacon with," Gorgas reported on April 6. He had received word that the white workers at the ore bank "would leave if they did not get bacon"; they were sending the beef "back as fast as we sent it up to them."[58] Weaver got a supply of bacon over to Etna in time to prevent a mass exodus of the white laborers, but soon they were voicing another complaint. The cornmeal they were receiving was of poor quality, they charged, although Gorgas added that the mules at Etna seemed to like it well enough.[59] "We have white hands, must give them money or Flour," he reminded Brady during the summer. "Please keep us supplied."[60]

Weaver was convinced that meat and grain were being consumed at an inordinate rate at Etna, and Gorgas had to explain on more than one occasion that he was issuing rations carefully. Weaver also suspected theft, and Gorgas promised to keep the trap door at the mill at Etna closed.[61] In the fall, the furnace office was "broken into / prized front door open," Gorgas noted ruefully.[62] Will Rex had commented earlier in the year that a farmer near Etna could not guarantee to deliver corn to the furnace because "he has to depend on white labor."[63] A somewhat analogous circumstance prevailed at the furnace itself, although the situation there was tempered by the presence of some two dozen slave workers. When Gorgas reported in late May that his mixed labor force "was moving at day light this morning," he also wrote, "hope it will continue."[64]

It was late July before Gorgas and Will Rex were able to get the furnace into blast. A familiar problem—low water—held production back during the late summer and early fall, but heavy rainfall in late September swelled Purgatory Creek.[65] "The rains play the mischief with our wag[on] & rail road," Gorgas noted, but he needed waterpower if he was going to make iron at a satisfactory pace.[66] By early October—very late in an ironmaster's year—the furnace was working extremely well, and Gorgas was hopeful he could maintain a high level of production over the next three months.[67] It had been a difficult year at Etna, and much of the trouble could be traced to the poor hiring season Brady and Gorgas had experienced when they had ridden "down the country" the previous December.

The demand for Buffalo Forge hammered iron continued strong through 1859, and Weaver could easily have sold well over 100 tons of his merchant bar that year. Having a ready market was one thing; fully supplying that market was quite another. The actions of Weaver's forgemen in 1859 provided Daniel Brady with ample evidence of the perils, uncertainties, and frustrations involved in trying to operate an industrial establishment with skilled slave labor.

In the summer and fall of 1859, Lee, Rocke & Company, the commission house that sold most of Weaver's bar iron in the Lynchburg area, sent a steady stream of orders to Buffalo Forge. Invariably, these merchants accompanied their memoranda for iron with pleas for prompt delivery. Their customers were becoming impatient, Lee, Rocke & Company told Brady in June and again in July.[68] "Please do not send any more orders until I send you what is ordered," Brady replied on July 18. "I have not been able to do anything for sometime, having a heavy harvest & then some repairs to [the] forge, so that I am just at work today."[69]

After waiting almost two weeks for the arrival of some metal, the Lynchburg merchants fired off another plea. "The orders we *now have* with you for Iron is [*sic*] all *badly wanted*," they wrote on July 30; "we would be *very glad* if you could send it along *pretty quick* and we will try to keep back any more for a while if you prefer *our doing so.*"[70] Brady managed to send off four tons of bar iron to them in mid-August, but that still left a number of back orders unfilled. "The forge has been stopped by repairs, & sick hands, but I hope to get along faster in the future," Brady explained.[71] Lee, Rocke & Company responded on August 29 that they had "lost the sale of several tons" of Buffalo Forge iron because they had none on hand. "Our customers are complaining *loudly* about the delay in getting their orders filled," they added several days later.[72]

By mid-September, the partners in the Lynchburg firm had become thoroughly exasperated with Brady's inability to deliver iron promptly. "We have succeeded in making a considerable inroad in the Iron Trade of this place, & it only remains now for you to dispatch our orders to secure it all or nearly so," they wrote on September 10. "Do you think you can fill orders next month, say October & after?"[73] Brady's reply undoubtedly brought cold comfort to the hard-pressed members of the Lynchburg mercantile house. "I cannot make the iron as fast as you order it," Brady answered, something Lee, Rocke & Company knew only too well. All Weaver's manager could promise for the future was to "do my best to fill orders as fast as I can." The delivery of nine tons of Buffalo Forge bar to the Lynchburg firm during September did not come close to satisfying their demand for Weaver's metal.[74]

The reasons Brady offered for not being able to produce iron at a faster pace—a heavy harvest, forge repairs, sick hands—were all legitimate, but they told only part of the story. There was an important element Brady did not mention in his correspondence with the Lynchburg merchants, a factor he kept confined to the pages of the recordbooks he religiously filled out day after day at Buffalo Forge. That element was the determination of the slave forgemen to work pretty much at their own pace and to do overwork only when they chose to do so. And then there were those days when they stubbornly refused to do any work at all.

From Brady's point of view, there was little question that his refiners— Sam Williams and Henry Towles—were a more reliable pair than his chaffery hammermen—Tooler and Harry Hunt, Jr. The surviving Buffalo Forge "Negro Books" do not extend past the beginning of 1858, and there are no anchony records for Weaver's principal forge, so it is impossible to trace the job performance of Sam Williams and Henry Towles in detail during this period. But Brady wrote the phrase "Sam and Henry at work" over and over again in his journal during 1859 and indeed for most—but not all—of the antebellum and Civil War period.

Only once in 1859, in the late spring and early summer, did Brady indicate that his forge operations were being impeded by a shortage of anchonies. That shortage came because during a two-week period at the end of May and the beginning of June, Sam and Henry had taken alternate weeks off. Brady indicated that Sam was sick on May 30 and 31. On June 1, Brady wrote "Sam Williams well, but not at work," and the next day he noted "Sam at forge but not at work." Henry Towles and Jim Garland made anchonies until Sam returned to his usual post at the finery on Saturday, June 4, but the following Monday, Henry Towles was on the sick list; he was "still sick" and off the job for over a week. Jim Garland served as Sam's underhand during Henry's absence, but it was clear that productivity sagged badly during this period.[75] "I am out of refined iron," Brady reported on June 13, 1859.[76] Illness may have been the principal cause, but Brady seems to have felt that Sam could have done more during those two days he was at the forge but not working, and Henry's sick spell came at a rather suspicious time, just after Sam had been off the job for the better part of a week. A similar, and far more dramatic, sequence of events would occur at the refinery forge in the summer of 1860.

There was frequently no question at all in Daniel Brady's mind about the poor work habits of his chaffery forgemen. Brady depended heavily on Tooler and Harry Hunt, Jr., to fill the orders that came in from Lynchburg with increasing frequency as 1859 progressed, and these orders invariably called for specific descriptions of bar drawn to exact specifications. If one of Lee, Rocke & Company's customers wanted a ton of wagon tire measuring $1\frac{5}{8}$ inches in width and $\frac{5}{8}$ of an inch in thickness, another ton of tire iron

1 ¾ inches wide and ¾ of an inch thick, and a third ton of bar measuring 2 inches by 1 inch, then that was exactly what the customer wanted and that was the order Brady had to try to fill.[77] Tooler and Harry Hunt, Jr., were fully capable of executing these orders, but Brady could not always count on their cooperation.

The entries in the Chaffery Forge Iron Book, a massive volume in which forge managers recorded the daily work regimen of Weaver's hammermen for a period of over thirty years stretching from 1831 until 1862, frequently make fascinating reading. No entries are more revealing than those for Tooler and Harry Hunt, Jr., in 1859, and when the notations in Brady's journal for the same period are added in, we can see why Buffalo Forge merchant bar, much prized by blacksmiths, farmers, wagon builders, and commission merchants in Lynchburg and in the Valley, did not always get to market on time.

Things started off reasonably well in 1859. January and February were both good months, with Tooler and Harry Hunt, Jr., making needed forge repairs and putting in several weeks in which they drew substantial amounts of overwork. Their most productive week during this period was the one ending Saturday, February 5. They drew eighteen journeys of 560 pounds each—a total of 10,089 pounds of iron. Their combined task for the week was twelve journeys—6,720 pounds—so their output for this six-day period included 3,369 pounds of overwork.

The trouble started in March. "Harry Hunt sick, which stopped the chaffery," Brady wrote on Thursday, March 10. "Tooler not working." Harry did not return to the forge until Wednesday, March 16. While he was out, Tooler spent his time, in Brady's words, "playing," "playing," and "playing still." High water and major forge repairs also cut into production that month, and when spring came, it was time to get the all-important corn crop in the ground. During the first two months of the year, the chaffery forgemen had turned out over twenty tons of hammered iron; during March and April, output fell to just under thirteen tons.

May and June saw more of the same. The forgemen were drawn off frequently for field work, and whenever Tooler saw an opportunity for a day off, he seized the chance. Brady recorded Harry Hunt as sick on Wednesday, May 25, and Thursday, May 26. Both days, according to Brady's entries in the iron book and in his journal, Tooler spent his time fishing in the waters of Buffalo Creek. Forge output of bar for these two months totaled just over ten tons. Tooler and Harry Hunt, Jr., turned out a total of 175 pounds of "over iron" during the month of May; in June, they did not produce a single pound of overwork iron, a pattern that would be repeated month after month until the year was almost out. Only in December, just in time to boost their earnings prior to the Christmas holidays, did they have a week's work that approached those they had turned in back at the beginning of the year.

Daniel Brady seems to have reached something of an upper limit of frustration with his two chaffery forgemen on Tuesday, July 19. "Harry Hunt laid up broke down i.e. lazy, & humbugging," he wrote; Tooler was "playing." He made similar entries the following day, but then the day after that, Tooler and Harry Hunt, Jr., were back at work, and they remained at their forge for the balance of the week, and indeed for the remainder of the month.

Brady should have known his luck could not last. On Monday, August 1, Tooler, Henry Towles, and Henry Matthews were all off from work, sick, they claimed, but "humbugging" in Brady's estimation. Harry Hunt joined Sam Williams at the finery until Wednesday, when Tooler returned to work. Henry Towles was back on the job the next day. The following week, August 8 through 13, Tooler was down again. "Tooler sick. *Hum,*" Brady wrote in his journal on Monday; for the remainder of the week, he simply listed Tooler as "loafing." Harry Hunt, Jr., and Jim Garland manned the chaffery hammer that week.

Tooler's pattern of a week on followed by a week off persisted throughout the month of August. He put in a full week's work August 15 through 20, and he and Harry Hunt, Jr., drew 6,029 pounds of bar—over two and a half tons. The following week, August 22 through 27, Tooler, Harry Hunt, Jr., *and* Jim Garland were either "sick" or "loafing" for most of the week. The chaffery hammer was silent from Wednesday through Saturday, and the week's output was only 1,510 pounds of iron.[78]

"We regret your inability to fill our orders, as we have made strong efforts to obtain the trade, & about the time they are getting pretty straight we have to disappoint them & we fear it will have a further bad effect," Lee, Rocke & Company told Weaver on September 17, 1859.[79] The series of complaining letters the Lynchburg merchants wrote during the summer and early fall had absolutely no effect on the pace of production at Buffalo Forge. That pace was largely set by the slaves themselves. Field work, illness, and forge repairs figured in as well, as Brady pointed out, but more often than not, it came down to the willingness of Weaver's forgemen to push on with their work during the hottest months of the year. The chaffery hands in particular clearly had their own ideas about how far they would go.

Why did Weaver and Brady put up with this situation? The answer to that question is relatively simple. They had little choice. They were totally dependent on their slave artisans for their forge production, and that de-

pendence carried with it a strong set of imperatives: minimal use of coercion, maximum use of incentive, and if incentive failed, as seems to have
been the case at the chaffery forge during the hot summer months of 1859,
toleration of the slaves' preference for rest instead of overwork. Sometimes
the masters had to acquiesce in the slaves' decision not to work at all. The
industrial skills that Sam Williams, Henry Towles, Tooler, and Harry
Hunt, Jr., possessed forced Weaver to permit them to behave in ways he
never would have allowed his field hands to act.

Forge production almost always picked up once cool weather returned,
and 1859 was no exception. By the end of the year, Buffalo Forge had
produced almost ninety tons of hammered iron, an increase of some thirteen tons over the amount drawn during 1858. But Tooler's and Harry
Hunt's overwork for 1859 had dropped to just under five tons, compared
with close to nine tons the previous year.[80] The two slaves had opted for
more time off, and less income, in 1859; Weaver and Brady, whether they
liked it or not, had gone along with their decision.

Brady's diary indicates that the summer of 1859 was not a season of
unrelieved frustration. Henry Towles's wife, Ann, gave birth to a healthy
baby girl in mid-July. Wilhelmina Towles was born on July 14, a day,
Brady noted, when the temperature reached ninety-seven degrees at one
o'clock in the afternoon. The crops were bountiful that year, and when the
slaves finished cutting the rye by two in the afternoon on Saturday, July 2,
Brady gave the field workers some time off. "All hands rested the balance of
the PM," he wrote. A month or so later, a celebration was held at Buffalo
Forge. On Saturday, August 6, Joe, the forge carpenter, spent most of the
day making enough tables so that all the slaves could be seated for a meal;
"At 4 P.M. had a harvest dinner for all hands," Brady recorded.[81]

The celebratory dinner on August 6 marked the completion of only part
of the harvest season at Buffalo Forge in 1859. The corps of wheat, oats, rye,
and hay were all in, but the fields and fields of corn were still ripening in
the late summer sun. That harvest would begin in September, and winter
wheat would be planted from mid-September to early October. By the
second week in October, the field hands would finish sowing the wheat
crop and turn their attention to planting the rye that would be harvested
the following year.

The week that began on Monday, October 10, was a beautiful one in the
Valley. Clear, cool days followed one after another, ideal weather for outdoor work. Plow gangs moved through the fields every day that week as the
soil was prepared for the rye crop, and sowing began on Thursday, October
13. Garland Thompson, Jr., delivered his daily load of charcoal to the forge,
and Sam Williams and Henry Towles were at their refinery hammer as

usual, Monday through Saturday. As dusk fell on Saturday, October 15, Brady could look back on the week's work with satisfaction.[82]

Late Saturday night, a heavy frost spread over the Valley. There was a sharp chill in the air as the Buffalo Forge community awoke to a day of rest on Sunday, October 16.[83] That same day, 175 miles to the north, a band of abolitionists led by John Brown launched their attack on the United States arsenal and armory located at Harper's Ferry, Virginia.

2

———◆———

The Eve of War

Something akin to panic swept over much of the South in the wake of John Brown's raid, and the Valley of Virginia was no exception. Lexington's two weekly papers, the Whiggish *Gazette* and the Democratic *Valley Star*, carried full reports of the attack on the government installations at Harper's Ferry and published highly emotional editorials the following week. The *Gazette* saw the abolitionist agitation leading inevitably "to rebellion and civil war, to the overthrow of the constitution and to the dissolution of the Union. The disgraceful outrages which came of the abstract question of territorial sovereignty over the vexed subject in Kansas have, by the abettors of treason and the participants in murder, been transferred to the soil of Virginia," wrote the editor of Lexington's most conservative newspaper.[1]

The editorial in the *Valley Star* was even more strident. "We are no friends to Lynch Law, but if ever fair subjects for its exercise have been arrested, these are the men. We wonder they did not hang all of them at once." Upon calm reflection, however, the editor of the *Star* concluded that it was "better . . . that they shall have a fair trial, and be hung [*sic*] in accordance with the law."²

The law moved swiftly in the case of John Brown. His one-day trial for treason at Charlestown, Virginia, on November 2 concluded with the judge declaring that no reasonable doubt existed as to his guilt. His execution by public hanging was scheduled for Friday, December 2, 1859.³

The month prior to Brown's execution was filled with wild rumors in Virginia of armed attacks on the border, of fanatical attempts to rescue Brown, and of abolitionist plots to kidnap prominent citizens and members of their families and hold them as hostages for Brown's release.⁴ The Richmond *Enquirer,* in an editorial reprinted in the *Gazette,* urged the citizens of the commonwealth to arm themselves and organize "as patrols and guards, and as volunteer videttes."⁵

This was the mood among whites in the Valley as preparations began for a double wedding in the slave community at Buffalo Forge. Caroline Williams, the seventeen-year-old daughter of Sam and Nancy Williams, and Andrew Reid, a slave teamster belonging to Jacob Fuller of Lexington, were hoping to get married. So were fifteen-year-old Amy Banks, the daughter of Warder and Frances Banks, and James Carter, whose owner, Charles H. Locher, operated the cement works at Balcony Falls on the James River, a few miles south of Weaver's place. The process, as was always the case when one of Weaver's slaves wanted to marry off the property, could not go forward without the consent of the masters.

Jacob Fuller gave his permission on November 29. "Andy asks me to drop you a line in relation to him," Fuller wrote Weaver. "He is my property—has many good traits, is a good hand at work—has never been detected as far [as] I know in any thing mean or dishonest—is rather high tempered, yet not unmanageable." According to Fuller, Andrew had only one "weakness"—"he will take a dram when it comes his way"—but his master regarded him as an honest and truthful person. "He has my consent to get married provided the girl is what she should be," Fuller concluded.⁶

Locher wrote a brief, rather formal note a few days later: "My Cold Boy, named James Carter, has my free and full permission to marry your Colored woman Amy, with such privileges as you may see proper to grant having reference allways [*sic*] to his duties as a servant and obedience to his master."⁷ Weaver gave his consent, and the marriages were scheduled to take place at Buffalo Forge on Saturday, December 3, 1859.

Daniel Brady was away on a cattle drive to Richmond during the first part of the month, but one of the clerks at Buffalo Forge took note of the events that were occurring there. On Friday, December 2, 1859, "John Brown of Ossawatiamie [*sic*] Noteriety to [be] hung at Charlestown Va. to day, for Insurrection," he wrote in Brady's journal. The day was unusually warm and sultry for December, a sign that something worse was on the way. The rains came the next day, Saturday, and enveloped Buffalo Forge in a cold, biting drizzle that continued from early morning until well into the night. It was not the best day for a wedding, but it was the day Caroline Williams and Andrew Reid and Amy Banks and James Carter had chosen to be married. A double wedding, with both grooms coming from off the property, meant a large gathering of slaves; and the timing—the day after John Brown was hanged—was undoubtedly the reason a distinctly unwelcome group of uninvited guests turned up at Buffalo Forge that day. On Saturday, December 3, the Rockbridge County slave patrol came calling.[8]

Fear of possible slave rebellion was commonplace in the South in the aftermath of Brown's attack on Harper's Ferry, and whites argued that the only way to prevent such uprisings was through an overwhelming show of force and the immediate suppression of the slightest hint of insurrectionary activity. It was not work for the squeamish. We do not know what, if anything, Weaver's slaves said about John Brown, but one of them apparently said or did something the patrol did not like. The hated "paddyrollers," as the blacks called them, left Buffalo Forge after the wedding party broke up on Saturday, but they were back the next day.

Overnight the temperature plunged and the first snow of the season fell at Buffalo Forge. Sunday dawned bright and clear, one of those magnificent early-winter days in the Valley when the air is crisp and fresh and the cloudless sky forms a stunning contrast to the snow-covered Blue Ridge. The tranquility of this December day was soon shattered by the clatter of horses' hooves as the slave patrol rode up the hill to Weaver's house. Perhaps a snide remark had been directed their way the day before and had festered in the patrollers' minds during the night. Maybe it was nothing more than rumors of some loose talk among the slaves at the forge. It did not take much to set off the paddyrollers in the overheated atmosphere brought on by John Brown's raid. Whatever the reason, their return visit resulted in an ugly incident. The patrol singled out Henry Towles for punishment; the twenty-three-year-old forge hand was taken out, stripped, and whipped. Towles did not return to work until December 15, eleven days after the beating administered by the Rockbridge County patrol.[9]

The whipping of Henry Towles, one of Weaver's most dependable forge hands, was a stark reminder of a basic fact of life at Buffalo Forge. The black workers there, no matter how skilled, were still no more than chattel in the eyes of the law, a piece of human personal property subject to the disciplinary whims of the master and regularly constituted county authorities. Whether Weaver concurred in the patrol's decision to whip Towles is unknown; he probably could not have stopped them even if he wanted to. White repression of suspected slave insurrectionary activity during the 1850s was often vicious and brutal, and the whipping of Henry Towles was only one incident among many carried out by panic-stricken southern whites during the late antebellum era. This mindset was probably best summed up in an editorial that appeared in a Tennessee newspaper in 1856 when slave ironworkers along the Tennessee and Cumberland rivers were supposedly preparing to "rise," as the expression went, against the white population:

> The crimes contemplated should be atoned for precisely as though those crimes had been attempted and consummated. Fearful and terrible examples should be made, and if need be, the fag[g]ot and flame should be brought into requisition to show these deluded maniacs the fierceness and the vigor, the swiftness and completeness of the white man's vengeance. Let a terrible example be made in every neighborhood where the crime can be established, and if necessary, let every tree in the country bend with negro meat. Temporizing in such cases as this, is utter madness. We must strike terror, and make a lasting impression, for only in such a course can we find the guaranties [sic] of future security.[10]

* * *

For Weaver, John Brown's raid and the heightened antagonism it produced against the North meant a possible windfall for southern ironmasters and an edge in their long-standing competitive struggle with outside manufacturers. He decided to jump the price of Buffalo Forge iron to $100 per ton as of January 1, 1860, and told his Lynchburg commission merchants to accept no more orders at the old price.[11] Weaver was undoubtedly cheered by a brief item that appeared in the Lexington *Gazette* in early December. A northern businessman visiting Richmond reported "an intense feeling against the North" there. "As for business, it is impossible to do anything," the man was quoted as saying. "Merchants here talk as if they were definitely resolved not to buy anything of the North unless of necessity."[12] Weaver wasted no time testing the waters in the Virginia capital. Following the sale of 200 tons of Etna pig iron at $24 per ton in mid-December, he instructed his Richmond mercantile house to close no more deals at that price. The 200 tons already sold should be delivered, Weaver wrote, "& by that time there may be a chance for better prices, if people will agree to encourage our own production."[13]

As Christmas approached in 1859, the mood at Buffalo Forge was a

somber one. The whipping of Henry Towles undoubtedly cast a pall over
the slave quarters, and Towles's beating was followed closely by the outbreak of a serious smallpox epidemic in Lexington. The appearance of the
disease placed the residents there under quarantine, severed normal contact with the town, and contributed to a heightened sense of isolation
among both black and white at Weaver's place. James Davidson cautioned
Weaver against allowing Andrew Reid to call on his new wife until the
epidemic was over, and Weaver agreed. "It would be dreadful to get it in
my Family," Weaver wrote, and he asked Davidson "to see Fuller and
Andy on the subject." Weaver wanted to come in to Lexington for a visit
and was not worried for himself about smallpox because he had "had the
disease in the old Fashioned way." But he would have to bring Wilson
King, his manservant, with him, and that was too great a risk.[14]

The political climate was also dismal. The hostility between North and
South might turn out to be good for business, but Weaver took no pleasure
in the prospect that the Union itself might be destroyed. His northern birth
and family connections and his Whig politics were still strong influences on
him, but then so were his loyalties to Virginia and the slave system. James
Davidson's sentiments, expressed to Weaver in a long, gloomy letter written on Sunday, December 18, undoubtedly reflected the mood of both men.
"The times are truly out of joint," Davidson noted, "tho I think the Union
may yet be saved." If the "agitation" over the slavery question continued,
however, "a few more presidential elections, will seal its fate." There was
one bright spot on the political landscape—the recent election of John
Letcher of Lexington, a good friend of both Weaver's and Davidson's, to
the governorship of Virginia. Weaver was eager to call on the governor-
elect, and Davidson promised to let him know when Letcher was back in
town. But for the moment, Weaver was well advised to stay out of Lexington. Davidson reported the recent deaths of two young people from smallpox and the outbreak of a number of new cases. "Our streets look like
desolation," he concluded. "We have a prospect of a quiet town this winter."[15]

Several days later, Davidson again reported on the political climate. The
bitter sectional fight in Congress over who should be elected Speaker of the
House prompted Davidson to observe that "Members of Congress do not
know the feeling of the people." At the same time he seemed to take
considerable pleasure in the latest manifestation of southern resistance to
northern influence. "I see 300 medical students left Phila. in a body, & have
come to Richmond to finish their studies. The South is beginning to rely on
its own resources—and if she will profit by them, good may result to her."
The smallpox epidemic continued unabated, he went on to say; Lexington

was "desolate," and the disease was "spreading to the country." He advised Weaver to have all of his slaves vaccinated as soon as possible and warned him not to allow "any of your Furnace hands [to] stop in Town" on their way home for the holidays.[16]

The somber mood at Buffalo Forge became even bleaker five days before Christmas. Frances Matthews had given birth to a boy back in mid-November, and the baby had been named Henry after his father. At 8:30 in the evening on December 20, five-week-old Henry Matthews, Jr., died of jaundice. Little wonder that Brady noted in his diary that Christmas was a "very quiet day" at Buffalo Forge that year.[17]

On the evening of December 27, it began snowing in the Valley, and the next morning Buffalo Forge lay under a two-inch blanket of fresh snow. The snowfall seemed to herald a fresh start in both the master's residence and the slave cabins. At 8 A.M. on December 28, Emma Brady gave birth to a healthy baby girl, which she and Daniel named Sarah Elizabeth. The snow continued the next day, and once again at eight in the morning, another baby was born at Buffalo Forge, this time in the slave quarters. Betty Coleman gave birth to her second child, a girl, and both Betty and the baby were fine.[18] Sam and Nancy Williams now had a granddaughter as well as a grandson at Buffalo Forge.

These births brought an added bonus. Dr. Morgan, who had come over to attend to Emma Brady, arrived at Buffalo Forge with enough smallpox matter to vaccinate all of Weaver's slaves who had not previously been immunized against the disease. Daniel Brady inoculated the slaves on December 31, carefully recorded those immunizations that were "good" and "no go," and repeated the process some two weeks later for those whose first vaccinations had not taken. The Buffalo Forge community, white and black, was spared the ravages of smallpox, and the fortuitous arrival of the vaccination material may well have made the difference.[19]

December had been a time of stark contradictions for the slaves of Buffalo Forge. The month had begun with the marriage of four young people, and this happy occasion had immediately been followed by the brutal whipping of Henry Towles. Less than two weeks later, Henry and Frances Matthews had lost their baby. Then had come the long-awaited break from work—"All hands idle, keeping Christmas," Brady noted during the holidays—and the birth of Betty Coleman's baby girl.[20] These events spoke eloquently of the anguish and joy that mingled together in the lives of the black men and women at Buffalo Forge, and indeed in slave families and communities across the entire South.

Much of the history of American slavery could also be said to reside in the name of Betty Coleman's new baby. She and her husband called their newborn child Mary Caroline.[21] Her middle name was almost certainly given in honor of her Aunt Caroline, who had celebrated her marriage just three weeks earlier. What better way could there be for Betty to show love and respect for her sister and, in the process of naming her new child, to demonstrate the transcendent importance of the family to them all? The baby's first name, Mary, went back much farther in the history of the family, back to little Mary's great-great-grandmother. That Mary, mother of Sally Williams, grandmother of Sam Williams, was, of course, the woman taken by Thomas Mayburry when he and Weaver divided the "Wilson negroes" over two decades before. Memories of her, it seems fair to say, were still alive in the minds of her descendants at Buffalo Forge, a family that in 1859 spanned four generations.

The new year began very much as the previous one had ended, with the outbreak of new cases of smallpox in Lexington reinforcing the feeling of isolation at Buffalo Forge. On January 25, 1860, James Davidson described the situation in town as a "small pox panic," and he once again had to decline Weaver's invitation to come out for a visit.[22] Weaver, who would celebrate his seventy-ninth birthday in March, was largely confined to his residence during the winter months, and he felt Davidson's absence keenly. "I was sorry to hear of the . . . small pox," Weaver replied. "It debarred me of your company, which I was anticipating with great pleasure. I am getting along as usual and no cause of complaint—old time has dealt with me kindly," he continued. "The only back sett I have had this winter is the want of your company—I have been accustomed to it so long that it has become a *necessity.*" No cases of smallpox had occurred at Buffalo Forge, Weaver was happy to report, and he attributed their good fortune to what amounted to a virtual quarantine of his slave force. "We keep close quarters and avoid Company (black)," Weaver explained.[23]

Another difficult hiring season meant that Etna Furnace would again have to depend on a mixed force of black and white laborers. The furnace had stayed in blast through December and had produced close to 600 tons of pig iron in 1859, a very respectable showing considering the troubles Charley Gorgas and Will Rex had encountered earlier in the year.[24] They would experience a very similar set of circumstances in 1860. Once again, their operations would be plagued by periodic shortages of food and clothing, the unreliable performance of their white workers, and serious health and disciplinary problems with their slave laborers.

"Our [white] hands are here wanting *flour, coffee* & *tobacco,*" Gorgas informed Brady on April 2, 1860. "I have for the past month been putting them off—I am afraid they will leave in a body—& throw us behind—I am acting on *your* principle—obey orders though break owners," he went on to say; "please ask Uncle William to send some—I don't wish to worry him myself—I have been doing too much of it already. We by all means should have *something* to satisfy them if we wish to keep them."[25] It took 200 pounds of bacon per week to feed both the black and white hands at Etna, and the managers frequently ran short of that basic commodity as well.[26] Little wonder that Rex reported in the fall that "our chopping has not gone on as brisk as I had reason to suppose it would." The reason was that the white hands "damn them . . . wont stick."[27] Certainly part of the explanation for their unreliability lay in Weaver's failure to keep them supplied with items—bacon, flour, cornmeal, coffee, and tobacco—they had every reason to expect would be available on a regular basis.

Perhaps the most inexplicable shortage at Etna in 1860 was a totally inadequate supply of shoes for the laborers, many of whom were working in very difficult terrain. Early in the year, Charley Gorgas and Will Rex began sending a stream of letters to Buffalo Forge asking for sizes that would fit the workers. "If you have no No 12 or *13*—Why not buy—Spott *now* has been working sometime [without shoes]—We cant afford to have another sick hand—he has a very large foot—send a pair of 13 for Griffen," Gorgas wrote on March 11.[28] Spring passed, summer came, and the furnace managers were still anxiously awaiting the arrival of the much-needed footwear. "What are we to do for shoes?" Will Rex asked in late June. "Three of the Blk & some of the white hands at [the ore] bank are entirely out."[29]

When Brady finally did manage to send some shoes, he failed to provide a sufficient number of the larger sizes. On September 21, Rex informed him of the consequences:

> Some four or five of our Blk hands are entirely out of shoes. I will be obliged to buy 4 par [*sic*] in town. Spott is laying up at Bank for the want of a par. . . the bank is very wet—it is so rough they cannot work with out them. There was only 2 par of the last lot that would fit the negroes— they went to the bank. Two of the Car boy[s] is barefooted they will be layed up if they are not shod.[30]

Brady replied that the needed sizes had been ordered and would be sent as soon as they arrived, so Rex confined his purchase to "a little sole leather" with which to mend the slaves' shoes. But in mid-October, he asked Brady to "send up some shoes besides those small ones."[31] Money was very tight in the fall of 1860, and Weaver apparently wanted absolutely nothing bought locally for cash that could be purchased more cheaply elsewhere.

Ultimately his slave workers, particularly the miners, paid the price for this niggardly policy.

Not surprisingly, the slaves at Etna experienced serious health problems in 1860. An older man belonging to Weaver, a slave named Jordan, died in early May of what a local physician diagnosed as a "heart & stomach" ailment, but the most dangerous time came in the late summer and early fall.[32] "George & John & two of Susan's children Manda & a younger one are sick with Putria soar throat—George is very bad," Will Rex informed Weaver on August 15. The disease—diphtheria—spread rapidly among the black population at the furnace and by late August had reached epidemic proportions. "George died on Monday morning about 2 o'clock," Rex reported on August 27. "Lucy is right low yet, still she is not as bad as George was." John and Manda were much better, but two other slaves, Will and Tom, had definitely contracted the highly contagious disease. The doctor had treated them by burning their throats out with "costic." Louisa, the principal cook at Etna, had a sore throat, as did Will Rex, and the doctor had cautioned him to watch it carefully.[33] Diphtheria lingered at the furnace throughout September, and it was early October before Rex reported that almost everyone there, including himself, had recovered.[34]

Buffalo Forge was spared the disease because Weaver kept contact with the Etna hands to an absolute minimum and because he and Emma Brady had fortuitously canceled a planned trip to the northern part of the county in late September to visit Henry McCormick and his family. Weaver only learned of the presence of numerous diphtheria cases in that neighborhood in early October when he received a letter from McCormick. "I am not sorry that you and Mrs. Brady did not pay us a visit at this particular time because of the sore throat," McCormick wrote on October 10. "Mrs. Brady's dear little babe might have taken the sore throat, & died, & might have carried the disease home, & given it to your black children & then Mrs. Brady would have had a terrible time of it."[35] As the woman of the house, Emma Brady would have been responsible for nursing the sick, black and white, and McCormick was glad she had been spared that burden. McCormick's sympathy did not extend to the slave mothers, or fathers, at Buffalo Forge, who almost certainly would have lost children if diphtheria had been introduced into their community in 1860. When the dread disease did arrive there during the Civil War years, the results were catastrophic.

There were also discipline problems among the furnace slaves in 1860, as there had been in 1859. Will Rex gave a hint of one kind of difficulty the managers had experienced when he wrote Brady on January 21, 1860, that he had "hired Bill Cartmill for 135 dollars—he is to drive [ore] car or any other work we have for him—he beged [*sic*] to come back—I apprehend no stubborness on his part this year."[36]

Further evidence of disciplinary problems came during the summer. In August, Weaver once again sold a woman and her children who had been living at Etna. Since his policy was to sell slaves only when their behavior made such a course of action necessary, she had apparently committed a serious breach of conduct, although the nature of her offense is not spelled out in surviving records. Her name was Susan, she had originally been purchased by Weaver in 1847, and she was the woman who had come down with diphtheria in mid-August.[37] She and her four children were sold to a Lexington slave trader named George W. Johnson for $2,900 before she contracted the disease.[38]

The onset of her sickness, and the subsequent illness of two of her children, delayed the completion of the transaction until they had all recovered, and it was clear that she did not want to be sold away from Etna. "The sick are all well except Lucy," Rex told Brady in late September. "Susan says she dont feel well, but I think she is as well as she can be. She wants to stay as long as possible."[39] In October, Johnson offered to "take them as they are" for $2,250, which he claimed was "the most I can offer."[40] Weaver held out for more, and the two men finally settled on a price of $2,500 for Susan and her four children.[41] Weaver seems to have had no qualms about doing business with this particular slave trader, although he knew of Johnson's unsavory reputation. In 1859, Henry McCormick had told Weaver the slave dealer was "not worth a horse," and McCormick had speculated that Johnson was drunk when he had recently purchased a tavern in Lexington.[42]

Unquestionably the most explosive incident in 1860 involving the Etna work force came in the fall. It involved an act of slave violence directed against another slave, and Will Rex gave the details in a letter to Brady written on October 26. "Quite a serious affrey took place at the ore bank yesterday," Rex reported. "Bill Camasky struck John Sims in the head with a Wheel Barrow handle. They sent John down on the cars but he got so sick that he had to get off & Spott took him to G. Olphins where he is now lying & I suppose I will have to send a wagon after him." Bill Camasky was a slave belonging to Weaver; John Sims was Mary's son—Sam Williams's uncle—and he was owned by Henry McCormick, who had purchased him in 1854 at the sale of Matthew Bryan's estate. John had regularly been hired out to Weaver as a miner and furnace hand in the years following his acquisition by McCormick. "I have heard all that I know about it from the negroes," Rex went on to say, and if the reports were accurate, Bill Camasky "deserves a good thrashing, which I will give him. He is a self will[ed] stubborn nigger & nothing but the lash or fear of being sold has kep[t] him straight during the year."[43]

John Sims recovered from the blow, resumed work, and was back at Etna Furnace as a hireling in 1861. Bill Camasky was undoubtedly whipped, but he remained in Weaver's labor force until 1863. In October of that year he came in from the coaling grounds with syphilis and was sold the next month.[44]

Serious disciplinary problems were not confined to the furnace hands in 1860. The Buffalo Forge slaves gave Weaver and Brady great difficulty as well, and this time much more than "loafing" or "humbugging" was involved.

Two striking examples of slave resistance occurred at Buffalo Forge in the summer of 1860. One involved a twenty-eight-year-old field hand named William Green. The other involved Sam Williams.

In December 1854, Henry McCormick had attended the sale at Mount Torry Furnace in Augusta County where part of the property belonging to the estate of Matthew Bryan was being auctioned. McCormick had made two purchases for Weaver at this sale: a six-mule team, wagon, and gear which he bought for $587.75; and "Boy William Bot @ Mt Torry about 21 years of age" for whom he paid $975.00.[45] Weaver knew the slave William Green quite well. He had gone to work as a hireling at Buffalo Forge in the spring of 1854, and Weaver undoubtedly gave his friend McCormick instructions to buy the slave when William was returned to Mount Torry in time for the sale scheduled to take place at the end of the year.[46] Weaver's purchase of this slave was probably prompted by something more than his desire to acquire another prime hand. Among William Green's overwork purchases at Buffalo Forge in 1854 was a "Dress for Matilda," for which he paid $2.[47] This was a gift for his wife, and his wife was Matilda Thompson, a daughter of Garland Thompson, Sr. She was also the young woman Weaver had given to James Davidson's nine-year-old daughter Mary in 1849, when Matilda was seventeen. Four years later, in 1853, Matilda Thompson and William Green were married.[48] The children born to Matilda in the ensuing years grew up in the Davidson household in Lexington.

William worked at Buffalo Forge during 1855 and for part of the next year. In the summer of 1856, he was sent over to Etna, and he served as a furnace hand there until the spring of 1857.[49] At this point, James Davidson appears to have hired him so that he could be near Matilda and their children. William moved to the Davidson home in Lexington, and things seemed to go reasonably well for a while. But in the summer of 1859, an incident occurred there which placed his status as one of Davidson's servants in grave jeopardy.

On August 2, 1859, James Davidson wrote a detailed letter to Weaver in which he described an altercation which had taken place the previous evening between William and one of James Davidson's sons, Greenlee Davidson. This letter is a remarkable document on many grounds and deserves to be cited in full:

> Greenlee had a difficulty with William last night, and he [William] went off, saying that he would go down to you.
>
> About 11 oclock last night, Greenlee left the office & I remained, engaged writing. When he got home, he found William lying in the wood yard, very drunk—indeed drunker than usual. He endeavored to get him up into the kitchen. He replied impudently, as he has often done to me, *when drunk*. Greenlee became foolishly excited at the ravings of a drunken man & threatened to whip him up. But neither he nor Matilda could get him up. Greenlee came into the house & William followed him, calling for me. He gave more impudence & threatened Greenlee, when he struck William with the shovel a severe blow. They sent for me and I met them coming up—Greenlee on his way for an officer. I met William. He yielded to me. I took him back—but he would not go to bed & said he would go to you.
>
> I should not trouble you with this. But I wish you to speak *positively & firmly* to William or he will be of no more account to me. I told him if he went off I would never send for him—nor will I. When sober, he attends to my business well, but when drunk, as he often is, he is most impudent & unmanageable. Dont let him or any one at home but Brady know I have written this as it will prejudice the warnings & commands you may give him. You know how to talk to him & manage him & can now teach him a lesson. Greenlee was indiscreet in saying any thing to a drunken man, & he regrets now he had any thing to do with him and would now wish to leave me to manage him in my own [way.] His drunkenness will in the end cause me to part company with him. On account of his wife & children, this would be painful to me. If William would say to Greenlee, that he was drunk & did not know what he was doing, Greenlee would be kinder to him than ever. You might say so to him, in your own way. I shall never *coax* him again. He suits me well, & if he would keep sober would always have a good home. Keep this to yourself.[50]

On August 5, Brady wrote a brief note to Davidson informing him that Weaver had received his letter but that "Bill," as Weaver generally called him, had not arrived at Buffalo Forge, nor had they heard of him. "I hope he has returned home ere this," Brady added.[51]

If William did return to the Davidson home in Lexington, he did not remain there long. By early September, he was back at Etna working as a furnace hand and doing a job for which he was paid an allowance of $4 per month. He used part of his earnings to buy coffee, sugar, and tobacco, but he also bought buttons, thread, drill, linsey, and cotton cloth, which suggests strongly that he was purchasing items for Matilda. He finished the year at Etna, and in January 1860 Weaver brought him back to Buffalo Forge.[52]

William Green seems to have been a man who kept a tremendous amount of anger and rage bottled up inside. When his self-control was weakened by alcohol, however, his fury broke forth, and he placed both himself and his family at risk. There is no way to know if he was willing to apologize to Greenlee Davidson and return hat in hand to the Davidson household, but chances are he was not. That was probably why he was working at Etna in September 1859.

We can be certain of one thing, however. His anger was still the ultimate driving force behind his actions in the summer of 1860, a season when the resistance of a number of Buffalo Forge slaves—the forgemen in particular—tested the limits of Weaver's tolerance.

Brady recorded the by now familiar pattern of alternating forge work, agricultural work, and nonwork for Tooler and Harry Hunt, Jr., during the spring and early summer of 1860. The cooler months of January and February had generally been productive ones at the chaffery hammer as Tooler and Harry worked steadily until the beginning of March, when Tooler spent a week "playing," in Brady's estimation. Spring planting and the onset of the summer wheat harvest had drawn the two chaffery forgemen into the fields on a fairly regular basis, and Brady was probably not too surprised when Tooler decided to take the Fourth of July off. While most of the hands put in a full day's work, Tooler spent his Fourth "loafing & fishing."[53] What Brady could not have anticipated, however, were the actions of Sam Williams and Henry Towles in July and August of 1860.

Over the years, Brady had grown accustomed to the steady work habits of his refinery forgemen. Tooler and Harry Hunt, Jr., might be something less than reliable, but Sam Williams and Henry Towles were almost invariably pounding out anchonies unless the forge was flooded or down for repairs or the water was low or one of the men was truly sick or injured. But both Sam and Henry had their own ideas about when they had worked long enough and hard enough to deserve a break, and the summer of 1860 was such a time.

The two men manned their forge through some very warm days at the beginning of July, but by the middle of the month they had obviously had enough. Henry said he was too ill to work on Wednesday, July 18, and Brady apparently believed him. "Henry Towles sick," he recorded in his journal. Jim Garland was brought in to relieve Henry, and he and Sam put in a full day together. The next day, the temperature reached 100 degrees at one o'clock in the afternoon, and the heat in the forge must have been stifling. Henry did not show up for work that day, either. "Henry Towles sick i.e. loafing" was Brady's assessment. Sam and Jim Garland continued to work, so the forge had its supply of anchonies that day, but Sam was working under very trying conditions, and no one knew it better than he. Sam and Jim finished out the week, however, with "Henry Towles loafing" both Friday and Saturday.[54]

On Monday, July 23, it was Sam's turn, and he may not even have made a pretense of being sick. Henry returned to work that day; he could handle Sam's job, with Jim Garland's help. Sam was now "loafing," according to Brady, and he stayed out "loafing" the entire week. At the end of Sam's first week of rest, a period when the heat in the Valley had been particularly oppressive, Tooler and Harry Hunt, Jr., also took matters into their own hands. On Saturday, July 28, they carried out an act of industrial sabotage: "Tooler & Harry drew a few pounds & then broke down to loaf," Brady wrote. A point of diminishing returns had obviously been reached, and Brady decided about the middle of the day that there was no sense fighting it any longer: "All hands had a ½ [day] holiday."[55] From Weaver's and Brady's vantage point, Saturday, July 28, had been an exceedingly difficult day. The slaves undoubtedly took just the opposite view.

Sam's vacation was not over yet, however. He did not go back to work for three more weeks. From Monday, July 30, to Saturday, August 18, Brady regularly noted that Sam was "loafing" each day. He did not return to his post at the refinery forge until Monday, August 20. He had been off the job *four* full weeks.[56]

Sam returned to work as if nothing had happened. Jim Garland went back into the fields, and Sam and Henry Towles took up where they had left off a month or so earlier. As far as we know, neither Weaver nor Brady attempted to do anything to coerce him back to work earlier. Sam's vacation, if that word fits the occasion, seems to have been something he felt was due him. He had worked hard that year up to his four weeks of "loafing." His overwork accounts unfortunately do not go beyond 1858, but Weaver's cashbooks show a number of payments to him between late 1859 and the summer of 1860[57]:

December 24, 1859	To Sam	$10.00
February 11, 1860	"	5.00
March 25, 1860	"	10.00
May 10, 1860	"	1.00
July 10, 1860	"	5.00

It had taken a lot of extra pounds of iron to make that kind of money. And a month after he returned to work, he began receiving cash payments from Weaver again, a strong indication that he was working overtime after he rejoined Henry Towles at the refinery forge:

September 24, 1860	To Sam	$2.50
November 13, 1860	"	1.00
December 1, 1860	"	5.00

Perhaps most significant of all, his savings account, which Weaver was holding, was not touched during or after his month-long absence from his job.[58]

What this fascinating incident suggests is that Sam was fully aware of the power he possessed and the quite distinct limits of that power. He knew that his skills were critically important to his master and that this gave him a considerable amount of leverage in his dealings with Weaver and Brady. In his view, he deserved some time off, and he chose the hot, muggy dog days of July and August 1860 to take it. It was probably no accident that he did not leave his forge until Henry Towles returned. This kept the situation from assuming potentially dangerous and threatening dimensions. Since they were off one at a time, Jim Garland could come in to spell each one of them temporarily, and forge operations could continue. Ironmaking would not grind to a complete and costly stop because Henry was feigning illness and Sam was "loafing" back at his cabin. Thus Weaver and Brady would not be backed into a corner where they would be forced to crack down on their two refinery hands. Sam knew just how far he could go with his resistance, and he was careful to keep the situation under control.

At the same time, he had enough pride in himself to insist, through his actions, that there was a line beyond which he would not allow himself to be pushed. Months of steady labor, followed by forge work in temperatures reaching 100 degrees, comprised a step over that line. He took off for a month, and there were certainly risks attendant in that. But they would probably be manageable risks, and that was the way things turned out. By tolerating his absence, Weaver and Brady tacitly recognized that Sam had the power to force reasonable, limited, and temporary changes in his work regimen; they also silently acknowledged that, in a certain sense, he was justified in what he was doing. None of this fits the classic definition of what southern slavery was supposed to be: total dominance by the white master and total subservience by the black slave. But social institutions have a way of getting fuzzy around the edges, especially when they are as complex as the institution of human bondage.

Sam Williams won this confrontation, probably because of who he was and because his challenge to the system was guarded and oblique and had a limited objective—rest from work. William Green's case was quite a different matter. William's wife, Matilda, came out from Lexington in early July to help her sister through childbirth. Eliza Thompson King was expecting a baby, and Matilda was at Buffalo Forge on July 7, 1860, when Hannah, as Wilson and Eliza named their new daughter, was born.[59] Whether Matilda's presence at Buffalo Forge had any impact on her husband's subsequent course of action is unknown, but William's anger at living apart from his wife and children may well have been heightened by her visit. Early in the morning on Friday, July 27, William ran away from Buffalo Forge. The next day, July 28, was the day Tooler and Harry Hunt, Jr., sabotaged the forge and Brady gave all hands half the day off. Sam Williams was in the midst of his month-long absence from work at this time.[60]

Weaver wasted little time in sending an experienced party in pursuit of William. James E. Carson, the Augusta County slave trader, was given the job of hunting the runaway down. With William's wife and children back in Lexington, his capture was only a matter of time. On Tuesday, August 7, Carson brought "Bill Greenlee," as he was generally referred to in Weaver's records, back to Buffalo Forge in shackles. "Carson . . . to dinner," Brady wrote in his journal. "Sold Bill Greenlee." The price was $1,150.[61]

The slave trader apparently thought he had gotten a bargain. "Carson . . . told some person in town, so I understood, that he was offered 1400 for Bill after he bought him of you. He made his bragg that after he put the handcuffs on him he got him at his own price," Will Rex told Weaver in mid-August.[62] Carson may well have sold William to the Lexington party who offered the slave dealer a quick turnover on his money and a profit of $250. The probability that William's sale was a local one is suggested by a brief notation in the marriage register kept by the Freedmen's Bureau in Lexington after the Civil War: "William Green and Matilda Thompson as man and wife since 1853." William, born in Orange County, Virginia, and Matilda, a native of Rockbridge County, had come in to the local office of the Freedmen's Bureau in 1866 to record their marriage.[63]

If, as seems likely, William was indeed sold to a Lexington buyer in 1860, he was extremely fortunate. The week he was captured, the Lexington *Gazette* carried Carson's advertisement stating that he wished to buy "500 likely YOUNG NEGROES of both sexes, for the Southern market, for which I will pay the highest market prices in cash."[64]

Carson's appearance at Buffalo Forge on Tuesday, August 7, seems to have had no affect on Sam Williams. Weaver's master refiner had been "loafing" for two weeks when Carson brought William Green back, and if Sam were going to be intimidated into returning to work, the slave trader's visit should have done it. But Sam stayed off the job the remainder of that week and all of the next. His month-long absence from the finery clearly was not enough to convince Weaver that he should part with his most valuable forgeman.

William Green, in his late twenties and a "prime hand" in the language of the slave trade, was, from the perspective of Weaver's labor needs, still only a furnace and agricultural worker. Even more important, his defiance of the slave regime was open and direct and had an objective that no slaveholder could tolerate—freedom. Not surprisingly, Weaver brought the full force of the system swiftly and brutally down on him. The example of the unsuccessful runaway's being taken off in chains was immediately before the eyes of Sam Williams and every other slave at Buffalo Forge, and that was undoubtedly the way Weaver wanted it. Even Sam's status as a master refiner probably would not have protected him if he had carried his resistance as far as William Green took his.

William's attempt to escape and Sam's much more limited protest raise one of the ultimate questions about American slavery. What, in fact, was the better part of valor for a slave? Should one fight, confront, resist openly, run away, do everything one could to bring the system down? Or should one maneuver as best one could within the system, stay with one's family and try to help and comfort them, and attempt to carve out the best possible life, despite the physical and psychological confines of enslavement? These were questions each slave had to decide; they were not easily answered then and they are not easily answered now. But most, like Sam Williams, chose the latter course. To have done otherwise would have placed almost everything he loved in jeopardy. And Sam—husband of Nancy, father of Betty, Caroline, Ann, and Lydia, grandfather of Alfred and Mary Caroline Coleman, and son of Sally and Sam Williams, Sr.—had a great deal to lose.

In September 1860, one of the strangest in the myriad events that made up the mosaic of antebellum slave life at Buffalo Forge occurred. Joe, Tooler's brother and one of Weaver's skilled forge carpenters, died that month at the age of forty-seven under very puzzling circumstances. Joe seems to have been an important member of the slave community at Buffalo Forge. Scattered entries in Brady's journal suggest strongly that he was the slave preacher there and that he was fully literate. On April 22, 1859, Brady noted that Joe was "sawing & reading his bible" while he and another slave carpenter were making a body for a charcoal wagon. Two months later, Joe was "praying" while he was doing some carpentry work. Earlier in 1859, Brady had described Joe as "playing gentleman," and in September, when Brady was away from Buffalo Forge, that phrase was explained by one of the clerks: "Joe Gentleman with his linen coat on."[65] This was undoubtedly the coat in which Joe preached and conducted weddings. He also apparently could write; on September 19, 1854, Weaver's cashbook shows that Joe purchased a lead pencil.[66]

Unfortunately, the page that contains Joe's overwork account in the "Negro Book" kept at Buffalo Forge from 1850 to 1858 is missing, and the entries under his name in the earlier overwork ledgers are very brief. But we do know that he was married and that his wife lived across the Blue Ridge Mountains. "Joe started to see his wife on the old sorrell," Brady wrote on March 17, 1859; a week later, Brady noted, "Joe returned from down the country."[67] We also know that his wife's name was Rebecca. Her name is listed as Joe's "consort" in the Rockbridge County Death Register.[68]

"Joe made helve & loafed about his wedding affair," Brady recorded on Saturday, September 1, 1860. No marriage took place at Buffalo Forge that weekend, so Joe was apparently conducting a wedding ceremony somewhere in the neighborhood. The following Monday, September 3, Brady listed Joe as sick. His condition steadily worsened during the next ten days, and at seven o'clock in the evening on Thursday, September 13, Joe died. Brady gave the cause of his death as "Poison," and when Weaver supplied information to the county clerk for inclusion in the death register, he used the verb form—"poisoned"—to describe the cause of Joe's demise.[69]

It was not uncommon in the Old South for masters to cite poisoning as the reason for a slave's death when no other cause was readily apparent. This may have been the case here, but there is no way to know. If he was indeed poisoned, we have no way of ascertaining who administered the fatal dose and whether it was given accidentally or intentionally. The Rockbridge criminal court records are silent on the subject, and no notice was taken of the case in the local newspapers. The brief entries in Brady's journal and the scant information in the county death register provide all we know about his death. The only other reference in the records that might conceivably have anything to do with his passing is a small item in the cashbooks showing that a deadly substance was available at Buffalo Forge; Brady spent 50 cents to lay in a supply of rat poison in the summer of 1860.[70]

Weaver's and Brady's correspondence in the summer and fall of 1860 gave little indication that Buffalo Forge and the entire slave South were heading into the maelstrom of sectional conflict. Their chief concern seemed to be the falloff in their business that followed the turbulent political events of the spring and summer months. The breakup of the Democratic party at the Charleston convention in May had been followed by the Republican nomination of Abraham Lincoln later that month. When the northern and southern wings of the Democratic party reassembled in separate conventions in June, the result was two Democratic tickets: Stephen A. Douglas was the choice of the northern meeting; the southern assembly chose John C. Breckinridge of Kentucky. A fourth candidate, John Bell of Tennessee, was nominated by remnants of the old Whig party to campaign for the presidency under the banner of a new political organization known as the Constitutional Union party.

With the Democrats irrevocably divided into two warring factions, Lincoln's triumph in the fall election was virtually guaranteed. That result would represent the realization of one of the South's worst nightmares: the elevation of a "Black Republican" to the highest political office in the land.

"Hoping soon to have new orders," Brady wrote Lee, Rocke & Taylor, his Lynchburg commission house, on September 15, 1860.[71] The situation was exactly the reverse of the one that had prevailed in 1859 when Buffalo Forge could not keep up with the demand for its iron. Brady did not know it at the time, but when he sent two tons of bar to Lynchburg in mid-September, he had shipped his last major order to that market for 1860.[72]

It certainly came as no surprise to Weaver and Brady when Lee, Rocke & Taylor wrote in late October that "the business of our place is very dull at present, . . . & money matters are as close now as we ever saw them (1857 not excepted)." The cause was clear: "the pending Presidential election." Local banks had curtailed their discounting of commercial paper, and "everyone is holding off from making forward engagements until further developments." The merchants closed by expressing the fervent hope that "next month will pleasantly relieve the public mind of its present embarrassment, & things will glide along as heretofore."[73]

The next month, November 1860, brought the election of Abraham Lincoln. The day following the election, the palmetto flag was raised in Charleston, and South Carolina prepared to lead the march of the Deep South states out of the Union. "The tea has been thrown overboard, the revolution of 1860 has been initiated," editorialized the Charleston *Mercury* on November 8.[74] On December 20, 1860, the South Carolina convention passed an ordinance of secession, and six more states across the cotton South followed in quick succession. By February 1, 1861, the tier of states stretching from South Carolina to Texas had dissolved their ties to the Union.

The prevailing mood in Rockbridge County in the weeks following Lincoln's triumph was cautious, conservative, and opposed to precipitous action. The county, reflecting the long-standing Whig tradition in the area, had voted heavily for John Bell and the Constitutional Union ticket in the presidential canvas, and a public meeting was called by James D. Davidson and other prominent local citizens and political leaders to assemble in Lexington in early December "for the purpose of taking into consideration the State of the country." A heavy snowfall prevented this meeting from taking place at the appointed time, and it was rescheduled for Monday, January 7, the first day of the January court. A committee met in James Davidson's law offices to draft a series of resolutions for presentation to this meeting, and these resolutions undoubtedly formed the basis for much discussion at Buffalo Forge when Davidson and two of his sons came out to Weaver's residence for dinner on Sunday, December 23.[75]

The central point of the resolutions was a call for the peaceful redress of southern grievances within the framework of "the sacred Constitutional Union." The anti-slavery agitation in the North should cease, northern states should repeal their "Personal Liberty Bills" which were designed to impede the return of fugitive slaves to the South, and the federal government should refrain from resorting "to coercion against any seceding State." The resolutions closed by endorsing the call of Virginia governor John Letcher for a special session of the state legislature and his proposal for a general convention of all the states to work out a peaceful solution to the crisis.[76]

The basic thrust of these resolutions was certainly shared by Weaver and Brady. Neither man wanted Virginia to secede and both fervently hoped the Union could be saved. Their mood matched the season in the dreary secession winter of 1861, and many of their business correspondents shared their outlook. "Business dull very dull, money matters tight very tight and things politically look no better," a Richmond merchant wrote in January.[77] Lee, Rocke & Taylor, Weaver's Lynchburg commission house, echoed these sentiments the following month. "We see no ray of light in the political firmament, & really believe there is a determined purpose in the Republican Party to break up this old cherished Government, & we very much fear they will succeed," a member of the firm wrote on February 13.[78] Weaver agreed. "The times are gloomy enough, & no signs of daylight yet," Weaver replied on February 28. "We are anxiously looking for 'Old Abes' inaugural, as we can judge by that what kind of man he is."[79]

Weaver thought Lincoln's vague, ambiguous, and sometimes rambling "travelling speeches," made on his journey to Washington that month, did "no credit to him or his party."[80] The president-elect was telling crowds along his route that he opposed any invasion or coercion of the southern states but that enforcing federal laws and retaining control of federal property in the secessionist area did not come under the definition of coercion. On more than one occasion Lincoln referred to the crisis gripping the country as an "artificial" one, and he candidly admitted that he was avoiding explicit policy statements until his inauguration.[81] "We must still 'hope on, hope ever' for the best," Weaver wrote.[82]

Hope faded rapidly in the tense weeks following Lincoln's inauguration. His address had offered no guarantees to the South other than a pledge to refrain from interfering with slavery in those states where it already existed and a promise that the federal government would not initiate hostilities against the seceding states. "You can have no conflict, without being yourselves the aggressors," he said. At the same time Lincoln rejected the notion that the Union could be dissolved, and he made it clear that he was determined to see that federal laws were "faithfully executed in all the states." The editor of the Lexington *Gazette* lamented the endorsement of "the doctrine of coercion" in Lincoln's address but hoped that the president would "not . . . recommend to Congress the adoption of any coercive measure."[83]

The debate over the use of force could not remain a philosophical one for very long. The crisis was building to a flash point at Charleston Harbor, where a federal garrison continued to occupy Fort Sumter. In late March, Lincoln decided that both Fort Sumter and Fort Pickens at Pensacola, Florida, should be held.[84]

Weaver thought there was a chance that the ill wind blowing across the country might carry some good his way. "I would like you to see Mr. Archer of the Bellona Foundry, & see if you cannot get an order for cannon metal," Weaver instructed Shields & Somerville, his Richmond commission merchants, on April 4. "His grandfather Clarke used to buy Etna metal for that foundry," he reminded his sales agents. Several days later, he again pressed the Richmond merchants on the subject. "Let me hear from you as soon as you can about the cannon metal, as I would like to prepare for that kind of blast if I get an order," he wrote on April 8.[85] There was little doubt in Weaver's mind that ordnance would soon be in great demand, and he did not intend to let this potentially lucrative market for his pig iron slip away.

April began auspiciously at Buffalo Forge. The weather was still unseasonably cool, but the field hands began planting the corn crop on Monday, April 1, the same day the first blossoms appeared on the plum trees in Weaver's orchards. The apple and peach trees had blossomed the previous month, and bluebirds, robins, and red-winged blackbirds had all returned after their winter migration south. Bullfrogs had been heard croaking nightly from the mill pond for the past several weeks, a sure sign that spring was rapidly approaching. The weather remained cool and dry almost all week, and the planting had progressed nicely when rain fell on Saturday, April 6.[86]

The forgemen put in a remarkably productive week at the beginning of April. Sam Williams and Henry Towles manned the finery with their customary steadiness, and Tooler and Harry Hunt did not miss a beat either. In six days of work beginning on April 1, they drew eleven journeys totaling 8,600 pounds of bar, and of that amount 1,880 pounds had been overwork. It was far and away their best performance to date in 1861.[87] Extensive repairs at Weaver's flour mill were also nearing completion. He had installed new milling machinery, some of which he had purchased in Philadelphia, and what he referred to proudly as "a tip top mill," the "equal to any in the country," would soon be ready for production.[88]

The second week in April did not start well, however, and things grew steadily worse as the week progressed. On Monday, April 8, a steady drizzle fell, and on Tuesday it rained hard all day. "Forge full of water: no work," Brady wrote. Buffalo Creek was over the bridge at dawn, and Henry Matthews and Prince Towles, whose cabins stood on the far side of the creek, could not get to work. It was too wet to go into the fields, so the agricultural hands cleaned out a storeroom and did other odd jobs. The next day, Wednesday, was no better. A mixture of rain and wet snow came down nearly all day, the field hands could do little, and Sam Williams, Henry Towles, Tooler, and Harry Hunt, Jr., had to devote their time to cleaning up the forge. Some work got done on Thursday. It was clear and mild, and the field hands rebuilt fences washed out earlier in the week and the forgemen returned to their hammers. But any hopes Brady might have entertained that the week would end well were dispelled Friday morning.

Brady normally got up before 5 A.M. so that he could be on the move at dawn when the workday began. Friday, April 12, started out with clouds and rain, and things went downhill from there. The forge once again was stopped by high water, the field hands had to be called in by 3 P.M., and the bridge across the creek was impassable by evening. All in all, it was a gray, dank, dismal day at Buffalo Forge, a day well suited for the beginning of a civil war.[89]

About the time Brady and the slave force were waking up that Friday, a shell was arching through the sky over Charleston Harbor signaling the start of the most momentous bombardment in American history. Lincoln's attempt to resupply Fort Sumter by sea had prompted the Confederate authorities on April 11 to demand the surrender of the fort before the relief vessels could reach Charleston. The fort's commander, Major Robert Anderson, refused. At 4:30 A.M. the next day, Friday, April 12, a shot was fired from one of the Confederate guns as a signal to the other southern batteries to open fire.[90] The attack on Fort Sumter, and the American Civil War, had begun.

3

War

"Our glorious union is broken, never to be united," Weaver wrote shortly after the attack on Fort Sumter. "We have nothing to do but our best for our state: We must all help to row the boat."[1]

The Virginia convention moved quickly to join the Confederacy following the surrender of Fort Sumter and Lincoln's call to the states for 75,000 troops to suppress the insurrection. The delegates in Richmond adopted an ordinance of secession on April 17 which provided for a popular referendum on the issue the following month, but the convention's action effectively took Virginia out of the Union. The dramatically changed mood in the state after Lincoln's call for troops was certainly reflected in the editorial columns of the Lexington *Gazette*. The editor, who had previously urged restraint and had endorsed the conservative resolutions drafted by Davidson and other local citizens earlier in the year, now rejoiced that Virginians were free from "the corrupt, rotten, and abolitionized despotism of the Northern usurpers. Sink or swim, live or die, survive or perish, their destinies are now cast with the Southern Confederacy." The vote in Rock-bridge County in the May election was 1,728 in favor of secession, one opposed.[2]

Weaver and Brady wasted little time in taking a public stand in favor of Virginia and the South. On April 19, they gave $100 to help outfit a volunteer regiment that was being recruited in their neighborhood, and Brady sprinkled his letters with references to their southern sympathies and the worthlessness of "Black" Republicans in the North.[3] When the results of the statewide secession vote became known in May, a flag-raising ceremony was held at Buffalo Forge to mark the occasion.[4] The next month, Brady swore an oath of allegiance to the Commonwealth of Virginia and joined the Rockbridge County Home Guard, which was authorized to arrest and bring before the county authorities "all persons, white or black, whom they may have reason to suspect of improper purposes, or violation of the Ordinance of Secession."[5] William Weaver and Daniel Brady, two native Pennsylvanians, had clearly cast their lot with their adopted state and region.

Nowhere were their loyalties more clearly revealed than in their correspondence with southern merchants with whom they had done business for many years. Lee, Rocke & Taylor kept Weaver and Brady closely informed on Confederate troop movements through Lynchburg and the commercial climate there and passed along news of early military engagements. When "the *Infernal Yankees*" attacked Confederate positions at Big Bethel in eastern Virginia in June and were repulsed, the Lynchburg merchants commented that such blows would "send terror to the remainder of the white-livered heartless scamps" in the North and that the results of this battle were "only an indication of what will be their fate whenever they show their *cowardly scalps.*"[6]

"I was glad to hear of the fight at Bethel," Weaver replied on June 18, "& hope for a few more, with same results, when I reckon our northern enemies will kalkulate [*sic*] that it don't pay & be willing to let us separate in peace, for that must be the result, even if we have to fight for 20 years." Weaver had "great hopes of a reaction taking place in the north" against the war. He thought there were "many good & true men there, whose voices were overpowered by the fanatics & mob. I think you will see some signs of it, even in Congress," Weaver went on to say, particularly when the Lincoln administration asked for massive military appropriations and the taxes to fund them. Weaver made no reference to northern cowardice in his letter; he knew the Yankee character too well for that. His assessment was "touch their pockets & you touch their hearts."[7]

Weaver might well have been speaking of himself when he offered that comment. There was no question that his sympathies lay with the South and slavery in the struggle engulfing the nation in 1861. But that struggle also meant that there was money to be made, particularly by manufacturers who could supply articles that would clearly be in great demand. His inquiries made just before the firing on Fort Sumter about the market for cannon metal in Richmond produced a quick response from his commission merchants there. On April 16, 1861, R. B. Somerville & Company reported that both the Bellona Foundry and the Tredegar Iron Works *"want metal now & will continue to want,"* and the reason was simple and obvious: "the South must have guns." Virtually unlimited sales of gun metal could be made, but only if Weaver's pig passed the "test of strength" required of all iron used in manufacturing ordnance. Cannon would first have to be cast and test-fired to prove the quality of Weaver's metal. In addition, Dr. Junius L. Archer, the proprietor of the Bellona Foundry, expressed a decided preference for Bath as opposed to Etna pig.[8] Weaver knew that the ore banks at Bath Furnace were exhausted and there was virtually no chance that that property, which was rapidly returning to wilderness, would ever be productive again. If he were going to tap into the market for gun metal, it would have to be with Etna pig.

A week before the firing on Fort Sumter, Weaver's commission house in Richmond had reported that the market for pig was "very dull" there and that the top price offered locally for Etna iron was $22.50 per ton.[9] On April 24, 1861, Weaver offered to sell 100 tons of cannon iron to the Bellona Foundry for $42.50 per ton. "I will not guarantee it, but will send 25 tons for trial & if it does not suit the purpose, they need not take the balance of 100 tons," Weaver wrote. "If Dr. Archer agrees to my terms, please inform me at once, so that I can make the 25 tons as soon as the furnace starts." Etna would go into blast on June 1, Weaver reported, and he would need a decision from Dr. Archer as soon as possible so that he could make the necessary preparations.[10]

Weaver's offer and an urgent letter from R. B. Somerville & Company crossed in the mail. "We wrote you short time since about cannon metal— we can sell *either* now—city full of soldiers—the cry is *War War*," Somerville wrote on April 26.[11] Weaver replied that he was waiting for a decision on his offer, and that, in the meantime, the merchants should halt all sales: "the small lot of metal you have on hand you had better hold, as certainly if the present state of things last, metal must go up."[12]

Metal did indeed go up, but not as rapidly as Weaver wanted it to. Dr. Archer had paid $28 for gun metal from a furnace in Wythe County, Virginia, just before the war, and he balked at Weaver's prices. Weaver did not seem overly concerned. "If the blockade is enforced & maintained, metal must be scarce," he wrote on May 3.[13] Since there were very few blast furnaces still in operation in Virginia, he was fully confident that there was no need for him to accommodate himself to the market. The market would come to him soon enough.

Weaver did not have to wait long. On May 9, F. B. Deane, Jr., the principal founder in Lynchburg, wrote to inquire about buying a substantial amount of pig iron for general foundry use and asked if Weaver intended to put his furnace into production that year.[14] "My Etna Furnace will go in blast around the first June, after which I shall have metal for sale, but I want to get a high price for it," Weaver replied. "Evidently the prospects are good for the iron men to make a little money this year & it is really time, as they have been doing a losing business for some years. I will be glad to supply you when I make metal," Weaver concluded, "if we can agree upon a price."[15]

Deane was pleased to hear that Etna iron would be available, but he was anxious about the price Weaver planned to charge. Weaver was in no hurry to allay his anxiety. "Supply & demand governs prices," Weaver replied, "& I wish to get [the] best price I can. . . . If the war & blockade continues, metal will go very high."[16]

Deane found out just how high in mid-June. "I will sell you 10 tons metal at $40 per ton," Weaver wrote on June 11. That was a *cash* price, Weaver went on to say; no more selling on time or accepting notes which would have to be discounted before he could receive his money. And Weaver refused to promise to provide more than the ten tons at that price. Supply and demand, as he had put it earlier, would govern future charges.[17]

The Lynchburg founder was outraged. Weaver's price was "higher than your iron can be sold in any market in the world known to me," Deane wrote on June 15, and he found Weaver's terms of payment as objectionable as the price. "I never purchased a ton of iron for cash unless . . . the *interest* was deducted *from the regular 4 months market price*," he added, "nor I never will."[18]

Weaver made no reply to this letter. He was receiving ample inquiries about his pig iron from other parties, and he was in no hurry to rush his metal onto the market. When a Richmond stove manufacturer, Asa Snyder, asked Weaver in July to quote him a price on twenty-five tons of his best iron, Weaver was more than happy to oblige: $50 per ton cash, delivered in Richmond. Snyder, like Deane the previous month, declined the offer. "I have only advanced 10 per cent on my stoves," he wrote, "whilst your [*sic*] asking 75 per cent on your iron!" Weaver was unmoved by Snyder's protest. "I have not altered my views about the price of metal, & shall be happy to supply you," Weaver replied, "at $50 per ton."[19]

Weaver's waiting game paid off handsomely in the fall. F. B. Deane, Jr., was the first party to have to swallow his words. He told Weaver in August that he would pay $40 per ton for Etna iron if Weaver would sell it to him on four months' time. Weaver wrote back that his terms were what they had been earlier: $40 per ton, cash on delivery in Lynchburg. On September 5, Deane agreed to Weaver's terms and asked him to send the metal at once.[20] Asa Snyder wrote from Richmond six days later that he would pay Weaver's price of $50 per ton cash for a select lot of pig iron, and the tone of Snyder's correspondence was much different than it had been during the summer. "I trust my stoves may acquire even greater celebrity by being made with Virg^a Iron than they heretofore acquired with the choicest brands of Scotch pig," he told Weaver in late September. "I have no doubt the Etna metal will make as fine stove plates as the Scotch," Weaver replied amicably.[21] When Deane asked Weaver in October for more iron, he too had to pay $50 per ton.[22]

"I am satisfied that metal must advance still more, if the war continues, & I am not very anxious to sell," Weaver wrote in late September.[23] But he wanted to pay off a long-standing account—something over $3,000—with Somerville & Company for supplies the Richmond merchants had furnished him before the war, so he pressed on with sales at $50 per ton. By mid-October, Weaver had cleared most of this debt and was looking for a price increase.[24] "If you don't want to sell at 50$ name a price for any quantity not exceeding 50 to 100 Tons," Somerville & Co. wrote in October; "parties want it for finishing up contracts with the Confederate government—of course all sales are now for cash—which reduces charges & gives you your money *at once.*"[25] Weaver thought it over and decided to put another 100 tons on the market. The price was $50 cash for iron brought by his wagons to the boat basin of the James River and Kanawah Canal in Buchanan, two and a half miles from Etna Furnace. Somerville & Company were to pass their 2½ percent commission plus canal tolls and freight charges on to the buyer. Weaver wanted "a clear $5,000" when the 100 tons were delivered "at the canal bank in Buchanan."[26]

William S. Triplett, the proprietor of the Old Dominion Iron & Nail Works in Richmond, snapped up this iron the day Weaver's letter reached the commission house. Triplett was struggling to fill orders for the Confederate government and was desperate for metal. Weaver had his "clear $5,000" in hand the first week in November.[27]

William Weaver was making a fortune off his blast furnace in 1861, and his profits were enhanced by several fortuitous circumstances which had prevailed earlier in the year. Before the war began, the economy had been seriously deranged throughout Virginia, and, as a consequence, slave hirelings had been plentiful and cheap. Daniel Brady made a successful swing through the Spotsylvania County hiring region in late December 1860 and early January 1861, and additional slaves were available closer to the furnace well past January 1, the traditional end of the hiring season. Will Rex wrote Weaver on January 11 that a canal boat captain reported "Factory hands & Farm hands hired for forty to sixty Doll in Lynchburg," and that the streets of that city "were crowded with them when he left New Years day."[28]

Weaver had managed to hire only thirteen slaves the previous year at an average cost of $120 per hand. He hired over thirty hands for work in 1861 at an average cost of $113.50, and some had come much cheaper than that.[29] When a Spotsylvania County slave who had previously been hired out to Etna showed up at Buffalo Forge in mid-January looking for work, Brady was reluctant to take him on. "I dully [sic] received your note by Clayborn & regret that you sent him, as I had hired as many hands as I needed," Brady wrote the slave's owner on January 15. "Uncle hired several whilst I was away as low as $75." Since the slave had already made the long journey over the Blue Ridge, Brady agreed to hire him but offered only $90 for his services. The owner accepted the offer.[30] It was a buyer's market for hired slave labor in 1861, a dramatic change from the circumstances that had prevailed in recent years.

Equally important, many of these slaves had worked at Etna before and knew the routine there. "We have 20 black choppers in, & the same number of whites," Rex wrote Brady in late January. The white woodcutters were paid by the cord and provided supplemental labor; the slave hands were the key to an adequate supply of fuel. The slave chopper's task of nine cords per week multiplied by twenty hands was the wood that would fill most of the charcoal pits, and Rex reported that the critical first week had gone well. "Our black choppers so far have made their task at least those on the Furnace hill," he wrote on January 29. "The other their first week is just out. They have not ranked it yet."[31] In terms of both the number of hands hired and their initial performance, the year was off to a very promising start.

Weaver had made a decision prior to the 1861 blast that would have a profound impact on the furnace's production that year. He had decided to install hot-blast machinery at Etna. This process basically involved heating the blast of air that was sent into the furnace to help bring the mixture of iron ore, fuel, and limestone to the temperature needed to melt the ore. Pipes through which the blast passed were carried over the top of the furnace stack where they could be heated by the combustion of the waste gases emitted by the furnace itself. The hot-blast technique, first introduced in England in 1828 and brought to this country six years later, spread rapidly across the North in the years prior to the Civil War. It was much less common in the South, despite the increased efficiency the process brought to blast furnace operations. A standard treatise on iron manufacturing published in 1854 claimed that a charcoal-fired furnace equipped with hot-blast machinery could achieve dramatic savings in the amount of fuel consumed and increase the production of pig iron by as much as 50 percent.[32] Weaver, his entrepreneurial acumen undimmed at the age of seventy-nine, had picked an ideal moment to improve his furnace.

"We have the pipes all in but five, which we are now moulding—20 new pipes in all," Rex told Brady in late February; "it will take about Three days to finish the Hot blast," and they would "then be ready to try the blast thoroughly." By mid-March, the first charcoal pits were ready to be opened, a new hearth had been installed in the furnace, and the ore trains had begun arriving at the stack. Needed repairs to the furnace stonework were completed in early April, and Rex thought they could fire up before the end of the month.[33]

Weaver was in no hurry, however. "Uncle is not willing for us to go in blast untill the middle of May," Rex reported less than a week before the firing on Fort Sumter.[34] Weaver was waiting for an answer to his proposition to make cannon metal, and that answer would have a great deal to do with how the furnace would be operated in 1861. Ordnance manufacturers insisted that gun iron be produced in cold-blast furnaces, which would mean, of course, that the new hot-blast machinery at Etna could not be employed. When Weaver's offer to turn out cannon metal at $42.50 per ton failed to tempt the Richmond foundries, his decision was made for him. He would proceed as originally planned with maximum hot-blast production of metal for general foundry use and for the use of his own forge. The rapid escalation in the price of all grades of pig iron in the summer and fall of 1861 quickly demonstrated both the wisdom of Weaver's decision to install the hot-blast process and his good fortune in not locking himself into a fixed-price contract for gun metal.

The outbreak of the war thrust both Charley Gorgas and Will Rex into the midst of military organizational activity in Botetourt County. Both men went to considerable lengths to show their loyalty to the South. They attended a militia muster in Fincastle, the county seat, on April 27 and quickly discovered that their demonstration of southern sympathies had been a prudent move. A "Vigilance Committee" in Buchanan had ordered two natives of Pennsylvania who had been living in the town to leave immediately, and the same group had tried and imprisoned "a gambler who loafed about the town & who said something about the negroes raise-ing," Rex reported.[35] Gorgas even went so far as to sign up with a volunteer regiment organizing in Buchanan, but he had no intention of serving in the military. He immediately procured a substitute on the grounds that, as a recently married man, his first duty was to remain close to hearth and home.[36]

Charley Gorgas had married a local woman in August 1860. Charley was twenty-seven at the time, and he listed his total net worth in 1860 as $100 in personal property. His bride, Ann Sisson, was one of the richest women in Botetourt County. She was thirty-five at the time of the wedding, and she brought to their union considerable inherited wealth, including thirty-three slaves and a landed estate that included both rich farm land and ore banks which she leased out to ironmasters, including William Weaver, in need of supplemental deposits of iron ore.[37] It was a marriage to which Charley's Uncle William could readily give his blessing.

Gorgas received a brief scare following his military enlistment. According to Will Rex, the substitute Charley had hired was thinking of changing his mind. "I understand that a substitute can decline going, & that the principal he's held responsible," Rex told Brady in April; "if that be the case farewell to Charley as his substitute is like himself a newly married man." When the local volunteer regiments left the county in May, however, Charley remained at home, his place taken by a substitute. Will Rex managed to secure exemption from military duty during the summer as an individual whose services were needed in essential war production.[38]

"We fired the Furnace Wednesday evening about 2 o'clock," Rex informed Brady on Friday, May 24, and the white founder, a man named Parr, thought it would take about ten days for Etna to heat up to the point when they could begin producing iron. The founder also thought that they had "the best lot of Coal he ever seen, taking it through out—it is good hard coal." After some annoying leaks in the hot-blast pipes were plugged, the furnace settled into a steady pace of production in June. "We have a good blast, & it is hot also," Rex reported with considerable satisfaction.[39]

The same month the furnace began regular production, the local vigilance organization paid a visit to Etna. Will Rex described the circumstances that prompted their appearance at the furnace in a letter to Brady written on Saturday, June 22:

> I wrote to Uncle about a report here of the negroes intending to raise. The same evening that I wrote about 2 oclock about 10 or 15 of these town fellows came out—John W. Jones Esquire with them. Their [sic] had been 2 out in the morning want[ing] to take the negroes up whether evidence or not, but I objected to it—they then went back & sent out the

above 10 or 15. After examine [*sic*] the girl & Cart's wife, Jones thought it would be adviseable to take Jim & Mark to town. She said she had heard Jim tell Mark on Sunday evening under the cherry tree that they must all be ready the Sunday night following—they were going to kill the white people. Mark replied that he would have nothing to do with it—he then went in the house & told his mother—she gave a grunt & told him that would be awfull. They got nothing out of them they [Jim and Mark] came back next day before dinner so I do not think they will make a breake on that night if they had intended.[40]

The return of the two slaves to the furnace following their interrogation in town strongly suggests that no plot had been discussed among the work force at Etna. Ironworks, staffed by sizable numbers of adult male slaves, were frequent targets of suspicion when circumstances created fear and anxiety in neighboring white communities. Rumors had circulated in Lexington in 1858 that slaves at a nearby ironworks were plotting an insurrection, and the guard at the arsenal at the Virginia Military Institute had been doubled as a precaution.[41] The visit of the Rockbridge County patrol to Buffalo Forge at the time John Brown was hanged was symptomatic of the same type of panic. In 1856, an insurrectionary scare in the iron district along the border between Tennessee and Kentucky had led to the torture and lynching of a number of slaves working at blast furnaces, forges, and rolling mills along the Tennessee and Cumberland rivers.[42] So the rumors surrounding the Etna slaves following the outbreak of the Civil War could almost have been predicted. Fortunately, no slaves living at the furnace seem to have suffered because of the tremor of fear that ran through portions of the local white community in the summer of 1861.

There was some evidence of anxiety at Buffalo Forge as well. The departure from the area of the Rockbridge Grays, a unit recruited principally from within a five-mile radius of Weaver's place, stripped the immediate vicinity of a sizable number of able-bodied white men. This company left the county shortly after the firing on Fort Sumter and became part of what would soon become known as the "Stonewall Brigade," commanded by a former instructor from the Virginia Military Institute named Thomas Jonathan Jackson.[43] On April 23, Weaver asked Lee, Rocke & Taylor to send two Colt Navy revolvers, "or any gun," to Buffalo Forge as soon as possible. "We have arms but not enough for the place," he explained.[44] Before the war Weaver had allowed his slaves to take firearms, as many as four rifles, over to Highland Farm for hunting when they went to that remote location at harvest time.[45] It was a practice he did not repeat after the outbreak of hostilities in the spring of 1861.

The Colt six-shooters were totally sold out by the time Weaver's request reached Lynchburg, but his commission merchants promised to do what they could to supply him with pistols. "I shall be glad to get the revolvers, as they are a scarce article amongst us & may be needed," Weaver replied in early May.[46] Later that month, the Home Guard at Fancy Hill, four miles from Buffalo Forge, posted a $50 reward for a mysterious gray-haired man of Irish descent, dressed totally in black and carrying a black carpet bag, whom the Guard accused of "tampering with our slaves and endeavoring to excite a spirit of insubordination and servile insurrection."[47] During the summer, a Lexington slave, having been "cleared of the charge of inciting servile insurrection," received thirty-nine lashes at a public whipping for "making seditious speeches."[48] It was a time, whites clearly believed, to watch closely the actions of both slaves and strangers.

Brady recorded nothing of a suspicious nature in his journal during the days following the outbreak of the war. Tooler spent the week after the surrender of Fort Sumter "loafing," but that was largely because of heavy rains that flooded the forge and interrupted normal operations. The other forgemen spent this time cleaning up debris and making necessary repairs and returned to work as soon as conditions permitted. Tooler was back at his hammer the following week, and Brady gave no indication that anything out of the ordinary had transpired.[49]

Sunday, April 21, was clear and warm, the first real day of spring in the Valley. The workweek started on a sad note, however. On Monday, Amy Banks Carter, one of the young slave women who had been married at Buffalo Forge at the time John Brown was hanged, lost her firstborn child. John William Carter, five months old, died of "inflamation of the brain," in all likelihood encephalitis. The baby was buried the next day, and that evening Weaver sent Warder Banks, Amy's father and one of the regular teamsters at Buffalo Forge, into Lexington with his mule team and wagon to haul supplies for the state. The rest of the week passed uneventfully as the field hands proceeded with their corn planting and the forgemen were at their usual posts. Brady noted that the corn lots worked by Sam Williams, Sam Williams, Sr., and Henry Matthews were laid off during the week, and on Saturday, the agricultural workers, under the supervision of overseer Lewis Entsminger, planted "the boys lots."[50] Buffalo Forge seemed to be settling back into a routine indistinguishable from that which had prevailed before the war.

As the spring of 1861 turned to summer, the forgemen certainly gave no evidence that their work pattern had changed. Sam Williams and Henry Towles were at the finery almost without fail, and Tooler and Harry Hunt,

Jr., alternated weeks of steady labor and "over iron" with weeks in which one or both of them were either "sick" or "loafing" or "sick or loafing." There was nothing here with which Brady was not already thoroughly familiar. When the corn crop required cultivation or the hay was ready for mowing or the wheat for cradling, Brady did not hesitate to pull Tooler and Harry Hunt, Jr., out of the forge and send them into the fields, just as he had done in peacetime.[51]

Except it was not peacetime, of course, and rumors of war abounded. "Great excitement caused by a report that the enemy were marching on Lexington," Brady noted on June 5. It was, as he correctly indicated, "all humbug." Nonetheless, the "F.F.V.'s"—First Families of Virginia—had all been "dreadfully scared," while the "F.F.P.'s"—First Families of Pennsylvania—had been "not frightened."[52] In July, the rumors of war turned to bloody reality on the battlefield of Manassas in northern Virginia. The Rockbridge Grays, rallying behind "Stonewall" Jackson to help check the Union advance against the Confederate left flank, lost nineteen of sixty-four men in this engagement.[53]

One reason Brady was willing to shift Tooler and Harry Hunt to field work in the summer of 1861 was the virtual disappearance of any market for Buffalo Forge merchant bar. "We see no prospect for selling iron now & fear the sales will amount to but little if any are made at all," Lee, Rocke & Taylor wrote from Lynchburg in early June.[54] Weaver found this situation puzzling. The demand for his pig iron was so great that he could virtually name his own price, but his bar was a drug on the market. He saw this as a temporary aberration, however. He was confident that "if the war continues & our ports are blockaded, bar iron will have to advance as well as other things."[55]

Weaver kept Sam Williams and Henry Towles at their refinery hammer throughout the summer so that Tooler and Harry Hunt, Jr., would have an ample supply of anchonies once the market revived. Even when his iron house at Buffalo Forge was almost full, he refused to drop his price below $100 a ton, the rate he had established back in January, and he insisted that his commission merchants in Lynchburg make all sales for cash. Earlier, when Lee, Rocke, & Taylor pressed Weaver to sell off some of his iron in order to settle his account with them, Weaver informed them that he would pay off his debt for slave clothing and the like by sending them funds raised by the sale of Etna pig.[56] Weaver was not about to be stampeded into rash moves that would jeopardize profits he was confident would soon be forthcoming.

The break in the merchant bar market came late in the summer. On August 27, James Davidson forwarded to Weaver an urgent letter from

Major James L. Cooley, the Confederate quartermaster at Huntersville in Pocahontas County, west of Rockbridge. The army was in urgent need of horseshoes, mule shoes, and horseshoe nails. What could Weaver do to help?[57] Brady replied at once and told Davidson they could "probably send 500 mule shoes & nails sufficient for that quantity," but that delivery might be delayed because the slave teamster needed to transport the iron was not available. Charles Towles, Henry's brother, along with his wagon and four-mule team, had been impressed and was working for the quartermaster at Millboro Depot in Bath County.[58] Brady, writing over Weaver's signature, also got a letter off to Major Cooley. "I shall send you a lot of mule shoes say 500 & nails & will thank you to send me a certificate of their value, & I can then decide how many more I can furnish you," he wrote.[59] The same day, August 28, Brady noted in his journal: "Commenced making mule shoes for army."

The shoes, and the metal used in making them, would come from the slave ironworkers at Buffalo Forge. Weaver had two skilled blacksmiths in his shop in 1861. Henry Matthews, who was thirty-six years old and one of Weaver's most versatile slave hands, and Constant Towles, who was nineteen, would hammer out the mule shoes. They were assisted by two young apprentices, both of whom were in their early teens in 1861. One was a boy named Heb, a son of Warder and Frances Banks, born in 1848. The other was Louisa's son John. He had grown up at Etna Furnace, where his mother was the principal cook, and he had helped her with various kitchen chores until the summer of 1861. He was thirteen then, and Weaver obviously thought it was time for him to move on to more adult work.[60] If Weaver followed his usual practice, both Heb and John agreed to train as blacksmiths.

The iron house at Buffalo Forge was bulging with metal when the request for shoes came in, and the work proceeded steadily through September. Before the month was out, Captain W. L. Powell, the quartermaster at Millboro, placed an urgent order. "I wish you would send . . . as many horse shoes as two or three wagons can bring so soon as *possible*, as we are much in need of them at head quarters," Powell wrote on September 24. General Robert E. Lee was engaged in a difficult campaign trying to clear federal forces out of western Virginia, and many critically needed items were in short supply. "If you have not the shoes made and cannot do it in a very short time then send me the shoe iron," Powell asked.[61] Six days later, Brady sent two and a half tons of bar suitable for making horseshoes to Millboro Depot. The shoes, 840 of them neatly packed in six wooden boxes, followed in early October.[62]

The Confederate authorities readily paid the $127.50 bill for the shoes, but they adamantly refused to pay for the horseshoe iron. Weaver had charged the unheard-of price of $140 per ton for this metal. Ten days before he sent this iron to the army, Brady had shipped ten tons of bar to Lee, Rocke & Taylor priced at $100 a ton. When Brady went to Millboro in November to seek payment for this metal, all he received was an acknowledgment that the quartermasters had used the iron but that they declined paying for it "on account of the price."[63] Weaver's blacksmiths continued to hammer out both horse and mule shoes for the Confederate forces in western Virginia throughout the fall and winter of 1861, and when army quartermasters ordered another shipment of bar iron in December, Weaver again priced the metal at $140 per ton.[64] Brady had to go to Richmond during the Christmas holidays and file a claim with the quartermaster-general in order to secure a promise to pay for this iron, and it probably did not damage his case when Greenlee Davidson, then serving as an aid to Governor Letcher, agreed to act as Weaver's intermediary in receiving payment from the government.[65]

Weaver was quick to use his initial sales of bar iron to the Quartermaster Department to try to advance the market price in Lynchburg. "I have been selling . . . to the government at $140 per ton, which is the price I hold it at here," Weaver informed Lee, Rocke & Taylor on October 3. "Bar must be scarce in Richmond, or they would not come here for it," he added. In early November, Weaver ordered his Lynchburg merchants to halt all sales of Buffalo Forge iron until further notice. The following month, he dispatched a ton of bar, which he described as "A No. 1," to the merchants with instructions to "Cr. me with the highest price your market will bear, & advise me of the state of the market & prospects for iron."[66] The iron sold for $140 a ton. Little wonder Weaver reported in the fall of 1861 that he had paid off all his outstanding debts and that he did not intend to issue any more notes.[67] At the start of 1862, he raised the price of his bar to $150 per ton.[68]

Weaver made no inflationary adjustments in the slaves' rate of overwork compensation, however. The "Negro Books" for the war years have not survived, but Brady recorded the overwork of the chaffery forgemen in the iron book in which bar iron production and sales records were kept. Tooler was credited on December 25, 1861, with $23.76 for drawing 6¾ tons of extra iron during the year; the rate was $3.50 per ton, exactly what it had been in the prewar years. Harry Hunt, Jr., received $14.31 in overwork credit the same day for his part in making "over iron" that year; his rate was $2.50 per ton, which had long been the overwork pay scale for chaffery underhands. Jim Garland had periodically served as Tooler's helper during 1861, and he was also paid $2.50 per ton for his overwork.

Total forge production was up slightly from the previous year. The hammermen drew almost 77 tons of merchant bar in 1861 compared with just over 70 tons in 1860. But both these figures fell well below the 89½ tons Tooler and Harry Hunt, Jr., had made in 1859. The poor market for bar iron throughout most of 1860 and 1861 was reflected in the lower production figures for those two years. Weaver invariably took Tooler and Harry Hunt, Jr., out of the forge and set them to other tasks when sales were off, and he had done no different in 1861.[69]

Christmas was celebrated in the customary fashion at Buffalo Forge in 1861. All hands were keeping "Holiday," as Brady put it, from December 25 to January 1, and on Christmas Day a settling up of the slaves' overwork accounts took place. Brady made small cash distributions to almost every hand on the place, and several slaves drew impressive sums of money. Sam Williams received $16, Henry Towles $15. These were the two largest amounts given out that day, which undoubtedly reflected the long and steady hours these two men had worked throughout most of the year. The only other slave who drew a comparable sum was Nancy Williams. She, like Henry Towles, was paid $15 on December 25, 1861.[70]

Weaver tried several ways to make money in the flush times of late 1861 and early 1862, most of which were successful, one of which was not. The one significant failure was his effort to get rid of Bath Iron Works. He advertised the furnace for sale in the Richmond *Dispatch* in November 1861 along with 7,000 acres of adjoining land and Bath's reputation for producing "the best cannon metal in the State." Perhaps Weaver's statement that "The property will be sold cheap, and upon favorable terms," gave too much away.[71] No buyer immediately came forward, but Weaver's advertisement caught the eye of Commander George Minor of the Confederate Navy's Bureau of Ordnance and Hydrography. Minor wrote in mid-December to inquire if Weaver could supply 300 to 500 tons of blooms to the government for use in manufacturing boiler plate. Weaver had to decline the offer. He worked only two fires at Buffalo Forge and made 80 to 100 tons of bar a year, he told Minor. "The price of iron has been so low for many years that I have let my large forge, at Bath Furnace, go down, & it is now rotted to the ground."[72]

Weaver's best chance for realizing something from the Bath property probably came early in 1862. Greenlee Davidson reported from Richmond that Commander Minor was extremely anxious to have someone reopen Bath Furnace and make gun metal. Before the war, Minor had examined ordnance made with Bath iron for the United States Navy, and Minor told Davidson "that the metal made at that establishment was the best, for cannon purposes, that he ever inspected." Minor was ready to sign a contract for 5,000 tons of Bath pig at a price of $60 per ton. "Now is the time to sell the property," Davidson concluded; "if it is not sold to advantage now, it never will be."[73]

A possible buyer, and one very well known to Weaver, surfaced in Rockbridge County in January 1862. Sam Jordan, former partner in the firm of Jordan, Davis & Company, had signed a contract to supply the Confederate government with a large quantity of pig iron and blooms and was in the market for ironworks. On February 1, young Davidson wrote Weaver that Jordan and his brother "had carefully examined the ore banks on the Bath furnace property & ascertained from personal observation & from the information of persons who had formerly worked at the Furnace, that the banks had been almost totally exhausted." Yet Sam "seemed reluctant to conclude that the ore was exhausted," Davidson went on, and he had returned to Bath to take a second look. That visit only confirmed the conclusion Sam had reached after his first inspection: "that the supply of ore was inadequate to supply the furnace." He did, however, have a proposition to make. If Weaver would grant him permission to prospect for ore on the property at his own expense for a month and if he found abundant quantities of ore, he would purchase Bath Iron Works.

Davidson strongly encouraged Weaver to authorize Jordan to make the search. "The ore is the only element of value upon the property," Davidson pointed out. "The dams have been washed away. The Forge buildings have rotted down & all the other buildings upon the property are in a woeful state of dilapidation." The furnace stack was "about to tumble down & will have to be rebuilt before it can be operated." Davidson's conclusion was that if Weaver did "not sell to him you will probably lose the last chance."[74]

Weaver, perhaps because he knew what Jordan would (or would not) find, refused to allow any prospecting for ore. Weaver had a take-it-or-leave-it proposition for Sam: Purchase Bath at once for $12,000 (the price Weaver had been asking for the property all along) or stay off his land.[75] Jordan simply walked away from the deal.

Weaver made a final effort to sell Bath Iron Works at the end of 1862. This time, he directed his efforts at the Confederate States Navy. Weaver assured Commander Minor that the gun metal bank only needed a shaft to be sunk to the ore, and that the Bath property contained an "abundance of ore," enough "to last the furnace for years." Weaver explained that he was "getting too old to attend to the business being nearly 82" and that he would "be glad to dispose of the property." The price was $12,000.[76] Minor's lack of interest at a time when the Confederacy was desperate for iron probably reflected his knowledge of the true state of Bath's ore reserves. Bath Iron Works remained a desolate ruin throughout the Civil War.

A speculation which Weaver opened in late 1861 was much more successful than his attempt to unload Bath Iron Works. McDaniel & Irby, a commission house in Lynchburg with whom Weaver occasionally did business, approached him with a proposition in the latter part of 1861. Stuart Buchanan & Company, who operated the works at Saltville, Virginia, were in great need of pig iron. Would Weaver be willing to trade some Etna metal for salt? Weaver jumped at the chance to acquire a considerable quantity of salt, an item already in very limited supply and in great demand in the upper South. The deal called for Weaver to ship to Saltville 100 tons of Etna pig iron priced at $40 per ton. Stuart Buchanan & Company would pay for the iron in salt valued at $3 per sack. The first 50 tons of pig were to be paid for as soon as they reached Saltville; the other 50 tons of iron were to be paid for by three carloads of salt per week shipped immediately after the receipt of the first lot of iron. This arrangement was intended to guarantee that both parties would have their payment fully in hand at approximately the same time. Weaver, in return for his 100 tons of pig iron valued at $4,000, would receive $4,000 worth of salt; at $3 per sack, that translated into some 1,330 sacks of that increasingly scarce commodity.[77]

The initial shipment of salt, 800 sacks, reached Lynchburg promptly early in 1862. Weaver immediately sent 600 sacks to W. D. Tompkins & Brother, a commission merchant in Richmond, who sold it for prices ranging from $9.95 to $15 per sack even before it arrived in the city. "If you can get more of it we advise you to do so & send it on, as the people appear to be just getting excited & we can sell any quantity," Tompkins informed Weaver. In February, the Richmond merchants sent Weaver an accounting of their sales on his behalf. Gross receipts for 600 sacks of salt amounted to $6,136. After Tompkins & Brother subtracted freight, drayage, and storage costs and their 2½ percent commission, all of which came to $347.89, this initial sale left Weaver with net proceeds of $5,788.11.[78] He had already turned a nice profit on the deal, and he still had 530 sacks of salt due him.

When March came and Weaver had not received the balance of his salt, however, he became increasingly agitated. "I am much surprised to find that you have not yet fulfilled the contract," he told Stuart Buchanan & Company on March 11. "On my part the metal has been del'd some time & I am yet short in my receipts over 500 sacks salt. I presumed that I was making a contract with business men," Weaver went on to say, but "I have been wofully [sic] disappointed & have sustained a loss by the delay . . . I will thank you to inform me, if you intend delivering the balance & when."[79]

This letter produced neither the salt nor a reply from Stuart Buchanan & Company. Weaver's anger grew accordingly. He asked Lee, Rocke & Taylor in Lynchburg to check with one of the partners at McDaniel & Irby to see what was going on. "I want to know so as to take some action, as I have no idea of being treated like a child," Weaver fumed.[80]

On April 8, 1862, Weaver dispatched another angry letter to Saltville. "You must recollect, that I sold you the metal at $40 per ton, when I was getting $65 per ton cash at the furnace, which makes the salt cost me nearly $5 per sack, & if I am not to get it until salt is down in price, I am losing much by the delay," Weaver wrote. "I will thank you to inform me if you intend to deliver the balance & when, as I should like to know something about it, not having heard from you (& your agents in Lynch. know nothing about it) for 2 months."[81]

This time Weaver received a reply. The branch railroad to the saltworks had been out of repair six to eight weeks and the partner who knew the details of their arrangement with Weaver was "very ill with fever," Stuart Buchanan & Company reported. "He and he alone knows the terms of your contract with us, & how much salt is yet due you. As soon as he is well enough you shall have your due," they promised. "And in the mean time rest assured that salt will not go lower." The company underlined the latter point by offering to guarantee Weaver against any losses he might incur "for 1/4 your profit." Weaver wanted no part of any such "guarantee." He wanted his salt.[82]

Weaver's salt began arriving in Lynchburg before the month was out, and by the end of May, all of his shipments had been received. Lee, Rocke & Taylor sold a considerable portion of this salt at the railway depot in Lynchburg for $15 a sack. Weaver had the balance sent on to him at Buffalo Forge for his own use and for delivery to parties in Rockbridge County to whom he had made sales. In November 1862, he sent five sacks to the Richmond market with instructions to W. D. Tompkins & Brother to put it up for auction if they thought that method of sale would bring the highest price. "Do not mention from whom you received it," Weaver instructed the Richmond commission merchants.[83]

It must have seemed to Weaver as if his first dreams for Buffalo Forge—his hope for quick profits during the War of 1812—were coming true. For someone who relished turning a trade as much as Weaver did, these were heady times indeed. Almost everything he touched turned to money in late 1861 and early 1862. He could not get around very well outdoors, but he was hardly "too old to attend to the business," as he disarmingly told Commander Minor when he was trying to sell Bath Iron Works to the Confederate Navy. Weaver was doing business and making deals like a man half his age.

Yet the Virginia iron industry had always had its ups and downs, as Weaver knew only too well. The times might be flush and it might be, as

Weaver wrote in 1862, "a good time to liquidate debts . . . as money is plenty," but he was already anticipating the changes that would occur at war's end. "When peace comes, which must come sooner or later money will be scarce," he predicted.[84] His one cause for anxiety during the first year of the war was Etna Furnace. Pig iron prices were soaring, but he could exploit that extraordinarily profitable market—and keep Buffalo Forge well stocked with pig metal—only so long as his furnace remained in production. And there were troubling signs at Etna as the furnace went into blast in 1861.

The quality and quantity of iron ore available at most Virginia furnace sites were invariably uncertain. Iron deposits occurred in scattered pockets along the ridges of the Blue Ridge and Alleghany mountains, and ironmasters frequently, and often with alarming suddenness, exhausted ore banks they once thought capable of being worked for years. Weaver had been having ore problems at Etna for some time prior to the outbreak of the war. He had been forced to use blasting powder almost constantly in the late 1850s, and by the summer of 1860, it took two to three kegs of powder a week to raise a sufficient quantity of ore. The dangers normally involved in this type of mining were increased by the configuration of the deposits. "The ore is full of pot holes & the Blast very often blow back," Rex warned Brady in June 1860.[85] Weaver conducted an extensive personal examination of his Etna lands in 1860 searching for iron deposits and leased an ore bank from Ann Sisson prior to her marriage to Charley Gorgas. John Sims, the hired slave who was Mary's son and one of the best miners at Etna, opened the leased bank under Weaver's instructions in the summer of 1860 and found a promising vein of ore.[86] But a year later, there were signs of trouble at every one of Weaver's sources at the furnace.

"Parr think[s] the ore is very poor—he says it will take a good deal to make a ton of iron," Will Rex informed Brady on June 1, 1861, as the founder was preparing to put the blast on the furnace. Rex thought with the newly installed hot-blast equipment that Etna could easily produce forty tons of pig iron per week, and he instructed Parr to turn out no less than thirty-five. The founder was unable to reach even that goal. Parr's prediction was coming true. "It takes a great deal of our ore to make a ton of metal," Rex admitted three weeks into the 1861 blast. From twenty-eight to thirty-two tons per week was the best the furnace could do.[87]

As the year progressed, Rex began to run short of both charcoal fuel and iron ore. The charcoal could be replinished; the ore could not. On November 19, 1861, he told Brady that he had only enough ore to last until December 7. Rex called it to the very day, and when it came, he reacted with a mix of emotions. "I have the metal all weighed up," he reported to

Brady on December 10, "& it is with great reluctance that I write the number but it must come—650 tons." Etna, even with the addition of the hot-blast machinery, had not come close to equaling the maximum levels of production Gorgas and Rex had achieved prior to the war. The reason was clear: "it was not in the ore & consequently it could not be got out," Rex wrote. "I for one thank God that we are through."[88]

It had been a trying twelve months. In addition to the ore problems, there had been the usual periodic shortages of bacon, corn, flour, clothing, and shoes during the year. Rex had largely taken over responsibility for the day-to-day operations at Etna in 1861, so the burden of dealing with these difficulties had fallen almost entirely on his shoulders.[89] Charley Gorgas seems to have spent much of the year adjusting to his new life as a member of the Botetourt County squirearchy. He had hired six slaves—formerly his wife's property, now his—to the furnace at the beginning of the year for $750, and in the fall, Rex wrote Brady that Charley wanted to know if Weaver would advance him $150 in order to pay his taxes; "he says he has not visible means of getting it except through him (rather bad for a Duke)," Rex pointed out gleefully.[90]

Just before the hirelings returned home for Christmas, Rex asked for a barrel of flour so that he could make a distribution to all the slave hands. "We have to give these boys a little," he told Brady.[91] Those "boys," as Rex referred to them, had been largely responsible for chopping the timber, firing the charcoal, mining the ore, and manning the furnace during the difficult blast of 1861. They had built coaling roads in the mountains in January when the ground was covered with snow, and they had hauled charcoal to the furnace in March when "the mountain [was] a sheet of ice." The slave keepers who stood day and night watches tending the furnace had worked under particularly hazardous conditions. "Please send us those aprons if you have them," Rex asked Brady on July 4, 1861; "if you have not got them send us 4 yds tow linen for the keepers—they want something to protect their pants from the fire & also to handle the hot Bars."[92] The slave hands deserved much more than a distribution of flour as the year drew to a close. Rex could not have produced a ton of iron without their labor in 1861.

Some of the slaves were probably especially glad Etna was closing down. Louisa, the longtime cook at the furnace, had been protesting for years about the amount of work she was required to do there, and in 1861 she obviously decided to do something about it. "Louisa . . . is continuously complaining & laying up with pains," Rex reported in June. He asked Brady if he "could . . . spare us a girl about 13 or 14 years old" to help Louisa with the cooking. They had to take Louisa's son John out of the kitchen because at age thirteen he was getting to be too old for that sort of duty. Louisa's nine-year-old daughter Lucy was too small to handle the heavy cooking utensils. "We will have to have a set of dishes casted if we keep her," Rex explained.[93] Louisa, fifty-two years of age and one of the original "Wilson negroes," was obviously a formidable presence at Etna.

So was John Sims. His longtime service as a miner at Etna had been invaluable to Weaver, but Sims paid a heavy physical price for carrying out his duties. "I had John Sims examined yesterday," Rex informed Brady on May 9, 1861. "The Dr says he has Rheumatic fevers & think he is or has been in a very dangerous condition . . . he can scarcely use his sholder cannot put on his coat without help."[94] Among other things, Sims had single-handedly sunk a fourteen-foot shaft in 1860 at the ore bank Weaver had rented from Ann Sisson, and it was his work that had led to the discovery of the iron deposits there. On December 19, 1861, Weaver's good friend Henry McCormick, Sims's owner since the sale of Matthew Bryan's estate in 1854, agreed to accept a $55 deduction in John's hire because of time lost during the year. The master and the employer had dealt with Sims's illness in a way that satisfied both parties. John Sims received thirty-seven pounds of flour and some sole leather with which to patch his shoes.[95]

With the completion of Etna's last blast in early December, the slaves began the laborious task of shutting down the property. The furnace machinery, the hot-blast equipment, and the ten-mile railroad to Retreat Bank were all dismantled prior to sale. Twenty-three tons of railroad iron, much of which was badly warped from years of heavy use, brought $120 per ton, the railroad spikes sold for 8 cents per pound. Every pound of scrap metal around the place was gleaned and brought back to Buffalo Forge. Weaver had stockpiled over 180 tons of Etna pig iron for his own use, but he knew his forgemen would eventually exhaust that reserve, and he wanted to make sure no iron of any kind was left behind. Weaver's principal teamsters—Garland Thompson, Warder Banks, and Charles Towles—were on the road whenever the weather permitted in late 1861 and early 1862 hauling to the canal the iron and machinery that had been sold or bringing items back to Buffalo Forge.[96] The furnace itself seemed to know it was dying. In February, Rex reported that a portion of the stack had settled about six inches and that rock had begun falling from a corner of the massive structure. Etna Furnace would never again make so much as a pound of pig iron. Its last duty was to serve as a kiln for burning some lime which Weaver thought might bring a good price on the Richmond market.[97]

During June 1862, the process of stripping Etna of everything of value was completed. Among the last people to leave the furnace were Will Rex and Louisa. She had stayed there to cook and to make sure that nothing belonging to her was left behind. Her diligence clearly annoyed Rex. On June 17, he told Brady that a few of her things would be coming down that day along with the house furniture from the principal residence, but he warned Brady that there was still a full load of her belongings at the furnace. Two days later Rex noted with some exasperation that "Louisa['s] things will not all go in [the] two horse wagon. (She has so much old plunder) I put hers in the big wagon with some articles on top which can be taken off. There is a large kettle here which she says is hers—she has it in the wagon."[98] Louisa, formidable to the end of her tour at Etna, would not be denied.

The closing down of the furnace was a critical loss for Weaver. It deprived him of the impressive income he had been receiving from pig iron sales, and it deprived Buffalo Forge of its only regular source of pig metal. Customers who had previously relied on Weaver for their pig iron besieged him with requests for metal in late 1861 and 1862. Brady, calling on merchants in Lynchburg just after Christmas, reported that he could sell 50 tons of Etna iron "at an awful price" if it were available.[99] By February, F. B. Deane, Jr., & Son, the Lynchburg founder, was in desperate need of pig. "Have you any more iron for sale & at what price: please reply by return mail," Deane asked urgently. Weaver told Deane what he was telling everyone else: "I have sold all the metal that I wish to spare from the forge."[100]

The consequences of Etna's demise for some important Richmond manufacturing concerns were dramatically illustrated by a letter Weaver received in the summer of 1862. "We have been brought pretty near the point that unless we can very soon get some Iron we must close our Works," wrote William S. Triplett of the Old Dominion Iron & Nail Works; "this we wish to avoid if possible as the Government is dependent upon us for several articles. I therefore write to you in perfect frankness to say we have no Iron, or next to none, and to enquire at what price you will send us, or make for us if you have not got it, 200 Tons Iron." Triplett admitted that he would "pay a high price to get it, but hope you will be as moderate as you can."[101]

Weaver used this inquiry to vent some frustration that dated back to the years before the war. "I have no metal for sale, nor am I making any, having closed my furnace last Christmas," Weaver informed Triplett. "My reason for relinquishing the furnace business was that Richmond was always a bad market & we could not compete with northern iron, as it always had a preference over our mountain iron & I had become tired of supplying an article at a loss." Weaver acknowledged that "the present price would pay well, but when the blockade is opened where will the profit be," he asked.[102] Weaver neglected to mention while he was grinding this old axe that Etna Furnace had consumed almost every pound of serviceable iron ore available to it and had ceased production for that reason and that reason alone.

The war news as 1862 began was almost uniformly depressing. "Fort Donelson has been captured by the Federals and much anxiety exists in the public mind," Lee, Rocke & Taylor reported in February.[103] James Davidson was particularly conscientious about passing on word of important developments. Brady, acknowledging the sense of isolation they felt at Buffalo Forge, had asked him to do so shortly after the firing on Fort Sumter, and Davidson did his best to keep them informed.[104] "The only topic now is the bad news from Roanoke Island, Tenn. & North Alabama," Davidson wrote in February. "We are being surrounded." His son Greenlee reported that "gloom overspread Richmond on receipt of the bad news from Roanoke, & business was pretty much suspended." Davidson correctly predicted the imminent passage of a conscription act by the Confederate Congress, but he added that substitutes would be allowed and thought "not many will have to go from Rockbridge."[105]

By late February, matters looked even worse. "The news is bad—bad indeed," Davidson told Weaver. "The Federals are carrying out their programme, of surrounding us on all sides." Norfolk was threatened from land and sea, and he thought there might be a federal army in the Shenandoah Valley before very long. "Sixty days will give us some insight into the future," he added.[106]

In the midst of these setbacks, Jefferson Davis was inaugurated as the first regularly elected president of the Confederate States. Governor Letcher, to whom Weaver regularly sent hams, flour, and other country delicacies, invited Weaver to come to Richmond for the inauguration and offered him a room in the Governor's Mansion if he would make the journey. "The trip will do you good & you will return home feeling like a new man," Greenlee Davidson wrote from the capital.[107] Weaver had to decline the governor's invitation. His mind was perfectly sharp, but his body was beginning to fail him and his mobility was limited.[108] There was also a great deal of business to attend to at Buffalo Forge in the winter of 1862.

The surging market for merchant bar made forge production a top priority for Weaver and Brady early in 1862. Weaver set the price at $150 per ton at the first of the year, went to $180 in February, and jumped to $200 per ton on May 1, 1862.[109] A year into the war, the price of Buffalo Forge hammered iron had doubled.

The forgemen started the year working steadily. Tooler and Harry Hunt, Jr., missed only one week's work in January—Tooler was "loafing," Harry Hunt was "sick"—and Sam Williams and Henry Towles kept the chaffery hammermen well stocked with anchonies. Two days were lost in the middle of the month when the forge flooded, and those two days when water stopped production were the precursors of many more to come.[110] Buffalo Forge would be plagued by either too much or too little water throughout much of 1862.

"The roads have been so bad that I cannot get coal, & my stock is exhausted," Weaver explained to a complaining customer on March 11. "I will let you know when I can draw iron again."[111] From March 1 to the end of the month, not a single pound of bar was made at Buffalo Forge, and even the refiners got a break. "Sam & Henry loafing, out of coal," Brady recorded on several occasions, and when the forgemen were not resting they were doing make-work jobs like piling castings and weighing up metal. About the only good things Daniel Brady could report in March were "Uncle William's birthday," his eighty-first, on March 8, and his own the following day, when he turned forty-one.[112]

April was little better. "I have not been able to make a pound of iron for 3 weeks, owing to high water," Brady informed Lee, Rocke & Taylor on April 26. Rain, snow, the forge filled with water, rivers too high to ford, no coal, slaves loafing—this was the stuff of Brady's journal that month.[113] With Buffalo Forge bar selling at $180 a ton, Weaver must have felt that nature was playing a particularly cruel trick on him.

May brought a temporary respite. Tooler and Harry Hunt, Jr., drew the year's first pounds of "over iron" during two good weeks at the start of the month. Tooler decided to "loaf" after that, but Jim Garland came in to work with Harry Hunt, Jr., so Weaver was able to fill a number of back orders.[114]

It did not take long for disaster to strike, however. On June 3 and 4, it rained steadily for twenty-four straight hours, and a wall of water came cascading down Buffalo Creek. A considerable portion of the forge dam was swept away. Brady sent the forgemen into the fields to mow hay and cradle wheat and did not even begin cutting logs to repair the dam until the end of the month.[115] "My forge dam is broken & I have not struck a blow for 5 weeks, & cannot tell when I will get to work," Weaver reported on July 11. At a time when Confederate quartermasters were pressing Weaver and Brady for all the horse and mule shoes they could make, Sam Williams was spending his time either "loafing," doing field work, helping to rebuild the dam, or looking after fifty horses and mules Weaver was pasturing, for a fee, for the Confederate Army.[116]

Production finally resumed in August. The forge had been down over two months when Sam Williams and Henry Towles returned to the finery and Tooler and Harry Hunt, Jr., drew two journeys on August 7. Weaver's price for a ton of bar was now $224. On September 1, he pegged it at $280 per ton, a month later he went to $336, and on November 1 he jumped the price to $448 per ton.[117] Weaver's explanation for these rapid price increases was simple: "everything has an upward tendency (except money)."[118] A Scottsville, Virginia, blacksmith who was building wagons under a contract with the Confederate government spoke for most of Weaver's customers when he wrote in November that he "was astonished at the advance in price."[119] On December 1, Weaver raised the price to $560 for a ton of Buffalo Forge hammered iron.[120]

The reaction of Weaver's customers to his price increases was certainly understandable. From their perspective, he was charging all the market would bear and then some: Throughout 1862, he consistently advanced the price of his bar at approximately double the overall rate of inflation in Virginia.[121] From Weaver's point of view, however, his increases were more than justified. As he liked to say, supply and demand govern price, and the demand for Buffalo Forge metal was, in fact, far greater than the supply.

Even at the prices Weaver was charging, he did not have an abundance of iron to sell. The repair of the forge dam had been followed by a period of low water, a frequent problem in the summer and early fall, and production had fallen off as a result.[122] It had, in many ways, been a difficult year for the masters at Buffalo Forge.

The slaves may well have taken a different view of things. A Union army under General Nathaniel Banks had appeared at the northern end of the Shenandoah Valley in March, just as James Davidson had predicted the previous month, and Buffalo Forge felt the impact of Banks's presence a hundred and fifty miles away. Over the next four months Confederate units under "Stonewall" Jackson fought a brilliant campaign in the Valley against the federal troops, but refugees came streaming past Buffalo Forge in the late winter and early spring. When they came, they brought their slaves with them. "Dr. Moorman, Col. Williamson, Capt. Potter, Capt. Henderson, 3 ladies, 3 children, 4 Negroes & 5 horses to supper & all night," Brady recorded on March 7. On April 28, "Col. Lockridge & 5 whites & 15 blacks camped here."[123] These slaves certainly brought news of the outside world to the Buffalo Forge black community.

In May, a Union raid against Jackson's River Depot in Alleghany County, just west of Rockbridge, gave whites in the Valley a clear picture of what would happen if the federals reached the area in force. The Union raiders "took a great many negroes, all that run to them & there were a great many," Will Rex reported on May 20.[124] Brady hoped that if the Confederates were able to defeat the Union forces under General George B. McClellan trying to capture Richmond in the spring and summer of 1862, it would "settle their business for them" and make the "Yanks . . . disposed for peace."[125] McClellan's attempt failed, but the Yanks were not about to sue for peace. The war went on, and its continuation enhanced the possibility that slavery might someday end.

The years of the Civil War were a time of mounting expectations among slaves everywhere in the South, and we can be reasonably sure that such was the case at Buffalo Forge. The blacks living there were isolated, to be sure, but that isolation was never perfect. Men like Garland Thompson and Harry Hunt, Jr., who were married to women who lived off Weaver's place, regularly went to visit their wives on weekends, and others, like Wilson King, made frequent trips to Lexington to run errands for Weaver and Brady.[126] Guests who came out to Buffalo Forge for Sunday dinner surely talked about the war. James Davidson was a regular visitor, and Governor Letcher dined with Weaver and the Bradys in July 1862.[127] Whites were notoriously careless about speaking freely in front of their slaves, and the house servants would have carried whatever news they managed to pick up back to family members and friends in the quarters. Hope would have been growing in the slave cabins that dotted the landscape around Weaver's house on the hill. But that hope would be tempered by grief and sorrow in the fall and winter of 1862, for that was a time when death began stalking the slave community at Buffalo Forge.

4

———◆———

Death

September 1862 seemed promising to Daniel Brady at first. Sam Williams and Henry Towles were doing their usual good job at the finery, and two weeks into the month neither Tooler nor Harry Hunt, Jr., had missed a day's work at the chaffery. Constant Towles and his helper, Louisa's son John, were manning the blacksmith shop while Henry Matthews went out to help the agricultural hands finish threshing the clover seed. A succession of dry pleasant days early in the month helped the field work go smoothly, although the absence of rain held forge production down. Tooler and Harry could generally draw only one journey a day because of low water. On September 6, a clear, warm early fall day in the Valley, Caroline Williams Reid gave birth to her second child. Caroline was Sam and Nancy Williams' daughter, and her marriage, occurring around the time of John Brown's execution and the whipping of Henry Towles, had taken place under less than ideal circumstances. The baby was a boy, and she and her husband named him William John Reid.[1] It may only have been a coincidence, but the baby's middle name was the same as one of the children taken by Thomas Mayburry in 1837. That boy was John Sims, Mary's son, and Caroline's great-uncle.

As far as Brady could tell, things also seemed to be going quite well for the Confederate cause. Lee's Army of Northern Virginia had checked Union general George B. McClellan's attempt to capture Richmond during the summer and had won an impressive victory at Second Manassas at the end of August. In September, Lee moved north. His army crossed the Potomac during the first week of that month, and on Monday, September 15, troops under "Stonewall" Jackson captured the federal garrison at Harper's Ferry. Some 11,500 Union soldiers surrendered to Jackson on that day, and the Confederates seized huge quantities of supplies. When Lee received word that Harper's Ferry had fallen, he began concentrating his scattered forces and established a line west of Antietam Creek near the Maryland village of Sharpsburg.[2]

On that same Monday, September 15, an important event in the history of the Brady family occurred. Daniel took his son, twelve-year-old Pat Brady, into Lexington to enroll him in Washington College. Emma was also pregnant that fall, with the baby due in the early spring. It was less than a year since she had lost a newborn child. Emma Belle Brady, born in October 1861, had lived only three days. The county records listed the cause of her death as "throat disease."[3] It was a precursor of things to come at Buffalo Forge.

Monday, September 15, 1862, was also the day Betty Coleman's four-year-old son, Alfred Elliott, complained of a sore throat. When Daniel Brady returned from Lexington and examined the boy, he saw unmistakable signs of impending disaster at Buffalo Forge. Alfred Elliott Coleman had diphtheria.[4] Since immunization and effective treatment were not available, it was bound to spread quickly, and no one, black or white, would be safe from its ravages.

Two days later, on Wednesday, September 17, the landscape turned red at Antietam. McClellan's Army of the Potomac launched a series of assaults on Lee's outnumbered forces, and in a day of savage fighting and incredible bloodshed over twenty thousand men were killed or wounded.[5]

Death also visited Buffalo Forge that month as diphtheria spread rapidly among Weaver's slaves. In rapid succession, Betty Coleman, Caroline Reid, and Lydia Williams, three of Sam and Nancy Williams' four daughters, came down with the disease. Betty's symptoms first appeared on Friday, September 19, and it was clear from the large yellow streaks extending deep into her throat that she had a severe case, much worse than her son's. When a membrane formed at the top of her throat, Brady cauterized it, and she vomited up large, leathery pieces of tissue. She died late in the afternoon on Wednesday, September 24. She was twenty-two years old and the mother of three small children, one of whom, Alfred Elliott, was fighting his own battle against diphtheria. Her father and his forge helper, Henry Towles, dug her grave in the slave cemetery at Buffalo Forge the next morning, and that afternoon, under a clear, cool autumn sky, she was buried. Brady gave all hands the afternoon off so that they could be present at her funeral. Sam was not asked to return to his forge until the following Monday.[6]

For over two months, diphtheria lingered at Buffalo Forge, and before it ran its course, fifteen of Weaver's slaves contracted the disease. Alfred Coleman, Caroline Reid, and Lydia Williams gradually recovered, although the caustic and turpentine with which their throats were treated must have caused them enormous pain. Three more slaves at Buffalo Forge did die of diphtheria following Betty's fatal attack, and before October had ended, her son was also dead. Alfred Elliott Coleman, perhaps weakened by his bout with diphtheria, died on October 31, 1862. Brady listed the cause of his death as an infestation of worms.[7] In the space of six weeks, Sam and Nancy Williams had lost their firstborn child and their oldest grandchild.

Among the slaves who died of diphtheria at Buffalo Forge that autumn was ten-year-old Wash Alexander Matthews, the oldest of Henry and Frances Matthews' five boys. His symptoms first appeared on October 12, and it soon became clear that he was gravely ill. On October 17, his father was given a day's respite from his duties as forge carpenter and head blacksmith, and he spent the day at his cabin across Buffalo Creek nursing his stricken son. The next day, a beautifully clear, crisp fall day in the Valley, Wash Matthews died. His brothers Phil, seven, and Bob, five, also came down with diphtheria but managed to pull through; the Matthews' other two sons, their twin boys Henry and Lewis, born three days before Christmas in 1860, were not touched at all by the disease.[8]

Several families seemed particularly at risk during this epidemic. In addition to Sam Williams's children and grandchildren and Henry Matthews's children, the Towles and Thompson families were both hard hit. Henry did not catch the disease, but two of his brothers, twenty-year-old Constant and seventeen-year-old Prince, did. So did Garland Thompson, Jr., and his brother Jim. John, Louisa's son and an apprentice in the blacksmith shop who regularly worked with Constant Towles, also came down with diphtheria.[9]

In the midst of this epidemic, another crisis had come. On Tuesday night, November 11, 1862, word reached Buffalo Forge that fire had broken out in the forge coalings several miles away. Brady immediately awakened six of the slave hands at the forge and led them to the coaling grounds. There they spent the rest of the night and most of the next day battling the blaze. Brady was forced to leave the fire before it was brought under control, however. He arrived back at Buffalo Forge by noon on Wednesday, November 12, several hours before the slaves came in. He had no choice— he had been stricken by diphtheria. He was confined to his bedroom for several weeks, but his attack was not fatal. When the slaves returned, bone-weary, to Buffalo Forge late Wednesday afternoon they learned that Constant Towles had died while they were away.

The slaves who had fought the fire hardly had time to recover from their exhausting ordeal when they were summoned back to the coalings. On Thursday, November 13, fire broke out in the smoldering pits again, and five of the six slaves who had battled the original blaze had to return. The sixth man, Griffin, had become ill and was left behind at the forge.

Tragic news once more awaited the men when they came back to Buffalo Forge on Friday, November 14. In their absence, Prince Towles, who had been fighting diphtheria for over a month and at one time had seemed on the verge of complete recovery, had succumbed. Brady, from his sickbed, did not have the heart to order his fire crew back to their normal jobs on Saturday. "All hands resting and loafing after the fire," he wrote in his journal on November 15, 1862.

Prince's death was not the last of the suffering experienced at Buffalo Forge that fall. Before November was over, Griffin, the slave who had not returned to the coalings fire a second time, was also dead. He died shortly before midnight on November 27 of "Inflammation of [the] bowels," according to the entries Brady made in the records. Brady failed to note whether Griffin's wife, who belonged to another Valley slaveowner and lived away from Buffalo Forge, was with her husband at the end. Chances are she was not. The last time Griffin had been to visit his wife had been in late October, a month before his death, when he had spent a long weekend with her.[10]

In less than two and a half months, six slaves had died at Buffalo Forge, and the only consolation was that it might have been much worse. Many more could have been struck down by diptheria, and there were other disasters that might have occurred. The renewed threat of smallpox in the Valley prompted Brady to vaccinate all the slave children at Buffalo Forge who had not been immunized against the disease on November 1, 1862, and to repeat the inoculation program the following January. Fortunately smallpox did not strike and add to the toll of sickness and death at the forge in late 1862.[11]

The fall of 1862, a season that brought great suffering and sadness to the

Buffalo Forge slave community, also brought the moment when Lincoln decided to issue the Preliminary Emancipation Proclamation. The public announcement came on September 22, five days after the Battle of Antietam. As of January 1, 1863, Lincoln wrote, "all persons held as slaves within any state, or designated part of a state, the people whereof shall then be in rebellion against the United States shall be then, thenceforward, and forever free."[12] The arrival of freedom would be agonizingly slow for slaves across much of the South, including those at Buffalo Forge, but Lincoln had planted the seeds of their ultimate deliverance.

The deaths in the Valley did not end that autumn with the passing of Weaver's six slaves. Charley Gorgas came down with a severe case of pneumonia and died at his home in Botetourt County on October 22, 1862.[13] He was twenty-eight years old. All of Charley's property went to his wife, and his estate, through a rather strange sequence of events, included Etna Furnace.

Weaver had long planned to leave his property to his relatives. His first will, drawn up in 1852, had instructed his executor to sell his land and slaves and to make cash disbursements to a lengthy list of heirs in Pennsylvania.[14] If Weaver had died while this will was in force, it would have meant the breakup of the Buffalo Forge slave community and the inevitable destruction of most, if not all, of the black families living there.

The arrival of the Bradys, Will Rex, and Charley Gorgas in Virginia over the next several years changed Weaver's plans drastically. In November 1857, he drafted a new will leaving the bulk of his estate to Emma Brady and Charley Gorgas, with Will Rex receiving one-half of the Etna Furnace property. Weaver also demonstrated a concern for his slaves in this document that had been totally absent from his first will. "It is further my wish that my legatees will treat my servants with humanity and kindness," he instructed in 1857.[15]

Three years later, on May 23, 1860, Weaver added a codicil to this will. It provided that Gorgas was to receive Etna Furnace and all of the surrounding land, which amounted to some 8,000 acres; Will Rex was given Turkey Foot farm, a 202-acre tract across Buffalo Creek, as well as three slaves: a woman named Matilda, who was twenty-two years old in 1860, and two men, Mark, who was thirty-four that year, and his brother Bill Dutch, who was nineteen.[16] After Charley Gorgas and Ann Sisson married in the summer of 1860, Weaver decided that before he died, he would give Charley Gorgas the Etna property. Weaver transferred full title to Etna Furnace and the adjoining land to Gorgas in March 1862.[17] Charley was the legal owner of the furnace, the woodlands, and the exhausted ore banks on the estate when he died in late October that same year.

Weaver did not get to Charley's funeral, and neither did Daniel Brady. Weaver was not up to the journey to Botetourt County, and Brady had his hands full with the diphtheria epidemic and the management of affairs at Buffalo Forge. But Emma very much wanted to go to her brother's funeral, as did Will Rex, who had managed Etna Furnace with Charley for several years. They left Buffalo Forge the day after Charley died and returned two days later.[18] According to family tradition, Will Rex joined Weaver in the library at Buffalo Forge and described the funeral and other events surrounding Charley's death. Weaver heard him out and then offered a comment of his own. "That Ann Sisson got my furnace damn slick," Weaver observed.[19]

Etna had left the hands of the family for good, and Weaver's affairs were changing in other ways that he did not like late in 1862. He was, for one, finding it increasingly difficult to sell iron to private parties. "I have been & am so pushed for iron for government use that I could not make any for your place," he told Lee, Rocke & Taylor in October 1862, but Weaver thought there might be another way to make some money in Lynchburg. "Let me know how the flour market is & if there is any danger of impressment if I were to send down a lot," he wrote. The merchants assured him that, for the time being at least, his flour would be safe there. "We hold near two thousand bbls," they added.[20]

As Christmas approached, private customers who needed Buffalo Forge iron in order to fill their contracts for various items put heavy pressure on Weaver and Brady to send them some metal. "I have been confined to my room with diphtheria for several weeks," Brady told one on December 1, but that was not the reason this party had not received their bar. "I have been unable to fill your order for iron, owing to the demand for government work," Brady explained. "It takes nearly all the iron I can make to supply . . . horseshoes, & did we not let them have it freely, it would be pressed, as they are now pressing all the iron at the furnaces in our neighborhood."[21] Weaver wrote Lee, Rocke & Taylor five days before Christmas that if he did not meet the government's demands, his metal "would be liable to seizure, as they have pressed all of S. F. Jordans & F. T. Andersons & *looked hard* at what metal I have."[22]

It was hardly the way Weaver and Brady expected to be able to do business. But economic conditions and market practices were changing radically in the Confederacy as total war engulfed the South. Quartermasters and military commanders began seizing urgently needed supplies long before the Confederate Congress passed an Impressment Act in March 1863 in an effort to bring some order and systemization to the practice.[23] Brady thought he had managed to buy some socks in Lexington in December 1862 to distribute to the slaves at Buffalo Forge as part of their regular winter clothing issue. After he had arranged for this purchase, however, the much-needed socks were taken by an army procurement agent. "I think it a pretty pass things have come to, when it will be necessary for a man, before purchasing anything to enquire, whether the goods are engaged to the army or any one else," Brady wrote James Davidson on December 17.[24] But that was the new order of things, and Weaver and Brady had little choice but to adjust. It was a painful process for them, particularly with Buffalo Forge bar bringing 30 cents a pound—$672 a ton—on the open market at the beginning of 1863.[25]

One reason Brady had wanted those socks, and other slave clothing, was the early onset of winter in 1862. Late November and early December had been exceptionally cold. Frigid weather settled in around Thanksgiving, and on November 29 the first snowfall of the season occurred. On December 5 it snowed and hailed all day; on December 7 the forge dam froze over; two days later the ice was thick enough for the slave hands to cut and haul nineteen loads of ice from Buffalo Creek and fill the icehouse by 4:30 that afternoon. From December 10 to December 20 the weather had been monotonously the same, as Brady recorded without fail in his journal, "clear and cold," though on December 21 (a Sunday and a day of rest for the slaves) he noted a change—"clear and very cold." In the midst of this bitter weather, Brady decided the time had come for hog-killing day; it took place at Buffalo Forge on Wednesday, December 10.[26]

The same day, December 10, Brady wrote the owner of two hired slaves to tell him that his men had recently been injured at Buffalo Forge. "Caesar has cut his leg, & Beverly his arm," Brady reported. "They cut themselves with axes, & the wounds are severe, but only flesh wounds—they are both disabled, & I cannot tell whether they will be able to work by January or not." Brady nevertheless wanted to keep the two men at Buffalo Forge for the next year's work. He was short of labor following the diphtheria epidemic and needed every available hand. "I am willing to pay the same hire, that I did last year, to commence from the time they are able to resume work," Brady offered. He closed this letter with a comment and a prediction regarding the military situation in eastern Virginia. "I observe that Burnside's army remains in status quo & do not make much progress in the 'onward March to Richmond,'" he wrote. "I do not feel any apprehension of their getting through by that route, but expect they will make an effort by James River, leaving Burnside to hold our army in check."[27]

Brady's strategic ideas had considerable merit, but his prediction was far off the mark. The Union Army, camped along the Rappahannock River east of Fredericksburg, did indeed seem stalled as the winter of 1862 set in.

But the new commander of the Army of the Potomac, General Ambrose Burnside, was determined to break the stalemate. On Thursday, December 11, the day after Brady made his prediction, Burnside's engineers laid pontoon bridges across the Rappahannock and federal forces began moving into Fredericksburg. The buildup of Union troops continued all the next day, and on Saturday, December 13, the battle of Fredericksburg opened in earnest. The Army of the Potomac hurled itself against Lee's well-entrenched divisions, and the result was a bloody and humiliating defeat for the powerful federal army. One Union observer described Fredericksburg as "a great slaughter pen"; it was as if hog-killing day had been moved to the battlefield, but this time the carnage was measured in human lives.[28]

As the year drew to a close at Buffalo Forge, Brady undertook a sad task. Normally, the settling up of the slaves' overwork accounts on Christmas Eve was a festive time, but things were different in 1862. Brady included in the settlements a distribution of the sums that the diptheria victims had earned prior to their deaths. He identified each of these payments as a "Legacy," and they went to the relatives of those who had died during the recent epidemic. Betty Coleman's earnings went to her father and mother, Sam and Nancy Williams. Each received $2.25. Constant and Prince Towles' overwork "legacies" went to their brothers, Henry, Charles, and Edgar, to Wilson King, and to Frances Matthews, Henry Matthews's wife. Slaves sometimes made loans to other slaves from their overwork accounts and something of that nature may have been involved here. As in the case of the payments of Sam and Nancy Williams, each of the disbursements was for $2.25.[29] This distribution clearly reflected the slaves' conviction that they held proprietary rights to their earnings while they were living; in death, these sums belonged to surviving members of their families.

Christmas Eve was also the day slave husbands who were married to women who did not live at Buffalo Forge left to join their families for the holidays. The traditional time for departure was at the end of the working day, and eleven of Weaver's slaves would be going off until New Year's Day. Garland Thompson, Jr., Tooler, and Harry Hunt, Jr., were among this group. Perhaps it was coincidental, but Tooler and Harry drew only a quarter of a journey on December 24 before their forge broke down. Brady did not indicate that they had deliberately sabotaged the forge, but he must have had his suspicions. The two forgemen departed with the others as scheduled.[30]

The closing down of Etna Furnace the previous year meant that Brady no longer had to go on a hiring trip over Christmas. A handful of hired slaves continued to work at Buffalo Forge as woodchoppers, colliers, and farm hands, but most of these men came from Rockbridge County and had been employed by Weaver for years. The few who came from "down the country," specifically from Orange and Spotsylvania counties, remained at Buffalo Forge that Christmas because of the presence of federal forces in that neighborhood following the Battle of Fredericksburg. Brady wrote their masters that the slaves were safer with him than they would be at home, and he rehired all of them for 1863.[31] Included in this number were Caesar and Beverly, the two men who had suffered axe wounds in December 1862. "Both your boys are doing well," Brady informed their owner on January 12; "their wounds [are] healing up very well, & if they do not catch cold in them will not be serious."[32] When he needed two additional hands in the spring, he secured them from a hiring agent in Richmond by promising that they would be used only for woodcutting and farm work. "I do not have any mining operations," Brady assured the agent.[33]

Christmas Day 1862 dawned with brilliant blue skies and mild temperatures, and although Brady termed it "a very dull day" in his journal, it must have been a doubly welcome break to the slaves of Buffalo Forge—relief both from their labor and from the cold which had gripped the Valley for so long. The traditional Christmas holiday was unchanged by the war. It lasted for a full week—until January 1—and Christmas Day was followed by three more just like it. The weather turned cooler on December 29 and remained cool through the end of the vacation, but skies were clear the entire time. The holiday and the pleasant weather of Christmas week surely must have been counted among the few blessings at Buffalo Forge during the bleak winter of 1862–63.

When January arrived, the slaves resumed work, and the weather soon turned anything but pleasant. Rain and snow came frequently and in abundance: January 6 "Cloudy until 9 o'clock, when it commenced raining and rained all day"; January 20 "Cloudy until 2 P.M. when it commenced snowing and continued all night"—the next morning the slaves awoke to find a seven-inch snowfall covering the ground at Buffalo Forge; January 28 "Snowed all day."

And even in this foul weather, Confederate authorities had insisted that Weaver and the other slaveowners of Rockbridge County meet their quota of hands for work on the Richmond defenses. So four slaves from Buffalo Forge—Sam Thompson, Bill Dutch, his brother Mark, and a hireling named Sam Salling—had to be taken four miles through that seven-inch snowfall on January 21 to be appraised at a country store and then sent on the next day, on foot, to the Confederate capital. On both days conditions were so bad that the two mule teams and wagons remaining at Buffalo Forge had laid up. (The third forge wagon, a four-mule team driven by Warder Banks, had been impressed on January 5 by army officials in Lex-

ington, and Banks and his team would not rejoin the work gang at Buffalo
Forge until three weeks later.) On January 22, Brady decided to ride with
the four men heading for Richmond as far as the pass in the Blue Ridge to
make certain they got over the mountains all right.

The weather in February was even worse. Snow, rain, and muddy fields
and roads kept the teams in their stable and the hands indoors much of the
month and contributed to a heavy incidence of sickness among the slave
force. Hardly a day passed without one or more slaves down with some sort
of illness, or pretending to be ill. Even Sam Williams was affected. "Sam
Williams sick," Brady noted on Monday, February 9, 1863, and the next
two days Williams was also "laid up." On Thursday, Friday, and Saturday,
however, Williams was just plain "loafing," in Brady's estimation, but he
was back at his refinery forge the following Monday.[34]

Toward the end of February, the wet weather had given two other slaves
a chance for a brief holiday. The low bridge connecting the forge with a
cluster of slave cabins on the other side of Buffalo Creek was covered with
water and impassable whenever the creek rose several feet. In the opinion
of Henry Matthews and his neighbor Prince Towles, the steady downpour
on the morning of Thursday, February 26, seemed likely to cut the forge
off from their homes, and they acted accordingly. "Rained hard until 12
o'clock. Flood in Buffalo," Brady commented in his journal. "Hy Matthews
sneaked over the creek before flood. Prince d[itt]o." Their vacation lasted
the next day as well: "Henry Matthews and Prince loafing at home. Water
high." The creek fell overnight and work resumed for the two men the
following day, Saturday, February 28.[35] Nothing in the surviving record
indicated that the two slaves were punished for something Brady obviously
considered a dereliction of duty.

The cold and sickly fall and winter of 1862–63 had not been without
some redeeming events at Buffalo Forge. There certainly was cause for
rejoicing during these months over the two births in the slave quarters in
which both mother and child came through in excellent shape. Amy Carter
had a healthy baby girl, Josephine, on October 2. And Ann Towles, Henry's
wife, safely delivered her fifth child, a daughter, Luanna, on January 25,
1863. One reason for the lack of complications in these two births may well
have been the presence of a black midwife at the deliveries. "Aunt Phillis,"
as Brady recorded her name in the records, came to Buffalo Forge to assist
Amy Carter in October 1862, and she returned the following January to
help Ann Towles have her baby. Brady gave Aunt Phillis $2 for each of
these visits, and he was obviously impressed by her skill.[36]

These births must have been particularly gratifying to Daniel and Emma
Brady, who knew all too well the risks involved in bringing babies into the

world. Emma had given birth to nine children since she had married in 1846. Only three of their children were still living in 1863. Twice she and her husband had tried to name a son after her Uncle William. Their first boy named William Weaver Brady had died in May 1856 when he was two and one half years old; their next child, also named William Weaver Brady, died the same day he was born in August 1857. Since that time she had had three more children, and only one, Sarah Elizabeth, had survived.[37] Perhaps those healthy newborn infants in the slave quarters were a good omen that things would go well in the mansion when her baby arrived in the spring.

The pressure on Buffalo Forge for iron was unrelenting during the early part of 1863. What little iron Brady could spare for private customers continued to skyrocket in price: 35 cents per pound on February 1, which worked out to $784 per ton—a figure, as had been the case throughout 1862, approximately double the overall inflation rate in Virginia.[38] But most of the forge's production went, as it had for some time, to the army. At the end of February, Brady made a substantial delivery of horseshoes and bar iron to the Quartermaster Department in Salem, Virginia—the bill came to $8,202.95 for 10 tons of bar and 3,000 horseshoes—but Brady warned that the order was incomplete and that future deliveries might be delayed. "I cannot make any nails for you, nor can I tell how many shoes I can make, as I shall be obliged to take my blacksmiths on the farm as soon as the weather is fit for farming operations," he wrote. Brady did promise to continue making horseshoes "as long as I can." The problem, as he explained it, was a shortage of labor. "We lost 6 negroes last autumn to diphtheria & I wish to buy some in their places." He expected "to go west for them," and he asked for a prompt remittance from the army so that he would have funds for the purchase. Brady closed by saying that "the writer's family is so *situated,* that he must go soon, or leave it some months."[39]

The family situation to which Brady referred was William Weaver's failing health. The new year brought alarming signs that he was slipping badly, and by March he was in an irreversible decline. His eighty-second birthday occurred on Sunday, March 8, a clear, warm day in the Valley. But every indication was that it would be his last.

March began auspiciously. Mild days at the beginning of the month gave welcome indication of the possibility of an early spring, and Brady had sent part of his forge and blacksmith force into the fields earlier than usual to help with preparations for the planting season. Sam Williams, Henry Towles, Tooler, and Harry Hunt, Jr., put in the potatoes during the first week in March, and then Hunt and Jim Garland from the smith shop joined the farm hands as the spring plowing began in earnest. The clear skies and mild temperatures on Monday, March 9, prompted Brady to order some of the livestock turned out to pasture, so he had Tooler, Wilson King, and Edgar Towles take fifty-one head of cattle across North River to Highland Farm.

Soon, however, there were signs that March might not live up to its promising beginnings. On Tuesday, March 10, the spring weather ended abruptly as a heavy snowfall blanketed the area. All farm hands and teams were forced to lay up until three that afternoon when Garland Thompson, Jr., Spotswood, and Charles Towles left Buffalo Forge with a wagonload of hay for the cattle at Highland Farm. The mild weather of early March gave way to a succession of cold, cloudy days, and on Monday, March 16, William Weaver took a serious turn for the worse.

Weaver's physician, Dr. Samuel T. Chandler, rode over from his home at Fancy Hill and was at Buffalo Forge all Monday night. He spent the next night there as well, and the night after that. Work went on as usual during these three days—Tooler and Harry Hunt, Jr., returned to their chaffery forge, the plow gangs went into the fields, and Sam Williams killed and butchered a hog. Then on Thursday, March 19, at eight in the morning, two hours after the workday had begun, the worst storm of the year set in. It started to hail, turned into snow, and snowed all day and all night and all the next day and night. On Saturday, the snow changed to rain and continued all day. The only outdoor tasks that got done at Buffalo Forge were the things that had to be done—clearing walks and feeding hogs and cattle—and even some of the inside work was halted. Brady recorded in his journal that all four of Weaver's forgemen—Sam Williams, Henry Towles, Tooler, and Harry Hunt, Jr.—spent Friday and Saturday "loafing," perhaps because the teams, all of which were snowbound, could not supply the forge with charcoal from the coaling ground. The weather was appropriate to the somber mood which must have prevailed at Buffalo Forge as William Weaver lay dying.

Dr. Chandler stayed until the end, although there was very little that he could do. He would ride out in the morning after breakfast to make such calls as had to be made, but he would return by late afternoon and would spend the night in the residence where he could be summoned at once if Weaver's condition worsened. The bleak weather continued. Monday, March 23, was cloudy and rainy; on Tuesday it rained the entire day; Wednesday the rains stopped, but the skies remained leaden. Work slowed to a crawl during these three days as a death watch fell over the entire community, black and white. The forgemen remained idle except for Henry Towles, who joined a group of farm hands and teamsters at some necessary woodchopping on Wednesday—the cold weather had sent the chopping gang back into the woods at the first of the week. Only the blacksmiths—Henry Matthews, Jim Thompson, Sam Grigsby, and Daniel—remained at their normal jobs, under constant pressure from Confederate supply officers for horseshoes.

On Wednesday, March 25, 1863, at 8:30 in the evening, William Weaver died. It had been almost fifty years since he had made the chance investment in the Valley iron properties that brought him to Virginia from his native Pennsylvania. It had been forty years since he had taken up what he thought would be a brief, temporary residence at Buffalo Forge. Now he would be laid to rest in a country churchyard in the Valley he had grown to love so dearly. All work was suspended at Buffalo Forge on Thursday and Friday. Dr. Chandler left after breakfast Thursday, and this time he did not come back. Later that day, the four slaves who had gone off in the January snow to work on the Richmond fortifications—Sam Thompson, Mark, Bill Dutch, and Sam Salling—returned to Buffalo Forge and learned that Weaver was dead.[40]

The sky remained cloudy on Thursday, but the weather broke in time for the funeral the next day. Friday, March 27, was a clear, cool spring day in the Valley, and many people turned out at nearby Falling Spring Presbyterian Church to pay their last respects to William Weaver. The size of the gathering—Brady, who was not given to hyperbole in his journal, simply called it "a large funeral"—might well have amused Weaver.[41] His hot temper, his ready willingness to haul anyone and everyone into court, and his reputation as a shrewd, tough-minded businessman were legend in Rockbridge County long before his death. But his immense wealth was equally legendary. Even with the loss of Etna Furnace, he still held over 12,000 acres of land at the time of his death, and he owned a labor force of seventy slaves in 1863—twenty-six men, fourteen women, and thirty children—that easily made him one of the largest slaveholders in the Valley.[42] Weaver himself had estimated three years before he died that his real and personal property was worth over $130,000, and that 1860 figure was in uninflated, prewar dollars.[43]

Some of the mourners may well have decided to attend the funeral when they saw what a lovely spring day Friday, March 27, was going to be, but it really was not all that surprising that a large crowd gathered for the services honoring Rockbridge County's leading ironmaster, or that notice of Weaver's death was taken across the Blue Ridge by the Lynchburg press.[44] An obituary published in the Lexington *Gazette* several days after the funeral accurately described the talent Weaver had displayed most often during his four decades in the Valley. "We had not long made the acquaintance of the deceased," the editor wrote, "until we discovered that he was a man of remarkable sagacity and judgment in whatever pertained to his business."[45]

As might be expected, Weaver had left his affairs in good order. On a bleak day back in early January, about the time his final illness set in, Weaver had drafted a new and final will. He wanted, first of all, to be buried next to his wife in the cemetery at Falling Spring Church. He instructed Daniel Brady, his executor, to see that a stone similar to the one that rested over his wife's grave be placed over his. He left $20,000 to William Weaver Rex, his grandnephew, and Weaver gave Will half of that sum at the time the will was drawn up in January. Daniel and Emma Brady's three children, Anne, Pat, and Sarah Elizabeth, each received bequests of $10,000 to be paid to them when they reached their twenty-first birthdays. Weaver gave Daniel Brady the 7,000-acre Bath Iron Works property. Small cash payments were to be made to his doctor, Samuel Chandler, and to one of his Philadelphia relatives, Lydia Fraley, the granddaughter and namesake of his beloved sister Lydia. The remainder of his real and personal property, including Buffalo Forge and all of his slave men, women, and children, he left to one person—his niece Emma Brady. Weaver made it clear in his will why he had decided to place most of his fortune in her hands. "As I have kept the great bulk of my estate together partly to provide for the comfort of my servants I desire that they shall be treated with kindness and humanity," he wrote.[46]

William Weaver was survived by a large group of relatives in Pennsylvania, but the list of kin living at Buffalo Forge at the time of his death was relatively brief—Daniel and Emma Brady, their three children, and Will Rex. Three weeks after Weaver died, the number of his descendants at Buffalo Forge increased by one. On April 17, 1863, Emma Brady gave birth to a fine, healthy baby, and the Bradys finally succeeded in naming one of their children after Emma's Uncle William. They named her Wilhelmina Weaver Brady.[47]

There is no way of knowing why this baby lived and some of the Brady's other newborn infants died, but it is just possible that Aunt Phillis had something to do with Wilhelmina's safe arrival on that balmy spring day in 1863. Brady sent for the black midwife as soon as Emma went into labor, and she arrived at Buffalo Forge in time to assist in the delivery. Undoubtedly Brady was very happy over the birth of his new daughter and greatly relieved that both his wife and the child had come through in such fine shape; he gave Aunt Phillis $10 for her part in helping to bring little Wilhelmina into the world.[48]

Work resumed at Buffalo Forge on the Saturday following Weaver's death, March 28. As he had indicated in his correspondence with Confederate quartermasters back in February, Brady pulled most of the ironworkers off their usual jobs during planting season. Sam Williams, Henry Towles, Tooler, and Harry Hunt, Jr., rejoined the agricultural hands following the break occasioned by Weaver's passing, and the blacksmiths also spent a considerable portion of their time in the fields during April. It was a damp spring, with heavy rains frequently forcing the slaves indoors and leaving the ground too wet to plow. These conditions, as had been the case since before the war, frequently provided occasions for widespread "loafing" by many of the slave hands, including Sam Williams and the rest of the forgemen. The entire Buffalo Forge community seemed to be taking a pause following Weaver's death.

By late April, things were pretty much back to normal. The four forgemen returned to their hammers on Monday, April 20, and although Tooler and Harry Hunt, Jr., did some additional agricultural work that spring, Brady wanted the forge back in operation, at least for a while. The blacksmiths left the fields even before the forge workers in order to resume production of horseshoes for the army.[49]

When it came time to mow the hay and cradle the wheat and oats during the summer months, however, the ironworkers spent a considerable amount of time helping to bring in these crops. The forge virtually shut down during the month of July 1863. The deaths of six slaves during the diptheria epidemic left Brady with a labor shortage he never managed to rectify. Another hand was lost in November 1863 when Bill Camasky, a coaling worker, was found to have syphilis and was sold.[50] Brady had Lee, Rocke & Taylor buy two slave men in Lynchburg in September 1863, but this purchase was made in order to meet a requisition for two slave hands to work on the Richmond fortifications. Brady bought the two men so that he would not have to send anyone from Buffalo Forge. One of the slaves promptly ran away from the Richmond earthworks and managed to reach Lynchburg before he was apprehended. Brady sold both slaves in December as soon as they completed their three-month tour of duty with the Confederate engineers.[51] Bill Camasky and these two fortification workers were the only ones Brady sold after Weaver's slaves passed into Emma's hands. It appears that they were honoring Weaver's request to treat his "servants . . . with kindness and humanity," as those terms were generally defined by masters in the slave society of the Old South.

It is impossible for us to know how the slaves at Buffalo Forge reacted to Weaver's death. Brady had been directing day-to-day operations for five years at the time Weaver died, so the work force certainly knew him well and was used to his management. Little seemed to change in the wake of Weaver's passing. Slaves continued to "loaf" on occasion, husbands still left the property regularly to visit their wives on weekends, pigs and calves were still distributed to the slave families at Buffalo Forge, and the slaves' corn lots remained theirs to cultivate and were regularly planted every spring. Brady continued the practice of declaring partial "holidays" on Saturdays during the planting and harvest season after the completion of important tasks.[52]

There is also some evidence that he made adjustments in overwork rates as the war continued and inflation spiraled ever upward. The absence of any "Negro Books" for the war years and of any forge production records after May 1862 makes generalizations regarding overwork pay tenuous, but the Buffalo Forge Cash Books have survived for this period and show monetary payments to the slaves that are suggestive. Prior to the summer of 1863, harvest money regularly distributed to the slaves after the crops of hay, wheat, and oats were gathered was always $1 for each hand. In August 1863, Brady raised the harvest payment to $2 per hand. Sam Salling, a hired slave who worked at Buffalo Forge throughout the war as a woodchopper and farm hand, drew cash to settle his overwork account just before going home every Christmas. In 1862, his payment on December 24 was $26.43; in 1863, it was $59.75; in 1864, it was an even $100. In the fall of 1864, Brady was paying the slaves 25 cents apiece for any surplus eggs they wished to sell, and he paid Sam Williams $30 for "chickens" at that time, although he failed to record the number of fowl he purchased from Sam. Brady also made small distributions of scarce items like tobacco and sugar to the slaves on occasion, particularly during planting season and at Christmas. All in all, the entries in the cashbooks indicate that the overwork system continued to function at Buffalo Forge as long as slavery lasted, and that Brady made at least modest increases in the rate of overwork compensation during the final two years of the war.[53]

No evidence exists that Brady turned to the whip or other forms of corporal punishment that Weaver seems to have shunned throughout most of his career as a Virginia ironmaster. There is no evidence, in fact, that the lash was ever employed at Buffalo Forge except by the Rockbridge County slave patrol in December 1859. Weaver's managers at Bath Iron Works and Etna Furnace sometimes whipped, or threatened to whip, slaves who had committed various offenses, but Weaver's most frequent response to serious infractions was to summon a local slave trader and arrange a swift sale of those men and women who had violated his rules of conduct. As mentioned, Brady's only sales were the two fortification workers and the man who had contracted venereal disease. The oral tradition handed down to the descendants of Garland Thompson's family indicates that the slaves held the same opinion of Brady that they did of Weaver: basically a decent man.[54]

A sad event that occurred in the summer of 1863 is suggestive of Brady's approach to slave discipline. Harry Hunt, Jr., and his wife Charlotte lost a child in 1863. Since Harry's wife lived away from Buffalo Forge, the details are sketchy, but Brady noted in his journal that on August 17 of that year, Harry left the property to attend the "funeral of his child." The Hunts had several children by this time; they had been married since 1856 and had two sons, Wilson and George, and a daughter, Mary, in addition to the child who died in 1863. On Saturday, August 29, twelve days after the funeral and after almost two weeks of steady work at the chaffery hammer, Brady noted that Harry did no work at all that Saturday because he was drunk. There is no indication that he was punished for this, and the chances are Brady understood very well what he was going through. Harry returned to work the following Monday.[55]

The strong impression conveyed by the surviving records is that Brady maintained Weaver's system of relying heavily on overwork compensation to motivate the black workers at Buffalo Forge and that he continued to look the other way when slaves "loafed" or committed other minor breaches of discipline.

Following Weaver's death, Brady began an immediate and systematic search for ways to protect the estate from the ravages of Confederate inflation. The spring of 1863 was a time of hope for the South, with Lee's victory at Chancellorsville in early May blunting the Union effort to defeat his Army of Northern Virginia and drive on to Richmond. But Lee's triumph was also a moment of tragedy for the Confederacy, because the battle of Chancellorsville cost the army the life of "Stonewall" Jackson. Wounded by a mistaken volley from his own men on the evening of May 2, Jackson died eight days later. Brady rode in to Lexington to attend Jackson's funeral services on Friday, May 15, and that somber occasion could only have confirmed in his mind the wisdom of looking for a safe haven for the resources Emma's Uncle William had left behind.[56]

One of his first steps was to renew the effort to dispose of Bath Iron Works. He placed a rather restrained advertisement in the Richmond *Enquirer* in April announcing the property for sale, but when no buyer came forward, he ran a second ad in July providing a more enthusiastic description of Bath's assets. The property had "water power . . . equal to any in the country," there was "an abundance of timber in the immediate neighborhood," and Bath possessed "valuable beds of Iron Ore, one of which is the best Ore for cannon metal in the Confederate States."[57] Once again, there were no takers. Brady would not make a cent out of his efforts to sell Bath Iron Works.

The real problem was finding investments that would hold their value during the war and perhaps provide financial security if the Confederacy went down to defeat. Less than a month after Weaver died, Brady asked one of Emma's cousins who lived in Richmond, a man named Joseph G. Dill, for some recommendations. Dill ran through a long list of items: tobacco, cotton, woolen goods, foreign exchange, gold. "The fact is it is all a lottery," he wrote, but added that "anything is better than having money idle." Dill knew Brady "felt a deeper interest in everything since it is yours. ... My advice is to buy *anything* not perishable and it will pay if the war lasts *but* no better than Gold probably would," he concluded. Later that spring, Dill told Brady of a recent outing he and a friend had made in Richmond. They had "a small snack of supper . . . and something to drink in the shape of [a] Julip, cost $13.00—and it was so indifferent we could not eat what was set before us. You don't know know any thing, Brady," Dill went on; "come down if you have a plethora of Confed. notes and you can get rid of them in short order."[58]

The deteriorating military situation in the summer of 1863 gave added impetus to Brady's quest for a safe financial haven. "The news is too heavy to report," Dill wrote from Richmond on July 8. "Lee in Penna. & Pemberton whipped at Vicksbg." Although confirmation of the fall of Vicksburg had not yet reached the Confederate capital, Dill held out little hope. "I suppose it has surrendered," he told Brady. There was no question at all about Lee's situation. His proud army had suffered a crippling defeat at Gettysburg on July 3, and the Confederate forces defending Vicksburg had, in fact, surrendered the city the next day. "This is the crisis in our affairs," Dill correctly predicted on July 10.[59] The Army of Northern Virginia managed to survive the battle of Gettysburg, but its offensive striking power could never be rebuilt. The loss of Vicksburg effectively split the South into two separate sections and gave the Union virtually unrestricted control of the entire Mississippi River. Gettysburg and Vicksburg provided ample evidence that the Confederacy faced, at best, an uncertain future, and Brady moved swiftly to transfer much of his Confederate currency into a tangible asset.

He decided on tobacco. He spent thousands of dollars in 1863, 1864, and early 1865 on tobacco stored in Richmond warehouses in an effort to put at least some of the family's funds in a commodity that would appreciate in price and find ready sale in the event of a Confederate collapse.[60] Only time would tell if Brady's decision was a wise one.

He had large amounts of Confederate money at his disposal as the war continued, but this income had a price tag of its own. Buffalo Forge came increasingly under government control. Part of that control derived from the passage of a series of Conscription Acts by the Confederate Congress beginning in the spring of 1862. Will Rex had secured a substitute before the initial act became law, and Brady, who was forty-one years old, fell outside the eighteen to thirty-five age limits set in the first bill. Brady's status changed abruptly in September 1862 when the draft was extended to include men up to forty-five years of age. Brady was exempt from military service, however, as long as he continued to manufacture iron for the army.[61]

Then, in 1864, government control over Brady's business and his freedom of movement tightened another notch. Both he and Will Rex were enrolled on the conscript lists for Rockbridge County, but they were detailed to Captain John Ellicott, an officer in the Confederate Nitre and Mining Bureau. This bureau, established by Congress in April 1863 to supervise the acquisition of iron and other metals needed by the military and to supply nitre required in the manufacture of gunpowder, became nothing less than a full-fledged partner in Brady's ironmaking enterprise. Captain Ellicott, who was in charge of the Virginia iron district, assigned Brady and Rex to duty at "Buffalo Forge Iron Works" as manufacturers of bar for the Confederate government.[62] And by 1864, Captain Ellicott had almost total control over their supply of pig iron as well.

Once Brady had exhausted the pig and scrap metal stockpiled at the time Etna Furnace went down, he found it impossible to obtain pig on the open market. The only way Brady and Rex could keep the forge, and their exemption from active military service, operative was to sign a contract with the Nitre and Mining Bureau. They entered into a formal agreement with the Bureau early in 1864.

Their contract called for Daniel C. E. Brady and William W. Rex, operating as the firm of Brady & Rex, to supply the government with a minimum of sixty tons of horseshoe iron during 1864. Deliveries were to begin no later than March 1, and monthly production was not to fall below six tons per month for the duration of the contract. The Nitre and Mining Bureau would supply Buffalo Forge with pig iron from local blast furnaces under its control; Brady & Rex would receive this metal at a set price of $124 per ton, a figure well below the current market value of pig iron. Buffalo Forge would convert this pig into horseshoe iron, and the partners would use this bar to fill requisitions from Confederate quartermasters. The firm of Brady & Rex would be allowed 41 cents a pound for their horseshoe metal, which worked out to $918.40 per ton. (The open-market price of Buffalo Forge merchant bar at this time was $1 per pound, $2,240 per ton.[63]) The cost of the pig metal furnished by the government would be deducted from the sums due Brady & Rex for their bar, and the firm would be paid through Captain Ellicott's office in Richmond. This contract, which carried the signatures of Brady, Rex, and Lieutenant Colonel I. M. St. John, chief of the Nitre and Mining Bureau, was dated January 1, 1864.[64]

"Enclosed please find the contracts signed," Brady wrote Captain Ellicott on February 6, 1864, "& inform us when we can get pig metal."[65] The forgemen had been running out scrap iron for some time prior to this, and by February 11, even that makeshift operation had ceased. In the absence of pig iron to run the forge, Sam Williams went to Brady's sawmill to work, and Henry Towles, Tooler, and Harry Hunt, Jr., joined the field hands. Sam, obviously looking for a way to increase his overwork earnings, worked all night sawing logs on a number of occasions in February, and the other forgemen shifted over to a crew composed largely of Brady's teamsters who were hauling logs to the mill. Moving heavy saw logs was dangerous work. On February 20, Charles Towles, Henry's brother, was "crushed by logs," Brady reported.[66] This accident apparently left him permanently crippled. In a descriptive list of slave workers at Buffalo Forge prepared for the Nitre and Mining Bureau in 1865, Brady noted that Charles Towles was "unsound."[67]

When late February arrived and no pig iron had been sent to Buffalo Forge, Brady became anxious. He asked Captain Ellicott when the metal would be provided, and this time he got a response in the form of an order to draw on local blast furnaces for a supply. Thirty tons of iron from Sam Jordan's Buena Vista Furnace arrived at Buffalo forge on March 17. Four days later, Sam Williams and Henry Towles fired up their forge, which had remained idle for well over a month. On Saturday, March 26, Tooler and Harry Hunt, Jr., drew two journeys of bar, the first iron produced by Brady & Rex under the new contract with the Nitre and Mining Bureau.[68]

The days of producing for the lucrative, and highly inflated, open market were over at Buffalo Forge. Charles H. Locher, who had formerly operated the cement works at nearby Balcony Falls, was in charge of the quartermaster's extensive blacksmith shop in Lynchburg, and he knew Buffalo Forge's productive capacities very well. On April 20, he instructed Brady "to deliver to us *all* the bar iron you manufacture under your contract. I hope you will obey *strictly* and to the letter the order," Locher added. "Every thing is moving now and requisitions are daily & numerous on me for transportation, and I am pressed sorely for Iron of all sorts." Locher closed by requesting Brady to "run your forge at night if possible." Three days later, Locher warned Brady again that Buffalo Forge was under firm and definite orders "for all the Iron you make to be turned over to me—fail not at your peril."[69]

Brady heeded this warning, but he made no effort to run Buffalo Forge at night. Coaling operations were delayed by wet weather in the late winter and early spring, and he barely had enough charcoal to operate the forge during the daylight hours. In late April, Brady told Captain Ellicott that "storms & high waters" had impeded operations for the past two months, but he assured the officer that Brady & Rex were "anxious to get up with our deliveries," and promised that they would "obey your instructions as to . . . [our] contract."[70]

In December 1864, John Ellicott, now a major in the Nitre and Mining Bureau, placed an extraordinary proposition before the firm of Brady & Rex. "The building of a new rolling mill of moderate capacity is in contemplation by the bureau, and various sites for the same have been proposed[,] examined and discussed," Ellicott wrote. Among the sites under consideration, "your forge (the Buffalo) stands prominent," the officer explained, and he invited the partners to come to Richmond "at once" to discuss the matter. Major Ellicott then went on to outline the terms under which this rolling mill would be built:

> The intention of the Department is to cause to be prepared as soon as possible and under the supervision of an officer all the necessary machinery, such as water wheel, rolls & housings, shears, castings for the requisite number of puddling & reheating furnaces of sufficient capacity, and in short everything essential to erect and start such an establishment as is proposed. All this work will be done by the Govt. just as though it were govt. work and will be paid for at Govt. prices.

If the Bureau and the firm could come to an agreement, the War Department would "turn over to you the said machinery, have it and the buildings erected, and charge for the same cost, taking in payment work to be done." Ellicott closed his communication by promising to provide "a sufficient quantity of pig iron . . . from your neighborhood to keep the establishment constantly in operation."[71]

Major Ellicott did not explain in this letter why the government was looking for a rolling-mill site in the Valley, but Daniel Brady and Will Rex could certainly read between the lines. The largest rolling mills in the Confederacy were those at the Tredegar Iron Works in Richmond; if Richmond should fall, the government would need an alternative source for bar iron in the upper South, and the Valley of Virginia might provide a safe location for such a facility.

Brady did go to Richmond later that month. His primary purpose was to collect a substantial sum of money from the Nitre and Mining Bureau for Buffalo Forge iron already furnished the government under the terms of his January contract, but the subject of the rolling mill undoubtedly came up when he met with Ellicott.[72] Nothing tangible emerged from this meeting, however. The Confederacy was nearing its death throes by December 1864 as William Tecumseh Sherman's forces completed their march to Savannah and the sea and turned north, and as U. S. Grant's formidable Army of the Potomac tightened its noose around Petersburg, the vital rail center that held the key to Richmond.

Yet Major Ellicott's proposal to Brady raises a critically important question about Buffalo Forge. Why had an ironmaking facility of the type this officer described in his letter—a modern rolling mill—not been built years earlier along the banks of the Buffalo? Why was wrought iron being produced there deep into the Civil War with basically the same technology that had existed at southern forges at the time of the American Revolution? Why had William Weaver, a hard-driving Yankee entrepreneur if there ever was one, largely ignored the technological innovations that had transformed the northern iron industry during the decades prior to the Civil War?

Certainly part of the explanation lay in the nature of Weaver's labor system. After he acquired and trained a group of skilled slave artisans in the 1820s and 1830s and had his ironworks functioning successfully, Weaver displayed little interest in trying to improve the technology of ironmaking at Buffalo Forge. The task and overwork systems brought the requirements of both the master and the slaves into some sort of balance, and once that balance had been achieved, Weaver's tendency was to keep doing things in old, familiar ways. The emphasis was on stability, not innovation. Slavery, in short, seems to have exerted a profoundly conservative influence on the manufacturing process at Buffalo Forge, and one suspects that similar circumstances prevailed at industrial establishments throughout the slave South.[73]

This failure to modernize earlier at Buffalo Forge had absolutely nothing to do with the talents and abilities of Weaver's slave artisans. Men like Sam Williams, Henry Towles, Tooler, and Harry Hunt, Jr., were highly skilled workers who turned out wrought iron that one Confederate contractor described as "the *best* I have *ever used*."[74] The problem was that they were unable, and were sometimes unwilling, to produce very much of it. The maximum capacity of a facility like Buffalo Forge was around 200 tons of bar iron per year; the annual capacity of a modern rolling mill like the one Major Ellicott proposed in December 1864 was measured in thousands of tons.[75] Buffalo Forge had retained the traditional tilt-hammer technology because Weaver had chosen to keep his slave forgemen doing things the way they always had. Now, in the twilight of the Confederacy, it was too late to modernize.

Spring was once again a season of death at Buffalo Forge in 1864. On Thursday, May 5, in the midst of the busy planting season, Sally Williams died. She was in her early sixties, and death appears to have come quickly to her. Brady listed the cause as "paralasys," undoubtedly a stroke. Her husband, Sam Williams, Sr., was alive at the time, although he was close to seventy years of age, was probably blind, and was apparently in frail health as well. When the appraisers went over Weaver's personal property in the spring of 1863, they had estimated Sally Williams to be worth $500, but they had listed Sam Williams, Sr., at no value. He had not been a member of the work force at Buffalo Forge for many years.[76]

Sam Williams was working at his refinery forge the day his mother died. Brady released him from his duties on the morning following her death, and later that day, Friday, May 6, she was buried in the slaves' cemetery at Buffalo Forge. It was a beautiful spring day.[77]

The slave cemetery, which stood in a grove of locust trees on a hill behind the mansion, commanded a magnificent view of the Valley—the pale haze of the Blue Ridge Mountains, the forests of oak, hickory, walnut, and cedar, the cleared fields, the waters of Buffalo Creek freshened by the spring thaw. There her wooden coffin was lowered into the earth, and a plain, uncarved shaft of limestone was set up to mark her grave.[78] She had been in the midst of her family and friends in the last days of her life, and they were doubtless there for her funeral—her husband, her son Sam, her daughter-in-law Nancy, her grandchildren, her great-grandchildren, her sister Louisa, her niece Lucy, and her nephews and their families. In 1815, as a young girl of thirteen or so, Sally Williams had been one of the "Wilson negroes," the first group of slaves purchased by Weaver in Virginia. Now Weaver the master and Sally Williams the slave had reached their final resting place in the Valley they both knew as home.

Had Sally Williams lived until the summer of 1864, she would have seen unmistakable signs that freedom was coming. On June 6, a Union force under General David Hunter occupied Staunton in Augusta County, just north of Rockbridge. Confederate forces seeking to check Hunter's advance fell back toward Rockfish Gap, a major passage through the Blue Ridge, in order to protect Charlottesville and central Virginia, and this movement opened the door to Lexington and the ironworks of Rockbridge County. On June 11, Hunter's men entered Lexington and proceeded to burn the Virginia Military Institute and Governor Letcher's residence. The Union troops set up camp and occupied the town for two days. On the morning of June 14, they broke camp and headed south.[79]

Brady knew they were coming. Refugees had begun arriving at Buffalo Forge as early as June 7 with news that Hunter was close by. Brady nevertheless kept the forge in operation and continued field work until June 11.

"Lexington occupied by Federal troops," Brady wrote that day. "All hands idle & over the river at farm." Brady had moved the slaves at Buffalo Forge across North River to Highland Farm, a mile east of the forge, in an effort to keep them from falling into the hands of Hunter's troops.[80]

Brady kept the slaves at Highland for four days while Hunter's forces swept through the lower half of the county. The federals' main object was to destroy all the blast furnaces in the area, and this turned out to be a fortunate circumstance for Buffalo Forge. Furnaces belonging to Sam Jordan and a number of other stacks in Rockbridge and Botetourt counties were burned, but the Union troops did not damage Buffalo Forge at all.[81] And if Brady had brought his colliers in when he moved the Buffalo Forge hands to Highland Farm, he probably would not have lost any slaves, either.

On June 12, Warder Banks, Bill Dutch, and Spotswood escaped to the federals. Banks was a teamster, Bill Dutch and Spotswood were coaling hands who had been working in the woods east of Buffalo Forge. Also managing to flee were two hirelings from Spotsylvania County, Beverly and Scipio, who were with the colliers (Beverly was one of the slaves who had suffered an axe wound at Buffalo Forge late in 1862). In addition, Will Rex was captured and held by Hunter's men. According to family tradition, Rex was off visiting a female acquaintance at the time of the Union raid and happened to be in the path of the advancing troops.[82]

"I regret to inform you that your boy Beverly went off with the enemy upon that raid through this county on 12 June," Brady wrote the slave's owner shortly after Hunter's men left the area. "I lost 3 of my own at the same time, & they captured Mr. Rex my manager, who they took off with them, on the ground of his being a detailed man. I was fortunate in escaping myself & sustaining no loss of other property," Brady added.[83] Hunter continued on to Lynchburg, which was too heavily defended for the federals to capture, prior to retreating into the Kanawha Valley in western Virginia. Will Rex did not manage to get back to Buffalo Forge until March 1865.[84]

When Warder Banks escaped in June 1864, he left behind a large family. His wife, Frances, and their seven children, the youngest of whom, Warder Jr., was two years old, were all taken to Highland Farm on June 12 and remained there until Brady considered it safe to return to Buffalo Forge. Spotswood was married to a woman who lived in the neighborhood of the forge, and she may or may not have joined her husband in his escape.[85] Warder Banks apparently did not return to Buffalo Forge at the end of the war. His name does not appear in any of the extensive postwar records kept by Brady.

The Buffalo Forge slave force resumed work on Wednesday, June 15.

The forge workers joined the field hands cultivating the corn crop and mowing hay that day and for most of the rest of the week. On Saturday, June 18, Sam Williams and Tooler returned to the forge to begin some repairs, and at the end of the workday, Garland Thompson, Jr., left to spend the weekend with his wife. Life at Buffalo Forge was returning to something approaching normal routine. The forgemen kept busy with repairs and agricultural tasks until Monday, July 11, when Brady noted that the "Forge started again." Sam Williams and Henry Towles resumed making anchonies that day, and Tooler and Harry Hunt, Jr., drew a journey of horseshoe iron for the Confederate quartermasters.[86]

Life at Buffalo Forge might have appeared routine on the surface, but Hunter's raid and the escape of five slaves were bound to have quickened the hope of freedom among the black men, women, and children still living there. The tragedy for Sam and Nancy Williams was that so many members of their family would not be there to see freedom come.

Death seemed to haunt the Williams family during the war years. Sam and Nancy lost their daughter Betty and their grandson Alfred Elliott Coleman during the diptheria epidemic in the fall of 1862. Sam's mother had suffered a stroke and died less than two years later. Then, in the fall of 1864, their twenty-year-old daughter Lydia, who was unmarried and was the nurse for the young Brady children, became seriously ill. She had typhoid fever, and her condition steadily worsened. On October 7, as Lydia neared death, her older sister, Caroline Williams Reid, gave birth to her third child, a girl. Caroline named her daughter Lydia Maydelene in honor of her stricken sister. Two days later, on Sunday, October 9, Lydia Williams died.[87]

The forge was idle Monday as Sam Williams and Henry Towles spent the day with their families. Henry undoubtedly shared the Williams' grief over the loss of their daughter, but he had another concern as well. His wife Ann was expecting a baby any day. On Tuesday morning, October 11, under a clear autumn sky, Sam and Nancy Williams and the rest of the Buffalo Forge slaves once again climbed the dirt road behind the mansion and buried one of their own under the locust trees on the hill. That same day, Ann Towles gave birth to a son, her sixth child, Clarence Henry Towles.[88]

The death of Lydia was not the last of the losses the Williams family suffered as the war neared its end. By early 1865, it was clear that Caroline Williams Reid was dying. She had "consumption," tuberculosis of the lungs, and there was no cure. She died on Thursday, January 12, 1865. Eight days later, Ann and Henry Towles lost their baby. Clarence Henry Towles died on January 20, 1865, of "spasms," according to the brief notation Brady made after his name in the slave recordbook.[89]

When Caroline Williams Reid died in January 1865, she left three small children at Buffalo Forge: Mary Martha, four; William John, two; and Lydia Maydelene, three months. They would be there in the spring of 1865 when slavery ended at Buffalo Forge and across the rest of the South. But so many members of Sam and Nancy Williams' family—Sally Williams, Lydia Williams, Betty and her son Alfred Coleman, and Caroline Williams Reid—would never know the taste of freedom. They had been so close, but for them release from bondage had come only with death.

5

Peace and
Freedom

Spring came late to the Valley in
1865. Damp, cold weather lasted well into March, and fields that Brady
knew were simply "too wet to plow" delayed the beginning of the planting
season at Buffalo Forge. Once the weather improved, however, the work
proceeded rapidly. Brady sent every available hand, including his forgemen, into the field, and before March was over the slaves had finished
sowing the crops of oats and clover and had begun planting the corn.[1]
Brady was intent on "making supplies," as Weaver used to say. Buffalo
Forge had virtually stopped making iron for the Confederacy.

The problems at the forge were twofold. The months of January and
February 1865 had been exceptionally wet, and the colliers had been unable to set their pits and begin making charcoal. Brady informed the Nitre
and Mining Bureau in early February that he could not commence coaling
until March, and on February 20, he told the Bureau that he would "not
have coal to haul for some time." The second problem was an acute shortage of pig iron. Brady asked Major Ellicott to hurry on some metal from

Sam Jordan's blast furnace in Amherst County so that Buffalo Forge could swing into production as soon as charcoal became available. Garland Thompson's coal wagon was standing idle and could be used to haul the iron from the North River Canal, Brady pointed out.[2] It was April 6, 1865, before a supply of pig iron reached Buffalo Forge[3]; three days later, on Sunday, April 9, Lee surrendered the Army of Northern Virginia at Appomattox Court House, across the Blue Ridge Mountains some fifty miles east of Buffalo Forge.

The end had come swiftly for the Confederacy. The government evacuated Richmond the previous Sunday, April 2, and Union troops occupied the city the next day. Before Confederate forces moved out of the capital, they had begun burning supplies, cotton, and tobacco stored in Richmond warehouses. Looting broke out, and soon the fires raged out of control.[4] Consumed in this conflagration were the thousands of dollars' worth of tobacco Brady had bought over the past two years. His last two purchases, in December 1864 and January 1865, had been substantial ones. He had gone to Richmond during those two months to secure payment from Major Ellicott for iron delivered to the government and had received over $35,-000 in Confederate treasury notes. He had immediately invested most of this cash in tobacco. Not a pound of his leaf escaped destruction in the fires that swept through Richmond the night of April 2.[5]

The surrender of Lee's army a week later rendered Brady's remaining Confederate money and bonds equally useless. He was holding over $34,-000 in cash at war's end and had several thousand dollars' worth of Confederate and Rockbridge County bonds in his possession as the executor of William Weaver's estate.[6] These notes and securities were now completely worthless. Brady's attempt to place Weaver's fortune in a position where it could survive the collapse of the Confederacy had failed.

A strange and almost eerie condition prevailed at Buffalo Forge following Lee's surrender. News of Appomattox reached Rockbridge County swiftly, and the Lexington *Gazette* noted on Thursday, April 13, that the surrender of the Army of Northern Virginia "is already known to most of our readers." But for well over a month, no Union troops showed up at Buffalo Forge, and work went on as though slavery had not ended. Sam Williams, Henry Towles, Tooler, and Harry Hunt, Jr., had done almost nothing but field work the entire month of March, but on Monday, April 10, Sam and Henry had gone back to their finery following the arrival of what turned out to be the last shipment of Confederate pig iron to reach Buffalo Forge. It took the two men several days to get ready, but on Saturday, April 15, they resumed production of anchonies at the refinery hammer; Tooler and Harry Hunt, Jr., remained with the field hands who had gone over to Highland Farm to plow and plant corn, and the two forgemen continued to do agricultural work for the rest of the month.[7]

The first signs that the slave system at Buffalo Forge was on the verge of disintegration came on Wednesday, April 12. A hired slave named Jack "left work" that day, as Brady phrased it, and his departure probably indicates the time word of the surrender of Lee's army reached the black community at Buffalo Forge. Work nevertheless went on. Garland Thompson, Jr., who had resumed his trips to the coaling grounds on April 7, continued to bring a daily load of charcoal to the forge, Henry Matthews and the other blacksmiths continued at their jobs, and Jim Thompson and the agricultural hands plowed and planted the fields at Highland Farm. On Saturday, April 15, Garland Thompson left to spend the weekend with his wife and family, but he returned to Buffalo Forge in time to resume work the following Monday.

And so it went. Buffalo Creek flooded on April 15, forcing some repairs to the forge dam the next week, but Sam and Henry Towles were back at the finery on Tuesday, April 18, and they continued to pound out anchonies for the remainder of the month. Tooler, Harry Hunt, Jr., and the agricultural workers finished at Highland Farm on Thursday, May 4, and then began plowing the fields around Buffalo Forge.[8]

Everything was to change in May, although the onset of freedom must have seemed tortuously slow to the black men, women, and children of Buffalo Forge. On Monday, May 8, five hirelings "ranaway," Brady wrote, and a week later, another hired worker left.[9] Certainly a major reason Weaver's former slaves did not quit work was the absence of a federal presence in the immediate area. With the breakdown in civil authority in the county, whites in both Lexington and the surrounding countryside organized armed patrols both to prevent lawlessness and to keep blacks in their place. One of these organizations was active in the vicinity of Buffalo Forge.

"A terrible thing occurred here today," Brady informed James Davidson on May 21. A man named Woods, a former overseer on a nearby farm, had stolen a horse and taken it to Alleghany County for sale. The owner of the horse tracked Woods down and applied to the local justice of the peace, James G. Updike, for an arrest warrant. When Updike stated that he had no authority to issue such a warrant, the owner asked for help from the local "Safety Club." The white patrol captured Woods, and while they were crossing one of Brady's Buffalo Forge farms, they "shot him through the head" and left him there on the ground. Brady considered the execution of Woods nothing less than murder and was appalled at this outbreak of "Lynch Law." He feared that friends of Woods would try to shoot the men responsible for killing him, "& then commences a desperate state of things," Brady wrote.[10] Under these conditions, Union troops would be welcome in Rockbridge County.

Federal authority was gradually being extended to all corners of Virginia during April and May, and military commanders were issuing a series of general orders pertaining to the freedmen. "Can you send me the paper containing Genl Hallecks last proclamation about Africa," Brady asked Davidson on May 21.[11] Henry W. Halleck had been named Commander of the Military District of the James following Appomattox, and his General Orders No. 6 appeared in the Lynchburg press on May 16, 1865. The general instructed all federal officers in the district to "use their influence to reconcile all differences between freedmen and their former masters." Halleck seemed particularly concerned that the former slaves would refuse to work. "All classes must be shown the necessity of planting and cultivating crops this spring and summer, in order to avoid want in the country," he wrote. Officers were to "assure freedmen that they will be required to labor for support of themselves and families, but they are also free to select their own employers and make their own bargains. They must be made to understand that Government will protect, but not support them," he continued. "Interest, as well as humanity, require that former masters of the colored race should unite in devising the best measures of ameliorating their condition, and for introducing some system of labor. To this end all military authorities will lend their aid," the order concluded.[12]

Brady made no attempt to act on these somewhat vague instructions when the workweek began on Monday, May 22. But he was worried on several counts. The only money he had at Buffalo Forge that was worth anything when the war ended was exactly $10 in specie. He was able to borrow $200 from a Lynchburg bank on May 15, but that would not last very long.[13] "My prospects are good for . . . supplies" he told Davidson on May 21, "but the change in labor may curtail them."[14]

A change in labor was long overdue at Buffalo Forge, and the black workers there knew it. The field hands were at Highland Farm the week of May 22, but the forge and blacksmith shop were running, Henry Matthews was operating the sawmill, and beginning on Tuesday, May 23, Garland Thompson, Jr., brought in his usual load of coal. Tooler had stopped work entirely, however. He had been "laid up" or "loafing" since May 8. Sam Williams and Henry Towles made anchonies that week, but the forgemen were preparing to follow in Tooler's footsteps. Jim Thompson had come in to take Tooler's place at the chaffery hammer, and he and Harry Hunt, Jr., drew two journeys on Tuesday, May 23. The next day, however, after drawing one journey of bar, they "threw down [their] hammer," Brady reported. On Thursday, May 25, Brady recorded that the first of Weaver's former slaves "ranaway." John, a sixteen-year-old helper in the blacksmith shop, left after pretending to be sick for most of the week.[15]

On Friday, May 26, 1865, slavery ended at Buffalo Forge. "Declared free by order of the military authorities," was all Daniel Brady wrote to describe the day of freedom there.[16] His words did no justice to the emotions of the black men and women who had labored at Buffalo Forge in bondage for so long.

The next day, Saturday, Brady noted "All hands quit work as they considered themselves free. I made a speech to them, and read the order No. 2 of Genl Gregg."[17] Brady did not write down what he said in his address, but subsequent events made clear that he told the newly freed blacks that he intended to keep the forge in production and to continue farming operations at Buffalo Forge. Those workers who wished to stay on could do so, and they would be paid on a piecework or wage basis depending on the specific position they held. Brady wrote that several other white men were present when he addressed the black community at Buffalo Forge. Will Rex was there; he had returned in late March following his capture and release by Hunter's troops. So was James G. Updike, the local justice of the peace, and three other men from the neighborhood, Alexander W. Hamilton, John D. Ewing, and Thomas Edwards. Whether these men were there as witnesses or to back Brady up in case he received a hostile reaction from the former slaves is not clear. None of these men appears to have been associated with the local "Safety Club," although Updike and Hamilton had both been captains in the Confederate Army and had served as the first two commanders of the Rockbridge Grays.[18]

The general orders that Brady read to the assembled workers and their families that Saturday had been issued on May 18 by General J. Irwin Gregg, the federal commander in Lynchburg, and they were published in the Lynchburg press five days later. Gregg went to considerable lengths to correct the "delusion" of many freedmen "that with their liberty they acquire individual rights in the property of their former masters, and that they are entitled to live with and be subsisted by them, without being obliged to labor or give any remuneration for their support." He then proceeded to spell out the rights the former slaves did possess, and he coupled this with a statement of their responsibilities:

> The operation of existing laws is to make *free*, but not to give them any claim whatever upon, or rights in connection with the property of former owners. They are at liberty to make any contract or agreement concerning themselves that a white man may, and equally bound to abide by it.

The former master had "the right to refuse them anything that he might deny to a perfect stranger," the orders continued, "and is not more bound to feed, clothe, or protect them than if he had never been their master." The freedmen might "remain with him if he and they both desire it, and agree on the terms, in which case each party is equally bound by the contract." The orders concluded by admonishing blacks "that they must work for their support now, the same as before they were free; in some instances, perhaps, even harder" and informed them that "destitute" rations would not be issued to able-bodied laborers unless they could show they had tried but were unable to obtain work. A final paragraph read:

> All colored persons living in the country, are informed that it is much better for them to remain there than to come to the already over-stocked city, and that they will not be permitted to come here for work or subsistence, unless they cannot obtain them where they are.[19]

Brady certainly wanted it clearly understood that the freedmen had no claims on his property, but he also wanted them to know that there were jobs for them at Buffalo Forge. The fact was, he desperately needed their labor. The crops in the ground, and any bar iron he could make and sell, were his only ready sources of income at the end of the war. With $10 in coin on hand and a modest loan from the bank in Lynchburg his only immediate monetary resources, Brady and his family faced disaster if his former slaves refused to work for him. He had supplies on hand—beef, bacon, cornmeal, flour, and the goods in the Buffalo Forge store—to maintain the work force, but it was up to them to decide whether to stay or go.

Each freedman, each family, had several factors to weigh. This was the only home most of them had ever known. Family ties were woven throughout the black community at Buffalo Forge and the surrounding countryside. The federal authorities were all but ordering them to continue working where they were, or to find work nearby, and to stay out of urban areas. Their choice was either to remain at a place with which they were familiar, among friends and family members they knew and loved, or to leave and face the uncertainties of the world beyond Buffalo Forge. Almost all chose to stay.

Thirty-seven men and women, almost the entire adult black work force at Buffalo Forge when emancipation occurred, accepted labor contracts from Brady that weekend. Among those who chose to stay on were all of the men, twenty-one in number, who had belonged to Weaver at the time of his death and who were still at Buffalo Forge when emancipation came. Four of Weaver's former slave women—Nancy Williams, Louisa, Frances

Banks, and Matilda—also agreed to individual contracts, as did twelve men who had been hired, primarily for woodchopping, at the beginning of the year. All agreements were for three months and were dated May 29, 1865.[20]

Sam Williams and Henry Towles received identical contracts. They would be paid $4 per ton for all the iron they refined and would furnish themselves "with everything" out of their wages. "Everything" meant food, clothing, housing, and firewood. Tooler and Harry Hunt, Jr., accepted contracts identical to those of the refiners, except that their "forge wages" were set at $3.50 per man for each ton of bar they drew. These wage rates were similar to the overwork pay scales dating back to before the war. Gone, however, were the tasks of slavery; the forgemen would now be paid for all the iron they produced.

Other forge workers received contracts as well. Henry Matthews agreed to work as a "blacksmith, rough carpenter, forge hand, or farm hand" for $15 per month, "he to supply himself with everything." Jim Thompson would be paid $8 per month and "rations of meat and bread" for working as a farm hand; should he be needed to spell one of the refiners or hammermen, he would be paid the appropriate forge wage. Garland Thompson, Jr., would continue to drive the charcoal wagon for $10 per month and rations of bread and meat.

Most of the farm hands—men like Charles Towles, Mark, and Bill and Sam Thompson—received the same contract: wages of $8 per month and weekly rations of meat and bread. Edgar Towles agreed to serve as a light wagoner and act as the Brady's carriage driver for $5 a month plus food. Some of the older farm workers, men like Prince Towles and Sam Grigsby, who was fifty-seven, would also be paid $5 a month and rations. The only woman who agreed to work as a farm hand, Matilda, was given similar compensation.

Two other women continued on in jobs they had held previously. Nancy Williams would act as the dairymaid at Buffalo Forge for $4 per month, "she to supply herself with everything." Louisa would cook for $4 a month and would receive her food; her daughter Lucy would "be clothed and fed for her labor." Frances Banks, whose husband, Warder, had escaped during Hunter's raid, initially agreed "to wash, help milk, and do anything else required of her" in return for Brady's commitment to furnish her and her children with food, clothing, a home, firewood, and medical care. Four of the Banks' children were also to work as part of this agreement. The space under this contract in the ledger containing the freedmen's accounts is totally blank, however, which indicates that she and her children left Buffalo Forge immediately. In all likelihood, she was trying to locate her husband and reunite the family.

Frances Banks' contract—work in return for maintenance but no money—was typical of several agreements that smacked heavily of a continuation of the old order of things. Wilson King's contract required him to work as a farm hand, his wife, Eliza Thompson King, to serve as a "washer-woman &c," and two of their older boys to act as coal stockers at the forge. Brady would furnish the entire family with food, clothing, housing, and fuel, but no wages would be paid. In the case of some of the elderly slave men, Brady simply promised that they would "be provided for as before the war." Not surprisingly, the men and women who held contracts of this sort were among the first to leave Buffalo Forge.[21]

"Commenced work on free labor," Brady wrote in his journal on Monday, May 29, 1865. Sam Williams and Henry Towles were back in the forge, as were Tooler and Harry Hunt, Jr. Tooler had not drawn a pound of iron for three weeks as slavery died a slow death at Buffalo Forge. On May 29, he and Harry Hunt turned out two journeys of bar. Garland Thompson, Jr., delivered a load of charcoal, and Henry Matthews did some work in the smith shop and jointed shingles. The weather was clear and cool, and Edward McFadden, Brady's longtime overseer, took the agricultural hands over to Highland Farm to work the corn crop.[22] The gang system of field labor, a distinctive aspect of antebellum southern agriculture, survived the end of slavery at Buffalo Forge as it did throughout much of the South in the immediate aftermath of the war.

Life and labor settled quickly into familiar patterns. Forge and field work went on steadily through the summer and early fall, as the oats, hay, and wheat were brought in and work started on the corn crop. Garland Thompson, Sr., returned to Buffalo Forge in June looking for work. Brady signed him on, but the terms must have been humiliating for the father of so many of the Buffalo Forge workers. "Commenced work June 12 for what he is worth," were the conditions of his employment as Brady recorded them. That turned out to be $5 per month, and Garland labored as a field hand only until the end of August. At that time he drew all of his earnings of $8.93—$8 in cash and 93 cents for thirty pounds of flour—and left Buffalo Forge. His daughter Eliza and her husband, Wilson King, and their children departed at the same time, and Brady recorded in his journal that they were moving to the vicinity of Bath Furnace, the area where Garland Thompson, Sr., had previously lived. The census of 1870 reported that Garland and Dicey Thompson and their children and Wilson King's family were living near one another in Walker's Creek Township, the section of Rockbridge County in which Bath Iron Works was located. Garland Thompson, Sr., who was sixty-five, and Wilson King, who was forty-seven, both listed their occupation as farm laborer.[23]

Daniel Brady's problems did not end with the retention of most of his labor force and the resumption of work. Under the terms of the Recon-struction Proclamation issued by President Andrew Johnson on May 29, 1865—the day work began "on free labor" at Buffalo Forge—Brady would not be able to receive amnesty simply by swearing an oath of future loyalty to the United States. A number of excepted classes were required to peti-tion the president for special pardons, and one of these categories consisted of persons who had participated in the rebellion and who held over $20,000 in taxable property. Brady fell into this category.

Daniel C. E. Brady's petition for presidential pardon was dated July 13, 1865. He gave his age as forty-four, identified himself as a native of Phila-delphia, and stated that he had moved to Rockbridge County, Virginia, in 1857. "He was never in the army," the petition went on, "but his Forge, under duress of impressment, made bar iron for the Confederate govern-ment after January 1864." Brady had taken the amnesty oath called for in the president's proclamation twice, at Lynchburg on June 9, 1865, and again in Lexington on July 8. "He wishes to continue his industrial pursuits as a loyal citizens [sic] of the United States, and to resume and preserve in good faith his allegiance to the Union and Constitution thereof," the peti-tion concluded. It was promptly endorsed by the Unionist governor of Virginia, Francis H. Peirpoint, and approved by President Johnson with a speed that was little less than astounding. The president signed Brady's pardon certificate on July 17, 1865.[24] His action effectively removed the possibility that Daniel and Emma Brady's property would be confiscated because of any aid Brady had rendered the rebel cause.

The conversion to free labor and the resumption of iron production initially brought a measure of prosperity back to Buffalo Forge. With farm-ers in need of iron and with transportation still seriously disrupted, ham-mered iron found a ready market both locally and across the Blue Ridge in Lynchburg in 1865 and early 1866. Brady obtained pig iron from Sam Jordan's Buena Vista and Amherst furnaces by agreeing to trade a ton of bar to Jordan for every four tons of pig furnished the forge.[25] This barter arrangement meant that Brady did not have to lay out any cash in order to secure a steady supply of metal for the forge.

When the forge resumed production in June 1865, Brady followed Weaver's long-standing practice of charging what the local traffic would bear, and he priced his iron at 10 cents per pound—$224 per ton—to customers in Rockbridge and surrounding counties. The next month, he raised the price to 12½ cents per pound, $280 a ton, for iron sold at the forge. He could not command these prices in Lynchburg, but "mountain iron" was bringing $130 to $135 per ton in that market in July, and in

August the price rose to 7 cents per pound, $156.80 per ton. By December 1865, Brady's commission house in Lynchburg had sold over twenty-four tons of Buffalo Forge iron at top market prices; these sales netted Brady almost $3,300 in much-needed cash.[26]

The forgemen were being paid at prewar wage rates, $4 per ton each for refining anchonies, $3.50 per ton each for drawing bar.[27] Brady, on the other hand, was receiving prices well above the $100 per ton his iron was bringing on the eve of the Civil War. But the black forge workers still managed to make a decent living for themselves during their first months of freedom.

On September 2, 1865, Brady credited Sam Williams and Henry Towles each with $100.05 for making just over twenty-five tons of anchonies during June, July, and August, and Sam received an additional $20 for taking care of the smokehouse. Both men had drawn against their earnings for bacon, cornmeal, flour, salt, molasses, tobacco, cloth, and an occasional pint of whiskey, an item they had been forbidden to purchase as slaves. Brady charged Sam $20 for three months' rent and firewood for his home; Henry Towles paid $2 per month rent for his cabin and $1 a month for firewood. Both men carried impressive sums of credit forward after this first balancing of their accounts in September 1865. Sam had earned $61.41 more than he had spent, and Henry had a credit of $50.67 on Brady's books. They continued to work steadily until the end of the year, and any extra work they did they were paid for. They each earned $2.75 for 2¾ days spent helping to clear debris out from behind the forge dam. Sam earned $1 for every day he put in at the sawmill. Together, they pounded out almost nineteen tons of anchonies between the time of the September settlement and the end of the year, which earned each of them $74.85. The pace of production slackened during the last four months of 1865, however, a reflection of the softening market for iron as the burst of demand induced by wartime shortages was met.[28]

Tooler and Harry Hunt, Jr., put in long hours as well. Tooler, who had taken a considerable amount of time off as a slave, did not miss a day's work in June, and neither did his forge partner. They drew twenty-three journeys of bar in their first month "on free labor" and also spent a week helping to bring in the wheat crop. Like the refiners, they carried credit balances forward at each point in the year when their accounts were totaled. In the fall, however, Tooler decided to leave Buffalo Forge. Perhaps he wanted to look for work closer to Lynchburg, where his wife had lived during slavery. For whatever reason, on October 28, 1865, he drew $20.25 in cash to close his account with Brady. Harry Hunt, Jr., took over his position at the chaffery, and Henry Matthews and Jim Thompson took turns serving as Harry's underhand for the remainder of the year.[29]

A number of Weaver's former slaves left Buffalo Forge in the summer and early fall of 1865, and most of these workers were farm hands. In addition to Garland Thompson, Sr., and Wilson and Eliza Thompson King, Bill and Sam Thompson pulled out during this period, as did Mark and Prince and Edgar Towles. Most of these men left after serving out their initial three-month contracts, but others, like Edgar Towles, "left without notice," as Brady recorded in the ledger in which the freedmen's accounts were kept. In every instance, they ended their time at Buffalo Forge with credit on the books, and most drew cash from Brady to settle their accounts. These sums ranged from the $6.17 which Prince Towles received in September to Bill Thompson's cash settlement of $11.44 the same month. None of these men had been reduced to any sort of debt peonage while they were in Brady's service. They were, however, working under conditions that were very similar to those that had existed under slavery. All were being issued weekly "rations of bread and meat" in addition to their monthly wages of $5 or $8. Most were doing gang labor in the fields under the same overseer who had supervised their work prior to emancipation. These men, it would appear, wanted more from their freedom than a continuation of life pretty much as they had known it at Buffalo Forge prior to May 26, 1865. Brady hired other freedmen from neighboring farms as replacements, but many of these men left at the end of the year.[30]

Like former slaveowners all across the South, Daniel Brady was forced to confront an evolving labor system in which blacks increasingly resisted the old forms of agricultural organization. The freedmen wanted their own land, but the federal government was uninterested in pursuing revolutionary land reform measures. In October 1865, the Freedmen's Bureau office in Lexington, which had opened the previous month, felt compelled to issued a printed circular in response to widespread rumors circulating among blacks in the area "that the United States Government will distribute lands among them after Christmas. *This is a delusive idea,*" the officer in charge warned.[31]

Land ownership would remain an unfulfilled dream for most former slaves in Rockbridge County and throughout the South. But if they could not own the land they worked, blacks wanted to work a plot of land where they could reap a greater proportion of the fruits of their own labor. Most of all, they were increasingly unwilling to move through the former masters' fields in gangs, cradling wheat, mowing hay, cultivating corn under the watchful eye of white supervisors. It took time for these new patterns to emerge, but the exodus of field hands from Buffalo Forge in the summer and fall of 1865 was a strong indication that the evolutionary process was already well under way.

The end of the year brought the usual Christmas holiday in 1865. The only difference in the first Christmas under freedom was that the break began earlier than usual. On Saturday, December 23, Brady wrote that McFadden and the field hands were "at work in mg: but all worked so badly that I stopped at noon."[32] Sam and Nancy Williams' celebration appears to have been particularly festive. Sam bought a gallon of whiskey on December 16, and just before Christmas he drew $10 in cash from his account. Nancy spent $2 of her money at the Buffalo Forge store on December 22 and the next day drew out $4 in cash and, for $1.50, purchased a turkey to cook for Christmas dinner.[33] That gathering undoubtedly included Sam's elderly father, their only surviving daughter, Ann, and the children left behind when Betty and Caroline died during the war years.

The pattern was the same throughout the Buffalo Forge black community that Christmas. Henry Towles: a pint of whiskey, $5 in cash, and a $3 store order. Harry Hunt: a plug of tobacco, $10 in cash, and a $10 store order. Jim Thompson: a pint of whiskey, $3 in cash, and twenty pounds of flour. Henry Matthews: a pint of whiskey, $10 in cash, and a $5 store order. Charles Towles, a farm hand: a pint of whiskey, a gallon of molasses, and store purchases of $3.50. The long-established tradition of men and women providing for their families at Christmas clearly carried over into freedom. The one new dimension was the ready availability of alcohol. The almost universal purchase of whiskey just before, and frequently during, the holidays suggests strongly that drinking was a significant aspect of this week-long Christmas break.[34] Such may have been the case at Buffalo Forge under slavery as well, but there is no indication in the surviving records to indicate that this was so.

Daniel and Emma Brady had cause to celebrate that christmas as well. There was a new baby in the household, Elliott Thomas Brady, born on January 8, 1865.[35] Wilhelmina Weaver Brady was a healthy two-year-old, and the other children, Anne, Pat, and Sarah Elizabeth, were all well. Will Rex had returned safely that spring and had taken over management of the Buffalo Forge store. And the entire complex—the forge, the flour mill, the grist mill, the blacksmith shop, the sawmill, the store, the barns and stables, and all of the housing—had escaped destruction. His draft animals had survived the war, his herds of cattle, sheep, swine, and poultry were intact. Brady's swift pardon for his wartime activities on behalf of the Confederacy meant that there was no chance that his property would be confiscated. He had managed to resume forge production and sales, he had brought in the crops that fall, and his flour mill offered an additional source of income. He had lost a number of field hands during the summer and fall, and Tooler had left the forge, but it looked as though he would be able to secure enough labor to plant and harvest his crops in the coming year. If he thought back to May when he had $10 in usable funds on hand and a $200 loan to serve as operating capital, he could certainly count his blessings.

One reason Brady's prospects looked reasonably bright for 1866 was the strong position the local commander of the Freedmen's Bureau had taken on labor agreements. In the fall of 1865, the officer in charge of the Lexington office, Lieutenant C. Jerome Tubbs, issued a printed circular containing explicit instructions for the area's black population. "All Freedmen are hereby directed immediately to enter into contracts for labor for the coming year," Tubbs ordered on October 20, 1865. The contracts were to be "just and reasonable," and he wanted it clearly understood "that the system of contracts is in no way connected with slavery—but is the system adopted by *free laborers* everywhere."[36] A month later, Tubbs again ordered the freedmen "immediately to enter into contracts for labor for the coming year" and warned that "any refusing to contract will be dealt with as Vagrants."[37] In agricultural areas all across the South, similar instructions went out that autumn. Land would not be distributed to the freedmen; they would, as General Gregg had bluntly informed them back in May, have to "work for their support . . . the same as before they were free; in some instances, perhaps, even harder."[38]

Brady's contracts fell under the Bureau's definition of "just and reasonable," and he began the year with a strong nucleus of William Weaver's former slaves. Those who had stayed on after the expiration of their initial three-month contracts continued working under the same terms for the balance of the year, and Brady simply carried those agreements over into 1866. Sam Williams, Henry Towles, Harry Hunt, Jr., Henry Matthews, and Jim Thompson would man the forge and would be available for field work when needed. Garland Thompson, Jr., would deliver charcoal and act as the principal teamster. Charles Towles and several other hands agreed to stay on as agricultural laborers. And Brady's work force was augmented by the return of several men who had left the previous summer. Sam Thompson and Edgar Towles came back in time to begin work as field hands when the new year's work began in January. And in the spring, Tooler returned.[39]

When Tooler came back to Buffalo Forge, he did not take up his old position at the chaffery hammer. The contract he agreed to on March 26, 1866, called on him to make wooden rails and haul timber. He would be paid $15 a month plus rations for hauling wood; he would receive 75 cents per hundred rails when he cut the wood from which they were made, 50 cents per hundred when the wood was already cut. Tooler began hauling timber on April 2, 1866, and the following day, Brady noted, he moved into a house on the property which Brady rented to him for $2 a month.[40]

We can only speculate on the reasons that brought men like Tooler, Sam

Thompson, and Edgar Towles back to Buffalo Forge in 1866. Ties to family and community may well have been a factor, and lack of opportunities and threatened abuse elsewhere in the county may also have been involved. Many whites in Rockbridge were openly hostile to the newly freed blacks, Lieutenant Tubbs reported in the fall of 1865. "There are a few people here that are well-disposed and willing to help the freedmen in making an honorable living, but the majority are selfish, stubborn men & try to take every advantage of the freedmen they can," he told his regional supervisor on October 30. "Occasionally one is bold enough to speak out plainly that as soon as the *Damned Yankees* [leave], they will shoot them like dogs." Tubbs concluded this report with a comment on the loyalty of most of the county's white citizens. "It is useless to speak of a Union sentiment for it does not exist in this section," he wrote. "Holy Water would as easily spring from a rock as loyal sentiments from their Rebellious hearts."[41]

In the spring of 1866, Tubbs's successor in the Lexington office of the Bureau, G. B. Carse, reported the existence of the "Fancy Hill Mutual Aid Club," a group of armed white men who patroled an area of the county not far from Buffalo Forge. Carse had obtained a copy of the rules and regulations of this "Vigilance Club," and he noted that the members threatened to convene a "committee of safety" to "determine the punishment of each party brought before the said club" for offenses such as stealing and failure to maintain peace and good order. This organization, clearly formed to intimidate the freedmen, was commanded by Colonel W. F. Poague, the same man who had led the "Safety Club" whose personnel had murdered the horse thief and left his body on one of Brady's farms in the spring of 1865.[42]

Given the hostile atmosphere toward the freedmen in many sections of Rockbridge County, Buffalo Forge may well have served as something of a haven for the black men and women living there during the early years of Reconstruction. The black oral tradition in the county that Daniel Brady was a decent man—"nice people" was the phrase James Thompson used to describe Weaver and Brady—suggests this possibility.[43] So does a letter written to Brady in 1871 by a former Union officer who had served in the area.

Captain J. W. Sharp commanded the Lexington office of the Freedmen's Bureau from December 1866 until January 1868. Three years after he left this position, he sent a warm letter of thanks to Brady. "You and your family were so kind to me when I was among you," Sharp wrote on May 16, 1871, "that I believe I am duty bound even after the long lapse of time that has intervened to return my thanks for your great courtesy." The spring flowers then blooming in Pennsylvania had reminded Sharp of a visit he had paid to the Bradys in May 1867 and of the horseback ride he had taken with a party including Anne Brady, who was nineteen years old at the time. They had ridden through the woods to Falling Spring Church and then back over the hills to Buffalo Forge, where Sharp had spent the night in the Brady's home. The former officer had vivid memories of the interior of the house, and the entire visit clearly had been one of the few bright social moments Sharp had experienced during his tour of duty in the Valley. "Do you recollect the day you patronised me at the Rockbridge Baths and again the evening Miss Brady so pleasantly saluted me when she was riding in the carriage with the Davidson girls?" he asked.[44]

In an area where, as one of Sharp's predecessors had so elegantly put it, Unionist sentiments were as commonplace as stones that spouted holy water, the Bradys and Buffalo Forge probably represented one of the freedmen's best hopes for physical security and fair treatment in the chaotic period following the end of slavery. The federal presence in Rockbridge and surrounding counties was minuscule: a few Freedmen's Bureau officers and a handful of enlisted men.[45] For those black men and women with families to support and protect both when freedom first came and during the years that followed, Daniel Brady was a known quantity, Buffalo Forge a secure and familiar place.

The strength of those black families was vividly demonstrated in 1866 when the Freedmen's Bureau office in Lexington opened a marriage register. Black men and women whose marriages had no legal standing under slavery could come into the office and record both the number of years they had been married and the names and ages of their children.[46] It was nine miles into Lexington from Buffalo Forge, and unless Brady loaned them a wagon, the trip would have to be made on foot. The newly freed husbands and wives of Buffalo Forge clearly thought the trip was worth whatever effort it required, because their names appear on page after page of this register (see page 353).

The list goes on, simple, dignified records that stand in marked contrast to the words Weaver used in 1853 to convey Garland Thompson's desire to marry: "My Boy Garland is smitten by one of your lasses, and nothing will content him but matrimony."[47] The patronizing and amused tone of Weaver's note tells us something about the ignorance and insensitivity he displayed on this occasion. It tells us nothing at all about the life Garland and Ester Thompson, married fourteen years and raising five children in 1866, had lived together. Their marriage registration and those of the other newly freed men and women at Buffalo Forge speak with a quiet eloquence of their feelings for one another and the ties that bound them irrevocably together in slavery and freedom.

Samuel Williams and Nancy Jefferson as man and wife since 1840

Samuel Williams	Born	Botetourt	Co.	Va.	age	46 yrs.
Nancy Jefferson	"	Rockbridge	"	"	"	49 "
Ann Williams	"	"	"	"	"	24 "

Henry Hunt and Charlotte Wade as man and wife since 1856—

Henry Hunt	Born	Rockbridge	Co.	Va.	age	32 yrs.
Charlotte Wade	"	"	"	"	"	28 "
Wilson "	"	"	"	"	"	9 "
Mary "	"	"	"	"	"	5 "
George "	"	"	"	"	"	7 "
Lucy "	"	"	"	"	"	3 "
Eliza "	"	"	"	"	"	1 "

Wilson King and Eliza Thompson since 1850 as man and wife—

Wilson Botetourt King	Born	Botetourt	Co.	Va.	age	43 yrs.
Eliza Thompson	"	Rockbridge	"	"	"	40 "
Charles B. King	"	"	"	"	"	13 "
James - "	"	"	"	"	"	11 "
Isabella "	"	"	"	"	"	9 "
Nanny "	"	"	"	"	"	7 "
Hannah "	"	"	"	"	"	5 "
William "	"	"	"	"	"	3 "

Garland Thompson and Ester Boldock since 1852 as man and wife—

Garland Thompson	Born	Rockbridge	Co.	Va.	age	36 yrs
Ester Boldock	"	"	"	"	"	32 "
John "	"	"	"	"	"	13 "
Ruben "	"	"	"	"	"	11 "
Adeline "	"	"	"	"	"	9 "
Eliza "	"	"	"	"	"	4 "
Garland "	"	"	"	"	"	1 "

In many ways, 1866 was a year of transition at Buffalo Forge. The refiners and hammermen went back to their posts when work resumed in January, but Brady soon discovered that the flush market for his merchant bar was over in Lynchburg. His first January shipment to Rocke & Murrell, his commission house there, brought 8 cents per pound, which translated into $180 per ton. By mid-January, the price had dropped to 7 cents a pound, and by the summer months it had fallen to 6 cents per pound, $135 a ton. During the last quarter of 1866, the commercial columns of the Lynchburg *Daily Virginian* reported that the local market for "mountain iron" was "very dull" at prices ranging from 5 to 5½ cents per pound.[48]

As the South's transportation system recovered from wartime destruction and less expensive bar from modern northern rolling mills began to flow into the region, Brady found his iron simply priced out of the market. He would never again see a day like the one in December 1865 when he received almost $3,300 from his Lynchburg commission house. Cash receipts from Rocke & Murrell during 1866 amounted to $712 in March, $882 in June, and then fell off sharply during the last six months of the year. Brady's final shipment to Rocke & Murrell, hauled by wagon to Miller's warehouse on the North River Canal on October 16, 1866, came to just under two tons. His last check from the Lynchburg merchants arrived two weeks later and was for $289.49. Brady, hoping to open a new market for his metal, tried shipping several tons to Baltimore via a steamboat line operating from Richmond, but that effort proved futile as well.[49] Buffalo Forge as an ironmaking enterprise was living on borrowed time as 1866 came to a close.

During the last seven months of 1865, their first on "free labor," Sam Williams and Henry Towles had each earned $174.90 in forge wages. If Buffalo Forge had been able to maintain production at the same rate during 1866, both Sam and Henry would have earned close to $350 that year. Their forge wages did not come close to that figure. Sam earned $228.60 producing anchonies in 1866, and Henry made $235.20; Henry's slightly higher earnings reflected some extra iron he made with Harry Hunt, Jr., just before Christmas in 1866. The chaffery, worked principally by Harry Hunt, Jr., and Jim Thompson in 1866, afforded similarly reduced earning power for the black hammermen at Buffalo Forge.[50]

With forge sales plummeting in the second half of 1866, Daniel Brady began an almost desperate search for new ways to make money. He decided during the year to plant grapevines at Buffalo Forge in the hope that eventually he could earn a substantial income from sales of wine and grapes. He spent $1,290 starting his vineyard in 1866, hired a vinedresser the following year, and during the late 1860s and early 1870s spent a total of over $5,000 planting and cultivating grapevines at Buffalo Forge.[51] These vineyards represented a substantial investment of Brady's increasingly scarce capital, but this enterprise never realized anything approaching his high hopes when he began.

Another project Brady launched in 1866 proved even more costly. In October, he and a man named Lorenzo Sibert of Augusta County entered into a partnership to mine manganese on some of the Brady's land. These manganese deposits had been discovered before the Civil War, but Weaver had not been interested in trying to work them. Brady jumped in where Weaver had refused to go. His contract with Sibert required Brady to put up the capital; Sibert would supervise the mining operations. The "Emma Mines," as Brady christened the manganese enterprise, opened in February 1867 and soon employed over twenty men, almost all of them white. Two blacks worked the Emma Mines, and one of these men, Sam Salling, had a connection to Buffalo Forge.[52] Weaver had hired him for a number of years as a woodchopper prior to the war, and he continued working for Brady in the same capacity after Weaver died. The decline in forge sales meant that charcoal was in much less demand at Buffalo Forge, so Salling's services as a provider of cordwood were no longer needed.

The manganese mine led to another major investment in 1866 and 1867. Sibert, it turned out, had come up with a process for making cast steel. Brady was fascinated. He took a half interest in Sibert's patent rights and leased California Furnace in northwestern Rockbridge County as a site for Sibert to conduct his experiments.[53] Brady also began borrowing to underwrite this enterprise. "I must have some little money to keep the furnace going," Brady told James Davidson on August 21, 1867. He had tried to borrow $1,200 to $1,500 the previous month "to start my steel experiment," but now he felt he could get along with less. "I enclose a note for $700 at 60 days & wish you see some of the directors of the Bank & ask them to discount it for me," he wrote Davidson. "I think the Bank ought to do it, as it is for the benefit of the whole county as well as myself that I am trying my steel experiment," he added.[54]

Brady managed to obtain the money to try the process, and he and Sibert hired thirteen men to work at California Furnace in the fall of 1867 when the tests got under way.[55] This endeavor, like the vineyard project and the manganese mine, was a failure. Brady wisely decided to cut his losses and abandon the attempt to manufacture steel. The "Emma Mines," after operating for less than three months, closed in the spring of 1867.[56] Brady and the freedmen who worked at Buffalo Forge in 1866 and 1867 were fast approaching the day when only one avocation would be left open to them.

The work contracts which Sam Williams, Henry Towles, Henry Matthews, and Jim Thompson signed with Brady on January 1, 1867, reflected this new reality. All stipulated that the men "agreed to perform farm or other work when needed" for the next twelve months in addition to their forge duties. They would be paid 62½ cents per day for field or other types of non-forge labor, the same rate Brady had paid for agricultural work the previous year. Forge wages remained the same: $4 per ton per man for refining, $3.50 per ton for each of the chaffery hammermen. All the work contracts that year stipulated that if either party wished to annul the agreement, "it shall be done only in the presence & with the consent of such officers of the Freedmen's Bureau as may have immediate jurisdiction in the district wherein the said parties reside." Every freedmen who signed a contract with Brady on New Year's Day 1867 did so in similar fashion:

his
Sam   X   Williams
mark

Sam Williams's contract had a number of special clauses. Sam agreed "to take charge of said Bradys smoke house, attend to issuing the rations, cutting up and curing meat &c." In return for performing these services, Brady would provide "said Sam with house & fuel free of charge." In addition, Sam had the right to "keep three hogs in a pen," and Brady promised the use of "a lot to raise corn to feed his hogs." This document also covered Nancy's work for the year. She would be paid $4 a month for a variety of jobs. Her duties were to "attend to the poultry, rendering tallow & lard, make candles & assist Mrs Brady in the house when needed." Will Rex and another man witnessed the agreement and certified that they "heard the above contract read to Sam Williams & he agrees thereto." All the other documents signed by the freedmen contained a certification using this language.[57]

Before Sam Williams agreed to work for Brady in 1867, however, there was some unfinished business to clear up. Sam's savings account, in Weaver's hands at the time of his death, had never been turned over to him. Beginning in 1861, Sam had regularly drawn off the 6 percent interest on his $100 deposit, but his last such withdrawal had occurred at the end of 1863. For three years, Brady had held his principal and Sam had taken nothing from his account. Whether this was by mutual agreement is unknown; the only records are the bookkeeping entries in a private ledger Brady kept at Buffalo Forge. But on January 1, 1867, the same day Sam made his mark on the work contract for the coming year, Brady agreed to give Sam $118 to close out his savings account—the $100 principal plus $6 in interest for each of the past three years. The timing certainly suggests that there was something in the nature of a *quid pro quo* here; Sam would continue to work at Buffalo Forge, but only if Brady made a satisfactory settlement with him. Brady's bond, dated January 1, 1867, and promising to pay Sam $118 "on demand," appears to have been such a settlement.[58]

The work force at Buffalo Forge during 1867 included many of Weaver's former slaves in addition to the forge crew of Sam Williams, Henry Towles, Jim Thompson, and Henry Matthews. Sam Thompson served as the principal blacksmith that year for $10 a month "& his rations." Garland Thompson, Jr., continued on as the head teamster and received $12 per month, rations, and a house "free of rent." Garland's two older boys, John, who was thirteen, and Ruben, who would turn twelve in 1867, were also to work for Brady during the year in return for "their food and clothing." Tooler hauled wood, made rails and hoop poles, and even drew a couple of tons of bar iron before the year was out, although Jim Thompson and Henry Matthews made most of the modest amount of bar—less than thirty tons—that was drawn at the chaffery hammer that year.[59]

Harry Hunt, Jr., did not go back to work for Brady in 1867, and for good reason. He had taken over for Tooler during 1866 as the principal hammer-man, earning almost $100 in forge wages and doing field work in the spring and summer months when Brady's demand for agricultural labor was par-ticularly heavy. On Christmas Eve 1866, he drew an extra journey of bar, undoubtedly to secure a little additional money for the holidays, and drew $10 in cash and bought fifty pounds of flour.[60] That evening, trouble broke out. "Henry Hunt (freedmen) complains that on the night of the 24th Inst. he was assaulted & cut with a knife by a Mr. McFadden," Captain Sharp of the Freedmen's Bureau wrote on December 27, 1866. Sharp's letter was addressed to James G. Updike, the county justice of the peace for the Buffalo Forge area and one of the white men who had been present when Brady addressed the freedmen at the time of emancipation. "I have the honor to request that you will take cognisance of the matter & see that justice is done to the party," Sharp continued. "It will be necessary that I should be present at the trial."[61] The assailant was probably Henry Clay McFadden, a relative of Brady's principal overseer at Buffalo Forge, Ed-ward McFadden.

No further mention of this incident occurs in the records of the Lexing-ton office of the Freedmen's Bureau, but it is probably indicative of the outcome of the trial, assuming one were held, that Harry Hunt left Brady's employment in 1867 while the McFaddens stayed on. Henry Clay McFadden traded regularly at the Buffalo Forge store in 1867 and 1868, and Edward McFadden continued as Brady's overseer.[62] Perhaps alcohol had been involved in this Christmas Eve assault; heavy drinking appears to have been very much a part of the holiday season at Buffalo Forge. Fortunately, Harry does not seem to have been seriously wounded. He called on Brady during January and collected the balance of the money due him for his past year's work, which amounted to $8.17.[63]

Harry Hunt's departure from Buffalo Forge in 1867 was symptomatic of the mounting reluctance of the freedmen to work under the direct supervision of white overseers and landowners. With ironmaking operations winding down at the forge in 1867, new arrangements would have to be made if Brady wanted to retain a black labor force to help him bring in the crops. He still needed an income and food for his own table; he also needed wheat for his flour mill, corn for his hogs, and hay for his mules, horses, cattle, and dairy herds. The failure of his manganese and steel-making enterprises in 1867, and the loss of the money he had sunk into these ventures, made it even more imperative that Brady work out some sort of system that would serve the basic interests of both parties. He had land, draft animals, seed, and very little capital at the end of 1867; the freedmen had their labor. The solution appeared to be sharecropping.

It was an inherently unfair bargain, but from the freedmen's perspective, working Brady's land on shares was preferable to working under Edward McFadden, or any other overseer for that matter. The system was a relatively simple one: A third share of the crop went to the landowner; a third share went to whoever provided the mules, seed, and farm implements; and a third went to the laborer. Since Brady possessed the first two, he took two-thirds of all the crops the freedmen would grow at Buffalo Forge. They kept the remaining third for themselves and gained a measure of independence in the process.[64] At least they would no longer be toiling under the eyes of white men. The land they worked did not belong to them, but those acres were the closest most ever came to owning a farm of their own. Sharecropping was also a road that led almost universally in one direction: toward a life of rural poverty.

Sharecropping came to Buffalo Forge in 1868 at almost exactly the same time that the freedmen there gained the right to vote. The political situation in Virginia was in considerable turmoil in 1867 and 1868 as Congress moved to check the excesses of conservative state governments in the South and to provide some measure of protection for the civil rights of blacks in the region. Reconstruction Acts passed in March 1867 and supplemented later that year divided the South into five military districts, commanded by army generals and subject to martial law. Southern states were required to summon constitutional conventions elected by universal manhood suffrage, and the governments established under those constitutions were to guarantee the vote to all black males twenty-one years of age and older. These Reconstruction Acts brought the ballot to the freedmen of Buffalo Forge.

In October 1867, Captain Sharp of the Freedmen's Bureau appointed Daniel Brady a voting registrar for the 1st Electoral District of Rockbridge County, which included Buffalo Forge.[65] Brady proceeded to open registration books, and Sam Williams, Henry Towles, Henry Matthews, Garland Thompson, Jr., Edgar Towles, and other black men from the area came in to swear that they were not disqualified from exercising the right of suffrage and to affix their mark to the registration oath.[66] This act undoubtedly had great symbolic meaning for the freedmen of Buffalo Forge, but it had almost no practical consequences for them. Virginia never underwent a period of radical rule similar to that experienced by other southern states, and the black population of Rockbridge County was too small to be a decisive force in local politics. In an election that was to set the pattern for the Reconstruction era, the county chose two Conservative white delegates to the convention to draft the new Virginia constitution despite the participation of the newly enrolled black voters.[67]

Indeed, the striking thing about the enfranchisement of the black men of Buffalo Forge was how little this supposedly revolutionary act seemed to affect their lives and their means of earning a living. Certainly their obtaining the vote paled into something approaching insignificance when compared with their failure to obtain land, and the means with which to work that land, in the immediate aftermath of the war. Lacking the resources needed to achieve economic independence in the rural South, the freedmen of Buffalo Forge were reduced increasingly to one of two choices if they wished to remain on the land most had known since childhood: They could stay on as agricultural laborers or they could stay on as sharecroppers.

The end of an era was reached at Buffalo Forge in 1868. During that year, Sam Williams and Henry Towles refined the last anchonies the forge would ever produce, just over five tons, and it was appropriate that Tooler was the principal hammerman who drew this iron into bars. Henry Matthews and Jim Thompson had both left early in 1868, so Henry Towles served as his underhand at the chaffery. In all probability, this iron was made to give Brady and the sharecroppers working his land a supply of iron to meet future needs. Sam Williams earned his last forge wages, $13.60, on November 18, 1868; Henry Towles and Tooler drew their last forge pay two weeks later.[68] Sam and most of the other freedmen who remained at

Buffalo Forge turned to sharecropping in 1868 as their principal means of earning a living.

The picture of the Buffalo Forge community provided by the census of 1870 was dramatically different than the one that had been sketched ten years before. In 1860, William Weaver, the owner of sixty-six slaves, had presided over an almost princely iron plantation. In 1870, Daniel C. E. Brady, farmer, indicated that the only industrial activity at Buffalo Forge took place in the flour and grist mills that stood down the hill from his residence. Emma and all the children were still there, and Frances Banks was back working as their cook. There was no mention in the census of the return of her husband, Warder. Sam and Nancy Williams occupied one of the brick cabins near the Bradys' home, and they had one other person living with them, their six-year-old granddaughter, Lydia Maydelene Reid. Henry and Ann Towles and their family lived next door, and Henry's brother, Edgar, also occupied a cabin nearby.[69] No other freedmen who had been part of the antebellum slave community at Buffalo Forge remained on the property.

One by one, the families had moved away. Almost all—Henry and Frances Matthews, Harry and Charlotte Hunt, Garland and Ester Thompson and the others—still lived in Rockbridge County, and some were fairly close to Buffalo Forge.[70] But what had once been the black community there had a new focus in the early 1870s.

In October 1871, Daniel Brady received $20 for a small piece of land about a mile south of Buffalo Forge. This tract, just over half an acre, was purchased by the trustees of the Buffalo Forge Colored Baptist Church for the purpose of erecting a church building and schoolhouse. Among the trustees of the church was Samuel Williams.[71]

Construction of the church had actually begun the previous year. Sam Williams and other freedmen in the area had put together a building fund of $307.29, an impressive sum for families whose livelihood depended on sharecropping and agricultural day labor. Work started on the foundation in September 1870, but the church structure was not completed until the summer of the following year. Brady agreed to hold the building fund and make dispersals as needed for the purchase of wood, nails, shingles, and hauling stone for the foundation. The final cost of the Mount Lydia Colored Baptist Church, as the freedmen called their place of worship, was $227.56. Brady returned the $79.73 remaining in the building fund to the trustees on September 25, 1871, and the following year he presented a silver pitcher and matching communion cups as a gift to Mount Lydia.[72] An indication of the active life of the church appeared in Brady's records four years later; "16 negroes baptized in Buffalo," he noted on Sunday, April 25, 1875.[73]

Sam Williams worked on Brady's land as a sharecropper from 1868 until 1874. His contract for 1873, his last with Brady, was probably typical of the yearly agreements the two men struck during the late 1860s and early 1870s:

> Leased to Sam Williams, as much as he can work, I to furnish the teams, seed & implements: he to furnish all labor. I let him have home & firewood free: he to get his firewood; he to have pasture for one cow free. He to pay ⅔ of all crops.

> D. C. E. Brady
> January 1, 1873

Also sharecropping on Brady's property that year were Henry Towles and Garland Thompson, Jr. In addition, four white farmers worked sections of Brady's land on a lease or share basis in 1873.[74] Sam consistently produced the largest crops on the place during these years, and 1873 was no exception. The 251 bushels of oats, 114 bushels of wheat, and 283½ bushels of corn Sam harvested that year Brady figured were worth $359.55. After the deduction of a small toll for threshing the oats and wheat, Sam's third was worth $117.35. Brady's share came to $233.76. No one else, white or black, sharecropping at Buffalo Forge that year came close to equaling these figures.[75]

In 1874, Sam and Nancy Williams moved to an adjoining farm owned by the Douglass family, and the Mount Lydia Church may well have had something to do with Sam's departure from Buffalo Forge. Andrew Franklin, a farm laborer on the Douglass property, and James Franklin, the miller at the flour mill there, were both trustees of the church, and other black families on the place were well known to Sam, including that of Henry Nash, the cooper who had staked his watch against Sam's watch in their 1853 bet over the existence of Sam's savings account.[76]

Sam and Nancy Williams became great-grandparents during their years on the Douglass farm. Their grandchild Mary Caroline Coleman, Betty's daughter, married a man named Steward Chandler in the summer of 1876. Mary Caroline would turn seventeen that year, her husband twenty-two. Their first child, a son, William, was born in October 1876; their second, a daughter, was born in 1878. Her name, Mary, carried a rich tradition in the Williams family, one that went back to the baby's great-great-great-grandmother.[77]

Another granddaughter was still living with Sam and Nancy during these years—Lydia Reid. In 1880 when the census taker made his rounds in the Natural Bridge District of Rockbridge County, he reported that

Samuel Williams, age sixty-one, a farm hand, Nancy Williams, sixty-three, a housewife, and Lydia Maydelene Reid, fifteen, were still making their home on the Douglass place.[78]

On May 31, 1878, the lead item in the "Local News" section of the Lexington *Gazette* carried a sad notice that Rockbridge County had lost one of its most distinguished citizens. "Rarely indeed has our community been so shocked and stunned as on Monday last, when the sudden and unexpected death of D. C. E. Brady, Esq., was announced in our town," the editor wrote. Death had come on May 27 without warning or previous illness, the *Gazette* went on to say, and the fifty-seven-year-old Brady would be sorely missed. He had represented Natural Bridge Township on the county Board of Supervisors since 1872, and had been elected by the board as its chairman in 1875. Brady had come to the area in 1857 to manage "the extensive business matters of his uncle, Wm. Weaver, Esq., a most active, energetic, intelligent farmer largely engaged and successfully also in the manufacture of iron, from which he realized a handsome property." Weaver's "large slave property" had been rendered "valueless" by the war, and the value of his estate was "sensibly diminished" thereby, the editor observed, but he praised Brady for managing Weaver's "estate very successfully to the time of his lamented death." Daniel Brady's funeral service and burial at Falling Spring Church on Wednesday, May 29, had been attended by "a large concourse of friends and acquaintances." The paper failed to report whether any black mourners had been in attendance.[79]

Emma Brady's death five years later came after a long illness. She died at Buffalo Forge on the morning of January 13, 1883, and, like her husband, she was fifty-seven years old at the time of her death. Her children were all living at home then. Anne Gertrude had turned thirty-five just ten days before her mother's death, Pat was thirty-two, Sarah Elizabeth was twenty-three, and the two youngest, Wilhelmina and Elliot Thomas, were nineteen and eighteen.[80] Emma's burial, like that of her husband and her Uncle William, took place at Falling Spring cemetery.

These years in the early 1880s appear to have been troubled ones for Sam and Nancy Williams as well. On January 2, 1882, Sam paid $25 to the county court so that he could become the legal guardian of Lydia Maydelene Reid.[81] He appears to have been trying to prevent his granddaughter from getting married. If that was his intent, the effort failed. On January 4, two days after Sam posted his guardian's bond, Lydia married a man named Charles Newman. Lydia was seventeen at the time of her marriage, her husband twenty-three. Their first child, a daughter, was born in November 1882, and she was named Mary Ann Newman.[82]

Six years later, Pat Brady noted in his diary that an arrest had been made in the neighborhood. Like his father, Pat was an inveterate recordkeeper and kept a daily journal in which he made note of events going on at and around Buffalo Forge. "Will Eads had C. Newman Cold. arrested for stealing Bacon," he wrote on April 20, 1888. "Sent on for trial, Geo. Zimmerman made arrest."[83] In an effort to locate the bacon which was alleged to have been stolen, Newman's house was searched. This search turned up silverware and a number of other stolen items. Newman was held in the county jail, and his trial was scheduled for early June.[84]

On Sunday, May 13, 1888, Nancy Williams died. It was a cool, clear day, Pat Brady noted, and she had been at "Watts school house," near the Natural Bridge Hotel, when the end had come. The weather turned cloudy and very cold on Monday, but the skies cleared in time for her funeral on Tuesday, May 15. Pat Brady, his wife, Marie, and his sister Anne attended the services for her at Mount Lydia Church that day, and her grandchildren and great-grandchildren were doubtless in attendance as well.[85] Nancy Williams was seventy-one years old at the time of her death. She had been the wife of Sam Williams since 1840, and there is little question that she had worked hard for almost all of her seventy-one years. She had also experienced great grief in her life with the deaths of three of her four children.

Less than a month after her funeral, Charles Newman, in the custody of the county jailor, stood before the Rockbridge Circuit Court charged with house-breaking. The prisoner was represented by counsel and pleaded not guilty. Several witnesses were called, but the trial lasted only one day, June 6. The jury found Newman guilty as charged. The following day, June 7, 1888, the judge sentenced him to two and a half years in the Virginia State Penitentiary.[86]

The next year, Sam Williams died. Pat Brady wrote on Friday, August 16, 1889, that he "went to Sam Williams Funeral in P.M." and that the skies were clear and the temperature was surprisingly moderate for a late summer day in the Valley.[87] Brady did not note the day of Sam's death, but it was probably Wednesday, August 14. Sam would have turned sixty-nine that year and may already have done so—the year of his birth, 1820, was recorded in the slave register at Buffalo Forge, but not the day.[88] His date of birth is only one of the many things we would like to know about this man but will never be able to ascertain. Sam and Nancy Williams never learned to read and write, so there are no family records to guide us.[89] As might be expected, no notice of his death was taken in the local press, so no obituary exists. Yet the broad outlines of his life in slavery and freedom are clear, and we can certainly say something about the sort of man he was.

Sam Williams was unquestionably a man of formidable intelligence and extraordinary skill. His prowess as both a forgeman and a farmer attests to that. He also lived a life filled with hard work and religious commitment, and he seems to have been unwavering in the support of his family. Everything we know about his life at Buffalo Forge suggests a man of strength who refused to allow slavery and racism to sap his manhood and his sense of pride in himself and his family. Sam Williams endured, and that was no mean accomplishment in a society that treated black men, women, and children as pieces of human property. But there is every indication that his life, and that of his wife, went beyond mere endurance. Sam and Nancy Williams, it seems fair to say, endured with dignity.

The Mount Lydia Church no longer stands, and today the cemetery site is covered with trees and a heavy growth of underbrush. But beneath these trees and under the dense carpet of honeysuckle, there are dozens of small triangular-shaped pieces of limestone. Almost certainly, one of these simple limestone markers rests over the grave of Sam Williams. It is equally certain that a similar stone on the grave nearest his marks the final resting place of Nancy, his wife. These stones are roughly carved and bear no inscriptions, but care was taken to anchor them solidly in the earth, with their peaks pointing gently toward the sky.

Epilogue

————◆————

Many of the buildings at Buffalo Forge remain standing today. The forge itself is gone, its stones apparently used to construct abutments for a nearby highway bridge that crosses Buffalo Creek on Virginia Route 608. But Weaver's handsome residence still dominates the landscape in this section of Rockbridge County, and the two brick slave quarters that went up in the late 1850s have survived. The Buffalo Forge store, the forge manager's house, the stone kitchen adjoining Weaver's home, the spring house, and various and sundry other outbuildings are also intact. These structures offer impressive visual reminders of the era when William Weaver, Daniel Brady, and the black men, women, and children of Buffalo Forge occupied this ground.

The property remains in the hands of the Brady family. Douglas E. Brady, Jr.—Daniel and Emma Brady's great-grandson—and his wife, Mary, have restored Weaver's home to its former stateliness, and Pat (as Douglas Brady is universally called in Lexington and surrounding Rockbridge County) has rebuilt the slave quarters—one single and one double cabin—in recent years. Many of William Weaver's books are still in the library, his imposing walnut bed occupies an upstairs bedroom, and his cane still hangs on a hook just inside the front door. It is very easy to forget the present as you move through the rooms of Pat and Mary Brady's gracious home at Buffalo Forge.

It is equally easy to imagine an earlier time when you cross the threshold of one of the brick cabins behind the Brady residence and enter what was once the slave's world. We know from postwar census records that Sam and Nancy Williams lived in one of these cabins after freedom came, and chances are they occupied the same home during the late antebellum and Civil War years as well. The spring house, where Nancy supervised dairy operations, is close by. A walk up the hill behind the slave quarters takes you to the site of the black cemetery, where the limestone grave markers still rest and where the view of the Blue Ridge Mountains to the east is nothing less than breathtaking. It is not at all hard in the midst of these surroundings to find your thoughts turning back to an earlier era. The challenge, and the intent of this book, is to try to imagine what life was like for the slaves of Buffalo Forge.

It is a difficult and risky proposition, this business of trying to re-create and understand the lives of the slaves. There is so much we can never know. But the impressive thing about the record of life and labor at Buffalo Forge is how much we can learn about what took place.

My purpose, in Charles Joyner's wonderful phrase, has been to "ask large questions in small places." I have tried to recapture the fabric of slavery at Buffalo Forge, to describe the texture of slave life there to the fullest extent possible. My approach has been to focus on individual slaves and their families—men like Sam Williams, Henry Towles, Tooler, Harry Hunt, Jr., Henry Matthews, and Garland Thompson—and to attempt to reconstruct their lives primarily from the surviving documentary evidence. By concentrating on their stories, I have tried to convey a sense of black life as it was lived at Buffalo Forge both before and after slavery.

I have also sought to tell the story of William Weaver and Daniel Brady because it was the interaction of the masters and the slaves that determined so much of what happened at Buffalo Forge. It was Weaver's early conviction that he could not run a profitable ironworks in the South without slave labor, which prompted him to purchase the "Wilson negroes" in 1815. It was his legal battle with Thomas Mayburry that led to the division of Mary's family in 1837. It was Weaver who sent his forge manager to help Harry Hunt and his family escape from Bath Iron Works. The list of ways in which Weaver influenced the course of slave life at Buffalo Forge is practically endless. And of course it was Weaver who set up the basic parameters of slavery at his installations by establishing a labor system that rested on a combination of coercion and reward. To attempt to write a history of slavery at Buffalo Forge without writing about the master would be telling only half the story.

The task and overwork systems, employed almost universally wherever industrial slavery occurred in the antebellum South, were intended by Weaver to maximize labor and productivity without undue reliance on force, or the threat of force. Force was the cement that held slavery together across the length and breadth of the Old South, but coercion had its limits, especially where something as difficult and demanding as ironmaking was involved.

The opportunity to earn overwork pay, in turn, provided Weaver's slaves with an absolutely critical weapon in their never-ending struggle against the dehumanizing aspects of their bondage. It gave them a tool that permitted them to do something for themselves, and for their families. It allowed Sam Williams to buy Christmas presents for Nancy and their children and furniture and a mirror for their home; it allowed Henry Towles to acquire the pants in which he was married; and it allowed Garland Thompson to purchase clothing for his sons as they passed from youth to adulthood. The overwork system was certainly a major reason slave hirelings were willing to leave their homes in the Virginia Tidewater and Piedmont, travel on foot across the Blue Ridge to Weaver's ironworks, and spend the year, or most of it, living and working apart from their families.

But the actions of men like Sam Williams, Henry Towles, Tooler, and Harry Hunt, Jr., also reveal the limits of Weaver's labor system. Resistance, work slowdowns, feigned illnesses, industrial sabotage—these were part of the Buffalo Forge story as well. Weaver and Brady seem to have had little choice but to go along when their slave forgemen decided they were going to take some time off from work. No such tolerance, however, was granted the more overt forms of resistance practiced by Weaver's slaves. Men like Arch, John Wilson, Lawson, and Bill Green—runaways all—were quickly hunted down, clapped in irons, turned over to a slave trader, and sold. In the end, there never was any real question about what it meant to be a slave.

If one theme stands out above all others in the history of Buffalo Forge, it is the transcendent importance of family in the lives of the slaves. It is there as you turn the pages of the "Negro Books," those extraordinarily valuable overwork ledgers that allow us a glimpse into the slaves' own world. It is there as you piece the names together in Sam Williams's family tree. It is there when the clerk in the National Archives brings you a slim volume and you open what turns out to be the Freedmen's Bureau Marriage Register for Rockbridge County. It is there in James Thompson's wonderful stories of slave life at Buffalo Forge. It is there in the photograph of Garland and Ester Thompson and their children.

Ultimately, the story of Buffalo Forge is about people caught up in that simplest and most complex of human institutions, chattel slavery. In its basic nature slavery was profoundly simple because it was so completely immoral; it allowed human beings of one race to hold human beings of another race as property. It is hard to imagine anything more evil and abhorrent than that. At the same time, slavery could be almost infinitely complicated in its day-to-day functioning. Something of that complexity, I hope, has been reflected in the pages of this book.

I have sometimes wondered if trying to reconstruct the history of Buffalo Forge was worth the years it took to ferret out the evidence and get the story down as fully and as accurately as I could. Buffalo Forge was, after all, only a very small corner of the antebellum South. I knew I had to write this book when I found John Rex's letter to James D. Davidson describing the wager between Sam Williams and Henry Nash—the bet these two men made in 1855 over whether or not Sam had a savings account in a Lexington bank. I recognized Sam Williams's name from his overwork accounts and from the entries in Daniel Brady's journals, which I had examined earlier, and I realized that the Buffalo Forge records would allow me to carry a study of slavery down to the level of individual slave workers. From that point on, my fate was sealed.

The question of whether or not I should have taken on this project was answered for me several years ago when I made a presentation based on this material at a predominantly black high school in Gary, Indiana. After I finished, a young man came up, thanked me for visiting his school, and told me that he had always been embarrassed by the subject of slavery. "It was just something I didn't want to talk about," he said, "that my ancestors had once been slaves." But, he went on, he did not think he would be so reluctant to talk about slavery in the future. "In fact," he added, "after hearing about the workers at Buffalo Forge, I feel like I'm descended from nobility."

Notes

INTRODUCTION

1. Charles B. Dew, *Ironmaker to the Confederacy: Joseph R. Anderson and the Tredegar Iron Works* (New Haven: Yale University Press, 1966).

2. Margaret R. Hafstad, ed., *Guide to the McCormick Collection of the State Historical Society of Wisconsin* (Madison: State Historical Society of Wisconsin, 1973), 63.

3. See Charles L. Perdue, Jr., et al., eds., *Weevils in the Wheat: Interviews with Virginia Ex-Slaves* (Charlottesville: University Press of Virginia, 1976), and George P. Rawick, ed., *The American Slave: A Composite Autobiography,* 41 vols. (Westport, CT: Greenwood Press, 1972, 1977, 1979).

PROLOGUE: Buffalo Forge, 1858

1. Weaver's ironworks are described in J. P. Lesley, *The Iron Manufacturer's Guide to the Furnaces, Forges and Rolling Mills of the United States* . . . (New York: John Wiley, 1859), 73, 181. Weaver's slaveholdings are given in Manuscript Slave Schedules, Rockbridge County, Virginia, Eighth Census of the United States, 1860, National Archives Microfilm Publications, M-653.

2. "Negro Hire," January 6, 1858, Buffalo Forge Journal, 1850–1859, Weaver–Brady

Papers, University of Virginia Library, Charlottesville (hereafter cited as Weaver–Brady Papers, Virginia).

3. On the quantity of land held by Weaver, see his property tax receipts in the James D. Davidson Papers, McCormick Collection, State Historical Society of Wisconsin, Madison.

4. "Weaver Family: Memo and Historical Notes," Weaver–Brady Papers in the possession of T. T. Brady, Richmond, Virginia (hereafter cited as Weaver–Brady Papers, T. T. Brady).

5. Ibid.; William Weaver to Daniel C. E. Brady, March 4, 1856, William Weaver Papers, Duke University Library, Durham, North Carolina (hereafter cited as Weaver Papers, Duke).

6. "Weaver Family: Memo and Historical Notes," Weaver–Brady Papers, T. T. Brady.

7. Ibid.

8. Weaver to Brady, August 27, 1855, Weaver Papers, Duke.

9. Weaver to Brady, February 19, 1856, Weaver–Brady Papers, T. T. Brady.

10. Weaver to Brady, February 28, 1856, ibid.

11. Weaver to Brady, March 4, 1856, Weaver Papers, Duke.

12. Weaver to Emma Brady, March 21, 1856, ibid.

13. "Weaver Family: Memo and Historical Notes" and Daniel C. E. Brady to James D. Davidson, June 27, 1867, Weaver–Brady Papers, T. T. Brady.

14. Daniel C. E. Brady, "Home Journal," 1858–60, Weaver–Brady Papers, Virginia; Daniel C. E. Brady, "Home Journal," 1860–65, McCormick Collection, State Historical Society of Wisconsin, Madison.

15. Buffalo Forge Farm Record Book, 1860–65, Weaver–Brady Papers, T. T. Brady.

16. See Arthur Cecil Bining, *Pennsylvania Iron Manufacture in the Eighteenth Century*, 2nd ed. (Harrisburg: Pennsylvania Historical and Museum Commission, 1973), 72–73.

17. Deposition of William Weaver, December 10, 1840, Case Papers, John Alexander *v.* Sidney S. Baxter, Administrator of John Irvine & Others, Superior Court of Chancery Records, Rockbridge County Court House, Lexington, Virginia. Weaver's cane is in the possession of D. E. Brady, Jr., Buffalo Forge, Virginia.

18. Bining, *Pennsylvania Iron Manufacture*, 72–73; deposition of John Doyle, February 7, 1840, Case Papers, Weaver *v.* Jordan, Davis & Co., Superior Court of Chancery Records, Rockbridge County Court House, Lexington, Virginia.

19. Buffalo Forge Negro Books, 1830–40, 1839–41, 1850–58, Weaver–Brady Papers, Virginia.

20. Bining, *Pennsylvania Iron Manufacture*, 73–74.

21. Buffalo Forge Iron Book, 1831–62, and Brady, "Home Journal," 1858–60, Weaver–Brady Papers, Virginia.

22. Brady, "Home Journal," 1858–60, ibid.

23. On the quality of Buffalo Forge iron see George W. Dawson to Weaver, May 30, 1862, ibid., and William D. Couch & Co. to Weaver, February 9, 1859, and McCorkle & Co. to Weaver, February 22, 1859, Weaver Papers, Duke.

I.1: William Weaver, Pennsylvanian

1. "Weaver Family: Memo and Historical Notes," Weaver–Brady Papers in the possession of T. T. Brady, Richmond, Virginia (hereafter cited as Weaver–Brady Papers, T. T. Brady); Martin Grove Brumbaugh, *A History of the German Baptist Brethren in Europe and America* (Elgin, IL: Brethren Press, 1899), 93, 95, 212, 265; Donald F. Durnbaugh, ed., *The Brethren in Colonial America* (Elgin, IL: Brethren Press, 1967), 86, 224–25.

2. Frank S. Mead, *Handbook of Denominations in the United States*, 5th ed. (Nashville:

Abingdon Press, 1970), 53–54; F. E. Mayer, *The Religious Bodies of America* (St. Louis: Concordia Publishing House, 1956), 400–402; Sydney E. Ahlstrom, *A Religious History of the American People* (New Haven: Yale University Press, 1972), 239–40; Anson Phelps Stokes, *Church and State in the United States,* 3 vols. (New York: Harper & Brothers, 1950), 2:121, 215; Roger E. Sappington, ed., *The Brethren in the New Nation* (Elgin, IL: Brethren Press, 1976), 256–76.

3. "Weaver Family: Memo and Historical Notes," Weaver–Brady Papers, T. T. Brady.

4. Ibid.

5. Ibid.

6. Johnson, Younger, & Otty to William Weaver, June 15, 1859, Weaver–Brady Papers, University of Virginia Library, Charlottesville.

7. "Weaver Family: Memo and Historical Notes," Weaver–Brady Papers, T. T. Brady; Brumbaugh, *History of the German Baptist Brethren,* 265.

8. Durnbaugh, ed., *Brethren in Colonial America,* 238–39.

9. Ibid., 214, 244; Brumbaugh, *History of the German Baptist Brethren,* 265; "Weaver Family: Memo and Historical Notes," Weaver–Brady Papers, T. T. Brady.

10. Weaver Family Genealogical Notes compiled by D. E. Brady, Sr., October 28, 1951 (typescript), Weaver–Brady papers in the possession of D. E. Brady, Jr., Buffalo Forge, Virginia (hereafter cited as Weaver–Brady Papers, D. E. Brady, Jr.); "Weaver Family: Memo and Historical Notes," Weaver–Brady Papers, T. T. Brady.

11. "The Answer of Thomas Mayburry to a Bill of Complaint exhibited against him . . . by William Weaver," November 28, 1825, Case Papers, Weaver *v.* Mayburry, Superior Court of Chancery Records, Augusta County Court House, Staunton, Virginia (hereafter cited as Case Papers, Weaver *v.* Mayburry); W. H. Kiblinger, "The Victoria Furnace," *Louisa County* [Virginia] *Historical Magazine,* 19 (Spring 1988), 15; Michael D. Thompson, *The Iron Industry in Western Maryland* (Morgantown, WV: the author, 1976), 66.

12. Deposition of Willoughby Mayburry, November 15, 1821, Case Papers, Wilson *v.* Mayburry & Weaver, Superior Court of Chancery Records, Augusta County Court House, Staunton, Virginia (hereafter cited as Case Papers, Wilson *v.* Mayburry & Weaver).

13. "Answer of Thomas Mayburry . . . ," November 28, 1825, Case Papers, Weaver *v.* Mayburry; "The Answer of Thomas Mayburry to a Bill of Complaint exhibited against him & William Weaver . . . by William Wilson," November 16, 1820, Case Papers, Wilson *v.* Mayburry & Weaver.

14. "Articles of Agreement . . . between William Wilson . . . & Thomas Mayburry & William Weaver . . . ," July 30, 1814, Jordan & Irvine Papers, McCormick Collection, State Historical Society of Wisconsin, Madison.

15. "Answer of Thomas Mayburry . . . ," November 28, 1825, Case Papers, Weaver *v.* Mayburry.

16. Deposition of Willoughby Mayburry, November 15, 1821, Case Papers, Wilson *v.* Mayburry & Weaver.

17. Thompson, *Iron Industry in Western Maryland,* 66–67.

18. "Answer of Thomas Mayburry . . . ," November 28, 1825, Case Papers, Weaver *v.* Mayburry.

19. "The Answer of William Weaver to a bill of complaint exhibited against him and Thomas Mayburry . . . by William Wilson," April 4, 1821, Case Papers, Wilson *v.* Mayburry & Weaver.

20. "Answer of Thomas Mayburry . . . ," November 28, 1825, Case Papers, Weaver *v.* Mayburry.

21. "Answer of William Weaver . . . ," April 4, 1821, Case Papers, Wilson *v.* Mayburry & Weaver.

22. Deposition of Thomas M. Jolly, September 21, 1821, ibid.; Bill of Complaint of William Weaver, November 19, 1825, Case Papers, Weaver *v.* Mayburry.

23. Bill of Complaint of William Weaver, November 19, 1825, Case Papers, Weaver *v.* Mayburry.

24. Ibid.

25. Ibid.

26. "Answer of Thomas Mayburry . . . ," November 28, 1825, ibid.

27. Bill of Complaint of William Weaver, November 19, 1825, and Thomas Mayburry to William Weaver, September 17, 1815, October 27, 1816, ibid.

28. Bill of Complaint of William Weaver, November 19, 1825, ibid.; "Answer of William Weaver . . . ," April 4, 1821, Case Papers, Wilson *v.* Mayburry & Weaver; "Weaver Family: Memo and Historical Notes," Weaver–Brady Papers, T. T. Brady.

29. Depositions of Lydia L. W. Gorgas, Hannah Leibert, Peter K. Gorgas, Mary Rex, and Peter Leibert, May 19, 1836, Case Papers, Weaver *v.* Jordan, Davis & Co., Superior Court of Chancery Records, Rockbridge County Court House, Lexington, Virginia (hereafter cited as Case Papers, Weaver *v.* Jordan, Davis & Co.). A printed copy of most of the documents pertaining to this case can be found in the Special Collections Department, Washington & Lee University Library, Lexington, Virginia.

30. "Weaver Family: Memo and Historical Notes," Weaver–Brady Papers, T. T. Brady; Weaver Family Genealogical Notes compiled by D. E. Brady, Sr., and "Statement of the Accounts of William Weaver Executor of . . . Abraham Weaver . . . ," November 5, 1836, Weaver–Brady Papers, D. E. Brady, Jr.

31. Mayburry to Weaver, October 8, 1815, Case Papers, Weaver *v.* Mayburry.

32. Bill of Sale between John S. Wilson and William Weaver, Philadelphia, October 24, 1815, ibid.

33. Deposition of James C. Dickinson, August 18, 1836, Case Papers, Weaver *v.* Jordan, Davis & Co.

34. Depositions of James Brawley, April 18–21, 1826, and John Danenhower, July 10, 1830, Case Papers, Weaver *v.* Mayburry.

35. Deposition of John S. Wilson, September 21, 1825, ibid.

36. Ibid.; see also John S. Wilson to Thomas Mayburry, March 1, 1825, ibid.

I.2: Mayburry & Weaver: Debt and Disappointment

1. Thomas Mayburry to William Weaver, October 18, 1815, and "The Answer of Thomas Mayburry to a Bill of Complaint exhibited against him . . . by William Weaver," November 28, 1825, both in Case Papers, Weaver *v.* Mayburry, Superior Court of Chancery Records, Augusta County Court House, Staunton, Virginia (hereafter cited as Case Papers, Weaver *v.* Mayburry).

2. An excellent description of blast furnace operations can be found in Arthur Cecil Bining, *Pennsylvania Iron Manufacture in the Eighteenth Century,* 2nd ed. (Harrisburg: Pennsylvania Historical and Museum Commission, 1973), 59–72; on the skills of Tooler and Bill, see deposition of Ambrose Campbell, May 15, 1826, Case Papers, Weaver *v.* Mayburry.

3. "Answer of Thomas Mayburry . . . ," November 28, 1825, Case Papers, Weaver *v.* Mayburry.

4. Mayburry to Weaver, September 17, 1815, ibid.

5. Deposition of Thomas Walker, clerk, Bank of Philadelphia, August 28, 1830, and Bill of Complaint of William Weaver, November 19, 1825, ibid.

6. Mayburry to Weaver, December 17, 1815, ibid.

7. Mayburry to Weaver, February 4, 1816, ibid.

8. Mayburry to Weaver, March 31, 1816, ibid.

9. Deposition of Daniel Hitner, January 9, 1826, ibid.

10. Deposition of Isaiah Wells, January 4, 1826, and William Powell, January 9, 1826, ibid.

11. Deposition of William Powell, January 9, 1826, ibid.

12. Depositions of Daniel Hitner and Peter Dager, January 9, 1826, and Thomas M. Jolly, January 4, 1826, ibid.

13. Weaver to Mayburry, August 30, 1821, ibid.

14. "The Answer of William Weaver to a bill of complaint exhibited against him and Thomas Mayburry . . . by William Wilson," April 4, 1821, Case Papers, Wilson *v.* Mayburry & Weaver, Superior Court of Chancery Records, Augusta County Court House, Staunton, Virginia (hereafter cited as Case Papers, Wilson *v.* Mayburry & Weaver).

15. Mayburry to Weaver, October 18, November 18, 1815, May 26, June 16, September 7, October 27, 1816, Case Papers, Weaver *v.* Mayburry.

16. Mayburry to Weaver, December 23, 1816, ibid.; see also Mayburry to Weaver, February 4, March 3, May 26, 1816, ibid.

17. Mayburry to Weaver, January 9, 1817, ibid.

18. Mayburry to Weaver, November 10, 1817, ibid.; see also Mayburry to Weaver, March 6, 1817, ibid.

19. Mayburry to Weaver, August 16, 1817, ibid.

20. Ibid.

21. Weaver to William Clarke, November 19, 1829, and Mayburry to Weaver, September 22, 1819, ibid.

22. Mayburry to Weaver, March 31, 1816, March 8, 1817, June 15, 1818, ibid.

23. Mayburry to Weaver, October 18, 1817, ibid.

24. Bill of Complaint of William Weaver, November 19, 1825, "Answer of Thomas Mayburry . . . ," November 28, 1825, and Mayburry to Weaver, December 19, 1817, ibid.

25. Thomas Mayburry to Jere W. Mayburry, November 10, 1817, and Thomas Mayburry to Weaver, December 19, 1817, ibid.

26. Mayburry to Weaver, October 18, December 19, 1817, ibid.

27. Mayburry to Weaver, November 10, 1817, ibid.

28. Mayburry to Weaver, December 19, 1817, February 2, March 29, 1818, ibid.

29. Mayburry to Weaver, March 29, 1818, ibid.

30. Mayburry to Weaver, April 15, June 1, July 16, November 29, 1818, ibid.

31. Mayburry to Weaver, November 29, 1818, ibid.

32. Mayburry to Weaver, January 20, 1819, ibid.

33. Ibid.

34. Mayburry to Weaver, September 22, 1819, August 19, 1821, ibid.; deposition of James Brawley, November 5, 1821, Case Papers, Wilson *v.* Mayburry & Weaver.

35. Weaver to Mayburry, August 30, 1821, Case Papers, Weaver *v.* Mayburry; "Statement of the Accounts of William Weaver Executor of . . . Abraham Weaver . . . ," November 5, 1836, Weaver–Brady Papers in the possession of D. E. Brady, Jr., Buffalo Forge, Virginia (hereafter cited as Weaver–Brady Papers, D. E. Brady, Jr.).

36. "Statement of Thomas Mayburry," October 1, 1821, and Mayburry to William Clarke, September 3, 1827, Case Papers, Weaver *v.* Mayburry.

37. Deposition of Daniel Hitner, January 9, 1826, ibid.; "Statement of the Accounts of William Weaver Executor of . . . Abraham Weaver . . . ," November 5, 1836, Weaver–Brady Papers, D. E. Brady, Jr.

38. Bill of Complaint of William Weaver, November 19, 1825, and deposition of Thomas Walker, clerk, Bank of Philadelphia, August 28, 1830, Case Papers, Weaver *v.* Mayburry.

39. See "Family Record," Peter K. Gorgas' Bible, "Family Record," Lydia L. Gorgas' Bible, and Weaver Family Genealogical Notes compiled by D. E. Brady, Sr., October 28, 1951 (typescript), Weaver–Brady Papers, D. E. Brady, Jr.; "Weaver Family: Memo and Historical Notes," Weaver–Brady Papers in the possession of T. T. Brady, Richmond, Virginia.

40. Mayburry to Weaver, June 15, 1822, Case Papers, Weaver *v.* Mayburry.

41. Mayburry to Weaver, September 25, 1822, ibid.

42. Mayburry to Weaver, October 2, 26, 1822, ibid.

43. Mayburry to Weaver, November 14, 1822, ibid.

44. "The Answer of Thomas Mayburry to a Bill of Complaint exhibited against him & William Weaver . . . by William Wilson," November 16, 1820, Case Papers, Wilson *v.* Mayburry & Weaver; Bill of Complaint of William Weaver, November 19, 1825, Weaver *v.* Mayburry.

45. Mayburry to Weaver, October 2, 1822, Case Papers, Weaver *v.* Mayburry.

46. Mayburry to Weaver, November 14, 1822, ibid.

47. Bill of Complaint of William Weaver, November 19, 1825, and deposition of John W. Danenhower, July 10, 1830, ibid.

I.3: Mayburry & Weaver: Dissolution and Division

1. Deposition of William Norcross, May 24, 1826, Case Papers, Weaver *v.* Mayburry, Superior Court of Chancery Records, Augusta County Court House, Staunton, Virginia (hereafter cited as Case Papers, Weaver *v.* Mayburry).

2. Deposition of John W. Danenhower, July 10, 1830, ibid.

3. Deposition of William Weaver, November 19, 1825, ibid.

4. Deposition of John Doyle, February 5, 1840, Case Papers, Weaver *v.* Jordan, Davis & Co., Superior Court of Chancery Records Rockbridge County Court House, Lexington, Virginia (hereafter cited as Case Papers, Weaver *v.* Jordan, Davis & Co.). A printed copy of most of the documents pertaining to this case can be found in the Special Collections Department, Washington & Lee University Library, Lexington, Virginia.

5. Deposition of John W. Danenhower, July 10, 1830, Case Papers, Weaver *v.* Mayburry.

6. Deposition of Thomas Mayburry, November 1, 1826, ibid.

7. Ibid., and deposition of Thomas C. Jolly, May 30, 1827, ibid.

8. "Forge Accounts," February 12, 1825, ibid.

9. Deposition of William Weaver, December 10, 1840, Case Papers, John Alexander *v.* Sydney S. Baxter, Administrator of John Irvine & Others, Superior Court of Chancery Records, Rockbridge County Court House, Lexington, Virginia (hereafter cited as Case Papers, Alexander *v.* Irvine's Administrator).

10. Bill of Complaint of William Weaver, November 19, 1825, Case Papers, Weaver *v.* Mayburry; Jacob Holgate to William Weaver, September 23, 1825, William Weaver Papers, Duke University Library, Durham, North Carolina (hereafter cited as Weaver Papers, Duke).

11. Bill of Complaint of William Weaver, November 19, 1825, and deposition of John W. Danenhower, July 10, 1830, Case Papers, Weaver *v.* Mayburry.

12. Bill of Complaint of William Weaver, November 19, 1825, "The Answer of Thomas Mayburry to a Bill of Complaint exhibited against him . . . by William Weaver," November 28, 1825, and deposition of John W. Danenhower, July 10, 1830, ibid.

13. "Answer of Thomas Mayburry . . . ," November 28, 1825, ibid.

14. Lease agreement between Thomas Mayburry and William Weaver, December 28, 1824, Bill of Complaint of William Weaver, November 19, 1825, and "Answer of Thomas Mayburry . . . ," November 28, 1825, ibid.

15. Bill of Complaint of William Weaver, November 19, 1825, "Answer of Thomas Mayburry . . . ," November 28, 1825, and deposition of John Doyle, July 10, 1830, ibid.

16. Bill of Complaint of William Weaver, November 19, 1825, and depositions of William Norcross, May 25, 1826, and John W. Danenhower, July 10, 1830, ibid.

17. Depositions of Charles B. Penn, July 7, 1826, and William Ross, April 14, 1826, ibid.

18. Deposition of William Ross, April 15, 1826, ibid. On Ross's career as a Virginia ironmaster, see deposition of William Ross, January 23, 1839, Case Papers, Weaver *v.* Jordan, Davis & Co.

19. Deposition of William Ross, April 14, 1826, Case Papers, Weaver *v.* Mayburry; "Articles of Agreement . . . between Thomas Mayburry and William Weaver . . . ," February 9, 1825, Weaver Papers, Duke.

20. Deposition of Thomas C. Jolly, July 27, 1826, and "Inventory Taken at U. Forge" [February 9, 1825], Case Papers, Weaver *v.* Mayburry.

21. The histories of the families that made up the group of slaves referred to in the records as the "Wilson negroes" has been pieced together from the following sources: "Answer of Thomas Mayburry . . . ," November 28, 1825, Bond of Thomas Mayburry for the forthcoming of slaves, December 20, 1828, depositions of William Ross, April 14, 1826, James Brawley, April 18–21, 1826, James T. Martin, May 23, 1826, William Norcross, May 25, 1826, and John W. Danenhower, July 10, 1830, ibid.; see also entries in Buffalo Forge Negro Books, 1830–40, 1839–41, 1844–50, and 1850–57, Weaver–Brady Papers, University of Virginia Library, Charlottesville (hereafter cited as Weaver-Brady Papers, Virginia).

22. Bill of William Weaver, August 9, 1827, Answer of Thomas Mayburry, October 12, 1831, Bond of Thomas Mayburry for the forthcoming of slaves, December 20, 1828, and deposition of John W. Danenhower, July 10, 1830, Case Papers, Weaver *v.* Mayburry.

23. Depositions of Ambrose Campbell, May 14, 1826, James Brawley, April 18–21, 1826, and Wilday Hughes, May 15, 1826, ibid.

24. Deposition of William Weaver, December 9, 1839, Case Papers, Alexander *v.* Irvine's Administrator.

25. "Articles of Agreement . . . between Thomas Mayburry and William Weaver . . . ," February 9, 1825, Weaver Papers, Duke.

26. Bill of Complaint of William Weaver, November 19, 1825, and deposition of John W. Schoolfield, May 22, 1826, Case Papers, Weaver *v.* Mayburry.

27. Weaver to Mayburry, May 12, 1825, ibid.

28. "Articles of Agreement . . . between Thomas Mayburry and William Weaver . . . ," February 9, 1825, Weaver Papers, Duke.

29. Deposition of John S. Wilson, September 21, 1825, Case Papers, Weaver *v.* Mayburry. See also John S. Wilson to Thomas Mayburry, March 1, 1825, ibid.

30. Deposition of Thomas Mayburry, April 23, 1839, Case Papers, Weaver *v.* Jordan, Davis & Co.

31. Deposition of Thomas Mayburry, April 22–23, 1839, ibid.

32. "Article of Agreement . . . between Thomas Mayburry . . . and William Weaver . . . ," January 19, 1827, Weaver Papers, Duke.

33. See page headings for January 1827 in Union Forge and Buffalo Forge Day Book, 1825–28, Weaver–Brady Papers, Virginia.

34. "Article of Agreement . . . between Thos. Mayburry & Wm. Weaver . . . ," August 3, 1836, Weaver Papers, Duke; deposition of Thomas Mayburry, April 22–23, 1839, Case Papers, Weaver *v.* Jordan, Davis & Co.

35. Deposition of Thomas Mayburry, April 20–23, 1839, Case Papers, Weaver *v.* Jordan, Davis & Co.; Deed Book R, Rockbridge County Court House, Lexington, Virginia, pp. 137–38, 249–50.

36. Deposition of Thomas Mayburry, April 23, 1839, Case Papers, Weaver *v.* Jordan, Davis & Co.; "Article of Agreement . . . between Thos. Mayburry & Wm. Weaver . . . ," August 3, 1836, Weaver Papers, Duke.

37. Deposition of James Brawley, April 18–21, 1826, Case Papers, Weaver *v.* Mayburry.

38. Deposition of John W. Danenhower, July 10, 1830, ibid.

39. "Article of Agreement . . . between Thos. Mayburry & Wm. Weaver . . . ," August 3, 1836, Weaver Papers, Duke.

40. "Answer of Thomas Mayburry . . . ," November 28, 1825, and deposition of James Brawley, April 18–21, 1826, Case Papers, Weaver v. Mayburry.

41. Bond of Thomas Mayburry for the forthcoming of slaves, December 20, 1828, ibid.

42. Deposition of William Weaver, August 15, 1842, Mayburry's Administrator v. Sophia C. Jolly, Case Papers, Superior Court of Chancery Records, Louisa County Court House, Louisa, Virginia.

I.4: Bath Iron Works

1. Article of agreement between William Weaver and Matthews & Harrison, September 17, 1825, Case Papers, Doyle v. Weaver, Superior Court of Chancery Records, Rockbridge County Court House, Lexington, Virginia (hereafter cited as Case Papers, Doyle v. Weaver); deposition of William Weaver, December 9, 1839, Case Papers, John Alexander v. Sydney S. Baxter, Administrator of John Irvine & Others, ibid. (hereafter cited as Case Papers, Alexander v. Irvine's Administrator); Oren F. Morton, *A History of Rockbridge County, Virginia* (Staunton, VA: The McClure Co., 1920), 170.

2. "The Answer of William Weaver to a bill exhibited against him . . . by John Doyle," December 15, 1831, Case Papers, Doyle v. Weaver.

3. Deposition of John W. Danenhower, October 23, 1837, ibid.

4. "The Answer of William Weaver to a bill exhibited against him . . . by John Doyle," December 15, 1831, ibid.

5. Deposition of William Weaver, December 10, 1839, Case Papers, Alexander v. Irvine's Administrator.

6. Caruthers & Alexander to Weaver, January 8, 1829, Weaver–Brady Papers, University of Virginia Library, Charlottesville (hereafter cited as Weaver–Brady Papers, Virginia).

7. Deposition of William Weaver, December 9, 1839, Case Papers, Alexander v. Irvine's Administrator.

8. Deposition of William Weaver, December 10, 1839, ibid.

9. Deposition of John Doyle, February 8, 1840, Case Papers, Weaver v. Jordan, Davis & Co., Superior Court of Chancery Records, Rockbridge County Court House, Lexington, Virginia (hereafter cited as Case Papers, Weaver v. Jordan, Davis & Co.). A printed copy of most of the documents pertaining to this case can be found in the Special Collections Department, Washington & Lee University Library, Lexington, Virginia.

10. Lewis Webb & Co. to Weaver, March 1, 1828, Weaver–Brady Papers, Virginia; Kathleen Bruce, *Virginia Iron Manufacture in the Slave Era* (New York: Century Co., 1930), 119.

11. Deposition of John Doyle, July 16, 1839, February 8, 1840, Case Papers, Weaver v. Jordan, Davis & Co.

12. Deposition of William Weaver, December 10, 1839, Case Papers, Alexander v. Irvine's Administrator; deposition of William Weaver, November 19, 1825, Case Papers, Weaver v. Mayburry, Superior Court of Chancery Records, Augusta County Court House, Staunton, Virginia (hereafter cited as Case Papers, Weaver v. Mayburry); "Statement of the Accounts of William Weaver Executor of . . . Abraham Weaver . . . ," November 15, 1836, Weaver–Brady Papers in the possession of D. E. Brady, Jr., Buffalo Forge, Virginia (hereafter cited as Weaver–Brady Papers, D. E. Brady, Jr.).

13. "Response of William Weaver to Bill of Complaint of M. Wilson & Wife in case of Wilson & Wife v. Barclays Heirs," April 13, 1848, Weaver–Brady Papers, Virginia; depositions of John Doyle, April 22, 1839, and Thomas Mayburry, April 23, 1839, Case Papers, Weaver v. Jordan, Davis & Co.

14. Deposition of William Weaver, December 10, 1840, Case Papers, Alexander v.

Irvine's Administrator; "Inventory taken at Buffalo Forge 1st February 1828," Weaver–Brady Papers in the possession of T. T. Brady, Richmond, Virginia (hereafter cited as Weaver–Brady Papers, T. T. Brady); John W. Danenhower to Weaver, January 10, 1829, and John Doyle to Weaver, March 31, April 15, May 12, July 29, 1829, William Weaver Papers, Duke University Library, Durham, North Carolina (hereafter cited as Weaver Papers, Duke); deposition of John Doyle, February 7, 1840, Case Papers, Weaver *v.* Jordan, Davis & Co.

15. Deposition of John Doyle, July 3, 1839, Case Papers, Weaver *v.* Jordan, Davis & Co.

16. Weaver to Doyle, April 28, 1827, January 7, 1828, Case Papers, Doyle *v.* Weaver; Doyle to Weaver, March 31, 1829, Weaver Papers, Duke.

17. Deposition of Jacob A. Wilhelm, July 22, 1836, Case Papers, Weaver *v.* Jordan, Davis & Co.; Weaver to Doyle, January 13, 1828, Case Papers, Doyle *v.* Weaver.

18. "The Answer of William Weaver to a bill exhibited against him . . . by John Doyle," December 15, 1831, and Weaver to Doyle, January 7, 13, 1828, Case Papers, Doyle *v.* Weaver; lists of hands hired for Bath Iron Works, January 13, 1829, January 16, 1830, January 24, 1830, Buffalo Forge Journal, 1828–34, Weaver–Brady Papers, Virginia; deposition of John Doyle, July 17, 1839, Case Papers, Weaver *v.* Jordan, Davis & Co.

19. Deposition of James Compton, February 5, 1840, Case Papers, Weaver *v.* Jordan, Davis & Co.; Weaver to Doyle, December 17, 1826, n.d. [November 1828], Case Papers, Doyle *v.* Weaver; James C. Dickinson to Weaver, January 2, 1828, James Rose to Weaver, January 2, 1828, and John Wiglesworth to Weaver, January 5, 1829, Weaver–Brady Papers, Virginia; John S. May to Weaver, November 10, 1828, Dickinson to Weaver, December 5, 1828, Robert Crutchfield to Weaver, January 4, 1829, and John Chew to Weaver, December 5, 1820, Weaver Papers, Duke; Tuyman Wyat to Jordan & Irvine, January 6, 1830, and Pattison Boxley to Jordan & Irvine, January 13, 1831, Jordan and Irvine Papers, McCormick Collection, State Historical Society of Wisconsin, Madison.

20. C. Wiglesworth to Weaver, December 31, 1828, Weaver Papers, Duke.

21. Elizabeth Callaway to Weaver, December 29, 1829, ibid.

22. Crutchfield to Weaver, January 4, 1829, ibid.

23. Crutchfield to Weaver, April 29, 1829, ibid.

24. William Staples to Weaver, January 4, 1830, Weaver–Brady Papers, Virginia.

25. Crutchfield to Weaver, January 10, 1830, Weaver Papers, Duke.

26. "The Answer of William Weaver to a bill exhibited against him . . . by John Doyle," December 15, 1831, and Doyle to Weaver, March 14, June 24, July 17, October 22, 1828, Case Papers, Doyle *v.* Weaver; Doyle to Abram W. Davis, December 1, 1828, and Doyle to Weaver, December 9, 1828, Weaver–Brady Papers, Virginia; Doyle to Weaver, May 5, July 29, November 17, 1829, Doyle to Davis, September 30, 1829, William W. Davis to Abram W. Davis, August 25, December 9, 1829, and William W. Davis to Weaver, November 5, 1828, December 4, 1829, Weaver Papers, Duke.

27. Doyle to Weaver, August 11, 1828, Case Papers, Doyle *v.* Weaver.

28. Doyle to Weaver, October 21, November 13, 1829, Weaver Papers, Duke; deposition of John Hill, August 18, 1836, Case Papers, Weaver *v.* Jordan, Davis & Co.

29. Depositions of William Hill, June 17, 1839, William Cash, June 20, 1839, and William Lusk, June 22, 1839, Case Papers, Weaver *v.* Jordan, Davis & Co.; "Inventory of Buildings at Bath Iron Works," June 14, 1839, Case Papers, Doyle *v.* Weaver.

30. Deposition of John Doyle, April 22, 1839, Case Papers, Weaver *v.* Jordan, Davis & Co.; "Memorandum of hired Negroes at Bath Iron Works for 1829," and Danenhower to Weaver, December 20, 1829, Weaver Papers, Duke.

31. W. E. Dickerson to Abram W. Davis, April 19, 1829, Weaver Papers, Duke; see also Wm. Watson for Joel W. Brown, Jailor, Charlottesville, to Postmaster, Lexington, April 29, 1829, and Dickinson to Weaver, May 29, 1829, Case Papers, Weaver *v.* Jordan, Davis & Co.

32. "The Answer of William Weaver to a bill exhibited against him . . . by John Doyle," December 15, 1831, Case Papers, Doyle *v.* Weaver.

33. Deposition of John Doyle, April 22, 1839, Case Papers, Weaver *v.* Jordan, Davis & Co.

34. Deposition of John Doyle, February 8, 1840, ibid.

35. "The Answer of William Weaver to a bill exhibited against him . . . by John Doyle," December 15, 1831, Case Papers, Doyle *v.* Weaver; deposition of James C. Dickinson, August 18, 1835, Case Papers, Weaver *v.* Jordan, Davis & Co.

36. Final Decree, April 17, 1851, Case Papers, Doyle *v.* Weaver.

37. Deposition of John Doyle, February 8, 1840, Case Papers, Weaver *v.* Jordan, Davis & Co.

38. Jno. W. Schoolfield to Weaver, January 28, 1830, Weaver Papers, Duke.

39. Deposition of Abram W. Davis, October 23, 1837, and John W. Danenhower, October 25, 1837, Case Papers, Doyle *v.* Weaver; deposition of William W. Davis, August 22, 1840, Case Papers, Alexander *v.* Irvine's Administrator; "Weaver Family: Memo and Historical Notes," Weaver–Brady Papers, T. T. Brady; William W. Davis to Weaver, April 16, July 22, August 13, 1826, Weaver Papers, Duke.

40. J. P. Lesley, *The Iron Manufacturer's Guide to the Furnaces, Forges and Rolling Mills of the United States* . . . (New York: John Wiley, 1859), 71, 182; "Weaver Family: Memo and Historical Notes," Weaver–Brady Papers, T. T. Brady; Weaver to Doyle, December 16, 1829, Case Papers, Doyle *v.* Weaver; "The Answer of Samuel F. Jordan, William W. Davis and Abraham [*sic*] Davis to a bill of complaint exhibited against them . . . ," October 5, 1835, Case Papers, Weaver *v.* Jordan, Davis & Co.; Margaret P. Jones, "Samuel Francis Jordan," 1951 (typescript), Weaver–Brady Papers, D. E. Brady, Jr.; deposition of Samuel F. Jordan, September 7, 1840, Case Papers, Alexander *v.* Irvine's Administrator.

41. Bill of complaint of William Weaver, June 1, 1835, Case Papers, Weaver *v.* Jordan, Davis & Co.

42. "Weaver Family: Memo and Historical Notes," Weaver–Brady Papers, T. T. Brady; depositions of Lydia L. W. Gorgas, Hannah Leibert, Peter K. Gorgas, Samuel V. Rex, Mary Rex, and Peter Leibert, May 19, 1836, Case Papers, Weaver *v.* Jordan, Davis & Co.

43. Deposition of John W. Danenhower, May 19, 1836, Case Papers, Weaver *v.* Jordan, Davis & Co.

44. Samuel F. Jordan reexamination of John Doyle, April 24, 1839, ibid.

45. "The answer of Samuel F. Jordan, William W. Davis and Abraham [*sic*] Davis to a bill of complaint exhibited against them . . . ," October 5, 1835, ibid.

46. Deposition of James C. Dickinson, August 18, 1836, ibid.

47. Bill of complaint of William Weaver, June 1, 1835, ibid.

48. Deposition of John Jordan, July 22–23, 1836, ibid.

49. Abram W. Davis to Weaver, July 24, September 3, 29, 1830, Weaver Papers, Duke; "Weaver Family: Memo and Historical Notes," Weaver–Brady Papers, T. T. Brady.

50. Abram W. Davis to Weaver, October 22, 1830, Weaver Papers, Duke.

51. Depositions of John Jordan, July 22, 1836, William Ross, January 23, 1839, John Doyle, April 22, 1839, William Hill, June 17, 1839, William Lusk, June 22, 1839, and James Compton, February 5, 1840, Case Papers, Weaver *v.* Jordan, Davis & Co.

52. "Jordan, Davis & Co. Dr. for Negro hire," January 24, 1830, Buffalo Forge Journal, 1828–34, and "a/c of Pigs made from new stack blast 1830," Bath Iron Works Ledger, 1828–34, Weaver–Brady Papers, Virginia; deposition of Jacob A. Wilhelm, July 22, 1836, Case Papers, Weaver *v.* Jordan, Davis & Co.; Jordan, Davis & Co. to Weaver, October 6, 1830, Jordan & Davis Papers, McCormick Collection, State Historical Society of Wisconsin, Madison (hereafter cited as Jordan & Davis Papers, McCormick Collection).

53. Deposition of James Compton, February 5, 1840, Case Papers, Weaver *v.* Jordan, Davis & Co.

54. Bill of complaint of William Weaver, June 1, 1835, and deposition of John Doyle, July 16, 1839, ibid.

55. Rose to Weaver, March 8, 1830, Weaver Papers, Duke.

56. Elizabeth Mathews to Weaver, March 29, 1830, ibid.

57. Jordan, Davis & Co. to Weaver, October 27, November 24, 1830, and Samuel F. Jordan to Weaver, December 7, 1830, Weaver Papers, Duke.

58. Dickinson to Weaver, October 21, 1830, Weaver–Brady Papers, Virginia.

59. Bill of complaint of William Weaver, June 1, 1835, and deposition of John Doyle, July 16, 1839, Case Papers, Weaver *v.* Jordan, Davis & Co.

60. Jordan, Davis & Co. to Weaver, March 25, August 11, 1830, and Jordan, Davis & Co. to Abram W. Davis, August 24, October 27, November 24, 1830, Weaver Papers, Duke.

61. Jordan, Davis & Co. to Weaver, September 8, 1832, ibid.

62. Depositions of Michael Ham and James H. Dixon, January 25, 1839, Joseph Miller, June 12, 1839, William Hill, June 17, 1839, and John Doyle, July 15, 1851, Case Papers, Weaver *v.* Jordan, Davis & Co.

63. Depositions of Anthony W. Templin, January 24, 1839, Michael Ham, January 25, 1839, Ira F. Jordan, March 4, 1839, John Doyle, April 20, 1839, and Thomas T. Blackford, November 7, 1839, ibid.; Jordan, Davis & Co. to Weaver, June 10, 1832, Weaver Papers, Duke.

64. Depositions of John Hill, August 18, 1836, March 2, 1839, Anthony W. Templin, January 24, 1839, John B. Johnson, June 12, 1839, William Cash, June 20, 1839, Thomas T. Blackford, November 7, 1839, and George M. Pennybacker, November 8, 1839, Case Papers, Weaver *v.* Jordan, Davis & Co.

65. Deposition of James Lowe, June 11, 1839, ibid.

66. Deposition of John Jordan, July 23, 1836, ibid.

67. Samuel F. Jordan to William W. Davis, April 2, 1851, Jordan & Davis Papers, McCormick Collection.

68. "Account of pig iron made and sent from Bath Furnace from . . . 1830 until . . . 1838 . . . ," June 7, 1840, Case Papers, Weaver *v.* Jordan, Davis & Co.; deposition of Samuel F. Jordan, September 7, 1840, Case Papers, Alexander *v.* Irvine's Administrator.

69. Jordan, Davis & Co. to Weaver, November 24, 1830, Weaver Papers, Duke.

70. "Account of pig iron made and sent from Bath Furnace from . . . 1830 until . . . 1838 . . . ," June 7, 1840, and Bill of complaint of William Weaver, June 1, 1835, Case Papers, Weaver *v.* Jordan, Davis & Co.

71. Jordan, Davis & Co. to Weaver, February 16, 1830, September 21, October 11, October 25, November 13, 1831, July 7, September 3, 1832, Weaver Papers, Duke; deposition of John Doyle, February 7, 1840, Case Papers, Weaver *v.* Jordan, Davis & Co.

72. Charles B. Dew, "David Ross and the Oxford Iron Works: A Study of Industrial Slavery in the Early Nineteenth-Century South," *William and Mary Quarterly,* 3rd Series, 31 (April 1974), 189–224; "List of Slaves at the Oxford Iron Works in Families and Their Employment, Taken 15 January 1811," William Bolling Papers, Duke University Library, Durham, North Carolina. See also Charles B. Dew, "Slavery and Technology in the Antebellum Southern Iron Industry: The Case of Buffalo Forge," in Ronald L. Numbers and Todd L. Savitt, eds., *Science and Medicine in the Old South* (Baton Rouge: Louisiana State University Press, 1989), 120.

73. Dew, "Slavery and Technology in the Antebellum Southern Iron Industry," 120; depositions of Joseph C. Barker, August 5, 1836, and John Doyle, February 7, 1840, and Bill of complaint of William Weaver, June 1, 1835, Case Papers, Weaver *v.* Jordan, Davis & Co.; "Names, births & c: of Negroes," Weaver–Brady Papers, T. T. Brady.

74. Abram W. Davis to Weaver, June 10, 1831, James D. Davidson Papers, McCormick Collection, State Historical Society of Wisconsin, Madison.

75. Deposition of John W. Danenhower, May 19, 1836, Case Papers, Weaver *v.* Jordan, Davis & Co.; Samuel F. Jordan to Abram W. Davis, June 17, 29, 1831, Weaver–

Brady Papers, Virginia; Abram W. Davis to Weaver, August 10, 1831, Weaver Papers, Duke.

76. Danenhower to Weaver, January 7, 1835, Weaver Papers, Duke.

77. Deposition of John W. Danenhower, May 16, 1836, Case Papers, Weaver *v.* Jordan, Davis & Co.; Danenhower to Weaver, May 10, 1833, Weaver Papers, Duke.

78. Danenhower to Weaver, May 10, 1833, Weaver Papers, Duke.

79. Danenhower to Weaver, January 7, 1835, August 10, 1854, Weaver Papers, Duke; entries for June 29, September 1, 1854, Etna Furnace Time Book, 1854–58, Weaver–Brady Papers, Virginia.

80. Tax receipts, Jordan, Davis & Co., 1830–34, Case Papers, Weaver *v.* Jordan, Davis & Co.

81. "The Names of the Different Founders [at Bath Furnace] and their Wages," and "Account of pig iron made and sent from Bath Furnace from … 1830 until … 1838 … ," June 7, 1840, ibid; Samuel F. Jordan to Weaver, March 25, 1832, Weaver Papers, Duke.

82. Samuel F. Jordan to Weaver, May 14, 1831, Weaver–Brady Papers, Virginia; Jordan, Davis & Co. to Weaver, June 10, 1832, William W. Davis to Weaver, July 7, 1832, Lewis Rawlings to Weaver or Jordan, Davis & Co., August 22, 1832, Abram W. Davis to Weaver, May 1, 1833, and Charles Perrow to Weaver, September 17, October 26, 1833, Weaver Papers, Duke.

83. Bill of complaint of William Weaver, June 1, 1835, Case Papers, Weaver *v.* Jordan, Davis & Co.

I.5: Weaver *v.* Jordan, Davis & Company

1. Bill of Complaint of William Weaver, June 1, 1835, Case Papers, Weaver *v.* Jordan, Davis & Co., Superior Court of Chancery Records, Rockbridge County Court House, Lexington, Virginia (hereafter cited as Case Papers, Weaver *v.* Jordan, Davis & Co.). A printed copy of most of the documents pertaining to this case can be found in the Special Collections Department, Washington & Lee University Library, Lexington, Virginia.

2. Ibid., and Agreement between William Weaver and Jordan, Davis & Co. (S. F. Jordan and Wm. W. Davis), April 4, 1834, ibid.

3. Agreement between William Weaver and Jordan, Davis & Co. (S. F. Jordan and Wm. W. Davis), April 4, 1834, ibid.

4. "The answer of Samuel F. Jordan, William W. Davis and Abraham [*sic*] Davis to a bill of complaint exhibited against them … ," October 5, 1835, ibid.

5. Ibid.

6. Jordan, Davis & Co. to Weaver, June 16, 1834, ibid.

7. Bill of Complaint of William Weaver, June 1, 1835, ibid.

8. "Notes for Argument of Plaintiff's Counsel," September 1842, ibid.

9. Deposition of Joseph C. Barker, August 5, 1836, ibid.

10. Ibid.

11. "Copy of Proposition made by Weaver to Jordan, Davis & Co.," February 12, 1835, William Weaver Papers, Duke University Library, Durham, North Carolina (hereafter cited as Weaver Papers, Duke).

12. Reply of Jordan, Davis & Co., February 24, 1835, Case Papers, Weaver *v.* Jordan, Davis & Co.

13. Bill of Complaint of William Weaver, June 1, 1835, and "Notes for Argument of Plaintiff's Counsel," September 1842, ibid.

14. James C. Dickinson to Weaver, December 2, 1832, ibid.

15. Deposition of James C. Dickinson, August 18, 1836, ibid.

16. Ibid.

17. Deposition of Mary Dickinson, August 19, 1836, ibid.

18. John W. Danenhower to Weaver, October 25, 1834, Weaver Papers, Duke.

19. Bill of Complaint of William Weaver, June 1, 1835, Case Papers, Weaver *v.* Jordan, Davis & Co.

20. Deposition of Don Q. Stokley, September 12, 1836, ibid.

21. Depositions of James C. Dickinson, August 18, 1836, Mary Dickinson, August 19, 1836, and John Jordan, July 22, 1836, ibid.

22. Deposition of John Jordan, July 23, 1836, ibid.

23. "The answer of Samuel F. Jordan, William W. Davis and Abraham [*sic*] Davis to a bill of complaint exhibited against them . . . ," October 5, 1835, ibid.

24. Bill of Complaint of William Weaver, June 1, 1835, ibid.

25. Deposition of Joseph C. Barker, August 5, 1836, ibid.

26. Depositions of Lydia L. W. Gorgas and Peter K. Gorgas, May 19, 1836, ibid.

27. Deposition of John Doyle, February 7, 1840, ibid.

28. "Exhibit CC . . . Profits, according to plaintiff's views," ibid.

29. Cause of the Circuit Superior Court of Law and Chancery, April 21, 1838, ibid.

30. Deposition of William Hill, June 17, 1839, ibid.

31. Eliza M. Potts to Weaver, March 1, 1835, Weaver Papers, Duke.

32. Deposition of Samuel F. Jordan, September 7, 1840, Case Papers, John Alexander *v.* Sydney S. Baxter, Administrator of John Irvine & Others, Superior Court of Chancery Records, Rockbridge County Court House, Lexington, Virginia (hereafter cited as Case Papers, Alexander *v.* Irvine's Administrator).

33. William Weaver cross-examination of Joseph Bell, June 21, 1839, and deposition of James H. Dixon, January 25, 1839, Case Papers, Weaver *v.* Jordan, Davis & Co.

34. Deposition of George M. Pennybacker, November 8, 1839, ibid.

35. William Weaver cross-examination of Joseph Bell, June 21, 1839, ibid.

36. "1st Report of Commissioner Chapin," March 14, 1840, ibid.

37. Cause of the Circuit Superior Court of Law and Chancery, September 22, 1842, ibid.

38. Petition of Samuel F. Jordan and William W. Davis to the Honorable Judges of the Court of Appeals of Virginia [1843], ibid.

39. Transcript certification of Samuel McD. Reid, Clerk, February 23, 1843, ibid.

40. James D. Davidson to Weaver, April 23, 1855, Weaver Papers, Duke; Statement, Jordan & Davis *v.* William Weaver, November 16, 1857, Weaver–Brady Papers, University of Virginia Library, Charlottesville (hereafter cited as Weaver–Brady Papers, Virginia).

41. Statement, Jordan & Davis *v.* William Weaver, November 30, 1857, Weaver–Brady Papers, Virginia.

42. Potts to Weaver, September 8, 1834, Weaver Papers, Duke; see also depositions of Lydia L. W. Gorgas, Hannah Leibert, Samuel V. Rex, Mary Rex, and Peter Leibert, May 19, 1836, Case Papers, Weaver *v.* Jordan, Davis & Co.

43. Margaret P. Jones, "Samuel Francis Jordan," 1951 (typescript), Weaver–Brady Papers in the possession of D. E. Brady, Jr., Buffalo Forge, Virginia; Daniel C. E. Brady, "Home Journal," 1858–60, Weaver–Brady Papers, Virginia; Daniel C. E. Brady to William W. Davis, September 26, 1861, Jordan & Davis Papers, McCormick Collection, State Historical Society of Wisconsin, Madison.

44. Abram W. Davis to Weaver, n.d. [1852], Weaver Papers, Duke.

45. Buffalo Forge Time Book, 1843–53, Weaver–Brady Papers, Virginia.

46. Indenture between Thomas Mayburry and Jordan & Davis, May 7, 1839, Deed Book W, pp. 324–26, Rockbridge County Court House, Lexington, Virginia.

47. Agreement between Samuel F. Jordan and William W. Davis, December 12, 1842, Weaver–Brady Papers, Virginia; Jones, "Samuel Francis Jordan."

I.6: The Master of Buffalo Forge

1. "Inventory taken at Union Forge" [1825], Weaver–Brady Papers in the possession of T. T. Brady, Richmond, Virginia (hereafter cited as Weaver–Brady Papers, T. T. Brady).

2. Union Forge Day Book, 1825–28, Weaver–Brady Papers, University of Virginia

Library, Charlottesville (hereafter cited as Weaver-Brady Papers, Virginia); depositions of William Norcross, August 22, 1840, and William Weaver, December 10, 1840, Case Papers, John Alexander *v.* Sydney S. Baxter, Administrator of John Irvine & Others, Superior Court of Chancery Records, Rockbridge County Court House, Lexington, Virginia (hereafter cited as Case Papers, Alexander *v.* Irvine's Administrator).

    3. Union Forge Day Book, 1825–28, and Buffalo Forge Ledger, 1825–28, Weaver–Brady Papers, Virginia; "Union Forge Balance Sheet," March 3, 1824, Case Papers, Weaver *v.* Mayburry, Superior Court of Chancery Records, Augusta County Court House, Staunton, Virginia (hereafter cited as Case Papers, Weaver *v.* Mayburry); depositions of William Weaver, December 10, 1839, December 10, 1840, and William Norcross, August 22, 1840, Case Papers, Alexander *v.* Irvine's Administrator; J. P. Lesley, *The Iron Manufacturer's Guide to the Furnaces, Forges and Rolling Mills of the United States* . . . (New York: John Wiley, 1859), 69, 180–81.

    4. William Weaver to John Doyle, October 12, 1827, Case Papers, Doyle *v.* Weaver, Superior Court of Chancery Records, Rockbridge County Court House, Lexington, Virginia (hereafter cited as Case Papers, Doyle *v.* Weaver).

    5. Doyle to Weaver, October 15, 1827, ibid.

    6. Weaver to Doyle, October 17, 1827, ibid.

    7. Deposition of Ludwell Diggs, August 8, 1826, Case Papers, Weaver *v.* Mayburry.

    8. Moses McCue to Weaver, July 3, 1829, William Weaver Papers, Duke University Library, Durham, North Carolina (hereafter cited as Weaver Papers, Duke).

    9. James C. Dickinson to Weaver, January 21, 1833, ibid.

    10. John W. Schoolfield to Weaver, February 28, 1828, ibid.

    11. Wm. C. McAllister to Weaver, February 22, 1830, ibid.

    12. Buffalo Forge Negro Book, 1830–40, Weaver–Brady Papers, Virginia.

    13. David S. Garland to Weaver, May 23, 1828, Weaver Papers, Duke.

    14. Deposition of John Jordan, July 22, 1836, Case Papers, Weaver *v.* Jordan, Davis & Co., Superior Court of Chancery Records, Rockbridge County Court House, Lexington, Virginia (hereafter cited as Case Papers, Weaver *v.* Jordan, Davis & Co.). A printed copy of most of the documents pertaining to this case can be found in the Special Collections Department, Washington & Lee University's Library, Lexington, Virginia.

    15. Weaver to James D. Davidson, July 13, 1852, Weaver–Brady Papers, Virginia.

    16. Davidson to Weaver, December 21, 1854, Weaver Papers, Duke.

    17. Davidson to Weaver, December 27, 1854, ibid.

    18. J. J. Fry to William W. Davis, June 19, 25, July 9, 21, 1855, William W. Davis Papers, University of Virginia Library, Charlottesville.

    19. Weaver to Davidson, November 4, 1849, James D. Davidson Papers, McCormick Collection, State Historical Society of Wisconsin, Madison (hereafter cited as Davidson Papers, McCormick Collection).

    20. Weaver to Davidson, April 6, 1852, ibid.

    21. Deposition of William Weaver, December 10, 1840, Case Papers, Alexander *v.* Irvine's Administrator; Buffalo Forge Iron Book, 1831–62, Weaver–Brady Papers, Virginia.

    22. Bath Forge Negro Books, 1839–42, 1846, Weaver–Brady Papers, Virginia; Bath Forge Anchony & Bar Iron Book, 1850–52, Weaver–Brady Papers, T. T. Brady.

    23. Deposition of John Doyle, February 8, 1840, Case Papers, Weaver *v.* Jordan, Davis & Co.

    24. Deposition of William Norcross, August 22, 1840, Case Papers, Alexander *v.* Irvine's Administrator.

    25. David Ross to Thomas Evans, June 24, 1812, David Ross Letterbook, 1812–13, Virginia Historical Society, Richmond (hereafter cited as Ross Letterbook). See also Charles B. Dew, "David Ross and the Oxford Iron Works: A Study of Industrial Slavery in the Early Nineteenth-Century South," *William and Mary Quarterly,* 3rd Series, 31 (April 1974), 216.

26. Ross to Robert Richardson, November 10, 1812, Ross Letterbook.

27. See Anthony F. C. Wallace, *Rockdale: The Growth of an American Village in the Early Industrial Revolution* (New York: W. W. Norton & Co., 1980), 150.

28. Deposition of John Doyle, February 8, 1840, Case Papers, Weaver *v.* Jordan, Davis & Co. See also Doyle to Weaver, January 6, 1853, Weaver Papers, Duke.

29. The best discussions of the overwork system are in Robert S. Starobin, *Industrial Slavery in the Old South* (New York: Oxford University Press, 1970), 99–103, and Ronald L. Lewis, *Coal, Iron, and Slaves: Industrial Slavery in Maryland and Virginia, 1715–1865* (Westport, CT: Greenwood Press, 1979), 119–27. See also Charles B. Dew, "Disciplining Slave Iron-workers in the Antebellum South: Coercion, Conciliation, and Accommodation," *American Historical Review,* 79 (April 1974), 405–10.

30. Deposition of Ira F. Jordan, December 10, 1839, Case Papers, Alexander *v.* Irvine's Administrator; depositions of John Jordan, July 22, 1836, James H. Dixon, January 25, 1839, Ira F. Jordan, March 4, 1839, and John Doyle, February 7, 1840, Case Papers, Weaver *v.* Jordan, Davis & Co.; Dew, "Disciplining Slave Ironworkers," 406.

31. Deposition of John Doyle, January 7, 1840, Case Papers, Weaver *v.* Jordan, Davis & Co.; Buffalo Forge Negro Books, 1830–40, 1839–41, 1844–50, Weaver–Brady Papers, Virginia.

32. Buffalo Forge Negro Books, 1830–40, 1839–41, 1844–50, 1850–57, and Etna Furnace Negro Book, 1854–61, Weaver–Brady Papers, Virginia.

33. Buffalo Forge Negro Book, 1830–40, ibid.

34. Ibid.

35. Buffalo Forge Negro Books, 1830–40, 1839–41, 1844–50, 1850–57, ibid.

36. Depositions of William Weaver, December 10, 1840, Ira F. Jordan, June 7, 1839, Robert J. Gilliam, April 4, 1843, William Cash, April 4, 1843, and James Shanks, April 5, 1843, Case Papers, Alexander *v.* Irvine's Administrator; depositions of William Durkee, July 27, 1826, and Charles W. Jolly, May 23, 1827, Case Papers, Weaver *v.* Mayburry.

37. See entries for clothing purchases in Buffalo Forge Journals, 1850–59 and 1859–66; Weaver to Lee, Rocke & Co., October 11, 1859, William W. Rex to Daniel C. E. Brady, December 23, 1859, and Weaver to Lee, Rocke & Taylor, November 13, 1860, Weaver–Brady Papers, Virginia; deposition of John M. Wilson, March 2, 1843, Case Papers, Alexander *v.* Irvine's Administrator.

38. Manuscript Slave Schedules, Eighth Census of the United States, 1860, National Archives Microfilm Publications, M-653; a sketch of the large, two-story cabin is in the possession of D. E. Brady, Jr., Buffalo Forge, Virginia.

39. Lewis Webb & Co. to Weaver, June 7, 1828, Weaver–Brady Papers, Virginia.

40. Webb & Co. to Weaver, March 28, 1829, ibid.

41. Henry Davis to Weaver, February 25, 1830, Weaver Papers, Duke.

42. John W. Schoolfield to Weaver, April 22, 1830, ibid.

43. Webb & Co. to Weaver, June 16, 1829, Weaver–Brady Papers, Virginia.

44. Schoolfield to Weaver, July 24, 1829, Weaver Papers, Duke.

45. Schoolfield to Weaver, December 7, 1829, ibid.

46. Schoolfield to Weaver, April 22, 1830, ibid.

47. Deposition of John Doyle, February 7, 1840, Case Papers, Weaver *v.* Jordan, Davis & Co.

48. Deposition of John Jordan, July 25, 1836, ibid; deposition of William Lusk, April 5, 1844, Case Papers, Alexander *v.* Irvine's Administrator.

49. Buffalo Forge Negro Book, 1830–40, Weaver–Brady Papers, Virginia.

50. Buffalo Forge Negro Books, 1830–40, 1844–50, 1850–57, ibid.

51. Buffalo Forge Negro Book, 1830–40, ibid.

52. Buffalo Forge Negro Book, 1850–57, ibid.; "List of Slaves at the Oxford Iron Works in Families and Their Employment, Taken 15 January 1811," William Bolling Papers, Duke University Library, Durham, North Carolina.

53. Buffalo Forge Negro Book, 1830–40, Weaver–Brady Papers, Virginia. Iron production was measured in tons of 2,240 pounds; a "hundredweight" of iron was 112 pounds, a "quarterweight" was 28 pounds.

54. Buffalo Forge Negro Book, 1830–40, Weaver–Brady Papers, Virginia.

55. Ibid.

56. Abram W. Davis to Weaver, September 25, 1830, Weaver Papers, Duke.

57. Buffalo Forge Negro Book, 1830–40, Weaver–Brady Papers, Virginia.

I.7: William Weaver, Virginian

1. "Article of agreement . . . between Thos. Mayburry & Wm. Weaver . . . ," August 3, 1836, John W. Schoolfield to William Weaver, October 28, 1834, and Samuel J. Henderson to Weaver, June 25, 1835, William Weaver Papers, Duke University Library, Durham, North Carolina (hereafter cited as Weaver Papers, Duke).

2. Weaver to James D. Davidson, June 12, 1848, Jordan & Irvine Papers, McCormick Collection, State Historical Society of Wisconsin, Madison.

3. William Ross to Weaver, June 15, 1830, Weaver–Brady Papers, University of Virginia Library, Charlottesville (hereafter cited as Weaver–Brady Papers, Virginia).

4. "Weaver Family: Memo and Historical Notes," Weaver–Brady Papers in the possession of T. T. Brady, Richmond, Virginia (hereafter cited as Weaver–Brady Papers, T. T. Brady).

5. T. T. Brady, "The Early Iron Industry in Rockbridge County," *Proceedings of the Rockbridge Historical Society,* 8 (1970–74), 50.

6. Depositions of William Weaver, December 10, 1840, and William Lusk, February 1, 1841, Case Papers, John Alexander *v.* Sidney S. Baxter, Administrator of John Irvine & Others, Superior Court of Chancery Records, Rockbridge County Court House, Lexington, Virginia (hereafter cited as Case Papers, Alexander *v.* Irvine's Administrator); depositions of Hugh Irvine, April 29, 1839, and William Lusk, June 4, 1839, Case Papers, Weaver *v.* Jordan, Davis & Co., Superior Court of Chancery Records, Rockbridge County Court House, Lexington, Virginia (hereafter cited as Case Papers, Weaver *v.* Jordan, Davis & Co.). A printed copy of most of the documents pertaining to this case can be found in the Special Collections Department, Washington & Lee University Library, Lexington, Virginia.

7. "Lydia Furnace . . . Negro hire for 1827," Union Forge–Buffalo Forge Day Book, 1825–28, Weaver–Brady Papers, Virginia.

8. Festus Dickinson to Weaver, February 12, 1828, Weaver Papers, Duke.

9. Dickinson to Weaver, March 8, 1828, ibid.

10. Dickinson to Weaver, January 15, 1829, ibid.

11. Dickinson to Weaver, February 2, 1829, Weaver–Brady Papers, Virginia.

12. William L. Ayres to James D. Davidson, December 12, 1855, James D. Davidson Papers, Duke University Library, Durham, North Carolina.

13. Weaver to Davidson, December 20, 1852, Weaver Papers, ibid.

14. William Weaver cross-examination of James Compton, July 3, 1839, Case Papers, Weaver *v.* Jordan, Davis & Co.

15. Deposition of John Doyle, February 5, 1840, ibid.

16. Deposition of Thomas Mayburry, April 23, 1839, ibid.

17. Weaver to John Jordan, December 15, 1851, Weaver–Brady Papers, Virginia.

18. Weaver to Davidson, February 7, 1852, ibid.

19. Weaver to Davidson, December 13, 1852, Weaver Papers, Duke.

20. "Weaver Family: Memo and Historical Notes," Weaver–Brady Papers, T. T. Brady.

21. Eliza W. Newkirk to Eliza Weaver, n.d. [1830], Weaver Papers, Duke.

22. Matilda Wallace to Mrs. William Weaver, December 26, 1831, ibid.

23. Weaver to J. J. Albright, January 9, 1850, ibid.

24. Weaver–Woodman Family Bible, Weaver–Brady Papers in the possession of D. E. Brady, Jr., Buffalo Forge, Virginia (hereafter cited as Weaver–Brady Papers, D. E. Brady, Jr.).

25. Weaver to Davidson, November 4, 1849, James D. Davidson Papers, McCormick Collection, State Historical Society of Wisconsin, Madison (hereafter cited as Davidson Papers, McCormick Collection).

26. Matilda Wallace to Mrs. William Weaver, November 8, 1831, Weaver Papers, Duke; obituary of Mrs. Eliza Weaver, Lexington *Gazette*, November 14, 1850.

27. Fragment of a letter written by Weaver, December 15, 1850, Weaver–Brady Papers, Virginia.

28. Weaver to Davidson, October 31, 1850, Davidson Papers, McCormick Collection.

29. Obituary of Mrs. Eliza Weaver, Lexington *Gazette*, November 14, 1850.

30. Weaver–Woodman Family Bible, Weaver–Brady Papers, D. E. Brady, Jr.

31. Daniel C. E. Brady to Weaver, August 8, 1854, Weaver Papers, Duke; Weaver to Davidson, May 18, 1856, Weaver–Brady Papers, Virginia.

32. Interview with D. E. Brady, Jr., Buffalo Forge, Virginia, October 7, 1977; interview with James Thompson, Glasgow, Virginia, December 13, 1977.

33. Interviews with James Thompson, Glasgow, Virginia, December 13, 1977, March 7, 1981.

34. Deposition of John Danenhower, July 10, 1830, Case Papers, Weaver *v.* Mayburry, Superior Court of Chancery Records, Augusta County Court House, Staunton, Virginia.

35. Abram W. Davis to Weaver, August 15, September 25, 1830, Weaver Papers, Duke.

36. Deed of conveyance, William Weaver to Mary Davidson, February 20, 1849, Deed Book CC, p. 390, Rockbridge County Court House, Lexington, Virginia.

37. Deed of conveyance, William Weaver to Clara Davidson, January 11, 1850, ibid. A copy of this deed can also be found in the Davidson Papers, McCormick Collection.

38. Buffalo Forge Time Book, 1843–53, Weaver–Brady Papers, Virginia.

39. Ibid.

40. Buffalo Forge Journal, 1850–59, ibid.

41. Ibid.

42. Weaver to Davidson, April 6, 1852, Davidson Papers, McCormick Collection.

43. Buffalo Forge Negro Book, 1850–57, Weaver–Brady Papers, Virginia.

44. "Farming of Mr. William Weaver, of Rockbridge County, Virginia," *Farmers' Register*, 10 (1842), 411–13. See also entries under "William Weaver," Rockbridge County, Virginia, in the Census of Agriculture, 1860 (microfilm copy in Virginia State Library, Richmond), and Henry A. McCormick to Weaver, July 27, 1855, Weaver–Brady Papers, Virginia.

45. See entries for June 1853, Buffalo Forge Time Book, 1843–53, Weaver–Brady Papers, Virginia, and Shields & Somerville to Weaver, July 14, 1854, Weaver Papers, Duke.

46. "William Weaver," Rockbridge County, Virginia, Census of Agriculture, 1860.

47. "Farming of Mr. William Weaver . . . ," 412.

48. Lexington *Gazette*, April 10, 17, 1845.

49. Ibid., April 17, 1845.

50. Ibid., May 1, 1845.

51. Ibid., April 9, 16, 1846.

52. Lexington *Valley Star*, December 12, 1850.

53. John W. Knapp, "Trade and Transportation in Rockbridge: The First Hundred Years," *Proceedings of the Rockbridge Historical Society*, 9 (1975–79), 229.

54. Weaver to Davidson, November 21, 1856, Weaver–Brady Papers, Virginia.

I.8: Etna Furnace

1. Buffalo Forge Negro Books, 1830–40, 1844–50, 1850–57, Weaver–Brady Papers, University of Virginia Library, Charlottesville (hereafter cited as Weaver–Brady Papers, Virginia).

2. W. H. Kiblinger, "The Victoria Furnace," *Louisa County* [Virginia] *Historical Magazine*, 19 (Spring 1988), 15–18; Mayburry's land purchases can be traced in Deed Books W, pp. 372–73, 409, and X, pp. 46–47, 56–57, 104–105, Louisa County Court House, Louisa, Virginia.

3. Bill of Complaint of William A. Gillespie, June 1, 1841, Case Papers, Thomas Mayburry's Administrator *v.* Sophia Jolly & Others, Superior Court of Chancery Records, Louisa County Court House, Louisa, Virginia (hereafter cited as Case Papers, Mayburry's Administrator *v.* Jolly); "Inventory and Appraisement of the personal Estate of Thomas Mayburry," August 13, 17, 1840, Will Book 10, p. 355, Louisa County Court House, Louisa, Virginia.

4. Bill of Complaint of William A. Gillespie, June 1, 1841, Case Papers, Mayburry's Administrator *v.* Jolly.

5. Ibid.; "Inventory and Appraisement of the personal Estate of Thomas Mayburry," August 13, 17, 1840, Will Book 10, p. 355, and "Thomas Mayburry dec'd. Settlement," Will Book 11, p. 190, Louisa County Court House, Louisa, Virginia.

6. "Thomas Mayburry dec'd. Settlement," Will Book 11, p. 190, Louisa County Court House, Louisa, Virginia.

7. Decree, September 16, 1842, Case Papers, Mayburry's Administrator *v.* Jolly.

8. "Thomas Mayburry dec'd. Settlement," Will Book 11, p. 190, Louisa County Court House, Louisa, Virginia. See also "Report of the Admr. of Thomas Mayburry dec'd. . . . ," April 1843, Case Papers, Mayburry's Administrator *v.* Jolly.

9. Indenture between William Weaver & Constant W. Newkirk, November 17, 1843, Deed Book Y, pp. 213–15, Rockbridge County Court House, Lexington, Virginia.

10. Deposition of John Doyle, July 15, 1851, Case Papers, Weaver *v.* Jordan, Davis & Co., Superior Court of Chancery Records, Rockbridge County Court House, Lexington, Virginia (hereafter cited as Case Papers, Weaver *v.* Jordan, Davis & Co.).

11. "Agreement . . . between William Weaver . . . and Samuel Sherrerd," August 14, 1845, Weaver–Brady Papers, Virginia.

12. William Weaver to Allbright Sherrerd & Co., January 21, 1850, William Weaver Papers, Duke University Library, Durham, North Carolina (hereafter cited as Weaver Papers, Duke).

13. Ibid.; Indenture between William Weaver and Samuel Sherrerd, February 1, 1847, Deed Book Z, pp. 426–30, Rockbridge County Court House, Lexington, Virginia.

14. Weaver to James D. Davidson, May 6, 1849, Cyrus H. McCormick Papers, State Historical Society of Wisconsin, Madison.

15. Ibid.

16. Indenture between Samuel Sherrerd and William Weaver, August 15, 1849, Deed Book AA, p. 349, and entry for September 11, 1849, Chancery Court Order Book 1847–52, Rockbridge County Court House, Lexington, Virginia.

17. Weaver to Allbright Sherrerd & Co., January 21, 1850, Weaver Papers, Duke.

18. Samuel McDowell Moore to Matthew Bryan, January 9, 1851, Matthew Bryan Correspondence, William Massie Collection, Barker Texas History Center, University of Texas at Austin; see also Moore to Bryan, September 24, 1851, ibid.

19. "Inventory of the personal Estate of Matthew Bryan Dec'd.," April 28, 1854, Will Book 13, pp. 83–85, Rockbridge County Court House, Lexington, Virginia.

20. Manuscript Slave Schedules, Rockbridge County, Virginia, Seventh Census of the United States, 1850, National Archives Microfilm Publications, M-432.

21. "Inventory of the personal Estate of Matthew Bryan Dec.d.," April 28, 1854.

22. "Matthew Bryan's Sale Bill," December 15, 1854, Will Book No. 13, p. 287, Rockbridge County Court House, Lexington, Virginia; John Crobarger's land purchases can be traced in Deed Books 48, p. 367, 49, p. 437, 52, p. 199, 53, p. 64, and 56, p. 290, Albemarle County Court House, Charlottesville, Virginia.

23. Manuscript Slave Schedules, Albemarle County, Virginia, Eighth Census of the United States, 1860, National Archives Microfilm Publications, M-653.

24. J. P. Lesley, *The Iron Manufacturer's Guide to the Furnaces, Forges and Rolling Mills of the United States* . . . (New York: John Wiley, 1859), 69–70; Manuscript Slave Schedules, Augusta County, Virginia, Eighth Census of the United States, 1860, National Archives Microfilm Publications, M-653.

25. Etna Furnace Negro Book, 1854–61, Weaver–Brady Papers, Virginia.

26. Richmond *Daily Dispatch,* January 7, 1854.

27. Deposition of John Doyle, July 15, 1851, Case Papers, Weaver *v.* Jordan, Davis & Co.; Bath Forge Bar Iron and Anchony Book, 1850–52, and entries under "Bath Forge" in Buffalo Forge Ledger, 1851–59, Weaver–Brady Papers in the possession of T. T. Brady, Richmond, Virginia (hereafter cited as Weaver–Brady Papers, T. T. Brady); Joseph L. Taylor to Weaver, February 5, 1854, Weaver Papers, Duke.

28. "Statement of purchase of Etna Furnace . . . by William Weaver and John & Thomas Cartmill . . . ," January 20, 1851, William W. Boyd to Davidson, February 6, 1851, Weaver to Davidson, February 14, 1851, and "Deed . . . between William Weaver . . . & Thomas Cartmill & John Cartmill . . . ," March 3, 1851, Weaver Papers, Duke.

29. See entries for March 29–31, September 24–28, 1853, Buffalo Forge Time Book, 1843–53, Weaver–Brady Papers, Virginia; Lesley, *Iron Manufacturer's Guide,* 73.

30. Newkirk to Davidson, September 1, 1853, Weaver–Brady Papers, T. T. Brady.

31. "Report of the Committee appointed to enquire into and report on the condition of the Coal and Iron Trades," Richmond *Whig,* December 17, 1850.

32. Prices were regularly quoted in the commercial columns of the Richmond press; see, e.g., Richmond *Daily Dispatch,* July 1, September 1, October 28, 1859.

33. Conveyance of John & Thomas Cartmill to William Weaver, October 20, 1853, Deed Book 32, p. 636, Botetourt County Court House, Fincastle, Virginia.

34. James Watkins to Francis T. Anderson, August 13, 1849, Francis T. Anderson Papers, Duke University Library, Durham, North Carolina; deposition of James Watkins, July 15, 1851, Case Papers, Weaver *v.* Jordan, Davis & Co.; James K. Watkins to Weaver, January 3, 1854, Weaver Papers, Duke.

35. Hiring authorization for James Watkins, November 25, 1853, Weaver–Brady Papers, Virginia; Weaver to Davidson, January 23, 1854, James D. Davidson Papers, McCormick Collection, State Historical Society of Wisconsin, Madison (hereafter cited as Davidson Papers, McCormick Collection); see opening entry in Etna Furnace Journal, 1854–57, Special Collections Department, Washington & Lee University Library, Lexington, Virginia (hereafter cited as Etna Furnace Journal, 1854–57, Washington & Lee).

36. Weaver to Davidson, January 23, 1854, Davidson Papers, McCormick Collection.

37. Etna Furnace Time Book, 1854–58, Weaver–Brady Papers, Virginia; "Memorandum of Cash Due Negroes," December 1854, Weaver Papers, Duke.

38. Etna Furnace Time Book, 1854–58, Weaver–Brady Papers, Virginia.

39. Ibid.

40. Depositions of Isaac Peterson, August 18, 1836, June 18, 1839, and Ira F. Jordan, March 4, 1839, Case Papers, Weaver *v.* Jordan, Davis & Co.; James Coleman to Weaver, February 19, 1856, Weaver Papers, Duke; Etna Furnace Time Book, 1854–58, Weaver–Brady Papers, Virginia.

41. Weaver to Davidson, May 20, 1854, Weaver–Brady Papers, Virginia.

42. Daniel C. E. Brady to Weaver, August 8, 1854, Weaver Papers, Duke.

43. Etna Furnace Time Book, 1854–58, Weaver–Brady Papers, Virginia.

44. "Memorandum of Cash Due Negroes," December 1854, Weaver Papers, Duke.

45. T. R. Towles to Weaver, November 27, 1854, ibid.

46. Mary E. Gregory to Weaver, December 29, 1854, ibid.

47. O. L. Chewning to Francis T. Anderson, December 14, 1855, Anderson Family Papers, University of Virginia Library, Charlottesville.

48. See entries for Etna Furnace, May 31, 1854, Buffalo Forge Journal, 1850–59, Weaver–Brady Papers, Virginia.

49. Etna Furnace Time Book, 1854–58, ibid.

50. John K. Watkins to Weaver, July 30, 1854, Weaver Papers, Duke.

51. P. R. Griggs to Weaver, November 20, 1854, ibid.

52. "Hands at Etna Furnace 1855," Etna Furnace Time Book, 1854–58, Weaver–Brady Papers, Virginia.

53. Davidson to Weaver, December 17, 1854, James D. Davidson Papers, Duke University Library, Durham, North Carolina.

54. Weaver to Davidson, January 10, 1855, Davidson Papers, McCormick Collection.

55. Weaver to Davidson, January 18, 1855, Jordan & Irvine Papers, McCormick Collection, State Historical Society of Wisconsin, Madison.

56. Newkirk to Weaver, January 4, 1855, Weaver Papers, Duke.

57. Etna Furnace Time Book, 1854–58, Weaver–Brady Papers, Virginia.

58. Ibid.

59. Weaver to Davidson, July 12, 1855, Weaver–Brady Papers, Virginia.

60. "Hands at Etna Furnace 1855," Etna Furnace Time Book, 1854–58, ibid.

61. Etna Furnace Negro Book, 1854–61, ibid.

62. Ibid.

63. Ibid.

64. Etna Furnace Time Book, 1854–58, ibid.

65. Etna Furnace Negro Book, 1854–61, ibid.

66. Etna Furnace Time Books, 1854–58, 1855–61, ibid.

67. Weaver to Brady, August 27, 1855, Weaver Papers, Duke.

68. Etna Furnace Journal, 1854–57, Washington & Lee; Etna Furnace Ledger, 1854–57, Weaver–Brady Papers, Virginia.

69. Lee, Rocke & Co. to Weaver, January 8, 1859, and Buffalo Forge Iron Book, 1831–62, Weaver–Brady Papers, Virginia.

70. Henry A. McCormick to Weaver, December 29, 1855, ibid.

71. "1856 arrival of hands," Etna Furnace Time Book, 1854–58, ibid.

72. Weaver to Brady, March 13, 1856, Weaver–Brady Papers, T. T. Brady.

73. "Weaver Family: Memo and Historical Notes," ibid.; Weaver to William W. Rex, March 4, 1854, Peter K. Gorgas to Weaver, April 13, 1854, and John A. Rex to Weaver, July 28, 1856, Weaver Papers, Duke.

74. Weaver to Brady, March 4, 1856, Weaver Papers, Duke.

75. Etna Furnace Time Book, 1854–58, Weaver–Brady Papers, Virginia; Weaver to Brady, March 21, 1856, Weaver Papers, Duke.

76. Weaver to Brady, March 4, 1856, Weaver Papers, Duke.

77. Weaver to Brady, February 19, 28, March 13, 1856, Weaver–Brady Papers, T. T. Brady.

78. "Weaver Family: Memo and Historical Notes," ibid.

79. Weaver to Brady, February 28, March 13, 1856, ibid.

80. Weaver to Brady, August 27, 1855, Weaver Papers, Duke.

81. William W. Rex to Weaver, May 21, 1856, ibid.

82. Etna Furnace Time Book, 1855–61, Weaver–Brady Papers, Virginia.

83. Ibid., and Etna Furnace Ledger, 1854–57, ibid.; Etna Furnace Journal, 1854–57, Washington & Lee.

84. Etna Furnace Time Book, 1855–61, and Etna Furnace Ledger, 1854–57, Weaver–Brady Papers, Virginia; "Memo Cash to Negroes," December 23, 1857, Weaver Papers, Duke.

85. Towles to Weaver, November 11, 1857, Weaver Papers, Duke; "Negro Hire for 1857," Buffalo Forge Journal, 1850–59, Weaver–Brady Papers, Virginia.

86. Charles K. Gorgas to Weaver, November 17, 1857, Weaver Papers, Duke.

87. Gorgas to Weaver, November 29, 1857, ibid.

88. Etna Furnace Time Book, 1854–58, and Etna Furnace Negro Book, 1856–60, Weaver–Brady Papers, Virginia.

89. Etna Furnace Negro Books, 1854–61, 1856–60, ibid.; "Memo Cash to Negroes," December 23, 1857, Weaver Papers, Duke.

90. Etna Furnace Negro Book, 1856–60, and "Negro Hire 1860" and "Negro Hire 1861," Buffalo Forge Journal, 1859–66, Weaver–Brady Papers, Virginia.

91. Etna Furnace Time Book, 1854–58, and entry for September 1, 1855, Buffalo Forge Cash Book, 1849–62, ibid.

92. Etna Furnace Time Book, 1854–58, ibid.

93. William W. Rex to Brady, March 22, 1862, ibid.

94. Etna Furnace Time Book, 1855–61, and Etna Furnace Ledger, 1854–57, ibid.; Etna Furnace Journal, 1854–57, Washington & Lee.

95. "Weaver Family: Memo and Historical Notes," Weaver–Brady Papers, T. T. Brady; Brady to Weaver, April 27, 1854, Weaver Papers, Duke.

96. Brady to Davidson, June 27, 1867, Weaver–Brady Papers, T. T. Brady.

97. "Weaver Family: Memo and Historical Notes," ibid.

98. Daniel Brady's handwriting appears on documents at Buffalo Forge beginning in November 1857; see docket on letter from Robert Coleman to Weaver, November 4, 1857, Weaver–Brady Papers, Virginia.

99. Weaver to Davidson, March 4, 1858, and entries for January–March 1858, Buffalo Forge Journal, 1850–59, ibid.

100. Ibid.; "Weaver Family: Memo and Historical Notes," Weaver–Brady Papers, T. T. Brady.

101. See, e.g., the Lexington *Valley Star*, March 25, April 1, 1858.

102. The first section of Brady's "Home Journal" covers the period from March 15, 1858, to September 30, 1860, and can be found on the interior pages of a volume labeled Bath Iron Works Day Book, 1849–59, Weaver–Brady Papers, Virginia; the second and third volumes of Brady's "Home Journal," covering the period from October 1, 1860, to June 30, 1865, are in the McCormick Collection, State Historical Society of Wisconsin, Madison.

II.1: Sam Williams

1. John A. Rex to James D. Davidson, February 25, 1855, James D. Davidson Papers, McCormick Collection, State Historical Society of Wisconsin, Madison (hereafter cited as Davidson Papers, McCormick Collection). Henry Nash is identified as a cooper in "A list of Male Free Negroes in the S. W. District of Rockbridge County, Va., between the ages of 18 and 50 years," August 7, 1861, James D. Davidson Papers, Washington & Lee University Library, Lexington, Virginia. See also Manuscript Free Schedules, Rockbridge County, Virginia, Eighth Census of the United States, 1860, National Archives Microfilm Publications, M-653.

2. Davidson's notation is on the reverse of Rex to Davidson, February 25, 1855, Davidson Papers, McCormick Collection.

3. Bill of Sale between John S. Wilson and William Weaver, Philadelphia, October 24, 1815, and Bond of Thomas Mayburry for the forthcoming of slaves, December 20, 1828, Case Papers, Weaver *v.* Mayburry, Superior Court of Chancery Records, Augusta County Court House, Staunton, Virginia (hereafter cited as Case Papers, Weaver *v.* Mayburry); "Names, births &c: of Negroes," Weaver–Brady Papers in the possession of T. T. Brady, Richmond, Virginia (hereafter cited as Weaver–Brady Papers, T. T. Brady); "An appraisement of the goods and chattels of William Weaver, deceased," June 1, 1863, Weaver–Brady

Papers, University of Virginia Library, Charlottesville (hereafter cited as Weaver–Brady Papers, Virginia).

4. "Names, births &c: of Negroes," Weaver–Brady Papers, T. T. Brady.

5. "An appraisement . . . ," June 1, 1863, Weaver–Brady Papers, Virginia.

6. William W. Davis to Weaver, July 7, 1832, William Weaver Papers, Duke University Library, Durham, North Carolina (hereafter cited as Weaver Papers, Duke).

7. Mayburry described his movements in detail when he gave a deposition in Weaver's suit against Jordan, Davis & Co.; see deposition of Thomas Mayburry, April 20, 1839, Case Papers, Weaver v. Jordan, Davis & Co., Superior Court of Chancery Records, Rockbridge County Court House, Lexington, Virginia (hereafter cited as Case Papers, Weaver v. Jordan, Davis & Co.).

8. "Article of agreement . . . between Thos. Mayburry & Wm. Weaver . . . ," August 3, 1836, Weaver Papers, Duke.

9. Ibid.; deposition of Thomas Mayburry, April 23, 1839, Case Papers, Weaver v. Jordan, Davis & Co.

10. Buffalo Forge Negro Books, 1830–40, 1844–50, Weaver–Brady Papers, Virginia.

11. Buffalo Forge Negro Book, 1830–40, ibid.

12. "Descriptive List of Negroes hired . . . , Confederate States Nitre and Mining Service, 1865," Weaver–Brady Papers, T. T. Brady.

13. Buffalo Forge Negro Book, 1830–40, Weaver–Brady Papers, Virginia.

14. Buffalo Forge [Bath Forge] Negro Book, 1839–41, and Buffalo Forge Negro Book, 1830–40, ibid.

15. Marriage Register for Rockbridge County, Sub-District "A," 6th District, Virginia, Records of the Bureau of Refugees, Freedmen and Abandoned Lands, Record Group 105, National Archives, Washington, D.C. (hereafter cited as Marriage Register for Rockbridge County, Freedmen's Bureau Records, RG 105, NA).

16. Bath Forge [Bath Furnace] Negro Book, 1839–42, Weaver–Brady Papers, Virginia.

17. "Names, births &c: of Negroes," Weaver–Brady Papers, T. T. Brady.

18. Buffalo Forge [Bath Forge] Negro Book, 1839–41, Weaver–Brady Papers, Virginia. For a detailed description of this process, see W. McKee Evans, *Ballots and Fence Rails: Reconstruction on the Lower Cape Fear* (Chapel Hill: University of North Carolina Press, 1967), 195–96.

19. Buffalo Forge [Bath Forge] Negro Book, 1839–41, and Bath Forge [Bath Furnace] Negro Book, 1839–42, Weaver–Brady Papers, Virginia.

20. Ibid.

21. Buffalo Forge [Bath Forge] Negro Book, 1839–41, ibid.

22. Marriage Register for Rockbridge County, Freedmen's Bureau Records, RG 105, NA; "Names, births &c: of Negroes," Weaver–Brady Papers, T. T. Brady.

23. Buffalo Forge Negro Book, 1844–50, Weaver–Brady Papers, Virginia. For Sam's return to Buffalo Forge in the spring of 1842, see entry for May 7 of that year in Buffalo Forge Time Book, 1830–43, ibid.

24. Minutes of the Lexington Baptist Church (typescript), Manly Memorial Baptist Church, Lexington, Virginia. I am indebted to E. Lynn Pearson, a graduate fellow at the Stonewall Jackson House in Lexington in 1989, and to Professor Charles W. Turner of Washington & Lee University for calling this reference to my attention.

25. The best description of the conversion experience is in Mechal Sobel, *Trabelin' On: The Slave Journey to an Afro-Baptist Faith* (Princeton: Princeton University Press, 1988), 108–19.

26. See entry for August 29, 1834, Buffalo Forge Iron Book, 1831–62, Weaver–Brady Papers, Virginia.

27. Interview with Mrs. Mamie Dunn, Glasgow, Virginia, March 11, 1981.

28. See entries for April 22, 23, 25, June 4, September 27, 1859, September 1, 1860,

Daniel C. E. Brady "Home Journal," 1858–60, Weaver–Brady Papers, Virginia.

29. Buffalo Forge Negro Books, 1844–50, 1850–57, ibid.

30. Ibid.

31. See entry for April 27, 1853, Buffalo Forge Time Book, 1843–53, ibid.

32. Buffalo Forge Time Book, 1843–53, Buffalo Forge Cash Book, 1853–63, entries for November 13, 20, 1858, March 17, April 8, November 5, 1859, Daniel C. E. Brady "Home Journal," 1858–60, and Buffalo Forge Negro Book, 1850–57, Weaver–Brady Papers, Virginia; Daniel C. E. Brady "Farm Notebook," 1859–68, Weaver–Brady Papers, T. T. Brady.

33. Buffalo Forge Time Book, 1843–53, Buffalo Forge Cash Book, 1853–63, and Buffalo Forge Negro Book, 1850–57, Weaver–Brady Papers, Virginia.

34. See, e.g., "An appraisement . . . ," June 1, 1863, ibid.

35. Buffalo Forge Negro Book, 1850–57, ibid.

36. See Table A-2, Consumer Price Indexes, United States, in John J. McCusker, *How Much Is That in Real Money? A Historical Price Index for Use as a Deflator of Money Values in the Economy of the United States* (Worcester, MA: American Antiquarian Society, 1992), 328, 332.

37. Buffalo Forge Negro Books, 1844–50, 1850–57, Weaver–Brady Papers, Virginia.

38. D. C. E. Brady Private Ledger, Weaver–Brady Papers in the possession of D. E. Brady, Jr., Buffalo Forge, Virginia (hereafter cited as Weaver–Brady Papers, D. E. Brady, Jr.).

39. Buffalo Forge Cash Book, 1853–63, Weaver–Brady Papers, Virginia.

40. Brady Farm Notebook, 1859–68, Weaver–Brady Papers, T. T. Brady.

41. McCusker, *How Much Is That In Real Money?*, 328, 332.

42. Brady Private Ledger, Weaver–Brady Papers, D. E. Brady, Jr.

43. Ibid. The history of their savings accounts can be traced by following the entries under their names in: Buffalo Forge Ledger, 1851–59, Weaver–Brady Papers, T. T. Brady; Buffalo Forge Ledger, 1859–78, Weaver–Brady Papers, D. E. Brady, Jr.; Buffalo Forge Journal, 1859–66, Weaver–Brady Papers, Virginia; and Buffalo Forge Journal, 1866–78, Weaver–Brady Papers, D. E. Brady, Jr.

44. "Names, births &c: of Negroes," Weaver–Brady Papers, T. T. Brady.

45. Betty's husband's first initial was given at the time one of their children married in 1876; see marriage registration of Mary C. Coleman and Steward Chandler, July 27, 1876, Register of Marriages, Book 1A, 1865–89, Rockbridge County Court House, Lexington, Virginia.

46. "Mr. Weaver Dr to D. L. Morgan," January–May, 1858, Weaver Papers, Duke.

II.2: Henry Towles

1. Deposition of John Doyle, February 7, 1840, Case Papers, Weaver *v.* Jordan, Davis & Co., Superior Court of Chancery Records, Rockbridge County Court House, Lexington, Virginia.

2. "Names, births &c: of Negroes," Weaver–Brady Papers in the possession of T. T. Brady, Richmond, Virginia (hereafter cited as Weaver–Brady Papers, T. T. Brady). See also marriage registration for Edgar Towles, December 31, 1876, Register of Marriages, Book 1A, 1865–89, Rockbridge County Court House, Lexington, Virginia. Prince Towles is sometimes identified as "Prince Tolles River"; see, e.g., list of shoes distributed in 1854 in Buffalo Forge Negro Book, 1850–57, Weaver–Brady Papers, University of Virginia Library, Charlottesville (hereafter cited as Weaver–Brady Papers, Virginia).

3. David Tinder to William Weaver, March 10, 1828, and "Memorandum of hired negroes at Bath Iron Works for 1829," William Weaver Papers, Duke University Library, Durham, North Carolina (hereafter cited as Weaver Papers, Duke).

4. Buffalo Forge Negro Books, 1830–40, 1850–57, Weaver–Brady Papers, Virginia.

5. "Names, births &c: of Negroes," Weaver–Brady Papers, T. T. Brady.

6. "Descriptive List of Negroes hired . . . , Confederate States Nitre and Mining Service, 1865," Weaver–Brady Papers, T. T. Brady.

7. Buffalo Forge Negro Book, 1850–57, Weaver–Brady Papers, Virginia.

8. Ibid.

9. Buffalo Forge Time Book, 1843–53, and Buffalo Forge Negro Book, 1850–57, ibid.; "Names, births &c: of Negroes," Weaver–Brady Papers, T. T. Brady.

10. "Names, births &c: of Negroes," Weaver–Brady Papers, T. T. Brady.

11. Register of Births, Book 1, 1853–70, Rockbridge County Court House, Lexington, Virginia.

12. Buffalo Forge Negro Book, 1850–57, Weaver–Brady Papers, Virginia.

13. Register of Births, Book 1, 1853–70, and Register of Deaths, Book 1, 1853–70, Rockbridge County Court House, Lexington, Virginia.

14. Buffalo Forge Negro Book, 1850–57, Weaver–Brady Papers, Virginia.

15. "Names, births &c: of Negroes," Weaver–Brady Papers, T. T. Brady.

16. Buffalo Forge Negro Book, 1850–57, Weaver–Brady Papers, Virginia.

II.3: Tooler

1. Buffalo Forge Negro Book, 1830–40, Weaver–Brady Papers, University of Virginia Library, Charlottesville.

2. Ibid.

3. Buffalo Forge [Bath Forge] Negro Book, 1839–41, Buffalo Forge [Bath Furnace] Negro Book, 1839–42, and Buffalo Forge Negro Books, 1830–40, 1844–50, 1850–57, ibid.

4. Buffalo Forge Wood Book, 1831–41, Buffalo Forge Negro Book, 1830–40, and Buffalo Forge Iron Book, 1831–62, ibid.

5. Buffalo Forge Time Book, 1843–53, ibid.

6. Buffalo Forge Negro Book, 1830–40, ibid.

7. Ibid.

8. See entries for July 3, 1847, February 12, 1848, Buffalo Forge Iron Book, 1831–62, entries for October 23, 27, 1851, April 26, July 3, 8, September 3, 8, 1852, Buffalo Forge Time Book, 1843–53, and Buffalo Forge Negro Book, 1830–40, ibid.

9. Buffalo Forge Negro Books, 1830–40, 1844–50, ibid.

10. See entries for March 11, July 22, 1837, Buffalo Forge Iron Book, 1831–62, and entries for July 31, September 13, 15, 16, 27, 1852, Buffalo Forge Time Book, 1843–53, ibid.

11. Buffalo Forge Negro Book, 1830–40, ibid.

12. Buffalo Forge Negro Book, 1844–50, ibid.

13. Ibid.

14. Buffalo Forge Negro Books, 1844–50, 1850–57, ibid.

15. Buffalo Forge Iron Book, 1831–62, and Buffalo Forge Negro Books, 1844–50, 1850–57, ibid.

16. Buffalo Forge Iron Book, 1831–62, ibid.

17. Ibid., and Buffalo Forge Negro Book, 1850–57, ibid.

18. Buffalo Forge Negro Book, 1850–57, ibid.

19. Buffalo Forge Iron Book, 1831–62, ibid.

II.4: Harry Hunt, Jr.

1. "List of Slaves at the Oxford Iron Works in Families and Their Employment, Taken 15 January 1811," William Bolling Papers, Duke University Library, Durham, North Carolina (hereafter cited as Bolling Papers, Duke).

2. Buffalo Forge Negro Book, 1830–40, Weaver–Brady Papers, University of Vir-

ginia Library, Charlottesville (hereafter cited as Weaver–Brady Papers, Virginia).

3. Ibid.; Buffalo Forge [Bath Forge] Negro Book, 1839–41, and entry for "Bath Forge Dr.," January 15, 1839, Buffalo Forge Journal, 1834–41, ibid.

4. Buffalo Forge Time Book, 1830–43, ibid.; "List of Slaves at the Oxford Iron Works . . . ," Bolling Papers, Duke.

5. Buffalo Forge [Bath Forge] Negro Book, 1839–41, Weaver–Brady Papers, Virginia.

6. Buffalo Forge Time Book, 1830–43, and Buffalo Forge Negro Book, 1844–50, ibid.

7. Buffalo Forge Iron Book, 1831–62, and Buffalo Forge Negro Book, 1844–50, ibid.

8. "Descriptive List of Negroes hired . . . , Confederate States Nitre and Mining Service, 1865," Weaver–Brady Papers in the possession of T. T. Brady, Richmond, Virginia (hereafter cited as Weaver–Brady Papers, T. T. Brady).

9. Buffalo Forge Negro Books, 1844–50, 1850–57, Weaver–Brady Papers, Virginia.

10. Ibid.; Marriage registration of Harry Hunt and Charlotte Wade, Marriage Register for Rockbridge County, Sub-District "A," 6th District, Virginia, Records of the Bureau of Refugees, Freedmen and Abandoned Lands, Record Group 105, National Archives, Washington, D. C.

11. Buffalo Forge Iron Book, 1831–62, and Buffalo Forge Time Book, 1843–53, Weaver–Brady Papers, Virginia.

12. Buffalo Forge Negro Books, 1844–50, 1850–57, and entries for December 27–28, 1853, Buffalo Forge Cash Book, 1853–63, ibid.

13. William Weaver to James D. Davidson, November 2, 1853, James D. Davidson Papers, McCormick Collection, State Historical Society of Wisconsin, Madison.

14. "1853 November Court," Rockbridge County Court Minute Book, 1852–54, Rockbridge County Court House, Lexington, Virginia, 189, 197–200.

15. Ibid., 199.

16. Ibid., 197.

17. Ibid., 200–201.

18. Buffalo Forge Iron Book, 1831–62, Weaver–Brady Papers, Virginia.

19. Ibid., and Buffalo Forge Negro Book, 1850–57, ibid.

20. "Descriptive List of Negroes hired . . . 1865," Weaver–Brady Papers, T. T. Brady.

21. "An appraisement of the goods and chattels of William Weaver, deceased," June 1, 1863, Weaver–Brady Papers, Virginia.

II.5: Henry Matthews

1. The range of Matthews's activities can be traced in the Buffalo Forge Iron Book, 1831–62, Buffalo Forge Time Book, 1843–53, Buffalo Forge Negro Books, 1844–50, 1850–57, Buffalo Forge Smith Shop Book, 1863–66, and D. C. E. Brady, "Farm & Home Journal," 1858, all in the Weaver–Brady Papers, University of Virginia Library, Charlottesville (hereafter cited as Weaver–Brady Papers, Virginia); information on the replacement of forge anvil blocks can be found in the deposition of William Weaver, December 10, 1839, Case Papers, John Alexander v. Sidney S. Baxter, Administrator of John Irvine & Others, Superior Court of Chancery Records, Rockbridge County Court House, Lexington, Virginia.

2. Buffalo Forge Negro Books, 1830–40, 1844–50, 1850–57, and entries for November 1–3, 1853, Buffalo Forge Time Book, 1843–53, Weaver–Brady Papers, Virginia; see also death registration for Charles Crosby [*sic*], October [*sic*] 1853, Register of Deaths, Book 1, 1853–70, Rockbridge County Court House, Lexington, Virginia.

3. Buffalo Forge [Bath Forge] Negro Book, 1839–41, Bath Iron Works Negro Book, 1846, and Buffalo Forge Negro Book, 1844–50, Weaver–Brady Papers, Virginia.

4. "Descriptive List of Negroes hired . . . , Confederate States Nitre and Mining

Service, 1865," Weaver–Brady Papers in the possession of T. T. Brady, Richmond, Virginia (hereafter cited as Weaver–Brady Papers, T. T. Brady).

5. "Names, births &c: of Negroes," ibid.; death registration for Charles Crosby [*sic*], October [*sic*] 1853, Rockbridge County Register of Deaths, Book 1, 1853–70; Buffalo Forge Negro Books, 1830–40, 1844–50, and 1850–57, Weaver–Brady Papers, Virginia.

6. Buffalo Forge Negro Book, 1830–40, and Buffalo Forge [Bath Forge] Negro Book 1839–41, Weaver–Brady Papers, Virginia.

7. Bath Iron Works Negro Book, 1846, ibid.

8. "Names, births &c: of Negroes," Weaver–Brady Papers, T. T. Brady.

9. Buffalo Forge Iron Book, 1831–62, and Buffalo Forge Negro Book, 1844–50, Weaver–Brady Papers, Virginia.

10. Buffalo Forge Negro Books, 1844–50, 1850–57, ibid.

11. Buffalo Forge Time Book, 1843–53, ibid.; death registration for Charles Crosby [*sic*], October [*sic*] 1853, Rockbridge County Register of Deaths, Book 1, 1853–70.

12. Buffalo Forge Negro Book, 1850–57, Weaver–Brady Papers, Virginia.

13. Ibid.; "Names, births &c: of Negroes," Weaver–Brady Papers, T. T. Brady.

14. Mary Ellen Matthews's death registration stated that she was seven months old when she died on September 1, 1856; see Rockbridge County Register of Deaths, Book 1, 1853–70.

15. Ibid.

16. See Todd L. Savitt, *Medicine and Slavery: The Diseases and Health Care of Blacks in Antebellum Virginia* (Urbana: University of Illinois Press, 1978), 63–64, 128–29, and Savitt, "Slave Health and Southern Distinctiveness," in Savitt and James Harvey Young, eds., *Disease and Distinctiveness in the American South* (Knoxville: University of Tennessee Press, 1988), 140.

17. Buffalo Forge Iron Book, 1831–62, and Buffalo Forge Negro Book, 1850–57, Weaver–Brady Papers, Virginia.

II.6: Garland Thompson and His Family

1. Buffalo Forge Iron Book, 1831–62, and Buffalo Forge Negro Books, 1830–40, 1844–50, 1850–57, Weaver–Brady Papers, University of Virginia Library, Charlottesville (hereafter cited as Weaver–Brady Papers, Virginia).

2. "Names, births &c: of Negroes," Weaver–Brady Papers in the possession of T. T. Brady, Richmond, Virginia (hereafter cited as Weaver–Brady Papers, T. T. Brady). Eliza Thompson's birthdate is indicated in her marriage registration; see Marriage Register for Rockbridge County, Sub-District "A," 6th District, Virginia, Records of the Bureau of Refugees, Freedmen and Abandoned Lands, Record Group 105, National Archives, Washington, D.C. (hereafter cited as Marriage Register for Rockbridge County, Freedmen's Bureau Records, RG 105, NA); Matilda Thompson's birthdate is indicated in Deed of conveyance, William Weaver to Mary Davidson, February 20, 1849, Deed Book CC, p. 390, Rockbridge County Court House, Lexington, Virginia.

3. Buffalo Forge Negro Book, 1830–40, Weaver–Brady Papers, Virginia.

4. Buffalo Forge Negro Book, 1844–50, ibid.

5. "Names, births &c: of Negroes," Weaver–Brady Papers, T. T. Brady.

6. Buffalo Forge Negro Book, 1850–57, Weaver–Brady Papers, Virginia.

7. Marriage Register for Rockbridge County, Freedmen's Bureau Records, RG 105, NA.

8. Buffalo Forge Negro Book, 1844–50, Weaver–Brady Papers, Virginia.

9. Interview with James Thompson, Glasgow, Virginia, December 13, 1977.

10. "Descriptive List of Negroes hired . . ., Confederate States Nitre and Mining Service, 1865," Weaver–Brady Papers, T. T. Brady.

11. Interview with James Thompson, December 13, 1977.

12. Ibid.

13. Samuel Sydney Bradford, "The Ante-Bellum Charcoal Iron Industry of Virginia" (unpublished Ph.D. dissertation, Columbia University, 1958), 127 *n.*45; interview with D. E. Brady, Jr., Buffalo Forge, Virginia, October 7, 1977.

14. Interview with James Thompson, March 7, 1981.

15. Buffalo Forge Iron Book, 1831–62, and Buffalo Forge Negro Book, 1844–50, Weaver–Brady Papers, Virginia.

16. Buffalo Forge Negro Book, 1844–50, ibid.

17. David Ross to William J. Dunn, January 1813, David Ross Letterbook, 1812–13, Virginia Historical Society, Richmond; see also Charles B. Dew, "David Ross and the Oxford Iron Works: A Study of Industrial Slavery in the Early Nineteenth-Century South," *William and Mary Quarterly,* 3rd Series, 31 (April 1974), 207.

18. Buffalo Forge Negro Books, 1844–50, 1850–57, Weaver–Brady Papers, Virginia.

19. Interviews with James Thompson, December 13, 1977, March 7, 1981.

20. See entry for George Obenchain, "William Weaver Ledger Bath Forge 1849," in Buffalo Forge Cash Book, 1849–62, and George Obenchain to William Weaver, November 27, 1849, Weaver–Brady Papers, Virginia.

21. Interview with James Thompson, December 13, 1977.

22. Buffalo Forge Iron Book, 1831–62, and Buffalo Forge Negro Books, 1844–50, 1850–57, Weaver–Brady Papers, Virginia.

23. See Manuscript Population Schedules, Rockbridge County, Virginia, Tenth Census of the United States, 1880, National Archives Microfilm Publications, T-9; Ann O. Davis to William W. Davis, February 4, 1858, Jordan & Davis Papers, McCormick Collection, State Historical Society of Wisconsin, Madison (hereafter cited as Jordan & Davis Papers, McCormick Collection).

24. Mary Dickinson to Ann O. Davis, August 22, 1848, William W. Davis Family Papers, University of Virginia Library, Charlottesville (hereafter cited as Davis Family Papers, Virginia).

25. See bond of William W. Davis to Mary Dickinson for hire of Garland, Daniel & Johnny, December 29, 1853, Jordan & Davis Papers, McCormick Collection.

26. Mary Dickinson to Ann O. Davis, August 22, 1848, Davis Family Papers, Virginia.

27. Mary Dickinson to Ann O. Davis, August 28, 1852, ibid.

28. Last Will & Testament of Mary Dickinson, October 1, 1855, Will Book 14, p. 354, Louisa County Court House, Louisa, Virginia.

29. Hire bonds of William W. Davis to Mary Dickinson, December 29, 1853, January 27, 1855, Jordan & Davis Papers, McCormick Collection.

30. James C. Davis to William W. Davis, January 5, 1856, Davis Family Papers, Virginia.

31. Article of agreement between William W. Davis and Matthew M. Bryan and James C. Davis, February 13, 1856, Jordan & Davis Papers, McCormick Collection.

32. C. Davis to William W. Davis, December 20, 1856, ibid.

33. Ann O. Davis to William W. Davis, February 4, 1858, ibid.

34. Last Will & Testament of Mary Dickinson, October 1, 1855, Will Book 14, p. 354, Louisa County Court House, Louisa, Virginia.

35. Ann O. Davis to William W. Davis, February 4, 1858, Jordan & Davis Papers, McCormick Collection.

36. J. Cole Davis to William W. Davis, December 27, 1854, ibid.

37. J. Cole Davis to William W. Davis, January 7, 1856, ibid.

38. James C. Davis to William W. Davis, January 5, 1856, Davis Family Papers, Virginia.

39. Ann O. Davis to William W. Davis, February 4, 1858, Jordan & Davis Papers, McCormick Collection.

40. Manuscript Slave Schedules, Rockbridge County, Virginia, Eighth Census of the United States, 1860, National Archives Microfilm Publications, M-653.

41. Daniel C. E. Brady, "Home Journal," 1860–65, McCormick Collection, State Historical Society of Wisconsin, Madison.

42. Ann O. Davis to William W. Davis, February 8, 1864, Jordan & Davis Papers, ibid.

43. Manuscript Population Schedules, Rockbridge County, Virginia, Ninth Census of the United States, 1870, National Archives Microfilm Publications, M-593.

44. Marriage registration of Wilson Botetourt King and Eliza Thompson, Marriage Register for Rockbridge County, Freedmen's Bureau Records, RG 105, NA; "Names, birth &c: of Negroes," Weaver–Brady Papers, T. T. Brady.

45. Buffalo Forge Negro Book, 1850–57, Weaver–Brady Papers, Virginia.

46. Ibid.

47. Manuscript Population Schedules, Rockbridge County, Virginia, Ninth Census of the United States, 1870, National Archives Microfilm Publications, M-593.

48. Buffalo Forge Negro Book, 1850–57, Weaver–Brady Papers, Virginia.

49. See entries in Daniel C. E. Brady, "Home Journal," 1858–60, ibid.

50. Marriage registration of Garland Thompson and Ester Boldock, Marriage Register for Rockbridge County, Freedmen's Bureau Records, RG 105, NA.

51. William Weaver to Alfred Douglass, October 7, 1853, Weaver–Brady Papers, Virginia.

52. Interview with James Thompson, December 13, 1977.

53. Marriage Register for Rockbridge County, Freedmen's Bureau Records, RG 105, NA.

54. See entries in Brady, "Home Journal," 1858–60, Weaver–Brady Papers, Virginia.

55. "Descriptive List of Negroes hired … 1865," Weaver–Brady Papers, T. T. Brady.

56. Interview with James Thompson, March 7, 1981.

III.1: The Late Antebellum Years

1. William Weaver to James D. Davison, March 4, 1858, Weaver–Brady Papers, University of Virginia Library, Charlottesville (hereafter cited as Weaver–Brady Papers, Virginia).

2. Davidson to Weaver, January 6, 1858, William Weaver Papers, Duke University Library, Durham, North Carolina (hereafter cited as Weaver Papers, Duke).

3. Weaver to Davidson, January 7, 1857 [*sic*], James D. Davidson Papers, McCormick Collection, State Historical Society of Wisconsin, Madison (hereafter cited as Davidson Papers, McCormick Collection).

4. "Negro hire," January 6, 1858, Buffalo Forge Journal, 1850–59, Weaver Brady Papers, Virginia.

5. William D. Couch & Co. to Weaver, February 9, 1859, Weaver Papers, Duke; Buffalo Forge Iron Book, 1831–62, Weaver–Brady Papers, Virginia.

6. Daniel C. E. Brady, "Home Journal," 1858–60, and "Farm & Home Journal," 1858, and Buffalo Forge Iron Book, 1831–62, Weaver–Brady Papers, Virginia.

7. Brady, "Home Journal," 1858–60, and "Farm & Home Journal," 1858, ibid.

8. Ibid.

9. Ibid., and Buffalo Forge Iron Book, 1831–62, ibid.

10. Brady, "Home Journal," 1858–60, ibid.

11. Ibid., and Brady, "Farm & Home Journal," 1858, ibid.

12. Brady, "Home Journal," 1858–60, and Buffalo Forge Iron Book, 1831–62, ibid.

13. Brady, "Home Journal," 1858–60, ibid.

14. Buffalo Forge Iron Book, 1831–62, ibid.

15. The exact total due was $8,235; see "Negro Hire," January 6, 1858, Buffalo Forge Journal, 1850–59, ibid.

16. Brady, "Home Journal," 1858–60, ibid.

17. Buffalo Forge Iron Book, 1831–62, ibid.

18. Ibid.

19. Brady, "Home Journal," 1858–60, ibid.

20. Ibid.

21. Ibid.

22. Ibid., and Buffalo Forge Iron Book, 1831–62, ibid.

23. Brady, "Home Journal," 1858–60, ibid.; "Weaver Family: Memo and Historical Notes," Weaver–Brady Papers in the possession of T. T. Brady, Richmond, Virginia (hereafter cited as Weaver–Brady Papers, T. T. Brady).

24. "Names, births &c: of Negroes," Weaver–Brady Papers, T. T. Brady; Marriage Register for Rockbridge County, Sub-District "A," 6th District, Virginia, Records of the Bureau of Refugees, Freedmen and Abandoned Lands, Record Group 105, National Archives, Washington, D.C.

25. Brady, "Home Journal," 1858–60, Weaver–Brady Papers, Virginia.

26. Buffalo Forge Iron Book, 1831–62, ibid.

27. Brady, "Home Journal," 1858–60, ibid.

28. Ibid.

29. Charles K. Gorgas to Weaver, October 25, 1858, Weaver Papers, Duke.

30. Buffalo Forge Journal, 1850–59, and F. B. Deane, Jr., & Son to Weaver, January 13, 1859, Weaver–Brady Papers, Virginia; see also Shields & Somerville to Weaver, February 8, 1859, ibid.

31. Brady, "Home Journal," 1858–60, ibid.

32. Ibid.; Roy P. Basler, ed., *The Collected Works of Abraham Lincoln*, 8 vols. (New Brunswick, NJ: Rutgers University Press, 1953), 3:1–37.

33. Brady, "Home Journal," 1858–60, Weaver–Brady Papers, Virginia; Basler, ed., *Lincoln Works*, 3:51.

34. Brady, "Home Journal," 1858–60, Weaver–Brady Papers, Virginia; Basler, ed., *Lincoln Works*, 3:254.

35. Lexington *Valley Star*, November 11, 1858.

36. William W. Rex to Weaver, January 8, 1859, Weaver–Brady Papers, Virginia.

37. Greenlee Davidson to James D. Davidson, January 9, 1859, Davidson Papers, McCormick Collection.

38. Gorgas to Weaver, February 3, 1859, Weaver–Brady Papers, Virginia.

39. Lee, Rocke & Co. to Weaver, January 8, 1859, ibid.

40. Irby & Saunders to Weaver, January 29, 1859, ibid.

41. Thomas G. Godwin to Weaver, September 26, 1859, and Buffalo Forge Iron Book, 1831–62, ibid.

42. Shields & Somerville to Weaver, February 8, May 10, 1859, F. B. Deane, Jr., & Son to Weaver, March 28, April 2, 7, 1859, and James Boyd & Co. to Weaver, September 30, 1859, ibid.

43. Rex to Brady, February 18, 19, 1859, ibid.

44. Etna Furnace Negro Book, 1856–59, ibid.

45. J. E. Carson to Weaver, March 12, 1859, Weaver Papers, Duke.

46. Carson to Weaver, May 30, 1859, ibid.

47. Buffalo Forge Cash Book, 1853–63, Weaver–Brady Papers, Virginia.

48. Brady, "Home Journal," 1858–60, ibid.

49. Carson to Weaver, June 27, 1859, Weaver Papers, Duke.

50. Weaver to Carson, July 2, 1859, Weaver Letterbook, Weaver–Brady Papers, Virginia.

51. Brady, "Home Journal," 1858–60, ibid.; Carson to Weaver, July 9, 1859, Weaver–Brady Papers, T. T. Brady.

52. Carson to Weaver, July 25, 1859, Weaver–Brady Papers, Virginia.

53. Brady, "Home Journal," 1858–60, and Buffalo Forge Cash Book, 1853–63, ibid.

54. Henry A. McCormick to Weaver, July 21, 1859, ibid.
55. Brady, "Home Journal," 1858–60, ibid.
56. McCormick to Weaver, November 19, 1859, ibid.
57. Gorgas to Weaver, March 29, 1859, ibid.
58. Gorgas to Weaver, April 6, 1859, ibid.
59. Gorgas to Weaver, May 6, 1859, ibid.
60. Gorgas to Brady, August 11, 1859, ibid.
61. Gorgas to Weaver, April 11, May 29, 1859, ibid.
62. Etna Furnace Time Book, 1859–61, ibid.
63. Rex to Brady, March 4, 1859, ibid.
64. Gorgas to Weaver, May 24, 1859, ibid.
65. Gorgas to Weaver, July 27, August 4, September 15, 1859, and Gorgas to Brady, August 11, 1859, ibid.
66. Gorgas to Weaver, September 22, 1859, ibid.
67. Gorgas to Weaver, October 6, 1859, ibid.
68. Lee, Rocke & Co. to Weaver, June 7, 9, July 14, 1859, ibid.
69. Brady to Lee, Rocke & Co., July 18, 1859, Weaver Letterbooks, ibid.
70. Lee, Rocke & Co. to Weaver, July 30, 1859, ibid.
71. Brady to Lee, Rocke & Co., August 16, 1859, Weaver Letterbooks, and Buffalo Forge Iron Book, 1831–62, ibid.
72. Lee, Rocke & Co. to Weaver, August 29, September 3, 1859, ibid.
73. Lee, Rocke & Co. to Weaver, September 10, 17, 1859, ibid.
74. Brady to Lee, Rocke & Co., September 20, 1859, Weaver Letterbooks, and Buffalo Forge Iron Book, 1831–62, ibid.
75. Brady, "Home Journal," 1858–60, ibid.
76. Brady to Lee, Rocke & Co., June 13, 1859, Weaver Letterbooks, ibid.
77. See Lee, Rocke & Co. to Weaver, June 7, 1859, ibid.
78. The pattern of forge work and production in 1859 can be traced in the Buffalo Forge Iron Book, 1831–62, and Brady, "Home Journal," 1858–60, ibid.
79. Lee, Rocke & Co. to Weaver, September 17, 1859, ibid.
80. Buffalo Forge Iron Book, 1831–62, ibid.
81. Brady, "Home Journal," 1858–60, ibid.
82. Ibid., and Buffalo Forge Iron Book, 1831–62, ibid.
83. Brady, "Home Journal," 1858–60, ibid.

III.2: The Eve of War

1. Lexington *Gazette,* October 27, 1859.
2. Lexington *Valley Star,* October 27, 1859.
3. Lexington *Gazette,* November 10, 1859.
4. Ibid., November 24, 1859.
5. Ibid.
6. Jacob Fuller to William Weaver, November 29, 1859, William Weaver Papers, Duke University Library, Durham, North Carolina (hereafter cited as Weaver Papers, Duke).
7. Charles H. Locher to Weaver, December 3, 1859, Weaver–Brady Papers in the possession of T. T. Brady, Richmond, Virginia (hereafter cited as Weaver–Brady Papers, T. T. Brady).
8. Daniel C. E. Brady, "Home Journal," 1858–60, Weaver–Brady Papers, University of Virginia Library, Charlottesville (hereafter cited as Weaver–Brady Papers, Virginia).
9. Ibid.
10. Clarksville *Jeffersonian,* December 3, 1856. See also Charles B. Dew, "Black Iron-

workers and the Slave Insurrection Panic of 1856," *Journal of Southern History,* 41 (August 1975), 321–38.

11. Weaver to W. D. Couch, November 18, 1859, and to Lee, Rocke & Co., November 9, 1859, Weaver Letterbooks, Weaver–Brady Papers, Virginia.

12. Lexington *Gazette,* December 8, 1859.

13. Weaver to Shields & Somerville, December 16, 1859, Weaver Letterbooks, Weaver–Brady Papers, Virginia.

14. Weaver to James D. Davidson, December 16, 1859, ibid.

15. Davidson to Weaver, December 18, 1859, James D. Davidson Papers, Duke University Library, Durham, North Carolina (hereafter cited as Davidson Papers, Duke).

16. Davidson to Weaver, December 22, 1859, ibid.

17. Brady, "Home Journal," 1858–60, Weaver–Brady Papers, Virginia; Register of Deaths, Book 1, 1853–70, Rockbridge County Court House, Lexington, Virginia.

18. Brady, "Home Journal," 1858–60, Weaver–Brady Papers, Virginia; "Weaver Family: Memo and Historical Notes," and "Names, births &c: of Negroes," Weaver–Brady Papers, T. T. Brady.

19. See vaccination record on flyleaf of Buffalo Forge Journal, 1859–66, and Brady, "Home Journal," 1858–60, Weaver–Brady Papers, Virginia.

20. Brady, "Home Journal," 1858–60, ibid.

21. "Names, births &c: of Negroes," Weaver–Brady Papers, T. T. Brady.

22. Davidson to Weaver, January 25, 1860, Weaver Papers, Duke.

23. Weaver to Davidson, January 27, 1860, James D. Davidson Papers, McCormick Collection, State Historical Society of Wisconsin, Madison (hereafter cited as Davidson Papers, McCormick Collection).

24. William W. Rex to Brady, December 31, 1859, Weaver–Brady Papers, Virginia.

25. Charles K. Gorgas to Brady, April 2, 1860, Weaver Papers, Duke.

26. Gorgas to Weaver, February 2, April 20, 1860, Rex to Brady, May 29, 1860, and Rex to Weaver, August 7, 1860, ibid.

27. Rex to Brady, October 2, 26, 1860, ibid.

28. Gorgas to Brady, March 11, 1860, ibid.

29. Rex to Brady, June 29, 1860, ibid.

30. Rex to Brady, September 21, 1860, ibid.

31. Rex to Brady, September 26, October 13, 1860, ibid.

32. Gorgas to Weaver, May 1, 1860, ibid.; Brady, "Home Journal," 1858–60, Weaver–Brady Papers, Virginia.

33. Rex to Weaver, August 15, 27, 1860, Weaver Papers, Duke.

34. Rex to Brady, September 7, 21, 26, October 2, 1860, ibid.

35. Henry A. McCormick to Weaver, October 10, 1860, Cyrus H. McCormick Papers, McCormick Collection, State Historical Society of Wisconsin, Madison.

36. Rex to Brady, January 21, 1860, Weaver Papers, Duke.

37. Her purchase price is given in an entry dated January 22, 1847, Buffalo Forge Journal, 1845–50, Weaver–Brady Papers, Virginia.

38. Johnson's check for $2,900, dated August 14, 1860, was returned to him on October 31; see entry for October 31, 1860, Buffalo Forge Cash Book, 1853–63, ibid.

39. Rex to Brady, September 26, 1860, Weaver Papers, Duke.

40. George W. Johnson to Weaver, October 29, 1860, ibid.; see also Johnson to Weaver, August 19, 1860, ibid.

41. See entry for October 31, 1860, Buffalo Forge Cash Book, 1853–63, Weaver–Brady Papers, Virginia.

42. McCormick to Weaver, February 14, 1859, ibid.

43. Rex to Brady, October 26, 1860, Weaver Papers, Duke.

44. See entry for October 24, 1863, Daniel C. E. Brady, "Home Journal," 1860–65, McCormick Collection, State Historical Society of Wisconsin, Madison (hereafter cited as

Brady, "Home Journal," 1860–65, McCormick Collection). Bill Camasky was sold November 25, 1863; see "Names, births &c: of Negroes," Weaver–Brady Papers, T. T. Brady.

45. See entry for December 27, 1854, Buffalo Forge Journal, 1850–59, Weaver–Brady Papers, Virginia.

46. Buffalo Forge Negro Book, 1850–57, ibid.

47. Ibid.

48. Marriage Register for Rockbridge County, Sub-District "A," 6th District, Virginia, Records of the Bureau of Refugees, Freedmen and Abandoned Lands, Record Group 105, National Archives, Washington, D.C. (hereafter cited as Marriage Register for Rockbridge County, Freedmen's Bureau Records, RG 105, NA).

49. Buffalo Forge Negro Book, 1850–57, and Etna Furnace Negro Book, 1856–59, Weaver–Brady Papers, Virginia.

50. Davidson to Weaver, August 2, 1859, ibid.

51. Brady to Davidson, August 5, 1859, Weaver Letterbooks, ibid.

52. Etna Furnace Negro Book, 1856–59, ibid.

53. Buffalo Forge Iron Book, 1831–62, and Brady, "Home Journal," 1858–60, ibid.

54. Brady, "Home Journal," 1858–60, ibid.

55. Ibid.

56. Ibid.

57. Buffalo Forge Cash Book, 1853–63, ibid.

58. See account of Sam Williams in Buffalo Forge Ledger, 1859–1878, Weaver–Brady Papers in the possession of D. E. Brady, Jr., Buffalo Forge, Virginia.

59. Brady, "Home Journal," 1858–60, Weaver–Brady Papers, Virginia; "Names, births &c: of Negroes," Weaver–Brady Papers, T. T. Brady.

60. Brady, "Home Journal," 1858–60, Weaver–Brady Papers, Virginia.

61. Ibid.; see entry for August 7, 1860, Buffalo Forge Cash Book, 1853–63, ibid.

62. Rex to Weaver, August 15, 1860, Weaver Papers, Duke.

63. Marriage Register for Rockbridge County, Freedmen's Bureau Records, RG 105, NA.

64. Lexington *Gazette,* August 2, 9, 1860.

65. See entries for April 18, 22, 23, 25, June 4, September 27, 1859, Brady, "Home Journal," 1858–60, Weaver–Brady Papers, Virginia.

66. Buffalo Forge Cash Book, 1853–63, ibid.

67. Brady, "Home Journal," 1858–60, ibid.

68. Register of Deaths, Book 1, 1853–70, Rockbridge County Court House, Lexington, Virginia.

69. Brady, "Home Journal," 1858–60, Weaver–Brady Papers, Virginia; Register of Deaths, Book 1, 1853–70, Rockbridge County Court House, Lexington, Virginia.

70. See entry for July 2, 1860, Buffalo Forge Cash Book, 1853–63, Weaver–Brady Papers, Virginia.

71. Brady to Lee, Rocke & Taylor, September 15, 1860, Weaver Letterbooks, ibid.

72. Buffalo Forge Iron Book, 1831–62, ibid.

73. Lee, Rocke & Taylor to Weaver, October 29, 1860, Weaver Papers, Duke.

74. E. B. Long, *The Civil War Day by Day: An Almanac, 1861–1865* (Garden City, NY: Doubleday & Co., 1971), 3–4.

75. Lexington *Gazette,* November 8, December 6, 20, 1860, January 10, 1861; Brady, "Home Journal," 1860–65, McCormick Collection.

76. Lexington *Gazette,* December 20, 1860.

77. Waggoner, Hill & Archer to Weaver, January 21, 1861, Weaver–Brady Papers, Virginia.

78. Lee, Rocke & Taylor to Weaver, February 13, 1861, ibid.

79. Weaver to Lee, Rocke & Co., February 28, 1861, Weaver Letterbooks, ibid.

80. Ibid.

81. Long, *Civil War Day by Day*, 35, 37, 39, 41.

82. Weaver to Lee, Rocke & Co., February 28, 1861, Weaver Letterbooks, Weaver–Brady Papers, Virginia.

83. Lexington *Gazette*, March 14, 1861; Lincoln's inaugural address was printed in its entirety in this issue.

84. Long, *Civil War Day by Day*, 51.

85. Weaver to Shields & Somerville, April 4, 8, 1861, Weaver Letterbooks, Weaver–Brady Papers, Virginia.

86. Brady, "Home Journal," 1860–65, McCormick Collection; *Comprehensive Farm Record* [1860–65], Weaver–Brady Papers, T. T. Brady.

87. Brady, "Home Journal," 1860–65, McCormick Collection; Buffalo Forge Iron Book, 1831–62, Weaver–Brady Papers, Virginia.

88. Weaver to W. D. Tompkins & Brother, February 28, 1861, Weaver Letterbooks, Weaver–Brady Papers, Virginia.

89. Brady, "Home Journal," 1860–65, McCormick Collection.

90. Long, *Civil War Day by Day*, 55–57.

III.3: War

1. William Weaver to Lee, Rocke & Taylor, April 23, 1861, Weaver Letterbooks, Weaver–Brady Papers, University of Virginia Library, Charlottesville (hereafter cited as Weaver–Brady Papers, Virginia).

2. Lexington *Gazette*, May 20, 1861.

3. See entry for April 19, 1861, Buffalo Forge Cash Book, 1853–63, and Weaver [Daniel C. E. Brady] to W. D. Thompkins & Brother, April 29, 1861, Weaver Letterbooks, Weaver–Brady Papers, Virginia.

4. See entry for May 27, 1861, Daniel C. E. Brady, "Home Journal," 1860–65, McCormick Collection, State Historical Society of Wisconsin, Madison (hereafter cited as Brady, "Home Journal," 1860–65, McCormick Collection).

5. See entry for June 22, 1861, ibid.; Oren F. Morton, *A History of Rockbridge County, Virginia* (Staunton, VA: The McClure Co., 1920), 133.

6. Lee, Rocke & Taylor to Weaver, June 14, 1861, William Weaver Papers, Duke University Library, Durham, North Carolina (hereafter cited as Weaver Papers, Duke).

7. Weaver to Lee, Rocke & Taylor, June 18, 1861, Weaver Letterbooks, Weaver–Brady Papers, Virginia.

8. R. B. Somerville & Co. to Weaver, April 16, 1861, Weaver Papers, Duke.

9. Shields & Somerville to Weaver, April 4, 1861, Weaver–Brady Papers, Virginia.

10. Weaver to Somerville & Co., April 24, 1861, Weaver Letterbooks, Weaver–Brady Papers, Virginia.

11. Somerville & Co. to Weaver, April 26, 1861, Weaver Papers, Duke.

12. Weaver to Somerville & Co., April 29, 1861, Weaver Letterbooks, Weaver–Brady Papers, Virginia.

13. Weaver to Somerville & Co., May 3, 1861, ibid.; see also Somerville & Co. to Weaver, April 16, 1861, Weaver Papers, Duke.

14. F. B. Deane, Jr., & Son to Weaver, May 9, 1861, Weaver–Brady Papers, Virginia.

15. Weaver to Deane, Jr., & Son, May 11, 1861, Weaver Letterbooks, ibid.

16. Weaver to Deane, Jr., & Son, May 30, 1861, ibid.; see also Deane, Jr., & Son to Weaver, May 27, 1861, Weaver–Brady Papers, Virginia.

17. Weaver to Deane, Jr., & Son, June 11, 1861, Weaver Letterbooks, ibid.

18. Deane, Jr., & Son to Weaver, June 15, 1861, Weaver–Brady Papers, Virginia.

19. Weaver to Asa Snyder, July 12, 29, 1861, Weaver Letterbooks, ibid.; Snyder to Weaver, July 22, 1861, Weaver Papers, Duke.

20. Deane, Jr., & Son to Weaver, August 8, 1861, and Weaver to Deane, Jr., & Son, August 15, 1861, Weaver Letterbooks, Weaver–Brady Papers, Virginia; Deane, Jr., & Son to Weaver, September 5, 1861, Weaver Papers, Duke.

21. Snyder to Weaver, September 11, 1861, and Weaver to Snyder, October 3, 1861, Weaver Letterbooks, Weaver–Brady Papers, Virginia; Snyder to Weaver, September 28, 1861, Weaver Papers, Duke.

22. Deane, Jr., & Son to Weaver, October 12, 22, 1861, Weaver Papers, Duke; Weaver to Deane, Jr., & Son, October 15, 1861, Weaver Letterbooks, Weaver–Brady Papers, Virginia.

23. Weaver to George Reid, September 20, 1861, Weaver Letterbooks, Weaver–Brady Papers, Virginia.

24. Somerville & Co. to Weaver, April 16, 1861, Weaver Papers, Duke; Weaver to Somerville & Co., May 1, July 20, September 12, 20, 25, October 21, 1861, Weaver Letterbooks, Weaver–Brady Papers, Virginia.

25. Somerville & Co. to Weaver, October 17, 1861, Weaver Papers, Duke.

26. Weaver to Somerville & Co., October 21, 1861, Weaver Letterbooks, Weaver–Brady Papers, Virginia.

27. Somerville & Co. to Weaver, October 24, 1861, and William S. Triplett to Weaver, October 29, 1861, Weaver Papers, Duke; Weaver to Somerville & Co., October 28, November 4, 1861, Weaver Letterbooks, and Somerville & Co. to Weaver, November 7, 1861, Weaver–Brady Papers, Virginia.

28. William W. Rex to Weaver, January 11, 1861, Weaver–Brady Papers, Virginia.

29. See entries for "Negro Hire," 1860, 1861, Buffalo Forge Journal, 1859–66, ibid.

30. Robert F. Willoughby to Brady, January 8, 28, 1861, and Brady to Willoughby, January 15, 1861, Weaver Letterbooks, ibid.

31. Rex to Brady, January 29, 1861, ibid.

32. Peter Temin, *Iron and Steel in Nineteenth-Century America: An Economic Inquiry* (Cambridge, MA: M.I.T. Press, 1964), 58–59; Charles B. Dew, "Slavery and Technology in the Antebellum Southern Iron Industry: The Case of Buffalo Forge," in Ronald L. Numbers and Todd L. Savitt, eds., *Science and Medicine in the Old South* (Baton Rouge: Louisiana State University Press, 1989), 111–12.

33. Rex to Brady, February 28, March 7, 15, 25, 26, April 1, 1861, Weaver–Brady Papers, Virginia.

34. Rex to Brady, April 6, 1861, ibid.

35. Rex to Brady, April 27, 30, 1861, Weaver Papers, Duke.

36. Rex to Brady, April 18, 1861, ibid.

37. Gorgas Family Bible, Weaver–Brady Papers in the possession of D. E. Brady, Jr., Buffalo Forge, Virginia; Manuscript Free Schedules and Manuscript Slave Schedules, Botetourt County, Virginia, Eighth Census of the United States, 1860, National Archives Microfilm Publications, M-653; J. H. Michener to Weaver, August 17, 1860, Weaver Papers, Duke.

38. Rex to Brady, April 18, May 14, August 3, 1861, Weaver Papers, Duke.

39. Rex to Brady, May 24, June 19, 26, 1861, Weaver–Brady Papers, Virginia.

40. Rex to Brady, June 22, 1861, Weaver Papers, Duke.

41. Morton, *History of Rockbridge County,* 123.

42. Charles B. Dew, "Black Ironworkers and the Slave Insurrection Panic of 1856," *Journal of Southern History,* 41 (August 1975), 321–38.

43. Morton, *History of Rockbridge County,* 126; see entry for April 20, 1861, Brady, "Home Journal," 1860–65, McCormick Collection; Lexington *Gazette,* May 23, 1861.

44. Weaver to Lee, Rocke & Taylor, April 23, 1861, Weaver Letterbooks, Weaver–Brady Papers, Virginia.

45. "Provisions, &c, taken by harvest hands," June–August, 1853, Buffalo Forge Time Book, 1843–53, ibid.

46. Lee, Rocke & Taylor to Weaver, May 4, 1861, Weaver Papers, Duke; Weaver to Lee, Rocke & Taylor, May 9, 1861, Weaver Letterbooks, Weaver–Brady Papers, Virginia.

47. Lexington *Gazette,* May 23, 1861.

48. Morton, *History of Rockbridge County,* 133.

49. Brady, "Home Journal," 1860–65, McCormick Collection.

50. Ibid.; "Names, births &c: of Negroes," Weaver–Brady Papers in the possession of T. T. Brady, Richmond, Virginia (hereafter cited as Weaver–Brady Papers, T. T. Brady).

51. Brady, "Home Journal," 1860–65, McCormick Collection.

52. Ibid.

53. Morton, *History of Rockbridge County,* 126.

54. Lee, Rocke & Taylor to Weaver, June 8, 1861, Weaver–Brady Papers, Virginia.

55. Weaver to Lee, Rocke & Taylor, May 3, 1861, Weaver Letterbooks, ibid.

56. Weaver to Lee, Rocke & Taylor, June 11, September 6, 12, 1861, ibid.

57. Major James L. Cooley to Weaver, August 19, 1861, Weaver Papers, Duke; James D. Davidson to Weaver, August 27, 1861, James D. Davidson Papers, Duke University Library, Durham, North Carolina (hereafter cited as Davidson Papers, Duke).

58. Brady to Davidson, August 28, 1861, James D. Davidson Papers, McCormick Collection, State Historical Society of Wisconsin, Madison (hereafter cited as Davidson Papers, McCormick Collection); Brady, "Home Journal," 1860–65, McCormick Collection.

59. Weaver [Brady] to Cooley, August 28, 1861, Weaver Letterbooks, Weaver–Brady Papers, Virginia.

60. Brady, "Home Journal," 1860–65, McCormick Collection, and Rex to Brady, June 1, 1861, Weaver–Brady Papers, Virginia; "Names, births &c: of Negroes," Weaver–Brady Papers, T. T. Brady.

61. Quartermaster W. L. Powell to Weaver, September 24, 1861, Davidson Papers, McCormick Collection; E. B. Long, *The Civil War Day by Day: An Almanac, 1861–1865* (Garden City, NY: Doubleday & Co., 1971), 117, 120.

62. Bill, "2½ tons Bar Iron Bot: of Wm. Weaver," September 30, 1861, Davidson Papers, McCormick Collection; bill, "Horse Shoes Bot: of Wm. Weaver," October 9, 1861, Daniel C. E. Brady Account, Confederate Citizens File, War Department Collection of Confederate Records, Record Group 109, National Archives, Washington, D. C. (hereafter cited as Brady Account, Confederate Citizens File, RG 109, NA).

63. Endorsement of Cooley, November 13, 1861, on bill of Weaver, September 30, 1861, Davidson Papers, McCormick Collection; receipt of Brady for payment for horseshoes, November 13, 1861, Brady Account, Confederate Citizens File, RG 109, NA; entries for November 13–15, 1861, Brady, "Home Journal," 1860–65, McCormick Collection, and Buffalo Forge Iron Book, 1831–62, Weaver–Brady Papers, Virginia.

64. Brady, "Home Journal," 1860–65, McCormick Collection, and accounts for Capt. E. S. Tutwiler, Buffalo Forge Journal, 1859–66, and Weaver to Tutwiler, October 29, 1861, Weaver Letterbooks, Weaver–Brady Papers, Virginia.

65. Brady, "Home Journal," 1860–65, McCormick Collection; Greenlee Davidson to Weaver, December 31, 1861, January 10, 1862, Weaver Papers, Duke.

66. Weaver to Lee, Rocke & Taylor, October 3, November 9, December 10, 1861, Weaver Letterbooks, Weaver–Brady Papers, Virginia.

67. Weaver to Lee, Rocke & Taylor, October 26, 1861, ibid.

68. Buffalo Forge Iron Book, 1831–62, ibid.

69. Ibid.

70. Brady, "Home Journal," 1860–65, McCormick Collection; Buffalo Forge Cash Book, 1853–63, Weaver–Brady Papers, Virginia.

71. Richmond *Dispatch,* November 2, 1861.

72. Commander George Minor to Weaver, December 16, 1861, Weaver Papers, Duke; Weaver to Minor, December 20, 1861, Weaver Letterbooks, Weaver–Brady Papers, Virginia.

73. Greenlee Davidson to Weaver, December 31, 1861, Weaver Papers, Duke.

74. Greenlee Davidson to Weaver, February 1, 1862, Weaver–Brady Papers, Virginia.

75. James D. Davidson to Weaver, February 4, 1862, ibid.

76. Weaver to Minor, December 20, 1862, January 1, 1863, Weaver Letterbooks, ibid.

77. Lee, Rocke & Taylor to Weaver, December 3, 1861, and Weaver to Lee, Rocke & Taylor, April 26, 1862, and to Stuart Buchanan & Co., April 26, 1862, Weaver Letterbooks, ibid.

78. W. D. Tompkins & Brother to Brady, January 10, 18, 1862, Weaver Papers, Duke; Tompkins & Brother to Weaver, February 13, 1862, Weaver–Brady Papers, Virginia.

79. Weaver to Stuart Buchanan & Co., March 11, 1862, Weaver Letterbooks, Weaver–Brady Papers, Virginia.

80. Weaver to Lee, Rocke & Taylor, March 27, 1862, ibid.

81. Weaver to Stuart Buchanan & Co., April 8, 1862, ibid.

82. Stuart Buchanan & Co. to Weaver, April 12, 1862, Weaver Papers, Duke; Weaver to Lee, Rocke & Taylor, April 26, 1862, Weaver Letterbooks, Weaver–Brady Papers, Virginia.

83. Lee, Rocke & Taylor to Weaver, April 24, May 24, 1862, and Weaver to Stuart Buchanan & Co., April 26, 1862, to Lee, Rocke & Taylor, May 18, 1862, and to Tompkins & Brother, November 20, 24, 1862, Weaver Letterbooks, Weaver–Brady Papers, Virginia.

84. Weaver to O. H. Perry, October 22, 1862, ibid.

85. Rex to Brady, June 29, 1860, ibid.

86. Etna Furnace Time Book, 1855–61, and Etna Furnace Negro Book, 1854–61, ibid.; see also entries for May 16, 19, 1861, Brady, "Home Journal," 1860–65, McCormick Collection.

87. Rex to Brady, June 1, 21, July 9, August 9, 1861, Weaver–Brady Papers, Virginia; Rex to Brady, June 22, August 3, 13, 20, 1861, Weaver Papers, Duke.

88. Rex to Brady, August 20, 31, October 8, November 19, 1861, Weaver Papers, Duke; Rex to Brady, December 10, 1861, Weaver–Brady Papers, Virginia.

89. Rex to Brady, June 15, 19, September 21, November 30, 1861, Weaver–Brady Papers, Virginia; Rex to Brady, August 3, 8, 31, October 8, 10, 26, November 2, 1861, Weaver Papers, Duke.

90. "Negro Hire," 1861, Buffalo Forge Journal, 1859–66, Weaver–Brady Papers, Virginia; Rex to Brady, October 17, 1861, Weaver Papers, Duke.

91. Rex to Brady, December 19, 1861, Weaver Papers, Duke.

92. Rex to Brady, March 21, 1861, ibid; Rex to Weaver, January 8, 1861, Rex to Brady, July 4, 1861, and Etna Furnace Time Book, Weaver–Brady Papers, Virginia.

93. Rex to Brady, June 1, 1861, Weaver–Brady Papers, Virginia; see also Charles K. Gorgas to Weaver, March 18, 1858, Weaver Papers, Duke.

94. Rex to Brady, May 9, 1861, Weaver–Brady Papers, Virginia.

95. Etna Furnace Time Book, 1855–61, and Etna Furnace Negro Book, 1854–61, ibid.; endorsement dated December 19, 1861, on hire bond of Weaver to Henry A. McCormick, January 1, 1861, Jordan & Irvine Papers, McCormick Collection, State Historical Society of Wisconsin, Madison; William W. Boyd to Francis T. Anderson, December 15, 1859, Anderson Family Papers, University of Virginia Library, Charlottesville.

96. Rex to Brady, December 12, 14, 1861, January 31, February 1, 4, March 20, 22, May 8, 30, June 12, 1862, Rex to Weaver, January 7, 21, 24, 1862, and Lee, Rocke & Taylor to Weaver, February 11, 1862, Weaver–Brady Papers, Virginia; entries for February 20, April 3, 1862, Buffalo Forge Journal, 1859–66, and Weaver to Lee, Rocke & Taylor, February 13, 1862, Weaver Letterbooks, ibid.; Rex to Brady, May 27, 1862, Weaver Papers, Duke.

97. Rex to Brady, February 13, 1862, and Tompkins & Brother to Weaver, February 15, 1862, Weaver–Brady Papers, Virginia; Weaver to Tompkins & Brother, February 11, 1862, Weaver Letterbooks, ibid.

98. Rex to Brady, June 17, 19, 1862, ibid.

99. Rex to Weaver, January 7, 1862, ibid.; see also Deane, Jr., to Weaver, November 11, 1861, and William S. Triplett to Weaver, November 23, 1861, Weaver Papers, Duke; Deane to Weaver, December 1, 1861, Somerville to Weaver, January 21, 30, 31, 1862, and Snyder to Weaver, February 7, 1862, Weaver–Brady Papers, Virginia.

100. Deane, Jr., & Son to Weaver, February 3, 1862, and Weaver to Deane, Jr., & Son, February 15, 1862, Weaver Letterbooks, Weaver–Brady Papers, Virginia; see also Weaver to Somerville, February 15, 1862, ibid.

101. Triplett to Weaver, August 21, 1862, Weaver Papers, Duke.

102. Weaver to Triplett, August 25, 1862, Weaver Letterbooks, Weaver–Brady Papers, Virginia.

103. Lee, Rocke & Taylor to Weaver, February 17, 1862, ibid.

104. Brady to James D. Davidson, June 24, 1861, Davidson Papers, McCormick Collection.

105. James D. Davidson to Weaver, February 12, 1862, Davidson Papers, Duke.

106. James D. Davidson to Weaver, February 20, 1862, ibid.

107. Greenlee Davidson to Weaver, January 10, 1862, Weaver Papers, Duke; see also John Letcher to Weaver, February 4, August 27, 1862, ibid., and Weaver to Letcher, September 30, 1862, Weaver Letterbooks, Weaver–Brady Papers, Virginia.

108. Brady to McCormick, May 27, 1862, Weaver Letterbooks, Weaver–Brady Papers, Virginia.

109. Buffalo Forge Iron Book, 1831–62, and Weaver to Thomas G. Godwin, February 5, 1862, and to George W. Dawson, May 27, 1862, Weaver Letterbooks, ibid.

110. Brady, "Home Journal," 1860–65, McCormick Collection; Buffalo Forge Iron Book, 1831–62, Weaver–Brady Papers, Virginia.

111. Weaver to Lee, Rocke & Taylor, March 11, 1862, Weaver Letterbooks, Weaver–Brady Papers, Virginia.

112. Brady, "Home Journal," 1860–65, McCormick Collection; Buffalo Forge Iron Book, 1831–62, Weaver–Brady Papers, Virginia.

113. Weaver [Brady] to Lee, Rocke & Taylor, April 26, 1862, Weaver Letterbooks, Weaver–Brady Papers, Virginia; Brady, "Home Journal," 1860–65, McCormick Collection.

114. Buffalo Forge Iron Book, 1831–62, Weaver–Brady Papers, Virginia.

115. Brady, "Home Journal," 1860–65, McCormick Collection.

116. Weaver to Lee, Rocke & Taylor, July 11, 1862, and to Capt. J. G. Paxton, April 17, 1862, Weaver Letterbooks, and Paxton to Weaver, March 3, 1862, Weaver–Brady Papers, Virginia; Paxton to Weaver, May 21, 1862, Weaver Papers, Duke; Brady, "Home Journal," 1860–65, McCormick Collection.

117. Brady, "Home Journal," 1860–65, McCormick Collection; Weaver to John H. Price, August 23, September 3, 1862, to A. L. Boyd, October 1, 1862, and to George W. Dawson, November 3, 1862, Weaver Letterbooks, and Dawson to Weaver, December 8, 1862, Weaver–Brady Papers, Virginia.

118. Weaver to Dawson, December 13, 1862, Weaver Letterbooks, Weaver–Brady Papers, Virginia.

119. Dawson to Weaver, November 12, 1862, ibid.; see also Dawson to Weaver, February 12, 1862, ibid.

120. Weaver to Dawson, December 13, 1862, Weaver Letterbooks, ibid.

121. This estimate is based on the average value of one dollar in gold in Richmond as compared with Confederate treasury notes each month during 1862; see Richard C. Todd, *Confederate Finance* (Athens: University of Georgia Press, 1954), 198.

122. Weaver to Lee, Rocke & Taylor, October 14, 1862, Weaver Letterbooks, Weaver–Brady Papers, Virginia.

123. Brady, "Home Journal," 1860–65, McCormick Collection.

124. Rex to Brady, May 20, 1862, Weaver Papers, Duke.

125. Brady to James D. Davidson, April 22, 1862, Davidson Papers, McCormick Collection.

126. Brady, "Home Journal," 1860–65, McCormick Collection; Brady to James D. Davidson, January 19, 1863, Weaver–Brady Papers, Virginia.

127. See entries for May 31, December 15, 1861, July 14, 26, 1862, Brady, "Home Journal," 1860–65, McCormick Collection.

III.4: Death

1. Daniel C. E. Brady, "Home Journal," 1860–65, McCormick Collection, State Historical Society of Wisconsin, Madison (hereafter cited as Brady, "Home Journal," 1860–65, McCormick Collection); "Names, births &c: of Negroes," Weaver–Brady Papers in the possession of T. T. Brady, Richmond, Virginia (hereafter cited as Weaver–Brady Papers, T. T. Brady).

2. E. B. Long, *The Civil War Day by Day: An Almanac, 1861–1865* (Garden City, NY: Doubleday & Co., 1971), 261–66; Stephen W. Sears, *Landscape Turned Red: The Battle of Antietam* (New York: Popular Library, 1983), 169–70, 177–79.

3. Brady, "Home Journal," 1860–65, McCormick Collection; "Weaver Family: Memo and Historical Notes," Weaver–Brady Papers, T. T. Brady; Register of Deaths, Book 1, 1853–70, Rockbridge County Court House, Lexington, Virginia.

4. "Diptheria & Sore Throat 1862," Brady, "Home Journal," 1860–65, McCormick Collection.

5. Sears, *Landscape Turned Red,* 327; Long, *Civil War Day by Day,* 267–68.

6. Brady, "Home Journal," 1860–65, McCormick Collection.

7. Ibid.; "Names, births &c: of Negroes," Weaver–Brady Papers, T. T. Brady.

8. Ibid.

9. "Diptheria & Sore Throat 1862," Brady, "Home Journal," 1860–65, McCormick Collection.

10. "Names, births &c: of Negroes," Weaver–Brady Papers, T. T. Brady; Brady, "Home Journal," 1860–65, McCormick Collection.

11. "Vaccination," 1859–63, Buffalo Forge Journal, 1859–66, Weaver–Brady Papers, University of Virginia Library, Charlottesville (hereafter cited as Weaver–Brady Papers, Virginia).

12. Roy P. Basler, ed., *The Collected Works of Abraham Lincoln,* 8 vols. (New Brunswick, NJ: Rutgers University Press, 1953), 5:434.

13. Gorgas Family Bible, Weaver–Brady Papers in the possession of D. E. Brady, Jr., Buffalo Forge, Virginia (hereafter cited as Weaver–Brady Papers, D. E. Brady, Jr.).

14. Last will and testament of William Weaver, April 14, 1852, Weaver–Brady Papers, T. T. Brady.

15. Ibid., November 17, 1857.

16. Ibid., codicil of May 23, 1860; "Names, births &c: of Negroes," ibid.

17. Deed, William Weaver to Charles K. Gorgas, March 29, 1862, Deed Book 34, p. 836, Botetourt County Court House, Fincastle, Virginia.

18. Brady, "Home Journal," 1860–65, McCormick Collection.

19. Interview with D. E. Brady, Jr., Buffalo Forge, Virginia, October 7, 1977.

20. William Weaver to Lee, Rocke & Taylor, October 14, 1862, Weaver Letterbooks, and Lee, Rocke & Taylor to Weaver, October 18, 1862, Weaver–Brady Papers, Virginia.

21. Weaver [D. C. E. Brady] to Jones & Miller, December 1, 1862, Weaver Letterbooks, ibid.

22. Weaver to Lee, Rocke & Taylor, December 20, 1862, ibid.

23. Richard D. Goff, *Confederate Supply* (Durham: Duke University Press, 1969), 41–42, 96–102.

24. Brady to James D. Davidson, December 17, 1862, James D. Davidson Papers, McCormick Collection, State Historical Society of Wisconsin, Madison (hereafter cited as Davidson Papers, McCormick Collection).

25. Weaver to Newton Switzer, January 1, 1863, Weaver Letterbooks, Weaver–Brady Papers, Virginia.

26. Brady, "Home Journal," 1860–65, McCormick Collection.

27. Weaver [Brady] to James Stewart, December 10, 1862, Weaver Letterbooks, Weaver–Brady Papers, Virginia.

28. Long, *Civil War Day by Day,* 294–95.

29. Entries for December 24, 1862, Buffalo Forge Cash Book, 1853–63, Weaver–Brady Papers, Virginia.

30. Brady, "Home Journal," 1860–65, McCormick Collection.

31. Weaver [Brady] to Thomas R. Towles, October 31, December 20, 1862, to Stewart, October 31, November 24, 1862, Weaver Letterbooks, and "Negro Hire 1863," Buffalo Forge Journal, 1859–66, Weaver–Brady Papers, Virginia.

32. Weaver [Brady] to Stewart, January 12, 1863, Weaver Letterbooks, Weaver–Brady Papers, Virginia.

33. Brady to Sam A. Robinson, April 23, 1863, ibid.

34. Brady, "Home Journal," 1860–65, McCormick Collection.

35. Ibid.

36. Ibid.; "Names, births &c: of Negroes," Weaver–Brady Papers, T. T. Brady; Buffalo Forge Cash Book, 1853–63, Weaver–Brady Papers, Virginia.

37. "Weaver Family: Memo and Historical Notes," Weaver–Brady Papers, T. T. Brady.

38. Weaver [Brady] to F. T. Glasgow, February 13, 1863, Weaver Letterbooks, Weaver–Brady Papers, Virginia; Richard C. Todd, *Confederate Finance* (Athens: University of Georgia Press, 1954), 198.

39. Brady to Major J. G. Paxton, February 27, 1863, Weaver Letterbooks, and entry for February 27, 1863, Buffalo Forge Journal, 1859–66, Weaver–Brady Papers, Virginia.

40. Brady, "Home Journal," 1860–65, McCormick Collection.

41. Ibid.

42. "An appraisement of the goods and chattels of William Weaver, deceased," June 1, 1863, Weaver–Brady Papers, Virginia.

43. Manuscript Free Schedules, Rockbridge County, Virginia, Eighth Census of the United States, 1860, National Archives Microfilm Publications, M-653.

44. Lynchburg *Daily Virginian,* April 1, 1863.

45. Lexington *Gazette,* April 8, 1863.

46. Last will and testament of William Weaver, January 8, 1863, William Weaver Papers, Washington & Lee University Library, Lexington, Virginia.

47. "Weaver Family: Memo and Historical Notes," Weaver–Brady Papers, T. T. Brady.

48. Entry for April 17, 1863, Buffalo Forge Cash Book, 1853–63, Weaver–Brady Papers, Virginia.

49. Brady, "Home Journal," 1860–65, McCormick Collection.

50. See entry for October 24, 1863, ibid; "Names, births &c: of Negroes," Weaver–Brady Papers, T. T. Brady; entry for November 25, 1863, D. C. E. Brady, Private Journal, Weaver–Brady Papers, D. E. Brady, Jr.

51. Receipts for purchase of slaves Daniel and William, September 26, 1863, and "Names, births &c: of Negroes," Weaver–Brady Papers, T. T. Brady; entry for Lee, Rocke & Taylor, October 10, 1863, Buffalo Forge Journal, 1859–66, Weaver–Brady Papers, Virginia; entry for December 23, 1863, Buffalo Forge Cash Book, 1863–76, Weaver–Brady Papers, D. E. Brady, Jr.; Brady to Davidson, December 9, 1863, Davidson Papers, McCormick Collection.

52. Brady, "Home Journal," 1860–65, McCormick Collection; Brady, "Farm Note-book," 1859–68, Weaver–Brady Papers, T. T. Brady.

53. Buffalo Forge Cash Book, 1853–63, Weaver–Brady Papers, Virginia; Buffalo Forge Cash Book, 1863–76, Weaver–Brady Papers, D. E. Brady, Jr.

54. Interview with James Thompson, Glasgow, Virginia, March 7, 1981.

55. Brady, "Home Journal," 1860–65, McCormick Collection; marriage registration of Henry Hunt and Charlotte Wade, Marriage Register for Rockbridge County, Sub-District "A," 6th District, Virginia, Records of the Bureau of Refugees, Freedmen and Abandoned Lands, Record Group 105, National Archives, Washington, D.C.

56. Long, *Civil War Day by Day,* 344–46; Brady, "Home Journal," 1860–65, McCormick Collection.

57. Richmond *Enquirer,* April 24, July 10, 1863.

58. Joseph G. Dill to Brady, April 27, May 20, 1863, William Weaver Papers, Duke University Library, Durham, North Carolina (hereafter cited as Weaver Papers, Duke).

59. Dill to Brady, July 8, 10, 1863, ibid.

60. Entry for October 10, 1863, Buffalo Forge Cash Book, 1853–63, Weaver–Brady Papers, Virginia; entries for March 24, December 8, 1864, January 4, 5, 31, 1865, Buffalo Forge Cash Book, 1863–76, and Daniel C. E. Brady, Executor's Ledger, Estate of William Weaver, Deceased, Weaver–Brady Papers, D. E. Brady, Jr.

61. Rex to Weaver, March 7, 1862, and Weaver [Brady] to Lee, Rocke & Taylor, March 27, 1862, Weaver Letterbooks, Weaver–Brady Papers, Virginia; exemption papers, D. C. E. Brady, August 17, 1863, Weaver–Brady Papers, T. T. Brady; Goff, *Confederate Supply,* 42, 93–95.

62. Detail papers, D. C. E. Brady, February 12, May 12, June 20, 1864, Weaver–Brady Papers, T. T. Brady; Goff, *Confederate Supply,* 32, 64.

63. Buffalo Forge Journal, 1859–66, Weaver–Brady Papers, Virginia. By early 1864, inflation had finally caught up with the price of Buffalo Forge merchant bar. It took $20 to $20.50 in Confederate treasury notes to buy a dollar in gold at Richmond banks in January 1864; in February, it required $22.50 to $25 in notes to purchase a gold dollar. Buffalo Forge iron at the beginning of the war was priced at $100 a ton, which makes it a relatively simple matter to compare the price of Weaver's and Brady's iron with the overall inflation rate in Virginia. A table comparing the value of a dollar in gold with Confederate currency is given in Todd, *Confederate Finance,* 198.

64. "Contract for Iron," Brady & Rex and I. M. St. John, Lieut. Colonel and Chief of the Nitre and Mining Bureau, January 1, 1864, Weaver–Brady Papers, T. T. Brady.

65. Brady & Rex to Capt. John Ellicott, February 6, 1864, Weaver Letterbooks, Weaver–Brady Papers, Virginia.

66. Brady, "Home Journal," 1860–65, McCormick Collection.

67. "Descriptive List of Negroes hired . . . , Confederate States Nitre and Mining Service, 1865," Weaver–Brady Papers, T. T. Brady.

68. Brady & Rex to Ellicott, February 20, 1864, Weaver Letterbooks, Weaver–Brady Papers, Virginia; Ellicott to Brady, March 1, 1864, Weaver Papers, Duke; Brady, "Home Journal," 1860–65, McCormick Collection.

69. Charles H. Locher, A. Q. M., to Brady, April 20, 23, 1864, Weaver Papers, Duke.

70. Brady & Rex to Ellicott, April 29, 1864, Weaver Letterbooks, Weaver–Brady Papers, Virginia.

71. Ellicott to Brady & Rex, December 14, 1864, Weaver Papers, Duke.

72. Brady, "Home Journal," 1860–65, McCormick Collection; entries for December 1864, Daniel C. E. Brady, Executor's Ledger, Estate of William Weaver, Deceased, Weaver–Brady Papers, D. E. Brady, Jr.

73. For a fuller discussion of this issue, see Charles B. Dew, "Slavery and Technology

in the Antebellum Southern Iron Industry: The Case of Buffalo Forge," in Ronald L. Numbers and Todd L. Savitt, eds., *Science and Medicine in the Old South* (Baton Rouge: Louisiana State University Press, 1989), 107–26.

74. George W. Dawson to Weaver, May 30, 1862, Weaver–Brady Papers, Virginia.

75. See deposition of Samuel F. Jordan, September 7, 1840, Case Papers, John Alexander *v.* Sidney S. Baxter, Administrator of John Irvine & Others, Superior Court of Chancery Records, Rockbridge County Court House, Lexington, Virginia; Charles B. Dew, *Ironmaker to the Confederacy: Joseph R. Anderson and the Tredegar Iron Works* (New Haven: Yale University Press, 1966), 87–89.

76. Brady, "Home Journal," 1860–65, McCormick Collection; "Names, births &c: of Negroes," Weaver–Brady Papers, T. T. Brady; "An appraisement of the goods and chattels of William Weaver, deceased," June 1, 1863, Weaver–Brady Papers, Virginia.

77. Brady, "Home Journal," 1860–65, McCormick Collection.

78. Ibid.; the limestone grave markers are still in place at the slave cemetery at Buffalo Forge.

79. Long, *Civil War Day by Day*, 516–21; Oren F. Morton, *A History of Rockbridge County, Virginia* (Staunton, VA: The McClure Co., 1920), 129–30.

80. Brady, "Home Journal," 1860–65, McCormick Collection.

81. Dew, *Ironmaker to the Confederacy*, 165; Brady to Stewart, July 7, 1864, Weaver Letterbooks, Weaver–Brady Papers, Virginia.

82. Brady, "Home Journal," 1860–65, McCormick Collection; interview with D. E. Brady, Jr., Buffalo Forge, Virginia, October 7, 1977.

83. Brady to Stewart, July 7, 1864, Weaver Letterbooks, Weaver–Brady Papers, Virginia.

84. Long, *Civil War Day by Day*, 523–26; entry for March 26, 1865, Brady, "Home Journal," 1860–65, McCormick Collection.

85. "Names, births &c: of Negroes," Weaver–Brady Papers, T. T. Brady; Brady, "Home Journal," 1860–65, McCormick Collection.

86. Brady, "Home Journal," 1860–65, McCormick Collection.

87. Ibid.; "Names, births &c: of Negroes," Weaver–Brady Papers, T. T. Brady.

88. Brady, "Home Journal," 1860–65, McCormick Collection; "Names, births &c: of Negroes," Weaver–Brady Papers, T. T. Brady.

89. Ibid.

III.5: Peace and Freedom

1. Daniel C. E. Brady, "Home Journal," 1860–65, McCormick Collection, State Historical Society of Wisconsin, Madison (hereafter cited as Brady, "Home Journal," 1860–65, McCormick Collection).

2. Brady & Rex to Captain R. C. Morton, February 5, 1865, and Brady to Major John Ellicott, February 20, March 20, 1865, Weaver Letterbooks, Weaver–Brady Papers, University of Virginia Library, Charlottesville (hereafter cited as Weaver–Brady Papers, Virginia).

3. Entry for April 6, 1865, Buffalo Forge Journal, 1859–66, ibid.

4. E. B. Long, *The Civil War Day by Day: An Almanac, 1861–1865* (Garden City, NY: Doubleday & Co., 1971), 664.

5. Entries for December 1864, January 1865, Buffalo Forge Cash Book, 1863–76, entries under "Nitre & Mining Bureau," 1864–65, Buffalo Forge Ledger, 1859–75, and entries for December 1864–April 1865, Daniel C. E. Brady, Executor's Ledger, Estate of William Weaver, Deceased, Weaver–Brady Papers in the possession of D. E. Brady, Jr., Buffalo Forge, Virginia (hereafter cited as Weaver–Brady Papers, D. E. Brady, Jr.).

6. Entries for April 1865, D. C. E. Brady, Executor's Ledger, Estate of William Weaver, Deceased, ibid.

7. Brady, "Home Journal," 1860–65, McCormick Collection.

8. Ibid.

9. Ibid.; "Hire for 1865," Buffalo Forge Journal, 1859–66, Weaver–Brady Papers, Virginia.

10. Daniel C. E. Brady to James D. Davidson, May 21, 1865, James D. Davidson Papers, McCormick Collection, State Historical Society of Wisconsin, Madison (hereafter cited as Davidson Papers, McCormick Collection); see also entry for May 21, 1865, Brady, "Home Journal," 1860–65, McCormick Collection.

11. Brady to Davidson, May 21, 1865, Davidson Papers, McCormick Collection.

12. Lynchburg *Daily Virginian,* May 16, 1865.

13. Entries for May 1, 15, 1865, Buffalo Forge Cash Book, 1863–76, Weaver–Brady Papers, D. E. Brady, Jr.

14. Brady to Davidson, May 21, 1865, Davidson Papers, McCormick Collection.

15. Brady, "Home Journal," 1860–65, McCormick Collection.

16. Entry for May 26, 1865, Buffalo Forge Journal, 1859–66, Weaver–Brady Papers, Virginia.

17. Brady, "Home Journal," 1860–65, McCormick Collection.

18. Ibid.; Oren F. Morton, *A History of Rockbridge County, Virginia* (Staunton, VA: The McClure Co., 1920), 425.

19. Lynchburg *Daily Virginian,* May 23, 1865.

20. Buffalo Forge Negro Book, 1865–73, Weaver–Brady Papers, Virginia.

21. Ibid.

22. Brady, "Home Journal," 1860–65, McCormick Collection.

23. Buffalo Forge Negro Book, 1865–73, Weaver–Brady Papers, Virginia; Daniel C. E. Brady, "Home Journal," 1865–73, Weaver–Brady Papers in the possession of T. T. Brady, Richmond, Virginia (hereafter cited as Weaver–Brady Papers, T. T. Brady); Manuscript Population Schedules, Rockbridge County, Virginia, Ninth Census of the United States, 1870, National Archives Microfilm Publications, M-593.

24. Daniel C. E. Brady, Pardon and Amnesty File, Records of the Adjutant General's Office, Record Group 94, National Archives, Washington, D.C.

25. Samuel F. Jordan to Brady, January 23, 29, May 21, July 23, October 11, 1866, William Weaver Papers, Duke University Library, Durham, North Carolina (hereafter cited as Weaver Papers, Duke).

26. Buffalo Forge Journal, 1859–66, Weaver–Brady Papers, Virginia; Lynchburg *Daily Virginian,* July 3, August 9, 1865.

27. Buffalo Forge Negro Book, 1865–73, Weaver–Brady Papers, Virginia.

28. Ibid.

29. Ibid.

30. Ibid.; Brady, "Home Journal," 1865–73, Weaver–Brady Papers, T. T. Brady.

31. "Circular," Lexington, Virginia, October 20, 1865, Book A, Letters Sent, 1865–66, Records of Sub-District "A," 6th District, Virginia, Records of the Bureau of Refugees, Freedmen and Abandoned Lands, Record Group 105, National Archives, Washington, D.C. (hereafter cited as Freedmen's Bureau Records, RG 105, NA).

32. Brady, "Home Journal," 1865–73, Weaver–Brady Papers, T. T. Brady.

33. Buffalo Forge Negro Book, 1865–73, Weaver–Brady Papers, Virginia.

34. Ibid.

35. "Weaver Family: Memo and Historical Notes," Weaver–Brady Papers, T. T. Brady.

36. "Circular," Lexington, Virginia, October 20, 1865, Book A, Letters Sent, 1865–66, Records of Sub-District "A," 6th District, Virginia, Freedmen's Bureau Records, RG 105, NA.

37. "Circular," Lexington, Virginia, November 20, 1865, ibid.

38. Eric Foner, *Reconstruction: America's Unfinished Revolution, 1863–1877* (New York: Harper & Row, 1988), 153–64.

39. Buffalo Forge Negro Book, 1865–73, Weaver–Brady Papers, Virginia.

40. Ibid.

41. Lieutenant C. Jerome Tubbs to Captain W. Stores How, October 30, 1865, Book A, Letters Sent, 1865–66, Records of Sub-District "A," 6th District, Virginia, Freedmen's Bureau Records, RG 105, NA.

42. Letter of G. B. Carse, Lexington, Virginia, May 8, 1866, Register of Letters Received, Lynchburg, Virginia, 1865–67, 6th District, Virginia, ibid.; Brady to Davidson, May 21, 1865, Davidson Papers, McCormick Collection.

43. Interview with James Thompson, Glasgow, Virginia, March 7, 1981.

44. J. W. Sharp to Brady, May 16, 1871, Weaver–Brady Papers, T. T. Brady.

45. See Special Order No. 8, November 23, 1865, and "Report of Officers and Enlisted Men on duty in Sub-District 'A,' " Book A, Letters Sent, 1865–66, Records of Sub-District "A," 6th District, Virginia, Freedmen's Bureau Records, RG 105, NA.

46. Marriage Register for Rockbridge County, ibid.

47. William Weaver to Alfred Douglass, October 7, 1853, Weaver–Brady Papers, Virginia.

48. Buffalo Forge Journal, 1859–66, ibid.; Lynchburg *Daily Virginian,* September–December, 1866.

49. Buffalo Forge Journal, 1859–66, Weaver–Brady Papers, Virginia; "Account Sales Iron made by Rocke & Murrell," July 1865–October 1866, and "Iron Receipts, Millers Warehouse, mouth Buffalo," March–December 1866, Weaver Papers, Duke.

50. Buffalo Forge Negro Book, 1865–73, Weaver–Brady Papers, Virginia.

51. Daniel C. E. Brady, Executor's Ledger, Estate of William Weaver, Deceased, Weaver–Brady Papers, D. E. Brady, Jr.; Contract with Antoine Bernard, vinedresser, November 1, 1867, Weaver–Brady Papers, T. T. Brady.

52. Agreement with Lorenzo Sibert, October 30, 1866, Weaver–Brady Papers, T. T. Brady; Emma Mines Time Book, 1867, Weaver–Brady Papers, Virginia.

53. Assignment of Patent Rights, Lorenzo Sibert to Daniel C. E. Brady, March 12, 1867, and lease of California Furnace by Brady & Sibert, July 8, 1867, Weaver–Brady Papers, T. T. Brady.

54. Brady to Davidson, July 4, August 21, 1867, Davidson Papers, McCormick Collection.

55. "California Furnace Sept. 1867," account filed in Brady, "Farm Notebook," 1859–68, Weaver–Brady Papers, T. T. Brady.

56. Emma Mines Time Book, 1867, Weaver–Brady Papers, Virginia.

57. Work contracts dated January 1, 1867, all in Weaver–Brady Papers, T. T. Brady.

58. See entries under "Sam Williams" in Daniel C. E. Brady, Private Ledger, and in Buffalo Forge Ledger, 1859–78, and entry under "Sam Williams Cr.," August 30, 1867, Buffalo Forge Journal, 1866–78, all in Weaver–Brady Papers, D. E. Brady, Jr.

59. Work contracts dated January 1, 1867, Weaver–Brady Papers, T. T. Brady; Buffalo Forge Negro Book, 1865–73, Weaver–Brady Papers, Virginia.

60. Buffalo Forge Negro Book, 1865–73, Weaver–Brady Papers, Virginia.

61. Sharp to Captain J. G. Updike, December 27, 1866, Letterpress Copy Book, Letters Sent, 1866–68, Sub-District "A," 6th District, Virginia, Freedmen's Bureau Records, RG 105, NA.

62. Buffalo Forge Store Day Book, 1867–68, Weaver–Brady Papers, Virginia; Brady, "Farm Notebook," 1859–68, Weaver–Brady Papers, T. T. Brady.

63. Buffalo Forge Negro Book, 1865–73, Weaver–Brady Papers, Virginia.

64. See entries for 1868–73, Brady, "Home Journal," 1865–73, Weaver–Brady Papers, T. T. Brady.

65. Sharp to Brevet Colonel Chapin, October 20, 1867, Letterpress Copy Book, Letters Sent, 1866–68, Sub-District "A," 6th District, Virginia, Freedmen's Bureau Records, RG 105, NA.

66. See registration oaths in Weaver–Brady Papers, Virginia.

67. Lexington *Gazette & Banner,* October 16, 20, 1867; Richard Lowe, *Republicans and Reconstruction in Virginia, 1856–70* (Charlottesville: University Press of Virginia, 1991), 176–77.

68. Buffalo Forge Negro Book, 1865–73, and entries for April 22, 1868, Buffalo Forge Store Day Book, 1867–68, Weaver–Brady Papers, Virginia.

69. Manuscript Population Schedules, Rockbridge County, Virginia, Ninth Census of the United States, 1870, National Archives Microfilm Publications, M-593; Manuscript Returns, Virginia, United States Census of Manufacturers, 1870 (microfilm copy, Virginia State Library, Richmond).

70. Most lived in the Natural Bridge section of the county, which included Buffalo Forge; see Manuscript Population Schedules, Rockbridge County, Virginia, Ninth Census of the United States, 1870, National Archives, Microfilm Publications, M-593.

71. Deed between Daniel C. E. Brady and Samuel Williams et al., Trustees of the Buffalo Forge Colored Baptist Church, October 9, 1871, Deed Book MM, pp. 37–38, Rockbridge County Court House, Lexington, Virginia.

72. "Col. Baptist Church of Buffalo Forge, Va." account with Daniel C. E. Brady, 1870–71, Weaver–Brady Papers, T. T. Brady; the silver pitcher bears the inscription "Presented to Mt. Lydia Baptist Church, Buffalo Forge, 1872," and, according to James Thompson, the pitcher and cups were given to the church by the Bradys (interview with James Thompson, Glasgow, Virginia, March 7, 1981). The pitcher and cups are now owned by Meshach Thompson of Glasgow, Virginia, James Thompson's son.

73. Brady, "Home Journal," 1875, Weaver–Brady Papers, T. T. Brady.

74. Contracts for 1873, Brady, "Home Journal," 1865–73, ibid.

75. See entries for August 1, 1873, and "1873 Cash Value of Rent," ibid.

76. Buffalo Forge Farm Book, 1874–82, Weaver–Brady Papers, D. E. Brady, Jr.; Manuscript Population Schedules, Rockbridge County, Virginia, Tenth Census of the United States, 1880, National Archives Microfilm Publications, T-9.

77. Marriage Registration of Steward Chandler and Mary C. Coleman, July 27, 1876, Register of Marriages, Book 1A, 1865–89, and Birth Registration of William H. A. Chandler, October 10, 1876, and Mary L. Chandler, August 15, 1878, Register of Births, No. 1, 1853–77, Rockbridge County Court House, Lexington, Virginia.

78. Manuscript Population Schedules, Rockbridge County, Virginia, Tenth Census of the United States, 1880, National Archives Microfilm Publications, T-9.

79. Lexington *Gazette & Citizen,* May 31, 1878.

80. Ibid., January 18, 1883; "Weaver Family: Memo and Historical Notes," Weaver–Brady Papers, T. T. Brady.

81. Guardian Bond of Lydia Reed, January 2, 1882, Will Book No. 24, 1881–84, p. 34, Rockbridge County Court House, Lexington, Virginia.

82. Marriage Registration of Charles Newman and Lydia Reid, January 4, 1882, Register of Marriages, Book 1A, 1865–89, and Birth Registration of Mary Ann Newman, November 1882, Register of Births, No. 2, 1878–96, ibid.

83. C. A. Brady, "Farm & Home Journal," 1888, Weaver–Brady Papers, D. E. Brady, Jr.

84. Commonwealth *v.* Charles Newman, Circuit Court Order Book, 1887–90, pp. 185, 191, Rockbridge County Court House, Lexington, Virginia.

85. C. A. Brady, "Farm & Home Journal," 1888, Weaver–Brady Papers, D. E. Brady, Jr.

86. Commonwealth *v.* Charles Newman, Circuit Court Order Book, 1887–90, pp. 191, 197, Rockbridge County Court House, Lexington, Virginia.

87. C. A. Brady, "Farm & Home Journal," 1889, Weaver–Brady Papers, D. E. Brady, Jr.

88. "Names, births &c: of Negroes," Weaver–Brady Papers, T. T. Brady.

89. Sam Williams marked all surviving documents requiring his signature with an "X," and the manuscript census returns for 1870 indicated that neither Sam nor Nancy Williams could read or write; see Manuscript Population Schedules, Rockbridge County, Virginia, Ninth Census of the United States, 1870, National Archives Microfilm Publications, M-593.

Index

Aaron (slave), 101
Abram (WW's hireling), 70
Absolom (WW's hireling), 119
agriculture, 4, 9, 11, 30, 110, 135–36, 149,
    242–48, 251, 262, 276
    after Civil War, 339–40, 345, 347, 355–56, 358
    in Civil War, 296, 297, 312, 322–23, 331, 338
    in late antebellum years, 242–48, 251, 262,
        284, 285
    organization of, 242–44
    sharecropping, 358–59, 361
    WW's success at, 136
alcohol, 31, 67, 99, 100, 114, 275–76, 349
Alexander, William, 241
Allen Collier (WW's slave), 110, 119–20
Amherst County hiring market, 69, 75
Amy (Mary's daughter), 25–26, 53, 172, 188, 205
Anderson, Francis T., 151–52, 252, 317
Anderson, Robert, 286
Anthony (Peter Griggs's slave), 152–53
Antietam, battle of, 316

Appomattox Court House, surrender at, 339
Arch (WW's slave), 134–35, 206, 367
Archer, Junius L., 284, 289

Banks (Carter), Amy, 243, 247, 265–66, 296, 321
Banks, Frances, 243, 298, 335, 343–45, 360
Banks, Heb, 298
Banks, Nathaniel, 310
Banks, Warder, 243, 296, 298, 306, 320–21, 360
    escape of, to Union forces, 335, 344
Banks, Warder, Jr., 335
Baptists, see Dunkers
bar iron, merchant bar, 65, 260
    in Civil War, 297–99, 300, 308, 310
    market and prices of, 47, 50, 56, 64, 66, 112,
        148, 154, 157, 257–58, 297–98, 299, 308,
        310, 354
    traded for pig iron, 55
    WW's monopoly of, 64–65
    see also iron, iron working
Barker, Joseph, 85–87

Bath (Lydia) Furnace, 54–55, 63, 67
Bath Iron Works, 70, 77–78, 79, 92–93, 142,
  149
  attempted sale of, 300–301, 328
  Buffalo Forge pig iron supplied by, 64, 66, 72,
    73, 78, 82, 84–85, 142, 143, 147
  D. Brady's inheritance of, 325
  food and clothing shortages at, 69–70, 76, 82
  forge closed at, 147
  forge erected at, 66, 67, 100, 101
  furnace dam at, 74, 75
  iron ore at, 70, 76–77, 82, 147, 300–301
  John Doyle's management of, 63–64, 65, 66,
    67, 69–71, 76, 79, 100
  under Jordan, Davis & Company, 71–82, 129,
    173
  location of, 59, 63
  profits of, 70, 91–92
  repairs at, 74–75
  Samuel Sherrerd's purchase of, 143
  sold to Jordan, Davis & Company, 73
  and WW's dispute with Jordan, Davis &
    Company, 83–96
  WW's repossession of, 92, 106, 176, 199
  WW's repurchase of, 143, 147
Bath Iron Works, slaves at, 75, 76, 79
  eating arrangements of, 76
  hiring of, 74, 75–76, 81, 124
  punishment of, 327
  quarters of, 70, 76
  runaway, 70, 75, 82
Baxter, John, 102, 115, 117–18, 175
Belinda, Old (slave), 198
Bell, John, 282, 283
Bellona Foundry, 65, 284, 289
Ben (Elizabeth Mathews's slave), 75
Beverly (WW's hireling), 318, 320, 335
Bible, 15–16
Big Bethel, Va., fighting at, 288
Bill (Tooler, Sr.'s son), 25, 26, 31, 41, 52–53, 54,
  59
  flight and capture of, 43, 44
  infirmity and death of, 60, 192
Billy (hireling), 154
Bob (Tooler, Sr.'s son), *see* Robert
Boldock (Thompson), Ester, 218–19, 229, 352,
  353, 360, 368
Booker (James Callaway's slave), 150
Brady, Anne Gertrude "Nanny" (WW's
  great-niece), 6, 8, 165, 249, 325, 349, 352,
  362, 363
Brady, Bonnie, xv
Brady, Charles Patrick Augustus "Pat" (WW's
  great-nephew), 6, 8, 9, 313, 325, 349, 362,
  363

Brady, Daniel C. E. (WW's nephew-in-law), 9,
  10, 150, 157, 158, 172, 189, 190–91, 203, 207,
  210, 217, 219, 269, 321–22, 349
  arrival of, in Virginia, xiv, 8, 159, 165, 185, 242
  assessment of slaves by, 259
  after Civil War, 339–62
  in Civil War, 292–339
  Confederacy supported by, 288
  Confederate contract with, 330–31
  on county Board of Supervisors, 362
  death of, 362
  diphtheria of, 315
  former slaves addressed by, 342
  home journal of, xiv, xvi, 163, 166–67, 179,
    224
  in late antebellum years, 242–85
  new business ventures sought by, 354–56
  Pat Brady's education and, 313
  Philadelphia businesses of, 164
  portrait of, 227
  poverty of, after Civil War, 341
  presidential pardon granted to, 346, 349
  recruited by WW, xiv, 4–8, 158–59, 164–65,
    185
  on secession and Civil War, 283, 297
  slave hiring and, 250, 252, 292, 318, 319
  slave list of, xvi
  and slaves' avoidance of work, 261, 276–78
  slaves' view of, 327, 351, 352
  at Stonewall Jackson's funeral, 328
  vaccinations given by, 269
  on vigilante justice, 340–41
  as voting registrar, 359
  wartime investments sought by, 329
  after WW's death, 324–62
  as WW's executor, 325
Brady, Douglas E., 211
Brady, Douglas E., Jr. "Pat," xv, 365–66
Brady, Elliott Thomas (WW's great-nephew),
  349, 362
Brady, Emma Belle, 313
Brady, Emma Matilda Gorgas (WW's niece),
  269, 313, 321–22, 346, 349, 360
  arrival of, in Virginia, xiv, 8, 159, 165, 185, 242
  Charles Gorgas's death and, 317
  death of, 362
  illness of, 248–49
  portrait of, 228
  recruited by WW, xiv, 4–8, 158, 164–65, 185
  sick tended by, 272
  in WW's will, 316, 325
Brady, Leah Cecilia Elliott, 164
Brady, Marie, 363
Brady, Mary, xv, 365–66
Brady, Patrick, 164

Brady, Sarah Elizabeth (WW's great-niece), 269, 322, 325, 349, 362
Brady, Thomas Forest (WW's great-nephew), 249
Brady, Tom, xv, xvi
Brady, Wilhelmina Weaver (WW's great-niece), 325, 349, 362
Brady, William Weaver (WW's great-nephew) (born 1853), 6, 8, 164, 322
Brady, William Weaver (WW's great-nephew) (born 1857), 8, 164–65, 322
Brady & Rex, 330, 332
Brandus (WW's hireling), 68
Brawley, James, 59–60, 68
Breckinridge, John C., 282
Brien (white hammerman), 36
Brown, John, 263, 264–66, 295
Bryan, James, 99
Bryan, Matthew, 141, 144–46, 149, 156, 274, 306
Stuart Buchanan & Company, 302–3
Buena Vista Furnace, 96, 252, 331, 346
Buffalo (Union) Forge:
    acquisition of, 19–21
    ambrotypes of, 225–26
    Bradys recruited for, xiv, 4–8, 158–59, 164–65, 185
    in Civil War, 295–339
    after Civil War, 339–62
    Confederate demands for iron of, 322, 324, 329–33, 338–39
    difficulties meeting demand at, 257–62
    diphtheria outbreak at, 313–15, 319, 326, 336
    in early years after dissolution of Mayburry & Weaver, 65, 66, 68, 69–70, 71
    Eliza Weaver's dislike for, 129
    Emma Brady's inheritance of, 325
    on eve of Civil War, 264–70, 274–86
    fire at, 314–15
    forge dam at, 39, 246, 309, 310, 340, 347
    individual stories of slaves at, 171–219
    during Jordan, Davis & Company years, 72, 74, 75, 81
    last iron work at, 359
    in late antebellum years, 241–63
    layout and location of, xiii, 5, 10
    low stockpiles at, 69–70
    managed by WW and Mayburry, 47, 48, 49, 50, 52
    photographs of, 230–33, 235–36
    present condition of, 365–66
    price of, 20, 41–42
    production level of, 65
    proposed rolling mill for, 332–33
    under rental arrangement, 49, 50
    repairs to, 29, 33
    research on, xiii–xviii
    slave cemetery of, 235–36, 366
    slave quarters at, 10, 111–12, 230–33, 243, 365
    slaves purchased for, 25–28
    store of, 47, 365
    strong demand for iron of, 257–62
    water problems at, 40, 41, 246, 309
    in WW and Mayburry's disputes, 54–62
    in WW's absence, 29, 33, 36–37, 39, 40, 41, 42
    after WW's death, 324–62
    WW's fondness for, 123
    see also pig iron, for Buffalo Forge; slaves
Buffalo Forge Cash Books, 327
Bureau of Ordnance of Hydrography, Confederate Navy, 300
Burnside, Ambrose, 318–19
Byrd (James Callaway's slave), 150

Caesar (WW's hireling), 318, 320
California Furnace, 355
Callaway, James, 150
Camack, Ben, 155, 156
Camack, Colonel, 155
Camack, Dick, 155
Camack, Dudley, 155, 156
Camack, Reubin, 155, 156
Camack, Tom, 155, 156
Camasky, Bill, 273–74, 326
canal politics, 136–37
cannon iron, 65, 289–90, 293
Carse, G. B., 351
Carson, James E., 254–56, 279–80
Carter, Amy Banks, 243, 247, 265–66, 296, 321
Carter, James, 265–66
Carter, John William, 296
Carter, Josephine, 321
Cartmill, Bill, 251, 272–73
Cartmill, John, 147, 251
Cartmill, Thomas, 147, 153, 154, 251
Cato (WW's hireling), 43, 44
Catoctin Furnace, 20–21
Chancellorsville, battle of, 328
Chandler, Mary, 361
Chandler, Mary Caroline Coleman, 270, 361
Chandler, Samuel T., 323, 324, 325
Chandler, Stewart, 361
Chandler, William, 361
charcoal making, 31, 110, 119–20, 135, 149, 331–32
Charles (Amy's son), see Matthews, Charles
Charleston Mercury, 282
Christmas holidays:
    after Civil War, 349
    working through, 177, 193

Christmas holidays (*continued*)
    work suspended for, 30, 31, 32, 78, 110, 119,
        269, 300, 319
Civil War, 287–339
    fighting in, 288, 297, 298, 308, 310–11, 313,
        318–19, 329, 333, 334–35
    general economic conditions in, 327, 328, 329
    hostilities preceding, 264–68, 282–86
    iron market during, 290–91, 297, 299, 303–4,
        307–8, 310, 317–18
Clarke, John, 65, 284
Clifton Forge, 72, 73, 100, 112
clothing, 69–70, 76, 82, 111, 270–72, 305, 318
Coleman, A., 185
Coleman, Alfred Elliott, 185, 249, 313–14, 336,
    337
Coleman, Elizabeth Williams "Betty," 176, 181,
    185, 249, 255, 269–70, 313
    death of, 313–14, 319, 336, 337, 349
Coleman (Chandler), Mary Caroline, 270, 361
Compromise of 1850, 166
Congress, Confederate, 308, 317, 329–30
Congress, U.S., 268, 358–59
Conscription Acts, Confederate, 308, 329–30
Constitutional Union party, 282, 283
Cooley, James L., 298
Cosby (Amy's husband), 205
"Cosby," Charles, *see* Matthews, Charles
Crews, Joshua, 162
Crobarger, John, 146
Crutchfield, Robert, 68, 69

dams, forge:
    at Buffalo Forge, 39, 246, 309, 310, 340, 347
dams, furnace:
    at Bath Works, 74, 75
    at Etna Furnace, 31
Danenhower, John Weaver (WW's nephew), 45,
    46, 49, 60, 64, 71, 72, 79–81, 88, 89, 90, 132
    ousted from Jordan, Davis & Company, 79–80
Danenhower, Rachel Weaver (WW's sister), 45
Daniel (Mary Dickinson's slave), 216
Davidson, Clara, 133–34
Davidson, Greenlee, 252, 275, 299, 300–301, 308
Davidson, James D., xiv, 94, 143, 148
    D. Brady's correspondence with, 318, 341, 355
    invited to Buffalo Forge, 270
    John Rex's correspondence with, 171, 172,
        183, 368
    public meeting for union called by, 283, 287
    on smallpox epidemic, 268–69
    on troubles preceding Civil War, 268
    visits of, 311
    William Green's drunkenness and, 274–75
    WW's correspondence with, 94, 104–5,

        122–23, 126, 128–30, 131, 143, 149, 150,
        153, 155, 201, 241, 242, 268–69, 270,
        297–98, 308, 310
    WW's gifts to daughters of, 133–34, 209
Davidson, Mary, 133–34, 209, 274
Davis, Abram Weaver (WW's nephew), 24,
    71–72, 74, 75, 79–80, 81, 83–92, 127, 129,
    133, 158
    Jordan, Davis & Company left by, 92
    Sam Jordan's conflict with, 83–84
    WW's reconciliation with, 95–96
Davis, Ann Overton Dickinson (WW's
    niece-in-law), 88–89, 95, 104, 178
    Mary Dickinson's slaves and, 213, 215, 217
Davis (Jordan), Hannah (WW's niece), 72, 89, 95,
    133, 178
Davis, James Cole (WW's great-nephew), 214,
    215–16
Davis, Jefferson, 308
Davis, Margaret Weaver (WW's sister), 24, 71
Davis (Rex), Mary Ann (WW's niece), 158
Davis, Stephen (WW's brother-in-law), 24
Davis, William Weaver (WW's nephew), 24,
    104–5, 133, 158, 178, 199, 213, 214
    with Jordan, Davis & Company, 71, 72, 74, 79,
        80, 81, 83–84, 173
    with Jordan & Davis, 92–97, 140
    marriage of, 88–89
    Mary Dickinson's slaves and, 215–18
    and WW's conflict with Jordan, Davis &
        Company, 83–95, 127, 128, 129, 176
    WW's reconciliation with, 95
Davy (WW's free black hireling), 68
F. B. Deane, Jr. & Son, 250, 253, 290, 291, 307
Democratic party, 66, 158, 251, 264, 282
Dennis (Festus Dickinson's slave), 124, 125
Derest, Jim, 119
Dick (William Davis's slave), 104–5
Dickinson, Ann Overton, *see* Davis, Ann Overton
    Dickinson
Dickinson, Cole, 125
Dickinson, Festus, 124–26
Dickinson, James C., 75–76, 88–89, 90, 93
Dickinson, Mary, 89, 90, 93, 213, 214–15
    slaves of, after her death, 215–18
Dickinson, Roscoe, 215
Dill, Joseph G., 329
diphtheria, 272, 273, 313–15, 319, 326, 336
disease, 70, 207, 326, 336
    diphtheria, 272, 273, 313–15, 319, 326,
        336
    smallpox, 268–69, 270, 315
Douglas, Stephen A., 166, 251, 282
Douglass, Alfred, 219
Douglass family, 361

Doyle, John, 123, 142
  at Bath Iron Works, 63–64, 65, 66, 67, 69–71,
    76, 79, 100
  on free vs. slave labor, 106, 107
  in Weaver v. Jordan, Davis & Company, 92,
    127, 187, 188
Dred Scott decision, 251
Dunkers, 15–16, 17, 130
  slavery opposed by, 16, 22, 28, 42
Dutch, Bill, 316, 320, 324, 335
dysentery, 70

Easton, Betsy, 115, 116
Easton, Phill, 51, 52, 99, 100, 101, 102, 106,
    115–17, 132
  death of, 117
  purchase of, 98
economic conditions, general, 66, 327, 328, 329
  see also iron, iron working
Edwards, Thomas, 342
elections of 1828, 66
elections of 1832, 66
elections of 1858, 251
elections of 1860, 282–84
Eliza (Clara Davidson's slave), 133–34
Ellen (Mary's daughter), 53, 60, 61, 97, 173, 207
  after Mayburry's death, 140, 141–42, 143–44,
    145, 146
Ellicott, John, 330, 331, 332, 333, 338–39
Elliott (Brady), Leah Cecilia, 164
Emancipation Proclamation, 316
Emma Mines, 355
Empy, William, 99, 115
Entsminger, Lewis, 296
Etna Furnace, 46, 67, 81, 132, 253
  acquisition of, 19
  Ann Sisson Gorgas's inheritance of, 316–17
  blast at (1816), 33
  blast at (1855), 155
  Charles Gorgas recruited for, 4, 6, 8, 158,
    159
  Charles Gorgas's management of, 160, 161,
    163, 164, 165, 242, 250, 270–71, 305
  in Civil War, 289–95, 302–7
  closing and dismantling of, 304–7, 319
  description of, 29–30
  discipline problems at, 272–74
  after dissolution of Mayburry & Weaver, 53,
    54
  on eve of Civil War, 270–74
  food and clothing shortages at, 270–72, 305
  furnace dam at, 31
  health problems at, 270, 272
  hot-blast machinery at, 292–93, 294, 305
  location of, xiii–xiv, 3

  managed by WW and Mayburry, 48, 49, 50,
    52
  photograph of, 237
  pig iron supplied to Buffalo Forge by, 50,
    53–55, 63, 149, 163, 242
  price of, 20, 41–42
  railroad from Retreat bank to, 147–48, 149,
    150, 153, 154, 155, 159, 306
  rebuilding of, 22, 23, 29, 32
  under rental arrangement, 49, 50
  Samuel Sherrerd's purchase of, 142–44, 149
  store of, 37
  water lacking at, 257
  white workers at, 257, 270–71
  in WW and Mayburry's disputes, 54–62
  in WW's absence, 32, 33, 41, 42
  WW's management of, after repurchase,
    147–64
  WW's repurchase of, 147–48
Etna Furnace, slaves at, 25, 26, 30–31, 41, 99,
    147, 149–63, 254–55, 256–57, 273–74, 305,
    319
  in Civil War, 305
  difficulties in obtaining of, 252
  hazardous duties and, 160–61
  incentives for, 150–51, 161–62
  in late antebellum years, 242, 250–52
  overwork system and, 151, 155–56, 162–63
  punishment of, 162, 327
  runaway, 43, 44, 160, 161, 162
  slaves' preference and, 151, 161–62
  time off purchased by, 162
"Etnas," *see* Williams, Charles; Williams, Sam,
    Jr.; Williams, Washington
Ewing, John D., 342

Falling Spring Presbyterian Church, 324, 325,
    362
  photograph of cemetery of, 235
Fancy Hill Mutual Aid Club, 351
Fannie, Old (Mary Dickinson's slave), 216
Farmers' Register, 136
Fleming, Solomon, 99, 100, 113, 117, 205
food, 69–70, 76, 82, 111, 257, 270–71, 318
Fort Sumter, 284, 285–86
Fraley, Lydia (WW's great-niece), 325
Frank (Peter Griggs's slave), 152, 153
Franklin, Andrew, 361
Franklin, James, 361
Fredericksburg, battle of, 318–19, 320
free black iron workers, 68, 99, 115, 171
Freedmen's Bureau, 348, 350, 351–52, 356,
    357–58, 368
Freeport Doctrine, 251
Fuller, Jacob, 265, 268

Garland (WW's slave), *see* Thompson, Garland, Sr.

Garland, David S., 103

"Garlands," *see* Thompson, James; Thompson, Samuel; Thompson, William

Georgianna (Mary's daughter), 25–26, 53, 172

Gettysburg, battle of, 329

Gibraltar (Mayburry's) Forge, 59, 96–97, 100, 101, 140, 173, 213, 214, 216

Gilmore, Ben, 102, 121

Glenwood Furnace, 151–52, 252

Gooch, Jim, 201–2

Goochland, Billy, 103

Gorgas, Ann Sisson (WW's niece-in-law), 294, 304, 306, 316–17

Gorgas, Charles K. (WW's nephew):
  Confederacy supported by, 293–94
  death of, 316–17
  Etna Furnace managed by, 160, 161, 163, 164, 165, 242, 250, 270–71, 305
  Lawson cursed by, 254
  marriage of, 294, 305
  recruited for Etna Furnace, 4, 6, 8, 158, 159
  slave hiring and, 242, 250, 252
  white workers and, 257
  in WW's will, 316

Gorgas, Emma Matilda, *see* Brady, Emma Matilda Gorgas

Gorgas, Lydia Weaver (WW's sister), 6, 43, 158, 164, 325
  portrait of, 228

Gorgas, Peter K. (WW's brother-in-law), 43, 164

Grace Furnace, 251–52

Grant, Ulysses S., 333

Granville (Sarah McDowell's slave), 104

Green, Matilda Thompson, 133–34, 209, 274, 275, 276, 279

Green, William, 274–76
  drunkenness of, 275
  flight and sale of, 279–80, 367

Gregg, J. Irwin, 342

Gregory, Mary E., 151

Griffin (WW's slave), 163, 271, 315

Griggs, Peter R., 152, 153

Grigsby, Sam, 324, 344

gun metal, 65, 289–90, 293

Halleck, Henry W., 341

Hamilton (Mary's son), 53, 60, 61, 97, 173, 207
  after Mayburry's death, 140, 141, 145, 146

Hamilton, Alexander W., 342

Harper's Ferry, Va.:
  Confederate capture of, 313
  John Brown's attack on, 263, 264–66

Harry (Ellen's husband), 144

Henry (Amy's son), *see* Matthews, Henry

Highland Farm, 135, 340

Hill, John, 77

Holmes, Jack, 119

"Home Journal" (Brady), xiv, xvi, 163, 166–67, 179, 224

horses and mules:
  shoes for, 298–99, 322, 324, 330
  WW's pasturing of, 309

"House Book," xvii, 174

Hunt, Billy, 51, 52, 79, 86, 98, 100, 115, 199
  appraisal of, 52
  death of, 199
  Oxford Iron Works training of, 101, 102, 198, 212

Hunt, Charlotte Wade, 200–201, 328, 353, 360

Hunt, Eliza, 353

Hunt, George, 328, 353

Hunt, Billy, 79, 198, 199, 203
  dispute over ownership of, 85–87, 88–94, 213

Hunt, Harry, Jr., 198–203, 212, 246, 319, 328, 353
  agricultural work of, 243, 244, 297, 326, 331, 339–40
  alleged assault on, 357–58
  apprenticeship of, 198, 200
  birth of, 198
  at Buffalo Forge, 11, 79, 105, 107, 157, 166, 191, 197, 207, 247, 261, 285, 310, 312, 323, 336, 341, 345, 347, 350, 354
  after Civil War, 339–40, 341, 344, 345, 347, 349, 350, 354, 357–58, 360
  D. Brady's assessment of, 259
  departure of, 357–58, 360
  dispute over ownership of, 85–87, 88–94, 213
  eye injury of, 201, 203
  illnesses of, 248, 260
  labor contracts and earnings of, 344, 350, 354
  marriage of, 200–201, 311, 328
  monetary value of, 203
  overwork and purchases of, 200, 201, 206, 249, 260, 296–97, 299, 309
  physical appearance of, 200
  sabotage and, 279, 319
  skill of, 3, 262, 333
  testimony of, in murder case, 201–2
  work missed by, 260–61, 276, 277, 296–97, 309, 323, 341
  work rate of, 247, 300

Hunt, Harry, Sr. "Hal," 100, 106, 176, 193, 198, 199, 200
  at Bath Iron Works, 79
  dispute over ownership of, 85–87, 88–94, 213
  overwork and purchases of, 199–200, 201
  Oxford Iron Works training of, 79, 101, 102, 198, 212
  productivity of, 106

valued at zero dollars, 203
WW's purchase of, 79, 99, 100
Hunt, Lucy, 353
Hunt, Mary, 328, 353
Hunt, Nanny, 198
Hunt, Old (slave), 198
Hunt, Wilson, 201, 328, 353
Hunter, David, 334–35, 342
Hunter, John, 141

Impressment Act, Confederate, 317
infant mortality, 250
inflation, in Civil War, 328, 329
investments, wartime, 329
Irby & Saunders, 253
iron, iron working:
  Confederate demands for, 322, 324, 329–33, 338–39
  continuous operation in, 30
  exact specifications in, 259–60
  jobs in, 204, 209
  market and prices of, after Civil War, 346–47, 354
  market and prices of, before Civil War, 3, 11, 35, 38, 39, 47, 50, 56, 64, 65, 66, 71, 112, 148, 154, 157, 159, 160, 241–42, 246, 250, 252–53, 257–62, 267, 282, 283
  market and prices of, during Civil War, 290–91, 297, 299, 303–4, 307–8, 310, 317–18
  in North vs. South, 148
  as precarious business, 123
  quality of, 112–13, 242
  techniques of, 10–11, 30, 31, 246, 292–93, 333, 355
  see also bar iron, merchant bar; Lynchburg market; pig iron; Richmond market
iron ore, 65, 66, 159, 304
  at Bath Iron Works, 70, 76–77, 82, 147, 300–301
  at Contrary Creek, 140
  on land rented from Ann Sisson, 306
  at Retreat Furnace, 147, 150, 159–60, 161
Isaac (WW's hireling), 69

Jack (WW's hireling), 340
Jackson, Andrew, 66, 137
Jackson, Thomas Jonathan "Stonewall," 295, 310, 313, 328
James River and Kanawha Canal, 136–37, 291
Jefferson, Nancy, *see* Williams, Nancy Jefferson
Joe (Tooler, Sr.'s son), 11, 25, 26, 27, 52, 99, 105, 179, 192, 244, 262
  death of, 280–81
  preaching of, 280–81
John (Louisa's son), 298, 305–6, 312, 314, 342
John (Mary's son), *see* Sims, John

Johnson, Andrew, 346
Johnson, George W., 273
Jolly, Thomas, 100
Jones, John W., 294–95
Jordan (WW's slave), 272
Jordan, Davis & Company, 71–82, 129, 158, 173
  family's view of WW's conflict with, 95
  John Danenhower ousted from, 79–80
  Sam Jordan's departure and return to, 83–84
  WW's dispute with, 83–96, 104, 127, 128, 129, 187, 213
Jordan, Elizabeth Leibert Keen (WW's niece), 95
Jordan, Hannah Davis (WW's niece), 72, 89, 95, 133, 178
Jordan, John, 72, 73–74, 76, 78, 82, 90, 100, 104
  canal politics and, 137
  WW's dispute with, over land use, 128–29
Jordan, Samuel F. (WW's nephew-in-law), 153, 199, 252, 317, 331, 335, 339, 346
  Abram Davis's conflict with, 83–84
  church founded by, 178
  first marriage of, 72, 89, 133
  with Jordan, Davis & Company, 72, 73, 74, 76, 78, 79, 81, 83–84
  with Jordan & Davis, 92–97, 140
  second marriage of, 95
  temper of, 78
  WW's attempted sale of Bath to, 301
  and WW's dispute with Jordan, Davis & Company, 83–95, 104, 127, 128, 129, 176
  WW's reconciliation with, 95
Jordan & Davis, 92–97, 140
Jordan & Irvine, 73, 112
B. J. Jordan & Company, 241
Joyner, Charles, 366

Kansas, slave issue in, 165–66, 264
Kansas-Nebraska Act (1854), 166
Keen (Jordan), Elizabeth Leibert (WW's niece), 95
King, Anne Gertrude "Nanny," 249, 353
King, Charles B., 218, 353
King, Eliza Thompson, 209, 210, 211, 218, 249, 279, 345, 348, 353
King, Hannah, 279, 353
King, Isabella, 218, 353
King, James, 218, 353
King, William, 353
King, Wilson Botetourt, 210, 218, 248, 311, 319, 323, 345, 348, 353

land reform, lack of, 348, 350, 359
Lawson (WW's slave), 254–55, 367
Lee, Robert E., 298, 313, 319, 328, 339
Lee, Rocke & Company, 253, 258, 261

Lee, Rocke & Taylor, 282, 283, 288, 295, 297, 299, 308, 309, 317
Lee & Johnson, 135
Letcher, John, 268, 283, 299, 308, 311, 334
Lexington Baptist Church, 178–79
Lexington *Gazette,* 131, 137, 142, 145, 264, 267, 279, 284, 287–88, 324, 339, 362
Lexington *Valley Star,* 264–65
Lincoln, Abraham, 166, 251, 285–86, 288, 316
    elected president, 282–84
livestock, 9, 110, 136, 244, 248, 250, 323
    slaughtering of, 248, 249–50, 318, 323
Locher, Charles H., 265, 331
Louisa (Mary Dickinson's slave), 216
Louisa (Mary's daughter), 25–26, 53, 54, 58, 59, 60, 61, 139, 172, 173, 210, 211, 272, 298
    after Civil War, 343–44
    Etna's closing and, 305–7
    husband of, 60–61
    WW's rejection of offer for, 256
Louisa County hiring market, 67, 76, 154
Lowe, James, 77–78
Lucy (Louisa's daughter), 272, 273, 306, 344
Lydia Furnace, *see* Bath Furnace; Bath Iron Works
Lynchburg *Daily Virginian,* 354
Lynchburg market, 3, 11, 47, 64, 66, 113, 135, 136, 157, 242, 246, 249, 250, 253, 258, 259–60, 267, 297, 299, 302, 346–47, 353

McAllister, William C., 102
McClellan, George B., 311, 313
McCormick, Cyrus Hall, xiv
McCormick, Henry A., 146–47, 156, 157, 256, 272, 273, 274, 306
McCue, Moses, 99, 101
McDaniel & Irby, 302–3
McDowell, Sarah, 104
McFadden, Edward, 345, 349, 357
McFadden, Henry Clay, 357–58
Mack, Alexander (WW's great-grandfather), 15
Mack, Alexander, Jr. "Sander" (WW's grandfather), 15, 17–18
Mack, Hannah, *see* Weaver, Hannah Mack
Mack, Sarah (WW's aunt), 17, 18
Madison, James, 137
Manassas, first battle of, 297
Manassas, second battle of, 313
manganese mining, 355
Manuel (Festus Dickinson's slave), 124, 125
maps:
    of Buffalo Forge, 5
    of Virginia and Rockbridge County, 245
marble quarry, 34, 42

Mark (Bill Dutch's brother), 316, 320, 324, 344, 348
marriage:
    Dunker rules of, 18
    former slaves' registration of, 352–53
    miscegentic, 174–75
    between slaves, xvii, 25–26, 176, 189–90, 219, 265–66, 352–53
Martha (WW's slave), 244
Mary (Sally Williams's mother), 53, 54, 58, 59, 60, 61–62, 97, 141, 172, 270
    after Mayburry's death, 140
    purchase of, 25–27
    separation of family of, 61–62, 173, 185, 207, 366
Mary Ann (John Crobarger's slave), 145, 146
Mathews, Elizabeth, 75
Matilda (WW's slave), 316, 344
Matthews, Bob, 314
Matthews ("Cosby"), Charles, 53, 205, 206
Matthews, Frances, 205, 206–7, 269, 314, 319, 360
Matthews, Henry, 53, 204–7, 212, 296, 314
    agricultural work of, 296, 312, 355–56
    after Civil War, 340, 344, 345, 347, 349, 350, 355–56, 357, 359, 360
    departure of, 359, 360
    illnesses of, 259, 261
    at iron work and carpentry, 11, 27, 107, 166, 197, 201, 202, 203, 246, 298, 324, 340, 345, 347–48, 350, 357
    name of, 205
    overwork and purchases of, 135, 205–7
    physical appearance of, 205
    at sawmill, 341
    slaughtering by, 248
    work missed by, 285, 321
    work rate of, 247
Matthews, Henry, Jr. (born 1859), 269
Matthews, Henry, Jr. (born 1860), 314
Matthews, Lewis, 314
Matthews, Mary Ellen, 207
Matthews, Philip Cosby, 207, 314
Matthews, Wash Alexander, 205, 206, 314
Mayburry, Eleanor, 54, 61
Mayburry, Thomas, 38, 66, 123, 133
    capital lacked by, 23–24, 38, 45
    Contrary Creek property of, 140
    death and estate of, 140–41
    deposition of, 127–28
    disputes with WW, after dissolution of partnership, 54–62, 63
    at Gibraltar Forge after dissolution, 59, 96–97, 100, 101, 140, 173
    iron works acquired by, 19–21

iron works managed by, in WW's absence, 29–45
and ownership of "Wilson negroes," 27, 47–48, 49, 51–52, 57–61, 85, 90, 139, 140, 173, 185, 188, 270, 313, 366
repairs and renovations undertaken by, 29–30
secret salary taken by, 49
slave hiring and, 32, 33, 35, 36, 37, 38–39, 40–41
on slavery, 22–23
Virginians distrusted by, 37
WW's dissolution of partnership with, 46–54
WW's first meeting with, 19
WW's generosity mocked by, 132
WW's lawsuits with, 56–60
WW's purchase of slaves from, 98
see also Buffalo Forge; Etna Furnace
Mayburry, Willoughby, 19, 20–21
Mayburry & Weaver, 20
  agricultural operations of, 30
  business established by, 21–28
  dissolution of, 46–54
  financial problems of, 32–33, 35, 37–38, 42, 43, 44, 45, 46, 55, 56
  managed by Mayburry, in WW's absence, 29–45
  properties acquired by, 19–21
  slave hiring and, 32, 33, 35, 36, 37, 38–39, 40–41, 47
  slaves purchased by, 22–23, 25–28
  slow sales of, 35, 38, 39, 47
  William Wilson's lawsuit against, 44
Mayburry's Forge, *see* Gibraltar Forge
merchant bar, *see* bar iron, merchant bar
Mexican-American War, 138, 165
Mies van der Rohe, Ludwig, xviii
Millboro Depot, 298–99
Millin (WW's slave), 255–56
mills, grain, 9, 285, 360
Minor, George, 300, 301
miscegenation, 174–75
Monroe, James, 137
Moore, Samuel McDowell, 144, 146
Morgan, Daniel, 185, 202, 206, 248, 269
Mossy Creek Furnace and Forge, 99
Mount Lydia Colored Baptist Church, 360, 361, 363, 364
  photographs of cemetery of, 236
Mount Torry Furnace, 274
mules, *see* horses and mules
Murphy (white forgeman), 35

Nash, Henry, 171, 172, 183, 361, 368
Navy, Confederate, 300, 301

"Negro books," 114–20, 135, 140, 155, 156, 180, 181–82, 190–91, 193, 199, 205, 209, 259, 299, 327, 367–68
Nevil, William, 99
Newkirk, Constant W. (WW's nephew-in-law), 141–42, 143, 148, 153–54
Newkirk, Elizabeth, *see* Weaver, Elizabeth Newkirk Woodman
Newman, Charles, 362, 363
Newman, Lydia Maydelene Reid, 336, 337, 360, 361–62
Newman, Mary Ann, 362
Niece (white forgeman), 35
Nitre and Mining Bureau, Confederate, 330, 331, 332, 338
Norcross, William, 99, 106

Obenchain, George, 212–13
Old Dominion Iron & Nail Works, 253, 291, 307
oral history, xvi, xvii, 129, 132, 208, 210–11, 212–13, 219, 327, 351
Orange County hiring market, 67, 151, 160, 320
overwork system, 108–21, 135, 151, 155–56, 162–63, 174, 328, 333, 367
  adjustments for inflation in, 327
  slaves' death and, 319
  see also specific slaves
Oxford Iron Works, 79, 101, 102, 106–7, 198, 212

Parr (white founder), 294, 304
patrol, vigilante, after Civil War, 340–41, 351
Peirpont, Francis H., 346
Pemberton, John, 329
Penn, Charles B., 51–52
Pennsylvania, fighting in, 329
Phill, Blacksmith (slave), 101–2
Phillis, Aunt (black midwife), 321, 325
pig iron, 10–11, 20
  after Etna's closing, 307
  Etna's production of, in Civil War, 289–95, 302–7
  market and prices of, *see* iron, iron working
  origin of term, 30
  traded for salt, 302–3
pig iron, for Buffalo Forge, 139, 140, 157
  Bath's production of, 64, 66, 72, 73, 78, 82, 84–85, 142, 143, 147
  after Civil War, 346
  during Civil War, 330, 331, 338, 339
  Etna's production of, 50, 53–56, 63, 149, 163, 242
  shortage of, 63, 65
Pittsylvania County hiring market, 32, 154
Placker, D. H., ambrotypes by, 224–25

Poague, John, 201
Poague, William F., 201, 351
politics, local and national, 66, 165–66, 251,
    264–68, 282–86, 358–59
Powell, W. L., 298
Preisz, John, 17, 18
Prince (Mary Towles's slave), 160, 161

Quakers, 16

railroad, from Retreat bank to Etna Furnace,
    147–48, 149, 150, 153, 154, 155, 159, 306
Rebecca (Joe's wife), 281
Rebecca (Tooler, Sr.'s wife), 25, 52, 152, 179,
    192
Reconstruction Acts (1867), 358–59
Reconstruction Proclamation, 346
Reid, Andrew, 265–66, 268
Reid, Caroline Williams, 178, 181, 255, 268, 270,
    312, 336
  death of, 336, 337, 349
  illness of, 313, 314
  wedding of, 265–66
Reid (Newman), Lydia Maydelene, 336, 337,
    360, 361–62
Reid, Mary Martha, 337
Reid, William John, 312–13, 337
religion, 178–79, 360
  see also Dunkers
Republican Party, 166, 251, 282, 288
Retreat Furnace, 22, 42, 67
  acquisition of, 19–21
  iron ore at, 147, 150, 159–60, 161
  railroad to Etna Furnace from, 147–48, 149,
    150, 153, 154, 155, 159, 306
Rex, John A. (WW's great-nephew), 157–58, 171,
    172, 183, 368
Rex, Mary Ann Davis (WW's niece), 158
Rex, Samuel V. (WW's nephew-in-law), 158
Rex, William Weaver (WW's great-nephew),
    157–58, 159, 161, 163, 253–54, 272, 273–74,
    279, 292, 293, 304–5, 306–7, 311, 332
  captured by Union forces, 335
  Charles Gorgas's funeral and, 317
  after Civil War, 342, 349, 356
  Confederacy supported by, 293–94
  Confederate conscription and, 293–94, 330
  Confederate contract with, 330–31
  slave hiring and, 242, 251, 252
  white labor and, 257, 270, 271
  in WW's will, 316, 325
Richmond, Va., xiii
  defense and capture of, 320, 324, 332, 339
  fighting for, 313, 318–19
Richmond *Dispatch,* 300
Richmond *Enquirer,* 265, 328

Richmond market, 3, 11, 47, 50, 65, 66, 71,
    112–13, 136, 153, 160, 164, 242, 250, 253,
    284, 289, 291, 293, 303, 307–8
  WW's complaint about, 307–8
Robert (Mary Towles's slave), 160–61, 163–64
Robert (Tooler, Sr.'s son), 25, 26, 53, 54, 98, 105,
    192, 193
Rockbridge Baths, 63
Rockbridge County:
  map of, 245
  slave patrol of, 266–67, 295, 327
Rockbridge County Home Guard, 288
Rockbridge Grays, 295, 297
Rocke & Murrell, 354
Rodenheizer, Henry, 156
Ross, David, 79, 101, 106–7, 212
Ross, William, 52
Ruffin, Edmund, 136
runaways, 43, 44, 70, 75, 82, 134–35, 160, 161,
    162, 163, 253–54, 255–56, 279–80

Safety Club, 340–41, 342, 351
St. John, I. M., 331
Salem, Va., Quartermaster Department at,
    322
Salling, Sam, 320, 324, 327, 355
Sally (Mary's daughter), *see* Williams, Sally
salt, pig iron traded for, 302–3
Saltville, Va., 302–3
Sam (hireling), 69
Sam (Poagues' slave), 201–2
Sam, Jr., *see* Williams, Sam, Jr.
sawmill, Buffalo Forge, 331, 341, 347
Schoolfield, John W., 113, 117
Scipio (WW's hireling), 335
secession, 282–86
Seward, William Henry, 166
Shanks & Patton, 251–52
sharecropping, 358–59, 361
Sharp, J. W., 351–52, 359
Sharpsburg, battle of, 313
Shaw, Lorenzo, 146
Sherman, William Tecumseh, 333
Sherrerd, John, 142, 143–44, 149
Sherrerd, Samuel, 142–44, 149
Shields & Somerville, 160, 284
shoes, 69–70, 76, 271–72
Sibert, Lorenzo, 355
Sims, John, 53, 60, 61, 97, 140, 141, 145, 146–47,
    173, 207, 304, 306, 313
  Bill Camasky's attack on, 273–74
  illness of, 306
Sisson (Gorgas), Ann (WW's niece-in-law), 294,
    304, 306, 316–17
slave insurrection, fears of, 266–67, 294–95, 296
slave patrol, 266–67, 295, 327

slavery:
  Dunkers' opposition to, 16, 22, 28, 42
  Emancipation Proclamation and, 316
  Mayburry on, 22–23
  mounting national hostilities over, 264–68
  national debate over, 138, 165–66, 251
  technological innovation slowed by, 333
slaves:
  alcohol and, 31, 114, 275–76
  after Civil War, 339–42
  coming freedom and, 334, 336
  consent of, to WW's purchase, 103, 105
  cost advantage of, over whites, 107
  and dispute with Jordan, Davis & Company,
    85–87, 88–94, 213
  Eliza Weaver as viewed by, 132
  escape of, to Union forces, 335
  firearms denied to, 295
  food and clothing provided for, 69–70, 76, 82,
    111, 270–71, 318
  freedom bought by, 102, 121
  freedom officially given to, 342
  freedom taken by, 340
  given as gifts, 89, 133–34, 209, 274
  impressment of, during Civil War, 320–21
  individual stories of, 171–219
  James Cole Davis's attitude toward, 216–17
  jobs of, 30–31, 52–54, 187–88, 204, 209
  maintenance costs for, 65
  marriage and, xvii, 25–26, 176, 189, 219,
    265–66, 352–53
  of Mary Dickinson, after her death, 215–18
  murder case involving, 201–2
  names of, 139–40, 155, 174, 181–82, 205, 207,
    210, 219, 270, 312–13, 361
  overwork payments of, after death, 319
  photographs of cabins of, 230–33
  photographs of cemeteries of, 235–37
  power gained by, through skills, 191, 259–62,
    278–79
  punishment of, 107–8, 212–13, 274–75, 327, 328
  purchase of, 22–23, 25–28, 66, 98–105, 120,
    188, 189, 208, 274
  quarters of, 10, 70, 76, 111–12, 230–33, 243,
    365
  religion of, 178–79, 360
  resistance by, 163, 367
  reunited by sale, 214, 274
  runaway, 43, 44, 70, 75, 82, 134–35, 160, 161,
    162, 163, 253–54, 255–56, 279–80
  sabotage and, 108, 279, 367
  sale as punishment of, 108, 110, 134–35,
    254–56, 273, 279–80, 326, 327
  varied experience lacked by, 106–7
  violence among, 273–74
  whipping of, 212–13, 266–67, 268, 269

  WW as viewed by, 132–35
  WW's arrangements for, after his death, 7,
    8–9, 158, 159, 316, 325, 326
  WW's examination of, before purchase, 104–5
  WW's hiding of, from family, 28, 42
  see also Bath Iron Works, slaves at; Etna
    Furnace, slaves at; overwork system;
    "Wilson negroes"
slaves, former, 339–64
  cabins of, 360
  D. Brady's address to, 342
  departure of, 340, 345, 347–48, 359, 360
  hostility toward, 351
  labor contracts and earnings of, 343–45, 347,
    348, 350, 355–56
  marriages registered by, 352–53
  return of, 350–51
  rights of, 342–43
  right to vote of, 358–59
  sharecropping by, 358–59, 361
slaves, hired, 23, 32, 33, 35, 36, 37, 38–39, 40–41,
    66, 74, 99, 100–101, 246
  in Civil War, 291–92, 318, 319–20
  consent of, to WW's hiring, 69, 151, 153,
    161–62, 367
  cost of, 65, 119, 125, 149, 214, 292
  escape of, to Union forces, 335
  Festus Dickinson and WW's argument over,
    124–26
  freedom taken by, 340
  at Gibraltar Forge, 214
  hiring markets for, 67–70; see also specific
    markets
  illness and injuries of, 70
  runaways among, 43, 44, 70, 160, 161, 162,
    253–54
  subsequent purchase of, 104
  see also Bath Iron works, slaves at; Etna
    Furnace, slaves at
smallpox epidemics, 268–69, 270, 315
Snyder, Asa, 291
Somerville, R. B., 289
R. B. Somerville & Company, 289, 291
Sophia (WW's slave), 152
Spotswood (WW's slave), 335
Spotsylvania County hiring market, 67, 69, 101,
    157, 242, 250, 292, 320
Staples, William, 69
Stout, William, 141
Stuart, Aaron, 253–54
Supreme Court, U.S., 251
Susan (WW's slave), 272, 273
syphilis, 274, 326

tar burning, 176–77
Taylor, Creed, 202

Templeton, Jenny, WW's purchase of, 99
Templeton, Sam, 99, 100
Terry (slave), 105
textile factory, 34, 72, 90
Thompson, Adeline, 219, 353
Thompson, Alice, 218
Thompson, Betsy, 218
Thompson, Dicey, 213–18, 345
Thompson, Eliza (Garland, Jr.'s daughter), 353
Thompson (King), Eliza (Garland, Jr.'s sister),
    209, 210, 211, 218, 249, 279, 345, 348, 353
Thompson, Ester Boldock, 218–19, 229, 352, 353,
    360, 368
Thompson, Frank, 218
Thompson, Garland, III, 353
Thompson, Garland, Jr., xvi, 105, 209, 210, 246,
    319, 336, 340, 353, 367
  agricultural work of, 323, 355–56
  after Civil War, 340, 341, 344, 345, 350,
    355–56, 357, 359, 360, 361
  departure of, 360
  diphtheria of, 314
  marriage of, 311, 336, 340, 352
  photograph of, 219, 229, 368
  physical appearance of, 210–11
  as sharecropper, 361
  teamster work of, 218–19, 243, 244, 262, 306,
    339, 340, 341, 345, 350, 357
Thompson, Garland, Sr., xvi, 11–12, 166, 208–19
  after Civil War, 345, 348
  first wife of, 209–10
  Mary Dickinson's death and, 215–18
  oral tradition on, 210–11, 212–13
  overwork and purchases of, 209, 213
  purchase of, 102, 208
  second wife of, 213–14
  sold by WW, 208, 214
  whipping story about, 212–13
Thompson ("Garland"), James (Garland, Jr.'s
    brother), 209, 211, 214
  agricultural work of, 11, 197, 247, 322, 340
  after Civil War, 340, 344, 347–48, 349, 350,
    354, 357, 359
  departure of, 359
  diphtheria of, 314
  at iron work, 11, 105, 197, 247, 248, 259, 261,
    276–77, 309, 324, 341, 347–48, 350, 354,
    357
  name of, 210
  overwork and purchases of, 212, 218, 299
  work refused by, 341
Thompson, James (Garland, Jr.'s grandson),
    xv–xvi, 132, 133, 210–11, 212–13, 219, 352,
    368
  photograph of, 229
Thompson, John, 219, 353, 357

Thompson (Green), Matilda, 133–34, 209, 274,
    275, 276, 279
Thompson, Rachael, 218
Thompson, Ruben, 219, 353, 357
Thompson, Samuel (born about 1863), 218
Thompson ("Garland"), Samuel (born early
    1840s), 209, 210, 211, 217–18, 219, 320, 324,
    344, 348, 350–51
Thompson ("Garland"), William, 209, 210, 211,
    217–18, 219, 344, 348
Tinder, David, 188
tobacco, D. Brady's investment in, 329, 339
Tom (Constant Newkirk's slave), 142, 143
Tom (hireling), 154
W. D. Tompkins & Brother, 302, 303
Tooler, Jr., 25, 26, 52, 99, 192–97, 200, 246, 319
  agricultural work of, 243, 244, 297, 322, 323,
    326, 331, 339–40
  at Buffalo Forge, 11, 27, 79, 105, 107, 157, 166,
    191, 203, 207, 209, 212, 213, 242, 248, 285,
    310, 312, 323, 336, 345, 347, 359
  after Civil War, 339–40, 344, 345, 347, 349,
    350, 357, 359
  D. Brady's assessment of, 259
  departure of, 347, 349
  illnesses of, 246, 249, 261
  injuries of, 195, 246–47
  labor contracts of, 344, 350
  marriage of, 194
  overwork and purchases of, 193–97, 206, 249,
    260, 296–97, 299, 309
  return of, 350
  sabotage and, 279, 319
  skill of, 3, 262, 333
  work missed by, 260–61, 276, 277, 296–97,
    309, 323, 341
  work rate of, 247, 300
Tooler, Sr., 25, 26, 31, 41, 52, 53, 98–99, 100, 139,
    179, 193–94
Towles, Ann, 189–90, 191, 262, 321, 336–37, 360
Towles, Charles, 188, 189, 243, 298, 306, 319,
    344, 349, 350
  crippling injury of, 331
Towles, Clarence Henry, 336–37
Towles, Constant, 188, 244, 298, 314, 319
Towles, Cornelia, 190
Towles, Edgar, 188, 189, 319, 323, 344, 348,
    350–51, 360
Towles, Hannah Frances, 190
Towles, Henry, 187–91, 200, 212, 246, 319, 321,
    323, 336–37
  agricultural work of, 322, 326, 331, 339,
    355–56
  Betty Coleman's grave dug by, 314
  at Buffalo Forge, 11, 27, 107, 157, 166, 197,
    207, 242, 244, 246, 259, 262–63, 278, 285,

296, 297, 309, 310, 312, 331, 336, 340, 341, 345, 347, 350, 354, 357, 359
cash distribution to, 300
after Civil War, 339, 340, 341, 344, 345, 347, 349, 350, 354, 355–56, 357, 359, 360, 361
D. Brady's assessment of, 259
diphtheria avoided by, 314
illnesses and injuries of, 247, 261
labor contract and earnings of, 344, 347, 350, 354, 355–56
marriage of, 189–90
monetary value of, 203
overwork and purchases of, 190–91, 367
physical appearance of, 188–89
as sharecropper, 361
skill of, 3, 262, 333
slave patrol's whipping of, 266–67, 268, 269
work missed by, 276–77, 323
Towles, Joseph, 189–90
Towles, Luanna, 321
Towles, Mary C., 160–61
Towles, Prince, 188, 285, 321, 344, 348
Towles, Prince, Jr., 188, 314, 315, 319
Towles, Sally, 188
Towles, Thomas R., 160–61
Towles, Wilhelmina, 262
Tredegar Iron Works, xiii, 148, 250, 253, 289, 332
Triplett, William S., 253, 291, 307
Tubbs, C. Jerome, 350, 351
tuberculosis, 336
typhoid fever, 336

Union Forge, see Buffalo Forge
Updike, James G., 340, 342

vaccinations, 269
Vesuvius Furnace, 59, 141, 144–45, 149, 173
Vicksburg, battle of, 329
Victoria Furnace, 140
Vigilance Committee, 293–94
vineyard, planting of, 354–55
Virginia:
Civil War fighting in, 288, 297, 298, 310–11, 313, 318–19, 329, 334–35
Federal control of, 341, 342, 352
map of, 245
military units from, 293–94, 295, 297
politics in, 136, 268
secession and, 283, 287–88
slave insurrection feared in, 294–95
Virginia Military Institute, 295, 334
voting rights, 358–59

Wade (Hunt), Charlotte, 200–201, 328, 353, 360
War of 1812, 18–19, 66, 137, 138

water supply, 40, 41, 246, 257, 309
Watkins, James K., 134, 135, 149, 196
Watkins, John K., 152, 153
Watson, Major, 119
Weaver, Abraham (WW's brother), 24
WW's management of estate of, 24, 34, 42–43
Weaver, Abraham, Jr. (WW's nephew), 42
Weaver, Adam (WW's father), 15, 16–17
Hannah's illicit meeting with, 17–18
illness and death of, 23, 24, 28, 32
Weaver, Alexander (WW's brother), 18
Weaver, Elizabeth Newkirk Woodman (WW's wife), 6, 79, 82, 88, 122
courtship and marriage of, 74
death of, 131
ghost of, 132
photograph of gravestone of, 235
WW's relationship with, 129–32
Weaver, Hannah Mack (WW's mother), 15, 16
Adam's illicit meeting with, 17–18
illness and death of, 24, 28, 32, 33
Weaver, John (WW's brother), 18
Weaver, Lydia, see Gorgas, Lydia Weaver
Weaver (Davis), Margaret (WW's sister), 24, 71
Weaver (Danenhower), Rachel (WW's sister), 45
Weaver, Sarah (WW's sister), 43
Weaver, William (WW):
Abraham's estate managed by, 24, 34, 42–43
background and childhood of, 4, 15–18
Bath Iron Works sale attempted by, 300–301
birth of, 18
boats of, 194, 201
Bradys and Charles Gorgas recruited by, xiv, 4–8, 158–59, 164–65, 185
during Civil War, 287–311, 316–17
Confederacy supported by, 288
declining health and death of, 308, 322–24
early ventures of, 4, 18–19
Elizabeth married by, 74
estate of, 324
and Etna Furnace in 1840s and 1850s, 142–64
Etna Furnace repurchased by, 147–48
Etna managed by, after repurchase, 147–67
on eve of Civil War, 264–86
Festus Dickinson's argument with, 124–26
funeral of, 324–25
health of, 7, 132, 158, 322–24
invited to Jefferson Davis's inauguration, 308
iron works acquired by, 19–21
iron works expanded by, after dissolution of partnership, 66
John Doyle dismissed by, 70–71
John Doyle's lawsuit against, 71
and Jordan, Davis & Company, 71–82
Jordan, Davis & Company dispute with, 83–96, 104, 127, 129, 187, 213

Weaver (*continued*)
    in late antebellum years, 241–63
    library of, 366
    loans obtained by, for Mayburry & Weaver,
        32–33, 43, 46
    loneliness of, 8, 129, 270
    marriage of, 6, 74, 129–32
    Mayburry & Weaver dissolved by, 46–54
    Mayburry's disputes with, 54–62, 63
    Mayburry's first meeting with, 19
    Mayburry's lawsuits with, 56–60
    military sales of, 65, 284, 289–99, 317, 322
    move of, to Virginia, 45
    as opinionated and temperamental, 123–24
    Pennsylvania businesses of, 34
    in Philadelphia as Mayburry manages iron
        works, 29–45
    in Philadelphia in early 1830s, 74, 78, 79, 82,
        122, 129
    photograph of gravestone of, 235
    photographs of residence of, 231, 233–34
    physical appearance of, 17, 123
    political career of, 34, 136–38
    portrait and ambrotypes of, 223–24
    relatives and business associates' opinion of,
        64–65, 95, 123–29, 324
    religion and, 15–16, 17, 22, 28, 42, 130
    reputation of, in hiring market, 68–69
    residence of, 231, 233–34, 365
    Samuel Sherrerd sued by, 143
    on secession and Civil War, 283, 284, 287,
        288–89
    slave management of, 105–21, 261–62, 278,
        328, 333, 366–67
    slavery as viewed by, 22–23, 134, 254, 352
    slaves' view of, 132–35, 327, 351
    spa visited by, 256
    sued by Abraham's widow and father-in-law,
        34, 42
    technological innovation ignored by, 333
    Virginia loved by, 122–23
    wealth of, 3–4, 123, 127, 130
    weapons sought by, 295–96
    wills of, 316, 325
Weaver, William, Jr. (WW's nephew), 42
Weaver v. Jordan, Davis & Company, 87–95,
    104, 127, 128, 129, 187, 213
Weaver v. Mayburry, 57–58
Lewis Webb & Company, 112, 125
Weir, Mrs. (Eleanor Mayburry's daughter), 54,
    61
Whig party, 136, 137, 158, 166, 264, 268, 282, 283
white iron workers, 22, 31, 99
    alcohol use among, 67, 99, 100
    at Etna, 257, 270–71
    food complaints of, 257

    greater skill of, 106
    Mayburry's request for, 40
    unreliability of, 36, 41, 66–67, 99, 100, 252,
        271
    WW's elimination of, 106, 120, 197
white woodcutters, 292
William (Mary Towles's slave), 160, 161
Williams, Ann, 178, 180, 181, 349, 353
Williams, Caroline, *see* Reid, Caroline Williams
Williams ("Etna"), Charles, 105, 139, 172, 174,
    179, 180, 189
Williams, Elizabeth (Sam, Jr.'s sister), 53, 172,
    174, 176
Williams, Elizabeth "Betty" (Sam, Jr.'s daughter),
    see Coleman, Elizabeth Williams "Betty"
Williams, Lydia, 178, 181, 243, 247, 255
    illness and death of, 313, 314, 336, 337
Williams, Mary, 53, 172, 174
Williams, Nancy Jefferson, 176, 177, 180, 248,
    269, 319, 336, 353, 367
    cash distribution to, 300
    after Civil War, 343–44, 349, 356, 360, 361–62,
        366
    death of, 363
    savings account of, 183–84
Williams, Sally, 25–26, 53, 54, 58, 59, 60, 61, 139,
    172, 173–74, 178, 180, 188, 334
    death of, 334, 336, 337
Williams ("Etna"), Sam, Jr., 53, 139, 171–86, 246,
    349, 367
    agricultural work of, 322, 326, 339, 355–56
    apprenticeship of, 175
    assessment of, 363–64
    Betty Coleman's death and, 314, 319
    birth of, 172
    at Buffalo Forge, 10, 11, 27, 105, 107, 157, 166,
        188, 197, 199, 242, 244, 247, 285, 309, 310,
        312, 331, 334, 336, 340, 341, 345, 347, 350,
        354, 357, 359
    cash distribution to, 300
    after Civil War, 339, 340, 341, 344, 345, 346,
        349, 350, 354, 355–56, 357, 359, 360,
        361–62, 366
    D. Brady's assessment of, 259
    death of, 363
    departure of, 361
    illnesses of, 259
    injury of, 246
    labor contract and earnings of, 344, 346, 350,
        354, 355–56
    marriage of, 176, 190
    name of, 181–82, 205
    overwork and purchases by, 172, 175–77,
        179–83, 190, 191, 277, 278, 327, 331,
        367
    physical appearance of, 174–75

Sally William's death and, 334
savings account of, 171–72, 183–84, 278,
    356–57, 368
at sawmill, 331
as sharecropper, 361
skill of, 3, 262, 333
slaughtering by, 248, 249–50, 323
work missed by, 276–79, 321, 323, 326
Williams, Sam, Sr., 53, 60, 105, 140, 172, 180,
    296
    disability of, 172–73, 334
Williams ("Etna"), Washington, 105, 139, 172,
    174, 179, 180
Willoughby, Bill, 162
Willoughby, Dabney, 162
Willoughby, Jack, 162
Willoughby, Jim, 162
Wilmot, David, 165–66
Wilmot Proviso, 165–66
Wilson, John, 134, 367
Wilson, John S., 20, 25–26, 42, 47, 52, 192
    deposition of, on sales of slaves, 57, 58, 60

Wilson, William:
    death of, 48
    heirs of, 65
    Mayburry & Weaver's debt to, 22, 24, 34–35,
        38, 39, 44
    Mayburry & Weaver sued by, 44
    properties acquired from, 19–21, 41–42, 58
"Wilson negroes," 27, 28, 41, 42, 44, 51–55, 132,
    192, 204, 210, 211, 366
    dispute over ownership of, 27, 47–48, 49,
        51–52, 57–61, 85, 90
    division of, 61–62, 139, 173–74, 185, 188, 207,
        270, 366
    fate of, 139–47
women, slave, role of, 26
woodcutting, 31, 110, 149–50, 152, 193–94, 211,
    248, 292, 323
Woodman, Constant, 130
Woodman, Elizabeth Newkirk (WW's wife), *see*
    Weaver, Elizabeth Newkirk Woodman
Woods (white overseer), 340
Wright, Harry, xv